Fifteen Famous Latin Americans

FIFTEEN FAMOUS LATIN AMERICANS

Helen Miller Bailey

Chairman
Social Science Department
East Los Angeles College

María Celia Grijalva

Utah Street School
Los Angeles City School System

CALIFORNIA STATE SERIES
published by
CALIFORNIA STATE DEPARTMENT OF EDUCATION
Sacramento, 1973

Cover photos courtesy of ARTES DE MEXICO.
Title page photo by Lee Boltin

Design by Arthur F. Soares

Fifteen Famous Latin Americans

Helen Miller Bailey and María Celia Grijalva

PRENTICE-HALL INTERNATIONAL, INC., London
PRENTICE-HALL OF AUSTRALIA, PTY. LTD., Sydney
PRENTICE-HALL OF CANADA, LTD., Toronto
PRENTICE-HALL OF INDIA PRIVATE LTD., New Delhi
PRENTICE-HALL OF JAPAN, INC., Tokyo

A Word About the Book

It would be hard to count all the people who have a part in the story of any country. There are the leaders in government, the builders, and the planners. The teachers are important, and the artists, as well as the writers and the musicians. The people in this book come from different countries, and lived at different times. But each of them had an important contribution to make. Some were rich and well-educated. Some were poor. One boy walked 42 miles so he could go to school. Another lost a hand in an accident, and yet he grew up to be a famous painter. You will read about a man who was born a slave and became the leader of his country. You will meet a priest who started a revolution because he wanted to help his people. If anyone ever teases you because you are shy, remember Lucila Godoy. She was such a quiet little girl that her teachers thought she was a slow pupil. Now they are forgotten, but her name is famous.

Life was not easy for any of these people. In this book, you can read their words, share their thoughts. Rich or poor, black, brown, or white, they were alike in a very important way. You will see that they were real people, with real problems—just like you.

Before meeting these people, you will spend a little time "south of the border." You are going to walk through a page of history. Let the words of the text lead you as you travel back in time one hundred and sixty years. Some of you will be reading about your own ancestors. Others will be entering a world quite new to them. For all, it is a chance to relive a story that happened long ago in Mexico.

If any of the words, or the Spanish subtitles, are strange to you, you can find their meaning in the glossary. You may want to find out more about the people and their times. The section listing books, films, and records, on page 176, will help you here. Each story is followed by questions. The answers to some of the questions can be found in the story. Others you will want to discuss with your class. Some may make you curious, leading you to discover things you never knew before.

A number of consultants have been very helpful in the preparation of this book. We would like to express our thanks to:

Rudolph Acuña — Chairman, Mexican American Studies
San Fernando State College

E. Bradford Burns — Department of History
University of California at Los Angeles

Leonardo de Morelos — Department of Spanish and Portuguese
Columbia University

Lic. Antonio Arriaga — Director, National Museum of History
Chapultepec Castle, Mexico City

Charles Lucas — Formerly University of the Americas
Mexico City

Juan O'Gorman — Mexican architect and artist who painted the mural, *The Birth of Mexican Nationality*, in Independence Hall, Chapultepec Castle

Contents

The Mural in the Castle

On the next four pages, you will see part of a mural painted on the wall of a castle in Mexico City. In 1866, the castle was the home of the Emperor Maximilian and his wife Carlotta. Later on in this book, you will read about their sad fate. Chapultepec Castle stands high on a hill in the largest park in Mexico City. It is said that Carlotta wanted to watch her husband as he rode on horseback from the castle to the government buildings. A wide road was built all the way to the center of Mexico City. Today this road is the beautiful Paseo de la Reforma. In 1940, the castle became Mexico's National Museum of History.

One of the rooms in the museum is called Independence Hall. This mural is painted on a curved wall in that room. It is well over 16 feet high and extends for more than 50 feet around the wall. As you walk along this curved wall, you feel as if part of Mexico's exciting history was coming to life around you. The mural is called *The Birth of Mexican Nationality*. It was painted in 1960-1961 by Juan O'Gorman. O'Gorman's father left Ireland and came to Mexico. There he married a girl who was also named O'Gorman. Their families were related, but she and her parents had been born in Mexico.

Juan was born on July 6, 1905. He grew up to be an architect as well as a painter. Anyone who knows Juan O'Gorman will tell you about the house he designed for himself. It is carved out of a gray volcanic cliff. The living room is a natural cave in the rock. Mosaics cover a ceiling and decorate the walls. Mosaics are pictures or designs made of colored stones. O'Gorman travels all over Mexico to find these stones.

Perhaps he is most famous for the mosaics that decorate the library of the University of Mexico. Nowhere in the world is there a building like this. O'Gorman designed it to look like an enormous box. He covered all four sides with mosaics. They tell the story of Mexico from its very earliest days to the present. Through all his work, O'Gorman has tried to give his people pride in the history of their country.

Do you remember the name of the room where this mural is painted? What does "Independence Hall" suggest about the picture? When did Mexico begin her struggle for independence? Look at the first section of the mural, facing page viii. The way the people are dressed may give you a hint. Notice the soldier in the front of the picture. He is in the uniform of a Spanish soldier of the colonial period. Some of the men and women in this section of the mural are wearing fine and expensive clothes. Who are they? They are probably nobles and landowners. The man in the red robes is a bishop. They must be important, or rich, or both. If they are rich, why do you suppose they look so unhappy? Can you figure out the reason for this?

We know that the colonies of Spain were governed by a viceroy. The viceroy was appointed by the king. He had a great deal of power. The man sitting down holding a sword is a viceroy. The viceroy lived in a beautiful palace. Many lords and ladies lived there, too. Do any of the ladies in the mural look as if they lived at the court of the viceroy? You will read a story in this book about a young girl who lived at the viceroy's palace. What kind of life do you think she led there? Later on you will find out how she liked it.

At this time, the people of Mexico were divided into groups. The people who had been born in Spain, but came to Mexico to live, belonged to the first group. They were called *peninsulares*. Another name for them was *gachupines*, or "those who wore spurs." The *peninsulares* had money and power.

The next group were the *criollos*. They were people of Spanish blood who were born in Mexico. Some were rich and owned large haciendas, but they could never hope to be as important as the *peninsulares*. Often the wife of a *peninsular* would travel to Spain before her child was born. Then the baby would be born in Spain, and would not be a *criollo*. Another group was called *mestizos*. The *mestizos* had a mixture of Spanish and Indian blood in their veins. Last of all, and usually poorest of all, were the Indians.

Look at the little Indian girl holding her mother's skirt. What kind of home do you think she may have lived in? The man with the black hood is talking to the soldier about the prisoner. What do you think about this kind of punishment? What can you tell about the way the Indians were treated, just by looking at this picture? Does it give you some idea of why the people in Mexico wanted their freedom?

Look at the building in the second section of the mural. Have you ever seen anything like it? The artist, who is also an architect, has painted an imaginary state building. It is crowned with church towers of different shapes and colors. Can you find a statue of a horse and rider? A Spanish captain is sitting proudly on his horse. Perhaps O'Gorman was thinking of the statue called the Iron Horse. This is a famous statue of Charles IV of Spain. It has stood in three different places, but never on

top of a building! Today it stands in a busy section of Mexico City, with all the traffic of the city rushing by.

In front of this building is a group of men pictured with books, papers, and a globe. What do you think they did for a living? Many of these learned men were thinking and writing about the problems of their country.

The man on the right of the group has his back turned to the others. He is looking off in another direction. Do you suppose he is thinking about the coming struggle? His name is Father Servando Teresa de Mier, and he wrote a book about the wars of independence. He wanted Mexico to free herself from Spain. Because of his ideas, he was sent to Spain and put in prison. He escaped and came back to Mexico, but was put in prison again. This happened over and over, but no jail could hold him for long. In spite of all Father Mier's misfortunes, he lived to be an old man. He had the joy of seeing a republic established in Mexico. He was honored by his country, and elected to a seat in the congress. One day the old priest had the feeling that he would not live very much longer. He went to visit all his friends to invite them to his funeral. Imagine their amazement when he died the very next day!

All the men shown here were forerunners of the struggle for independence. They were the writers and thinkers of the period. They spread the ideas of self-government and equality. José Joaquín Lizardi is there. He is called "The Mexican Thinker." That was the name of the newspaper he started. He wrote many articles explaining these new ideas of freedom. Because of his writings, he, too, was in and out of jail. One had to be a brave person to speak out for true democracy.

Baron Alexander von Humboldt is the first man on the left in the

group behind the cross. He was a German scientist and explorer. The books he wrote about his journeys in Latin America are famous. The Humboldt current off the coast of Peru is named for him. He spent much time in Mexico. In one of his books, he praised the young men in the university for their interest in science.

Standing in front of Father Mier is a rather untidy looking man with his eyeglasses pushed up on his head. He is Father Miguel Ramos Arizpe. When he spoke out for independence, he was persecuted and arrested. Later he was freed. In 1824, he wrote a short essay on Mexico's constitution. All these men used their intelligence and their learning to fight injustice. What is happening to the Indians in the mural? Do you understand why these men wanted to help them?

In the third section, the scene changes. Instead of words, the weapons are swords and even sticks and stones. We see a flaming torch and banners. What is happening? The man holding the torch seems to be a priest. He is shouting something. In this book, you will find out all about the shout—*El Grito*—of this famous priest. If you look closely at the red and black banner you will find his name. In his story you will learn why one banner has a picture of Our Lady of Guadalupe.

Notice the man holding that banner. This is Father Hidalgo, too. The artist has shown some of these people in more than one pose. Do you see a priest wearing sandals? He is Father Maldonado. Standing behind him is an officer named Captain Aldama. Aldama was in the viceroy's army, but he wanted Mexico to be free of Spain. Father Maldonado started two different newspapers. He supported the revolutionaries, and he called Hidalgo a "new Washington."

Notice the pretty young woman in back of Captain Aldama. She is

have started when it did. Her husband◆ is in the mural, too. He is the white-haired man standing near the long table. Perhaps you can find him in the picture on pages xiv and xv. In his hand he holds a rolled up document. He was an official of Querétaro, south of Dolores, where the *Grito* was sounded. His title was Corregidor. As you will learn, the secret society met in his home to plan the revolt. The Spaniards became suspicious. They forced him to take them to the home of one of the plotters. When they searched, they found guns and ammunition. The secret was out! They put the Corregidor in prison.

Doña Josefa was locked in a room in her home, the Palacio of the Corregidor. As soon as the soldiers left, she started stamping on the floor. This was the only way she could send a message to one of the rebels hiding in a room below. The rebel ran out to pass on the warning that the plot was discovered. You will have to read the story to find out what happened next. But if you should ever visit Querétaro, go to the Palacio of the Corregidor. There you will see a plaque on the floor, on the very spot where Doña Josefa stamped her foot.

Do you remember the story of Paul Revere? The young officer standing underneath the red and black banner is Captain Ignacio Allende.■ Could he be called the Paul Revere of Mexico? Why? You will find the answer in the story of Father Hidalgo. The town where he was born is called San Miguel Allende. His home

Gertrudis Bocanegra.● She and her husband worked for the independence movement. One day she was arrested. Unfortunately, she was carrying papers that proved she was a spy for the revolutionaries. She was shot by a firing squad. The Plaza Gertrudis Bocanegra in the town of Pátzcuaro is named for this heroine of the people.

Do all the people in this part of the mural look the same? How many types of faces do you see? What explains this variety? Why are all these people gathered together here? One of the women is Doña Josefa Ortiz de Domínguez.▲ You will meet her in our story of Father Hidalgo. If it were not for her, the revolt may not

still stands at Cuña de Allende. A sign over the door reads: "Here was born he who is known everywhere." Mexico is proud of the handsome revolutionary hero.

Did it occur to you that the red and black banner  looks like a pirate flag? It was sent to the revolutionaries by Jean LaFitte, the famous pirate from New Orleans. He had ships in the Gulf of Mexico at this time. They flew the flags of the Latin American nations that were revolting against Spain. The words "La Doliente de Hidalgo" were added later. The banner became a symbol of sorrow for the death of Father Hidalgo. LaFitte also sold some guns to the Mexicans. Near the end of his life he went to live in the Yucatán peninsula. Some of the people living there today are descended from Jean LaFitte.

Gathered around Captain Allende are some of the men who joined the independence movement. One is Nicolás Bravo, standing next to the Corregidor. Can you find him on the cover of your book? Later on, Bravo became Mexico's first vice-president. The men around Allende stand for all the people who were poor and downtrodden—the Indians, the *mestizos*, and the blacks. These people were ready to fight for a better life. But they were not soldiers, they were peasants and slaves. What chance would they have against the well-trained Spanish soldiers?

The last section of the mural shows us a more peaceful scene. The lady on the white horse is Leona Vicario. She had an uncle who was loyal to the Spanish government, and

who spoke out against the revolution. But his son died fighting for independence, and his niece, Leona, gave up her life for the same cause. She had married another revolutionary, Andrés Quintana Roo. They were always being hunted down by the Spanish soldiers. Her baby girl was born while Leona was hiding in a mountain cave. Finally they were captured and put in prison. Leona's husband could have escaped, but he gave himself up to try to save her from execution. A territory in Mexico is named Quintana Roo in their honor.

In the front of this section, a group of men are seated at a long table. They are organizing the first

Congress. The man standing in front of the group is José María Morelos y Pavón. The city of Morelia is named for him. If you think the man behind him looks like Morelos, you are absolutely right. Again the artist has shown a man in two roles. Morelos was a priest, and he was also a general. Like Father Hidalgo, he was not a soldier by choice. Both of these leaders fought for a cause. The revolt seemed to be the only way to make a better life for their people.

They say Morelos was "as brave as a lion and wise as a fox." You will usually see him pictured with a white cloth tied around his head. He suffered from very bad headaches. To ease the pain, he always wrapped

his head with a towel. Morelos was very clever at planning, and he won many victories. In 1813, he opened the first Congress at Chilpancingo, a town north of Acapulco. He planned a government in which all races would have equal rights. He told the people to stop calling themselves Indians and *mestizos*. He said they should think of themselves simply as Mexicans.

The ideas of Morelos were the basis for Mexican reforms for the next hundred years. But by this time, the country was tired of war. Many people wanted peace, even if it meant a Spanish victory. They turned against Morelos and joined the royalists. Morelos and the men who formed his congress had pitched their camp on a steep hill. They were surprised at night by the Spanish soldiers who stormed the hill. The revolutionaries were defeated. The general let himself be captured so the others could escape. He ordered Nicolás Bravo to guide the congressmen to safety. In this way, he thought the new government might be saved.

Morelos was shot in 1815. His government was disbanded. Many patriots were captured. The revolution was almost over. There were still bands of fighters led by men like Bravo, Pedro Ascencio, and Valerio Trujano. The last two men are shown on horseback, near Leona Vicario. These bands of guerrilla fighters were ragged and half-starved, and they needed a strong leader to unite them.

Two leaders would not admit defeat. One called himself Guadalupe

Victoria. He is the officer Morelos is pointing to. For two and a half years, Guadalupe Victoria  hid from the Spanish soldiers. He lived in the hills, eating whatever fruits he could find. A thousand men looked for him and couldn't find him. He became a legend. Years later, he was Mexico's first president. The other leader was Vicente Guerrerro, the handsome young officer you see here, riding on a tan horse with a white mane. The viceroy offered him a command in the Spanish army if he would give up. Guerrerro refused. He had served under Morelos, and he believed in that great man's ideas. He kept on fighting for what looked like a lost cause. Today you can see his name written in gold on the Hall of Sessions in Mexico City. He is one of the great heroes of independence.

Behind Guerrerro is the Banner of Morelos. The Latin words mean "With eyes and claws one can achieve victory." What else do you see on this banner? Do you see the same symbol on another banner? What country has this symbol on its national flag? The story of this eagle goes all the way back to the Aztecs. Their legend tells of a god who led his people to an island in a lake. There they saw an eagle perched on a cactus plant. In this place, they built a great city. In the story of Bernal Díaz, you will learn more about this city.

The water of the lake was not fresh enough to drink. In the hills were springs bubbling with clean water. The Aztecs built stone aqueducts to carry the water from the springs to the city. Other aqueducts were built later on, in different parts of Mexico. Many of the stone arches stand today. O'Gorman has painted them in the background of his mural. He shows you the mountains and the lakes of Mexico, the old haciendas and the fortresses. Notice the sun rising over the new nation in the third picture. The sun is important in the Aztec legends. For Mexicans, it is a symbol of national identity.

The people you have seen in this mural are a part of the exciting story of Mexico. As you read this book, you will meet others. Some are Mexicans, some are from the other Latin American countries. Each one has a special story to tell.

Where and When

Fifteen famous Latin Americans! When and where did each one live? This map and time line will show you.

Do you know when Benito Juárez lived? Find his name at the left of the time line. The dates at the bottom of the chart show he was born in 1806 and died in 1872. You probably know some of the things that were happening in the world at that time. For example, the United States was torn by the Civil War from 1861 to 1865.

One of our famous Latin Americans is missing from the list: Quetzalcoatl. His story starts years before the beginning of our time line. Was he a real person? When you read the first story, you will find out.

The map of Latin America has names printed on certain countries. If you want to know where Pedro II was born, find his name on the map. For Bernal Díaz, we show you where his story took place instead of the country of his birth. He was born in the Old World. However, Díaz, like the rest of these famous people, had a part to play in the making of the New World.

	1500	1550	1600	1650	1700
BERNAL DÍAZ	1492 (?)		1584		
GARCILASO DE LA VEGA		1539		1616	
SISTER JUANA DE LA CRUZ					1651 1695
ALEIJADINHO					
TOUSSAINT L'OUVERTURE					
MIGUEL HIDALGO					
JOSÉ SAN MARTÍN					
SIMÓN BOLÍVAR					
BENITO JUÁREZ					
PEDRO II					
JOSÉ CLEMENTE OROZCO					
HEITOR VILLA-LOBOS					
GABRIELA MISTRAL					
OSCAR NIEMEYER					

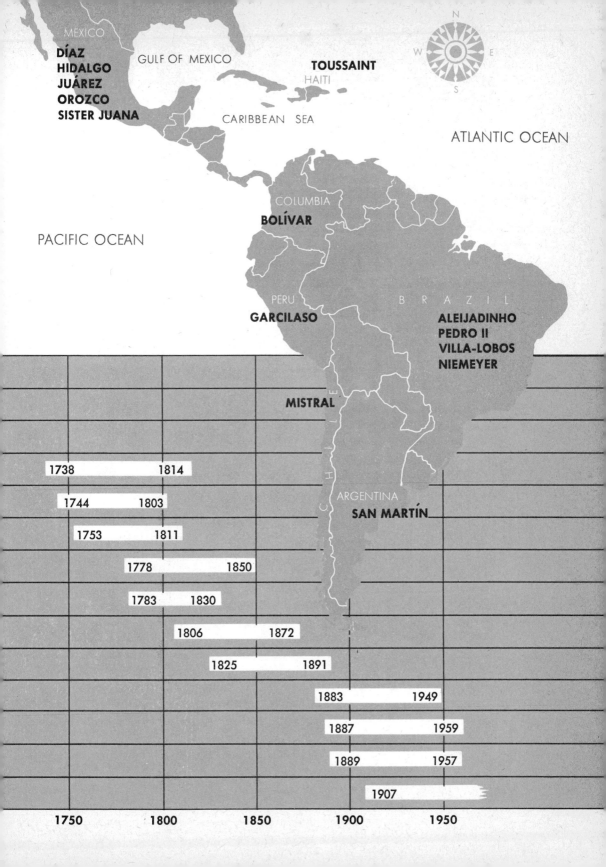

MEXICO

DÍAZ
HIDALGO
JUÁREZ
OROZCO
SISTER JUANA

GULF OF MEXICO

TOUSSAINT
HAITI

N

CARIBBEAN SEA

ATLANTIC OCEAN

PACIFIC OCEAN

COLUMBIA
BOLÍVAR

PERU
GARCILASO

B R A Z I L
ALEIJADINHO
PEDRO II
VILLA-LOBOS
NIEMEYER

MISTRAL

C H I L E

ARGENTINA
SAN MARTÍN

1738	1814			
1744	1803			
1753	1811			
1778		1850		
1783	1830			
	1806	1872		
	1825	1891		
		1883	1949	
		1887	1959	
		1889	1957	
		1907		

| 1750 | 1800 | 1850 | 1900 | 1950 |

THE NEW WORLD

Latin America stretches from the Rio Grande all the way to the tip of South America. People have lived in this land for thousands of years. They wove textiles and made pottery, and still do. They planted seeds and grew crops. They built great cities. Mexico City stands today on the very place where the Aztecs built a big city. They called it Tenochtitlán. Hundreds of thousands of Aztecs lived in this island city long before Columbus came to the New World.

In the peninsula of Yucatán, and in the high central valley of Mexico, were other big cities. The Incas of Peru built cities in the Andes Mountains. Their capital, Cuzco, was filled with unbelievable riches. In all these cities were large stone temples honoring the gods. The Maya people of Guatemala built temples higher than any cathedral in Europe. Pictures carved on the temples and paintings on the walls tell us about the ancient religion and customs of these early people.

Did you know that Cortés conquered the Aztec kingdom with 600 men? Fifteen years later, Pizarro landed in Peru with 180 soldiers. They captured Atahualpa, head of the great Inca Empire. Can you explain how so few white men could have defeated the Indian people? The story of Quetzalcoatl may give you part of the answer.

Much of the civilization of the Incas and the Aztecs was destroyed. The explorers claimed the lands and riches of the Indians for their own countries. Spain and Portugal decided to divide the New World between them. An imaginary line was drawn through the middle of the Atlantic Ocean. It was not known that a part of South America extended out into the ocean beyond this line. This is why Brazil was settled by the Portuguese. It is the only Portuguese-speaking nation in Latin America.

Many of the conquerors stayed in the new colonies and married Indian girls. More and more settlers came from Europe. Much hard work had to be done on the farms and plantations, and in the mines. The Spaniards and Portuguese put the Indians to work for them. They also brought in thousands of black people from Africa to work as slaves.

The colonies grew fast. When Jamestown and Plymouth were tiny villages, Mexico City and Lima were already big cities. The Spanish governors lived in palaces. There were colleges where sons of Spanish noblemen could be educated. Bahía in Brazil was a large port town. Its buildings were as fine as some of those in Lisbon. Priests and missionaries came to teach the people of Latin America. They brought their Catholic religion and the learning of the Old World with them. São Paulo, Brazil, is one of the towns that grew up around a mission school.

And now we shall read about this New World, from its beginnings in the legend of Quetzalcoatl to the time of the struggle for independence from the kings of Europe. We shall see the New World through the eyes of some interesting people.

1

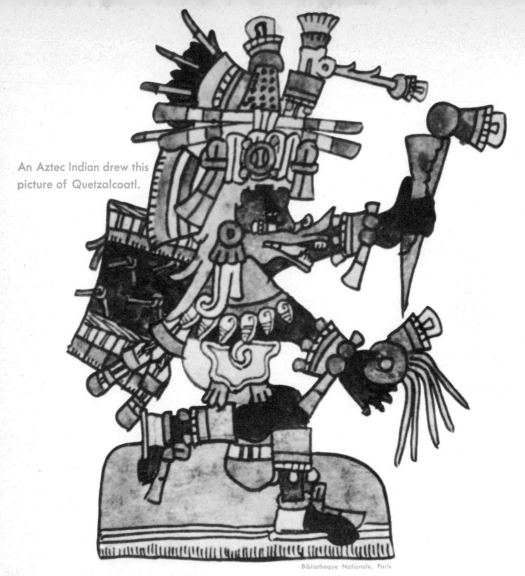

An Aztec Indian drew this picture of Quetzalcoatl.

Quetzalcoatl

Years and years ago there were beautiful cities in the high valley of central Mexico. Teotihuacán (Tay-oh-tee-whah-kahn') was the largest of these cities. It fell into ruins, but some of the buildings are still there. One of these was a temple built to honor a god. He had a body like

2

a snake, or serpent. But instead of scales he had red and green feathers. The people thought his feathers were like those of a long-tailed bird called a *quetzal* (ket'-sahl). Their word for snake was *coatl* (kwah'-tal). So they called their god *Quetzalcoatl,* or Feathered Serpent.

The people of Teotihuacán also built pyramids to the Sun and to the Moon. They used gold and silver and precious stones to make jewelry. They knew how to make clay figures and brightly decorated pottery.

Many different stories are told about Quetzalcoatl, the Feathered Serpent god. And there was another Quetzalcoatl, a king who was named for the god. The life of the man Quetzalcoatl is wrapped in the mystery of the old legends. The legends have mixed the deeds of the real person with those of the god. No two of the stories are alike. Here is one of them.

About a thousand years ago, the people of Teotihuacán left their beautiful city. We don't know whether they were conquered by an enemy or driven away because of lack of food.

About forty miles from Teotihuacán, another great city was built. It was called Tula (Too'-lah). Here the Toltec (Tohl'-teck) people built a temple with narrow

Carl Frank

This giant statue of a Toltec soldier stood on top of a pyramid at Tula. With others like it, it held up the roof of a temple.

QUETZALCOATL   3

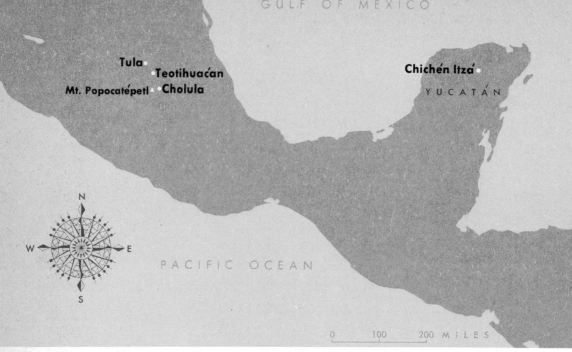

GULF OF MEXICO

Tula
Teotihuacán
Mt. Popocatépetl Cholula

Chichén Itzá
YUCATÁN

N
W   E
S

PACIFIC OCEAN

0   100   200 MILES

flights of steps up the sides. Artists carved jaguars and eagles on the walls. There were also carvings of feathered serpents, in honor of Quetzalcoatl. The king named his baby son after the god. This little boy grew up to become king of the Toltecs. The great city of Tula was his capital. His people were happy and contented. They sang a song about their king:

> In Quetzalcoatl all these
> Trades and arts had their beginnings.
> He, the master workman, taught them
> All their trades and handicraft work.
> Fashioned they the sacred emeralds,
> Melted they both gold and silver
> Other trades and arts they mastered.

But Quetzalcoatl had a wicked uncle who drove him out of Tula. His uncle's soldiers burned the city. The ruins can still be seen today.

Quetzalcoatl and his warriors marched across the valley all the way to the foot of the great volcano Mount Popocatépetl (Poh-poh-kah-tay'-peh-tal). Finally they came to another valley farther south. There Quetzalcoatl became king at a city called Cholula (Choh-loo'-lah). The largest pyramid in the New World was built at Cholula. Deep inside the pyramid is a room. On the wall of this room is a painting of a handsome young god. He has a serpent's body and he is wearing feathers on his head—Quetzalcoatl! The people of Cholula added a verse to the song about the king:

> There in grandeur reared his temple,
> Reared aloft its mighty ramparts
> Reaching upwards to the heavens
> Wondrous stout and tall the walls were,
> High the skyward-climbing stairway
> With its steps so long and narrow
> That there scarce was room for stepping.

A group of Toltec soldiers left this city and went to the coast. There they learned to build long canoes which held twenty men each. In these, they went by sea to the Yucatán (Yoo-kah-tahn') Peninsula. After fighting with the tribes they met on the coast, the Toltecs marched inland.

They came to the town of Chichén Itzá (Chee-chen' Eet-sah'). This name means "well of the Itzás." The Itzás were descendants of the Maya. The Maya were an ancient people who had a highly developed civilization.

Today, in the ruined city that once was Chichén Itzá, a tall pyramid is still standing. Here, too, is a small inside room with a wall painting. It shows warriors decorated with feathers and snakes' heads. Do you suppose King Quetzalcoatl ordered this pyramid to be built? Other buildings at Chichén Itzá have carvings of jaguars and eagles, just like those on the temple at Tula.

Chichén Itzá became a large city under the rule of Quetzalcoatl. The people were proud of their king, and they carved many pictures of him. Because he was the only king who ever had a beard, their name for him was "The Bearded One."

The Toltecs and the Maya people of Chichén Itzá learned from each other. Quetzalcoatl and his followers taught the people

These are the steps of Quetzalcoatl's Temple at Teotihuacán. The fierce looking serpents' heads, with their open mouths, seem to be guarding the steps.

6

This tall pyramid at Chichén Itzá is called El Castillo. Each of its four sides has 91 steps leading to a square temple at the top.

how to make gold jewelry and temple bells and showed them new ways of building. On the other hand, the Mayans had a lot to teach the Toltecs. For many years they had been carving in wood and stone. They had a number system and used a kind of picture writing. They even built a high tower so they could climb to the top and study the stars. They knew the longest and shortest days of the year, and could predict an eclipse of the sun. Their weavers showed the Toltecs how to make cloth with gay designs, and how to make beautiful carvings.

But Quetzalcoatl longed to see Teotihuacán again. He promised the people of Chichén Itzá that he would return. He started out, but his fleet of canoes vanished, and he was never heard from again. The Itzá people lived in Yucatán for three centuries after Quetzalcoatl went away. Then for years the city of Chichén Itzá lay deserted in the forest.

The people in Yucatán and the people in the central valley of Mexico never forgot Quetzalcoatl. He had been a king, a teacher, and a hero. Their memories of him were all mixed up with the old stories of the god. The last verse of the song says:

> He, the wind that's ever blowing;
> He, the guide that's ever marching,
> Sweeping clean the floor of heaven;
> He of all the gods the master.

Surely Quetzalcoatl, the Bearded One, was a real person. In time he became a legend. It is part of the religion of all the Indian peoples of ancient Mexico. His promise was never forgotten.

Left: Pottery figure of a Mayan soldier-priest. The Maya were short husky people with sloping foreheads, long black hair, and dark eyes. We learn about them from their sculpture and paintings. Right: This picture was painted on a temple wall. It shows prisoners being brought before a war chief. The Maya made headdresses out of the feathers of the quetzal.

Peabody Museum, Harvard Univ

Museum of the American Indian

Left: The Mayan earth god decorates this pottery bowl. The designs around the top were a form of picture writing. Right: The Mayan maize god. Maize, or Indian corn, was their principal crop.

They believed that some day he would come back. On the wings of the wind, he would come from across the eastern sea. The Maya in Yucatán abandoned Chichén Itzá. Hundreds of years later, people called the Aztecs came to live in the valley where Teotihuacán and Tula lay in ruins. They believed in the promise also.

At last came a day when the promise seemed to come true. A bearded one came from far across the eastern sea. Had Quetzalcoatl returned? The answer is part of another chapter in the history of these people.

9

Vocabulary

pyramid   jaguar   rampart
legend   grandeur   descendant

Thinking It Over

1. Why is the information about Quetzalcoatl called a legend?

2. Do you know any other legends?

3. Explain to the class the difference between a legend and a story.

4. Explain the difference between a legend and history.

5. Why does the song on page 4 call Quetzalcoatl a master workman?

6. What does the legend say about Cholula? How does the pyramid at Cholula show that there might be some truth in the legend?

7. What is the meaning of Chichén Itzá? Who were the Itzá people?

8. What is inside the pyramid at Chichén Itzá? Why is this important?

9. How do we know that the Toltecs and the Maya learned from each other?

10. Read the last verse of the song (page 8). How is the king Quetzalcoatl remembered by the people?

Map Study

1. Locate the peninsula of Yucatán.

2. Locate Guatemala and Honduras. Name the other Central American countries.

3. Locate each of the places mentioned in the story of Quetzalcoatl.

4. There are ruins of other ancient cities in Mexico and Central America. Try to locate Mitla, Monte Albán, Tikal, Palenque, Copán.

5. Pretend that you are a tour conductor. Work out a tour for someone who wishes to see the ruins of all these ancient cities.

6. Suppose the Spaniards had never come to the New World. Do you think the ancient cities would still be important places? Describe how they might look today.

Activities

1. Build a model of a pyramid, using cardboard boxes or clay.

2. Make a painting or crayon drawing of a feathered serpent.

3. Make a calendar different from ours. Divide the year any way you wish. Make up names for the months or seasons.

4. Using modelling clay, carve a border design for an ancient temple or pyramid.

5. Divide your class into two groups, Toltecs and Maya. The Maya group will show the Toltec group how to weave cloth with gay, colorful designs. First, they will draw the pattern. Next, transfer it to graph paper. If your school has a craft shop with a loom, weave a square of cloth, following the pattern.

Bernal Díaz

In the year 1492, Spaniards first saw the New World. In the very same year, a boy named Bernal Díaz (Behr'-nahl Dee'-ahs) was born in Spain. His family lived in a small town. They were not very rich, but Bernal Díaz was able to go to school. There he learned to read and write. He loved adventure stories, especially those about the New World. Naturally, Bernal Díaz wanted to be an

veyothpan.

Soldado y Escritor

explorer some day. He didn't know that years later he would be writing the story of his own adventures.

As soon as he was old enough, he went to seek his fortune in Panama. He had heard that gold and pearls were found there. He said to himself: "Why couldn't a boy from a small town find

One of the men on the expedition with Bernal Díaz acted as Cortés' secretary. He drew these pictures in order to keep a record of the gifts given to Cortés by the Aztecs. The girl standing with Cortés is an Aztec princess. You will read about her in this story.

13

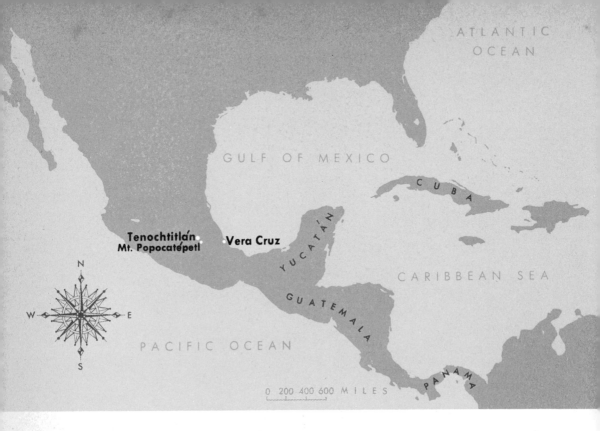

a fortune in Panama?" At this time, Bernal Díaz was so tall and handsome that his friends called him "the elegant one." But he found no pearls in Panama. So he sailed away to Cuba.

The governor of Cuba had heard about a city in Mexico as rich and beautiful as any in China or India. He put Captain Hernando Cortés (Air-nahn'-doh Kohr-tays') in command of an expedition. In his book, Bernal Díaz tells us that Cortés was "a young man skilled in the use of all weapons, very bold and strong. His face was dark and serious, with a short square beard. He could be stern, yet he was soft-spoken and never used bad language even when angry."

Of course, Bernal Díaz joined Cortés. They had about five hundred men, but only sixteen horses. Bernal Díaz would have liked to own a horse, but he was too poor. Only a few horses had been brought from Spain to the New World. It cost a lot of money to buy one. So he had to be a foot soldier.

All the men and horses were loaded aboard eleven ships. At the last minute, the governor of Cuba decided to name another captain. Cortés was very angry. He said he would no longer obey the governor. Against orders, they sailed away from Cuba. When they needed fresh water, they anchored near an island off the coast of Yucatán. Here they found a Spaniard named Aguilar (Ah'-ghee-lahr). He had been shipwrecked eight years before. For all those years he had lived among the Maya as a slave. He had learned their language. You can imagine how glad he was to be rescued. It was lucky for Cortés, too. With Aguilar to translate, Cortés could speak with the Maya Indians. Setting sail again, they took Aguilar with them. They saw villages along the coast. At some of these, Cortés' men fought with the Indians. When the horses came ashore, the Indians were frightened. They had never seen a horse. To them, the horse and rider looked like one big animal! They gave up quickly when they were charged on by these terrifying creatures.

After the Indians were defeated, they brought gifts to the Spaniards. They gave them golden earrings and bracelets, and tiny animal figures made of gold. The Spaniards asked where the gold came from. They heard more and more about a beautiful kingdom in a valley beyond the mountains. The Indians also gave Cortés slaves to work for him. One of the slaves was really an Aztec princess. These Indians had kidnaped her from her own people. Cortés called her Marina (Mah-ree'-nah) and Bernal Díaz tells us she was smart as well as beautiful.

Sailing along the coast, Cortés came to a good harbor. Here he founded the city of Vera Cruz. Today it is Mexico's biggest port. At this time, some of the men planned to return secretly to Cuba. Cortés learned of the plot. He ordered the ships to be burned. Now no one could desert the expedition. Counting the sailors from the ships, there were now about six hundred men under Cortés.

As a young man, Cortés heard many stories about the New World. He was a student at the University of Salamanca when he decided to leave Spain and seek his fortune.

Montezuma (Mohn-tay-soo'-mah), the emperor of the Aztecs, heard about the expedition. His messengers told him that the leader was bold and strong. And he had a beard! Montezuma thought about the old legend handed down by the Toltec and the Maya Indians. Was this the Bearded One from across the eastern sea? Could it be Quetzalcoatl? He sent runners to Cortés, carrying gifts. They had a message: "Our lord, the great Montezuma, sends you these presents. He says he is sorry for the hard journey you and your men have made. He is pleased you have come such a great distance to see him. But you must not come any closer toward Mexico. He begs you as a favor to go back where you came from."

Among the gifts were large plates of gold and silver, and cloth decorated with embroidery and feathers. When the Spaniards saw these treasures, they were even more determined to march to Montezuma's capital.

Now indeed, Díaz wished he had a horse! He had to travel on foot for more than two hundred miles. It was an almost steady climb. They struggled through jungles and across deserts. Steep mountain trails brought them to the high windy plains. They passed through small villages. Marina could talk to these Aztec Indians in her own language. When she was a prisoner of the Maya Indians, she learned their language. So she could speak to Aguilar in Mayan and tell him what the Aztecs were saying. Then he translated this into Spanish for Cortés. In this way, they learned that many of the Indian tribes hated Montezuma. He forced them to pay heavy taxes. Every year they had to send young men to the capital. Some became slaves. Others were sacrificed to the Aztec gods. So there were many Indians willing to join Cortés.

Finally they came to the "smoking mountain," Popocatépetl. Many of the Spaniards had never seen a volcano. But something even more marvelous lay ahead. As they went through the mountain pass they could hardly believe their eyes! There, in a beautiful valley, was the Aztec capital. Many years later, Bernal Díaz recalled: "We were amazed when we saw so many cities and villages built in the waters of a lake, and those straight level streets and bridges with open gates leading into Mexico City. We said

This is a drawing of the Great Temple on the plaza of Tenochtitlán. Mexico City's Zócalo now stands here. Workers building the new subway have found many objects from the time of the Aztecs.

17

American Museum of Natural History

Museo De America, Madrid

Montezuma is about to welcome Cortés. The Aztec emperor really believed that Cortés was the great god Quetzalcoatl. According to the Aztec priests, this was the very year Quetzalcoatl had promised to return. If it were not for that, perhaps Cortés and his small army would not have been able to conquer the Aztec empire.

that it was like the enchanted things told in the books we had read in our youth. Huge towers, temples, and stone buildings rose from the edge of the water. Some of the soldiers even asked whether the things we saw were not a dream."

Of course the Aztecs did not call their capital Mexico City. Their name for it was Tenochtitlán (Tay-nohsh-teet-lahn′). It was built on an island in the middle of a lake. Bridges led to it, and great wide causeways. In the picture on page 17, you can see the plaza of Tenochtitlán as it may have looked to Bernal Díaz and the other Spaniards.

Montezuma decided to come to the edge of the lake and welcome Cortés. He was sure Quetzalcoatl had returned. Díaz describes the meeting: "Montezuma was carried in a chair on the arms of noblemen. The chair was under a rich cover of green colored feathers, with much gold and silver embroidery. The Great Montezuma was wonderfully dressed. His shoes were of gold and the top parts of them had precious stones . . . The Great Montezuma was about forty years old. He had a slender figure with copper colored skin. His face was serious, but his eyes seemed friendly and tender. . . . When Cortés saw him, they came to meet each other. Montezuma welcomed him. Cortés told Marina to wish him good health. Then Montezuma spoke other polite words to him. He gave us messengers. They took us to live in some large houses, where there were apartments for us all. All these rooms were coated with shining cement, and were swept clean and decorated with many, many flowers. Montezuma said to Cortés, 'You and your brothers are in your own house; rest awhile.'"

At this point, Cortés hoped to win the city without a battle. But he knew his men were in a dangerous position. The city was built like a fortress. Montezuma could close off the bridges and causeways. This would separate the Spaniards from their Indian friends. So Cortés plotted against Montezuma, and soon his men held him as their prisoner. Now the king was in their power. The Spaniards began to take gold, silver, and precious stones for themselves. They set up a Christian altar in an old Aztec temple. These things made the people very angry. They felt that Montezuma was weak to allow the Spaniards to act this way. A feeling of great unrest swept through the city.

Several months passed. Then Cortés received word that nineteen Spanish ships had arrived at the coast. This meant trouble. The governor of Cuba wanted his men to seize Cortés. Cortés had to divide his men. Some stayed in Tenochtitlán. Bernal Díaz with the other men marched to the coast. He tells us that Cortés sent gifts of gold to the men from Cuba. He knew this would tempt them to join him. Sure enough, they refused to obey their officers. They marched back with Cortés.

Meanwhile the Spaniards who had stayed behind were having trouble. While Cortés was away the Aztecs were told they could celebrate the feast of one of their gods. Priests and warriors had come to the great temple in the plaza. As Spanish soldiers watched, they chanted and sang and danced. Suddenly the Spaniards attacked them. A war cry went up. Other Aztecs joined the warriors in the plaza. They drove the Spaniards back into their apartments.

When Cortés returned, there was a bitter fight: "Cannons and muskets were not enough against them, or hand-to-hand fighting, or killing thirty or forty of them every time we charged. They still fought on with more energy than at the beginning." Montezuma climbed to a rooftop and tried to calm his people. They hurled stones at him. He was badly hurt. A few days later, he died. His own people had turned against the great Montezuma.

Now the Spaniards had to escape from the city. Some of the men were greedy for gold. They stole as much as they could carry. But then, they couldn't find their way out of the island city.

Historians believe this two-headed serpent was among the treasures given to Cortés by Montezuma.

The British Museum

The Aztecs were chopping down the bridges. Many Spaniards, weighted down with gold, fell into the water. Bernal Díaz got safely across one of the bridges. He says: "It was raining and two of the horses fell into the lake." He didn't try to carry away any gold. But he does tell us that he "snatched four precious stones and hid them under my armor. These stones are highly prized among the Indians. Later on the price of them helped a lot in healing my wounds and getting food."

It was a night Cortés would never forget. The next morning he sat in the shade of a tree on the shore of the lake. This is the tree of La Noche Triste (Lah Noh'-chay Tree'-stay), the Sad Night. It still stands there today.

What would Cortés do now? He certainly couldn't go back to Cuba. But he had lost so many men. Could he ever take the city? He led his little band to a friendly Indian town. Here, with the help of the Indians, they made plans. They built thirteen heavy boats. After working for almost a year, they were ready for another siege.

With their boats, they were able to cross the lake. They fought on the bridges and on the causeways. They forced their way into the city itself. Once again, the Aztecs defended their city bravely. But this time, the Spaniards were able to cut off their food supply. Women, children, and soldiers were starving. Their homes and buildings were destroyed, one by one. Still the struggle went on. Cuauhtémoc (Kwah-tay'-mohk), a nephew of Montezuma, was

Helen Miller Bailey

The tree of La Noche Triste. Cortés wept under the tree, despairing of ever conquering the Aztec Indians.

now the Aztec ruler. At last, he was captured by the Spaniards. This ended the bitter fighting. After ninety-three days of agony, the ruined city was silent.

Bernal Díaz was hurt twice during the fighting. "When the attack began," he remembered, "many Indians laid hold of me. But I managed to get my arm free and saved myself with some good thrusts of my sword. I was badly wounded in that arm. While trying to hold one of the bridges I was very badly wounded by a lance thrust in the throat near my windpipe. I was in danger of dying from it and I have the scar on my throat to this day."

Díaz had certainly found adventures beyond his wildest dreams. He was given some land in Guatemala (Guah-tay'-mah'-lah) as a reward for his part in the conquest. There he lived with his children and grandchildren. When he was a very old man, he

At one of their fiestas, the Indians of Guatemala do the Dance of Conquistadores. They wear masks and have make-believe battles between the Spanish conquerors and the Indians.

decided to put his adventures into a book. He called it *The True History of the Conquest of New Spain.* At the very beginning, he wrote: "I will describe quite simply . . . that which I have myself seen and the fighting I have gone through . . . I am now an old man, over eighty-four years of age, and I have lost my sight and my hearing. As luck would have it, I have gained nothing of value to leave my children and grandchildren except this true story. They will soon find out what a wonderful story it is."

We can read this wonderful story, too. Cortés and his men and the fierce Aztecs seem to come to life as we travel back in time with Bernal Díaz.

Vocabulary

expedition   volcano   celebrate
translate   fortress   plaza
embroidery   causeway   agony

Thinking It Over

1. How did Aguilar and Marina help Cortés?
2. Why did Cortés destroy the ships in Vera Cruz harbor?
3. Montezuma thought Cortés was a god. Explain this by referring back to your story of Quetzalcoatl.
4. Montezuma welcomed Cortés and his men into the city as his guests. Why did Cortés leave?
5. Describe what happened on "The Sad Night." Was it sad for Cortés? For the Aztecs? For both? Explain your answer.

BERNAL DIAZ   23

Quoted material reprinted by permission from *The Discovery and Conquest of Mexico* by Bernal Diaz del Castillo, © 1956 by Farrar, Straus & Giroux, Inc.

Other Leaders

1. When he was in Panama, Díaz may have met the famous explorer, Balboa. Find out as much information as you can about Balboa. Prepare a report for the class.

2. When Cortés had to leave Montezuma's city, he put Pedro de Alvarado in charge. When the Spaniards attacked the Aztecs, Cortés blamed Pedro. Try to find some information about Pedro de Alvarado.

3. Cuauhtémoc was Montezuma's nephew. Why is he honored in Mexico today?

4. Marco Polo had been to China three centuries before the time of Cortés. Try to find a book in the library which tells you how he described the wonderful cities he found. Choose a passage to read to the class.

Map Study

1. Trace the route of Bernal Díaz' adventures from the time he arrived in Cuba.

2. Locate the place where they found Aguilar.

3. Bernal Díaz lived for many years in Guatemala. Find out the distance between Mexico City and Guatemala. How long do you think it would take him to make the journey on foot?

4. Try to find a book which describes Mexico City today. Locate the following on a street map of the city:

a park used by the Aztec emperors	(Chapultepec Park)
a monument in honor of Cuauhtémoc	(on the Paseo de la Reforma)
site of the ancient temple	(National Cathedral)
site of the ancient plaza	(Zócalo)

Activities

1. Try to find some information on life in Guatemala today, and in the time of Bernal Díaz. Do the people live differently?

2. Suppose an old Aztec warrior was telling the story of the conquest to his grandson. What might he say?

3. Imagine a story that might have been told by Aguilar when he was an old man. Tell the story to your class.

4. Cortés wants to find out from an Aztec Indian why his family hates Montezuma. He can't understand the man's language. Choose four of your classmates to play the parts of Marina, Aguilar, Cortés, and the Indian. How can they solve this problem?

5. Select one of your classmates to act the part of Cortés. Another student is Montezuma. The rest of the class must decide which side they would rather be on, and explain their reasons.

6. Montezuma thought Cortés was a god. To understand his feelings, try to imagine how you might feel if a flying saucer landed in front of your house. Write down a description of what your feelings and actions might be. Would everyone react in the same way? Why? Have the class discuss each student's reactions.

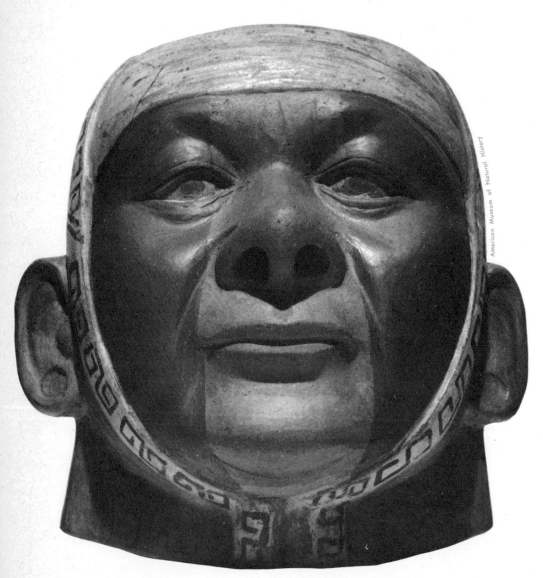

People lived in Peru long before the Incas came. They liked to make clay
water jugs and drinking cups which were really portraits of people they knew.

Garcilaso de la Vega
Historiador de los Incas

In the book by Bernal Díaz, we can read about the conquest of the Aztecs in Mexico. To learn about the conquest of Peru, we turn to a book written by Garcilaso de la Vega (Gahr-see-lah'-soh day lah Vay'-gah).

His father, Don Sebastián de la Vega (Dohn Say-bahs-tee-ahn' day lah Vay'-gah), was one of the knights who came to the New World from Spain. He belonged to a noble family. In Peru he met and fell in love with a beautiful Inca princess. She was a cousin of Atahualpa (Ah-tah-whahl'-pah), King of the Incas. When she became a Christian, she took the name Isabel.

It was the custom of the Incas to bury tools, ornaments, and other objects with their dead people. This golden mask was found on a mummy.

Photo by Charles Uht/The Museum of Primitive Art

27

Machu Picchu

Cuzco

PACIFIC
OCEAN

ATLANTIC
OCEAN

Extent of the Inca Empire

0   200   400   600   M I L E S

On April 12, 1953, bells rang out in Cuzco, in both the Inca Temple of the Sun, and in the Christian church. Princess Isabel and Don Sebastián had a son, Garcilaso de la Vega. There was a great feast to honor the new baby. He was one of the first children born in the New World with both Spanish and Inca blood. Both sides of the family were proud and happy. It represented the mixing of two great peoples. Garcilaso was a "new American."

Garcilaso and his parents lived in a house on the plaza. In his book, Garcilaso tells us that "on feast days the leading nobles of Cuzco gathered there. They watched the games, contests, and bullfights from a balcony that ran just above the main door."

Garcilaso enjoyed all this excitement. When friends and relatives came to visit, he listened to all they had to say. His mother's relatives spoke of the Inca kings and the glories of the past. Then the Spanish knights would talk about their adventures. They described the unforgettable meeting between Atahualpa, the king of the Incas, and the Spaniards led by Pizarro (Pee-sah'-roh). This was the story they told.

Atahualpa was spending the summer at a place about ten days ride from the Inca capital at Cuzco. The Spaniards came inland from the coast to find him there. Atahualpa sat upon a golden throne. He had thousands of Indians with him, but they carried no weapons. Atahualpa did not want them to harm the strangers. He wanted to receive the Spaniards peacefully. He spoke to them slowly, through an interpreter.

Suddenly, the Spanish soldiers attacked. It was as if a thunderbolt had struck! Thousands of Incas were killed. Some were trampled to death by the horses. Others were trapped when a wall fell down. The Inca nobles tried to protect their ruler. It was no use. The king became a prisoner.

Atahualpa, surrounded by his people, meets Pizarro. Minutes later, the Spaniards attacked.

Now the king knew that the Spaniards were greedy for the treasures of the Incas. So he thought of a way to win his freedom. He stood next to the wall of the room where he was imprisoned. He raised his arms high above his head. Then he told the guard to draw a red line around the walls at that height. He promised to fill the room, right up to that line, with gold and silver. The Spaniards agreed to free him if he could do this in two months.

The beauty of all these ornaments meant little to the Spaniards. Pizarro had them melted down so the gold and silver could be divided up. Historians think the ransom amounted to about 13,265 pounds of gold and 26,000 pounds of silver.

Atahualpa sent runners to every corner of his kingdom. They were to bring back all the treasures they could find. They collected cups and pitchers, jewelry and even statues. Anything made of gold or silver was to be melted down for the ransom of the king. But two months went by, and the room was not filled. The Spaniards were impatient. Pizarro was afraid to trust Atahualpa. Suppose he were raising an army, instead of collecting treasures? So Pizarro sent spies to Cuzco.

The spies learned about the king's half-brother, Huáscar (Whah´-scahr). Both brothers wanted to be king. But Atahualpa had seized the throne, and his men were holding Huáscar captive. The Incas in charge of Huáscar sent word to Atahualpa. They thought the Spaniards would plot to free Huáscar. As soon as Atahualpa heard this, he ordered his men to put his half-brother to death. He did not know that he himself would soon face a terrible death.

When Pizarro's spies returned, they told tales of the wonders they had seen. The capital at Cuzco had beautiful palaces and temples. They could scarcely believe the treasures they saw. The Spaniards decided that Atahualpa stood between them and all this wealth. Besides, there was no room for both a Spanish and an Inca king. So Pizarro decided to bring the Inca ruler to trial for the crime of murdering his half-brother.

A young Indian named Felipillo (Fay-lee-pee'-yoh) knew how to speak Spanish. He was the interpreter at the trial. Felipillo was in love with a girl from the royal court. He knew he could never marry her as long as Atahualpa lived. So he spread false stories. He said that Atahualpa was plotting to kill the Spaniards. Twelve charges were made against Atahualpa. He denied everything. He begged the judges not to believe what the traitor Felipillo said. But the Inca ruler was condemned to die. Atahualpa asked to be baptized. He knew that, as a Christian, he would be put to death by strangling. Otherwise, he would have been burned to death. After Atahualpa's death, the Spanish leader Pizarro became the ruler of Peru. This was the sad story Garcilaso heard about the end of the Inca empire.

An Inca princess wearing her native costume. Peruvians have always been proud of their skill at weaving colorful cloth.

Photo Claude Arthaud, Paris

Garcilaso listened to all these stories. He says in his book: "They were more exciting to me than most fairy tales are to little children." His father had hired a man to live in the family home and teach Garcilaso to read and write Spanish. When he was eleven, he was sent to a school run by priests. There he was educated with the sons of other Spanish noblemen. They all had to study Spanish history. As time went on, Garcilaso also began to think about the history of his mother's people, the Incas. He tells us: "When I was sixteen years old, I went to ask my uncle, my mother's eldest brother, how he knew all these stories. 'Inca, my uncle, you have no written records,' I said. 'The Spaniards have books. They know their entire history. I would like to know all of our history. It may be forgotten before it is ever written down.' 'My nephew,' answered my uncle, 'I am glad you wish to hear these things, for then someone among the Spaniards will remember our history in his heart.' Then my uncle told me the tales of the first of the Inca kings, and I took the stories down in notes."

Garcilaso often went with his father on business around the city. Don Sebastián was the mayor of Cuzco, and Garcilaso helped him in his work. In this way, he met many important people from Spain. Some of them had taken part in the conquest of Peru. They were glad to tell the boy about their adventures.

Garcilaso was also able to talk to the Indians who still lived in Cuzco. He asked them many questions. They told him about the old ceremonies in the temples. They described the old ways of planting and harvesting. All this Garcilaso took down in his notes.

Don Sebastián died when Garcilaso was nineteen. It was his wish to be buried in his native country. Garcilaso felt he should take his father's body to Spain. Just before he left, he visited a room under an old temple. There he found the mummies of three kings. It was an amazing sight. Garcilaso tells us: "All these bodies

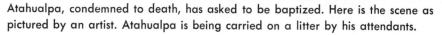

Atahualpa, condemned to death, has asked to be baptized. Here is the scene as pictured by an artist. Atahualpa is being carried on a litter by his attendants.

were so well preserved that not a hair, not an eyebrow, not even a lash was missing. They were dressed in their royal garments and were seated Indian fashion . . ."

Later, these mummies were carried through the streets so all the people could see them. Both Spaniards and Indians took off their hats as the mummies were carried by. The Indians cried as they remembered their kings who were once so powerful. Once again Garcilaso felt pride in his Inca past. He said: "It is to be

GARCILASO DE LA VEGA 33

Luckily, the Spaniards did not find all the Inca treasures. These are made of silver. The animals, an alpaca and a llama, were important to the Inca way of life. The long soft fur of the alpaca was used for weaving warm clothing. The llama could carry cargo for long distances.

regretted that the Incas had no writing, for all the rest of what they knew disappeared with them . . ."

After a long hard journey, Garcilaso arrived in Spain. He arranged for his father to be buried. His Spanish uncles thought he should serve in the king's army. Garcilaso became a captain. After a number of years, he told a friend, "I am tired of fighting Arabs. I have nothing but wounds and debts from the wars. I will go to a monastery and write about the Incas. A career of writing will give me more lasting fame than any victory in war."

It was forty years since he had left Peru. Luckily, he had kept his notes with him all that time. Now at last he was ready to write the history of his mother's people. He called his book *The Royal Commentaries*. By the time he finished, there were ten volumes. In the beginning he told how the Incas founded the city of Cuzco. His uncle had told him the old legend: "Our Father the Sun . . . decided to send one of his sons and one of his daughters from heaven to earth . . . and he gave them a rod of gold . . . 'Go where you will,' he said to them, 'and whenever you stop to eat or to sleep, plunge this rod into the earth. At the spot where, with one single thrust, it disappears entirely, there you must establish and hold your court.'"

After several tries, the rod sank into the earth. There they built a temple. The land was wild and lonely, and the people lived like beasts. The two children of the Sun became their rulers. They taught the people "how to live, how to clothe and feed themselves like men instead of like animals."

In each volume, Garcilaso described the rule of one of the Inca kings. He told of their deeds and the laws they made. He praised the Inca people's knowledge. The children had to learn everything by heart. This was necessary because the Incas had never made up any system of writing. Even so, these amazing people understood arithmetic, geography, and medicine. They had even learned about the stars. He wrote out some of their poems, and described their music and plays. He told how the Inca kings gave the farmers land, and how the land was irrigated. They had to learn ways of draining and fertilizing the land before they could grow good crops. He described forts and palaces and temples. He was so proud of the Incas that he may have made their civilization seem even better than it really was. Some accounts of the Spanish conquest are a little different from his. But he left a complete

The Spaniards never found Machu Picchu, a fort 10,000 feet up in the Andes. Its terraces and staircases are built of stones carefully fitted together. Inca builders did not use mortar, and their tools were not strong enough for stone-cutting. Yet the stones fitted together perfectly.

record of the Inca story. He spent twenty years writing *The Royal Commentaries,* finishing it just before he died. He was an old man of seventy-seven.

Garcilaso de la Vega never returned to Peru. On his tombstone in Spain are these words: "The Inca Garcilaso, distinguished man of a famous family, a man who deserves to be remembered forever." It says nothing about Peru. But the people of Peru have never forgotten him. His book can be found in their libraries. The young people study the story of his life. They can walk along Garcilaso Street in Cuzco today, and they play soccer in a stadium named for him. He will long be remembered in the country of his birth.

36

Vocabulary

noble   mummy   career

baptize   preserved   commentary

execute   monastery   distinguished

ceremony

Thinking It Over

1. What two languages did Garcilaso speak before he was twelve years old?
   How did he happen to know them both?
   Which one did he learn to read and write? Why?
   Is it good to be able to understand more than one language? Why?

2. Tell the story of the death of Atahualpa. How did so few Spaniards win the kingdom of the Incas so easily? All this happened before Garcilaso was born. How did he know the story?

3. Why was Garcilaso's book, *The Royal Commentaries,* so important?

4. Why do you think the Incas never developed a system of writing?
   How do you think they kept track of what happened?

5. Reread the part of the story that tells of the conquest of the Incas. Now go back to your story of Bernal Díaz. Reread the part that describes the conquest of the Aztecs. How were they alike? How were they different?

Other Leaders

1. Try to find enough information about Cortés and Pizarro so that you can compare the two men. Which was fairer in his treatment of the Indians?

2. Hernando de Soto came to Peru with Pizarro. He then went on to explore in North America. Find out more about him.

3. Recall what you found out about Pedro de Alvarado, who was with Cortés in Mexico City. He also visited Pizarro in Peru. Can you find out how that happened?

4. One of Pizarro's men was named Pedro de Valdivia. Try to get some information about him. Where did he go after the conquest of Peru. What cities did he found? You might like the story of an Indian boy who worked for Pedro de Valdivia. His name is Lautaro. Try to find his story.

Map Study

1. Locate Cuzco and Lima on a map of South America. Read the article on Cuzco in the encyclopedia. Prepare a report on what Cuzco is like today.

2. Your class may plan a project on the Andes Mountains. Form five groups. Each group will obtain information on one of the following topics:

> Location and physical features
> Volcanoes and glaciers
> Rivers and lakes
> Transportation
> People

3. Locate Machu Picchu on a map of Peru. Why has it been called a "lost city"? Who lived there? Do you suppose Garcilaso ever saw it?

Activities

1. With your teacher's help divide your class into three groups: Incas, Aztecs, and Mayas. Each group is to get information

about these ancient people. Each group will choose two members to represent the group. These students will report on the information gained to the class.

2. Bernal Díaz and Garcilaso tried to tell exactly what they saw and heard and did. Yet we cannot be sure that their books tell us what really happened. Can you explain this? What does this tell you about recorded history?

Think of an event that happened to you at the beginning of the school term. Write a description of it. Now show your story to someone who shared this experience with you. Do they remember it the same way? Can you explain this?

Select a Class Historian who will keep an accurate record of class activities for a week.

Choose a certain school day about a month ago. Write down the events of that day, exactly as you remember them. Then compare your account with others in the class.

3. Write a paragraph on the following:
If you were Atahualpa, what would you have done when Pizarro arrived? Different students may play the role of Atahualpa as they have imagined it. In each instance another student plays the part of Pizarro.

Sister Juana Inés de la Cruz Poeta y Monja

In 1664, Mexico City was the largest city in the New World. The viceroy who lived there was very interested in art and in all kinds of books. Writers from Spain, France, and Italy came to visit his court. One day there was to be a party for some Spanish poets. They knew some of their poems would be read aloud. But a surprise was in store for them. A little thirteen-year-old girl had been invited. She was to read some of her own poetry to these famous writers! Her name was Juana Inés de Asbaje (Wah'-nah Ee-nays' day Ahs-bah'-hay). She was the daughter of a wealthy landowner in a town south of Mexico City.

Years later, Juana told about her childhood: "I was only three years old when my mother sent my older sisters to a school for little girls in Puebla (Pway'-blah). I was full of mischief and wanted to tease my older sisters. So I went to school with my sisters without telling my mother. At the school, I found out that they were going to learn to read books. I wanted to learn to read more than anything else in the whole world. I told the teacher a lie. I said that my mother had sent me to school, too.

"The teacher did not believe me. But she did let me try to read. She soon saw that I really wanted to learn. The teacher was pleased and helped me to learn quickly. No one told my mother. The teacher wanted to surprise her by showing how much I had learned. I did not tell my mother because I was afraid that she would spank me. And the Indian girls that worked for my mother did not tell her. Mother thought that they were caring for me at home every day, but I was really at school.

"But I thought I was very bad, so I made myself do without something I liked. When cheese was passed at the table for supper, I did not take any for many months. I liked cheese so much that I felt it was a punishment to go without any."

Of course, Juana's parents soon found out that she was going to school. They were amazed to hear how smart their little daughter was. Instead of scolding her, they let her have all the books she wanted. But they thought she should learn the usual things also. In those days, girls were taught to make fine lace and to embroider. Juana and her sisters learned to play the harp. While the grown-ups visited and talked, young girls were supposed to sit quietly and do their embroidery.

Juana and her sisters probably dressed like this little girl. This painting hangs in Mexico's National Museum of History.

Mexico City as it looked in 1695. Part of the new subway follows the causeways that connected the island city with the mainland.

But this was not enough for busy little Juana. She had an idea: "When I was about seven, and already knew how to read well, I was much more clever than I needed to be in sewing. I saw that this was the only learning girls would ever get. I heard somewhere that in the city of Mexico there were high schools and a college in which science was taught. No sooner had I heard this than I began to plead with my mother. I wanted her to let me dress in boy's clothes and go to live with some relatives in Mexico City. Then I could go to school there to get ready for college. Only boys went to these schools. But mother would not let me go. Then all of our family moved to Mexico City into a fine house belonging to our grandfather."

Now Juana was really happy. She said: "I could finally do some of the things that I really wanted. I read many kinds of books that belonged to my grandfather. He thought this was wrong for a girl to do, and said I should be punished. But nothing they did to me was able to stop me. I memorized many things I read.

The viceroy is riding in his coach in a procession. Many women have set up stands to sell flowers, fruit, and good things to eat.

People who knew my grandfather in Mexico City were surprised at me because I used such big words and knew so many different things. They thought a child my age would just be learning to talk correctly."

The amazing little girl could read Latin as well as Spanish. At this time, most of the important books came from Europe, and many were written in Latin. Juana's grandfather owned such books. She wanted to be able to read them. "I set myself to learn Latin and I was allowed to take twenty lessons. I had hoped to have beautiful long curly hair like my older sisters. But when I saw that at first I was learning Latin slowly, I cut off all my hair. I did not think at the time that it was right that a head so slow in learning Latin should be covered with pretty hair. When I could read Latin well, I let my hair grow again."

Juana's grandfather was a good friend of the viceroy. He arranged for her to live in the viceroy's palace. There she would meet many noblemen from Spain. Perhaps, one day, she would

Quoted material reprinted from the *Bulletin of the Pan American Union*.

marry one of them. So she became lady-in-waiting to the wife of the viceroy. Juana was just thirteen years old, and she was very pretty.

The viceroy's wife was very kind to her little lady-in-waiting. Juana liked her so much that she wrote some poems for her. When the viceroy read them, he couldn't believe that Juana had written them. He sent for her and asked her many questions. He was amazed at her answers. She knew even more than he did about the great poets in Spain. He asked her to write a poem for the party he was giving. That is how it happened that the little girl read her own poetry to the famous Spanish writers.

The viceroy was very proud of Juana. He spoke of her to professors at the University of Mexico. They wondered if she was good at mathematics, too. So the viceroy called a meeting of forty of these professors. Juana came before them. They laughed when they saw how small she was. Juana smiled, and began to answer their questions. She solved every problem. She did not even have to work them out on paper!

Time passed, and many of the wealthy men at the court wanted to marry the lovely Juana. She was afraid that her grandfather would wish her to marry one of the rich old noblemen. But it is said that she fell in love with a boy of her own age. She became secretly engaged to the young man she loved. But her family would not allow them to marry. No one knows what happened. Juana never told the story of her love in any of her writings. It was one thing for the little Juana to go to school without her parents' permission. But in Mexico at that time, a young lady would not dare marry unless her parents approved.

This was a sad time for Juana. She was not interested in the life at the court. It was not proper for a daughter of a wealthy family to work. Finally, she went to a friend for advice. This friend

The National Cathedral of Mexico was built in the time of Cortés. It faces the Zócalo, Mexico City's beautiful public plaza. The Zócalo covers the site where the Aztecs had their main square. The emperor's palace and the Great Temple once stood there.

was in charge of a large convent in Mexico City. The nuns who lived there taught in the church schools. Her friend thought Juana might be happier in the convent. She could help train the nuns to be good teachers. There would be plenty of time for her to study and to write poetry. She would no longer be bored by life in the viceroy's court.

So Juana went to live at the convent, and became a nun. Now she would be called Sor Juana Inés de la Cruz (Soar Wah'-nah Ee-nays' day lah Kroos), or sister Juana. The first thing she did was to start a library at the convent. With the help of her grandfather and the viceroy, she collected almost 4,000 books. No other library in Mexico City had so many books. She also collected maps.

They showed the parts of the New World discovered by the Spaniards. Sister Juana made more exact drawings of these maps. She wrote many beautiful poems, and even made up music to fit the words.

She wrote a book about science and music. It was printed in Europe, and many people read it. After this, learned people in Spain and France were anxious to read all her writings. Sister Juana became famous. Professors from the university came to see her. Scientists wanted to meet her. Officials from the viceroy's court visited her, and an artist in Mexico City painted her portrait. She was young, beautiful, and very learned.

The bishop became worried. He did not think women should be interested in science. And he could not understand why a nun should write poems about love and sunshine and flowers. He was afraid Sister Juana was not paying enough attention to religion. Juana did not want to get her convent in trouble with the Bishop. She felt that perhaps she should give more time to her prayers. So she made a big sacrifice. She gave up her studies. She wrote no more poetry. She sold her entire library and all her musical instruments. Sister Juana gave the money from this to help a home for orphan girls.

Two years later, an epidemic of smallpox hit Mexico City. There was no such thing as vaccination in those days. Many people died. Sister Juana helped care for the nuns who caught the disease. She also went to the poor section of the city. There she found many poor Indian children sick with smallpox. They were just lying in the streets. Each day, she carried children back to the convent. She was able to save many of them.

Soon, Sister Juana herself fell sick with the dreadful disease. She was worn out from nursing others. Now there was no one well enough to care for her. In two days, she died.

Almost three hundred years have passed, but Sister Juana is not forgotten. She is one of the best-loved poets of the Spanish colonial period. Her poems are written in lovely, musical Spanish. In one of them, "The Dream," she tells how it feels to wake at sunrise:

> The sun draws up just below the horizon,
> Spilling over the rim in rays of pure light.
> Thousands of rays like darts of golden metal
> Shoot into the sky of sapphires gleaming bright.
> Now things on earth are glowing with brilliant colors,
> It is the ending of night and the day's break.
> The whole hemisphere is sparkling with radiance.
> The world is full of sunlight! Now I am awake!

Vocabulary

viceroy	mathematics	bishop
plead	convent	sacrifice
lady-in-waiting	nun	epidemic
professor		

Thinking It Over

1. List all the subjects you study in school. Now list the things you would study if you were a girl in the time of Sister Juana. Which do you prefer? As a young person, would you rather be living now, or in the days of Sister Juana? Girls and boys may have different opinions here. Why?
2. Why did Juana go to live in a convent? What else could she have done?
3. Write a different ending for the story of Juana. Suppose:
   (1) She married her sweetheart without her parents' permission.
   (2) She married a wealthy Spanish nobleman.

Map Study

1. Locate the city of Puebla on a map of Mexico.
2. Locate Mexico City. Notice its elevation. Does this tell you anything about the climate of Mexico City? What large mountains can be seen from Mexico City? From Puebla? Why is there snow on them all year, even though they are in the tropics? Could Juana have answered these questions?

Activities

Divide your class into two sections. You may decide which section you wish to join. Each section works together on one of the following:
   a. Make up some poems. Can you translate them into Spanish? Read both versions to the class.
   b. Complete a research project on scientists who lived between 1500 and 1750.

Aleijadinho
Desde Esclavo hasta Escultor

The churches of Latin America are famous for their beauty. They are the symbols of the religion and learning that the missionaries brought to the New World. They are richly decorated with paintings, carvings, and statues. We know that some of the work was done in Portugal, Spain, and Italy by well-known artists. These works of art were brought to the New World by wealthy men. They wanted their churches to be as beautiful as those in Europe.

The most famous artist in the entire New World, during these colonial times, was born in Brazil. He was the son of a slave woman, and his name was Antônio Francisco Lisboa (Ahn-tohn-ee-oh Frahn-sees'-koh Lees-boh'-ah). But he was called Aleijadinho (Ahl-ay-jah-deen'-yoh) "Little Cripple." Today he is remembered by that name.

At that time, ship captains from all over went to Africa to buy slaves. They sold these people to the colonists in Brazil. Many of these slaves had been farmers in Africa. They knew how to spin and weave cotton cloth. They decorated their cooking pots with bright designs. They could make wood carvings. They were much more talented than the Indians who lived in the forests of Brazil. Millions of these people were sold into slavery.

One of these slaves was a young woman who knew how to cook and keep house. She was brought to Bahía (Bah-ee'-ah), a city on the coast of Brazil. There she was sold to a man named Manuel Lisboa (Mahn-well, Lees-boh'-ah). He had come to Bahía from Portugal. He could paint, carve, and even build churches. Many of his statues of saints decorated the churches in Portugal.

Now our story takes us far inland, to a place called Minas Gerais (Mee'-nahs Jay-rah'-eesh), or General Mines. Gold was discovered here. Brazil had its "Gold Rush" just as did our own West. Prospectors and gamblers started a city called Vila Rica (Vee'-lah

Left: The statue of the Prophet Isaiah stands on a pedestal, tall against the sky. It is one of the twelve statues of the prophets carved by Aleijadinho.

Some little boys in choir robes are drinking at a fountain in Ouro Preto. The city has changed very little since the days of Aleijadinho.

Ree'-kah), "rich city." It was what we would call a "boom town." Later the name was changed to Ouro Preto (Ow'-roh Pray'-toh). This means "black gold," and it referred to the pure, dark gold found there.

Time passed, and Ouro Preto changed from a rough boom town to a beautiful city. The families of the first miners built big homes. They wanted to build churches, too. They sent to Bahía for a man who was well known for designing churches—Manuel Lisboa.

He stayed in Ouro Preto and became very prosperous. Young men were anxious to be his helpers. His work shop was like an art school. Some of his students were the children of slaves. They learned how to plaster church walls to make them ready for the mural paintings. They could do some of the simple wood carvings. One boy learned faster than any of the others. This was Aleijadinho, Lisboa's own son. Aleijadinho's mother was the young slave girl Manuel had bought in Bahía. The boy never grew very tall, and he had a crooked back. But he was a born artist. When he was quite young, he could draw designs in color without his father's help.

Lisboa continued to design and build churches. Aleijadinho worked along with him. They worked together on the church of Our Lady of Mount Carmel. Lisboa died before it was finished, and his son took over the work. He did so well that visitors still go to Ouro Preto to see this beautiful church.

Aleijadinho did more and more work in Ouro Preto. Sometimes he was asked to do over churches. At other times, he drew up plans for new churches. He decorated the inside of these churches, too. When he wanted to carve a statue of one of the old prophets or saints, he asked old men to pose for him. He often chose poor slaves who did backbreaking work in the mines, as models for his statues.

Sculptors come from miles away to study statues of the twelve prophets. Aleijadinho spent nine years carving them.

ALEIJADINHO 53

Aleijadinho was becoming famous. Art students came to him from different cities in Brazil, and even from Portugal. His best students were two African boys who had been sold in the slave market in Bahía. Aleijadinho freed them. They became so skillful that they were able to carve many of the large statues—except for the faces. Then Aleijadinho, who never grew tall, would climb a ladder. This was the only way he could reach the heads of the tall statues. When Aleijadinho finished carving the faces, the statues seemed to spring to life.

Then a terrible thing happened. Aleijadinho felt his hands becoming stiff. It was harder and harder for him to hold his hammer and chisel. These were the tools he used to carve his curly-headed angels and wrinkled old prophets. Poor Aleijadinho! He had caught a dreadful disease. It may have been leprosy. There

The courtyard of the church where the statues of the Prophets stand. It is located in the city of Congonhas.

was no known cure for it in those days. What was he to do? It was as if a great opera singer discovered that he was losing his voice. Aleijadinho would rather die than give up his work.

His two African students helped him as much as they could. He told them to tie a chisel to his left hand, and a hammer to the right. In this difficult way, he continued to carve.

It is hard to believe, but Aleijadinho did some of his best work during this period. A wealthy mine owner lived in a town near Ouro Preto. He wanted to be remembered as a generous man. He asked Aleijadinho to carve twelve tall statues of Old Testament prophets. Each was made from a single block of stone. They stand in the courtyard of the church to this day. Beside these, there are wooden statues of Christ, the apostles, and some Roman soldiers. One group is arranged to show the Last Supper. Others, called the Stations of the Cross, show the people who were there when Christ was carrying His cross.

While Aleijadinho was working on this project, there was a lot of unrest in the area. The people knew about the revolutions in France and in North America. They, too, wanted to break away from their mother country, Portugal. They knew that the revolutionaries in France wore pointed caps. So the young men of Minas Gerais started dressing this way. It was a sign that they were against the government. Their leaders were arrested, and one of them was put to death.

Aleijadinho pretended to know nothing about all this. He was busily working on the statue of the prophet, Amos. When the statue was finished, Amos was wearing a pointed cap! Evidently Aleijadinho was on the side of the rebels. The governor's soldiers came to question him. He became angry at the soldiers, and shouted at them to go away. He wanted to finish the statue of Isaiah. When the statue was complete, the face was that of an old man, crying out in anger. The people said it showed Aleijadinho's anger against the government.

The last years of Aleijadinho were sad ones. The disease had paralyzed him. He lost his sight. He died, a penniless, lonely, old man. Legends about Aleijadinho grew. We cannot really be sure of all the facts. But we do know he was a genius. The whole town of Ouro Preto, where he was born, is now a national monument. This means that no one can make any changes in the buildings. And the statues he carved are preserved for all to see and to wonder at.

Vocabulary

symbol   national monument
mural painting   prosperous
leprosy

Thinking It Over

1. Why were black people from Africa brought to Brazil to work as slaves?

2. Compare Vila Rica with a boom town of the American West or Alaska. Bring to class some pictures of statues. Are they like those carved by Aleijadinho? Are they different? How? Which do you like best? Why?

Other Leaders

Divide your class into six groups. Each group is to find information on one of the following men, and tell the class what they learned.

Father José de Anchieta   Tiradentes
Father Manoel de Nobrega   Diogo Álvares (Caramarú)
Pedro Álvares Cabral   Tomé de Sousa

Map Study

1. Find the distance between the shoulder of Brazil (near Recife) and the West Coast of Africa. Did this have any effect on the history of Brazil?
2. Compare the size of Brazil to the size of the United States. Compare the physical features of the two countries.
3. Locate Bahía, Ouro Preto, Minas Gerais on the map of Brazil.

Activities

1. The city of Taxco in Mexico is preserved as a national monument. Try to find it on a map. Why is it so preserved? What United States cities are kept as national monuments? Try to find pictures of these cities, and bring them to class.
2. You may not be able to carve out of wood, as Aleijadinho did, but you can try soap sculpture. Try to shape and mold a figure out of a large bar of soft white soap.
3. The people in Brazil spoke the Portuguese language. Why was this so?

THE STRUGGLE FOR FREEDOM

As you know, the thirteen colonies in North America fought the Revolutionary War to gain their independence. They had been ruled by England for nearly 200 years, and they wanted their freedom. Patrick Henry shouted "Give me liberty or give me death!" George Washington organized an army and led the fighting. Many men are remembered for their part in that struggle.

Thirty years later, the colonies of Latin America began their struggle for freedom. Each country had its heroes. Simón Bolívar was the George Washington of Latin America. He dreamed of forming the new nations into one great country, just as the colonies of North America formed the United States. This never happened, but Venezuela, Ecuador, Peru, Bolivia, and Colombia owe their independence to Bolívar. José San Martín drove the Spaniards out of Chile. Through the efforts of San Martín and Bolívar, the rule of Spain in Latin America finally ended.

Ideas about freedom and equality came from France as well as from North America. From 1789 to 1792, the people of France revolted against unjust taxes and bad government. France had only one colony in the New World. It was led to freedom by Toussaint L'Ouverture and became the nation of Haiti.

In Mexico, Father Hidalgo, a priest in a small village, cried out for independence. His words are as famous in Mexico as the words of Patrick Henry are in this country.

The story of Brazil is different from all the others. Brazil belonged to Portugal. Yet the son of Portugal's king helped Brazil gain its independence. Later, the grandson of that king became Emperor. He ruled Brazil wisely and well until he was an old man.

By 1850, there were eighteen independent countries in Latin America. The people of Brazil spoke Portuguese; the Haitians spoke French; the rest were Spanish-speaking. The United States was friendly to all these nations. In fact, in 1823 President Monroe said that the United States would not allow the European powers to interfere with the new Latin American nations. This was the famous Monroe Doctrine. Freeing these colonies from the mother countries was only a start.

Other problems lay ahead. The new nations had to learn to stand alone. The heroes of independence did not always make good presidents. The people were not trained to run their own government. Civil wars broke out between the different political leaders.

These wars weakened the new nations. Trade was cut down; mines were closed; jobs were scarce. Large estates, called haciendas, were owned by rich families. Often the owner lived in the city and an overseer managed the hacienda. The poor people, descendants of Indians and slaves, worked on these haciendas. They got little or no money for their hard work. Most of them were no better off than the poor had been in Father Hidalgo's day.

One of these Indians managed to get an education. His name was Benito Juárez, and he is a real hero to most Mexicans today. Mexico honors him as we honor Abraham Lincoln, because he held his country together through a bitter civil war.

In this section, you will find the story of each of these heroes of independence.

Simón Bolívar
Libertador

In the city of Caracas (Kah-rah'-kahs), in what is now Venezuela, lived a little boy named Simón Bolívar (See-mohn' Boh-lee'-vahr). He owned land worth four million dollars. But he had lost something worth more than all the money in the world. His parents died when he was very young. When they died, he became the owner of a big house, many slaves, and large sugar plantations. His uncles managed all this wealth for Simón and took good care of him.

Simón was a lively, mischievous child who often ran away from home. He made life miserable for his teachers. Simón's uncle wanted him to learn science, history, and mathematics, so he hired a young man from Spain to teach the restless little boy. Simón grew to love this man, Simón Rodríguez (See-mohn' Roh-dree'-gays), as if he were his father. He was a good teacher, and he was interested in what was happening all over the world. He taught his pupil about the revolutions in America and in France. When Simón Bolívar grew up, he wrote to his old teacher: "You have molded my heart for liberty, justice, greatness, and beauty. You were my pilot. You cannot imagine how deeply engraved upon my heart are the lessons you taught me."

With Señor Rodríguez (Seen-yore' Roh-dree'-gays) to teach him, Simón became a good student. He liked sports, too, and he enjoyed the parties at the governor's palace. When Simón was sixteen, his uncle thought the young man should visit Spain. Simón went to Madrid. He was

Simón Rodríguez.

The Pan American Union

invited to the king's court. Here, too, he went to parties and dances. But the young noblemen at the court looked down on Bolívar. He was born in the colonies, so they felt he wasn't as good as they were. One day, he was playing tennis with Crown Prince Ferdinand. By accident, Simón hit the prince on the head with his racquet! Years later, it amused him to think about this. Little did the two boys on the tennis court know that one day Bolívar would take from Ferdinand "the most precious jewel in his crown," the city of Caracas.

While he was at the Spanish court, Simón Bolívar met the Countess María Teresa (Mah-ree'-ah Tay-ray'-sah). She was a beautiful girl of sixteen. It didn't bother her in the least that this handsome young man was born in the colonies. They fell in love. The king allowed them to marry. Simón took his lovely bride back to his plantation in Caracas.

But their happiness did not last long. An epidemic of yellow fever broke out in Caracas. María Teresa caught the disease. She was one of the first to die in the epidemic.

Bolívar wrote: "I loved my wife very much. Upon her death I vowed never to marry again." He traveled to Europe to try to forget his sorrow. There he met his old teacher, Señor Rodríguez. They traveled together in France, Austria, and Italy. They must have discussed many things. Señor Rodríguez knew of Bolívar's wish to see Caracas freed from Spain. He used to teach the young Simón how other countries had fought for their freedom. While they were in Rome, they climbed a hill. From there, they had a wonderful view of the ancient city. The sight made him think of his own city. He made a promise: "I will never allow my hands to be idle, nor my soul to rest until I have broken the chains which tie us to Spain."

He went back to Caracas. There he formed a secret society. Many friends were ready to join him. All of them were anxious to drive the Spaniards out of their city.

Just at this point, an event across the ocean gave them unexpected help. The French Emperor, Napoleon, had conquered Spain. He put the Spanish king and Crown Prince Ferdinand in jail. Then he sent French officials to Caracas. They had orders to take the place of the Spanish governor. Bolívar and his friends forced the French to leave. They pretended to be loyal to the Spanish king. Of course, what they really wanted was to free Caracas from both the Spanish and the French.

In 1811, Caracas and the area around it was declared a republic. Francisco Miranda (Frahn-sees'-koh Mee-rahn'-dah) was named President. He was one of the leaders of the revolution. Bolívar led the army. It was a hard time for the new republic. Most of the citizens did not really want to break away from Spain.

Also, Spain controlled many cities in South America. Spanish soldiers were stationed in forts along the coast near Caracas.

Then, during Easter Week, 1812, a terrible earthquake hit Caracas. Many people thought it was a punishment from God. "Down with the Republic!" they shouted. When Bolívar tried to help an old lady trapped in the ruins, an angry mob of people attacked him. After the earthquake, Spanish soldiers came to Caracas. They put President Miranda in prison, but Bolívar managed to escape. The republic was dead.

Next he went to the part of South America we now call Colombia. Here Bolívar helped the people rise up against their governor. He returned to Caracas. With his soldiers, he drove the Spanish out. The people forgot how they had hated him after the earthquake. Now they lined the streets to cheer him. They called him their liberator. Girls threw roses in front of his horse as Simón Bolívar rode into the city.

Meanwhile, in Europe, Napoleon had been defeated. The old Spanish king had died in prison. Crown Prince Ferdinand became King of Spain. New Spanish governors were sent out to South America. Once again, Bolívar and his men had to go into hiding.

He went to the island of Jamaica in the Caribbean. While there, he worked out a plan. He wanted to form a union something like the United States. The cities of Caracas, Bogotá (Boh-goh-tah'), Quito (Kee'-toh), and Lima (Lee'-mah) would belong. He wrote letters about this plan to his friends. He said: "Our new nation should be called Colombia, as a sign of gratitude to the discoverer of the New World." This was Bolívar's dream.

Two years went by. Finally he was able to get back to Venezuela. He called an army of patriots together. They found a route across the high Andes. No explorer had ever been there before. Bolívar's army of 2,000 men came out of the mountains near the

Bolívar is the central figure in this mural by Martínez Delgado. He is proclaiming the constitutional government of Colombia. The mural is in the National Congress Building in Bogotá, Colombia.

city of Bogotá. There they took the Spanish soldiers by surprise and defeated them. The date, August 7, 1819, is still celebrated in South America.

Later, Bolívar's men drove the Spanish troops out of Caracas. Once again, it was declared a republic. The people of Caracas joined those of Bogotá. They formed a new nation, Gran Colombia. Bolívar was the president.

But other cities in South America were still ruled by Spanish governors. Bolívar felt Colombia could not truly be a nation until these cities were also free. He marched south with his army to the area we now call Ecuador (Eh'-kwah-dohr). A brave young lieutenant named Sucre (Soo'-kray) went on ahead. He and his men freed the city of Quito. Bolívar marched on to take the seaport, Guayaquil (Guy-ah-keel). Now all of Ecuador was free.

At Guayaquil, Bolívar met another great liberator, José de San Martín (Hoh-sáy day Sahn Mahr-teén). You will hear more about him soon. Both men wanted to drive out the Spaniards. Bolívar was the more popular leader. Perhaps that is the reason San Martín told his men to join Bolívar's army. This army was now made up of soldiers from all over South America. They marched to a town called Ayacucho (Iy-ah-koo'-choh), in Peru. There, in one single morning, they defeated the whole Spanish army. The war for Spanish American independence was over. Spain no longer ruled any land in South America. The date was December 9, 1824.

Now Bolívar went to La Paz (Lah Pahs'), a mining town high in the Andes. Once again, he was greeted with shouts of joy and bouquets of flowers. Bolívar thought La Paz should be independent. He wrote up a constitution, with a bill of rights. In his honor, the people of La Paz named their new country Bolivia.

The trip back to Bogotá took many weeks. Bolívar had to travel on horseback over steep mountain trails. When he arrived, there was nothing but bad news for him. While he was away, his Colombian union was falling apart. Caracas had left the union to set up the new nation of Venezuela. The people of Peru wanted to break away. Ecuador separated from Colombia. And in a short time, Bolivia changed the constitution he had written. Bolívar realized that victory in war did not guarantee a strong nation.

There was little left of Bolívar's dream of a United States of South America. Only Colombia remained. Bolívar was still president, but he was no longer a hero. People were angry because so many young men had died, fighting to free the other South American cities. And there were many people who had lost their homes in the fighting in Colombia.

The vice president of Colombia was jealous of Bolívar. He hired some men to kill President Bolívar, but Bolívar escaped. He climbed out of a window and hid all night underneath a bridge. He stood in icy cold water. The next day friends helped him to get out of the city. He had escaped with his life, but not for long. All those long journeys through the Andes had tired him out. When he was in Bolivia, with its high altitude, he had caught a bad cold. Now he was coughing all the time.

He had lost his great wealth and his property in his lifelong fight for liberty. Now he knew he was dying. Was it all in vain?

Bolívar's friends called a doctor. He said to the doctor: You came to Colombia from Europe. Why did you come?"

Bolívar Peak in the Andes in Venezuela. The snowy pass is more than 15,000 feet high.

"I came to find liberty in South America," answered the doctor.

"I fought to bring liberty to the New World," said Bolívar, "but those of us who fought for liberty in South America have accomplished nothing. It has been as if we had tried to plough the ocean to plant seeds, and the waves washed our seeds out as fast as we planted them."

Twelve years after Bolívar's death, there was peace in some of the countries he had founded. It was decided that the Great Liberator should be honored. His coffin was dug up and brought to Caracas. Crowds came to honor his memory. Officials came from all over the world. Bolívar's coffin was placed in a horse-drawn carriage. Not roses this time, but funeral wreaths were thrown in front of the horses as they moved slowly along. The president of Venezuela read Bolívar's words: "Fellow South Americans, you saw my efforts to establish liberty where tyranny had ruled. I gave my fortune and my life for this country. I have hoped for no other glory than the freedom of this entire region. My last wishes are for the happiness of all the people in these nations."

And so, the seeds he tried to plant finally took root.

Vocabulary

mold	loyal	patriot	tyranny
vow	liberator	plough	

Thinking It Over

1. When did Bolívar probably decide to fight for the independence of South America?

2. Who may have given Bolívar ideas of liberty?

3. Simón Bolívar is called the George Washington of South America. How are these two men alike? What problems did each one face?

4. Why did Bolívar want to call the new union Colombia?

5. August 7 and December 9 are important dates in the history of South America. Why?

6. Can you plant seeds in the ocean? What did Bolívar mean when he said: "It has been as if we had tried to plough the ocean to plant seeds . . ."

Other Leaders

Prepare a report on José de Sucre.

Map Study

1. Trace or draw a map of South America. Show the countries as they are today. Using your story as a guide, mark the routes that Bolívar and his army took.
2. What nations were won from Spain by Bolívar? Mark the capital of each.

Activities

1. Bolívar's secret society was called the Lautaro Society. The password to get into the meetings was "Lautaro." Why did Bolívar use that name?
2. Pretend you are Simón Bolívar. Write a short letter to a friend telling of your plan for a union of Latin American countries.
3. Many African nations have become independent in recent times. Members of the class may volunteer to find information on Ghana, Nigeria, Tanzania, Kenya, Uganda. Prepare a report for the class covering these points:

>Who have been their leaders?
>Have they been dictators?
>Have they "ploughed the ocean"?

Have another group of students report on Cambodia, Laos, and Vietnam. In a class discussion, compare their problems of poor people, few schools, and lack of self-government with the problems Bolívar faced.

José San Martín
Héroe de la Argentina

José de San Martín was born in Argentina. This is the man who met Simón Bolívar at Guayaquil. If it were not for that meeting, the story of Peru might have been quite different. San Martín's long-range plan, like Bolívar's, was to free the countries of South America from Spain.

Try to find the city of Buenos Aires (Bway'-nohs Iy'-rays) on your map. If you follow the Uruguay (Oo-ruh-gwaih') River for 500 miles, you will come to the place where the San Martín family lived. José's father had been sent by the king of Spain to govern the Indians in the area. The Spanish priests had founded a mission there. They had taught the Indians to live in houses and to farm the land. Then the missionaries left, and José's father became the governor. The family lived in the house built for the mission fathers. There was a beautiful garden, and a grove with hundreds of orange trees. Inside the house was a room filled with books left behind by the priests.

The San Martíns were very happy living here. It was warm and pleasant all year. José played in the garden, and swam in the river with the Indian boys. They liked to watch the boats sailing down the river to Buenos Aires. The Indians grew cotton and sugar and oranges. José's father was in charge of shipping these products to Spain. He was a good governor, and the Indian people were happy and contented.

When José was eight, his father was promoted. He became a colonel in the king's army, and the San Martín family went to Spain to live. José had just learned to read, and was beginning to enjoy the books in the mission library. Now he would be going to school in Spain. The carefree days when he played on the river banks were gone forever. He was sent to a special school for boys who were going to be army officers. There he studied grammar, mathematics, geography, and science. José had to learn to use a

Left: At the port of Guayaquil, a monument marks the spot where San Martín and Bolívar had their historic meeting.

sword, and he spent many hours practicing with his instructor. When he was fifteen, he went to sea as a marine. By the time José had become a captain, Napoleon had invaded Spain. Captain San Martín was put in charge of a band of guerrilla fighters. They were trained to fight in the mountains against Napoleon's forces.

But José's heart wasn't in it. He knew that the Spanish king was just as much of a dictator as Napoleon. He didn't want to die in the mountains of Spain, fighting for a king he didn't respect. He kept thinking of his happy childhood in Argentina. That was his true country. Years later, he wrote: "In 1811 I was serving in the Spanish army and had already spent twenty years of honorable service. I heard of the Revolution in South America. I no longer wanted to be an officer in the Spanish army. I wanted to

promote the liberty of my native land. So I sailed for Buenos Aires in the beginning of 1812. From that time on I gave all of my time and effort to the cause of Spanish America." Now San Martín would join the great struggle for independence. He knew that many of the Spanish laws were unfair to the colonists. No longer were they willing to be ruled by a great power across the sea.

When he arrived at Buenos Aires, he was disappointed. The town did not seem nearly as big as he had remembered it. After all, he was just eight years old when he left there. It was still just a group of one-story houses strung along the muddy banks of the Rio de la Plata. The waters of the port were so shallow that his boat could not come in to the shore. San Martín and the other passengers were taken in by rowboat. Then they rode on oxcarts with wheels eight feet high. These carts pulled passengers and cargo through the mud at the river mouth. Finally, they got to the plaza of the little town.

In those days, Buenos Aires could not compare with cities like Caracas, Lima, Bogotá, or Mexico City. But this muddy little town was already independent. With the help of soldiers from other towns, the people had driven the Spanish governor out. But they did not have a regular, well-trained army of their own. San Martín offered to train the young men of Buenos Aires. His experience in the Spanish army could be helpful now. At first, the officials of the city did not accept his offer. They knew that his father had been a Spanish governor. They were afraid José might be a spy sent from Spain. When he married an Argentine girl and made his home in Buenos Aires, they decided he was a South American at heart. They realized that he was eager to work for the freedom of his native land.

Just at this time, Spain threatened to attack the city from Montevideo (Mohn-tay-vee-day'-oh). The officials went to San

Museo Histórico Nacional, Buenos Aires

José de San Martín. This oil painting of the handsome general can be seen in the National Historical Museum at Buenos Aires.

Martín for help. No one in Buenos Aires knew as much about guerrilla war as he did. Other towns in the grassy plains, or pampas, of South America joined forces with Buenos Aires. Men from each of these towns met, and on July 9, 1816, they declared their independence from Spain. They called their nation "The United Provinces." Fifty years later it became known as the United Provinces of Argentina.

San Martín was commander in chief of the army of the new nation. There were some who thought they did not need an army.

Spanish troops had been gone from the area for some time. But José San Martín knew there was still danger. There were Spanish soldiers in Chile, across the Andes to the west. To the northwest was the strong Spanish headquarters in Lima, Peru. Napoleon had just been defeated at Waterloo. And Crown Prince Ferdinand was now king of Spain. All this San Martín knew. He was sure Ferdinand would be sending thousands of fresh troops to Peru and to Chile. The officials in Buenos Aires laughed at San Martín's fears. After all, they said, Lima was 2,000 miles away, with a high mountain range between them. Let the Spaniards hold Lima forever, for all they cared. But San Martín realized, just as Bolívar did, that "Spain must be driven out of South America completely, or we will never be free."

So he made a plan. He asked to be made governor of Mendoza (Main-doh'-zah). If you look at your map, you will see why he chose Mendoza. It lay in the foothills of the Andes, less than 300 miles from Chile. That meant less than 300 miles from the Spanish troops! But the mountain passes from Mendoza to Chile were covered with snow. The trail was wide enough for only one mule. Many lives had been lost in these mountains. Could an army get through? For San Martín, the answer was "Yes!" He said, "To cross into Chile with a small, well-disciplined army is my course. There can be no other."

The people of Mendoza agreed to the plan. Everyone helped the cause. Young men volunteered for the army. Women wove cloth and dyed it blue for uniforms. They sold their jewelry to raise money. Blacksmiths worked long hours making guns and cannons out of iron, and shoeing horses and mules. The Indians in the Andes helped in their own way. They spread false stories to the Spaniards in Chile. They pretended to be fighting San Martín. Instead, they were showing him how to get through the high mountain passes. They took secret messages from San Martín to the patriots in Chile.

The officials at Buenos Aires knew of San Martín's plan. They sent a troop of volunteers to join his army. When these men arrived, they brought good news. San Martín's wife had had a baby daughter several months before. The thought of the happiness which was waiting for him back in Buenos Aires spurred San Martín on.

At last, the army was ready. Mules were loaded with guns and cannons. They even carried a cable bridge to be used to get across deep ravines. Thousands of cattle had been killed to provide food for the soldiers. The meat was cut into strips and dried so that it would last during the long march. Men, horses, and mules started out. Nearly half the mules and horses died on the way, but the men got through. In a month's time, they were in Chile. Later, San Martín recalled: "Crossing the Andes had been a triumph in itself. The soldiers had marched 200 miles along craggy peaks and deep narrow chasms. It was a victory because the mountains were conquered. It was also a victory because the enemy had been surprised and frightened."

The Indians had done their job well. Many of the Spanish soldiers were guarding the wrong pass because of the false reports the Indians had sent. San Martín's army was joined by the patriots in Chile. Together, they fought and won at the village of Chacabuco (Chah-kah-boo'-koh). It was February 12, 1817, and Chile was declared a free nation. However, one more battle had to be fought a year later before Chile was really free.

San Martín's next goal was to free Peru. He managed to get twenty-four ships. Loaded with men, horses, and supplies, this was his "invasion fleet." They sailed up the coast, and landed near Lima. The viceroy knew the people were glad to see San Martín's

San Martín's army at Mendoza. They had to fight their way over the Andes before they could fight the Spaniards.

men. To avoid a battle, he ordered the Spanish soldiers to leave the city and go to their forts in the mountains. Then the people crowded into the streets, shouting for independence. The bells rang out. San Martín was named the "Protector of Peru." But he knew Peru was not safe. Thousands of Spanish soldiers were waiting in the mountains. His army was not strong enough to fight them. Somehow, the Spaniards would have to be defeated.

That is why San Martín went to meet Bolívar at Guayaquil. If the two liberators combined their armies, he thought, perhaps they could drive the Spaniards out forever. Near the inn where

JOSE DE SAN MARTIN

One of the soldiers of San Martín's army. He is dressed for the long, cold march across the Andes.

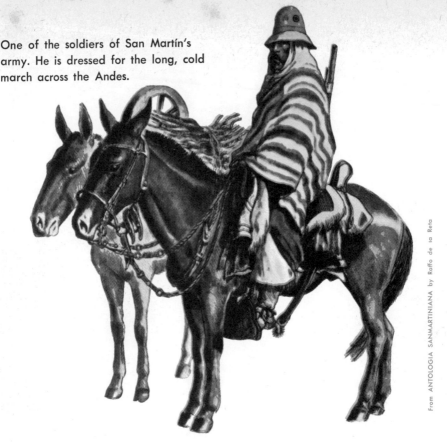

From ANTOLOGIA SANMARTINIANA by Raffo de la Reta

they met secretly, there is a monument now. The picture on page 70 shows you the statue of San Martín and Bolívar shaking hands. You already know the outcome of that meeting.

When San Martín returned to Lima, he said good-bye to the people: "I have seen the independence of Peru and Chile. I have taken the banner under which Pizarro enslaved the Incas. My promise to the countries for which I fought is fulfilled." Then he sailed back to Chile. But when he arrived, no one welcomed him. The officials were angry because their young men, now under Bolívar, were still fighting in Peru. With only an Indian to guide him, and two mules, San Martín sadly left the country. He went back through the mountain pass to Mendoza. The people there still looked up to San Martín. They wanted him to live there. He went on to Buenos Aires to get his wife and daughter, and bring them back to Mendoza.

But it was not to be! His young wife had died. The little girl, Mercedes (Mehr-say'-dees), was living with her grandparents. The people in Buenos Aires were unfriendly toward San Martín. They said many lives had been lost in the fighting, and much money spent. He had come back, but he did not bring the young men with him. He felt lonely and unwelcome. He didn't even want to go back to Mendoza. So he took Mercedes and sailed away to France.

In Paris, he met an old friend from his school days in Spain. He learned that the Spanish government was giving a pension to the officers who had fought against Napoleon. San Martín had spent his life helping the countries of South America free themselves from Spain. Yet in his old age they forgot him. The small pension from the Spanish king was just enough for him to live quietly in Paris and send Mercedes to school. When she married, he made his home with her. He enjoyed his books, and visits from old friends. San Martín never returned to Argentina. His death in 1850 went unnoticed in Buenos Aires. Years later, the story of San Martín was printed in the Argentine newspapers. Then Argentina remembered her hero. His body was brought home and buried in the cathedral at Buenos Aires. Streets, plazas, and schools now bear the name of this great liberator.

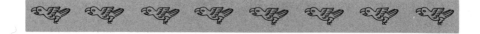

Vocabulary

guerrilla war   craggy peaks   protector
headquarters   chasm   fulfill
cable bridge   invasion   pension
ravine

Thinking It Over

1. Why did San Martín think that the people of Buenos Aires needed an army?
2. How did the whole city of Mendoza help San Martín?
3. Why is the battle at the village of Chacabuco important to the story of Chile?
4. Tell why San Martín met Bolívar at Guayaquil. What happened to San Martín because of this meeting?
5. Refer to your story of Bolívar. What was the battle that took place after the two leaders met at Guayaquil? Why was it important?

Other Leaders

Divide your class into four groups. Each group is to find information on one of the following men, and tell the class what they learned:

José Artigas
Antonio Páez
Bernardo O'Higgins
Francisco Miranda

Activities

1. One student may read to the class the description of San Martín's preparations for the crossing of the Andes. The students who worked on the Andes Mountain project (Garcilaso story) can explain the need for these preparations. If possible, bring in some pictures to class to add interest to the discussion.

2. Describe the reasons for the meeting between Bolívar and San Martín. Write a conversation the two leaders might have had. Two students may act the parts of Bolívar and San Martín, using the most interesting conversation.

Miguel Hidalgo

Artes De Mexico

Padre de la Independencia Mexicana

On most nights, the little towns of Mexico are quiet and peaceful. But once a year, on the stroke of midnight, all the church bells ring out. The mayor stands on the steps of the church or the town hall and calls out, as loud as he can, "Long live independence, long live Mexico!" This takes place in every village, and in the big cities, too. It is the *"Grito"* (Gree'-toh), the shout for independence. On the next day, September 16, there are parades and celebrations all through the country. It is Mexico's national holiday.

The story of the *Grito* takes us back to the year 1810. That was the year Father Miguel Hidalgo (Mee-ghel' Hee-dahl'-goh) sounded the *Grito*, the first call for the independence of Mexico.

Miguel Hidalgo lived on a large ranch called a hacienda (hah-see-ehn'-dah) where his father was the manager. He had four brothers, and they often worked in the fields with the Indian peasants. They planted corn, picked cotton, and helped bring it into the sheds. Here the women did the spinning and weaving, and made the cotton into cloth. Miguel came to know the Indians well. As hard as he worked, he knew they worked even harder.

When Miguel was fourteen, his father sent him away to school. He was a good student, and he liked to give speeches and take part in debates. He was so clever at winning debates that his classmates nicknamed him "The Fox." He passed his tests with such high marks that his professor sent him a letter. It said: "You get the main points of the books you read, as a bee gets honey from a flower. Therefore, I will call you the hardworking bee. With joy in my heart, I foresee that you will become a light placed in a candlestick, or a city set up on a hill."

Miguel went on with his studies because he wanted to be a priest. He was given the job of teaching in a Catholic college. After becoming a priest, he was made head of the college. At this

Left: The slaves in chains are reaching out to Father Hidalgo, who is giving them their freedom. Juárez and Morelos are shown in the lower part of this mural painted by Orozco.

time, all the college textbooks were written in Latin. They were old-fashioned and out of date. Father Hidalgo wanted his students to learn more about what was happening in the world. He allowed them to have debates about the government. He encouraged them to try out new ideas. However, the officials of the government, and of the church, were not pleased with this. Father Hidalgo was considered a bad influence on the students. He was forced to give up his work at the college.

Now Father Hidalgo began to work as a pastor. He lived in a number of small towns and villages. The people he served were mostly Indian farm workers. Father Hidalgo remembered well the hard work on the ranch. But he had been the manager's son, and he was able to get an education. These workers had no chance at such a future. They were really not much better off than slaves. They worked long hours, and were scarcely able to feed their families. Father Hidalgo decided he would do everything he could to help these people better themselves.

He was living in a little village called Dolores (Doh-loh'-rays). There was a church, the priest's house, a town plaza, and a jail. The priest's house was built around a patio, in the Spanish

Cowboys herding cattle on a hacienda in Mexico. As a boy, Father Hidalgo lived on one of these big ranches.

Artes De Mexico

The village of Dolores may have had a market place like this one. What do you think is happening here?

style. Some of the rooms were used for church activities. In the patio, Father Hidalgo held classes every night. His house became a kind of community center. On feast days, there were parties in the patio with music and dancing. Everyone was invited—Indian and white, rich and poor. Father Hidalgo was a man who loved people, and he joined in their fiestas. He taught them to play the guitar, and to form singing groups. He also liked to read and discuss books and ideas with his friends.

This good parish priest also started a craft program for the Indians. He set aside a place where carpenters could make and sell tables and chairs. There was a blacksmith shop where the young men could learn to work with metals. Another group made beautiful pottery out of the clay in the hills nearby. Indians from other villages came to Dolores to learn these skills.

Father Hidalgo had other plans to help the Indians make a better living. He had them plant grapevines. When the grapes were harvested, he taught them how to make wine. He planted twenty mulberry trees which an uncle had brought back from China. In five years he had a hundred mulberry trees. Silkworms ate the leaves, just as his uncle had seen them do in China. Then they spun their cocoons. The Indian women learned how to unwind the thread from the silkworm cocoons. They became skilled at weaving the thread into beautiful silk cloth.

The Father had hoped that programs like these would spread throughout Mexico. In this way, the Indians could look forward to a better way of life. But some of his programs ran into trouble. The merchants in Spain heard that the colonists were growing grapes, and making wine. They heard about the new silk industry. These efforts would hurt their business. So they had a law passed to forbid these industries. The government ordered soldiers to chop down the mulberry trees. They even burned out the roots to put the Indians out of the silk business forever. They discouraged them from raising grapes and making wine.

Father Hidalgo became very bitter when all his efforts to help the Indians came to nothing. On a trip to Mexico City, he heard many people complaining about the unfairness of the government.

The craft of making pottery is still important in Mexico today. Some villages and towns are famous for the kinds of pottery they make.

The people who were born in Mexico were discriminated against. Only Spaniards had government jobs. They treated the Mexicans as lower class people. There were many reasons for the people of Mexico to be dissatisfied. They knew of the revolutions in America and in France, and they felt that Mexico should also be independent. Secret societies were formed by people who wanted to plot against the Spanish government. This is what Bolívar was doing in Venezuela.

Miguel Hidalgo joined such a club, and soon became its leader. Ignacio Allende (Eeg-nah´-see-oh Ah-yen´-day), a young officer in the Spanish army, was a member. So was the wife of an important town official! Her name was Doña Josefa (Dohn´-yah Hoh-say´-fah), and some of the secret meetings were held right in her living room. They planned to start their revolt on December 12, the feast of Our Lady of Guadalupe (Gwah-dah-loo´-pay). She is the patron saint of Mexico, and great fiestas would be held in all the towns on that day. Somehow, the officials discovered the plan. Doña Josefa heard that the government was going to arrest the leaders of the revolt. She got word to Allende. He galloped furiously to Dolores, to warn Father Hidalgo. It was September 15, 1810.

Some of the Indian people were having a party at Father Hidalgo's patio. Everyone was having a good time, singing and dancing. Suddenly Captain Allende arrived, and broke the news to Hidalgo. The priest spoke to his people: "Do not be unworthy of the independence movement. Do not act like frightened children. My friends, we have no choice but to attack the Spaniards now."

He rang the church bell as a signal for the rest of the people of Dolores to gather together. From all over the village, sleepy people came to the church. Father Hidalgo led them inside. He

This is the way an artist pictured the scene at Dolores the night Father Hidalgo gave the *Grito*, the famous shout for independence.

said: "My children, the day has come. Do you want to be free? Will you make the effort to get back from the hated Spaniards the lands stolen from our forefathers three centuries ago?" These were ordinary people from the village and countryside. They were farmhands and servants, water carriers and cowboys. They shouted, "Down with bad government! Long live independence!"

This was the *Grito de Dolores*, the shout for independence.

By daylight of September 16, this crowd of people began to march. They were armed with knives, hoes, and a few rusty guns. Hidalgo and Allende led them to a large city called Guanajuato (Gwah-nah-whah'-toh). There were silver mines nearby, and many wealthy Spaniards lived there. When they heard that the patriots were coming, the Spaniards hid in a big stone building. It was a warehouse for storing grain, but it was as strong as a fort. They took everything they could carry with them—money, jewelry, and ornaments of gold and silver.

Father Hidalgo's army now had 50,000 men. They attacked the warehouse. The Spaniards had cannons, and they fired into the crowd of patriots. Then Hidalgo's men set fire to the thick wooden doors. The men inside threw grenades out of the windows, killing some more of the rebels. After a short fight, the rebels took the warehouse. They killed most of the Spaniards inside. Then they swept through the city, robbing the wealthy homes. When they found brandy, they drank it. When they found beautiful clothes, they put them on. There was looting and destruction for several days. After years of being overworked and underpaid, the Indians took bitter revenge on the Spaniards.

When the news reached Mexico City, people were deeply shocked. They wanted independence, but not this way. They denounced Father Hidalgo's followers. But there were many in Mexico who supported the revolutionary movement. Soon many towns were controlled by rebels.

Captain Allende and Father Hidalgo knew they had a hard job ahead. Could they train the Indian peasants to be disciplined soldiers? They must teach them not to kill helpless people, not to steal and destroy the towns they captured. They grouped the Indians into squads. Some were foot soldiers; some had horses. They had four cannons, two of which were homemade. These were put on oxcarts. Now they began their march toward Mexico City. All along the way they gathered more men, until they numbered 80,000.

North of the capital, they met and fought a well-trained Spanish army. Nearly 2,000 of the rebels were killed or wounded, yet they forced the Spaniards to retreat. Captain Allende thought they should march on and attack Mexico City. But Father Hidalgo knew the capital was well defended. Perhaps he felt his troops were not yet ready. Or perhaps he was afraid he could not control them if they did take the city. At any rate, he decided not to attack Mexico City.

Instead, he went to Guadalajara (Gwah-dah-lah-hah'-rah). The governor had left the city, and the people wanted to set up a republic. They welcomed Father Hidalgo with a ceremony in the cathedral. A big parade wound through the city. People shouted and waved flags. And Father Hidalgo rode in the governor's carriage!

One of Father Hidalgo's first acts was to announce that all the slaves in Mexico were to be freed. This was the year 1810, more than fifty years before Abraham Lincoln's Emancipation Proclamation. He also told the people they should stop paying taxes to Spain. And they could now produce their own wine, tobacco, and silk, instead of importing them from Spain. He made this announcement: "Let us establish a congress representing all the cities, towns, and villages of this country. Our law makers will treat us all like brothers. They will do away with poverty. They will build up industry. The richest products of our fertile

The Cathedral of Guadalajara. A statue of Father Hidalgo stands nearby. He is holding a scroll which announces the end of slavery in Mexico.

soil will be for the use of all of us. Within a few years, we, the people of Mexico, will enjoy all the things which nature has given to our beautiful land."

When word of these reforms reached Mexico City, the Spaniards took action. About 6,000 well-equipped soldiers were sent to Guadalajara. Father Hidalgo's plan was to stop the Spanish soldiers before they reached the city. His men would guard a bridge on the edge of town. They had some cannons made of wood. Their gunpowder was carried on oxcarts and covered with straw matting. The men could hide in tall dry grass on the hills above the bridge.

There was a terrible battle. Suddenly a shell struck one of the rebel ammunition wagons. It blew up with a roar. Many of the patriots were killed by the explosion. Soon the whole hillside was in flames. Those who weren't burned were choked and blinded by the smoke. Panic broke out, and men ran in all directions. Ten

91

Again Orozco shows Father Hidalgo with the suffering people. The mural is painted in the Governor's Palace in Guadalajara.

Photo by Manuel Alvarez Bravo

thousand died on that hillside. Ten thousand more were taken prisoner by the Spaniards. Father Hidalgo's dreams went up in those flames. And the independence of Mexico was set back ten years.

Father Hidalgo and Captain Allende escaped and marched north with the remaining soldiers. Perhaps they could get help and make a new start. But they didn't get far. On the way, they were captured by Spanish soldiers. Now there was no escape possible. The two leaders were taken to the nearest Spanish governor. Their hands and feet were chained, and they were heavily guarded. The trip took four weeks, on muleback, through the rugged country.

When they reached a town far to the north, there was a trial. Father Hidalgo tried to save Allende's life. He said: "I placed myself at the head of the revolution, raised armies, made ammunition and cannon and appointed the officers of the government. I alone was to blame." But even so, Allende was shot as a traitor.

Because he was a priest, Father Hidalgo was treated differently. First, the bishop took away his right to perform priestly duties. Then Father Hidalgo was taken to the Spanish governor. He was asked if he was sorry for what he had done. His reply was, "I mourn day and night for these Mexicans who have been killed in my cause." The governor sentenced him to death. But Father Hidalgo did not seem frightened. He talked and joked with his jailers. They brought him a guitar, and he played and sang songs. On the walls of his cell, they found poems he had written in charcoal, the night before his death. In them, he thanked his jailers for their kindness to him, and blessed them.

When Father Hidalgo was brought before the firing squad, he blessed each of the soldiers. He assured them that some day, independence would come to Mexico. Then he was shot. It was the morning of July 31, 1811, less than a year since the first *Grito de Dolores.*

Mexico's dream of freedom did not die with Father Miguel Hidalgo. It finally came true in 1821. Many men fought and died for it. Miguel Hidalgo was one of the best loved. The church bell he rang became Mexico's liberty bell. His *Grito* was the first battle cry for independence. Because of it, September 16, 1810, is the most famous date in the history of Mexico.

Vocabulary

debate	mulberry	grenade
influence	cocoon	rebel
pastor	discriminate	revenge
fiesta	forefather	ammunition
craft		

Thinking It Over

1. Why were the officials displeased with Father Hidalgo when he was a college teacher?
2. How did Father Hidalgo help the Indians when he lived in Dolores?
   Do you think his ideas were good? Why?
   Why didn't these plans work out?
3. Why were the people of Mexico dissatisfied?
4. How did Father Hidalgo plan to free Mexico from Spain?

5. Compare Father Hidalgo's army to the Spanish army.

6. How did the people of Guadalajara treat Father Hidalgo? What was he able to do there?

7. Do you think Father Hidalgo accomplished anything for Mexico?

Other Leaders

Divide your class into three sections. Each section is to find information about one of the following men:

> Ignacio Allende
> José Morelos
> Augustín Iturbide

Map Study

Locate the following towns on a map of Mexico:

Dolores	Zacatecas
Guanajuato	Chihuahua
Morelia	San Miguel de Allende
Guadalajara	

Activities

1. What connection is there between the silk industry and mulberry trees? Perhaps you can get some information on silk worms from a nature study center, or from the biology department of a high school. Try to find out about the manufacture of silk cloth in Japan today.

2. Is Hidalgo's *Grito de Dolores* of September 16 celebrated any-where in the United States? Are any other Mexican holidays celebrated in the U.S.? What can you find out about these celebrations? Are some Puerto Rican holidays celebrated where you live? Some holidays of other nationalities? If so, describe them for the class.

3. Can you think of any other historic ride that might compare with Allende's? Describe it to the class.

4. Can you think of any other *Gritos* in history? Have there been any in your lifetime?

5. Make up a conversation for a secret meeting between Father Hidalgo, Doña Josefa, and Allende. Choose three classmates to play the parts.

6. Plan conversation and action for the following scene: Allende arrives at Father Hidalgo's patio where a party is going on. He has a warning for Father Hidalgo. The class may plan such a party, with Mexican songs, dances, and decorations.

7. Suppose Father Hidalgo were living in your neighborhood to-day. Can you think of any changes he would try to make?

On his first voyage to the New World, Columbus discovered a beautiful island which he named Hispaniola (Iss-pahn-yoh′-lah). The island has had an exciting history. At one time, it was headquarters for the Spanish and English pirates who roamed the Carribean. Later on, Spain gave up part of the island to the French. When settlers arrived from France, they called the new colony Saint Domingue (Sant Doh-mang′). It grew very fast. Towns became cities. Roads and bridges were built. Mountain slopes were cleared and became coffee plantations. Large amounts of coffee and sugar were grown. Ships sailed off to Europe, loaded with these products. Then they sailed back, bringing European goods to the wealthy planters.

There was much work to be done in the busy colony. Some of the land was owned by Frenchmen who never even saw Hispaniola. They hired managers to run their plantations. But these managers didn't do the hard work. They went to the slave markets and bought slaves. Thousands of black people were brought from Africa and sold into slavery. They worked from dawn to dark. If they didn't work hard enough to satisfy the masters, they were beaten. Many died after four or five years of this treatment. But slave labor was cheap—there was always another boatload due to arrive from Africa.

One plantation where the slaves were not treated cruelly was called Bréda (Bray′-dah). The owner allowed the children of his slaves to learn reading and writing. Toussaint Bréda (Too′-san Bray′-dah) lived here. He was born on the religious holy day called All Saints' Day. In French, it is called *Toussaint*. That is how he got his first name. Like other slaves, his last name was the name of the plantation where he belonged.

When he was little, Toussaint did not have to work. He could go swimming in the river, and play with the other children. His

Rare Book Room/The New York Public Library

This is the way an artist imagined the scene when Columbus arrived at the island of Hispaniola.

father was coachman at Bréda, so Toussaint was allowed to ride the master's horses. One day, he and his brother went horseback riding. Toussaint fell off the horse. He broke a finger. The bone was not set properly. When the finger healed, it was curled out like a question mark.

Life at Bréda was better than at most plantations. Compared to other slaves, Toussaint was lucky. But one day, his little sister was taken away. She was only eight years old, but she had been sold to another planter. Her own father and mother could do nothing about it. Toussaint began to realize what it meant to be a slave. Even a well-treated slave had no control over his own life. Soon after that, Toussaint was put to work in the fields. But he managed to keep up his reading. He borrowed books from the manager of Bréda, and from a priest he knew. In one book he read something he would always remember. It was written by a Frenchman who had visited the colony. He warned the planters, ". . . your slaves will throw off the loads that weigh upon them. The Negroes only lack a leader. Where is that great man to be found? He will appear, we cannot doubt it . . . The name of this man will be blessed forever."

When his father, the coachman, was too old to work, the master of Bréda gave the job to Toussaint. Driving the coach was much better than working in the burning sun. One day, Toussaint was sent on an errand to one of the large towns. There he saw a scene he could never forget. A black man was being put to death in the town plaza, where everyone could watch him suffer. Toussaint learned the story. The man had visited France. There he had heard the slogan of the French Revolution: Liberty, Equality, and Fraternity. He came back to Saint Domingue with news of the revolution in France. He found a number of followers willing to fight for these same ideas. When the governor heard about their plans, he sent a large force of soldiers to teach the black men a lesson. The leader was captured. This was the man who was put to death. Toussaint realized that the man died for the cause of liberty.

The ideas of liberty and equality began to spread. A slave rebellion broke out. It was the largest and most important slave rebellion in the Western Hemisphere. Some plantations were looted and burned, and the managers and their families were killed. A whole section of Saint Domingue was ruined. Toussaint had been left in charge of Bréda plantation while the master was away. He drove the master's wife to a town where she would be safe. Then he took his own family to the Spanish part of the island. When they were settled, he went back to Saint Domingue. He organized a large army of rebellious slaves. He was determined to free all of his people.

This rebellion was only the beginning. For several years, there was fighting and bloodshed in all of Saint Domingue. Across the ocean, Spain and England were fighting bitterly against France because of the revolution going on there. English and Spanish troops fought in Saint Domingue against the French soldiers still there. A French official came from Paris in the name of the new revolution. He said the slaves were free. Toussaint's army stayed on the side of the French.

Toussaint was a great leader. His men respected him. When they went hungry, he went hungry. When they had to work hard, he was working right beside them. He joked and laughed with them, and kept up their courage. He seemed to have no fear for himself. Because they looked up to him, Toussaint's men were willing to follow his commands. He knew how bitterly they hated their cruel masters. Yet, when they captured an area, he allowed no burning or looting. And they obeyed his orders. He was no longer known as Toussaint Bréda. The French word for "opening" is *L'Ouverture* (Loo'-vehr-tour), and this is the name he took. It was a symbol of his dream—to open up a new life for his people.

Finally, the British were driven out. When the officer representing France left for Paris, Toussaint was put in charge of the colony. One day, he was visiting the northern part of Saint Domingue. He knew this was the area where his sister had been sent. That was forty years before, and they had not seen each other since. He sent out scouts among the freed slaves. They finally found her.

"It isn't possible," she told the messenger, "that my skinny little brother is now the ruler of the colony. Does one of his fingers curl upward? If it does, that can only be my Toussaint." She was taken to meet her brother. He was able to give her a pension and to help her children. Her son came to work for Toussaint, and her daughters went to live at Bréda.

Somehow, Toussaint had always found time for reading and learning. He had educated himself, and prepared himself to be a leader. For the short time he was in power, he accomplished wonders. He had the war-torn cities rebuilt, and the crops replanted. Almost all children were sent to school. Blacks, whites, and people of mixed blood were treated equally. He built up trade with the United States. An American official wrote: "Perfect peace has been restored to this colony. Former slaves are now working on the plantations for wages. The governor himself, a black man and former slave, is using the wisest measures to bring order and prosperity. Agriculture and trade are beginning to revive." A visitor from France said: "He has restored and improved the cities. He has built roads and replaced bridges destroyed during the fighting. He has made sure that Negroes and whites are given equal justice in the law courts. He has founded schools for the Negro children. He himself gives prizes to the best scholars. The amount of work this unusual man does is amazing."

On a hillside near Cap Haitien is a monument to the heroes of Haiti. Toussaint stands in front, with Dessalines and Christophe behind him. Soldiers and flag bearers are on each side.

Toussaint had sent his sons to school in France. "My sons will learn to read and write and act as gentlemen," he said. Toussaint himself lived like a gentleman. He gave receptions for important visitors from other countries. White planters and merchants were happy to be invited to these parties. They would chat politely with blacks who had been their slaves a few years before. When Toussaint arrived, everybody became quiet. The ruler of Saint Domingue wore a plain uniform with a few medals. As he went through the hall, officers saluted him. Men bowed to him, and ladies curtsied. He had the respect and loyalty of all his people.

Toussaint wrote a constitution for Saint Domingue. It did away with slavery forever. It also made Toussaint governor for life. Napoleon Bonaparte was ruling France at this time, and Toussaint sent him a copy of the constitution. But Napoleon had plans for Saint Domingue. He wanted to carve out an empire in the New World. The money from Saint Domingue's crops would pay the cost of supplying his army. He was told that the profits were higher when the slaves worked the plantations. So Napoleon decided to restore slavery. A war fleet would soon be on its way.

When Toussaint learned this, he sent a message to Napoleon: "You should hear of the prosperity of agriculture and commerce under my rule. It is by my work that I want to be judged. I have taken up arms for the liberty of the people of my color. Of all the nations, France alone proclaimed liberty for us. Now she can no longer do as she pleases with it. Liberty belongs to us. We shall know how to defend it or die."

Napoleon's answer was: "I will not leave an officer's uniform on a single black!" He went ahead with his plan. It had three steps:

1. The French general, Leclerc (Luh-claírk'), was to pretend to be Toussaint's friend.

2. He was to see that the black army was broken up. Then French troops could control the colony.

3. He was to arrest Toussaint.

Then Leclerc would rule Saint Domingue. He would return the plantations to the owners, and the blacks would again be slaves.

As it happened, Toussaint's sons were returning from their school in France. Napoleon gave them a letter for their father. When he read it, Toussaint was puzzled. It sounded like a friendly letter. Yet here was Leclerc, bringing an army to Saint Domingue.

One of Toussaint's generals was a former slave named Henri Christophe (Ahn-ree' Krees'-toff). His job was to keep the French fleet from landing. He even set fire to the port city. The French soldiers finally landed, but the war did not last long. Before one battle, a French general said to his men: "They are only slaves you have to fight today; they will flee in every direction. You have

The year is 1798 and Toussaint is in control of Saint Domingue. Here he is asking the English officers to leave the island.

not come eighteen hundred miles across the sea to allow your-selves to be beaten by slaves."

But the black soldiers won the battle. Many of Leclerc's men were killed or wounded. Then the rainy season came, and with it came yellow fever. The people of Saint Domingue were immune. But thousands of French soldiers became ill and died. Their army grew steadily weaker.

Toussaint knew that continuing the war would only mean more death and suffering. Peace talks were begun. Meanwhile, Leclerc managed to win over to his side Christophe and some other generals. He made them officers in the French army. This weakened Toussaint's position.

Now we come to step three in Napoleon's plan. Toussaint was invited to dinner at the home of a French officer. He trusted the man, and accepted. As soon as he entered the house, soldiers surrounded it. Suddenly the door opened. A French officer, armed with a pistol and a sword, came in. Behind him was a group of soldiers. As Toussaint leaped to his feet, he was warned: "If you resist, you are a dead man. Your power in Saint Domingue is at an end. Hand over your sword."

The soldiers took Toussaint's sword, and tied his hands be-hind his back. He was taken to the harbor and rowed to a war-ship. Then he was placed in a cabin and closely guarded. Several days later, his wife and sons were brought to the ship. The entire family was to be sent to prison in France. When he boarded the ship, Toussaint said: "In overthrowing me they have only cut down the tree of Negro liberty in Saint Domingue. It will shoot up again, for it is deeply rooted and its roots are many."

During the journey to France, Toussaint wrote to Napoleon: "Doubtless I owe this treatment to my color. But my color has not prevented me from serving my country with loyalty. Does the color of my skin affect my honor or my bravery?" As soon as the ship landed, Toussaint sent more letters. He was worried about his family. "I alone am responsible," he wrote.

Napoleon's orders were that the family would be separated. Toussaint was allowed to see them once more, to say goodbye. Then he was sent to a prison in the mountains near Switzerland. Toussaint was strong, and had never been sick, but he was not used to this climate. He had to live in a cold, damp cell. He soon became ill and died.

In Saint Domingue, there was another great uprising. Leclerc died of yellow fever. The French were finally driven out. Napoleon had to give up his plan for an empire in the New World. He agreed to sell a vast area of land to the United States. This was the Louisiana Purchase.

Saint Domingue became independent on January 1, 1804. One of Toussaint's generals, Jean Jacques Dessalines (Zhahn Zhahk Deh'-sahl-een), was the head of the new nation. He changed its name to Haiti, an Indian word meaning "mountainous."

Haiti was not only the first nation in Latin America to gain independence. She was also the first country to free her slaves. And so, in the life of Toussaint L'Ouverture we have the answer to a question. It was the question he had read when he was a young man: "The Negroes only lack a leader. Where is that great man to be found?"

As ruler of Haiti, Dessalines became the first head of an independent nation in Latin America. He was called "The Tiger" and ruled as an absolute dictator.

The Pan American Union

Vocabulary

plantation   reception   resist
coachman   prosperity   uprising
rebellion   immune

Thinking It Over

1. Refer back to your story of Aleijadinho. Compare his early life with Toussaint's. How are they alike?
2. Suppose you were Toussaint. What would you have done when the slave rebellion started?
3. Why is the story of Toussaint's broken finger important?
4. How did Toussaint prepare himself to be a leader?
5. What place of importance does Haiti hold in the Latin American fight for independence?

Other Leaders

Divide your class into five sections. Each section may choose one of the following men, and find as much information as possible about his part in Haiti's fight for independence:

> Thomas Jefferson
> LeClerc
> Napoleon Bonaparte
> Jean Jacques Dessalines
> Henri Christophe

Map Study

1. Locate the cities of Cap Haitien and Port-au-Prince.
2. Toussaint was put in prison at the fort of Joux in the Jura Mountains. On a map of Europe locate these mountains. Why

do you think Toussaint became ill so soon after being put in this prison?

3. On a map of the United States, find the area of the Louisiana Purchase. How many states grew out of this territory?

Activities

1. Look up some information on the French Revolution. Who was King? If no revolution had taken place in France, do you think Haiti would have begun its move toward independence?

2. How was the cause of yellow fever finally discovered? Is this disease a danger in the Caribbean today?

3. Refer to the section "Other Leaders." Have your class choose one student from each of the five sections. That student is to address the class as if he were Bonaparte, Jefferson, etc.

4. Prepare a report on present day life in Haiti. Try to find magazine or newspaper articles, and if possible, bring to class articles such as Haitian wood carvings. Be sure to include in your report answers to the following questions:

    a. Why do you think the people are not more prosperous?
    b. Why do so few of them speak clear French?
    c. Why are there so few school books?
    d. Why have the Haitians had so little contact with Spanish-Americans?

Pedro II
Emperador del Brasil

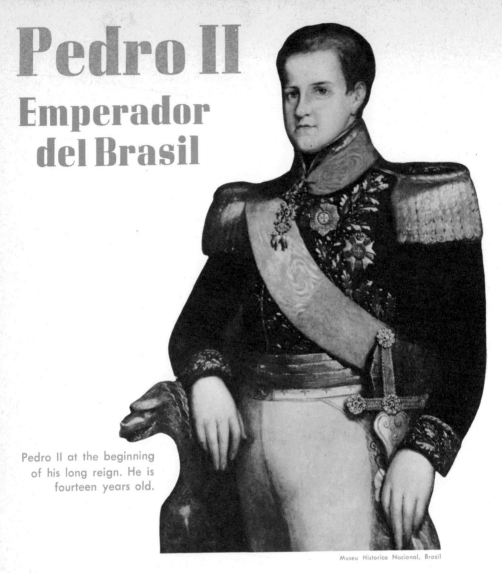

Pedro II at the beginning of his long reign. He is fourteen years old.

Museu Historico Nacional, Brazil

"Long live Pedro the Second, Emperor of Brazil!" shouted the excited crowd. Rio de Janeiro (Ree-oh day Jah'-nay-roh) was gay with flags and streamers. It was an April day in 1831, and all the streets were decorated with flowers. A parade, with horses and carriages, passed in front of the City Palace. People in the carriages threw flowers up at the palace balcony. On the balcony, standing on a chair so that he could see over the railing, was the new emperor. He was five years old! He smiled and waved to the crowds. In back of him stood the men who were going to help him rule the land.

How did it happen that Brazil had a little boy as its ruler? Why did this country have an emperor instead of a president? To answer these questions, we must go back to Portugal, and the year 1807. In that year, the ruler of Portugal was Prince John. His mother was the queen, but she was not well enough to rule the country. Napoleon's armies were marching through Europe, and they were on their way to Portugal. Prince John did not want to be captured by the French. He decided to leave the country and to take the whole government with him.

Statesmen, priests, soldiers, lords, and ladies packed up as much as they could. Together with the royal family, they boarded ships in Lisbon harbor. They didn't look very much like lords and ladies. It was pouring rain, and their fancy clothes were ruined. Some were carrying packages wrapped in newspaper. In the excitement, many of their trunks were left on the dock. They had little time to spare. When the French arrived in Lisbon, the sails of the Portuguese ships were just disappearing out to sea.

The small fleet headed for Brazil, Portugal's big colony in Latin America. Eight weeks later the ships arrived at Bahía. The people welcomed the royal family. Some of the lords and ladies were still wearing the laces and velvets they had on when they rushed away from Portugal. They had to borrow fresh clothes from the colonists. After a short time, they sailed on to Rio de Janeiro. Rio was the capital of colonial Brazil. Even then, it was a beautiful town.

It took six years to drive the French out of Portugal. Eventually, John had to go back and rule the mother country. His son, Pedro I, was in his early twenties. He stayed in Brazil to rule in his father's place. His father, King John, knew that almost all the people of Brazil wanted their country to break away from Portugal. He told his son Pedro I that he should lead the Brazilians in gaining their independence. When John left, he gave Pedro this advice: "If Brazil must separate herself from Portugal, let it be under you rather than under some unknown adventurer."

A year later, Pedro acted on his father's advice. He was making a tour of one of the provinces of Brazil. A horseman galloped up with a message. The news was bad: the Portuguese government was demanding more control over Brazil. Pedro pulled up his horse sharply. "Off with these emblems, soldiers," he commanded. He tore the Portuguese colors from his uniform and threw them on the ground. Waving his hat in the air, he shouted "Independence or death!" The date was September 7, 1822. Brazil has celebrated it ever since as her Independence Day.

Pedro I was crowned in Rio as Emperor of Brazil. The new nation was made up of seventeen provinces, with a constitution and a congress. Independence had been won without a battle. When his father, King John, died, Pedro I of Brazil was invited back to Portugal. Some of the Portuguese people wanted him to rule from their capital, Lisbon. But the Brazilians were afraid that

Brazil's first Independence Day. At the little stream of Ypiranga, Pedro I shouts "Independence or Death"—the *Grito de Ypiranga.*

Museu Paulista, Brazil

this would mean the end of their independence. As time went on they felt Pedro I was taking too much interest in Portugal. They became angry. One night great mobs of people gathered in the streets of Rio. It seemed there would be fighting and bloodshed. Pedro I decided to give up the throne of Brazil. He wrote a letter to his people, asking that his five-year-old son be made emperor. A few days later he sailed for Portugal.

This is how a five-year-old boy came to be an emperor in the New World. Pedro I had left a careful plan for his son's education. Advisors would help Pedro II rule the country until he was older.

It was a good thing young Pedro liked to study. This is the way he spent most of his days. He got up at six every morning, and went to church for Mass. After breakfast, his lessons started. He studied geography, science, mathematics, and history. He also had French and English lessons. By the time he was grown up, he had learned to speak fourteen languages!

Every day at lunch advisers and officials ate with him. They talked to him about problems of government. They encouraged him to ask questions about his country. After lunch, Pedro had to take a nap for two hours. When he woke up, he had to do his homework for the next day. At 4:30 P.M. he went horseback riding. Lessons in drawing, piano, and dancing had to be squeezed in somehow. Very often, important visitors came to dinner. The little boy had to sit at the head of the table and be polite to them.

While Pedro was studying hard, there was unrest and civil war in Brazil. But statesmen believed there was a way to end this unrest. If Pedro could be crowned at once, the country would feel united. But Pedro was only fourteen. The law said that he had to be eighteen years old to be crowned emperor. However, this fourteen-year-old boy was very grown-up for his age. He had more education than many of his advisers. For years he had been trained to be a good ruler. "I wish to be crowned now!" he said, and so it was decided.

Once again, Pedro came out on the palace balcony. The people cheered him as they had when he was five years old. This time he spoke to them: "Brazilians, the hopes of the nation have come true. A new age is beginning! May it be one of union and pros-

Pedro II, Emperor of Brazil, and his wife, the Empress Thereza. Brazil still honors him as a national hero.

Museu Histórico Nacional, Brazil

THE STRUGGLE FOR FREEDOM

perity! May we be worthy of such a great blessing." For three days, the Brazilians celebrated the crowning of their young emperor, Pedro II.

Pedro worked and studied harder than ever. The only fun he had was horseback riding. It was a lonely life, but he was too busy to feel sorry for himself. When he was eighteen, a bride was chosen for him. This was the custom at that time. She was Princess Thereza (Tay-ray'-zah) of Italy. Pedro had never met her, but he had seen a pretty picture of her. A date was set for the wedding, and a big fiesta was planned. Pedro could hardly wait for the princess to arrive.

When Pedro saw Thereza for the first time, he was disappointed. The artist who painted her picture had made her prettier than she really was. But Thereza was a loving person with a good disposition. They had a happy marriage. Pedro soon forgot his romantic dreams of a beautiful princess. At last the lonely young emperor had a companion to share his busy life.

When a baby son was born to the young couple, all of Brazil celebrated. Then a little girl, Princess Isabel, was born. Pedro and Thereza were very happy. But they had their share of sadness, too. The little boy died. Later, another son was born. He, too, died as a baby. Pedro wrote a poem which tells of his sorrow:

> Twice already I have suffered death
> For the father dies who sees his son die.
> On me has fallen the saddest of fates,
> In tender infancy I lacked father and mother,
> And now my little sons are dead.*

Pedro II ruled Brazil wisely and well for almost fifty years. There was peace in the land. Pedro II built the first railroads in Brazil. High schools and colleges were started, and museums and

* Reprinted from *Don Pedro the Magnanimous* by Mary Wilhelmine Williams. Permission granted by University of North Carolina Press.

libraries built. He encouraged people from Europe to settle in Brazil. There was much work to be done. The coffee industry was just beginning. Rubber from the Amazon region became an important product.

The emperor wanted to free all the slaves in Brazil. But he moved slowly. He was afraid that the rich slaveowners would start a civil war. First he freed the slaves he had owned. Then he declared that no more slaves could be brought into Brazil. Later he passed a law giving freedom to any child born to a slave. He wanted the young black people to get an education and find good jobs. He hoped that in this gradual way, slavery in Brazil would disappear.

Princess Isabel, Pedro's oldest daughter, was growing up. Now she was old enough to take his place while he was away. Pedro and Thereza decided to take a trip to Europe. The Emperor wanted to travel in disguise, but everyone recognized the tall, handsome, bearded man. The royal couple was expected to visit other kings and queens. But Pedro really wanted to meet all sorts of people. He talked to business men and factory workers. He wanted to learn ways to make Brazil an up-to-date country.

Pedro also visited the United States. On the ship he asked some Americans to teach him to speak English with a "Yankee accent." He planned to see something new and interesting every single day. It is amazing how much of the country he saw. He traveled by railroad all the way from New York to San Francisco. He sailed in a small boat all around San Francisco Bay to see how it compared to Rio's harbor.

Then Pedro returned to the east coast. He visited Boston. The first person he asked to see was the poet Longfellow. Pedro liked his poems, and had translated some of them into Portuguese. A few weeks later, Pedro was invited to a sort of world's fair in Phila-

Jean Debret drew this picture of a street scene in Brazil. Born in Paris, this artist lived and worked many years in Brazil during the time of Pedro I.

delphia. Among the new inventions shown was the telephone. Alexander Graham Bell was explaining it. Pedro had met Bell in Boston, where the inventor was teaching a class of deaf children. Pedro was interested in his methods. At the fair, he asked Bell to let him try the telephone. Bell went to the other end of the exhibit hall. Pedro could hear his voice on the telephone. "Good heavens, it talks!" he exclaimed.

While he was in America, Pedro wanted to visit factories and farms, and schools. "He wants to see the great world as a simple traveler, not as a king," wrote his friend Longfellow. "He is a hearty, pleasant, noble person."

Again, the Emperor went home with many new ideas for Brazil. He hoped to improve the cities. He wanted to fill the great empty spaces of the land with people. He wanted to see his country grow. But Pedro was no longer young. He had a disease called diabetes. His doctor advised him to go to Europe for treatment. Again, he turned over the government to Princess Isabel. Isabel thought the process of freeing the slaves in Brazil was too slow. With one stroke of the pen, she freed every slave in the country. When Pedro heard the news, he was proud. He was very ill, yet he told his wife: "Telegraph immediately to Isabel and give her my blessing. Send my congratulations to the nation and the Congress. What a great people the Brazilians are!"

Soon Pedro was well enough to return. He was welcomed by his people. But there was discontent in the air. The rich plantation owners were angry over the loss of their slaves. Another group wanted to make Brazil a republic without an emperor. Leaders of this group planned a quiet revolt. Late at night, they came to Pedro. They asked him and his family to go with them to the harbor. He didn't realize what was happening. A few people waved as he rode through the almost empty street. They thought he was just taking a drive before bedtime. But it was Pedro's last drive in Rio de Janeiro. He and his family were put on a ship. Soon they were out of the harbor and on the way to Portugal. The next day the people of Brazil were shocked when they heard about the plot.

Pedro and Thereza were broken hearted. If only he had been allowed to speak to the people, they would have wanted him to stay. He believed they would have kept him as their Emperor as long as he lived. But he never tried to go back. He said: "I shall never scheme to return, nor let anyone lead a plot in my name."

A month later, Thereza died. The Emperor was alone. He continued to study languages and geography. He wrote letters to friends all over the world. Famous writers and world travelers came to see him. And after two years, he, too, died. When news of the Emperor's death reached Brazil, people cried openly in the streets. Years would pass before the country was as well-governed again. Today, the people of Brazil honor the memory of Pedro the Second. He brought his country almost sixty years of peace and progress. Those years were Brazil's Golden Age.

Vocabulary

emperor	worthy	infancy
carriage	custom	industry
province	fate	republic
emblem		

Thinking It Over

1. Pretend you are one of the people who sailed away from Portugal with Prince John. Write a letter to a friend, telling how you felt. You may want to write about:

   Your experiences on the dock and on the ship
   Your opinion of Napoleon
   Your feelings about leaving your home country
   What you expected to see in Brazil

2. Pedro I was at a place called Ypiranga when he shouted: "Off with these emblems, soldiers!" Have a group of students act out this *Grito de Ypiranga*. Then have a group of students act out the *Grito de Dolores*.

3. Make up a daily program or schedule for the young Pedro II. Compare his day with yours. Would you like to change places? Why?

4. List the things Pedro II did for Brazil. Tell why each was important.

5. Divide the class into three groups. Each group will find information on one of the following topics. One student will be chosen to report to the class.

> The freeing of the slaves in Brazil
> The freeing of the slaves in the United States
> How do Brazilians feel about black people today?

After the reports have been made, you may wish to have a class discussion comparing attitudes in the United States with those in Brazil.

6. Pedro II invited people from Europe to settle in Brazil. Why do you think he did this? How is this similar to United States history in the 1870's?

Other Leaders

Try to find some information on these Brazilian leaders:

> José Bonifacio
> Joaquim Nabuco
> Getúlio Vargas

Map Study

1. Draw a map of Brazil. What are the largest cities there today? What is important about each one? How are cities in northern Brazil different from those in southern Brazil? Why are there no cities in the deep interior?

2. Pretend you were in charge of planning Pedro II's trip to the United States. Try to find out how much time he would need to travel across the country. Draw a map showing some of the stops he made.

Activities

Plan class projects on how coffee and rubber are grown and marketed today. Prepare maps showing where they are grown. Explain how they are harvested and how they are marketed. List the uses of each. Try to find pictures, articles, and advertisements to bring to class.

Benito Juárez Desde Pastor hasta Presidente

The Pan American Union

Orozco shows Juárez in a red cloud of victory after the 1857 revolution. Below him are the men he defeated, carrying the body of Maximilian.

Our story starts when Benito Juárez (Bay-nee'-toh Whah'-rays) was twelve years old. He was an orphan, and lived with his uncle. He took care of his uncle's sheep. For this, he was given a few corn cakes each day, and a blanket to sleep on. The family was very poor, and their home was a hut made of mud and straw.

Later he told about the little village in the hills of Mexico: "My village was so small, it had hardly twenty families. In those times hardly anyone was concerned with the education of youth. So there was no school. And there one hardly ever heard Spanish." The people were Zapotec (Sah'-poh-tehk) Indians. They had their own language, and they did not understand Spanish.

One day, while Benito was herding the sheep, he met some mule drivers. They had come from the nearest city, Oaxaca (Wah-hah'-kah). The men talked about the beautiful churches and homes, and the busy markets in the city. Benito listened, wide-eyed. Only after they left did he realize that one of his sheep was missing. How could he ever explain to his uncle? He promised his uncle that some day he would pay for the sheep. Years later, he wrote: "I fled from my house and walked on foot to the city of Oaxaca, where I arrived on the night of the same day." He didn't mention that the distance he walked that day was forty-one miles!

Some parts of Mexico look much as they did when Juárez was born in a little Zapotec village in the hills of the Sierra Madre.

Benito had a good reason for going to Oaxaca. He knew that parents who could afford it sent their children to live in Oaxaca so they could go to school. Benito wrote, "I became convinced that I could learn only by going to the city. I often urged my uncle to take me to Oaxaca. He did not do so. But he gave me hopes that some day he would take me there." Benito gave up those hopes. He decided to go to Oaxaca by himself.

Helen Miller Bailey

Zapotecan girls from the mountain valley of Ixtlan. They are at a fiesta where they will dance for the governor of Oaxaca. The embroidered designs on their dresses and their necklaces and bracelets are bright and colorful.

Benito knew one person in Oaxaca. He had an older sister who had left the village some time before. She worked for a rich family in Oaxaca. As soon as he arrived, he tried to find her. He met some Indians who knew her. They told him where she lived. When he found the house, it was so beautiful he was afraid to go to the front door. He went around to the back, and timidly knocked. His sister opened the door, but she didn't know him. It was a long time since they had seen each other. When she realized it was her young brother, Benito, she was glad to see him. Let him tell us what happened next: "I stayed in the house of Don Antonio Maza (Dohn Ahn-tohn'-ee-oh Mah'-sah) in which my sister, María Josefa (Mah-ree'-ah Hoh-say'-fah), was serving as a cook. During those first days, I was given a job by Don Antonio. At that time,

A folk dancer from the area where Juárez was born. He is wearing a costume for a dance called the *Plumeros*. Does his feathered headdress remind you of anything?

there lived in the city a religious and honorable bookbinder. He was named Don Antonio Salanueva (Dohn Ahn-tohn'-ee-oh Sahl-ah'-nway'-vah). He was interested in the education of youth. He received me into his house, offering to send me to school, so that I could learn to read and write. In this way, I found myself settled in Oaxaca." Of course, Benito wrote these words years later, when he had children of his own. He wanted them to know how it was when he was a boy. The book he wrote is called *Notes for My Children*.

Try to imagine what an experience this was for Benito Juárez. It was the first time the little Indian boy had been to the city. In all his dreams, he had never pictured such beautiful houses. And here he was, living in one! Even the work he did must have seemed strange to him. He "washed down the floors, ran errands, built the fire, watered plants in the patio, washed dishes, and waited on Don Antonio Salanueva at the table."

BENITO JUAREZ   123

In two years' time, Benito learned how to read and write, and to speak Spanish. Señor Salanueva could see that he was a good student. He decided to send Benito to the secondary school, and then to a college for priests. He thought it would be wonderful for the young Indian lad to become a priest. Then he could go back to the mountain village and help his people. Perhaps he would be another Father Hidalgo!

Benito studied at this college for seven years. Then a new college opened at Oaxaca. Benito realized that he did not want to be a priest. Don Antonio gave him permission to transfer to the new college. Now he would study law. The Indian people were not treated fairly in the courts. They needed lawyers to defend them and protect their rights.

While Benito was at law school, an important general named Santa Anna (Sahn'-tah Ahn'-nah) came to Oaxaca. He was honored at a dinner. Benito and other students acted as waiters. Benito did not know then that one day he and Santa Anna would be enemies. Benito became a successful lawyer in Oaxaca, and was made a judge. He still visited the Maza family. These were the people who had helped him when he first came to Oaxaca. They were really proud of this important man. They would never forget the day the barefoot Indian boy, tired and hungry, came knocking at their door. Now Benito asked permission to marry their daughter, Margarita (Mahr-gah-ree'-tah). She had known him all her life, and admired him. He was twenty years older than she, and not very handsome. In fact, Margarita said: "He is very homely, but very good." She was happy to become his wife.

Four years after his marriage, Juárez became Governor of the State of Oaxaca. He made many changes. Schools were built, and teachers trained to staff them. Only through education could the poor climb out of their poverty. He hoped that some day no Indian child would have to walk forty-one miles for the chance to go to school. There were other improvements, too. Roads and bridges were built. Juárez made sure that the government money was used wisely.

At this time, Santa Anna was President of Mexico. He was against everything Juárez wanted to do for the people. He called Juárez an ignorant Indian. Santa Anna said that Juárez encouraged the poor to make war on the rich. His soldiers arrested Juárez, and put him in prison. After twelve horrible days, he was put on a ship and sent to Havana. From there, he went to New Orleans where he lived in exile for over a year. He had no money, and it was hard to get work. He learned how to make cigars, and sold them on the streets at night. The little money he made was hardly enough for food. "Sometimes I went fishing in the Mississippi," he wrote. "When I had good luck, the catch lightened my misery."

A rebellion broke out against Santa Anna. At last, Juárez and the other exiles could return to Mexico. Santa Anna was forced to leave the country, and a new government took over. Juárez was given a high position. Now he could help to make important changes. He wrote what is known as the *Ley Juárez* (Lay Whah'-rays) or Juárez Law. This law reduced the power of the church and the military. It made everyone equal in the courts. A new constitution was written. It included ideas from the Juárez Law, and other changes planned to help the poor people. Many of these were the reforms that Father Hidalgo had fought for long ago.

Many people opposed the new constitution. Church leaders, military officers, and many wealthy people were against it. As soon as it was adopted, rebellions broke out. There was fighting in Mexico City. One president was forced out, and another one elected. At the same time, Juárez declared himself the President. Now Mexico had two presidents. A civil war, the War of the Reform, raged for three dreadful years. The other president was in Mexico City, so Juárez directed the government from the city of Vera Cruz. It seemed as if peace would never come.

While the war was raging, Napoleon III of France saw his opportunity. He would try to get control of Mexico. A number of Mexicans were in favor of having their country ruled by a king. They thought he would have more conservative ideas than Juárez. Napoleon suggested that they visit a young Austrian prince named Maximilian. Maximilian said he would be happy to rule Mexico, but only if the people wanted him as their king.

Napoleon sent French troops to prepare the way for Maximilian. Now the Mexican soldiers had to defend their country against the French. On the 5th of May, 1862—*Cinco de Mayo* (Seen'-koh day My'-yoh), the ragged patriots won a battle. In memory of that victory, *Cinco de Mayo* is a national holiday in Mexico. But more French troops landed, and the Mexicans were finally defeated. Juárez had been welcomed back to Mexico City as President a couple of years before. Now French soldiers were marching to the capital. He had to leave again. The great square in front of the National Palace was filled with sorrowful people. It was sundown. President Juárez stood on the balcony as the Mexican flag was slowly lowered. Then the flag was handed to Juárez. He lifted it to his lips. Suddenly, in a loud voice, he shouted, "Viva México!" (Vee-vah Meh'-hee-koh). The people took up the cry. "Viva México" echoed through the square. They hoped that "the little Indian," as they called Juárez, would soon be back in the capital as their President.

Ten days later, the French army took Mexico City. As the French troops advanced, Juárez moved farther north. After a year of this, he decided to send his family to the United States. Once again, Juárez had to say good-bye to his loved ones.

Maximilian was Archduke of Austria and Carlotta was a Belgian princess. They were still in Europe when these portraits were painted. The handsome young couple planned to wear these beautiful clothes when they were crowned Emperor and Empress of Mexico.

Maximilian was told that the followers of Juárez were a small minority. Maximilian and his pretty wife, Carlotta, believed that most of the people of Mexico wanted them. A welcoming parade was staged. People were hired to cheer and throw flowers in front of their carriage. They moved into Chapultepec (Chah-pool'-tay-pehk) Castle, high on the hill overlooking Mexico City. Today,

BENITO JUAREZ 127

The Aztecs worshiped their rain god on the hill where Chapultepec Castle is built. Years later a Christian chapel was built there. In turn it became a fortress, a military school, a Presidential Palace, and finally, a museum.

visitors to Mexico can wander through the castle. Carlotta's gold-inlaid furniture is still there. Carlotta loved to dress up for dances and parties given by the rich people of Mexico City. She and her handsome husband rode in a golden coach pulled by six white horses. Maximilian tried to be a good ruler. But he never really understood the Mexicans or their problems. Maximilian and Carlotta never even knew that most of their "subjects" really considered Benito Juárez the true head of Mexico.

Juárez' army continued to fight the French troops. The fighting moved south, closer and closer to Mexico City. Napoleon was having troubles at home, so he decided to take his soldiers out of Mexico. This left Maximilian and Carlotta unprotected. Carlotta thought she could talk Napoleon into changing his mind. She went all the way to Paris to see him. But it did no good. Poor Carlotta couldn't stand all this misfortune. She had to be put in a mental hospital. For sixty years, she waited for Maximilian to send for her. She never knew her husband's fate. Shortly after she left, he was captured and shot by a firing squad. It was a sad end to the romantic life that Carlotta and Maximilian had expected. They had trusted and believed in Napoleon III, but he betrayed the young couple.

After Maximilian was executed, Juárez returned to Mexico City. He was dressed in a plain black suit and a black stove-pipe hat like the one Lincoln wore. He rode in a black carriage drawn by two horses. How different from Carlotta's fancy coach! Both coaches stand side by side in Chapultepec Castle today. Meanwhile, Juárez' family had arrived in Mexico from the United States. They had not been together for three years. The President had a happy reunion with his wife and four of their children. There was sadness too—while they were in exile, two of their sons had died. In the United States, Doña Margarita won admiration and respect for herself and for her country. High officials in Washington, D.C., were kind and helpful. The Juárez family had many hard years of struggle and separation. Now they could hope for a life which would be peaceful.

Juárez served Mexico as its president until his death. He was almost seventy years old. Unfortunately, his work was not finished. He had hoped to bring about the changes provided for in the constitution. He had planned to give all the children a chance to go to school. He encouraged the country to build up industry. Most of Mexico's problems were still unsolved. Many people lived in poverty and ignorance. Not long after the death of Juárez, Mexico was under the control of a military dictator. Many years were to pass before his country would see the peace and progress Juárez had hoped for. But today, Benito Juárez is a real hero to most Mexicans. He was the soul of the reform. He will always be remembered as a champion of the people.

Vocabulary

bookbinder   ignorant   reform
poverty   exile   encourage

Thinking It Over

1. Make up a conversation between Benito Juárez and his sister, María Josefa. He has just arrived in Oaxaca. You may want them to talk about:

> Benito's reasons for coming to Oaxaca
> Benito's journey
> María Josefa's life in Oaxaca
> Their plans for Benito

2. List the reforms Juárez made while he was governor. Are there any places where some of these reforms are needed today? What can we do to bring about needed reforms?

3. What role did Santa Anna play in the life of Juárez.

4. Try to find the following information on Napoleon III:

> How did he influence the history of Mexico?
> What was his plan?
> Why did he call his troops home from Mexico?
> Compare his plan to that of Napoleon Bonaparte in the story of Toussaint.

5. Why is May 5 an important day in Mexican history? Is that day celebrated anywhere in the United States?

6. Juárez is sometimes called the "Lincoln" of Mexico. In a short talk, explain the reason for this.

7. Describe one of the important turning points in the life of Juárez.

Other Leaders

Find information on one of the following persons. Prepare a short talk, in which you will describe an important event in the life of that person.

> Abraham Lincoln
> Santa Anna
> Maximilian
> Carlotta
> Porfirio Díaz

Map Study

Find the following cities on a map of Mexico:

> Ciudad Juárez   Vera Cruz
> Oaxaca   Mexico City

Activities

1. Choose one member of your class to write a letter to a travel agency or to the Mexican Tourist Bureau. Ask them to send you some pictures of Oaxaca. Try to find the following information:

   > What old ruins are in Oaxaca?
   > How did the ancestors of Juárez live there before the time of Columbus?

   How do Indians in that region celebrate fiestas today?

2. Try to find pictures of the Castle of Chapultepec and bring them to class. The name Chapultepec refers to a hill known as the "Hill of the Grasshopper." Try to find out what was built here during the time of Montezuma.

THE ARTS IN THE NEW NATIONS

Today the Latin American nations are important in world affairs. Brazil is the center of the coffee industry. The great Amazon Basin is now being settled. Rio de Janeiro, São Paulo, and Bahía are busy modern cities. Brazilian architects have built a new capital in an area that was wilderness not too long ago. Would it surprise you to know that Brazil's people, who speak Portuguese, outnumber all the Spanish-speaking people in South America?

Argentina has become world famous as a center of the beef industry. Frozen beef from Argentina leaves Buenos Aires every day in big ships bound for Europe. People from Italy, Spain, Poland, England, and Switzerland have settled in Argentina. Buenos Aires is more modern than most cities in the United States.

Mexico has become as developed a nation as Argentina and Brazil. No longer do poor Indian peasants work for nothing. The reforms Father Hidalgo and Juárez worked for have finally come about. But many problems must still be solved.

In the Latin American countries, the rich people are very rich, and the poor people are very poor. It is hard for people to change from the old ways of living to life in an industrial society. Families from the country farms or from the big plantations move in to the cities. Often they are able to find jobs, but many of them have to live in shantytowns and slums. Homes must be built for these people. Sometimes their children do not have decent clothes to wear to school, or even enough to eat. Some way must be found so that each person will have enough to eat, clothes to wear, a home, and the chance to get an education.

The Latin American nations, along with the United States, belong to the Organization of American States. Representatives of each nation meet in a building in Washington, D.C. It is called the Pan American Union. Here the different countries work together to try to find answers to their problems.

Latin America is a land of contrasts. Jet planes fly to the big cities. Railroads have been built across the Andes. The Pan American Highway runs from Bogotá, Colombia, to Santiago, Chile. Engineers are planning new airfields and building more roads. Yet, driving along these roads you will pass sleepy villages. The modern world has not changed them. You may see a little boy leading a mule burdened down with a load of firewood. A woman walks to a nearby stream. On her head she balances a basket, filled with the family wash.

Do you like snowy mountain peaks, or hot sandy beaches? Latin America has both. It has the longest river in the world, and a waterfall higher and wider than Niagara. It has ancient pyramids and modern skyscrapers.

It is no wonder that this beautiful land has its painters and poets, its musicians and its architects. You will meet four of them now. Each one has something to say to you about Latin America.

José Clemente Orozco
Muralista de Fama Mundial

Orozco painted Quetzacoatl as a blue-eyed, bearded man. In back of him, the old Aztec gods parade across the sky. The God of Fire is rising out of a volcano. Below Quetzacoatl are the pyramids of Teotihuacán. Some of the Aztecs in the front of the mural are sleeping, others are talking together.

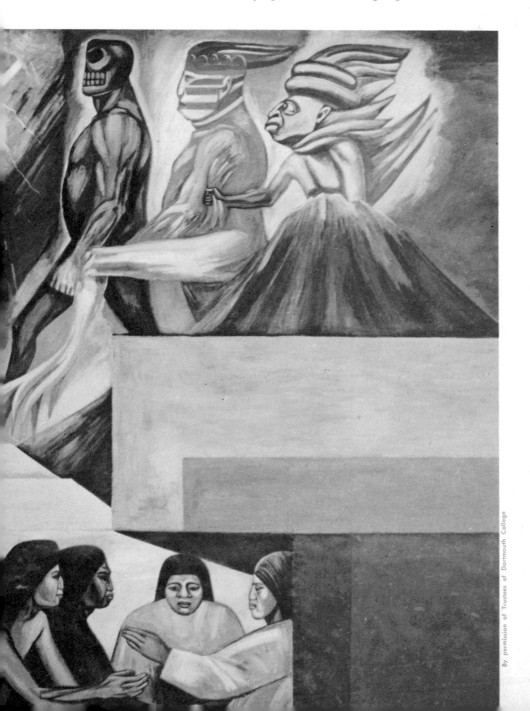

135

Can you imagine a boy with only one hand, and poor eyesight, becoming a great painter? Such is the story of José Clemente Orozco (Hoh-say' Clay-mayn'-tay Oh-rohs'-koh). He was born in Mexico in 1883. His father had been a wealthy man, but his business failed. The family had to move from their home near Guadalajara to rented rooms in Mexico City. Across the street was a printing shop.

Clemente spent a lot of time watching the artist at work in the printing shop. The artist drew pictures on metal plates, using a sharp tool. This is called engraving. Black and white pictures were printed from the plates. Then the artist's helpers used stencils to color in the pictures. When he wrote the story of his life, José Clemente Orozco said: "This was my awakening to the existence of the art of painting. This was the push that first set my imagination in motion and impelled me to cover paper with my earliest little figures."

Clemente begged his mother to let him take drawing lessons. She took him to the director of an art school. She asked if her son could attend classes at night. The director said: "Why, this little child is hardly old enough to be in primary school." When he looked at some of Clemente's pictures, he said: "Well, he can come and sit with the evening classes. But he cannot enroll, because he is so young." Clemente's family was proud of the little boy. His sister, Rosa, said: "He faithfully carried out the professor's directions. Before many weeks had passed, the academy's director called at our home. He came to inform my mother that her young son was drawing better than the older students. To the director's amazement, he was drawing even better than many of the teachers. At this point, Clemente was regularly enrolled in the art school. My mother made him an artist's smock with long sleeves to protect his clothes from the paint and charcoal."

Clemente's art lessons went on until he finished primary school. Then he received a scholarship to the School of Agriculture. No more art school for Clemente! His family did not have very much money, and art school was expensive. He would have to study subjects like surveying and irrigation. His father thought this would be better training for his son. One part of his course was interesting to Clemente. He had to draw maps showing exactly how the fields were laid out. Naturally, he was very good at this. By the time he was seventeen, he was earning money by making these maps for the government.

Next, he went to a school of architecture. At least, as an architect, he could use his talent for drawing. But, more than anything else, he wanted to be an artist. Then came tragedy. One day, Clemente and some friends tried an experiment. They wanted to make powder for fireworks. Suddenly, the chemicals exploded in Clemente's hands. Rosa told a friend that "every effort was made to save his left hand. But at last the doctors had to amputate it at the wrist. For all the days of his life, the palm of his powerful right hand showed deep scars. His vision also was weakened as a result of the accident. He had to wear thick glasses all the rest

Although Orozco is most famous for his murals, he has done many paintings on canvas as well. Here you see him, working on a painting called "Landscape."

Rapho-Guillumette

of his life." Yet years later Orozco said, "After the terrible accident I felt a sense of relief. Now at last I was free to become a painter."

A few years after his accident, Clemente left school and began to work full time as an artist. Half of the money he earned he gave to his mother. He used part of his earnings to pay for art lessons. He went to class for five hours almost every night. Most of Clemente's teachers were from Europe. They thought that all art students should learn by copying the old European masters. But one of the teachers, Dr. Atl (Ah'-tull), was a Mexican who had been educated in Italy. He told the students about the works of Michelangelo and Leonardo da Vinci. He described the beautiful paintings on the walls of the churches in Italy. These paintings are called frescoes. Dr. Atl encouraged the young artists to experiment with this kind of painting. He also suggested using scenes from Mexico's history. He felt this would help the Mexican people to take pride in their past.

The year was 1910—one hundred years after Father Hidalgo's *Grito* for independence. There was to be a big celebration. An art show was set up. But all the pictures in the show were from Spain! The Mexican artists were furious. They set up their own art show. In it were paintings and sculptures of Mexico, showing its people, its heroes, and its history. The exhibit was a success. Clemente and some other artists were asked to decorate a school with frescoes. They were all ready to start when a revolution broke out.

It was a rebellion against the dictator, Porfirio Díaz (Pohr-fee'-ree-oh Dee'-ahs). He was the man who came to office after Juárez. He ruled Mexico for thirty years. For the poor people, times were as bad as they had been under the old Spanish rule. A few people owned almost all the land. Foreigners were better off in Mexico than the Mexicans themselves. It was as if Father Hidalgo and Juárez had never existed. The rebellion led to a civil

This painting by Orozco is called *Zapatistas*. It shows the men who joined the rebellion against Porfirio Díaz. Their leader, Emiliano Zapata, wanted the land to be divided among the people.

war. Men fought to divide the land more equally. They wanted to bring democracy to Mexico. Soldiers, farmers, and cowboys fought each other bitterly. People were left homeless; children went hungry. More and more men died in the fighting. And yet, the war went on for almost ten years. It became too dangerous to live in Mexico City. Orozco moved to another town. There he worked for a newspaper, drawing cartoons. As he watched the hardship and suffering caused by the revolution, he became more and more discouraged. Then he was warned that the government officials were angry at his newspaper cartoons. At this point, he decided to leave Mexico and go to the United States.

JOSE CLEMENTE OROZCO 139

He did not return to Mexico until 1920, when the revolution ended. The new president tried to improve conditions in Mexico. He and his officials wanted the Mexican people to be proud of their country. The man in charge of education had a good idea. He wanted to cover the walls of schools and government buildings with paintings. They would show scenes from Mexican history. In this way, the Mexicans could learn about their heroes and the history of their country. Of course, he wanted Mexican artists to do the painting.

This fresco is being painted on a wall in Chapultepec Castle. Sheets of tracing paper are rolled up near the top. On the lower part of the wall, you can see the outlines which the artist will fill in. A workman has just put fresh plaster on the unfinished part of the mural.

140

This was what José Clemente Orozco always wanted to do. He read all he could find about the methods used by Michelangelo in painting frescoes. He talked with builders and plasterers. Then he was ready to begin. First he made sketches on large sheets of paper. The pictures had to be big enough to cover a whole wall. The wall was coated with fresh white plaster. On the wall he traced the outlines of the figures in his picture. Then a workman covered a section of the wall with a very thin coat of plaster. The outlines still showed through. Orozco had to paint his picture while the plaster was wet. He worked on a section at a time. Part of the time, he worked on a scaffold to reach to the top of the wall. He mixed his own paints, and poured each color into a small bucket. These were hung on a frame which he hooked over the stub of his left arm. Then he climbed on the scaffold, holding on with his right hand. He had to hold his brushes in his teeth! Fresco painting is such hard work that very few artists attempt it. Yet Orozco, with only one hand, became one of the greatest fresco painters of all time.

For seven years, Orozco painted scenes from his country's history on the walls of new buildings in Mexico. The pictures were not pretty. Some of them showed the horrors of war. He painted thin, hungry children, wounded soldiers, weeping mothers. The murals were Orozco's way of telling the people that war is evil. Visiting Americans came back to the United States with stories of this great artist. Then Pomona College in California asked him to paint a mural for one of its buildings. He came to California, and lived with the students at the college. They helped him mix paint and put the thin wet plaster on the section he worked each day. The mural showed a Greek god bringing fire down from the sky as a gift to the people on earth. All the people around the god looked thin, hungry, and unhappy. Many of the students objected.

This is a detail from the mural painted by Orozco at Pomona College, California, in 1930.

Orozco explained to the students that most of the people in the world have always been hungry and unhappy.

Art experts in the United States were impressed by Orozco's mural. Newspaper articles were written, praising his work. Then Orozco received a letter from Dartmouth College, in New Hampshire. The directors there asked him to paint a series of murals in the library. Orozco brought his wife and three children to New Hampshire. It was their first visit to this part of the United States. The children loved the cold New England winter, and all the snow. They went sledding and ice skating. While they were enjoying themselves, their father was busily at work. He covered the walls of the Dartmouth Library with big sweeping pictures of Quetzalcoatl. He showed the great pyramids of the Aztecs. In these wall paintings, you can follow the story of the coming of the

Spaniards to Mexico under Cortés. Some of the paintings show our modern machine-age world. All of them are filled with powerful figures, painted in violent colors.

When Orozco had the chance to go to Europe, he studied the great frescoes of Michelangelo and Leonardo da Vinci. He came back to Mexico full of new ideas. He was kept busy all the rest of his life, doing the work he loved. He painted a series of scenes from the life of Father Hidalgo. In the pictures, the Mexican people are stretching out strong hands to Father Hidalgo, who reaches out to hold up the banner of freedom. His hands are shown large and strong, too. Many of the figures in Orozco's paintings have powerful hands. Perhaps because of his accident, Orozco saw a man's hands as a symbol of strength.

Chapultepec Castle, where Maximilian and Carlotta had lived, was to be a museum. Orozco was asked to paint a mural in it. It shows scenes from the life of Benito Juárez, and his struggle against Maximilian. Orozco had hardly finished this when he had more jobs to do. Low-rent apartment houses had just been built. Orozco was to paint murals on the outside walls. He was also working on some school buildings.

The year was 1949 and Orozco was 65 years old. He was happily working on several jobs at once. He still did all the work himself, even when it meant climbing high up on the scaffolding. One day he felt tired. He was working on the housing project, painting a gay, colorful picture called "Spring." For the first time in his life he stopped before finishing a section. He climbed down and went to lie on the grass. One of his sons came to help him home. During the night, Orozco's tired heart just stopped beating.

All Mexico mourned him. Mexico City's largest newspaper printed an edition called "Our Homage to Orozco." They called him the "most creative artist in the whole Western Hemisphere."

He caught the very spirit of Mexico. All of her history and all of her people are in his paintings. And as long as those buildings stand, the story of Mexico will not be forgotten.

Vocabulary

impel

surveying

irrigation

architecture

fresco

scaffold

homage

creative

Thinking It Over

1. How did José Orozco's accident happen? How did it change his life?
2. Do you think all paintings should be pretty to look at? What did Orozco think? What did Orozco picture in his murals?
3. What murals by Orozco can be seen in the United States?
4. Describe the method he used in painting murals.
5. How did Orozco show his love for Mexico?

Other Leaders

Choose one of the following men and prepare a report on his life:

Álvaro Obregón

Porfirio Díaz

Diego Rivera

José Vasconcelos

Pancho Villa

Emiliano Zapata

Activities

1. If possible, visit a local newspaper or printing company. Or you may get some information on printing and engraving from an encyclopedia. Be prepared to tell the class what you learned. Try to find newspaper or magazine clippings to make your talk more interesting.

2. Using poster paints and large sheets of wrapping paper, make a mural for your classroom wall. The mural should have a theme. You may vote on the theme. It might be one of these:

> One of the stories in this book
> Neighborhood activities
> Coming events in your school
> Games and sports

3. Are there any murals in the public buildings in your city or town? If possible, visit one of these and prepare a report for your class. Some students may wish to photograph or sketch these murals.

4. Get some information on Michelangelo and his fresco paintings.

5. Are there any art schools in your city? Try to get some information on scholarships for students who are interested in art.

Gabriela Mistral

Open Air School by Ramon Alva Guadarrama, photo by Manuel Alvarez Bravo

Ramón Alva Guadarrama painted this mural in a school building in Mexico City. The school was designed and built by Juan O'Gorman.

What could you tell about the author after reading the above poem? If you guessed that she loved children, you were right. If you guessed that she loved the clouds, the stars, and all of nature, you were right again. The poem was written by a woman who was a school teacher as well as a poet. She was born in a small town in Chile. Her father had been a wandering poet and singer who was part Spanish and part Indian. He had come down from the high Andes to teach at a village school in the valley.

Maestra y Poeta

There he met and married a pretty young lady from a rich family. They had a baby girl, Lucila Godoy (Loo-see′-la Goh-doy′).

One day, when Lucila was about four, her mother dressed her in a beautiful blue dress. It was trimmed with lacy ruffles. Then she put flowers in her daughter's hair. Lucila was going to visit her wealthy grandmother. When they arrived, the grandmother made fun of Lucila. She said the little girl looked like an Indian. She said she couldn't be proud of a child whose father was a worthless man from the hills. Lucila began to cry. All her life she remembered how her grandmother hurt her feelings that day.

Lucila was very proud of her father. He taught in the village school, and he could make up songs and verses. He was always asked to sing these songs at the village fiestas. Lucila liked to go with him. She knew all his songs by heart and loved to sing along with her father. But Señor Godoy knew his wife's relatives looked down on him. They felt that the marriage was a mistake. He became depressed and discouraged and he started to drink a great deal. He stayed away from his job for days at a time. Finally he left home. Lucila never saw her father again.

Lucila's mother had to go to work. She was a school teacher, too, and she helped the shy little girl with her lessons. Lucila went to the village school. She was so timid and quiet the teacher thought she was dull. But Lucila was far from dull. By the time she was fifteen, she had finished school. Each little town had a school, but it was hard to find teachers. Another village, twelve miles away, needed a teacher. They had thirty-eight children in the eight grades of their school. They offered the job to Lucila. Every morning, she walked or rode horseback through the countryside to the school. Sometimes she stayed late to prepare lessons or mark papers. Then she walked home by the light of the stars. Lucila was a good teacher. She invented games so the children would have fun while they were learning. She made up verses to help them with their reading. Even arithmetic was fun when Lucila taught it.

When she was eighteen, Lucila fell in love with a young man who worked for the railroad. They became engaged and planned to marry. Lucila was happy. She loved children, and she hoped to have a large family some day. But the young man thought he didn't have enough money to get married. It was his job to collect fares from the railroad passengers. He "borrowed" some of this money and used it to bet on the horse races. He was sure he would win. Then he could give back the money he had stolen. With the rest of his winnings, he could buy nice things for Lucila. But instead of winning, he lost. He knew his theft would be discovered. The thought of the disgrace was too much for him. The desperate boy killed himself.

When Lucila was told that her sweetheart had died in this tragic way, she was heartbroken. She could not bear to go on living in the village where everyone knew the sad story. She and her mother moved to a larger town. There she went on with her studies, and became a high school teacher.

From the time she was a little girl, Lucila loved poetry. Her father's poems and songs were part of her childhood memories. She had already begun to write poetry herself. She wrote about the beauties of the countryside, about her pupils, and about her lost love. A poetry contest was to be held in Santiago (Sahn-tee-ah'-goh), the capital city of Chile. She decided to enter it, but

149

The University of Chile in Santiago is the largest college in Chile. Santiago is a beautiful city with many parks. It was founded in 1541 by one of Pizarro's men, Pedro de Valdivia.

DPI/Jerry Frank

she was shy about using her own name. She decided to make up a "pen name." What should it be? She thought and thought. Some of her father's songs told about the angel Gabriel. He was a messenger between God and men. Once she read a poem which mentioned the wind that blows through southern France. It is called a *mistral*. She put them together: "Gabriela Mistral (Gah-bree-ay'lah Mees-trahl)." She liked the musical sound of it, and it had poetic meaning. That would be her "pen name."

Lucila, as Gabriela Mistral, won first prize in the contest. She was supposed to come and accept a gold medal. But if she did, everyone would know that Gabriela Mistral was really Lucila Godoy! So she asked a friend to take her place. Lucila slipped quietly into the meeting and sat in a back seat. She was so nervous that her hands and feet were like ice. No one recognized her. We are told that she had an air of "loneliness and mystery." Imagine how thrilled Lucila was to hear the applause when the poems of Gabriela Mistral were read! From now on she would use her new name.

Gabriela Mistral did not remain unknown for long. Her poems and writings were printed in newspapers and magazines. People also realized that she was an excellent teacher. School officials became interested in the games she made up to teach spelling and arithmetic. She was asked to explain her methods to young teachers. Her fame spread beyond her own country. This was 1922, when the government of Mexico was trying to improve the schools. Many teachers were needed. Gabriela was asked to go there to train Mexican girls to be teachers. She was glad for any opportunity to help children. She was so well thought of in Mexico that a new school was named for her.

A professor at Columbia University in New York read some of her poems to his classes. So many students asked for copies that he wrote to Gabriela. He asked for permission to put all her poems in a book. She agreed, and the book was printed in the United States. It was sold not only here, but in the Latin American countries, and even in Spain. The government of Chile was very proud of Gabriela Mistral. In 1923, it gave her the title of "Teacher of the Nation." In 1926, the President of Chile sent her to Europe to work with the League of Nations. She helped to translate poems and stories of different countries so that all the world could read and enjoy them.

These school children are visiting a museum in Mexico City. Gabriela Mistral spent some time in Mexico, training young girls to be teachers.

Gabriela went on to do many things. She taught Spanish in colleges in the United States. She served as Chilean consul in various countries in Europe. It was her job to help Chileans who were in trouble while in a foreign country. It was very unusual for a Latin American woman to have a job like this. Gabriela also gave lectures to teachers in other countries. But her main interest was in children. While she was consul in Lisbon, she studied Portuguese. She wanted to be able to speak to the school children there, and in Brazil. She wrote this letter to some children in Rio after a visit there: "I am grateful to you for the day I spent in your school. We exchanged stories of your childhood and mine. We tossed the stories from hand to hand like playthings as we chatted together like members of one family. I liked your songs about your own people, your forests, your wilderness, and your parks. You are the children of the New World."

An artist named López Mesquita painted this picture of Gabriela Mistral in 1935, while she was serving as consul in Madrid, Spain.

Courtesy of the Hispanic Society of America

Gabriela Mistral looks happy as she shakes hands with Adlai Stevenson. They are being honored at Columbia University, New York. In 1952, Stevenson ran for the office of President of the United States.

Gabriela's poems and articles were translated into many languages. They were read all over the world. Then, in 1945, a wonderful thing happened. The Nobel Prize for Literature was awarded to Gabriela Mistral! To receive this honor is the dream of every writer. Who would have thought the little country school teacher would be the first Latin American to receive the Nobel Prize? She went to Stockholm, Sweden, for the award. The King and Queen honored her at a dinner. An American reporter described her as "a tall, handsome woman with strong features, dark hair, and a charming smile."

She died twelve years later. Her life had been busy and satisfying. She was interested in all sorts of things—art, religion, politics. She wanted to awaken everyone to the importance of truth and goodness, justice and morality. But most of all she was interested in children. All the love she would have given to children of her own, she spent on children all over the world.

Vocabulary

disgrace   tragic   morality
desperate   consul

Thinking It Over

1. What kind of person do you think Gabriela's grandmother was? Why did she laugh at Gabriela? How do you think this may have affected Gabriela's life?
2. How did Gabriela's misfortunes help shape her life?
3. Why did she change her name from Lucila Godoy to Gabriela Mistral?
4. In what other places besides Chile did she teach? What other important jobs did she hold?
5. Why is she remembered? What made her great?
6. Do you think her life was happy or sad?

Other Leaders

Following is a list of well-known women. See if you can find out why they are famous:

Madame Calderón   Vikki Carr
   de la Barca   Emily Dickinson
Marie Curie   Señora Salomé Ureña de
Señora González Videla   Henríquez
Amelia Earhart   Althea Gibson
Indira Gandhi

Activities

1. Make up a poem about your friends, your family, your school, or your teacher.

2. Interview one of the teachers in your school. Ask the following questions:

   > How did you happen to become a teacher?
   > What kind of training did you have to have?
   > Have you thought of any new methods to use in your teaching?

   Report to the class the result of your interviews. There may then be a class discussion, comparing Gabriela's experience with that of present day teachers.

3. What would you have to do to become a teacher? Try to get some information on scholarships available for students interested in teaching.

4. Make up a pen name for yourself. Write a short paragraph explaining why you chose that name.

5. What writer from Latin America has recently won the Nobel Prize for literature? Get some information on his life and work.

6. Can you translate into Spanish the poem which opened our story?

7. Try to find some other poems by Gabriela Mistral. (These can be found in a book called *Selected Poems of Gabriela Mistral* translated by Langston Hughes, Indiana University Press, 1957.) Choose a poem which has a special appeal for you. Memorize it, or read it to the class. Can you translate it back into Spanish?

Heitor Villa-Lobos Creador de Música

✿ Every school child in Rio was getting ready for the "big sing." They were celebrating Brazil's Independence Day, September 7. It was springtime in Brazil, and all the children were dressed in white. The boys wore white shirts. If a girl did not own a white dress, her mother made her one.

That morning, the children marched class by class from all the schools in the city. Their teachers led them to the big soccer stadium. There, high on a platform, stood the famous Brazilian composer, Heitor Villa-Lobos (Hay′-ee-tohr Vee′-yah Loh′-bohs). He was going to lead them in a concert. The teachers were nervous because the children had never studied music in school. But Villa-Lobos was not worried. He didn't think children should learn about music from books. He said children should "learn melody and feel harmony not by rules on paper, but by the sounds in their ears."

This is what he did: When he held his fingers up, he wanted the children to go up the musical scale. When he held them down, they were to go down the scale. One finger meant one step up or down, two fingers meant two steps. All 25,000 children sang out loud and clear. They followed the movements of his hands without any trouble. All the songs they sang that day were by Villa-Lobos himself. They were songs about the forests, the rivers, and the towns of Brazil. Some were about Brazilian birds singing, and Brazilian children playing. A song the younger children loved told about a little steam engine puffing along near the edge of the jungle.

The "big sing" was so successful that the teachers asked Villa-Lobos to teach them his methods. President Vargas (Vahr′-gahs) of Brazil set up a music school for teachers. Villa-Lobos taught there, and wrote music books that the children could understand

and enjoy. He believed that every child could learn to sing and to enjoy good music.

From the time Heitor Villa-Lobos was a little boy, his parents knew he was musical. His father was a music teacher who played the violin and the cello. Heitor could name any note his father played. He could even translate the sounds he heard around him to notes on the scale. He could pick out on the piano the very note that matched the twang of a rubber band, or the "ping" of a knife on an empty glass. When he was old enough to read and write, his father taught him how to write musical notes. Now he could keep track of all the songs he had in his head. He heard music in the sounds of Rio de Janeiro, the capital of Brazil, where he lived. Factory whistles, trolley cars rattling in the streets, honking automobile horns—Villa-Lobos put them all in his songs.

His father died when Heitor was only eleven years old. In order to stay in school, he now had to make some money. Luckily,

Heitor Villa-Lobos is playing an instrument used in Brazilian folk music. It is called a *Piu*. The musical sound is made by lengthening and then loosening the string, as he is doing here.

he had already learned to play several instruments. He was able to get a part-time job with an orchestra. Heitor enjoyed popular music, but he was especially interested in the folk songs of Brazil. When he finished high school, he wanted to study this kind of music. There was only one way to do this. He had to travel around the country and listen to all the folk songs. The songs in the north were different from the songs in the south. Most of them had never been written down.

One day he saw an ad in the newspaper. A group of scientists were going to survey the Amazon River Valley. They would take young men with them if they could share the expenses. Heitor knew this was his opportunity! But he needed money. He asked his mother if he could sell his father's collection of music books. She said it would be all right, but she couldn't imagine why he would want to go exploring. He was a musician, not a scientist!

Heitor joined the expedition. They sailed along the coast of Brazil to Belém (Bay-laym'), at the mouth of the Amazon. Here they boarded a river steamer. The scientists wanted to map the streams that flowed into the Amazon. Heitor was interested in the Indian villages along the river. This was country that had never been explored. The Indians were living just as their ancestors did, before the Portuguese ever came.

The sounds that Heitor heard were very different from the sounds of Rio. The water lapping against the boats made its own rhythm. Wild jungle birds screeched overhead. The dark nights were alive with the calls of animals. The Indians had their own special music. They used hollow gourds with dried seeds rattling inside. They made small wooden boxes and filled them with pebbles for a different sound. Drums were made by stretching animal skins over clay pots. Villa-Lobos wrote down all the Indian songs. He watched their dances, and learned their old legends.

When the time came for the scientists to return, Villa-Lobos did not go with them. Instead, he sailed slowly down the Amazon, stopping at every village along the way. He played his cello in exchange for food and lodging. And he listened to the songs of the people and copied them down. Finally he got back to Belém. He stayed in this area for several years. He worked his way down to Bahía, playing in theaters or in orchestras to support himself. It was carnival time in Bahía when he arrived. In each section of the city, the people made up a new song for the carnival. Then they put on costumes and masks, and paraded through the streets, singing and dancing. Usually all the new carnival songs were forgotten once the carnival was over. But Villa-Lobos wrote them all down. He wrote arrangements for violin, cellos, horns, and drums, so the folk music could be played by an orchestra.

Besides collecting folk songs, Villa-Lobos wrote hundreds of original musical pieces. When he returned to Rio, he gave a concert, playing his own music. But very few people appreciated his talent. He had to take a job with an orchestra in a movie theater. These were the days of silent films. Theater owners hired musicians to play "mood music" to fit the story on the screen. One lucky day, Artur Rubinstein, a famous pianist, dropped into the theater. Rubinstein was making a concert tour in South America. When he heard some of Villa-Lobos' exciting music, he asked to meet the composer. Villa-Lobos arrived at Rubinstein's hotel—with his whole orchestra! The longer they played, the more enthusiastic Rubinstein became. He knew this was real talent. He suggested that Villa-Lobos go to Paris for more training. Rubinstein persuaded the government to give him the necessary money, and Villa-Lobos went to France. He studied there for a year. But he really wanted to show the European musicians what he himself had done. He spent several years in Europe giving concerts in

Some Indians of Brazil still live a primitive life. These musicians are using the same kind of instruments their ancestors used.

The Pan American Union

The young girls below are taking part in a colorful carnival in Rio de Janeiro.

Black Star

161

different countries. He became "the fresh new voice from the New World." His music was different from anything the Europeans had ever heard.

Villa-Lobos was a famous man when he returned to Brazil. He then began the Independence Day concerts for the school children. He had great energy and enthusiasm. He was conducting orchestras all over South America, teaching and composing. No one seems to know how many musical pieces he wrote. His works include operas, ballets, symphonies, and music for movies. A lot of his work was done especially for children. He wrote a musical fairy tale, and a piece which is a list of toys and dolls. He wrote some of his pieces so that they would be easy enough for a child to play on the piano.

One day, an American writer showed Villa-Lobos a picture of the New York City skyline. He asked the composer if he could "set the picture to music." Villa-Lobos actually traced the ups and downs of the buildings on graph paper. Then he turned this graph into musical notes. Naturally, he called the piece "The New York

This is the New York skyline which Villa-Lobos "set to music." Across it are a few bars of music he wrote. Do you think you would be able to hear music in the sounds of a big city?

Skyline." It was played at the New York World's Fair in 1940. A few years later, Villa-Lobos came to the United States, and had his first look at the famous skyline. In the United States, musicians held a "Villa-Lobos Week." Symphony orchestras played his works and Villa-Lobos conducted. Some of the pieces called for the Indian drums and gourd rattles. Villa-Lobos knew other orchestras would not have these odd instruments, so he brought them with him. Then he had to teach the musicians how to play them. He considered the United States his second home. He liked its people, its skyscrapers—and its ice cream!

All the honors he received did not change Villa-Lobos. He wasn't really interested in becoming rich and famous. His main interest was his music. Beyond that, he was a good-natured man who enjoyed playing billiards with his friends, smoking big cigars, and making jokes. Once he was invited to a dinner party. In his honor, Brazil's national dish, feojada (fay-oh-jah'-dah), was served. Villa-Lobos enjoyed it so much, he wrote a musical piece to praise it. The piece had four parts: Flour, Meat, Rice, Beans. Of course, these were the ingredients of feojada!

Villa-Lobos always worked quickly and the noisier it was, the better he liked it. He could concentrate anywhere. He said that if he wrote in a quiet place, his music would be slow and sad. He especially liked to have children playing near him when he was composing.

In 1954, Villa-Lobos took part in a big music festival in Venezuela. Ten concerts were planned, and all the music was written by Latin Americans. Music lovers came from all over the world. Never before had so much important Latin American music been played at one time. The government of Venezuela had often given money as prizes for horse races and auto races. This time, they decided to encourage young Latin American musicians.

Prizes amounting to $20,000 were awarded to a Mexican, a Cuban, and an Argentinian. Villa-Lobos was one of the judges. He said: "This festival is as important as Columbus' discovery of America. The only difference is that he came from one hemisphere to discover another, and in this case, a hemisphere is discovering itself."

Villa-Lobos had always said he would live to be a hundred. But that was a promise he couldn't keep. He died in 1959 when he was 72 years old. Musicians all over the world were sad. "His big family," as he called all the people of Brazil, knew they had lost someone special. One of them said: "In all his music there was a piece of Brazil, the Brazil that he loved so much and knew like the palm of his hand. In Villa-Lobos' music one can read all the history and geography of Brazil."

Vocabulary

cello	composer	symphony
gourd	concert	ballet
carnival	opera	ingredients

Thinking It Over

1. What do you know about the musical scale? How did Villa-Lobos teach the scale to 25,000 children at once?
2. What type of music was Villa-Lobos eager to collect? Why?
3. What kinds of instruments were used to play the folk music of Brazil? Do you have any of these instruments in your school?

Activities

1. Do you have a musical program in your school? If you can read music, explain to the class the way it is done.

2. Hold a community sing in your school. Perhaps your school orchestra knows some of Villa-Lobos' music.

3. Listen to some recordings of Villa-Lobos. Can you "read all the history and geography of Brazil" in the music? Why do you think the people of Brazil enjoy Villa-Lobos' music?

4. Read about the Mexican composer Carlos Cháves. Be prepared to tell the class what you learned.

5. What are some American "folk songs"? Why is folk music popular in America today?

6. Refer to the poems you and your classmates wrote for the story of Gabriela Mistral. Choose two or three of these poems. Working as a group, try to set them to music. Students who play a musical instrument may play the song for the class.

Oscar Niemeyer

The Pan American Union

Creador de una Ciudad

Brazil has an "instant" capital. It sprang up in the wilderness about 500 miles from Rio de Janeiro, the old capital. Many of its beautiful buildings were designed by Oscar Niemeyer (Nee-my'-er). He is a Brazilian architect, and his work is known all over the world. The reason he has a German-sounding name is that his grandfather came to Brazil from Germany. Oscar's father married a Brazilian girl. They had six children, and Oscar was the youngest.

As a schoolboy, Oscar was more interested in sports than in his studies. Soccer is a popular sport in Brazil, and Oscar was on his school's soccer team. Years later someone asked Oscar why his school marks were so poor. Oscar said: "I surely had a good time when I was a boy. I only liked to play soccer and to draw pictures of buildings and street scenes."

Even after finishing high school, Oscar continued to enjoy life. He went to work in his father's business, but he was not interested in a career. He kept up his soccer, and went fishing and swimming as often as he could. When he was nineteen, he met the girl he wanted to marry. The time had come to settle down and choose a career. He had always enjoyed drawing pictures of buildings. Perhaps this made him decide to be an architect. After studying at a school in Rio, he managed to get a job with a well-known architect, Lúcio Costa (Lou'-see-oh Kohs'-tah). At first, Costa did not want to hire Oscar. He told the young man that he could not pay him very much money. Then, Costa tells us, Oscar "turned the tables on me and suggested paying for the

The Department of Education, Rio de Janeiro. This is the building that Niemeyer and the other young architects of Lúcio Costa's company worked on, under the direction of Le Corbusier.

right to work with me." This amazed Costa. He couldn't imagine why Oscar Niemeyer was so determined to be an architect.

For quite a while, Oscar did not do any outstanding work. Then, in 1936, things began to change. The Costa company was asked to design an important building in Rio. A famous European architect, Le Corbusier (Luh Kohr-boos'-ee-ay), came to Brazil to work on the project. Costa picked some of his young architects to work with Le Corbusier. But Oscar was not one of those picked. The usually timid, quiet young man went to Costa and "practically demanded that he be included on the team." Again Costa gave in to Oscar.

Perhaps working with Le Corbusier inspired Oscar Niemeyer. Whatever it was, something happened to him. He began to change from an average architect to an outstanding one. The building planned with Le Corbusier became famous. It is an example of modern architecture at its best. It is raised from the ground on pillars twenty feet tall. Part of the building is covered with blue and white tiles in seashell patterns. A wall of glass looks out on the bay of Rio de Janeiro. A light blue sunshade controls the glare of Rio's tropical sun. The building looks as though it is floating in air.

168

In 1942, Niemeyer was given a project of his own. The mayor of Belo Horizonte (Bay-loh Ohr-ee-sohn'-tay) realized that his city was becoming overcrowded. He wanted a suburb built on the shores of a man-made lake. He asked Oscar Niemeyer to design some of the buildings. Niemeyer was careful not to spoil the lovely countryside. His buildings became part of the beautiful scenery, and actually added to it.

By now Niemeyer was a well-known architect. He was asked to design all sorts of buildings—hotels, banks, offices, homes, schools. In 1947, he went to New York. A group of architects was to work out the design for the United Nations buildings. They came from many different countries, and Niemeyer represented Brazil.

In 1955, Juscelino Kubitschek (Joo-shay-leen'-oh Koo'-bee-check) was elected President of Brazil. This was the man who had been mayor of Belo Horizonte. He had been very pleased with Niemeyer's work there, and they were good friends. During his election campaign, Kubitschek promised to build a new capital for Brazil. This was not a new idea. It had been suggested back in the days of Pedro II, and even earlier. The very name, Brasília (Brah-see'-lee-ah), had been chosen years ago. When Brazil first became a republic, a large area was set aside for the capital. It was a forest wilderness halfway between the Atlantic coast on the east and the Bolivian border on the west. Every time a new constitution was written, it said that the capital would be moved inland. But in all these years nothing had been done. Rio de Janeiro was still the capital. It was a beautiful city, but it was becoming overcrowded and clogged with traffic. Squeezed between the mountains and the sea, Rio had no place to expand.

President Kubitschek decided the time had come to move the capital inland. He would make the dream of Brasília come true.

Niemeyer explains his project for Brasília to visiting United States architects.

But it would be a tremendous job. Who would be able—and willing—to accept the challenge? He chose Oscar Niemeyer. There were many questions to be answered. How should the streets be laid out? Where should the government buildings be placed? Many people would be working and living in Brasília. Where should the homes be built? What about railroads, bus terminals, an airport? How do you turn a wilderness into a modern city? Where do you begin?

Niemeyer began by gathering ideas from many architects. A competition was held to choose a master plan for Brasília. Judges considered the plans of more than sixty Brazilian architects. The winner was Lúcio Costa, the man who gave Niemeyer his first job! Costa's plan was very interesting. You could call it a symbol of the Air Age. Imagine the shadow of a huge airplane on the ground. The main east-west avenue of the city is the body of the plane. The north-south streets are the wings. In the wing area are the homes. The government buildings are placed on the wide main avenue. A nearby river was dammed to make a lake which curves around the city.

As soon as Costa's plan was accepted, work began. Bulldozers pushed their way through the wilderness. Then they were used to clear the underbrush away so a small airport could be built. Men and supplies were flown into the area. When a road to Belo Horizonte was ready, trucks went back and forth day and night.

Back in Rio, many young architects worked with Niemeyer. From his drawings, they made small scale models of each building. These were glued on a big green board. Streets and avenues were laid out just as they would be in the real city. President Kubitschek came to the architects' office to see the model. It was a dream beginning to come true. In December, 1957, he gave a party to celebrate Niemeyer's fiftieth birthday. At the party he said: "Oscar Niemeyer has undertaken the most daring work of city planning and architecture in our history, the construction of Brasília."

The following week, Niemeyer and his wife left their beautiful home in Rio. They would be living in a wooden shack in the wilderness while he supervised the building of the city. An American reporter came to Brasília to interview Niemeyer and Costa. He talked to them at the building site.

"It isn't really a city yet, just a framework," said Costa.

"Everything we have done here is really quite simple," said Niemeyer. "I have tried to make the buildings beautiful. Beauty lasts."

"We haven't had much time," Costa added. "We started less than three years ago. All the plans had to be simple and straightforward."

"We may be making mistakes," Niemeyer admitted, "but we are in such a big hurry. That hotel you are staying in had to be designed in a week."

By now Niemeyer was driven by one idea—to finish Brasília. He said: "Until I began work on Brasília, I thought of architecture as a way to make a living, as an exercise to be practiced in a sporting spirit—nothing more. Now I live for Brasília."

He could see it all in his mind. He hoped that all the workers would stay on and make their homes in Brasília. All sorts of jobs would open up for them. Bus drivers would be needed, gardeners, restaurant owners, and shop keepers. He hoped that the people would have a better life in Brasília than in the crowded cities. Streets were planned for safe driving. Children would have plenty of space to play. He even thought ahead to the need for high schools. There would be one high school for every five elementary schools. This was important to Niemeyer. In Brazil's big cities, very few children could go to a free high school. In Niemeyer's plan, all the children in Brasília would be able to get a good education.

On April 21, 1960, Brazil's Congress held its first meeting in Brasília. It was just three years, one month, and five days after the master plan had been chosen. The President was living in the beautiful presidential palace. More government workers and their families were arriving every day. Over half of the buildings designed by Niemeyer were finished. Kubitschek was anxious to have the government move to Brasília before he left office. This meant building seven days a week, 24 hours a day.

When Kubitschek's term was over, this work slowed down. The men who succeeded Kubitschek were not as interested in the new capital. It was harder for the working people to find jobs. These were slow years for Brasília.

In 1964, there was a revolution, and General Castello Branco (Kah-stay'-yoh Brahn'-koh) became President. He believed that the great inland area of Brazil should be developed. Work in Brasília moved ahead again. More apartments and homes were built. Congressmen and businessmen brought their families to live in the new capital.

Six years later, Niemeyer was still designing buildings for Brasília. Various foreign countries wanted him to help plan their embassies. The city has not yet been finished, and some of Niemeyer's ideas have not worked out just as he planned. For example, he designed one group of homes so that the back yards were close together. The front of each house faced the open country, and had a lovely view. But when the people moved in, they had their own ideas. They decided they would rather face their neighbors. So they used the back of the house as if it were the

These government buildings in Brasília are located on the Plaza of the Three Powers. This name refers to the legislative, the executive, and the judicial powers of the government. The building with the huge "cup" on the roof is the Congress building.

DPI/Jerry Frank

front. However, Niemeyer can be proud of all his work. He says: "Brasília is the city of the future. It will be better than Rio de Janeiro, Bahía, and Belo Horizonte. It will help us develop the central plateaus and the Amazon valley. It will turn the attention of our whole nation to the great unsettled area of Brazil."

This is the dream of Oscar Niemeyer. Because of his genius, Brazil's capital is one of the most beautifully arranged cities in the world.

Vocabulary

inspired	tremendous	supervise	plateau
pillars	competition	embassies	

Thinking It Over

1. Describe an incident that helped shape the life of Oscar Niemeyer.
2. What did the mayor of Belo Horizonte do when his city became overcrowded? Can this problem always be solved in this way? Are there any other solutions? What happens if the problem is not solved?
3. Why did Brazil need a new capital? Why is the location of Brasília important? If the capital of the United States were moved to Kansas, how would it affect this country?
4. How did Niemeyer plan for the children in this new city?

Other Leaders

Try to find some information on one of the following:

Juscelino Kubitschek   Le Corbusier
Lúcio Costa

Map Study

1. On a map of Brazil, locate the following:

The state of Mato Grosso   Belo Horizonte
The state of Amazonas   Brasília
The state of Goiás

Activities

1. Juscelino Kubitschek was pleased with the buildings Niemeyer planned for the suburb. What are some advantages and disadvantages of planning a whole community or town?
2. Architecture has changed over the years. Prepare a report comparing modern architecture and Gothic architecture. Try to find pictures to illustrate your report.
3. Name some famous architects working in the United States. Are there any in your own city?
4. Some other countries have planned their capital cities. Read about how Washington, D.C. was planned. Find out all you can about the Australian capital of Canberra.
5. Oscar Niemeyer helped design the United Nations buildings in New York. What are some of the activities there this year?
6. Name some colleges which have courses in architecture. Are there any in your own state? Are there scholarships available?

Books, Films, and Records 🐢 🐢 🐢 🐢 🐢 🐢 🐢

Books About the Indian People

These books will help you to learn more about the ancient peoples:

Baity, Elizabeth C., *Americans Before Columbus*. New York: Viking Press, Inc., 1961. This is a book which you would like to keep in your classroom and use for checking facts about the ancient peoples. It has a good chart to show the time when each of the ancient cities was important.

Bleeker, Sonia, *The Aztec, Indians of Mexico*. New York: William Morrow & Co., Inc., 1963. *The Maya, Indians of Central America*. New York: William Morrow & Co., Inc., 1961. *The Inca, Indians of the Andes*. New York: William Morrow & Co., Inc., 1960. Books by an author who spent many months visiting the places where these ancient people lived.

Glubok, Shirley, *The Art of Ancient Peru*. New York: Harper & Row Publishers, Inc., 1966. This book consists of photographs of Inca art work.

Von Hagen, Victor, *Maya, Land of the Turkey and the Deer*. Cleveland: World Publishing Co., 1960. This author has explored the Mayan ruins.

These are books about young people who lived in the ancient Indian cities:

Alegría, Fernando, *Lautaro*. New York: Farrar, Straus & Giroux, Inc., 1944. This is a story about the adventures of Lautaro, an Indian boy who led his people to defeating the Spaniards.

Bennett, Rowena, *Runner for the King*. Chicago: Follett Publishing Co., 1963. In this story of the Incas, the young hero carries messages from Cuzco to the distant provinces.

Clark, A. N., *Secret of the Andes*. New York: Viking Press, Inc., 1952. An adventure story which describes how the Incas lived.

Fuller, Lois, *Jade Jaguar Mystery*. Nashville: Abingdon Press, 1962. This story takes place at the time of the Aztecs.

Books About Explorers

Each of these books contains several stories about Spanish explorers:

Blacker, Irwin R., *The Bold Conquistadores*. Indianapolis: Bobbs-Merrill Co., Inc., 1961. The last three stories in this book are about men you did not read about in your own book: Cabeza de Vaca, Coronado, de Soto.

Buehr, Walter, *The Spanish Conquistadores in North America*. New York: G. P. Putnam's Sons, 1962. In this book you can read more about Cortés. There are also stories on Columbus, Montezuma, Balboa, de Soto, and Father Junípero Serra, who founded the missions in California.

Each of these books is about just one explorer. They are all by the same interesting writer, Ronald Syme, and all published in New York by William Morrow & Co., Inc.:

Balboa, Finder of the Pacific (1956)

Cortez of Mexico (1951)

De Soto, Finder of the Mississippi (1957)

Francisco Coronado and the Seven Cities of Gold (1965)

Francisco Pizarro, Founder of Peru (1963)

Magellan, First Around the World (1957)

Vasco de Gama, Sailor Towards the Sunrise (1959)

These two books are stories written by the explorers themselves:

Meredith, Robert and E. Brooks Smith, editors, *The Quest of Columbus, An Exact Account of the Discovery of America*. Boston: Little, Brown and Co., 1966. This book includes some of Columbus' own writings.

Wojciechowska, Maia, *Odyssey of Courage, The Story of Cabeza de Vaca*. New York: Atheneum Publishers, 1965. Twenty years after Cortés, Cabeza de Vaca was shipwrecked on the coast of Texas. He lived for eight years among the Indians, and walked all the way to a Spanish town just north of Mexico City. This book tells about his journey.

Books About the Spanish Colonies and Their Struggle for Independence

These books are adventure stories about Spanish colonial times:

Bishop, Claire, *Martin de Porres, Hero*. Boston: Houghton Mifflin Co., 1954. A story of a Negro boy in colonial Peru who wanted to learn to heal sick people.

O'Dell, Scott, *The King's Fifth*. Boston: Houghton Mifflin Co., 1966. This story is about a seventeen-year-old boy who went on an expedition in northern Mexico to hunt gold for the Spaniards.

Here are two books about Simón Bolívar:

Baker, Nina, *He Wouldn't Be King, The Story of Simón Bolívar*. New York: Vanguard Press, Inc., 1941.

Carse, Robert, *Glory Haul*. New York: G. P. Putnam's Sons, 1962.

Some true-life stories of the days of the new nations before 1900:

Baker, Nina, *Juárez of Mexico*. New York: Vanguard Press, Inc., 1942. If you liked the story about Juárez in your book, you will enjoy reading this one.

Brown, Rose, *The Story of Alberto Santos-Dumont*. New York: Charles Scribner's Sons, 1953. Here you can read about a famous Brazilian inventor.

Raine, Alice, *Eagle of Guatemala*. New York: Harcourt, Brace & World, Inc., 1947. The hero of this book was president of Guatemala when it was a new nation.

Vance, *Ashes of Empire*. New York: E. P. Dutton & Co., 1959. A story of Maximilian and Carlotta, who tried to rule Mexico.

Books About Life in the Modern Latin American Nations

These books are about several different nations:

Fideler, Raymond and Carol Kvande, *South America*. Michigan: Fideler Co., 1963. This is a book which you can use to look up facts about South America.

Goetz, Delia, *South America*. Michigan: Fideler Co., 1958. *Neighbors to the South*. New York: Harcourt, Brace, and World, Inc., 1956. These two books tell about all the nations this author has visited.

Joy, C. R., *Young People of South America*. New York: Duell, Sloan & Pearce, 1963. Here you can read about people your own age in twelve different countries.

This is a series of fast reading books about young people in different countries:

Carter, William, *The First Book of Bolivia*. New York: Franklin Watts, Inc., 1963.

Epstein, S. & B., *The First Book of Mexico*. New York: Franklin Watts, Inc., 1955.

Markun, Patricia, *The First Book of Central America and Panama*. New York: Franklin Watts, Inc., 1963.

Sheppard, Sally, *The First Book of Brazil*. New York: Franklin Watts, Inc., 1962.

These two books are longer stories called *The Life in Other Lands Series*:

May, Stella, *Brazil*. Michigan: Fideler Co., 1959.

Ross, Patricia, *Mexico*. Michigan: Fideler Co., 1962.

These three books are fast-reading stories about the life of young people in cities and villages:

Breetveld, Jim, *Getting to Know Brazil*. New York: Coward-McCann, Inc., 1960.

Gomez, Barbara, *Getting to Know Mexico*. New York: Coward-McCann, Inc., 1959.

Kepple, Ella, *Three Children of Chile*. New York: Friendship Press, 1961.

Two books that will tell you about modern Mexican leaders as well as the early heroes:

Hancock, Ralph, *Mexico*. New York: The Macmillan Company, 1964. Be sure to read the stories on the modern presidents, Obregón and Calles, and the modern Mexican musician, Carlos Chávez.

McNeer, May, *The Mexican Story*. New York: Ariel Books, 1953. Look in this book for leaders of Mexico after Benito Juárez.

Fast-Reading Adventure Stories About Individual Young People

Cavanna, Betty, *Carlos of Mexico*. New York: Franklin Watts, Inc., 1964.

Cavanna, Betty, *Chico of Guatemala*. New York: Franklin Watts, Inc., 1963.

Cavanna, Betty, *Pepe of Argentina*. New York: Franklin Watts, Inc., 1962.

Desmond, Alice, *Jorge's Journey*. New York: The Macmillan Company, 1942. A book about life on a Brazilian coffee plantation.

Fleming, Patricia, *Rico, The Young Rancher*. Boston: D. C. Heath & Co., 1942. This story takes place in Chile.

Malkus, Alida, *Citadel of a Hundred Stairways*. Holt, Rinehart & Winston, Inc., 1961. A mining story in Peru.

Tarshis, Elizabeth, *Village That Learned to Read*. Boston: Houghton Mifflin Co., 1941. A story about how a new school was founded in a small Mexican town.

Pamphlets Which Can Be Bought for a Few Cents from the Pan American Union, Washington, D. C., 20006.

Your class can write to the Pan American Union for an up-to-date list of the pamphlets. Some of these are:

The Aztecs	*José Artigas*	*José San Martín*
The Incas	*Simón Bolívar*	*The Amazon*
The Mayas	*Bernardo O'Higgins*	*The Christ of the Andes*

Coronet Films, Sales Department, Coronet Building, Chicago, Ill. 60601.

Early American Civilizations, 13½ minutes, color; b&w. Shows you the Teotihuacán Pyramid of the Sun, the Aztec Calendar stone, Mayan carvings, and Incan weavings. Explains the influences of these cultures upon our own culture.

The Mayas, 11 minutes, color; b&w. Follows the Mayans from Tikal to Uxmal and Chichén Itzá. Tells about their achievements in agriculture, sculpture, astronomy, and mathematics.

The Aztecs, 11 minutes, color; b&w. Shows pre-Aztec ruins and reconstructions. Shows the lagoons and canals, the market place and religious temples of the Aztecs.

The Incas, 11 minutes, color; b&w. Shows life in a Peruvian Indian village today. Tells about the Incan civilization, their government, and their economic system.

A Boy of Mexico; Juan and His Donkey, 11 minutes, color; b&w. Through the story of Juan, we learn some of the ways of life in rural Mexico.

Mexican Village Life, 13½ minutes, color; b&w. Manuel lives in a village in central Mexico. We visit him at school, and at home with his family. We go with them to the weekly market day in the village.

Bolívar: South American Liberator, 11 minutes, color; b&w. You will visit Venezuela, Ecuador, Peru, and Colombia and learn more about the life of Bolívar.

McGraw-Hill Book Company, Text-Film Division, 327 West 41st Street, New York, N. Y. 10036.

Brazil, 20 minutes, color; b&w. We visit Salvador and Recife, tour Belo Horizonte, and compare Rio de Janeiro with Brasília. We meet a family of Sao Paulo, and learn what they think is ahead for Brazil.

Peru, 17 minutes, color; b&w. Our film study begins with an Indian shepherd boy high in the Andes. We visit parts of the country the boy has never seen: Cuzco, Machu Picchu, and Lima.

Sound Filmstrips

Doubleday and Company, Inc., School and Library Division, Garden City, N. Y. 11530.

Yucatán—Land of the Mayas, color, 70 frames. Shows different modes of life of a Spanish, a Mayan, and a Mestizo family.

Fiesta Time—Mexico, color, 58 frames. The *Cinco de Mayo,* famous Mexican fiesta, is featured. Shows colorful parades, rodeos, Indian gymnasts, and handicraft exhibits..

The Aztecs and Cortés, color, 51 frames. Shows the Aztecs as they lived in what is now Mexico City. We learn about their defeat by the Spaniards.

The Life of Benito Juárez, b&w, 34 frames. Tells the story of the pureblooded Indian boy who became one of the great presidents of Mexico.

Stanley Bowmar Company Inc., 4 Broadway, Valhalla, N. Y. 10595.

Living in Mexico: City and Town, 4 color filmstrips, 4 records (12″ 33⅓ rpm) guide. The set gives you a complete picture of life in Mexico today.

Mexico—The Country and Its People, 4 color filmstrips, 2 records (10″ 33⅓ rpm) guide. Pre-Columbian, Spanish Colonial, and Modern Mexico.

Society for Visual Education, Inc., 1345 Diversey Parkway, Chicago, Ill. 60614.

Living in Mexico Today, Set of 4 filmstrips, 2 records, 4 guides.

Northern Mexico and the Central Highlands, 16 minutes, 45 frames. You will learn about early civilizations—Aztec and Spanish, and you will see mountain villages and industrial areas.

The Historical Triangle—Mexico City, Cuernavaca, and Puebla, 14 minutes, 36 frames. Shows Aztec, Spanish, and modern-day ways of life in three major cities.

Taxco, A Spanish Colonial City, 11 minutes, 35 frames. You will visit a beautiful old city, now preserved as a national monument.

Southern Mexico, The Lowlands, and the Yucatán Peninsula, 12 minutes, 34 frames. Shows Mayan as well as Spanish influence on various areas.

Children's Music Center, 5373 West Pico Boulevard, Los Angeles, Calif. 90019.

Living in Mexico Today, kit of 7 color filmstrips, 7 LP records, guide. Each record has one side in Spanish and one side in English, 2½ hours of narration.

Warren Schloat Productions, Inc., Pleasantville, New York 10570.

Mexican Americans, one in a set of 6 color filmstrips and 6 records:

Minorities Have Made America Great: Set II. This filmstrip tells the history of the Spanish explorers and of the Aztec and Pueblo Indians. Mexican influences on and contributions to life in the United States.

Stanley Bowmar Company, Inc., 4 Broadway, Valhalla, N. Y. 10595.

Mexican Town, Population 14,000, 4 color filmstrips. A 1964 production of the life of children in the town of San Miguel de Allende.

Children of Latin America, 6 color filmstrips, guide.
   Vacation on the Pampas—Argentina
   Chico Learns to Read—Brazil
   José Harvests Bananas—Guatemala
   Market Day at Cusco—Peru
   Fiesta Day—Mexico
   The Silver Studded Belt—Chile

Jam Handy School Service, 2781 East Grand Boulevard, Detroit, Michigan 48211.

Mexico—Yesterday and Today, series in color.
   The Aztecs
   Cortés Conquers the Aztecs
   Indians of Mexico Today
   Mexican Town and Country Life
   Native Mexican Handicrafts
   Mexico City

Records You Might Like to Hear

Children's Music Center, 5373 West Pico Boulevard, Los Angeles, Calif. 90019.

Folk Songs of Latin America, set of 12″ LP record and 2 filmstrips in color.

Good Neighbors, album of 3 LP records (7″). A fiesta of Latin American folk dances with directions.

Latin American Folk Dances, 12″ LP record. Eight dances with instructions.

Realm of the Incas, 12″ LP record. Pre-Columbian and native instruments used for Chant to the Sun. Instruments are shown on album cover.

Little Train of Caipira, 12″ LP record. Villa-Lobos uses Brazilian folk songs to develop a musical picture of the journey of a little Brazilian train.

Spotlight on Latin America, 12″ LP record. Narration and songs about Mexico, Brazil, Chile, Indians, etc.

Glossary

agony   Pain of body or mind.

ammunition   Bullets, shells, gunpowder.

Andes   A high mountain range in South America.

architecture   The art of planning buildings.

ballet   A kind of dance.

baptize   To sprinkle a person with water as a sign of washing away sin.

bishop   A clergyman of high rank.

bookbinder   A person who works at fastening the pages of a book into a cover

boom town   A town that grows up in a few months.

cable bridge   A bridge held up by strong thick ropes made of wires twisted together.

career   Occupation; lifetime job.

carriage   Wheeled vehicle for carrying people, usually pulled by horses.

carnival   A time of feasting and merry-making, a public amusement show, often with booths and games.

causeway   A raised road over wet ground or water.

cello   A stringed musical instrument larger than a violin.

celebrate   To observe a special occasion with certain ceremonies.

ceremony   A set manner of conducting an important occasion; A certain act to be done on special occasions.

chasm   A deep opening in the earth.

coachman   A man who drives a coach or carriage.

183

cocoon A silk case spun by a caterpillar to live in while it changes into a butterfly or moth.

commentary A series of notes or explanations.

competition A contest.

composer A writer of music.

concert A musical entertainment.

consul A person appointed by a government to help his countrymen in a foreign land.

convent A place where a group of women live together and devote themselves to a religious life.

craft Skill, especially in making things by hand.

craggy peaks Pointed mountain tops with steep, rough rocks.

creative Having the power to create or invent.

criollo A person born in Mexico, whose parents were Spanish.

custom Any usual action or habit.

debate A formal argument, according to rules, in which each side of a question is presented before an audience.

descendant A person born of a certain family or group.

desperate Not caring what happens because hope is gone.

discriminate To treat differently because of race, religion, etc.

disgrace Loss of honor or good name.

distinguished Great, well-known.

embassy Residence or office of an ambassador.

emblem Symbol, sign of an idea; something that represents an idea.

embroidery Fancy designs sewn on material.

emperor The ruler of an empire.

epidemic The rapid spreading of a disease in an area.

execute To put to death according to law.

exile Banishment; living away from one's home or country as a punishment.

expedition A journey for a special purpose such as exploration.

fate That which happens to a person in his life.

fiesta A religious festival, or a lively party in a Spanish-speaking country.

forefather A person from whom one is descended.

fortress Place of safety; place built with walls for defense; fort.

fresco Picture painted on damp, fresh plaster.

fulfill To carry out a promise.

gachupín A person living in Mexico who had been born in Spain.

grandeur Greatness, splendor.

gourd The fruit of a certain plant. When dried, gourds have hard shells and seeds which rattle.

grenade A small bomb thrown by hand.

grito The Spanish word for a shout; a loud cry.

guerrillas Fighters who hide and carry on a "hit and run" war.

guerrilla war An irregular war fought by independent bands.

hacienda A large ranch or estate.

headquarters The place from which orders are sent out.

homage Respect; honor.

ignorant Knowing little or nothing.

immune Protected against; safe from.

impel To drive or push forward.

industry Any kind of business or trade.

infancy Babyhood.

influence Power of persons or things to act on others.

ingredient Any one of the things that make up a mixture.

inspired Stirred deeply; aroused to action.

invasion Act of forcing one's way in.

irrigation Supplying land with water by means of ditches.

jaguar A fierce animal like a leopard.

lady-in-waiting A lady who attends a queen or princess.

legend A story handed down from the past which may be part history and part myth.

leprosy A disease causing loss of feeling, swellings and sores on the skin. The flesh wastes away.

liberator A person who sets free.

loyal True and faithful.

mathematics The study of numbers, amounts, measurements, shapes, sizes, etc. (includes arithmetic, algebra, and geometry).

mestizo A person born in the New World with one Indian parent and one Spanish parent.

monastery A building where a group of men live and devote themselves to a religious life.

morality The rightness or wrongness of an action.

mother country A country in which one is born; a country that owns colonies.

mummy A dead body preserved from decay.

mural painting A picture painted on a wall.

national monument Something set up by a country to keep a person or event from being forgotten.

noble High and great by birth or title; of a high position.

nun A woman who lives a life of prayer and worship, usually in a convent. Some nuns teach, others care for the sick.

opera A play with most of the lines sung instead of spoken.

pampas The broad treeless plains of Argentina.

pastor A minister or priest in charge of a church or parish.

patriot A person who loves and supports his country.

peasant A poor farmer who works on the farm of a rich landlord.

peninsular A person born in Spain, who had come to Mexico to live.

pension An amount of money paid to a person by a government or by a former employer, after the person has stopped working.

pillar A column made of stone, wood or metal, and used to hold up a floor or roof of a building.

plantation A large farm on which only one crop is grown, such as cotton, tobacco, sugar or rubber.

planter A man who owns or runs a plantation.

plateau A high area of flat land.

plaza A public square in a city or town.

plead To give reasons for or against something; to beg earnestly.

plough Another way of spelling plow; a big heavy instrument for turning over the soil.

preserved Kept from harm or change.

professor A teacher in a college.

prosperity Success; good fortune.

province A division of a country.

pyramid A solid structure with triangular sides meeting at a point, and a flat base.

rampart A wide bank of earth, often with a wall on top, built around a fort to help defend it.

ravine A long, deep, narrow valley.

rebel A person who resists or fights against authority instead of obeying.

rebellion Revolt, a fight against government.

reception A party; an entertainment usually to greet or welcome someone.

reform Improvement; a change for the better.

republic A nation or state in which the citizens elect representatives to manage the government.

resist To oppose; to act against; to fight back against.

revenge The act of paying back a wrong or injury; returning evil for evil.

sacrifice The act of offering something to God; giving something up.

scaffold A temporary platform on which workmen may stand.

supervise To watch over the work of; to oversee.

surveying The science of measuring the boundaries of land.

symbol Anything used as a sign for something else.

symphony A long musical composition for an orchestra.

tragic Very sad.

translate To change from one language to another.

tremendous Very large; of great importance

tyranny Cruel or unjust use of power.

uprising A revolt.

volcano A mountain which spews out steam, ashes and melted rock.

viceroy A person ruling in place of the king.

vow A solemn promise.

worthy Having worth or merit.

Index

PROLEGOMENA TO ETHICS

BY THE LATE

THOMAS HILL GREEN, M.A., LL.D.

FELLOW OF BALLIOL COLLEGE
AND WHYTE'S PROFESSOR OF MORAL PHILOSOPHY
IN THE UNIVERSITY OF OXFORD

EDITED BY

A. C. BRADLEY, M.A.

FORMERLY FELLOW OF BALLIOL COLLEGE AND PROFESSOR OF POETRY
IN THE UNIVERSITY OF OXFORD

FIFTH EDITION

WITH A PREFACE BY

E. CAIRD, M.A., Hon. D.C.L.

MASTER OF BALLIOL COLLEGE, OXFORD

OXFORD
AT THE CLARENDON PRESS
1906

HENRY FROWDE, M.A.

PUBLISHER TO THE UNIVERSITY OF OXFORD

LONDON, EDINBURGH, NEW YORK

TORONTO AND MELBOURNE

PREFACE TO THE FIFTH EDITION

I HAVE been asked to say a few words of Preface to the new and cheaper edition of Green's Prolegomena, the merits of which as an introduction to Ethics are generally recognised. The Prolegomena may be described as a new treatment of the fundamental questions of Ethics, from an idealistic point of view, somewhat modified from that of Kant. The problem from which Green, like Kant, starts is the apparent opposition between (a) the ordinary conception of the world, as a system of causally connected objects in space and time, which is presupposed by physical science, (b) and what seem to be the fundamental ideas of morality and religion, the ideas of God, freedom, and immortality. If man, like all the other objects of our empirical knowledge, is merely one part of the world of objects which act and react upon each other, according to fixed general laws, what room is left for the assertion of his moral freedom, or for any higher destiny which distinguishes him from the other creatures? and how can we regard him as other than a conditioned finite being, a link in the chain of conditioned being, or as having a direct living relation to a God who is regarded not as a part, but as the principle, source, and end of the whole system? Morality and religion seem to attribute to man an individual independence, and a relation to the absolute Being which no merely finite object could possess. If we follow out the ordinary methods of physical science, we seem reduced either to deny the moral responsibility of man and the existence of God, or to assert both on grounds which we should not admit in any other case.

a 2

Now Green, like Kant, endeavours to show that in ordinary experience and in physical science we usually ignore or abstract from a principle which, nevertheless, is always present in all our knowledge, and that therefore such science does not deal with the ultimate reality of things, but only with phenomena; i. e. with things partially understood, or not apprehended in their whole reality. When, however, we detect this principle in relation to which all phenomena exist and are known, the result is both to vindicate the ways of knowing that characterise science and ordinary experience within their proper sphere, and at the same time to establish our right to apply the principles of morality and religion to the absolute reality. Hence, our ordinary experience and science rest upon a principle which, when recognised, carries us beyond such experience and science. Kant, indeed, maintains that it does not do this in the way of knowledge, but only opens the way for a faith which may guide us in practice. It can, in his view, prevent us from conceiving our experience as more than a knowledge of phenomena, but cannot enable us to change such partial knowledge into an apprehension of the real nature of things. Green, on the contrary, holds that when we see phenomenal objects in relation to their principles, we acquire a knowledge of what they are in themselves. Both, however, agree that our moral consciousness does take account of that principle, and that, as a consequence, we are entitled to postulate the moral freedom of man, and the existence of God, as primary truths on which we can base our existence as spiritual beings. And Green endeavours to work out the consequences of these principles in relation to morality.

In the Second Book of the Prolegomena, therefore, he treats man's practical life as a realisation of freedom, and endeavours to show in what sense freedom is realised, firstly, in man's action generally; and secondly, in a narrower sense, in actions that are morally good. What is meant by saying that man is free in all his practical activity? and what is meant by saying that he is free only when his action conforms to the moral ideal? The first question is answered by showing that all action from motive is essentially free or self-determined action; the *second*, by showing that man is truly realising *himself* only when the motive of his action is the moral ideal. The moral ideal, it is then contended, is not truly represented by Hedonism as the sum of pleasures, either for the individual, or 'the greatest number'. It involves, however, the complete realisation and satisfaction of the capacities of the individual, and it involves also the idea of a common good, in the attainment of which all moral beings may co-operate. After a full criticism and rejection of Hedonism in all its forms, Green proceeds to show the agreement of his own view of the moral ideal with that developed in the philosophy of Plato and Aristotle, both in their conception of virtuous activity as the chief good, and in their analysis of the special virtues; pointing out, however, that the conception of these virtues has been enlarged in modern times, under the influence of Christianity, and especially by the idea of the brotherhood of men. The Fourth and last Book of the Prolegomena discusses the practical value of moral philosophy, examining in particular the question how his own view enables us to deal with practical difficulties; how, in this point of view, it compares with other theories; and how, especially, it enables us to take account not only of the results, but of the motives of our action.

The difficulty which has been most felt by readers of the Prolegomena is that raised by the assertion that man must not be regarded merely as a result of certain previous conditions, but as a 'reproduction of itself by an eternal consciousness'; in other words, that he is literally 'made in the image of God.' And perhaps there are some valid objections to this way of stating the unity of the universal with the particular element in man's being; or, in other words, maintaining that we are obliged to think of him not merely as an object who is a particular part of this partial world, but also to regard him as a being in whom the principle of unity that underlies all the differences of the world becomes conscious of itself. But we have to consider that any valid theory of human nature must somehow explain the union of these two aspects of man's being, as, on the one hand, an individual object in the world, and on the other hand, a subject of knowledge and a moral being, who is capable of regarding and treating all objects, including himself, in relation to the whole to which he belongs. Thus, in knowledge and in morality, his point of view is not anthropocentric, but cosmocentric, or theocentric. For, in so far as he views the world from the point of view of his own individuality and acts with sole regard to it, his thought and his action are illegitimate. Hence those who view human life in a comprehensive way are apt to describe it antithetically, alternately emphasizing the different aspects in which it presents itself. This dualistic way of describing humanity is especially characteristic of Pascal. Thus he declares, 'it is dangerous to let man see too clearly how he is on a level with the animals, without showing him his greatness. It is dangerous to let him see too clearly his greatness, without his meanness. If he boasts himself, I abase him; if he abases himself, I exalt him. I contradict him continually, till he comprehends what an incomprehensible monster he is.'

Green's work may be described as an attempt to explain this antagonism, and especially to show that the conception of man, *sub specie aeternitatis*, may be taken as the basis of our view of him *sub specie temporis*. But it is by no means easy to find a fit mode of expression for this unity : a mode of expression that does not fall into one of the opposite forms of error ; a mysticism which loses man in God, or an individualism which forgets his relation both to God and to the world. Green at least has kept continually both of these aspects in view, and yet has been able to rise above the *via media* that remains perpetually ' in doubt whether to call him God or beast.'

Those who have a living remembrance of Green's personality will always feel that he has a special right to be heard on the subject of ethics, seeing that he was specially characterised by the intimate blending in him of idealism and practicality. If there was a third quality by which he was distinguished, it was by an intensely democratic or Christian tone of feeling that could not tolerate the thought of privilege, and constantly desired for every class and individual a full share in all the great heritage of humanity. Of this sentiment many illustrations may be found in the following pages. The practical consequences of Green's ethical principles are further developed in his Lectures on the Principles of Political Obligation.

E. CAIRD.

January, 1906.

EDITOR'S PREFACE TO THE FIRST EDITION

THE works by which Professor Green has hitherto been chiefly known to the general public are his *Introduction* to Messrs. Longmans' edition of Hume's Philosophical Works, and his articles in the *Contemporary Review* on some doctrines of Mr. Spencer and Mr. Lewes.

When in the year 1877 Mr. Green became Whyte's Professor of Moral Philosophy, his main desire was, both in his teaching and writing, to develope more fully and in a more constructive way the ideas which underlay his previous critical writings and appeared in them. The present treatise is the first outcome of that desire; and doubtless it would have been only the first but for the premature and unexpected death of the author in March, 1882.

Even the *Prolegomena to Ethics* (the title is the author's own) was left unfinished. The greater part of the book had been used, some of it twice over, in the Professorial lectures; and about a quarter of it (the first 116 pages) was printed in the numbers of *Mind* for January, April, and July, 1882. But, according to a letter of the author written not long before his death, some twenty or thirty pages remained to be added, and, though with this exception the whole was written out nearly ready for printing no part of it can be considered to have undergone the final revision.

At his death Mr. Green left the charge of the manuscript to me; and I have now only to explain the course I have followed in preparing it for publication.

The manuscript was written in paragraphs, but otherwise was continuous; and I may add that it was composed without regard to arrangement in Books and

Chapters. For that arrangement I am responsible, and also for the numbering and occasional re-division of the sections, and for the frequent division of a section into two or more paragraphs. I have also made the few corrections in expression which seemed to be necessary, and in one case I have ventured, for the sake of clearness, to transfer a passage from one place to another. References have been verified and supplied; translations of Greek quotations have been given, where their meaning was not obvious from the text; and a few notes have been added by way of explanation or qualification, for the most part only where a mark in the author's manuscript showed that he intended to reconsider the passage. The Editor's notes, except where they give merely a reference or translation, are enclosed in square brackets.

My desire throughout has been to make no changes except in passages which I felt sure Mr. Green would have altered had his attention been called to them. With the further object of rendering the work as intelligible as possible to the general reader I have ventured to print an analysis. Mr. Green would probably have followed the plan he adopted in the *Introduction* to Hume, and have placed a short abstract on the margins of the pages. I have thought it better to print my analysis as a Table of Contents, as that arrangement clearly separates my work from the author's, and will also probably be the most useful to those who care to read an analysis at all. Perhaps I may further suggest to any reader who is unaccustomed to metaphysical and psychological discussions that much of the author's ethical views, though not their scientific basis, may be gathered from the Third and Fourth Books alone.

It has been already explained that the book was left unfinished. But on the whole I thought it best to make no attempt to add anything, especially as the comparison

which occupies the last chapter seems to have reached
a natural conclusion. The reader will also find in the
text indications of subjects which were to have been discussed. In particular the author—at any rate at one
time—intended to introduce a criticism of Kant's ethical
views (see page 177). But I think this intention must
have been abandoned during the composition of the book,
and, as it is hoped that before long Mr. Green's published
writings will be collected and edited, together with a short
biography and selections from his unpublished manu-
scripts [1], it seemed best that the materials on this subject
furnished by the author's notes for lectures should be
reserved for a future occasion.

I have received material assistance in preparing the
present work for the press. Mrs. Green has compared
the whole of the book in proof with the original manuscript. Professor Edward Caird, of Glasgow University,
and Mr. R. L. Nettleship, Fellow of Balliol, read through
the proofs and the analysis and sent me many suggestions.
I feel, in particular, that but for Professor Caird's very
full and valuable notes the analysis must have been far
more imperfect than it remains. But it would seem to
me, and to those who have helped me, out of place to
express any gratitude for work given to a book which,
more than any writing of Mr. Green's yet published, may
enable the public outside Oxford to understand not only
the philosophical enthusiasm which his teaching inspired,
but the reverence and love which are felt for him by all
who knew him well.

A. C. BRADLEY.

University College, Liverpool,
    April, 1883.

---

[1] See *Works of T. H Green, edited with a Memoir by R. L. Nettleship*,
3 vols., Longmans, 1885-8. These volumes contain all Green's writings
except the *Prolegomena to Ethics*.

ANALYTICAL TABLE OF CONTENTS

INTRODUCTION

THE IDEA OF A NATURAL SCIENCE OF MORALS

BOOK I. Metaphysics of Knowledge

CHAPTER I

THE SPIRITUAL PRINCIPLE IN KNOWLEDGE AND IN NATURE

CHAPTER II

THE RELATION OF MAN, AS INTELLIGENCE, TO THE SPIRITUAL PRINCIPLE IN NATURE

CHAPTER II

THE RELATION OF MAN, AS INTELLIGENCE, TO THE SPIRITUAL PRINCIPLE IN NATURE

CHAPTER III

THE FREEDOM OF MAN AS INTELLIGENCE

BOOK II. The Will

CHAPTER I

THE FREEDOM OF THE WILL

CHAPTER II

DESIRE, INTELLECT, AND WILL

Desire

Desire and Will

Will and Intellect

BOOK III. The Moral Ideal and Moral Progress

CHAPTER I

GOOD AND MORAL GOOD

Pleasure and Desire

CHAPTER II

CHARACTERISTICS OF THE MORAL IDEAL

A. *The Personal Character of the Moral Ideal*

CHAPTER III

THE ORIGIN AND DEVELOPMENT OF THE MORAL IDEAL

A. Reason as Source of the Idea of a Common Good

CHAPTER IV

Virtue as the Common Good

CHAPTER V

THE DEVELOPMENT OF THE MORAL IDEAL— CONTINUED
D. *The Greek and the Modern Conceptions of Virtue*

BOOK IV.   The Application of Moral Philosophy to the Guidance of Conduct

CHAPTER I

THE PRACTICAL VALUE OF THE MORAL IDEAL

CHAPTER II

CHAPTER III

THE PRACTICAL VALUE OF A HEDONISTIC MORAL PHILOSOPHY

CHAPTER IV

THE PRACTICAL VALUE OF UTILITARIANISM COMPARED WITH THAT OF THE THEORY OF THE GOOD AS HUMAN PERFECTION

Mr. Sidgwick's view of Ultimate Good

PROLEGOMENA TO ETHICS

INTRODUCTION

1. A WRITER who seeks to gain general confidence scarcely goes the right way to work when he begins with asking whether there really is such a subject as that of which he proposes to treat; whether it is one to which enquiry can be directed with any prospect of a valuable result. Yet to a writer on Moral Philosophy such a mode of procedure is prescribed, not only by the logical impulse to begin at the beginning, but by observation of the prevalent opinions around him. He can scarcely but be aware that Moral Philosophy is a name of somewhat equivocal repute; that it commands less respect among us than was probably the case a century ago; and that any one who professes to teach or write upon a subject to which this name is in any proper or distinctive sense applicable, is looked upon with some suspicion.

There is, indeed, no lack of utterance in regard to the great problems of life or the rights and wrongs of human conduct. Nor does it by any means confine itself to what are commonly counted secular or 'positive' considerations. Guesses as to some

> sweet strange mystery,
> Of what beyond these things may lie,
> And yet remain unseen,

are announced with little reserve and meet with ready acceptance. These, we may say, are for the multitude of the educated, who have wearied of the formulas of a stereotyped theology, but still demand free indulgence for the appetite which that theology supplied with a regulation-diet. But the highest poetry of our time—that in which the most serious and select spirits find their food—depends chiefly for

its interest on what has been well called 'the application of
ideas to life;' and the ideas so applied are by no means
sensibly verifiable. They belong as little to the domain of
natural science, strictly so called, as to that of dogmatic
theology. A moral philosopher may be excused for finding
much excellent philosophy, in his special sense of the word,
in such poems as the 'In Memoriam' of Lord Tennyson and
Mr. Browning's 'Rabbi ben Ezra,' to say nothing of the more
explicitly ethical poetry of Wordsworth. Presented in the
rapt unreasoned form of poetic utterance, not professing to do
more than represent a mood of the individual poet, it is welcomed by reflecting men as expressing deep convictions of
their own. Such men seem little disturbed by the admission
to a joint lodgement in their minds of inferences from popu-
larised science, which do not admit of being reconciled with
these deeper convictions in any logical system of beliefs.

But if any one, alarmed at this dangerous juxtaposition,
and unwilling that what seem to him the deepest and truest
views of life should be retained merely on scientific suffer-
ance, seeks to find for them some independent justification,
in the shape of a philosophy which does not profess to be
a branch either of dogmatic theology or of natural science,
he must look for little thanks for his trouble. The most
intelligent critics had rather, it would seem, that the ideas
which poetry applies to life, together with those which form
the basis of practical religion, should be left to take their
chance alongside of seemingly incompatible scientific beliefs,
than that anything calling itself philosophy should seek to
systematise them and to ascertain the regions to which they
on the one side, and the truths of science on the other, are
respectively applicable. 'Poetry we feel, science we understand;'—such will be the reflection, spoken or unspoken, of
most cultivated men;—'theology professes to found itself
on divine revelation, and has at all events a sphere of its
own in the interpretation of sacred writings which entitles
it at least to respectful recognition; but this philosophy,
which is neither poetry nor science nor theology, what is it

but a confusion of all of these in which each of them is spoilt? Poetry has a truth of its own, and so has religion — a truth which we feel, though from the scientific point of view we may admit it to be an illusion. Philosophy is from the scientific point of view equally an illusion, and has no truth that we can feel. Better trust poetry and religion to the hold which, however illusive, they will always have on the human heart, than seek to explain and vindicate them, as against science, by help of a philosophy which is itself not only an illusion but a dull and pretentious one, with no interest for the imagination and no power over the heart.'

2. With such opinion in the air all around him, it must be with much misgiving that one who has no prophetic utterance to offer in regard to conduct, but who still believes in the necessity of a philosophy of morals which no adaptation of natural science can supply, undertakes to make good his position. He will gain nothing, however, by trying to sail under false colours, or by disguising his recognition of an antithesis between the natural and the moral, which can alone justify his claim to have something to say that lies beyond the limits of the man of science. It is better that he should make it clear at the outset why and in what sense he holds that there is a subject-matter of enquiry which does not consist of matters of fact, ascertainable by experiment and observation, and what place he assigns to morals in this subject-matter. In other words, at the risk of repelling readers by presenting them first with the most difficult and least plausible part of his doctrine, he should begin with explaining why he holds a 'metaphysic of morals' to be possible and necessary; the proper foundation, though not the whole, of every system of Ethics.

This has not been the method commonly pursued by English writers on the subject, and, in the face of present tendencies, is likely to seem something of an anachronism. To any one who by idiosyncrasy, or by the accident of his position, is led to occupy himself with Moral Philosophy, the temptation to treat his subject as a part of natural science is certainly a strong one. In so doing he can plead the authority of eminent names and is sure of intelligent acceptance; nor can he fail by patient enquiry to arrive at a theory of some phenomena of human life, which, though it may leave certain primary problems untouched, shall be not only plausible but true so far as it goes. He can reckon securely on having more to show for his life's work, when it comes to an end, than if he spent himself on questions which he may recognise as of real interest, but to which he will also be aware that experiment and observation, strictly so called, cannot afford an answer. It thus would not be wonderful that, with most enquirers and teachers, the interest once taken in Moral Philosophy should be mainly transferred to the physical science conveniently called Anthropology, even if the insufficiency of the latter to deal with the most important questions of Moral Philosophy were admitted.

This admission, however, has of late been fast coming to be thought unnecessary. That a physical science of Ethics is not intrinsically impossible, however difficult it may be rendered by the complexity, and inaccessibility to direct experiment, of its subject-matter; that there are no intelligible questions—no questions worth asking—as to human life which would be beyond the reach of such a science; this would seem to be the general opinion of modern English 'culture,' so far as it is independent of theological prepossessions. And it is natural that it should be so. The questions raised for us by the Moral Philosophy which in England we have inherited, are just such as to invite a physical treatment. If it is the chief business of the moralist to distinguish the nature and origin of the pleasures and pains which are supposed to be the sole objects of human desire and aversion, to trace the effect upon conduct of the impulses so constituted, and to ascertain the several degrees in which different courses of action, determined by anticipation of pleasure and pain, are actually productive of the desired result; then the sooner the methods of scientific experiment and observation are substituted for vague guessing and an arbitrary interpretation by each man of his own consciousness, the better it will be. Ethics, so understood, becomes to all intents and purposes a science of health, and the true moralist will be the physiologist who, making the human physique his specialty, takes a sufficiently wide view of his subject; who traces the influence of historical and political factors, or of what it is now the fashion to call the 'social medium,' in giving a specific character to those susceptibilities of pleasure and pain on which, according to the theory supposed, the phenomena of human action depend.

3. There were two elements, indeed, in the system of popular ethics inherited from the last century, which were long thought incompatible with its complete reduction to the form of a physical science. These were the doctrines of free-will and of a moral sense. Each, however, was understood in a way which suggested to the naturalist a ready explanation of its supposed claim to lie beyond his sphere. The moral sense, according to the accepted view, was a specific susceptibility to pleasure or pain in the contemplation of certain acts. What was the quality in the acts which excited this pleasure or pain in the contemplation of them? If it were something in the conception of which any originative function of the reason was implied, then the existence of the moral sense would have meant that there was a determining agent in the inner life of man, of which no natural history could be given. But those writers who had made most of the moral sense had been very indefinite in their account of the quality in action to which it was relative. The most consistent theory on the subject was Hume's. According to him the pleasure of moral sense is pleasure felt in the 'mere survey' of an act, independently of any consequences of the act to the person contemplating it; and that which occasions this pleasure is the tendency of the act to bring pleasure to the agent himself or to others[1]. Moral sense, in short, is a social

[1] Treatise on Human Nature, Book III, Pt. i. §§ 1, 2, and Pt. iii. § 1.

sentiment either of satisfaction in the view of such conduct as has been generally found to increase the pleasure or diminish the pain of others, or of uneasiness in the reverse, quite apart from any expectation of personal advantage or loss. It is thus properly not by the action of the person feeling it, but by that of others, that it is excited. An act of a man's own, necessarily proceeding, according to Hume, from some desire for pleasure which it satisfies or fails to satisfy, must have personal consequences for him, incompatible with that disinterested survey which alone yields the pleasure or pain of moral sense, properly so called. Sympathy, however, with the effect which he knows that his act produces on the moral sense of others, may modify the feeling which it causes to the doer of it. An act, in gratification of some passion, which he would otherwise look forward to as pleasant, may become so painful in anticipation from sympathy with the general uneasiness which he knows would arise upon the contemplation of it that, without any fear of punishment, he abstains from doing it.

4. Thus moral sense and sympathy jointly, as understood by Hume, serve plausibly to explain the office ordinarily ascribed to conscience, as the judge and possible controller in each man of his own acts. At the same time the lines are indicated along which a physical theory of ' conscience ' might be logically attempted. The problem which Hume bequeathed to a successor who adopted his principles was mainly to account for the twofold fact, that the mere survey of actions as tending to produce pleasures in which the contemplator will have no share, is yet a source of pleasure to him ; and that, among the pleasures taken into account in that estimate of the tendency of an action which determines the moral sentiment, are such as have no direct connexion with the satisfaction of animal wants. A theory which will account for this will also account for the affection of the agent by sympathy with the sentiment which the contemplation of his action excites in others. Can we find any scientific warrant for believing in a process by which, out of susceptibility to pleasures incidental to the merely animal life, there have grown those capacities for enjoyment which we consider essential to general well-being, and those social interests which not only make the contemplation of general well-being an independent source of pleasure, but also make the pleasure of exciting this pleasure—the pleasure of satisfying the moral sentiment of others—an object of desire so strong as in many cases to determine action? If we can, it would seem that we have given to our national system of ethics—the ethics of moral sentiment—the solid foundation of a natural science.

5. It is no wonder, therefore, that the evolutionists of our day should claim to have given a wholly new character to ethical enquiries. In Hume's time a philosopher who denied the innateness of the moral sentiments, and held that they must have a natural history, had only the limits of the individual life within which to trace this history. These limits did not give room enough for even a plausible derivation of moral interests from animal wants. It is otherwise when the history may be supposed to range over an indefinite number of generations. The doctrine of hereditary transmission, it is held, explains to us how susceptibilities of pleasure and pain, of desire and aversion, of hope and fear, may be handed down with gradually accumulated modifications which in time attain the full measure of the difference between the moral man and the greater ape. Through long ages of interaction between the human organism and the social medium in which it lives, there has been developed that 'sensibility of principle which feels a stain like a wound;' that faculty of moral intuition which not only pronounces unerringly on the social tendencies of the commoner forms of human action, but enables us in some measure to see ourselves as others see us; that civil spirit through which the promptings of personal passion are controlled even in the individual by the larger vision and calmer interest of society.

Thus it would seem that for the barren speculation of the old metaphysical ethics we should seek a substitute in a scientific 'Culturgeschichte'; in a natural history of man conducted on the same method as an enquiry into any other form of life which cannot be reduced to the operation of strictly mechanical laws. For the later stages of this history we have, of course, abundant materials in the actual monuments of human culture—linguistic, literary, and legal—and these, the physiologist may say, have yet to be considered in connexion with the data which his own science furnishes. It is true that, however far they carry us back, however great the variations of moral sentiment to which they testify, they do not bring us to a state of things in which the essential conditions of that sentiment were absent. The most primitive man they exhibit to us is already conscious of his own good as conditioned by that of others, already capable of recognising an obligation. But the theory of descent and evolution opens up a vista of possibilities beyond the facts, so far ascertained, of human history, and suggests an enquiry into the antecedents of the moralised man based on other data than the records which he has left of himself. Such enquiry, it is thought, will in time give us the means of reducing the moral susceptibilities of man to the rank of ordinary physical facts, parts of one system, and intelligible by the same methods, with all the natural phenomena which we are learning to know. Man will then have his ascertained place in nature, as perhaps the noblest of the animals, but an animal still.

6. When the moral sentiment has been explained on the principles of natural science, free-will is not likely to be regarded as presenting any serious obstacle to the same mode of treatment. By those of our national philosophers who have asserted its existence, it has generally been understood as a faculty of determining action apart from determination by motives; as a power, distinct alike from reason and from desire, which chooses between motives without being itself dependent on any motive. So crude a notion must long ago have given way before the questions of science, if there had not been a practical conviction behind

it which it failed fairly to interpret. What after all, it is asked, is any faculty but an hypostatised abstraction? A faculty is no more than a possibility. Whatever happens implies no doubt a possibility of its happening. Voluntary action implies a possibility of voluntary action, just as the motion of a billiard-ball implies a possibility of that motion; but the possibility in each is determined by definite conditions. In the case of the billiard-ball these conditions, or some of them, are so obvious that we do not think of treating the possibility of the ball's moving as a faculty inherent in the ball, and of ascribing the ball's motion to this faculty as its cause; although, as we know, when the causes of a motion are less apparent, the uninstructed are quite ready to ascribe it to a faculty or power in the moving body. In ascribing any voluntary action to a faculty in man, we are doing, it is said, just the same as in ascribing any particular motion to a faculty in the moving body. The fact is the particular voluntary action, which must be possible, no doubt, or it would not be done, but of which the real possibility consists in the assemblage of conditions which make up its cause. To include any faculty of action among these is merely to express our ignorance of what they are or our unwillingness to examine them. Among them, it is true, is the wish which happens to be predominant in the agent at the moment of action; but this, too, has its definite conditions in the circumstances of the case and the motives operating on the agent. It may be owing to the character of the agent that one of these motives gets the upper hand; but his character again is only a name for an assemblage of conditions, of which it may be scarcely possible for us completely to trace the antecedents, but which we are not on that account justified in assigning to a cause that is no cause, but merely a verbal substantiation of the abstraction of our ignorance. Human freedom must be understood in some different sense from that with which our anthropologists are familiar, if it is to stand in the way of the scientific impulse to naturalise the moral man.

7. We will suppose then that a theory has been formed which professes to explain, on the method of a natural history conducted according to the principle of evolution, the process by which the human animal has come, according to the terminology in vogue, to exhibit the phenomena of a moral life—to have a conscience, to feel remorse, to pursue ideals, to be capable of education through appeals to the sense of honour and of shame, to be conscious of antagonism between the common and private good, and even sometimes to prefer the former. It has generally been expected of a moralist, however, that he should explain not only how men do act, but how they should act: and as a matter of fact we find that those who regard the process of man's natural development most strictly as a merely natural one are as forward as any to propound rules of living, to which they conceive that, according to their view of the influences which make him what he is, man *ought* to conform. The natural science of man is to them the basis of a practical art. They seek to discover what are the laws—the modes of operation of natural forces—under which we have come to be what we are, in order that they may counsel us how to seek our happiness by living according to those laws.

Now it is obvious that to a being who is simply a result of natural forces an injunction to conform to their laws is unmeaning. It implies that there is something in him independent of those forces, which may determine the relation in which he shall stand to them. A philosopher, then, who would reconstruct our ethical systems in conformity with the doctrines of evolution and descent, if he would be consistent, must deal less scrupulously with them than perhaps any one has yet been found to do. If he has the courage of his principles, having reduced the speculative part of them to a natural science, he must abolish the practical or preceptive part altogether. Instead, for instance, of telling men of a greatest sum of pleasures which they ought to seek, and which by acting in the light of a true insight into natural laws they may attain, he will content himself with ascertaining, so far as he can, whether such and such a temperament under such and such circumstances yields more frequent, durable, and intense pleasures than such another temperament under such other circumstances. He will not mock the misery of him who fails, nor flatter the self-complacency of him who prospers, by speaking of a happiness that is to be obtained by conformity to the laws of nature, when he knows that, according to his own principles, it is a struggle for existence determined by those laws which has brought the one to his wretchedness and the other to his contentment. He will rather set himself to show how the phraseology of 'ought' and 'ought not,' the belief in a good attainable by all, the consciousness of something that should be though it is not, may according to his philosophy be accounted for. Nor, if he has persuaded himself that the human consciousness, as it is, can be physically accounted for, will he find any further difficulty in thus explaining that language of moral injunction which forms so large an element in its expression. He will probably trace this language to the joint action of two factors—to the habit of submission to the commands of a physical or political superior, surviving the commands themselves and the memory of them, combined with that constant though ineffectual wish for a condition of life other than his own, which is natural to a being who looks before and after over perpetual alternations of pleasure and pain.

8. The elimination of ethics, then, as a system of precepts, involves no intrinsic difficulties other than those involved in the admission of a natural science that can account for the moralisation of man. The discovery, however, that our assertions of moral obligation are merely the expression of an ineffectual wish to be better off than we are, or are due to the survival of habits originally enforced by physical fear, but of which the origin is forgotten, is of a kind to give us pause. It logically carries with it the conclusion, however the conclusion may be disguised, that, in inciting ourselves or others to do anything because it ought to be done, we are at best making use of a serviceable illusion.   And when this consequence is found to follow logically from the conception of man as in his moral attributes a subject of natural science, it may lead to a reconsideration of a doctrine which would otherwise have been taken for granted as the most important outcome of modern enlightenment.   As the first charm of accounting for what has previously seemed the mystery of our moral nature passes away, and the spirit of criticism returns, we cannot but enquire whether a being that was merely a result of natural forces could form a theory of those forces as explaining himself.   We have to return once more to that analysis of the conditions of knowledge, which forms the basis of all Critical Philosophy whether called by the name of Kant or no, and to ask whether the experience of connected matters of fact, which in its methodical expression we call science, does not presuppose a principle which is not itself any one or number of such matters of fact, or their result.

Can the knowledge of nature be itself a part or product of nature, in that sense of nature in which it is said to be an object of knowledge?   This is our first question.   If it is answered in the negative, we shall at least have satisfied ourselves that man, in respect of the function called knowledge, is not merely a child of nature.   We shall have ascertained the presence in him of a principle not natural, and a specific function of this principle in rendering knowledge possible.   The way will then be so far cleared for the further question which leads us, in the language of Kant, from the Critique of Speculative to that of Practical Reason : the question whether the same principle has not another expression than that which appears in the determination of experience and through it in our knowledge of a world—an expression which consists in the consciousness of a moral ideal and the determination of human action thereby.

BOOK I

CHAPTER I

THE SPIRITUAL PRINCIPLE IN KNOWLEDGE AND IN NATURE

9. THE question, Can the knowledge of nature be itself a part or product of nature? must not be confused with that commonly supposed to be at issue between spiritualists and materialists. It is one which equally remains to be put, in whatever way we understand the relation between body and mind. We may have admitted most unreservedly that all the so-called functions of the soul are materially conditioned, but the question how there come to be for us those objects of consciousness, called matter and motion, on which we suppose the operations of sense and desire and thought to be dependent, will still remain to be answered. If it could be admitted that matter and motion had an existence *in themselves*, or otherwise than as related to a consciousness, it would still not be by *such* matter and motion, but by the matter and motion which we know, that the functions of the soul, or anything else, can for us be explained. Nothing can be known by help of reference to the unknown. But matter and motion, just so far as known, consist in, or are determined by, relations between the objects of that connected consciousness which we call experience. If we take any definition of matter, any account of its 'necessary qualities,' and abstract from it all that consists in a statement of relations between facts in the way of feeling, or between objects that we present to ourselves as sources of feeling, we shall find that there is nothing left. Motion, in like manner, has no meaning except such as is derived from a synthesis of the different positions successively held by one and the same body; and we shall try in vain to render an account to ourselves of position or succession, of a body or its identity, except as expressing relations of what is contained in experience, through which alone that content possesses a definite character and becomes a connected whole.

What then is the source of these relations, as relations of the experienced, in other words, of that which exists for consciousness? What is the principle of union which renders them possible? Clearly it cannot itself be conditioned by any of the relations which result from its combining and unifying action. Being that which so organises experience that the relations expressed by our definitions of matter and motion arise therein, it cannot itself be determined by those relations. It cannot be a matter or motion. However rigidly, therefore, we may exclude from our explanations of phenomena all causes that are not reducible to matter and motion, however fully we may admit that the nature which we know or may know is knowable only under strictly physical laws, we are none the less in effect asserting the existence of something which, as the source of a connected experience, renders both the nature that we know and our knowledge of it possible, but is not itself physically conditioned. We may decide all the questions that have been debated between materialists and spiritualists as to the explanation of particular facts in favour of the former, but the possibility of explaining them at all will still remain to be explained. We shall still be logically bound to admit that in a man who can know a nature—for whom there is a 'cosmos of experience'[1]—there is a principle which is not natural and which cannot without a ὕστερον πρότερον be explained as we explain the facts of nature.

10. There are certain accepted doctrines of modern philosophy—*e.g.*, that knowledge is only of phenomena, not of anything unrelated to consciousness, and that object and subject are correlative—from which this conclusion seems to follow so inevitably, that any one who has adopted it must enquire anxiously why it is not more generally recognised. If nothing can enter into knowledge that is unrelated to

[1] I borrow the phrase from Mr. G. H. Lewes.

consciousness; if relation to a subject is necessary to make an object, so that an object which no consciousness presented to itself would not be an object at all; it is as difficult to see how the principle of unity, through which phenomena become the connected system called the world of experience, can be found elsewhere than in consciousness, as it is to see how the consciousness exercising such a function can be a part of the world which it thus at least co-operates in making; how it can be a phenomenon among the phenomena which it unites into a knowledge. Why then do our most enlightened interpreters of nature take it as a matter of course that the principle of unity in the world of our experience is something which, whatever else it is—and they can say nothing else of it—is at any rate the negation of consciousness, and that consciousness itself is a phenomenon or group of phenomena in which this 'nature' exhibits itself or results? And why is it that, when we have professedly discarded this doctrine, we still find it to a great extent controlling our ordinary thoughts? There must be reasons for this inconsistency, which should be duly considered if we would understand what we are about in maintaining that there is a sense in which man is related to nature as its author, as well as one in which he is related to it as its child.

11. The reader is probably acquainted with Kant's dictum that 'the understanding makes nature.' It gives no doubt a somewhat startling expression to the revolution in philosophy which Kant believed himself to have introduced, and which he compared to the change effected by the Copernican theory in men's conception of the relative positions of the earth and the sun. When we enquire, however, into the precise sense in which Kant used the expression, we find that its meaning is subject to a qualification which testifies to the difficulty experienced by Kant himself in carrying out the doctrine which the words seemed to convey. 'Macht zwar der Verstand die Natur, aber er schafft sie nicht.' The understanding 'makes' nature, but out of a material which it does not make. That material, according to Kant, consists in phenomena or 'data' of sensibility, given under the so-called forms of intuition, space and time. This apparent ascription of nature to a twofold origin—an origin in understanding in respect of its form as a nature, as a single system of experience; an origin elsewhere in respect of the 'matter' which through the action of understanding becomes a nature—cannot but strike us as unsatisfactory. Perhaps it may not be a doctrine in which we can permanently acquiesce, but meanwhile it represents fairly enough on its two sides the considerations which on the one hand lead us to regard nature as existing only in relation to thought, and those on the other which seem obstinately opposed to such a view.

12. To say with Kant that the understanding is the principle of objectivity, that only through understanding is there for us an objective world, is sure to seem at first sight the extreme of perversity. We have come to think of the understanding as specially an agency of our own, and of the objective world as specially that which is presented to us independently of any such agency; as that which we find and do not make, and by which we have to correct the fictions of our own minds. When we ask, however, whether any impression is or represents anything 'real and objective,' what exactly does the question mean, and how do we set about answering it? It is not equivalent to a question whether a feeling is felt. Some feeling must be felt in order to the possibility of the question being raised at all. It is a question whether a given feeling is what it is taken to be ; or, in other words, whether it is related as it seems to be related. It may be objected indeed that, though *some* feeling or other must be felt in order to give any meaning to the question as to the objectivity of the impression or its correspondence with reality, yet still this question may and often does mean merely whether a *particular* feeling is felt. This is true ; but a particular feeling is a feeling related in a certain way, and the question whether a particular feeling is really felt is always translatable into the form given—Is a feeling, which is undoubtedly felt, really related as some one thinking about it takes it to be? If an engine-driver, under certain conditions, permanent with him or temporary, 'sees a signal wrong,' as we say, his disordered vision has its own reality just as much as if he saw right. There are relations between combinations of moving particles on the one side and his visual organs on the other, between the present state of the latter and certain determining conditions, between the immediate sensible effect and the secondary impressions which it in turn excites, as full and definite—with sufficient enquiry and opportunity, as ascertainable—as in any case of normal vision. There is as much reality in the one case as in the other, but it is not the same reality : *i. e.*, it does not consist in the same relations. The engine-driver mistakes the effect of one set of relations for that of another, one reality for another, and hence his error in action. He may be quite innocent of a scientific theory of vision, but he objectifies his sensations. He interprets them as related in a certain way, and as always the same in the same relations; or, to use an equivalent but more familiar expression, as signs of objects from which he distinguishes his feelings and by which he explains them. Were this not the case, his vision might be normal or abnormal, but he would be incapable of mistaking one kind of reality for another, since he would have no conception of reality at all.

13. The terms 'real' and 'objective,' then, have no meaning except for a consciousness which presents its experiences to itself as determined by relations, and at the same time conceives a single and unalterable order of relations determining them, with which its temporary presentation, as each experience occurs, of the relations determining it may be contrasted. For such a consciousness, perpetually altering its views of the relations determining any experience under the necessity of combining them in one system with other recognised relations, and for such a consciousness only, there is significance in the judgment that any experience seems to be so and so, *i.e.*, to be related in a certain way, but really is otherwise related. We shall have afterwards [§ 19 and foll.] to consider the question whether the consciousness, for which alone this contrast of the real and the apparent is possible, has anything to do with the establishment of the relations in which it conceives reality to consist—whether the conception or reality has any identity with the act by which reality is constituted. But even if this latter question is waived or answered in the negative, there will still be an important sense in which understanding, or consciousness as acting in the manner described, may be said to be the principle of objectivity. It will be through it that there is *for us* an objective world; through it that we *conceive* an order of nature, with the unity of which we must reconcile our interpretations of phenomena, if they are to be other than 'subjective' illusions.

14. Of course it may very well be that many a man would disclaim any such conception, who is yet constantly acting upon the distinction between what he believes to be mere appearance and what he believes to be reality. But want of familiarity with the abstract expression of a conception, want of ability to analyse it, is no evidence that the conception is inoperative upon the experience of the person who, from this want of familiarity or ability, would say, if he were asked, that he had it not or knew not what it meant. The proof of the necessity of certain ideas has never been supposed, by any one who knew what he was about, to rest upon the fact that every one was aware of having them. Such a proof, to say nothing of the well-worked appeal to savages or the uneducated, would be at the mercy of every lively gentleman who was pleased to say that he searched his breast for such ideas in vain. The necessity of a conception, as distinct from the logical (or rather rhetorical) necessity of a conclusion contained in premisses already conceded, means that it is necessary to the experience without which there would not for us be a world at all; and there can be neither proof nor disproof of such necessity as is claimed for any conception, but through analysis of the conditions which render this experience possible. Unless the accuracy or sufficiency of the analysis can be disputed, the necessary character of the ideas which it exhibits as operative in the formation of experience, is unaffected by the inability of any one to recognise them in that abstract form to which the analysis reduces them, but which, just because they are operative in a concrete experience, is not the form of their familiar use.

Thus a man who is quite at home with the distinction between facts and fancies may think it strange to be told that the distinction implies a conception of the world as a single system of relations ; that this is the conception on the strength of which he constantly sets aside as fancy what he had taken to be fact, because he finds that the supposed relations, which for him formed the nature of the fact, are not such as can be combined with others that he recognises in one intelligible system. Such language may convey no meaning to him, but the question will still remain whether upon reflection the distinction can be otherwise accounted for. When we analyse our idea of matter of fact, can we express it except as an idea of a relation which is always the same between the same objects ; or our idea of an object except as that which is always the same in the same relations ? And does not each expression imply the idea of a world as a single and eternal system of related elements, which may be related with endless diversity but must *be* related still ? If we may properly call the consciousness which yields this idea 'understanding,' are we not entitled to say that understanding is the source of there being for us an objective world, that it is the principle of objectivity ?

15. So far we have only reached the conclusion that a conception, to which understanding is related as faculty to function, is the condition of our ability to distinguish a real from the unreal, matter of fact from illusion. It will be said perhaps that so much pains need not have been spent on establishing a proposition which in effect merely tells us that without a conception of an order of nature we could not conceive an order of nature. Is not this, it may be asked, either an identical proposition or untrue—an identical proposition, if understood strictly as thus put ; untrue, if taken to mean that the conception of an order of nature does not admit of being generated out of materials other than itself? Now it is just the difficulties in the way of explaining the origin of the conception in question out of anything else than judgments which presuppose it, that we wish to exhibit. They are the difficulties which beset any theory that would treat the knowledge of nature as itself the result of natural processes. It is through *experience* that every such theory must suppose the resulting know-ledge to be produced. But experience, as most students of philosophy must now be aware, is a term used in very different senses. In this case an experience which is to yield the required result must not be merely an experience in the sense in which, for instance, a plant might be said to experience a succession of atmospheric or chemical changes, or in which we ourselves pass through a definite physical experience during sleep or in respect of the numberless events which affect us but of which we are not aware. Such an experience may no doubt gradually alter to any extent the mode in which the physical organism reacts upon stimulus. It may be the condition of its becoming organic to intellectual processes, but between it and experience of the kind which is to yield a knowledge of nature there is a chasm which no one, except by confusion of speech, has attempted to fill. Or to speak more precisely, between the two senses of experience there is all the difference that exists between change and consciousness of change.

16. Experience of the latter kind must be experience of matters of fact *recognised as such*. It is possible, no doubt, to imagine a psychological history of this experience, and to trace it back to a stage in which the distinction between fact and fancy is not yet formally recognised. But there is a limit to this process. An experience which distinguishes fact from fancy cannot be developed out of one which is not, in some form or other, a consciousness of events as related or as a series of changes. It has commonly, and with much probability, been held that the occurrence of the unexpected, by exciting distrust in previously established associations of ideas, has at any rate a large share in generating the distinction of what seems from what is. But the shock of surprise is one thing, the correction of a belief quite another. Unless there were already a consciousness alike of the events, of which the ideas have become associated, as a related series, and of the newly observed event as a member of the same, the unfamiliar event might cause a disturbance of the nerves or the 'psychoplasm,' but there would neither be an incorrect belief as to an order of events to be corrected by it, nor any such correlation of the newly observed event with what had been observed before as could suggest a correction. But a consciousness of events as a related series—experience in the most elementary form in which it can be the beginning of knowledge—has not any element of identity with, and therefore cannot properly be said to be developed out of, a mere series of related events, of successive modifications of body or soul, such as is experience in the former of the senses spoken of. No one and no number of a series of related events can be the consciousness of the series as related. Nor can any product of the series be so either. Even if this product could be anything else than a further event, it could at any rate only be something that supervenes at a certain stage upon such of the events as have so far elapsed. But a consciousness of certain events cannot be anything that thus succeeds them. It must be equally present to all the events of which it is the consciousness. For this reason an intelligent experience, or experience as the source of knowledge, can neither be constituted by events of which it is the experience, nor be a product of them.

17. 'Perhaps not,' it may be replied, 'but may it not be a product of *previous* events?' If it is so, a series of events

of which there is no conscious experience must be supposed to produce a consciousness of another series. On any other supposition the difficulty is only postponed. For if the series of events which produces a certain consciousness of other events is one of which there *is* a consciousness, this consciousness, not being explicable as the product of the events of which it is the consciousness, will have in turn to be referred to a prior series of events ; and ultimately there will be no alternative between the admission of a consciousness which is not a product of events at all and the supposition stated—the supposition that the primary consciousness of events results from a series of events of which there is no consciousness. But this supposition, when we think of it, turns out to be a concatenation of words to which no possible connexion of ideas corresponds. It asserts a relation of cause and effect, in which the supposed cause lacks all the characteristics of a cause. It may be questioned whether we can admit anything as a cause which does not explain its supposed effect, or is not equivalent to the conditions into which the effect may be analysed. But granting that we may, a cause must at least be that to which experience testifies as the uniform antecedent of the effect. Now a series of events of which there is no consciousness is certainly not a set of conditions into which consciousness can be analysed. And as little can it be an antecedent uniformly associated with consciousness in experience, for events of which there is no consciousness cannot be within experience at all.

18. It seems necessary, then, to admit that experience, in the sense of a consciousness of events as a related series—and in no other sense can it help to account for the knowledge of an order of nature—cannot be explained by any natural history, properly so called. It is not a product of a series of events. It does not arise out of materials other than itself. It is not developed by a natural process out of other forms of natural existence. Given such a consciousness, the scientific conception of nature, no less than the every-day distinction between fact and fancy, between objective reality and subjective illusion, can be exhibited as a development of it, for there is an assignable element of identity between the two. But between the consciousness itself on the one hand, and on the other anything determined by the relations under which a nature is presented to consciousness, no process of development, because no community, can be really traced. Nature, with all that belongs to it, is a process of change : change on a uniform method, no doubt, but change still. All the relations under which we know it are relations in the way of change or by which change is determined. But neither can any process of change yield a consciousness of itself, which, in order to be a consciousness of the change, must be equally present to all stages of the change ; nor can any consciousness of change, since the whole of it must be present at once, be itself a process of change. There may be a change into a state of consciousness of change, and a change out of it, on the part of this man or that ; but within the consciousness itself there can be no change, because no relation of before and after, of here and there, between its constituent members—between the presentation, for instance, of point A and that of point B in the process which forms the object of the consciousness.

19. From the above considerations thus much at any rate would seem to follow : that a form of consciousness, which we cannot explain as of natural origin, is necessary to our conceiving an order of nature, an objective world of fact from which illusion may be distinguished. In other words, an understanding—for that term seems as fit as any other to denote the principle of consciousness in question—irreducible to anything else, 'makes nature' for us, in the sense of enabling us to conceive that there is such a thing. Now that which the understanding thus presents to itself consists, as we have seen, in certain relations regarded as forming a single system. The next question, then, will be whether understanding can be held to 'make nature' in the further sense that it is the source, or at any rate a condition, of there being these relations. If it cannot, we are left in the awkward position of having to suppose that, while the conception of an order of nature on the one side, and that order itself on the other, are of different and independent origin, there is yet some unaccountable pre-established harmony through which there comes to be such an order corresponding to our conception of it. This indeed might be urged as a reason for seeking some way of escape from the conclusion at which we have just arrived. But before we renew an attempt which has often been made and failed, let us see whether the objections to the other alternative—to the view that the understanding which presents an order of nature to us is in principle one with an understanding which constitutes that order itself—have really the cogency which common-sense seems to ascribe to them.

20. The traditional philosophy of common-sense, we shall find, speaks upon the point with an ambiguity which affords a presumption of its involving more difficulty than might at first sight appear. No one is more emphatic than Locke in opposing what is real to what we 'make for ourselves,' the work of nature to the work of the mind. Simple ideas or sensations we certainly do not 'make for ourselves.' They therefore and the matter supposed to cause them are, according to Locke, real[1]. But relations are neither simple ideas nor their material archetypes. They therefore, as Locke explicitly holds, fall under the head of the work of the mind, which is opposed to the real[2]. But if we take him at his word and exclude from what we have considered real all qualities constituted by relation, we find that none are left. Without relation any simple idea would be undistinguished from other simple ideas, undetermined by its surroundings in the cosmos of experience. It would thus be unqualified itself, and consequently could afford no qualification of the material archetype, which yet according to Locke we only

[1] Essay concerning Human Understanding, II. xii. 1.
[2] Ibid. II. xxv. 8.

know through it or, if otherwise, as the subject of those 'primary qualities' which demonstrably consist in relations[1]. In short, the admission of the antithesis between the real and the work of the mind, and the admission that relation is the work of the mind, put together, involve the conclusion that nothing is real of which anything can be said.

Our ordinary way out of the difficulty consists in keeping the two admissions apart, without, however, surrendering either. We maintain the opposition between the real and the work of the mind exactly as it was asserted by Locke; and if we are less explicit in accounting relations to be the work of the mind, it is not because we have any theory of the real which more logically admits them than does Locke's. Yet we have no scruple in accepting duly verified knowledge as representing reality, though what is known consists in nothing else than relations. We neither ask ourselves how it can be that a knowledge of relations should be a knowledge of reality, if the real is genuinely simple sensation or that which copies itself in simple sensation, nor what other account we can give of the real without qualifying the antithesis between the work of the mind and it. It is in fact from our adoption of this antithesis that we come to accept that identification of the real with simple sensation or its archetype which, as Locke was aware, implies the unreality of relations. But when in our processes of knowledge we have virtually recognised relations as constituting the very essence of reality, we do not reconsider our definition of the real in the light of this recognition. We do not lay our procedure in what we regard as knowledge of the real alongside Locke's view of the real, which is also ours, so as to ask whether they are consistent with each other. And hence we are not led to call in question the antithesis on which that view depends.

21. As it is a serious matter, however, to accept a view of the real which such a thinker as Locke could not reconcile with the reality of relations, and which logically

[1] Essay concerning Human Understanding, II. viii. 15 and 23; xxx. 2.

implies that knowledge is not of the real; and as on the other hand there is something in the opposition between the real and the work of the mind which seems to satisfy an imperative demand of common-sense; it becomes important to enquire whether we interpret that demand aright. Is there not a conception of the real behind the opposition in question, which seems to require us to accept it, but which in truth we misinterpret in doing so?

We constantly find Locke falling back on the consideration that of simple ideas ' we cannot *make* one to ourselves.' They 'force themselves upon us whether we will or no.' It is this which entitles them in his eyes to be accounted real. 'The work of the mind,' on the other hand, he considers arbitrary. A man has but to think, and he can make ideas of relation for himself as he pleases. Locke thus indicates what we may call the operative conception— operative as governing the action of our intelligence—which underlies the opposition between the real and the work of the mind. This is the conception which we have described already as that of a single and unalterable system of relations. It is not the work of the mind, as such, that we instinctively oppose to the real, but the work of the mind as assumed to be arbitrary and irregularly changeable.

22. In truth, however, there is no such thing. The very question, What is the real?—which we seem to answer by help of this opposition—is a misleading one, so far as it implies that there is something else from which the real can be distinguished. We are apt to make merry over the crude logic of Plato in supposing that there are objects, described as μὴ ὄντα, which stand in the same relation to ignorance as τὰ ὄντα to knowledge, and other objects, described as τὰ μεταξύ, which stand in a corresponding relation to mere opinion. Of this fallacy, as of most others that are to be found in him, Plato himself supplies the correction, but much of our language about the real implies that we are ourselves its victims. If there is a valid opposition between the work of the mind and something else which is not the

work of the mind, the one must still be just as real as the other. Of two alternatives, one. Either 'the work of the mind' is a name for nothing, expressing a mere privation or indeterminateness, a mere absence of qualities—in which case nothing is conveyed by the proposition which opposes the real or anything else to it : or, on the other hand, if it has qualities and relations of its own, then it is just as real as anything else. Through not understanding the relations which determine the one kind of object—that ascribed to the work of the mind—as distinct from those which determine the other—that ascribed to some other agency—we may confuse the two kinds of object. We may take what is really of the one kind to be really of the other. But this is not a confusion of the real with the unreal. The very confusion itself, the mistake of supposing what is related in one way to be related in another, has its own reality. It has its history, its place in the development of a man's mind, its causes and effects ; and, as so determined, it is as real as anything else.

23. It is thus in vain that we seek to define the real by finding, either in the work of the mind or elsewhere, an unreal to which it may be opposed. Is there, then, no meaning in an opposition which is constantly on our tongues? Undoubtedly that which any event seems to us to be may be—nay always is—more or less different from what it really is. The relations by which we judge it to be determined are not, or at any rate fall short of, those by which it is really determined. But this is a distinction between one particular reality and another ; not between a real, as such or as a whole, and an unreal, as such or as a whole. The illusive appearance, as opposed to the reality, of any event is what *that* event really is not ; but at the same time it really is something. It is real, not indeed with the particular reality which the subject of the illusion ascribes to it, but with a reality which a superior intelligence might understand. The relations by which, in a false belief as to a matter of fact, we suppose the event to be determined,

are not non-existent. They are really objects of a conceiving consciousness. As arising out of the action of such
a consciousness, as constituents of a world which it presents
to itself, they are no less real than are the actual conditions
of the event which is thought to be, but is not really, determined by them. It is when we reflect on the judgments in
which we are perpetually deciding that what has previously
been taken to be the reality of a particular event is a mere
appearance, *i.e.*, not the reality of that particular event —
or rather when we reflect on the language in which those
judgments have been expressed—that we come to speak of
the real, as an abstract universal, in contrast with another
abstract universal, the unreal. Thus for a contrast which is
in truth a contrast between two acts of judgment—the act of
judging an event to be determined by certain relations which,
according to the order of the universe, do determine it, and
that of judging it to be determined by relations other than
these—we substitute another, which exists merely in words,
but to which we fancy that we give a meaning by identifying
the unreal with the work of the mind, as opposed to a real
which has some other origin, we cannot say what.

24. What we have so far sought to show has been (1),
generally, that an attempt to define the real by distinction
from anything else is necessarily futile—the result of a false
abstraction from the distinction between the real nature of
one event or object and that of another—and (2), specially,
that the antithesis between the real and the work of the
mind is invalid, not because the real is the work of the
mind—whether it is so or not we have yet to enquire —but
because the work of the mind is real. The 'mere idea' of
a hundred thalers, to use the familiar instance, is no doubt
quite different from the possession of them, not because it
is unreal, but because the relations which form the real
nature of the idea are different from those which form the
real nature of the possession.

So much it was necessary to show, in order that the
enquiry, whether it is due to 'understanding' not merely

that we are able to conceive a nature but that there is such a thing as nature at all, might not be prejudiced by a preconception which would make it seem equivalent to an enquiry whether the real could be the work of the unreal. If now from the futile question, What is the real? which we can only answer by saying that the real is everything, we pass to one more hopeful—How do we decide whether any particular event or object is really what it seems to be, or whether our belief about it is true?—the answer must be that we do so by testing the unalterableness of the qualities which we ascribe to it, or which form its apparent nature. A certain hill appears to-day to be near : yesterday under different conditions of atmosphere it appeared to be remote. But the real nature of the event which took place in yesterday's appearance cannot, we judge, thus change. What it was really, it was unalterably. There may have been a change from that appearance to another, but not a change of or in whatever was the reality of the appearance. The event of yesterday's appearance, then, must have been determined by conditions other than those which determine to-day's. But if both appearances depended solely on the position of the hill, they would be determined by the same conditions. Therefore we must have been wrong in believing the hill to be so remote as we believed it to be yesterday, or in believing it to be so near as we believed it to be to-day, or in both beliefs : wrong in respect of the relation which we supposed to exist between the several appearances and the distance of the hill.

25. With sufficient time and command of detail it would not be difficult to show how the conviction here illustrated, that whatever anything is really it is unalterably, regulates equally our most primitive and our most developed judgments of reality—the every-day supposition of there being a multitude of separate things which remain the same in themselves while their appearances to us alter, and the scientific quest for uniformity or unalterableness in a law of universal change. Through a slight confusion of thought and expression, this conviction may issue either in the sensational atomism of

Locke or in the material atomism of popular science. A sen
sation is the unalterable effect of its conditions, whatever
those conditions may be. It is unalterably related to other
sensations. Our opinion about its conditions or relations
may vary, but not the conditions or relations themselves, or
the sensation determined by them. Hence when a man
looks into his breast, as Locke bids him do, simple feelings—
feelings apart from intellectual interpretations and combinations of them—seem alone unalterable in contrast with our
judgments about them. In truth the unalterableness belongs not to any simple feeling, for our feelings change every
moment upon us, but, as we have said, to the relation between it and its conditions or between it and other feelings ;
and such a relation is neither itself a feeling nor represented
in our consciousness by a feeling. This distinction, however, is overlooked. The unalterableness of the fact that
a certain feeling is felt under certain conditions, is ascribed to
the simple feeling, or simple idea, as such : and unalterableness being the test by which we ascertain whether what we
have believed to be the nature of any event is really so or
not, the simple feeling, which by itself cannot properly be
said to be really anything, comes to be regarded either as
alone real, according to the ideal form of sensationalism, or
as alone representing an external reality, according to the
materialistic form of the same doctrine.

On the other hand, reflection upon the 'perpetual flux' of
sensation suggests the view that it is not real in the same
sense as its material conditions. The old dictum ascribed
to Democritus—νόμῳ γλυκὺ καὶ νόμῳ πικρόν, νόμῳ θερμόν, νόμῳ
ψυχρόν, νόμῳ χροιή· ἐτεῇ δὲ ἄτομα καὶ κενόν [1]—expresses a way
of thinking into which we often fall. The reality which in
truth lies in the relations, according to one law or system
of relation, between feelings and their material conditions—
not in the material conditions abstracted from the feelings
any more than in the feelings abstracted from their material

[1] Sweet, bitter, hot, cold, colour, are by convention ; only atoms
and void are real.

conditions—we are apt to ascribe exclusively to the latter. We think obscurely of matter and motion as real in some way in which nothing else is. Nor do we stop here. The demand for unalterableness in what we believe to be real, when once we are off the right track of seeking it in a uniform law of change, leads us to suppose that the 'reality of things' is only reached when we have penetrated to atoms which in all changes of their motion and distribution remain intrinsically the same.

26. Let us consider now how we stand. We have rejected the question, What is or constitutes the real? as intrinsically unmeaning, because it could only be answered by a distinction which would imply that there was something unreal. The question arises, we have seen, out of an abstraction from our constant enquiry into the real nature of this or that particular appearance or event—an enquiry in which we always seek for an unchanging relation between the appearance and its conditions, or again for an unchanging relation between these and certain other conditions. The complete determination of an event it may be impossible for our intelligence to arrive at. There may always remain unascertained conditions which may render the relation between an appearance and such conditions of it as we know, liable to change. But that there *is* an unalterable order of relations, if we could only find it out, is the presupposition of all our enquiry into the real nature of appearances; and such unalterableness implies their inclusion in one system which leaves nothing outside itself. Are we then entitled to ask—and if so, are we able to answer—the further question, What is implied in there being such a single, all-inclusive, system of relations? or, What is the condition of its possibility? If this question can be answered, the condition ascertained will be the condition of there being a nature and of anything being real, in the only intelligible sense that we can attach to the words 'nature' and 'real.' It would no doubt still be open to the sceptic, should this result be attained, to suggest that the validity of our conclusion, upon our own showing, depends upon there really being such an order of nature as our quest of knowledge supposes there to be, which remains unproven. But as the sceptic, in order to give his language a meaning, must necessarily make the same supposition—as he can give no meaning to reality but the one explained— his suggestion that there really may not be such an order of nature is one that conveys nothing at all.

27. First, then, is there any meaning in the question just put? Having set aside as unmeaning the question, What is the real? can we be entitled to ask, What is implied in there being a nature of things? If the former question would have been only answerable on the self-contradictory supposition of there really being something other than the real from which it could be distinguished, will not the latter in like manner be only answerable on the equally impossible supposition of there being something outside the nature of things, outside the one all-inclusive system of relations, by reference to which this nature or system can be explained? To this we reply that the question stated is or is not one that can be fitly asked, according as the conception of nature, of a single all-inclusive system of relations, is or is not one that can stand alone, is or is not one that requires something else to render it intelligible. To suppose that this 'something else,' if nature were found unthinkable without it, is related to those conditions, of which the relation to each other forms the system of nature, in the same way in which these are related to each other, would no doubt be in contradiction with our account of this system as one and all-inclusive. It could not therefore be held to be related to them as, for instance, an invariable antecedent to an invariable sequent, or as one body to another outside it. But there would be no contradiction in admitting a principle which renders all relations possible, and is itself determined by none of them, if, on considera- tion of what is needed to constitute a system of relations, we found such a principle to be requisite.

28. This, then, is the consideration which we have now to undertake. Relation is to us such a familiar fact that we are apt to forget that it involves all the mystery, if it be a mystery, of the existence of many in one. Whether we say that a related thing is one in itself, manifold in respect of its relations, or that there is one relation between manifold things, *e.g.*, the relation of mutual attraction between bodies—and one expression or the other we must employ in stating the simplest facts—we are equally affirming the unity of the manifold. Abstract the many relations from the one thing, and there is nothing. They, being many, determine or constitute its definite unity. It is not the case that it first exists in its unity, and then is brought into various relations. Without the relations it would not exist at all. In like manner the one relation is a unity of the many things. They, in their manifold being, make the one relation. If these relations really exist, there is a real unity of the manifold, a real multiplicity of that which is one. But a plurality of things cannot of themselves unite in one relation, nor can a single thing of itself bring itself into a multitude of relations. It is true, as we have said, that the single things are nothing except as determined by relations which are the negation of their singleness, but they do not therefore cease to be single things. Their common being is not something into which their several existences disappear. On the contrary, if they did not survive in their singleness, there could be no relation between them—nothing but a blank featureless identity. There must, then, be something other than the manifold things themselves, which combines them without effacing their severalty.

29. With such a combining agency we are familiar as our intelligence. It is through it that the sensation of the present moment takes a character from comparison with the sensation of a moment ago, and that the occurrence, consisting in the transition from one to the other, is presented to us. It is essential to the comparison and to the character which the sensations acquire from the comparison, essential, too, to their forming an observable event or succession, that one should not be fused with the other, that the distinct being of each should be maintained. On the other hand, in the relation to which their distinctness is thus necessary they are at the same time united. But if it were not for the action of something which is not either of them or both together, there would be no alternative between their separateness and their fusion. One might give place to the other, or both together might be combined into a third; but a unity in which their distinctness is preserved could not be constituted without the relating act of an intelligence which does not blend with either.

The above is an instance of relation between sensations which, as brought into relation by intelligence, become sensible objects or events. But the same or an analogous action is necessary to account for any relation whatever—for a relation between material atoms as much as any other. Either then we must deny the reality of relations altogether and treat them as fictions of our combining intelligence; or we must hold that, being the product of our combining intelligence, they are yet 'empirically real' on the ground that our intelligence is a factor in the real of experience; or if we suppose them to be real otherwise than merely as for us, otherwise than in the 'cosmos of our experience,' we must recognise as the condition of this reality the action of some unifying principle analogous to that of our understanding.

30. As we have seen, the first of these alternative views, if consistently carried out, will not allow us to regard anything as real of which anything can be said, since all predication is founded on relation of some kind. It therefore naturally leads to the second. All that we in fact count real turns out to be determined by relations. Feeling may be the revelation or the test of the real, but it must be feeling in certain relations, or it neither reveals nor tests anything. Thus we are obliged to recognise a reality, at least of that kind which in our every-day knowledge and action we distinguish from illusion, in what is yet the work of the mind, or at any rate must be held to be so until relations can be accounted for without a relating act or that act referred to something else than the mind.   Hence with those who adhere to the opposition between the real and the work of the mind, and who at the same time cannot ignore the work of the mind in the constitution of relations, there arises a distinction between reality in some absolute sense—the reality of 'things-in-themselves,' which are supposed to be wholly exempt from any qualification through relating acts of the mind, but of which, for that reason, nothing can be known or said—and the 'empirical' reality of that which we distinguish from illusion, as standing in definite relations to the universe of our experience.

31. This distinction governs the theory of Kant.   It is more easy to point out the embarrassments and inconsistencies into which it leads him, than to get rid of the distinction itself.   Ordinary criticism of Kant, indeed, has not taken much heed of the distinction or of its perplexing results.   It has been too busy in refuting his doctrine that 'laws of nature' are derived from understanding, to enquire closely into his view of the relation between nature, in his sense of the term, and 'things-in-themselves.'   It has been gaining apparent triumphs, due to a misunderstanding of the question at issue, over the strongest part of his system, while it has left the weakest unassailed.   There have been abundant proofs of what was not in dispute, that our knowledge of laws of nature is the result of experience ; but the question whether phenomena could be so related as to constitute the nature which is the object of our experience without the unifying action of understanding is seldom even touched. Given an experience of phenomena related to each other in one system—so related that, whatever an object is really, or according to the fulness of its relations, it is unalterably—it is easy to show that our knowledge of laws of nature is derived from it.   Such experience in its most elementary form is already implicitly a knowledge that there are laws of nature, and only needs to be reflected on in order to become so explicitly.   When it has become so explicitly, the develop-

ment of the experience—through cognisance of relations of which there has previously been no experience, or of which the experience has not been reflected on—becomes a growing knowledge of what the laws of nature in particular are.

But the derivation of knowledge from an experience of unalterably related phenomena is its derivation from objects unalterably related in consciousness. If the relation of the objects were not a relation of them in consciousness, there would be no experience of it. The question then arises how a succession of feelings becomes such a relation of objects in consciousness. If a relation of objects existed or could be known to exist otherwise than for consciousness, this would not help to account for what has to be accounted for, which is wholly a process of consciousness. The feelings which succeed each other are no doubt due to certain related conditions, which are not feelings. But granting for the moment that these conditions and their relation exist independently of consciousness, in accounting for a multitude of feelings they do not account for the experience of related objects. Of two objects which form the terms of a relation one cannot exist as so related without the other, and therefore cannot exist before or after the other. For this reason the objects between which a relation subsists, even a relation of succession, are, just so far as related, not successive. In other words, a succession always implies something else than the terms of the succession, and that a 'something else' which can simultaneously present to itself objects as existing not simultaneously but one before the other.

32. Thus, in order that successive feelings may be related objects of experience, even objects related in the way of succession, there must be in consciousness an agent which distinguishes itself from the feelings, uniting them in their severalty, making them equally present in their succession. And so far from this agent being reducible to, or derivable from, a succession of feelings, it is the condition of there being such a succession ; the condition of the existence of that relation between feelings, as also of those other relations which are not indeed relations between feelings, but which, if they are matter of experience, must have their being in consciousness. If there is such a thing as a connected experience of related objects, there must be operative in consciousness a unifying principle, which not only presents related objects to itself, but at once renders them objects and unites them in relation to each other by this act of presentation; and which is single throughout the experience. The unity of this principle must be correlative to the unity of the experience. If all possible experience of related objects—the experience of a thousand years ago and the experience of to-day, the experience which I have here and that which I might have in any other region of space—forms a single system; if there can be no such thing as an experience of unrelated objects; then there must be a corresponding singleness in that principle of consciousness which forms the bond of relation between the objects.

33. It is such a principle that Kant speaks of sometimes as the 'synthetic unity of apperception,' sometimes simply as 'understanding.' For the reasons stated there seems no way of escape from the admission that it is, as he says, 'the basis of the necessary regularity of all phenomena in an experience[1]:' the basis, that is to say, not merely of our knowledge of uniform relations between phenomena, but of there being those uniform relations. The source of the relations, and the source of our knowledge of them, is one and the same. The question, how it is that the order of nature answers to our conception of it—or, as it is sometimes put, the question, whether nature really has, or, having, will continue to have, the uniformity which belongs to it in our conception—is answered by recognition of the fact that our conception of an order of nature, and the relations which form that order, have a common spiritual source. The uniformity of nature does not mean that its constituents are everywhere the same, but that they are

---

[1] Kant's Werke, ed. Rosenkranz, II. p. 114; ed. Hartenstein (1867), III. p. 585.

everywhere related ; not that 'the thing which has been is that which shall be,' but that whatever occurs is determined by relation to all that has occurred, and contributes to determine all that will occur.   If nature means the system of objects of possible experience, such uniformity necessarily arises in it from the action of the same principle which is implied in there being any relation between the objects of experience at all.   A relation not related to all other relations of which there can be experience, is an impossibility.   It cannot exist except as constituted by the unifying subject of all experienced relations, and this condition of its possibility implies its connexion with all other relations that are, or come to be, so constituted.   Every real relation, therefore, that is also knowable, is a necessary or 'objective' or unalterable relation.   It is a fact of which the existence is due to the action of that single subject of experience which is equally, and in the same way, the condition of all facts that can be experienced ; a fact which thus, through that subject, stands in definite and unchangeable connexion with the universe of those facts, at once determining and determined by them.

34.   The result of this view is to overcome the separation, which in our ordinary thinking we assume, between the faculty or capacity or subjective process of experience on the one side and the facts experienced on the other.   In first reflecting on our knowledge of a world, we always regard the facts known as existing quite independently of the activity by means of which they are known.   Since it is obvious that the facts of the world do not come into existence when this or that person becomes acquainted with them, so long as we conceive of no intellectual action but that which this or that person exercises, we necessarily regard the existence or occurrence of the facts as independent of intellectual action. Hence arises the antithesis between the known or knowable world and the subject capable of knowing it, as between two existences independent of each other, or of which the former is at any rate independent of the latter.   The mind is supposed to derive its materials from, and to act only in response to, the action of the world upon it ; but the relations which it establishes between the materials, so derived, in its processes of distinction and comparison, of conception, judgment, and discourse, are supposed to be quite different, and to have a different source, from the relations between things or matters of fact in the world known. Upon further reflection, however, the untenableness of this view becomes apparent. It renders knowledge, as of fact or reality, inexplicable. It leaves us without an answer to the question, how the order of relations, which the mind sets up, comes to reproduce those relations of the material world which are assumed to be of a wholly different origin and nature. Nor, as we pursue the analysis of the operations involved in the simplest perception of fact, are we able to detect any residuary phenomenon amounting to a fact at all, that can be held to be given independently of a combining and relating activity, which, if the antithesis between the work of the mind and the work of things be accepted, must be ascribed to the former.

35. The necessity, therefore, of getting rid of the antithesis in question forces itself upon us : and it is natural that the way of doing so, which at first sight most commends itself to us, should consist in treating the mind and its work as a secondary result of what had previously been opposed to it as operations of nature. The weakness of such a method is twofold. In the first place there is the objection upon which we have already dwelt and which may be put summarily thus : that 'nature' is a *process of change*, and that the derivation of a *consciousness* of change from such a process is impossible. Secondly, such an explanation of the work of the mind, if nothing is known of it otherwise, is an explanation of it by the inexplicable. It is taking nature for granted, and at the same time treating that as a result of nature which is necessary to explain the possibility of there being such a thing as nature. For nature, as a process of continuous change, implies something which is other than the changes and to which they are relative. As a system of related elements it implies a unity, through relation to which the elements are related to each other. But with the reduction of thought or spirit or self-consciousness to a result of nature, if such reduction were possible, we should be eliminating the only agent that we know as maintaining an identity with itself throughout a series of changes, or as a principle that can unite a manifold without cancelling its multiplicity. In so explaining spirit we should be rendering the basis of our explanation itself inexplicable.

36. From the Kantian point of view, the dualism of nature and knowledge is disposed of in a different way. They are not identified but treated as forming an indivisible whole, which results from the activity of a single principle. It is not that first there is nature, and that then there comes to be an experience and knowledge of it. Intelligence, experience, knowledge, are no more a result of nature than nature of them. If it is true that there would be no intelligence without nature, it is equally true that there would be no nature without intelligence. Nature is the system of related appearances, and related appearances are impossible apart from the action of an intelligence. They are not indeed the same as intelligence; it is not reducible to them nor they to it, any more than one of us is reducible to the series of his actions or that series to him ; but without it they would not be, nor except in the activity which constitutes them has it any real existence. Does this then imply the absurdity that nature comes into existence in the process by which this person or that begins to think ? Not at all, unless it is necessary to suppose that intelligence first comes into existence when this person or that begins to understand—a supposition not only not necessary, but which, on examination, will be found to involve impossibilities analogous to those which prevent us from supposing that nature so comes into existence.

The difference between what may be called broadly the Kantian view and the ordinary view is this, that whereas, according to the latter, it is a world in which thought is no necessary factor that is prior to, and independent of, the process by which this or that individual becomes acquainted with it, according to the former it is a world already determined by thought, and existing only in relation to thought, that is thus prior to, and conditions, our individual acquaintance with it. The growth of knowledge on our part is regarded not as a process in which facts or objects, in themselves unrelated to thought, by some inexplicable means gradually produce intelligible counterparts of themselves in thought. The true account of it is held to be that the concrete whole, which may be described indifferently as an eternal intelligence realised in the related facts of the world, or as a system of related facts rendered possible by such an intelligence, partially and gradually reproduces itself in us, communicating piece-meal, but in inseparable correlation, understanding and the facts understood, experience and the experienced world.

37. There are difficulties enough, no doubt, in the way of accepting such a form of 'idealism,' but they need not be aggravated by misunderstanding. It is simply misunderstood if it is taken to imply either the reduction of facts to feelings—impressions and ideas, in Hume's terminology—or the obliteration of the distinction between illusion and reality. The reduction of facts to relations is the very reverse of their reduction to feelings. No feeling, as such or as felt, is a relation. We can only suppose it to be so through confusion between it and its conditions, or between it and that fact of its occurrence which is no doubt related to other facts, but, as so related, is not felt. Even a relation between feelings is not itself a feeling or felt. A feeling can only be felt as successive to another feeling, but the terms of a relation, as we have seen, even though the relation be one of succession, do not succeed one another. In order to constitute the relation they must be present together; so that, to constitute a relation between feelings, there must be something other than the feelings for which they are equally present. The relation between the feelings is not felt, because it is only for something that distinguishes itself from the feelings that it can subsist. It is our cognisance of the successiveness or transitoriness of feelings that makes us object intuitively to any idealism which is understood to imply an identification of the realities of the world with the feelings of men. Facts, we are sure, are in some way permanent. They are not 'like the bubble on the fountain,' a moment here, then 'gone, and for ever.' But if they were feelings as we feel them, they would be so. They would not be 'stubborn things;' for as each was felt it would be done with. They would not form a world to which we have to adapt ourselves; for in order to make a world they must coexist, which feelings, as we feel them, do not.

But the idealism which interprets facts as relations, and can only understand relations as constituted by a single spiritual principle, is chargeable with no such outrage on common-sense. On the contrary, its very basis is the consciousness of objectivity. Its whole aim is to articulate coherently the conviction of there being a world of abiding realities other than, and determining, the endless flow of our feelings. The source of its differences from ordinary realism lies in its being less easily satisfied in its analysis of what the existence of such a world implies. The mere statement that facts are not feelings, that things are not ideas, that we can neither feel nor think except contingently upon certain functions of matter and motion being fulfilled, does not help us to understand what facts and things, what matter and motion, are. It does not enable us, when we seek to understand these expressions, to give them any meaning except such as is derived from experience, and, if from experience, then from relations that have their being only for an intelligent consciousness.

38. So far we have been following the lead of Kant in enquiring what is necessary to constitute, what is implied in there being, a world of experience—an objective world, if by that is meant a world of ascertainable laws, as distin-

guished from a world of unknowable 'things-in-themselves.'
We have followed him also, as we believe every one must
who has once faced the question, in maintaining that a
single active self-conscious principle, by whatever name it
be called, is necessary to constitute such a world, as the
condition under which alone phenomena, *i.e.* appearances
to consciousness, can be related to each other in a single
universe. This is the irrefragable truth involved in the proposition that 'the understanding makes nature.' But so
soon as we have been brought to the acceptance of that
proposition, Kant's leading fails us. We might be forward,
from the work thus assigned to understanding in the constitution of nature, to infer something as to the spirituality
of the real world. But from any such inference Kant would
at once withhold us. He would not only remind us that
the work assigned to understanding is a work merely among
and upon phenomena; that the nature which it constitutes
is merely a unity in the relations of phenomena; and that
any conclusion we arrive at in regard to 'nature' in this
sense has no application to 'things in themselves.' He insists, further, on a distinction between the form and matter
of 'nature' itself, and, having assigned to its 'form' an
origin in understanding, ascribes the 'matter' to an unknown but alien source, in a way which seems to cancel
the significance of his own declarations in regard to the
intellectual principle necessary to constitute its form. We
do not essentially misrepresent him in saying that by the
'form' of nature or, as he sometimes phrases it, 'natura
formaliter spectata,' he means the relations by which phenomena are connected in the one world of experience; by its
'matter,' or 'natura materialiter spectata,' the mere phenomena or sensations undetermined by those relations[1].
'Natura formaliter spectata' is the work of understanding;
but 'natura materialiter spectata' is the work of unknown
things-in-themselves, acting in unknown ways upon us.

[1] Kant's Werke, ed. Rosenkranz, II. p. 755; ed. Hartenstein (1867),
III. p. 133.

39. Now, if the distinction, thus drawn, between the form and matter of the world of experience were necessary or even admissible, the effect of tracing those relations between phenomena, which form the laws of nature as we know it, to the action of a spiritual principle, would simply have been to bring us to a dead-lock. The distinction implies that phenomena have a real nature as effects of things-in-themselves other than that which they have as related to each other in the universe of our experience : and not only so, it puts the two natures in a position towards each other of mere negation and separation, of such a kind that any correspondence between them, any dependence of one upon the other, is impossible. As effects of things-in-themselves, phenomena are supposed to have a nature of their own, but they cannot, according to Kant's doctrine, be supposed to carry any of that nature with them into experience. All the nature which they have in experience belongs to them in virtue of relations to each other which the action of the intellectual principle, expressly opposed to the action of things-in-themselves, brings about. The nature which a sensation is supposed to possess 'materialiter spectata,' as the appearance of a thing-in-itself, must not be confused with its nature as conditioned by a particular mode of matter and motion— the nature which the man of science investigates. It is probably from this confusion that Kant's doctrine of the relation between phenomena and things-in-themselves derives any plausibility which it may have for most of his readers : but, after what has been said above, a moment's consideration will show how unwarrantable according to his principles it is. The nature of a sensation, as dependent upon any motion or configuration of molecules, is still a nature determined by its relation to other data of experience—a relation which (like every other relation within, or capable of coming within, experience) the single self-distinguishing principle, which Kant calls understanding, is needed to constitute. It is not such a nature, but one to which no experience or interrogation of experience brings us any the nearer, that we must suppose to belong to the phenomenon as an appearance of a thing-in-itself, if Kant's antithesis is to be maintained.

And if phenomena, as 'materialiter spectata,' have such another nature, it will follow—not indeed that all our knowledge is an illusion in the ordinary sense of the term, for that implies a possibility of correction by true knowledge—but that there is no ground for that conviction of there being some unity and totality in things, from which the quest for knowledge proceeds. The 'cosmos of our experience,' and the order of things-in-themselves, will be two wholly unrelated worlds, of which, however, each determines the same sensations. All that determination of a sensible occurrence which can be the object of possible experience or inferred as an explanation of experience—its simple position of antecedence or sequence in time to other occurrences, as well as its relation to conditions which regulate that position and determine its sensible nature—will belong to one world of which a unifying self-consciousness is the organising principle : while the very same occurrence, as an effect of things-in-themselves, will belong to another world, will be subject to a wholly different order of determinations, which may have—and indeed, in being so described, is assumed to have—some principle of unity of its own, but of which, because it is a world of things-in-themselves, the principle must be taken to be the pure negation of that which determines the world of experience. If this be so, the conception of a universe is a delusive one. Man weaves a web of his own and calls it a universe ; but if the principle of this universe is neither one with, nor dependent on, that of things-in-themselves, there is in truth no universe at all, nor does there seem to be any reason why there should not be any number of such independent creations. We have asserted the unity of the world of our experience only to transfer that world to a larger chaos.

40. A tempting but misleading way out of the difficulty is to reduce the world of experience to dependence on that of things-in-themselves by taking the intellectual principle, which, in the sense explained, 'makes' the world of experience, to be not, as Kant considered it, an independent thing-in-itself, but itself a product of things-in-themselves. Our readiness to confuse things-in-themselves, as just pointed out, with the material conditions of sensation, may easily bring us to put the case in this way to ourselves. Certain combinations of moving matter, we are ready to believe, issue, by processes yet to be ascertained, in those living organisms which again, in reaction upon certain modes of motion, yield sensation ; and the sensitive subject, under a continuance of like physical influences, somehow grows into the intellectual subject of which the action is admitted to be necessary to constitute the 'cosmos of our experience.' But we have learnt Kant's lesson to very little purpose if we do not understand that the terms, which in such psychogenesis are taken to stand for independent agents, are in fact names for substantiated relations between phenomena ; relations to which an existence on their own account is fictitiously ascribed, but which in truth only exist for, or through the action of, the unifying and self-distinguishing spiritual subject which they are taken to account for. If this subject is to be dependent on things-in-themselves, something else must be understood by these 'things' than any objects that we know or can know ; for in the existence of such objects its action is already implied.

The question then arises whether, when we have excluded from things-in-themselves every kind of qualification arising from determination by, or relation to, an intelligent subject, any meaning is left in the assertion of a dependence of this subject upon them. Does not any significant assertion of that dependence, either as a fact or even as a mere possibility, imply a removal of the things-in-themselves from the region of the purely unknowable, and their qualification by an understood relation to the intelligent subject said to be dependent on them ? But if this is so, and if it is impossible for such a relation, any more than any other, to exist except through the unifying action of spirit, what becomes of the independence of the things-in-themselves? Are they not being determined by a spiritual action exactly of that kind which is being alleged to depend on them, and their exclusion of which is the one point expressed by their designation as things-in-themselves?

41. These considerations seem to preclude us, when once we have recognised the ground of distinction between a world of experience and a world of things-in-themselves, from any attempt to overcome that absolute separation between the two worlds, which Kant's doctrine implies, by treating the organising subject of the world of experience as in any sense a product of things-in-themselves. Kant himself lends no countenance to any such attempt; but on further reflection we may begin to question whether the view, which Kant himself gives, of the relation between things-in-themselves and the 'matter' of experience, or 'natura materialiter spectata'—the view out of which the whole difficulty arises—is not itself open to the same charge of inconsistency as that method of escape from its consequences which we have examined. When we say that sensations, or phenomena in respect of their mere 'matter,' are effects of things-in-themselves, we may exclude as carefully as possible all confusion of the things-in-themselves with the ascertainable material conditions, or formal causes, of feeling, but we cannot assert such a relation of cause and effect between the things and sensation without making the former a member of a relation which, as Kant himself on occasion would be ready to remind us, we have no warrant for extending beyond the world of experience, or for considering as independent of the intellectual principle of unity which is the condition of there being such a world. Causation has no meaning except as an unalterable connexion between changes in the world of our experience—an unalterableness of which the basis is the relation of that world throughout, with all its changes, to a single subject. That sensations therefore, the matter of our experience, should be connected as effects with things-in-themselves, of which all that can be said is that they belong to a world other than the world of our experience and are not relative to the subject to which it is relative, is a statement self-contradictory or at best unmeaning.

That Kant should not have seen this merely goes to show that his own doctrine, being the gradual conquest of his later years, had not obtained full possession of his mind. The antithesis between the real and the work of thought had still such command over him that, after he had himself traced the agency of thought in all that gives the world of experience a definite character, he still could not help ascribing to this world, in terms of the knowable, a relation to an unknowable opposite; though that very relation, if it existed, would according to his own showing bring the unknowable opposite within that world (dependent on an intelligent subject) from which it is expressly excluded.

42. At this point we may probably anticipate a rejoinder to some such effect as the following. It appears to be impossible to take the matter of experience to be the effect of things-in-themselves, since these things, if they are to be things-in-themselves, cannot be supposed to exist in a relation which only holds for the world of experience, as determined by an intelligent subject. But it must be equally impossible to consider it a product of the intelligent subject, to which, when we have allowed every function that can be claimed for it in the way of uniting in a related system the manifold material of sensation, we must still deny the function of generating that material. Yet we cannot ignore sensation. We cannot reduce the world of experience to a web of relations in which nothing is related, as it would be if everything were erased from it which we cannot refer to the action of a combining intelligence. After all our protests against Dualism, then, are we not at last left with an unaccountable residuum—an essential element of the real world of experience, which we cannot trace to what we regard as the organising principle of that world, but which is as necessary to make the world what it is as that principle itself? What do we gain by excluding other ways of accounting for it, if it is finally irreducible to the only agency by which we can explain the order of the world? Does it not remain a thing-in-itself, alien and opposite to anything that we can explain as the construction of intelligence, just as much as if it were admitted to be the product of an unknowable power?

43. The best hope of answering these questions lies in considering further how they arise. They are due to the abstraction of the 'matter' from the 'form' of experience. This abstraction we inevitably make in reflecting on the process by which we obtain such knowledge as we have, but it deceives us when we make it a ground for supposing a like separation of elements in the world of experience. It is true indeed, according to the doctrine previously stated, that the principle which enables us to know that there is a world, and to set about learning its nature, is identical with that which is the condition of there being a world; but it is not therefore to be imagined that all the distinctions and relations, which we present to ourselves—and necessarily present to ourselves—in the process of learning to know, have counterparts in the real world. Our presentation of them, as a part of our mental history, is a fact definitely related and conditioned in the reality of the world; but the distinctions presented may exist only for us, in whom the intellectual principle realises itself under special conditions, not in the world as it is in itself or for a perfect intelligence.

The distinction between the form and matter of experience is a distinction of this kind. In reflecting on the process by which we have come to know anything, we find that, at any stage we may recall, it consists in a further qualification of a given material by the consideration of the material under relations hitherto unconsidered. Thus as contrasted with, and abstracted from, the further formation which upon continued observation and attention it may acquire, any perception, any piece of knowledge, may be regarded as an unformed matter. On the other hand, when we look at what the given perception or piece of knowledge is in itself, we find that it is already formed, in more complex ways than

E

we can disentangle, by the synthesis of less determinate data. But there is a point at which the individual's retrospective analysis of the knowledge which he finds himself to possess necessarily stops. Antecedently to any of the formative intellectual processes which he can trace, it would seem that something must have been given for those processes to begin upon. This something is taken to be feeling, pure and simple. When all accretions of form, due to the intellectual establishment of relations, have been stripped off, there seem to remain the mere sensations without which the intellectual activity would have had nothing to deal with or operate upon. These then must be in an absolute sense the matter—the matter excluding all form—of experience.

44. Now it is evident that the ground on which we make this statement, that mere sensations form the matter of experience, warrants us in making it, if at all, only as a statement in regard to the mental history of the individual. Even in this reference it can scarcely be accepted. There is no positive basis for it but the fact that, so far as memory goes, we always find ourselves manipulating some data of consciousness, themselves independent of any intellectual manipulation which we can remember applying to them. But on the strength of this to assume that there are such data in the history of our experience, consisting in mere sensations, antecedently to any action of the intellect, is not really an intelligible inference from the fact stated. It is an abstraction which may be put into words, but to which no real meaning can be attached. For a sensation can only form an object of experience in being determined by an intelligent subject which distinguishes it from itself and contemplates it in relation to other sensations; so that to suppose a primary datum or matter of the individual's experience, wholly void of intellectual determination, is to suppose such experience to begin with what could not belong to or be an object of experience at all.

45. But the question we are here concerned with is not whether any such thing as mere sensation, a matter wholly unformed by intelligence, exists as a stage in the process by which the individual becomes acquainted with the world ; it is the question whether there is any such element in the world of knowable facts. Has nature—the system of connected phenomena, or facts related to consciousness, which forms the object of experience—a reality of that kind which Kant describes as 'natura materialiter spectata ;' a reality consisting of mere sensations, or sensations of which the qualities, whatever they may be, are independent of such determination as arises from the action of a unifying and self-distinguishing subject? Or has it in any other sense a 'matter' which does not depend on a combining intelligence for being what it is, as much as does the relation between my experience of to-day and that of my previous life?

Phenomena are facts related to consciousness. Thus, when we enquire whether there is such a thing in the world of phenomena as sensation undetermined by thought, the question may be considered in relation either to the facts, as such, or to the consciousness for which the facts exist. It may be put either thus—Among the facts that form the object of possible experience, are there sensations which do not depend on thought for being what they are? or thus— Is sensation, as unqualified by thought, an element in the consciousness which is necessary to there being such a thing as the world of phenomena?

46. After what has been already said, the answer to these questions need not detain us long. If it is admitted that we know of no other medium but a thinking or self-distinguishing consciousness, in and through which that unification of the manifold can take place which is necessary to constitute relation, it follows that a sensation apart from thought—not determined or acted on by thought—would be an unrelated sensation ; and an unrelated sensation cannot amount to a fact. Mere sensation is in truth a phrase that represents no reality. It is the result of a process of abstraction ; but having got the phrase we give a confused meaning to it, we fill up the shell which our abstraction has left, by reintroducing the qualification which we assumed ourselves to have got rid of. We present the *mere* sensations to ourselves as determined by relation in a way that would be impossible in the absence of that connecting action which we assume to be absent in designating them *mere* sensations. The minimum of qualification which we mentally ascribe to the sensation in thus speaking of it, is generally such as implies sequence and degree. A feeling not characterised either by its connexion with previous feeling or by its own intensity we must admit to be nothing at all, but at first sight we take it for granted that the character thus given to a feeling would belong to it just the same, though there were no such thing as thought in the world. It certainly does not depend on ourselves—on any power which we can suppose it rests with our will to exert or withhold—whether sensations shall occur to us in this or that order of succession, with this or that degree of intensity. But the question is whether the relation of time between one sensation and another, or that relation between a sensation and other possible modes of itself which is implied in its having a degree, could exist if there were not a subject for which the several sensations, or modes of the same sensation, were equally present and equally distinguished from itself. If it is granted that these relations, which constitute the minimum determination of a sensible fact, only exist through the action of such·a subject, it follows that thought is the necessary condition of the existence of sensible facts, and that *mere* sensation, in the sense supposed, is not a possible constituent in the realm of facts.

47. Or, if the consequence be disputed, the dispute can only turn on a secondary question as to the fitness of the term 'thought' to represent a function of which the essential nature is admitted. If by thought is necessarily understood a faculty which is born and dies with each man ; which is exhausted by labour and refreshed by repose ; which is exhibited in the construction of chains of reasoning, but not in the common ideas which make mankind and its experience one; on which the 'great thinker' may plume himself as the athlete on the strength of his muscles; then to say that the agency which makes sensible facts what they are can only be that of a thinking subject, is an absurd impropriety. But if it appears that a function in the way of self-consciousness is implied in the existence of relations, and therefore of determinate facts—a function identical in principle with that which enables the individual to look before and after, and which renders his experience a connected system—then it is more reasonable to modify some of our habitual notions of thought as exercised by ourselves than, on the strength of these notions, to refuse to recognise an essential identity between the subject which forms the unifying principle of the experienced world, and that which, as in us, qualifies us for an experience of it. It becomes time to consider whether the characteristics of thought, even as exercised by us, are not rather to be sought in the unity of its object as presented to all men, and in the continuity of all experience in regard to that object, than in the incidents of an individual life which is but for a day, or in abilities of which any man can boast that he has more than his neighbour.

48. Our question, then, in the first of the two forms suggested, must be answered in the negative. A fact consisting of *mere* feeling, in the sense supposed, is a contradiction, an impossibility. This does not of course mean that no being can feel which does not also think. We are not called on here to enquire whether there are really animals which feel but have not the capacity of thinking. All that the present argument would lead us to maintain would be that, so far as they feel without thinking, their feelings are not facts for them—for their consciousness. Their feelings *are* facts; but they are facts only so far as determined by relations, which exist only for a thinking consciousness and otherwise could not exist. And, in like manner, that large part of our own sensitive life which goes on without being affected by conceptions, is a series of facts with the determination of which, indeed, thought, as ours or in us, has nothing to do, but which not the less depends for its existence as a series of facts on the action of the same subject which, in another mode of its action, enables us to know them. But in saying this, it may be objected, we have already admitted that there is such a thing as a merely feeling consciousness; and, in the presence of this admission, what becomes of the denial to feeling of any separate or independent reality? The answer is that the distinction of the merely feeling consciousness is just this, that what it is really it is not consciously—that the relations by which it is really determined do not exist for it, but for the thinking consciousness on which it and they alike depend for being what they are. Its very characteristics as a merely feeling consciousness depend on conditions, in the universe of things, by which it would not be conditioned if it were really no more than it feels itself to be; if it were not relative to, and had not its existence for, another form of consciousness which comprehends it and its conditions.

49. In the second of the forms in which the question before us admits of being presented—Can sensation exist as an independent element in a consciousness to which facts can appear?—it has been virtually answered in being answered in the first. To that thinking subject, whose action is the universal bond of relation that renders facts what they are, their existence and their appearance must be one and the same. Their appearance, their presence to it, is their existence. Feeling can no more be an independent element in that subject, as the subject to which they appear, than it can be an independent element in it, as the subject through whose action they exist. It is true on the one hand, as has just been admitted, that in a great part of our lives we feel without thinking and without any qualification of our feelings by our thoughts; while yet, on the other hand, we are subjects to whom facts can appear, who are capable of conceiving a world of phenomena. But just so far as we feel without thinking, no world of phenomena exists for us. The

suspension of thought in us means also the suspension of fact or reality for us. We do not cease to be facts, but facts cease to exist for our consciousness. However then we may explain the merely temporary and interrupted character of the action of thought upon feeling in us, that temporary character affords no reason why we should hesitate to deny that feeling unqualified by thought can be an element in the consciousness which is necessary to there being such a thing as a world of phenomena.

50. Mere feeling, then, as a matter unformed by thought, has no place in the world of facts, in the cosmos of possible experience. Any obstacle which it seemed to present to a monistic view of that world may be allowed to disappear. We may give up the assumption that it needs to be accounted for as a product of things-in-themselves; or that, if not accounted for in this way, it still remains an unaccountable opposite to thought and its work. Feeling and thought are inseparable and mutually dependent in the consciousness for which the world of experience exists, inseparable and mutually dependent in the constitution of the facts which form the object of that consciousness. Each in its full reality includes the other. It is one and the same living world of experience which, considered as the manifold object presented by a self-distinguishing subject to itself, may be called feeling, and, considered as the subject presenting such an object to itself, may be called thought. Neither is the product of the other. It is only when by a process of abstraction we have reduced either to something which is not itself, that we can treat either as the product of anything, or apply the category of cause and effect to it at all. For that category is itself their product. Or rather, it represents one form of the activity of the consciousness which in inseparable union they constitute. The connexion between a phenomenon and its conditions is one that only obtains in and for that consciousness. No such connexion can obtain between that consciousness and anything else; which means that the consciousness itself, whether considered as feeling or considered as thought, being that by means of which everything is accounted for, does not in turn admit of being accounted for, in the sense that any 'whence' or 'why' can be assigned for it.

Any constituent of the world of possible experience we can account for by exhibiting its relation to other constituents of the same world ; but this is not to account for the world itself. We may and do explore the conditions under which a sentient organism is formed, and the various forms of molecular action by which particular sensations on the part of such an organism are elicited. We may ascertain uniformities in the sequence of one feeling upon another. In the life of the individual and the race we may trace regular histories of the manner in which a particular way of thinking has been affected by an earlier, and has in turn affected a later way ; of the determination of certain ideas by certain emotions, and of certain emotions by certain ideas. But in all this we are connecting phenomena with phenomena within a world, not connecting the world of phenomena with anything other than itself. We are doing nothing to account for the all-uniting consciousness which alone can render these sequences and connexions possible, for which alone they exist, and of which the action in us alone enables us to know them. We can indeed show the contradictions involved in supposing a world of phenomena to exist otherwise than in and for consciousness, and upon analysis can discern what must be the formal characteristic of a consciousness for which a system of related phenomena exists. So far we can give an account of what the world as a whole must be, and of what the spirit that constitutes it does. But just because all that we can experience is included in this one world, and all our inferences and explanations relate only to its details, neither it as a whole, nor the one consciousness which constitutes it, can be accounted for in the ordinary sense of the word. They cannot be accounted for by what they include, and being all-inclusive—at any rate so far as possible experience goes— there remains nothing else by which they can be accounted for. And this is equally true of consciousness as feeling and of consciousness as thought, for each in its reality involves the other.

51. We are now in a position to reconsider the restriction which Kant puts on the interpretation of his own dictum that 'understanding makes nature.' This with him means that understanding, as the unifying principle which is the source of relations, acts formatively upon feelings as upon a material given to it from an opposite source called 'things-in-themselves,' rendering them into one system of phenomena called 'nature,' which is the sole object of experience, and to which all judgments as to matters of fact relate. We demur to the independent reality, or reality as determined by something else than thought, which is thus ascribed to feeling. It is not that we would claim any larger function for thought than Kant claims for understanding as separate from feeling, supposing that separation to be once admitted. It is the separation itself that is in question. We do not dispute the validity of Locke's challenge to a man by any amount of thinking to produce a single 'simple idea' to himself. We admit that mere thought can no more produce the facts of feeling, than mere feeling can generate thought. But we deny that there is really such a thing as 'mere feeling' or 'mere thought.' We hold that these phrases represent abstractions to which no reality corresponds, either in the facts of the world or in the consciousness to which those facts are relative. We can attach no meaning to 'reality,' as applied to the world of phenomena, but that of existence under definite and unalterable relations ; and we find that it is only for a thinking consciousness that such relations can subsist. Reality of feeling, abstracted from thought, is abstracted from the condition of its being a reality. That great part of our sensitive life is not determined by *our* thought, that the sensitive life of innumerable beings is wholly undetermined by any thought of theirs or in them, is not in dispute : but this proves nothing as to what that sensitive life really is in nature or in the cosmos of possible experience. It has no place in nature, except as determined by relations which can only exist for a thinking consciousness. For the consciousness which constitutes reality and makes the world one it exists, not in that separateness which belongs to it as an attribute of beings that think only at times or not at all, but as conditioned by a whole which thought in turn conditions.

As to what that consciousness in itself or in its completeness is, we can only make negative statements. *That* there is such a consciousness is implied in the existence of the world; but *what* it is we only know through its so far acting in us as to enable us, however partially and interruptedly, to have knowledge of a world or an intelligent experience. In such knowledge or experience there is no mere thought or mere feeling. No feeling enters into it except as qualifying, and qualified by, an interrelated order of which a self-distinguishing subject forms the unifying bond. Thought has no function in it except as constantly co-ordinating ever new appearances in virtue of their presence to that one subject. And we are warranted in holding that, as a mutual independence of thought and feeling has no place in any consciousness on our part, which is capable of apprehending a world or for which a world exists, so it has none in the world-consciousness of which ours is a limited mode.

52. The purpose of this long discussion has been to arrive at some conclusion in regard to the relation between man and nature, a conclusion which must be arrived at before we can be sure that any theory of ethics, in the distinctive sense of the term, is other than wasted labour. If by nature we mean the object of possible experience, the connected order of knowable facts or phenomena—and this is what our men of science mean by it when they trace the natural genesis of human character—then nature implies something other than itself, as the condition of its being what it is. Of that something else we are entitled to say, positively, that it is a self-distinguishing consciousness; because the function which it must fulfil in order to render the relations of phenomena, and with them nature, possible, is one which, on however limited a scale, we ourselves exercise in the acquisition of experience, and exercise only by means of such a consciousness. We are further entitled to say of it, negatively, that the relations by which, through its action, phenomena are determined are not relations *of* it —not relations by which it is itself determined. They arise out of its presence to phenomena, or the presence of phenomena to it, but the very condition of their thus arising is that the unifying consciousness which constitutes them should not itself be one of the objects so related. The relation of events to each other as in time implies their equal presence to a subject which is not in time. There could be no such thing as time if there were not a self-consciousness which is not in time. As little could there be a relation of objects as outside each other, or in space, if they were not equally related to a subject which they are not outside ; a subject of which outsideness to anything is not a possible attribute ; which by its synthetic action constitutes that relation, but is not itself determined by it. The same is true of those relations which we are apt to treat as independent entities under the names matter and motion. They are relations existing for a consciousness which they do not so condition as that it should itself either move or be material.

53. If objection is taken to the interpretation of matter as consisting in certain relations, if its character as substance is insisted on, it remains to ask what is meant by substance. It is not denied that there are material substances, but their qualification both as substances and as material will be found to depend on relations. By a substance we mean that which is persistent throughout certain appearances. It represents that identical element throughout the appearances, that permanent element throughout the times of their appearance, in virtue of which they are not merely so many different appearances, but connected changes. A material substance is that which remains the same with itself in respect of some of the qualities which we include in our definition of matter—qualities all consisting in some kind of relation—while in other respects it changes. Its character as a substance depends on that relation of appearances to each other in a single order which renders them changes. It is not that first there is a substance, and that then certain changes of it ensue. The substance is the implication of the changes, and has no existence otherwise. Apart from the changes no substance, any more than apart from effects a cause. If we choose to say then that matter exists as a substance, we merely substitute for the designation of it as consisting in relations, a designation of it as a certain correlatum of a certain kind of relation. Its existence as a substance depends on the action of the same self-consciousness upon which the connexion of phenomena by means of that relation depends.

And the subject, of which the action is implied in the connexion of phenomena in one system of nature by means of this correlatum of change, is one that can itself be as little identified with that correlatum—with any kind of substance—as with the change to which substance is relative. It has already been pointed out that a consciousness, to which events are to appear as changes, cannot itself consist in those events. Its self-distinction from them all is necessary to its holding them all together as related to each other in the way of change. And, for the same reason, that connexion of all phenomena as changes of one world which is implied in the unity of intelligent experience, cannot be the work of anything which is the substance qualified by those changes. Its self-distinction from them, which is the condition of their appearance to it under this relation of change, is incompatible with its being so qualified. Even if we allow it to be possible that a subject, which connects certain appearances as changes, should itself be qualified by—should be the substance persistent in—certain other changes, it is plainly impossible that a subject which so connects all the appearances of nature should be related in the way of substance to any or all of them.

54. We may express the conclusion to which we are thus

brought by saying that nature in its reality, or in order to be what it is, implies a principle which is not natural. By calling the principle not natural we mean that it is neither included among the phenomena which through its presence to them form a nature, nor consists in their series, nor is itself determined by any of the relations which it constitutes among them. In saying more than this of it we must be careful not to fall into confusion. We are most safe in calling it spiritual, because, for reasons given, we are warranted in thinking of it as a self-distinguishing consciousness. In calling it supernatural we run the risk of misleading and being misled, for we suggest a relation between it and nature of a kind which has really no place except *within* nature, as a relation of phenomenon to phenomenon. We convey the notion that it is above or beyond or before nature, that it is a cause of which nature is the effect, a substance of which the changing modes constitute nature; while in truth all the relations so expressed are relations which, indeed, but for the non-natural self-conscious subject would not exist, but which are not predicable of it. If we employ language about it in which, strictly taken, they are implied, it must only be on a clear understanding of its metaphorical character.

On the other hand, there is no imperative reason why we should limit 'nature' to the restricted sense in which we have been supposing it to be used, if only the same sense can be covered by another term. If we like, we may employ the term 'nature' to represent the one whole which includes both the system of related phenomena and the principle, other than itself, which that system implies. But in that case, if we would avoid confusion, we must find some other term than nature to represent the system of phenomena as such, or as considered without inclusion of the spiritual principle which it implies, and some other term than 'natural' to represent that which this system contains. We are pretty sure, however, to fail in this, and 'nature' in consequence becomes a term that is played fast and loose with in philosophical writing. It is spoken of as an independent agent;

a certain completeness and self-containedness are ascribed to it; and to this there is no objection so long as we understand it to include the spiritual principle, neither in time nor in space, immaterial and immovable, eternally one with itself, which is necessary to the possibility of a world of phenomena. But it is otherwise if 'nature' is at the same time thought of, as it almost inevitably is, under attributes only applicable to the world of phenomena, and thus as excluding the spiritual principle which that world indeed implies, but implies as other than itself. In that case, to ascribe independence or self-containedness to it—if for a moment the use of theological language may be allowed which it is generally desirable to avoid—is to deify nature while we cancel its title to deification. It is to speak of nature without God in a manner only appropriate to nature as it is in God. Or— to employ language less liable to misleading associations—it is to involve ourselves in perpetual confusion by seeking for a completeness in the world of phenomena, the world existing under conditions of space and time, which, just because it exists under those conditions, is not to be found there. The result of the confusion will generally be that, being unable to discover any perfection or totality or independent agency among the matters of fact which we know, and having ignored the implication by those facts of a spiritual principle other than themselves, we come to assume that no perfect or self-determined being exists at all, or at any rate in any relation to us.

CHAPTER II

55. THE conclusion of the preceding chapter has brought
us to the question which lies at the root of ethical enquiry.
In what relation do we ourselves stand to the one self-
distinguishing subject, other than nature, which we find to
be implied in nature? To a certain extent an answer to this
question has been involved in the considerations which have
led to the conviction of there being such a subject. That if
we were merely phenomena among phenomena we could not
have knowledge of a world of phenomena, appears from
analysis of the conditions of an intelligent experience. Our
experience, we have seen, has two characteristics, of which
neither admits of being reduced to or explained by the other.
On the one hand it is an order of events in time, consisting
in modifications of our sensibility. On the other hand it is
a consciousness of those events—a consciousness of them as
a related series, and as determined in their relations to each
other by relation to something else, which is from the first
conceived as other than the modifications of our sensibility,
and which with growing knowledge comes to be conceived
as involving relations between objects that are not events at
all, and between events that preceded or lie beyond the
range of sentient life. But, as has been further pointed out,
a consciousness of related events, as related, cannot consist
in those events. The modifications of our sensibility cannot,
as successive events, make up our consciousness of them.
Within the consciousness that they are related in the way of
before and after there is no before and after. There is no
such relation between components of the consciousness as
there is between the events of which it is the consciousness.
They form a process in time. If *it* were a process in time,

it would not be a consciousness of them as forming such a process.

56. Thus that man is not merely a phenomenon or succession of phenomena, that he does not consist in a series of natural events, is implied in the fact that phenomena appear to him as they do, that for him or for his consciousness there is such a thing as nature. There are certain current phrases of modern psychology, which no doubt have their warrant in facts to be considered presently, but which, as commonly used, are apt to blind us to this essential characteristic of the position in which we stand towards the world we know. We use the term 'phenomena of consciousness' as if it covered the whole range of knowledge and morality—all our thought about the world, all our perceptions and conceptions of objects, all the ideas which we seek to realise in action. We speak of consciousness universally, without qualification or distinction, as a succession of states ; and the figure of the stream is the accepted one for expressing the nature of our spiritual life. Now it would be idle to deny that there is an appropriateness in a way of speaking which none of us can avoid, but it is important to call attention to that kind of activity undoubtedly exercised by us, implied in all distinctively intelligent or moral experience, to which it is wholly inappropriate.

If we reflect on what is contained in our knowledge, or in any conception or perception contributory to it, we shall see that the relation in which its constituents stand to each other is essentially different from the relation between stages of the process by which the knowledge or perception is arrived at. The figure of the stream may be applicable to the latter, though the more we think of it the less we shall find it so, but it is quite inapplicable to the former. Successive states of consciousness may be represented as waves of which one is for ever taking the place of the other, but such successive states cannot make a knowledge even of the most elementary sort. Knowledge is of related facts, and it is essential to every act of knowledge that the related facts should be present together in consciousness. Between the apprehensions of those facts, so far as they make up a certain piece of knowledge, there is no succession. I may have apprehended some of them, no doubt, before I apprehend the rest ; or, after having apprehended the latter, my consciousness may lose its hold on some apprehended before. In this sense different states of knowledge succeed each other in the individual, but not so the manifold constituents of that which in any act of knowledge is present to his mind as the object known ; not so the determinations of consciousness in which those constituents are presented, and which make up the complex act of knowledge. For a known object, as known, is a related whole, of which, as of every such whole, the members are necessarily present together ; and the acts of consciousness in which the several members are apprehended, as forming a knowledge, are a many in one. None is before or after another. This is equally the case whether the knowledge is of successive events or of the ' uniformities ' which are said to constitute a law of nature. For, as we have previously had occasion to point out, between the constituents of a knowledge of succession there can be no succession : so long as certain events are *contemplated* as successive, no one of them is an object to consciousness before or after another.

57. For this reason no knowledge, nor any mental act involved in knowledge, can properly be called a 'phenomenon of consciousness.' It may be *of* phenomena ; if the knowledge is of events, it is so. The attainment of the knowledge, again, as an occurrence in the individual's history, a transition from one state of consciousness to another, may properly be called a phenomenon ; but not so the consciousness itself of relations or related facts—not so the relations and related facts present to consciousness—in which the knowledge consists. For a phenomenon is a sensible event, related in the way of antecedence and consequence to other sensible events ; but the consciousness which constitutes a knowledge, or (if we may be allowed the use of a word which, though unfamiliar in this connexion,

avoids some ambiguity) the content of such consciousness, is not an event so related nor made up of such events. We cannot point to any other events, as we can in the case of a phenomenon proper, from antecedence or consequence to which it takes its character as an event.

As an instance, let us take a man's knowledge of a proposition in Euclid. This means a relation in his consciousness between certain parts of a figure, determined by the relation of those parts to other parts. The knowledge is made up of those relations as in consciousness. Now it is obvious that there is no lapse of time, however minute, no antecedence or consequence, between the constituent relations of the consciousness so composed, or between the complex formed by them and anything else. To call such knowing consciousness a phenomenon, in the ordinary meaning of a sensible event, is a confusion between it and the process of arriving at or losing it. That in the learning or forgetting a proposition of Euclid, as in the acquisition or loss of any other piece of knowledge, a series of events takes place, is plain enough; and such events may legitimately be called 'phenomena of consciousness.' But it must be noticed that when these events of the mental history come to be reviewed in intelligent memory or experience—when we know them as the connected facts of a history—their existence as in consciousness is no longer that of events. They do not succeed each other in time, but are present in the unity of relation, as much as are the parts of a geometrical figure which has been apprehended by, or taken into, an intelligent consciousness.

58. The discrepancy here pointed out, between the reality of consciousness as exhibited in knowledge and anything that can properly be called phenomena or successive states of consciousness, would be more generally acknowledged but for two reasons. One of these is the ambiguity attending all our terms expressive of mental activity—knowledge, conception, perception, &c.—which may denote events in our mental history, the passing into certain states of consciousness, as well as that of which in those states we are conscious, the content and object of consciousness. At the same time — and this is the second of the reasons referred to—this content or object is looked upon as existing quite otherwise than in or for consciousness ; as independent of it, though from time to time affecting it in a certain way and producing a certain state of consciousness. Hence it is only the successive changes in our apprehensive attitude towards the objects of our knowledge and experience that are commonly put to the account of consciousness. Its nature is not taken to be exhibited in the structure of those objects, any more than it would be if, instead of being objects known and experienced, they were 'things-in-themselves.' By perception is understood a modification of our sensibility in which some present external object is revealed to us. Conception we regard equally as an *occurrence* in consciousness ; and, though we suppose it to take place in the absence of any object at the time affecting the senses, we practically separate in our thoughts the conceived content or object from the conception, and imagine it vaguely as residing elsewhere than in consciousness. We thus avoid the necessity of facing the question how an object determined by relations can have its being in a consciousness which consists of a series of occurrences. Even 'knowledge,' though we often mean by it a system of known facts or laws, is apt to lose this sense when we speak of it as a form of consciousness. It then becomes merely the mental event of arriving at an apprehension of related facts. It does not represent the relation of the facts in consciousness. That there must be such a relation of them in consciousness, and that a consciousness consisting of events cannot contain such a relation, is a conclusion which we avoid by eviscerating knowledge of its content, and transferring this content from consciousness to 'external things.'

59. Even those who recognize the difficulty of extruding the object conceived or known, an object constituted by relations, from the consciousness which conceives or knows, and in consequence of describing conception and knowledge as mental events or phenomena, will be apt to ignore the

same difficulty in regard to *Perception.* The externality of
the perceived object to consciousness seems to be taken for
granted, even by those who would be quite ready to tell us
that the 'things' which we talk of conceiving are but 'nomi-
nal essences.' This arises from the connexion of perception with sensation, and from the real explicability of sensation by external impact. It is admitted on all hands that
there can be no perception without (in Locke's phraseology)
'actual present sensation.' The difference between a perception of the moon and any mere conception of it is that,
when it is perceived, although it is only in virtue of some
conception of relations that it is perceived as a qualified object, there is necessarily some present sensation which those
relations are conceived as determining. From this necessary presence of sensation in the act of perception, there
easily arises a confusion between the perceived object and
the exciting cause of sensation; which again leads to an
extrusion of the perceived object from the consciousness in
which perception consists, and to the view of it as an external something to which perception is related as an occurrence to its cause.

60. A little reflection, however, will show us that the
exciting cause, the stimulant, of the sensation involved in
a perception is never the object perceived in a perception.
It is necessary to a perception of colour that there should
be a sensation, arising out of a stimulus of the optic nerve
by a particular vibration of ether. That vibration, however
—the external exciting cause of the sensation—is not the
object perceived in the perception of the colour. That object, indeed, will not be the same for every percipient. It
will vary according to the extent of his knowledge and to the
degree of attention aroused in him in the particular case.
The perception may be no more than consciousness of the
fact that a particular colour is presented to him—a fact to
be aware of which is already to be aware of a certain rudimentary relation—or it may be a consciousness of various
relations by which this fact is determined. And the rela-

tions thus apprehended in the perception may vary, again, from those by which the colour is connected with accompanying appearances in superficial experience, to those less obvious ones which science has ascertained. It may thus come to include a knowledge that the sensation of light arises out of a certain relation between vibrations of ether and the optic nerve. If the perception is that of a man of science, observing light or colour for scientific purposes, it probably does so. Such knowledge is present to his mind in the perception. But it is a mere confusion to imagine that, in this or any other form of such a perception, the vibration of ether enters into the object perceived—into the content of the perception—in the same sense in which it acts as the exciting cause of the sensation ; or to suppose that this object or content is external to the percipient consciousness, as the stimulant matter is to the sentient organism.

The sentient organism to which the vibratory ether may be considered external is not consciousness, either as exercised in perception or in any other way, any more than the vibratory ether, as external, is the object perceived. Strictly speaking, it is not a vibratory ether but the fact consisting in the relation between this and the optic nerve—this fact as existing for consciousness—that enters into or determines the perceived object, as the scientific man perceives it. This fact, as forming part of the content of the perception, is wholly within consciousness; or, to speak more accurately, the opposition of without and within has no sort of application to it. A *within* implies a *without*, and we are not entitled to say that anything is without or outside consciousness ; for externality, being a relation which, like any other relation, exists only in the medium of consciousness, only between certain objects as they are for consciousness, cannot be a relation between consciousness and anything else. An affection of the sentient organism by matter external to it is the condition of our experiencing the sort of consciousness called perception ; a relation of externality between objects is often part of that which is perceived ; but in no case is there such a relation, any more than a relation of before and after, between the object perceived and the consciousness of it, or between constituents of that consciousness.

61. If, having got rid of the confusion between the stimulant of sensation and the perceived object, we examine the constituents of any perceived object—not as a 'thing-in-itself,' or as we may vainly try to imagine it to be apart from our perception, but as it actually is perceived—we shall find alike that it is only for consciousness that they can exist, and that the consciousness for which they thus exist cannot be merely a series of phenomena or a succession of states. For a justification of this statement we may appeal to the account given of perception by the accepted representatives of empirical psychology. 'Our perception of an animal or a flower,' says Mr. Lewes, 'is the synthesis of all the sensations we have had of the object in relation to our several senses [1].' This object itself, he tells us, is a 'group of sensibles'; which corresponds with Mill's account of it as a combination of 'permanent possibilities of sensation.' Such language is no doubt susceptible of a double interpretation, and it is only upon one of the two possible interpretations that it justifies the conclusion we shall draw from it. It is true also that this interpretation is not sanctioned by the writers mentioned, who seem not to distinguish the two interpretations, and avail themselves sometimes of the one, sometimes of the other. It is the only interpretation of the definition, however, that is really suitable to it as a definition of perception.

62. What exactly is it that is combined in the synthesis spoken of? Is it a synthesis of feelings as caused by the action of external irritants on the nervous system, or is it a synthesis of known and remembered facts that such feelings have occurred under certain conditions and relations? The two kinds of synthesis are perfectly distinct; and, though the former may be presupposed in perception, it is the latter alone which constitutes it in the distinctive

[1] *Problems of Life and Mind*, I. 191.

sense. It is true, no doubt, that an excitement of sensation by some present irritant may revive, in a fainter degree, feelings that have been previously associated with this sensation. But such a revival does not constitute a perception. It cannot result in a synthesis of the feelings as *feelings of an object*, or in the apprehension of a sensible fact, recognized as a symbol of many other related facts of which there would be experience if certain conditions on the part of a sentient subject were fulfilled—in other words, as a symbol of possibilities of sensation. If past feelings were reinstated merely as feelings, they could not properly be said to be combined in an object or in consciousness of an object at all, nor would their reinstatement be in any sense an inference, such as Mr. Lewes rightly holds to be involved in all perception [1]. They could only be combined, either in the way of producing and giving place to a further feeling, as little a consciousness of fact or object as any of them, or in the sense that their effects are accumulated in the nervous organism so as to modify its reactions upon stimulus. Anything more than this—any combination of the data of feeling as qualities of an object, or as facts related to a certain sensation, which the recurrence of that sensation may recall to us—implies the action of a subject which thinks of its feelings, which distinguishes them from itself and can thus present them to itself as facts.

Such action is as necessary to the original presentation of all that is recalled in perception, as to the incorporation of what is recalled in the total fact perceived. As we have seen, no feeling, as such or as merely felt, enters into the perceived object—not even the present sensation which is admitted to be a necessary condition of perception. It is not the sensation, but the fact, presented by the self-distinguishing subject to itself, that such a sensation is here and now occurring, occurring under certain relations to other experience—it is this that is the nucleus on which the recalled experience gathers, suggesting other possibilities of sensation, not them-

[1] Problems of Life and Mind, I. 257.

selves 'actual present sensations,' but no less present, as facts, than the fact that the given sensation is here and now being felt. The knowledge of such possibilities of sensation is doubtless in every case founded on actual sensation experienced in the past, but on this as on an observed fact, determined by relation to other like facts through the equal presence of all to a thinking subject. Except to an intelligence which has thus observed sensations as related facts, there can be no suggestion, upon the recurrence of one of them, that others are possible upon certain conditions being fulfilled.

The revival of the past sensations themselves, with whatever intensity, is no such suggestion. It may be that the excitement of sensation by an external stimulant, which is the occasion of perception, is always followed by a revival, with some less intensity, of the sensations known to be possible as accompaniments of the given sensation; but the knowledge of their possibility—the apprehension of the relation between their several possibilities, as facts, and the fact of the given sensation occurring—this, the essential thing in perception, is as different from the revival of the sensations themselves or their images as is the given sensation from the presentation of its occurrence as a fact. And on this difference depends the susceptibility of combination in a perceived object, of presentation as a many in one, which belongs to known possibilities of sensation, to known facts that certain feelings would occur under certain conditions, in distinction from feelings as felt. Manifold feelings may combine, as we have seen, in one result, but in that one result their multiplicity as feelings is lost. The constituents of a perceived object, on the contrary, whether we consider them qualities or related facts, survive in their multiplicity at the same time that they constitute a single object. The condition of their doing so is the self-distinction of the thinking subject from the data of sensation, which it at once presents to itself in their severalty as facts, and unites as *related* facts in virtue of its equal presence to them all.

63. It thus appears that the common objects of experience—not those 'things in general' which are sometimes supposed to be the object of conception, but the particular things we perceive, this flower, this apple, this dog—in the only sense in which they are objects to us or are perceived at all, have their being only for, and result from the action of, a self-distinguishing consciousness. As perceived, they consist in certain groups of facts, which again consist in possibilities of sensation, known to be related in certain ways to each other and to some given fact of sensation. The extent of the group in the case of each perception, and the particular mode in which the constituent facts are related, depend on the experience and training of the percipient, as well as on the direction of his mind at the time of the perception. In every case the relations by which the given sensation is determined in the apprehension of the percipient, are but a minute part of those by which it is really determined. The object which the most practised botanist perceives in his observation of a flower, is by no means adequate to the real nature of the flower. That real nature, indeed, if our previous conclusions have been true, must consist in relations of which consciousness is the medium or sustainer, though not consciousness as it is in the botanist. It is not, however, with the real nature of the flower, but with its nature as perceived —a fragment of the real nature—that we are here concerned; and it is relations of which the percipient consciousness is the sustainer, which exist only through its action, that make the object, as in each case the percipient perceives it, what it is to him. Facts related to those of which the percipient is aware in the object, but not yet known to him, can only be held to belong to the perceived object potentially or in some anticipatory sense [1], in so far as upon a certain development of intelligence, in a direction which it does not rest with the will of the individual to follow or no, they will become incorporated with it. But they become so incorporated with it only through the same continued action of a

[1] [See, however, § 69.]

combining self-consciousness upon data of sensation, through which this object, as the percipient already perceives it, has come to be there for him.

64. Common sense is apt to repel such statements as these, because they are taken to imply that we can perceive what we like; that the things we see are fictions of our own, not determined by any natural or necessary order. But in truth it implies nothing of the sort, unless it is supposed that our whole consciousness is a fiction of our own, of which it rests with ourselves to make what we please. Objects do not cease to be 'objective,' facts do not cease to be unalterable, because we find that a consciousness which we cannot alter or escape from, beyond which we cannot place ourselves, *for* which many things indeed are external to each other but *to* which nothing can be external, is the medium through which they exist for us, or because we can analyse in some elementary way what it must have done in order to their thus being there for us. It is not the conception of fact, but the conception of the consciousness for which facts exist, that is affected by such analysis.

So long as consciousness is thought to have nothing to do with the constitution of the facts of which we are conscious, it is possible to look upon it merely as a succession of events or phenomena 'of the inner sense.' The question how these inner events or successive phenomena come to perform a synthesis of themselves into objects is not raised, because no such work of synthesis is thought to be required of consciousness at all. The objects we perceive are supposed to be there for us independently of any action of our minds; we have but passively to let their appearances follow each other over the mental mirror. While this view is retained, the succession of such appearances and of the mental reactions upon them—reactions gradually modified through accumulated effects of the appearances—may fairly be taken to constitute our spiritual being. But it is otherwise when we have recognised the truth, that a sensation excited by an external irritant is not a perception of the irritant or

(by itself) of anything at all ; that every object we perceive is
a congeries of related facts, of which the simplest component,
no less than the composite whole, requires in order to its
presentation the action of a principle of consciousness, not
itself subject to conditions of time, upon successive appearances, such action as may hold the appearances together,
without fusion, in an apprehended fact.　It then becomes
clear that there is a function of consciousness, as exercised
in the most rudimentary experience, in the simplest perception of sensible things or of the appearances of objects,
which is incompatible with the definition of consciousness
as any sort of succession of any sort of phenomena.　Something else than a succession of phenomena is seen to be as
necessary in the consciousness that perceives facts, as it is
necessary to the possibility of the world of facts itself.

65. We have dwelt at length on this implication in ordinary
perception of a spiritual action irreducible to phenomena,
because the question whether and how far man is a part of
nature, is apt to be debated exclusively on what is considered
higher ground and, in consequence, without an admitted
issue being raised.　The transcendence of man is maintained on the ground of his exercising powers, which it may
plausibly be disputed whether he exercises at all.　The notion
that thought can originate, or that we can freely will, is at
once set down as a transcendental illusion.　There is more
hope of result if the controversy is begun lower down, with the
analysis of an act which it is not doubted that we perform.

Now, if the foregoing analysis be correct, the ordinary
perception of sensible things or matters of fact involves the
determination of a sensible process, which is in time, by an
agency that is not in time,—in Kant's language, a combination of 'empirical and intelligible characters,'—as essentially
as do any of those 'higher' mental operations, of which the
performance may be disputed.　The sensation, of which the
presentation as a fact is the nucleus of every perception, is an
event in time.　Its conditions again have all of them a history
in time.　It is true, indeed, that the relation between it and

its cause, if its cause is understood strictly as the sum of its conditions, is not one of time. The assemblage of conditions, 'external' and 'internal,' constitutes the sensation. There is no *sequence* in time of the sensation upon the assembled conditions. But the assemblage itself is an event that has had a determinate history ; and each of the constituent conditions has come to be what it is through a process in time. So much for the sensation proper. The presentation of the sensation, again, as of a fact related to other experience, is in like manner an event. A moment ago I had not so presented it : after a brief interval the perception will have given place to another. Yet the content of the presentation, the perception of this or that object, depends on the presence of that which in occurrence is past, as a fact united in one consciousness with the fact of the sensation now occurring ; or rather, if the perception is one of what we call a developed mind, on numberless connected acts of such uniting consciousness, to which limits can no more be set than they can to the range of experience, and which yield the conception of a world revealed in the sensation. The agent of this neutralization of time can as little, it would seem, be itself subject to conditions in time as the constituents of the resulting whole, the facts united in consciousness into the nature of the perceived object, are before or after each other.

66. We are not, however, fully stating the seemingly paradoxical character of everyday perception, in merely saying that it is a determination of events in time by a principle that is not in time. That is a description equally applicable to fact and to the perception of fact. For fact always implies relation determined by other relations in a universe of facts ; and such relations, again, though they be relations of events to each other in time, imply, as has been previously pointed out, something out of time, for which all the terms of the several relations are equally present, as the principle of the synthesis which unites them in a single universe. But, in thus explaining the ultimate conditions of the possibility of fact, we need not assign the events themselves, and the determination of them by that which is not an event—the process of becoming, and the regulation of it as an orderly process,—to one and the same subject; as if the events happened to and altered the subject that unites them, or as if the source of order in becoming itself became. We cannot indeed suppose any real separation between the determinant and the determined. The order of becoming is only an order of becoming through the action of that which is not in becoming; nor can we think of this order as preceded by anything that was not an order of becoming. We contradict ourselves, if we say that there was first a chaos and then came to be an order; for the 'first' and 'then' imply already an order of time, which is only possible through an action not in time. As little, on the other hand, can we suppose that which we only know as a principle of unity in relation, to exist apart from a manifold through which it is related. But we may avoid considering this principle, or the subject of which the presence and action renders possible the relations of the world of becoming, as itself in becoming, or as the result of a process of becoming. It seems to be otherwise with our perceiving consciousness. The very consciousness, which holds together successive events as equally present, has itself apparently a history in time. It seems to vary from moment to moment. It apprehends processes of becoming in a manner which implies that past stages of the becoming are present to it as known facts; yet is it not itself coming to be what it has not been?

67. It will be found, we believe, that this apparent state of the case can only be explained by supposing that in the growth of our experience, in the process of our learning to know the world, an animal organism, which has its history in time, gradually becomes the vehicle of an eternally complete consciousness. What we call our mental history is not a history of this consciousness, which in itself can have no history, but a history of the process by which the animal organism becomes its vehicle. 'Our consciousness' may mean either of two things; either a function of the animal organism, which is being made, gradually and with interruptions, a vehicle of the eternal consciousness; or that eternal consciousness itself, as making the animal organism its vehicle and subject to certain limitations in so doing, but retaining its essential characteristic as independent of time, as the determinant of becoming, which has not and does not itself become.   The consciousness which varies from moment to moment, which is in succession, and of which each successive state depends on a series of 'external and internal' events, is consciousness in the former sense.   It consists in what may properly be called phenomena; in successive modifications of the animal organism, which would not, it is true, be what they are if they were not media for the realisation of an eternal consciousness, but which are not this consciousness.   On the other hand, it is this latter consciousness, as so far realised in or communicated to us through modification of the animal organism, that constitutes our knowledge, with the relations, characteristic of knowledge, into which time does not enter, which are not in becoming but are once for all what they are.   It is this again that enables us, by incorporation of any sensation to which attention is given into a system of known facts, to extend that system, and by means of fresh perceptions to arrive at further knowledge.

68. For convenience sake, we state this doctrine, to begin with, in a bald dogmatic way, though well aware how unwarrantable or unmeaning, until explained and justified, it is likely to appear.   Does it not, the reader may ask, involve the impossible supposition that there is a double consciousness in man?   No, we reply, not that there is a double consciousness, but that the one indivisible reality of our consciousness cannot be comprehended in a single conception.   In seeking to understand its reality we have to look at it from two different points of view; and the different conceptions that we form of it, as looked at from these different points, do not admit of being united, any more than do our impressions of opposite sides of the same shield; and as we apply the same term 'consciousness' to it, from whichever point of view we contemplate it, the ambiguity noticed necessarily attends that term.

In any case of an end gradually realising itself through a certain organism a like difficulty arises. If we would state the truth about a living and growing body, we can only do it by the help of two conceptions, which we shall try in vain to reduce to a third. One will be the conception of the end, the particular form of life realised in the body—an end real and present, because operative, throughout the development of the body, but which we cannot identify with any stage of that development. The other will be that of the particular body, or complex of material conditions, organic to this end, as on the one hand dependent on an inexhaustible series of other material conditions, on the other progressively modified by results of the action, the life, to which it is organic. The particular living being is not less one and indivisible because we cannot dispense with either of these conceptions, if we would understand it aright, or because it is sometimes one, sometimes the other, of them that is predominant in our usage of the term 'living being.' In like manner, so far as we can understand at all the reality of consciousness, one and indivisible as it is in each of us, it must be by conceiving both the end, in the shape of a completed knowledge that gradually realises itself in the organic process of sentient life, and that organic process itself with its history and conditions. We have not two minds, but one mind; but we can know that one mind in its reality only by taking account, on the one hand, of the process in time by which effects of sentient experience are accumulated in the organism, yielding new modes of reaction upon stimulus and fresh associations of feeling with feeling; on the other, of the system of thought and knowledge which realises or reproduces itself in the individual through that process, a system into the inner constitution of which no relations of time enter.

69. If we examine the notion of intellectual progress common to all educated men, we find that it virtually involves this twofold conception of the mind. We regard it as a progress towards the attainment of knowledge or true ideas. But we cannot suppose that those relations of facts or objects in consciousness, which constitute any piece of knowledge of which a man becomes master, first come into being when he attains that knowledge; that they pass through the process by which he laboriously learns, or gradually cease to be as he forgets or becomes confused. They must exist as part of an eternal universe—and that a spiritual universe or universe of consciousness—during all the changes of the individual's attitude towards them, whether he is asleep or awake, distracted or attentive, ignorant or informed. It is a common-place indeed to assert that the order of the universe remains the same, however our impressions may change in regard to it; but as the common-place is apt to be understood, the universe is conceived in abstraction from consciousness, while consciousness is identified simply with the changing impressions, of which the unchanging order is independent. But the unchanging order is an order of relations; and, even if relations of any kind could be independent of consciousness, certainly those that form the content of knowledge are not so. As known they exist only for consciousness; and, if in themselves they were external to it, we shall try in vain to conceive any process by which they could find their way from without to within it. They are relations of facts, which require a consciousness alike to present them as facts and to unite them in relation. We must hold then that there is a consciousness for which the relations of fact, that form the object of our gradually attained knowledge, already and eternally exist; and that the growing knowledge of the individual is a progress towards this consciousness.

70. It is a consciousness, further, which is itself operative in the progress towards its attainment, just as elsewhere the end realised through a certain process itself determines that process; as a particular kind of life, for instance, informs the processes organic to it.   Every effort fails to trace a genesis of knowledge out of anything which is not, in form and principle, knowledge itself.   The most primitive germ from which knowledge can be developed is already a perception of fact, which implies the action upon successive sensations of a consciousness which holds them in relation, and which therefore cannot itself be before or after them, or exist as a succession at all.   And every step forward in real intelligence, whether in the way of addition to what we call the stock of human knowledge, or of an appropriation by the individual of some part of that stock, is only explicable on supposition that successive reports of the senses, successive efforts of attention, successive processes of observation and experiment, are determined by the consciousness that all things form a related whole—a consciousness which is operative throughout their succession and which at the same time realises itself through them.

71. A familiar illustration may help to bring home that view of what is involved in the attainment of knowledge for which we are here contending.   We often talk of reading the book of nature; and there is a real analogy between the process in which we apprehend the import of a sentence, and that by which we arrive at any piece of knowledge.   In reading the sentence we see the words successively, we attend to them successively, we recall their meaning successively.   But throughout that succession there must be present continuously the consciousness that the sentence has a meaning as a whole; otherwise the successive vision, attention and recollection would not end in a comprehension of what the meaning is.   This consciousness operates in them, rendering them what they are as organic to the intelligent reading of the sentence.   And when the reading is over, the consciousness that the sentence has a meaning has become a consciousness of what in particular the meaning is,—a consciousness in which the successive results of the mental operations involved in the reading are held together, without succession, as a connected whole. The reader has then, so far as that sentence is concerned, made the mind of the writer his own. The thought which was the writer's when he composed the sentence, has so determined, has so used as *organs*, the successive operations of sense and soul on the part of the reader, as to reproduce itself in him through them; and the first stage in this reproduction, the condition under which alone the processes mentioned contribute to it, is the conviction on the reader's part that the sentence is a connected whole, that it has a meaning which may be understood. This conviction, it is true, is not wrought in him by the thought of the writer expressed in that particular sentence. He has learnt that sentences have a meaning before applying himself to that particular one. Before any one can read at all, he must have been accustomed to have the thought of another reproduced in him through signs of one kind or another. But the first germ of this reproduction, the first possibility or receptivity of it, must have consisted in so much communication of some one else's meaning as is implied in the apprehension that he has a meaning to convey. It is through this elementary apprehension that certain functions of one man's soul, the soul of a listener or reader, become so organic to the thought of another, as that this thought gradually realises itself anew in the soul of the listener.

May we not take it to be in a similar way that the system of related facts, which forms the objective world, reproduces itself, partially and gradually, in the soul of the individual who in part knows it? That this system implies a mind or consciousness for which it exists, as the condition of the union in relation of the related facts, is not an arbitrary guess. We have seen that it is the only answer which we have any ground for giving to the question, how such a union of the manifold is possible. On the other side, our knowledge of any part of the system implies a like union of the manifold in relation; such a presentation of feelings as facts, and such a determination of the facts by mutual relation, as is only possible through the action upon feelings of a subject distinguishing itself from them. This being so, it would seem that the attainment of the knowledge is only explicable as a reproduction of itself, in the human soul, by the consciousness for which the cosmos of related facts exists—a reproduction of itself, in which it uses the sentient life of the soul as its organ.

72. Because the reproduction has thus a process in time for its organ, it is at once progressive and incapable of completion. It is 'never ending, still beginning,' because of the constant succession of phenomena in the sentient life, which the eternal consciousness, acting on that life, has perpetually to gather anew into the timeless unity of knowledge. There never can be that actual wholeness of the world for us, which there must be for the mind that renders the world one. But though the conditions under which the eternal consciousness reproduces itself in our knowledge are thus incompatible with finality in that knowledge, there is that element of identity between the first stage of intelligent experience— between the simplest beginning of knowledge—and the eternal consciousness reproducing itself in it, which consists in the presentation of a many in one, in the apprehension of facts as related in a single system, in the conception of there being an order of things, whatever that order may turn out to be. Just as the conviction that a speaker or writer has a meaning is at once the first step in the communication of his thought to a listener or reader, and the condition determining all the organic processes of reading and listening which end in the reproduction of the thought, so the conception described is at once the primary form in which that mind to which the world is relative communicates itself to us, and the influence which renders the processes of sensuous experience into organs of its communication. It is only as governed by the forecast of there being a related whole that these processes can yield a growing, though for ever incomplete, knowledge of what in detail the whole is.

73. There should by this time be no need of the reminder, that the evidence of the action of this fore-casting idea, in the several stages of our learning to know, does not depend on any account of it which the learner may be able to give. Whether he is able to give such an account or no, depends on the development of his powers of reflection; and the idea is at work before it is reflected on. The evidence of its action lies in results inexplicable without it. Nor must we imagine it, as the doctrine of innate ideas might lead us to do, antecedent in time to the processes of learning through which it realises itself, and which, in so doing, it makes what they are. This would be the same mistake as to suppose the life of a living body antecedent in time to the functions of the living body. It is inconsistent with the essential notion that the consciousness of a related whole, *so far as it is ours*, is an end realising itself in and determining the growth of intelligence. Thus when the question is raised, whether the conception of the uniformity of nature precedes or follows upon the inartificial or unmethodised exercise of induction, the answer must be either that it does both or that it does neither; or, better, that the question, being improperly put, does not admit of an answer. The conception of the uniformity of nature is one form of the consciousness on which we have been dwelling; and the processes of experience are related to it as respiration or the circulation of the blood is related to life. It is the end to which they are organic; but, at the same time, it is so operative in them that without it they would not be what they are. It is no more derivable from processes of sense, *as these would be without it*—from excitements and reactions of the nervous system—than life is derivable from mechanical and chemical functions of that which does not live. Under various expressions, it is the primary form of the intellectual life in which the eternal consciousness, the spirit for which the relations of the universe exist, reproduces itself in us. All particular knowledge of these relations is a filling up of this form, which the continued action of the eternal consciousness in and upon the sentient life renders possible.

CHAPTER III

THE FREEDOM OF MAN AS INTELLIGENCE

74. THROUGHOUT the foregoing discussion of the conditions of knowledge our object, it will be remembered, has been to arrive at some conclusion in regard to the position in which man himself stands to the system of related phenomena called nature—in other words, in regard to the freedom of man ; a conclusion on which the question of the possibility of Ethics, as other than a branch of physics, depends. Arguing, first, from the characteristics of his knowledge, postponing for the present the consideration of his moral achievement, our conclusion is that, while on the one hand his consciousness is throughout empirically conditioned,— in the sense that it would not be what at any time it is but for a series of events, sensible or related to sensibility, some of them events in the past history of consciousness, others of them events affecting the animal system organic to consciousness,—on the other hand his consciousness would not be what it is, *as knowing*, or as a subject of intelligent experience, but for the self-realisation or reproduction in it, through processes thus empirically conditioned, of an eternal consciousness, not existing in time but the condition of there being an order in time, not an object of experience but the condition of there being an intelligent experience, and in this sense not 'empirical' but 'intelligible.' In virtue of his character as knowing, therefore, we are entitled to say that man is, according to a certain well-defined meaning of the term, a 'free cause.' Let us reconsider shortly what that meaning is.

75. By the relation of effect to cause, unless the 'cause' is qualified by some such distinguishing adjective as that just employed, we understand the relation of a given event, either to another event invariably antecedent to it and upon

which it is invariably sequent, or to an assemblage of conditions which together constitute the event—into which it
may be analysed. Such a cause is not a 'free' cause. The
uniformly antecedent event is in turn dependent on other
events; any particular sum of conditions is determined by
a larger complex, which we at least cannot exhaust. But
the condition of the possibility of this relation in either
of its forms—the condition of events being connected in
one order of becoming, the condition of facts being united
in a single system of mutual determination—is the action of
a single principle, to which all events and facts are equally
present and relative, but which distinguishes itself from
them all and can thus unite them in their severalty. In
speaking of this principle we can only use the terms we
have got; and these, being all strictly appropriate to the
relations, or objects determined by the relations, which this
principle renders possible but under which it does not itself
subsist, are strictly inappropriate to it.

Such is the term 'cause.' So far indeed as it indicates
the action of something which makes something else what
it is, it might seem applicable to the unifying principle which
makes the world what it is. But we have no sooner so
applied it than we have to qualify our statement by the
reminder, that to the unifying principle the world, which it
renders one, cannot be something else than itself *in the
same way* as, to ordinary apprehension, a determined fact is
something else than the conditions determining it, or an
event caused something else than the antecedent events
causing it. That the unifying principle should distinguish
itself from the manifold which it unifies, is indeed the
condition of the unification; but it must not be supposed
that the manifold has a nature of its own apart from the
unifying principle, or this principle another nature of its
own apart from what it does in relation to the manifold
world. Apart from the unifying principle the manifold
world would be nothing at all, and in its self-distinction
from that world the unifying principle takes its character

from it; or, rather, it is in distinguishing itself from the world that it gives itself its character, which therefore but for the world it would not have.

76. It is true indeed of anything related as a cause to anything else on which it produces effects, that its efficiency in the production of those effects is an essential part of its nature, just as susceptibility to those effects is an essential part of the nature of that in which they take place. No group of conditions would be what they are but for the effect which it lies in them to produce, no events what they are but for the other events that arise out of them; any more than, conversely, the conditioned phenomenon, or necessarily sequent event, has a nature independent of its conditions or antecedents. Still every particular cause, whether agent or assemblage of conditions or antecedent event, has a nature, made for it by other agents, conditions, or antecedent events, which appears but partially in any particular effect; and again the patient or conditioned phenomenon or sequent event, in which that effect appears, has a nature other than that which it derives from the particular cause. Therefore in the determined world there is a sense in saying that a cause is something on which something *else* depends for being what it is, which no longer holds when the effect is the whole determined world itself, and the cause the unifying principle implied in its determinateness. There is nothing to qualify the determined world *as a whole* but that inner determination of all contained in it by mutual relation, which is due to the action of the unifying principle; nor anything to qualify the unifying principle but this very action, with the self-distinction necessary to it.

When we transfer the term 'cause,' then, from a relation between one thing and another within the determined world to the relation between that world and the agent implied in its existence, we must understand that there is no separate particularity in the agent, on the one side, and the determined world as a whole, on the other, such as characterises any agent and patient, any cause and effect.

within the determined world. The agent must act absolutely from itself in the action through which that world is
—not, as does everything within the world, under determination by something else. The world has no character but
that given it by this action; the agent no character but that
which it gives itself in this action.

77. This is what we mean by calling the agent a 'free
cause.' But the question at once arises whether, when we
have thus qualified the term 'cause' by an epithet which
effectually distinguishes it from any cause cognisable within
the world of phenomena, it still has a meaning for us. The
answer is that but for our own exercise of such causality it
would have none. But, in fact, our action in knowledge—
the action by which we connect successive phenomena in
the unity of a related whole—is an action as absolutely from
itself, as little to be accounted for by the phenomena which
through it become an intelligent experience, or by anything
alien to itself, as is that which we have found to be implied
in the existence of the universal order. This action of our
own 'mind' in knowledge—to say nothing of any other
achievement of the human spirit—becomes to us, when
reflected on, a *causa cognoscendi* in relation to the action
of a self-originating 'mind' in the universe; which we then
learn to regard as the *causa essendi* to the same action,
exercised under whatever limiting conditions, by ourselves.
We find that, quite apart from the sense in which all facts
and events, including those of our natural life, are determined
by that mind without which nature would not be, there
is another sense in which we ourselves are not so much
determined by it as identified by it with itself, or made the
subjects of its self-communication. *All* things in nature are
determined by it, in the sense that they are determined by
each other in a manner that would be impossible but for
its equal, self-distinguishing presence to them all. It is
thus that the events of our natural life are determined by it;
not merely the mechanical and chemical processes presupposed by that life, but the life itself, including all that can

properly be called the successive phenomena of our mental history. But to say that it is thus determined, though it is true of our natural life, is not the full account of it; for this life, with its constituent events or phenomena, is organic to a form of consciousness of which knowledge is the development, and which, if for no other reason than that it conceives time, cannot itself be in time. While the processes organic to this consciousness are determined by the mind to which all things are relative, in the sense that they are part of a universe which it renders possible, this consciousness itself is a reproduction of that mind, in respect, at least, of its attributes of self-origination and unification of the manifold.

78. It may be asked here, what after all is the conclusion as to the freedom of man himself to be drawn from these considerations in regard to knowledge. 'Granted,' it may be said, 'that the knowledge of nature is irreducible to a natural process, that it implies the action of a principle not in time, which you may call, if you please, an eternal mind; still you admit that man's attainment of knowledge is conditional on processes in time and on the fulfilment of strictly natural functions. These processes and functions are as essential to man, as much a part of his being, as his knowledge is. How then can it be said that the being itself, thus conditioned, is not a part of nature but is free? Or, if this statement is made and can be justified, must it not be left alongside of an exactly contrary statement? Do you not after all leave man still "in doubt to deem himself a God or beast;" still perplexed with the "partly this, partly that" conclusion, for which philosophy, if good for anything, should substitute one more satisfactory, but which, on the contrary, it seems merely to restate in a more prolix form?'

79. We answer that, if the foregoing considerations have any truth in them, we are not shut up in this ambiguity. To say that man in himself is *in part* an animal or product of nature, on the ground that the consciousness which distinguishes him is realised through natural processes, is not more true than to say that an animal is in part a machine, because the life which distinguishes it has mechanical structures for its organs. If that activity of knowledge on the part of man, to which functions provisionally called natural are organic, is as absolutely different from any process of change or becoming as we have endeavoured to show that it is, then even the functions organic to it are not described with full truth when they are said to be natural. For the constituent elements of an organism can only be truly and adequately conceived as rendered what they are by the end realised through the organism. The mechanical structure organic to life is not adequately conceived as a machine, though, for the purpose of more accurate examination of the structure in detail, it may be convenient to treat it as such. And, for a like reason, the state of the case in regard to a man is not fairly represented by saying that, though not merely an animal or natural, he is so in respect of the processes of physical change through which an intelligent consciousness is realised in him. In strict truth the man who knows, so far from being an animal altogether, is not an animal at all or even in part. The functions, which would be those of a natural or animal life if they were not organic to the end consisting in knowledge, just because they are so organic, are not in their full reality natural functions, though the purposes of detailed investigation of them—perhaps the purpose of improving man's estate— may be best served by so treating them. For one who could comprehend the whole state of the case, even a digestion that served to nourish a brain, which was in turn organic to knowledge, would be essentially different from digestion in an animal incapable of knowledge, even if it were not the case that the digestive process is itself affected by the end to which it is mediately relative. And, if this is true of those processes which are directly or indirectly organic to knowledge but do not constitute or enter into it, much more is it true of the man capable of knowledge, that in himself he is not an animal, not a link in the chain of natural becoming, in part any more than at all.

80. The question whether a man himself, or in himself, is a natural or animal being, can only mean whether he is so in respect of that which renders him conscious of himself. There is no sense in asking what anything *in itself* is, if it has no self at all. That which is made what it is wholly by relations to other things, neither being anything but their joint result nor distinguishing itself from them, has no self to be enquired about. Such is the case with all things in inorganic nature. Of them at any rate the saying 'Natur hat weder Kern noch Schale' is true without qualification. The distinction between inner and outer, between what they are in themselves and what they are in relation to other things, has no application to them. In an organism, on the other hand, the distinction between its relations and itself does appear. The life of a living body is not, like the motion of a moving body, simply the joint result of its relations to other things. It modifies those relations, and modifies them through a nature not reducible to them, not constituted by their combination. Their bearing on it is different from what it would be if it did not live ; and there is so far a meaning in saying that the organism is something in itself other than what its relations make it—that, while it is related to other things according to mechanical and chemical laws, it has itself a nature which is not mechanical or chemical. There is a significance, accordingly, in the enquiry what this nature in itself is, which there is not in the same enquiry as applied to anything that does not live. But the living body does not, as such, present its nature to itself in consciousness. It does not consciously distinguish itself from its relations. Man, on the other hand, does so distinguish himself, and his doing so is his special distinction. The enquiry, therefore, what he in himself is, must refer not merely to a character which he has as more, and other, than a joint result of relations to other things—such a character he has as simply living,—but to the character which he has as consciously distinguishing himself from all that happens to him.

81. Now this distinction by man of himself from events is no less essentially different from any process in time or any natural becoming than is the activity of knowledge, which indeed depends upon it. It is through it that he is conscious of time, of becoming, of a personal history; and the active principle of this consciousness cannot itself be determined by these relations in the way of time or becoming, which arise for consciousness through its action. The 'punctum stans,' to which an order of time must be relative that it may be an order of time, cannot itself be a moment or a series of moments in that order; nor can the 'punctum stans' *in consciousness*, necessary to the *presentation* of time, be itself a succession in consciousness. And that which is true in regard to the mere presentation of time is true also of everything presented in time, of all becoming, of every history. To be conscious of it we must unite its several stages as related to each other in the way of succession; and to do that we must ourselves be, and distinguish ourselves as being, out of the succession. Ἀνάγκη ἄρα ἀμιγῆ εἶναι τὸν νοῦν, ὥσπερ φησὶν Ἀναξαγόρας, ἵνα κρατῇ, τοῦτο δ᾽ ἐστίν, ἵνα γνωρίζῃ [1]. It is only through our holding ourselves aloof, so to speak, from the manifold affections of sense, as constant throughout their variety, that they can be presented to us as a connected series, and thus move us to seek the conditions of the connexion between them. And again, when the conception of such conditions has been arrived at, it is only through the same detachment of self from the succession of its experiences that we can conceive the conditions as united in their changes by an unchanging law, which, as determining the order of all events in time, is itself unaffected by time.

82. Thus, while still confining our view to man's achievement in knowledge, we are entitled to say that in himself, *i.e.* in respect of that principle through which he at once is a self and distinguishes himself as such, he exerts a free

---

[1] Mind, then, must be unmixed with anything else, as Anaxagoras says, in order that it may master things; that is, in order that it may know them. Arist. de anim. III. iv. 4.

activity,—an activity which is not in time, not a link in the chain of natural becoming, which has no antecedents other than itself but is self-originated. There is no incompatibility between this doctrine and the admission that all the processes of brain and nerve and tissue, all the functions of life and sense, organic to this activity (though even they, as in the thinking man, cannot, for reasons given, properly be held to be merely natural), have a strictly natural history. There would only be such an incompatibility, if these processes and functions actually constituted or made up the self-distinguishing man, the man capable of knowledge. But this, as we have seen, is what they cannot do. Human action is only explicable by the action of an eternal consciousness, which uses them as its organs and reproduces itself through them.

The question why there should be this reproduction, is indeed as unanswerable as every form of the question why the world as a whole should be what it is. Why any detail of the world is what it is, we can explain by reference to other details which determine it; but why the whole should be what it is, why the mind which the world implies should exhibit itself in a world at all, why it should make certain processes of that world organic to a reproduction of itself under limitations which the use of such organs involves— these are questions which, owing perhaps to those very limitations, we are equally unable to avoid asking and to answer. We have to content ourselves with saying that, strange as it may seem, it is so. Taking all the facts of the case together, we cannot express them otherwise. The unification of the manifold in the world implies the presence of the manifold to a mind, for which, and through the action of which, it is a related whole. The unification of the manifold of sense *in our consciousness* of a world implies a certain self-realisation of this mind in us through certain processes of the world which, as explained, only exists through it—in particular through the processes of life and feeling. The wonder in which philosophy is said to begin will not cease when this conclusion is arrived at; but, till it can be shown to have left some essential part of the reality of the case out of sight, and another conclusion can be substituted for it which remedies the defect, this is no reason for rejecting it.

83. Before proceeding, it may be well to point out that it is a conclusion which can in no wise be affected by any discovery, or (legitimately) by any speculation, in regard either to the relation between the human organism and other forms of animal structure, or to the development of human intelligence and the connexion of its lower stages with the higher stages of the intelligence of brutes. Having admitted that certain processes in time are organic in man to that consciousness exercised in knowledge which we hold to be eternal, we have no interest in abridging those processes. If there are reasons for holding that man, in respect of his animal nature, is descended from 'mere' animals—animals in whom the functions of life and sense were not organic to the eternal or distinctively human consciousness,—this does not affect our conclusion in regard to the consciousness of which, as he now is, man is the subject; a conclusion founded on analysis of what he now is and does. This conclusion could only be shaken by showing either that a consciousness of the kind which, for reasons already set forth, we describe as eternal, is not involved in knowledge, or that such a consciousness can in some intelligible way be developed out of those successions of feeling which can properly be treated as functions of the animal system ; and this must mean that it has some element of identity with them. That countless generations should have passed during which a transmitted organism was progressively modified by reaction on its surroundings, by struggle for existence, or otherwise, till its functions became such that an eternal consciousness could realise or reproduce itself through them—this might add to the wonder with which the consideration of what we do and are must always fill us, but it could not alter the results of that consideration. If such be discovered to be the case, the discovery cannot affect the analysis of knowledge—of what is implied in there being a world to be known and in our knowing it,—on which we found our theory of the action of a free or self-conditioned and eternal mind in man.

84. The question, however, of the development of the human organism out of lower forms is quite different from that of the relation between the intelligence exercised in our knowledge and the mere succession of 'impressions and ideas,' *i.e.* of feelings in their primary, or more lively, and in their secondary, or less lively, stage. Till some flaw can be shown in the doctrine previously urged, we must hold that there is an absolute difference between change and the intelligent consciousness or knowledge of change, which precludes us from tracing any development of the one into the other, if development implies any identity of principle between the germ and the developed outcome. When we speak of a development of higher from lower forms of intelligence, there should be no mistake about what we mean, and what we do not mean. We mean the development of an intelligence which, in the lowest form from which the higher can properly be said to be developed, is already a consciousness of change, and therefore cannot be developed out of any succession of changes in the sensibility, contingent upon reactions of the 'psychoplasm' or nervous system, however that system may have been modified by accumulated effects of its reactions in the past.

To deny categorically on this account that the distinctive intelligence of man, his intelligence as knowing, can be developed from that of 'lower' animals would indeed be more than we should be warranted in doing. We have much surer ground for saying what, in respect of our knowledge, we are than for saying what the animals are not. The analysis of what we do and have done in knowledge, which entitles us to certain conclusions as to what we must be in order to do it, is inapplicable to beings with whom we cannot communicate. If the animals have a consciousness corresponding to that which we exercise in knowledge, at any rate we cannot enter into it. Their actions, as observed from outside, would seem to be explicable without it—explicable as resulting from the determination of action by feeling and that of feeling by feeling, in other words as resulting from successive changes of the sensibility,—without any need for ascribing to them any consciousness of change, any synthesis of the modifications they experience as belonging to an inter-related world. We are thus warranted in saying that we have no evidence of the presence in 'brutes' of such an intelligence as that which forms the basis of our knowledge ; and that, *if it is absent,* there can, properly speaking, have been no development of our mind from such a mind as theirs. But this hypothetical negation is quite compatible with the admission that there may have been a progressive develop-ment, through hereditary transmission, of the animal system which has become organic to the distinctive intelligence of man ; that the particular modes of successive feeling upon which a unifying intelligence supervenes in man, rendering them for him into a related world, may be the result of a past experience on the part of beings in whom such intelli-gence had not yet supervened, and who were in that sense not human; and that certain modifications of the sensibility, arising from this pre-human history, may have been the con-dition, according to some unascertained law, of that super-vention of intelligence in man.

BOOK II

THE WILL

CHAPTER I

THE FREEDOM OF THE WILL

85. So far we have been dealing with what we may venture to call the metaphysics of experience or knowledge, as distinct from the metaphysics of moral action. We have been considering the action of the self-conditioning and self-distinguishing mind, which the existence of a connected world implies, in determining a particular product of that world, *viz.* the animal system of man, with the receptive feelings to which that system is organic,—in so determining it as to reproduce itself, under limitations, in the capacity for knowledge which man possesses. The characteristic of this particular mode of its reproduction in the human self is the apprehension of a world which *is*, as distinct from one which *should be*. It constitutes a knowledge of the conditions of the feelings that occur to us, and of uniform relations between changes in those conditions. But the animal system is not organic merely to feeling of the kind just spoken of as receptive, to *impressions*, according to the natural meaning of that term, conveyed by the nerves of the several senses. It is organic also to *wants*, and to impulses for the satisfaction of those wants, which may be in many cases occasioned by impressions of the kind mentioned, but which constitute quite a different function of the animal system.

These wants, with the sequent impulses, must be distinguished from the consciousness of wanted objects, and from the effort to give reality to the objects thus present in consciousness as wanted, no less than sensations of sight and hearing have to be distinguished from the consciousness of objects to which those sensations are conceived to be related. It has been sufficiently pointed out how the presentation of sensible things, on occasion of sensation, implies the action of a principle which is not, like sensation, in time, or an event or a series of events, but must equally be present to, and distinguish itself from, the several stages of a sensation to which attention is given, as well as the several sensations attended to and referred to a single object. In like manner the transition from mere want to consciousness of a wanted object, from the impulse to satisfy the want to an effort for realisation of the idea of the wanted object, implies the presence of the want to a subject which distinguishes itself from it and is constant throughout successive stages of the want.

So much is implied in the conversion of a want into the presentation of a wanted object, though the want be of strictly animal origin, and however slightly the object may be defined in consciousness. Every step in the definition of the wanted object implies a further action of the same subject, in the way of comparing various wants that arise in the process of life, along with the incidents of their satisfaction, as they only can be compared by a subject which is other than the process, not itself a stage or series of stages in the succession which it observes. At the same time as the reflecting subject traverses the series of wants, which it distinguishes from itself while it presents their filling as its object, there arises the idea of a satisfaction on the whole—an idea never realisable, but for ever striving to realise itself in the attainment of a greater command over means to the satisfaction of particular wants.

86. For the present we take no notice of any wanted objects but such as arise from the presentation by a reflecting subject to itself of wants that are of a purely animal origin. With the exception of the object consisting in a general satisfaction of such wants, we take no account as yet of wants that are of distinctively human origin, of wants that arise out of conceptions. The form of consciousness

[margin note: Distinction bet. the world of sense experience + the world of practice i.e. bet. what is + what should be.]

which we are considering does indeed differ absolutely from the mere succession of animal wants; but it so differs, not in respect of the presence of such wants as are not of animal origin, but in virtue of that distinction of self from the wants, through which there supervenes upon the succession of wants a consciousness—not a succession—of wanted objects. It is this consciousness which yields, in the most elementary form, the conception of something that *should be* as distinct from that which *is*, of a world of practice as distinct from that world of experience of which the conception arises from the determination by the Ego of the receptive senses. Whereas in perceptive experience the sensible object carries its reality with it—in being presented at all, is presented as real, though the nature of its reality may remain to be discovered,—in practice the wanted object is one to which real existence has yet to be given. This latter point, it is true, is one which language is apt to disguise. The food which I am said to want, the treasure on which I have set my heart, are already in existence. But, strictly speaking, the objects which in these cases I present to myself as wanted, are the eating of the food, the acquisition of the treasure; and as long as I want them, these exist for me only as ideas which I am striving to realise, as something which I would might be but which is not.

Thus the world of practice depends on man in quite a different sense from that in which nature, or the world of experience, does so. We have seen indeed that independence is not to be ascribed to nature, in the sense either that there would be nature at all without the action of a spiritual self-distinguishing subject, or that there could be a nature for us, for our apprehension, but for a further action of this subject in or as our soul. It is independent of us, however, in the sense that it does not depend on any exercise of our powers whether the sensible objects, of which we are conscious, shall become real or no. They are already real. On the other hand, it is characteristic of the world of practice that its constituents are objects of which

[marginal notes:]
Illustration of wld of exp.

Illustration of wld of practice

These two are differently "related" to man

1) Man & Exp. wld. Reality of its objs does not depend on man.

2) Objs of the wld of practice exist "as wanted" in man's consciousness bef they can become real.

the existence in consciousness, as wanted, is prior to, and conditions, their existence in reality. It depends on a certain exercise of our powers, determined by ideas of the objects as wanted, whether those ideas shall become real or no.

87. The same thing may perhaps be otherwise stated by saying that the world of practice—the world composed of moral or distinctively human actions, with their results— is one in which the determining causes are *motives ;* a *motive* again being an idea of an end, which a self-conscious subject presents to itself, and which it strives and tends to realise. Now, *prima facie,* as will be admitted on all hands, this causality of motives effectually distinguishes the world which moral action has brought, and continues to bring, into being, from the series of natural events. In the latter the occurrence of an event does not depend on an idea of the event, as a desired object, being previously presented. If then moral action is to be brought within the series of natural phenomena, it must be on supposition that the motives which determine it, having natural antecedents, are themselves but links in the chain of natural phenomena ; and that thus moral action, though distinguished from other kinds of natural event by its dependence on prior ideas, is not denaturalised, since the ideas on which it depends are themselves of natural origin.

The question whether this is so is the point really at issue in regard to the possibility and indispensableness of a Moral Philosophy which shall not be a branch of natural science ; or, if we like to put it so, in regard to the freedom of moral agents. It is not the question commonly debated, with much ambiguity of terms, between 'determinists' and 'indeterminists' ; not the question whether there is, or is not, a possibility of unmotived willing ; but the question whether motives, of that kind by which it is the characteristic of moral or human action to be determined, are of properly natural origin or can be rightly regarded as natural phenomena.

88. If the foregoing analysis be correct, even those mo-

tives (defined above) which lie nearest, so to speak, to animal wants are yet effectually distinguished from them and
from any kind of natural phenomena. No one would pretend to find more than a strictly natural event either in any
appetite or want incidental to the process of animal life, or
in the effect of such a want in the way of an instinctive
action directed to its satisfaction. But it is contended that
such appetite or want does not constitute a motive proper,
does not move to any distinctively human action, except as
itself determined by a principle of other than natural origin.
It only becomes a motive, so far as upon the want there
supervenes the presentation of the want by a self-conscious
subject to himself, and with it the idea of a self-satisfaction
to be attained in the filling of the want.

89. It is not indeed that the want is intrinsically altered,
or ceases to be a want, through the supervention upon it of
the moral motive, properly so called; but that, while it continues or ceases and begins again, there arises a new agency,
other than it, from its presence to a self-conscious subject
which takes from it an idea of an object in which self-satisfaction is to be sought. And the new agency, thus resulting,
is no more a natural event or process, or the product of any
such event or process, than is the self-consciousness to which
it owes its distinguishing character. We may illustrate the
state of the case from what takes place in physical life. A
chemical process does not cease to be a chemical process
because it goes on in a living organism, but it does become
contributory to a result wholly different from any which,
apart from a living organism, it could have yielded. On
the other hand, life is not a chemical or mechanical process
because chemical and mechanical processes are necessary to
the living body, unless such processes can by themselves
constitute life. No more is any moral action, or action from
motives, a natural event because natural want is necessary to
it, unless the self-consciousness, in and through which a motive arises out of the want, is itself a natural event or series
of events or relation between events.

90. That it is not so is scarcely less plain of self-consciousness, in that relation to want which yields a motive, than it is of it in that relation to sensation which yields perception and, through it, knowledge. Can that be an event or phenomenon, whether in the way of want or otherwise, which throughout the successive stages, the abatements and revivals, of a want presents the single idea of the self-satisfaction to be attained in its filling; which unites successive wants in the idea of a general need for which provision is to be made, and holds together the successive wants and fillings as the connected but distinct incidents of an inner life, as an experience of happiness or the reverse? Can it, again, be a *series* of events, either the series of which the connexion in an inner life thus arises through its action, or any other series? Can it, finally, be the connexion or *relation* thus arising, or any other relation? But when we have rejected all these alternatives, when we have said that the practical self-consciousness, which is the distinguishing factor in all motives, is not an event or series of events or relation between events, we have said that it is not <u>natural</u> in the ordinary sense of that term; not natural at any rate in any sense in which naturalness would imply its determination by antecedent events, or by conditions of which it is not itself the source.

Defines his use of the term natural.

91. If the reader is satisfied by these considerations that there is something more than natural in the motive to a moral or distinctively human action, he may be apt to assume—since there is no disputing the dependence on animal impulse at any rate of those elementary motives to which we have so far confined our view—that animal impulse is one component of the motive, while self-consciousness is another; that the moral agent is partly an animal, partly a rational or self-realising subject. But against such a view we should protest as much as previously [§ 68] against the notion that the presence of a double consciousness in man was implied in the distinction pointed out between the process of sensation in time and its determination by a subject

motive not to be taken as self consciousness + animal impulse

subtle.

not in time, as alike necessary to perception and knowledge. If it would be untrue to say of the functions of life that they are partly chemical, because without chemical processes they could not be exercised, it is even more untrue to say of a motive, in the proper sense, that it is partly animal, because, unless an animal want occurred, it would not arise. The motive is not made up of a want and self-consciousness, any more than life of chemical processes and vital ones. It is one and indivisible; but, indivisible as it is, it results, as perception results, from the determination of an animal nature by a self-conscious subject other than it; so results, however, as that the animal condition does not survive *in* the result.

The want, no doubt, may remain along with the new result—the motive, properly so called—which arises from its relation to self-consciousness, but it is not a part of it. Hunger, for instance, may survive along with the motive, involving some form of self-reference, which arises out of it in the self-conscious man—whether that motive be the desire to relieve himself from pain, or to give himself pleasure, or to qualify himself for work, or to provide himself the means of living,—but hunger neither is that motive nor a part of it. If it were, the resulting act would not be moral but instinctive. There would be no moral agency in it. It would not be the man that did it, but the hunger or some 'force of nature' in him. The motive in every imputable act for which the agent is conscious on reflection that he is answerable, is a desire for personal good in some form or other; and, however much the idea of what the personal good for the time is may be affected by the pressure of animal want, this want is no more a part or component of the desire than is the sensation of light or colour, which I receive in looking at this written line, a component part of my perception in reading it.

92. Whether our conclusion be accepted or no, it may be hoped that the point which it is sought to make good in regard to the distinctive character of motives has at least been made clear. What instinct is, whether there are in truth merely instinctive actions, is a question on which, though of late some men seem almost to have argued themselves into believing the contrary, there is much more room for doubt than there is as to the nature and reality of motives and the moral action determined by them. If we have to explain what we mean by instinct and instinctive action, we have to do it by excluding the essential characteristic of our own motives and motived action. By an instinctive action we mean one *not* determined by a conception, on the part of the agent, of any good to be gained or evil to be avoided by the action. It is superfluous to add, good *to himself;* for anything conceived as good in such a way that the agent acts for the sake of it, must be conceived as *his own* good, though he may conceive it as his own good only on account of his interest in others, and in spite of any amount of suffering on his own part incidental to its attainment. By a moral action, an action morally imputable or that can be called good or bad, we mean one that *is* so determined as the instinctive action is not. Clearly it is nothing but our knowledge of what moral or motived action is, that gives a meaning to the negation conveyed in the description of another sort of action as instinctive. Whether there in fact are actions, either done by ourselves under certain conditions or by other agents, that correspond to this negative description can never be known with the same intimate certainty with which it is known that actions belonging to our conscious experience are related to motives in that manner of which the negative forms the meaning of the description of any action as instinctive.

93. It is true that it makes no difference to the outward form of an action whether it is so related to a motive or no; whether it has a moral quality or—as would be the case, if it were determined *directly* by animal want—is merely instinctive, in the sense of not proceeding from a conception of personal good. It may have the same effect on the senses of an onlooker, the same nervous and muscular motions may be involved in it, the same physical results may follow

[margin notes:]
Instinctive action

moral action is determined by a conception

Instinctive is negative of moral.

We are not nearly so sure that we act instinctively as we are that we act morally.

Both types of action appear the same externally.

from it, in the one case as in the other. But it is not by
the outward form, thus understood, that we know what
moral action is. We know it, so to speak, on the inner
side. We know what it is in relation to us, the agents;
what it is as our expression. Only thus indeed do we know
it at all. In knowledge so derived, where from the nature
of the case our judgments are incapable of verification in
the ordinary sense by reference to matters of fact—for the
motive which an act expresses is not what we commonly
mean by a matter of fact—there is, no doubt, much liability
to arbitrariness in the interpretation of the self-consciousness
to which alone we can appeal. Against such arbitrariness,
it would seem, we can only protect ourselves by great circumspection in the adoption of our formulæ, so that they may
be as nearly adequate as possible to the inner experience
which we mean them to convey, and by constant reference
to the expression of that experience which is embodied, so
to speak, in the habitual phraseology of men, in literature,
and in the institutions of family and political life.

94. However insufficient such safeguards may be, it
remains the case that self-reflection is the only possible
method of learning what is the inner man or mind that our
action expresses ; in other words, what that action really is.
Judgments so arrived at must be the point of departure for
all enquiry into processes by which our actual moral nature
may have been reached, and into links of connexion between
it and that of animals otherwise endowed. Whatever the
result of such enquiries, it can only be through a confusion
that we allow them to affect our conclusions in regard to
the actuality of our conscious life. Our knowledge of what
that life is may not seldom entitle us to reject speculations
as to a process by which it has come about, on the ground
that such a product as can be legitimately traced from the
process is not the inner life which we know. But no inference from such supposed processes can entitle us to decide
that this life is not that which a sufficiently comprehensive
view of the evidence afforded by itself would authorise us in

taking it to be ; since the acceptance of this evidence as the given reality is the presupposition of any enquiry into a process by which the given reality has come to be.

95. It must be plainly admitted, then, that self-reflection is the basis of the view here given in regard to the distinctive character of the motives which moral actions represent. Any one making this admission will of course endeavour to conduct his self-reflection as circumspectly as possible, and to save it as far as may be from errors which personal idiosyncrasy might occasion, by constant reference to the customary expressions of moral consciousness in use among men, and to the institutions in which men have embodied their ideas or ideals of permanent good. In the interpretation, however, of such expressions and institutions self-reflection must be our ultimate guide. Without it they would have nothing to tell ; and it is to it, avowedly, that we make our appeal when we say that to every action morally imputable, or of which a man can recognise himself as the author, the motive is always some idea of the man's personal good—an idea absolutely different from animal want, even in cases where it is from anticipation of the satisfaction of some animal want that the idea of personal good is derived.

Now a motive so constituted, like the perception which answers to it in the sphere of speculative intelligence, clearly admits of being considered in seemingly opposite ways. Two seemingly incompatible, yet equally true, sets of statements may be made in regard to it ; which, however, are not really incompatible, because one relates to the motive in its full reality, which is not a sensible event, the other to a sensible event which is implied in it (as sensation is implied in perception) but is not it. The sensible event or phenomenon, implied in the motive, is, like every other event, determined by antecedent events according to natural laws. The motive itself, though it too is in its own way definitely determined, is not naturally determined. It is constituted by an act of self-consciousness which is not a natural event, an act in

---

Marginalia (left):

Importance of Self-reflection.

Without it there would be no morality.

By it a man is author; is morally imputable & responsible: it gives us the meaning of motive.

Seemingly opposite statements re this motive.

Explains the apparent contradiction.

Marginalia (right):

definition of motive on the self reflect view.

which the agent presents to himself a certain idea of himself—
of himself doing or himself enjoying—as an idea of which the
realisation forms for the time his good.   It is true that the
moral quality of this act, its virtue or its vice, depends on
the character of the agent.   It is this that determines what
the kind of personal good, which under any set of circumstances he presents to himself, shall be.   This character, in
turn, has had its history, just as a man's developed intelligence, as it at any time stands, has had a history.   But just
as this latter history, though to call it a history *of* an eternal
consciousness would be a contradiction, has yet taken its
distinctive nature, as a history of *intelligence*, from a certain
action of an eternal self-distinguishing consciousness upon
the processes of feeling ; so the history of human character
has been one in which the same consciousness has throughout been operative upon wants of animal origin, giving rise
through its action upon them to the specific quality of that
history.

96. The view which it is sought to convey may be made
more plain by an instance.   When Esau sells his birthright
for a mess of pottage, his motive, we might be apt hastily to
say, is an animal want.   On reflection, if by 'motive' is
meant that which an action represents or expresses, the
inner side of that of which the action is the outer, we shall
find that it is not so.   The motive lies in the presentation of
an idea of himself as enjoying the pleasure of eating the
pottage, or (which comes practically to the same thing) as
relieved from the pain of hunger.   Plainly, but for his
hunger Esau could have no such motive.   But for it his
presentation of himself as a subject of pleasure could have
taken no such form.   But the hunger is not the presentation
of himself as the subject of pleasure, still less the presentation of that particular pleasure as under the circumstances
his greatest good ; and therefore it is not his motive.   If the
action were determined directly by the hunger, it would
have no moral character, any more than have actions done
in sleep, or strictly under compulsion, or from accident, or

(so far as we know) the actions of animals. Since, however, it is not the hunger as a natural force, but his own conception of himself, as finding for the time his greatest good in the satisfaction of hunger, that determines the act, Esau recognises himself as the author of the act. He imputes it to himself, and it is morally imputable to him—an act for which he is accountable, to which praise or blame are appropriate. If evil follows from it, whether in the shape of punishment inflicted by a superior, or of calamity ensuing in the course of nature to himself or those in whom he is interested, he is aware that he himself has brought it on himself. Hence remorse, and with it the possibility of change of heart. He may 'find no place for repentance' in the sense of cancelling or getting rid of the evil which his act has caused; but in another sense the recognition of himself as the author of the evil is, in promise and potency, itself repentance.

97. 'But how,' it will be asked, 'does this analysis of Esau's motive affect the question of his moral freedom?' We admit at once that, if he is not free or self-determined in his motive, he is not free at all. To a will free in the sense of unmotived we can attach no meaning whatever. Of the relation between will and desire more shall be said in the sequel. For the present the statement may suffice, that we know of no other expression of will but a motive in the sense above explained, or, as it may be called to avoid ambiguity, a strongest motive. Such a motive is the will in act. The question as to the freedom of the will we take to be a question as to the origin of such a strongest motive.

98. The assertion that Esau's motive, and with it the action which expresses his character, is the joint outcome of his circumstances and character, however true it may be, throws little light on the matter, unless followed by some further analysis of the circumstances and character. One 'circumstance' no doubt is his hunger, and this has a definite physical history. The physiologist, with sufficient knowledge and opportunity of examination, could trace its determining antecedents with the utmost precision. But even this hunger, *as it affects Esau's action*, is not really what it would be in relation to a merely natural agent, any more than the visual sensation, which this flower conveys to an intelligent person who attends to it, is really the same as that which it conveys to a merely sentient animal. The want in the one case, the sensation in the other, may rightly be abstracted from the self-consciousness by relation to which, in the cases supposed, it is really determined, for the purpose of investigating those natural conditions and antecedents which are unaffected by that relation; but it must not be forgotten that there *is* an abstraction in so treating it, and that, when the moral bearing of the want is in question, the abstraction may become misleading. The circumstances which in combination with character affect moral action, just because they are so combined, are no longer what they would be merely as circumstances. They are not like forces converging on an inert body which does not itself modify the direction of the resulting motion. Thus even a circumstance in itself and in its antecedents so strictly physical as hunger, if it is Esau's hunger, the hunger of an agent morally endowed, has in effect a quality not determined by natural antecedents.

Of the other circumstances bearing on Esau's action, or of the most important among them, it could not be admitted that they are merely physical at all, even in their origin or antecedents as distinct from their bearing on his act. We may perhaps classify them roughly under three heads—the state of his health, the outward manner of his life (including his family arrangements and the mode in which he maintains himself and his family), and the standard of social expectation on the part of those whom he recognises as his equals. All these have their weight in affecting the result which his character yields under the pressure of animal want, but they are all of them influences which have come to be what they are through processes in which human character or will has been an essential factor. Just as the result to which they contribute in his conduct only arises from the particular mode in which the self-presenting and self-seeking Ego in him reacts upon them, so it is only through previous conduct similarly determined, on his own part or that of others, that such circumstances have taken their actual shape. Their formation at every stage has indeed been affected by events which, like the particular experience of hunger in Esau's case, have each had their definite chain of physical antecedents ; but it has only been as determined by relation to the human self that these events have yielded the given result in the shape of these particular circumstances. In the last resort, then, we are thrown back on the question of the character of the agency so exerted, alike in the formation of those circumstances by which the motive expressed in any moral action is affected, and in that reaction of the man upon the circumstances which actually yields that motive.

99. When we thus speak of the human self, or the man, reacting upon circumstances, giving shape to them, taking a motive from them, what is it exactly that we mean by this self or man ? The answer must be the same as was given to a corresponding question in regard to the self-conscious principle implied in our knowledge. We mean by it a certain reproduction of itself on the part of the eternal self-conscious subject of the world—a reproduction of itself to which it makes the processes of animal life organic, and which is qualified and limited by the nature of those processes, but which is so far essentially a reproduction of the one supreme subject, implied in the existence of the world, that the product carries with it under all its limitations and qualifications the characteristic of being an object to itself. It is the particular human self or person, we hold, thus constituted, that in every moral action, virtuous or vicious, presents to itself some possible state or achievement of its own as for the time its greatest good, and acts for the sake of that good. The kind of good which at any point in his life the person presents to himself as greatest depends, we admit, on his past experience—his past passion and action—and on circumstances. But throughout the past experience he has been an object to himself, and thus the author of his acts in the sense just stated. And as for the circumstances, in the first place they only affect his action through the medium of that idea of his own good upon which he makes them converge; and, secondly, in respect of that part of them which is most important in its bearing on conduct, they themselves presuppose personal, self-seeking [1] agency of the kind described.

100. It will probably be objected that it makes no practical difference to the moral freedom of the individual, whether or no the circumstances by which he is influenced are of strictly natural or of specially human origin, so long as it is not to the individual's own action that they are due. That there is a sense of 'freedom,' indeed, in which it is very differently affected by such a 'circumstance' as hunger or imminent death, and by such another 'circumstance' as the customs and expectations of a society to which the individual belongs, will hardly be disputed. The freedom of an action must be taken to mean simply its imputability in the juristic sense, if it is alleged that it makes no difference to its freedom whether the agent is influenced in doing it by the circumstance of pressing physical need, or by the circumstance that his honour is appealed to by his family or his state. Before taking further notice, however, of the very various senses in which freedom is asserted of man, and of the relation in which our doctrine stands to them, it will be well to guard against further liability to misapprehension in respect of the doctrine itself [2].

'Do you mean,' it may be asked, 'to assert the existence of a mysterious abstract entity which you call the self of

---

[1] The distinction between that sort of self-seeking which is the characteristic of all action susceptible of moral attributes, and that which is specially characteristic of bad moral action, will be considered in the sequel.

[2] [The author must have determined, after this paragraph was written, to omit the fuller account of the different senses of 'freedom' which was sometimes given in his lectures and is promised here. It is now printed in the second volume of Green's *Works*, edited by R. L. Nettleship.]

a man, apart from all his particular feelings, desires, and thoughts—all the experience of his inner life?' To such a question we should reply, to begin with, that of 'entities' we know nothing, except as a dyslogistic term denoting something in which certain English psychological writers seem to suppose that certain other writers believe, but in which, so far as known, no one has stated his own belief. That the self, as we conceive it, is in a certain sense 'mysterious' we admit. It is in a sense mysterious that there should be such a thing as a world at all. The old question, why God made the world, has never been answered, nor will be. We know not why the world should be; we only know that there it is. In like manner we know not why the eternal subject of that world should reproduce itself, through certain processes of the world, as the spirit of mankind, or as the particular self of this or that man in whom the spirit of mankind operates. We can only say that, upon the best analysis we can make of our experience, it seems that so it does. That in thus reproducing itself, however, it remains an 'abstract' self, apart from the desires, feelings, and thoughts of the individual man, is just the notion we seek to set aside. Just as we hold that our desires, feelings, and thoughts would not be what they are— would not be those of a man—if not related to a subject which distinguishes itself from each and all of them; so we hold that this subject would not be what it is, if it were not related to the particular feelings, desires, and thoughts, which it thus distinguishes from and presents to itself. If we are told that the Ego or self is an abstraction from the facts of our inner experience—something which we 'accustom ourselves to suppose' as a basis or substratum for these, but which exists only logically, not really,—it is a fair rejoinder, that these so-called facts, our particular feelings, desires, and thoughts, are abstractions, if considered otherwise than as united in the character of an agent who is an object to himself. The difficulty of saying what this all-uniting, self-seeking, self-realising subject is—the 'mystery' that belongs to it—arises from its being the only thing, or a form of the only thing, that is real (so to speak) in its own right; the only thing of which the reality is not relative and derived. For this reason it can neither be defined by contrast with any co-ordinate reality, as the several forms of inner experience which it determines may be defined by contrast with each other; nor as a modification or determination of anything else. We can only know it by a reflection on it which is its own action; by analysis of the expression it has given to itself in language, literature, and the institutions of human life; and by consideration of what that must be which has thus expressed itself.

101. Having said that the self, as here understood, is not something apart from feelings, desires and thoughts, but that which unites them, or which they become as united, in the character of an agent who is an object to himself, we have implied that there is a sense in which the self has a history, though there is another in which it has none. As has already often enough been pointed out, the eternal subject, which is the condition of there being a succession in time, cannot itself exist as a succession. And its reproduction of itself in man carries with it the same characteristic, in so far as the man presents himself to himself as the subject to which the experiences of a life-time and, mediately through them, the events of the world's history are relative. Such presentation is a timeless act, through which alone man can become aware of an order of time or becoming, or can be capable of such development as can rightly be called moral; of which it is an essential condition that it be united by a single consciousness. On the other hand, just as there is a growth of knowledge in man, though knowledge is only possible through the action in him of the eternal subject, so is there a growth of character, though the possibility of there being a character in the moral sense is similarly conditioned. It grows with the ever-new adoption of desired objects by a self-presenting and, in that sense, eternal subject as its personal good. The act of adoption is the act of a subject which has not come to be; the act itself is not in time, in the sense of being an event determined by previous events; but its product is a further step in that order of becoming which we call the formation of a character, in the growth of some habit of will.

102. We can only express this state of the case by saying that the form in which the self or Ego at any time presents a highest good to itself—and it is on this presentation that conduct depends—is due to the past history of its inner life; but that, throughout, to make this history there has been necessary an action of the Ego, which has no history, has not come to be, but which is the condition of our being conscious of any history or becoming. The particular modes in which I now feel, desire and think, arise out of the modes in which I have previously done so; but the common characteristic of all these has been that in them a subject was conscious of itself as its own object, and thus self-determined. Whatever influences have determined it have done so through, or as taken into, its self-consciousness.

It is to the Ego thus constituted, conscious of its nature—of all that makes it what it is, temper, character, ability—as its own, that new feelings and desires occur from moment to moment, upon the suggestion (to use the most general term) of circumstances. Just as feelings may, and constantly do, come and go without being attended to, so desires constantly arise and pass without exciting any reaction on the part of the Ego, without its placing itself in an attitude of acceptance or rejection towards them. In that case no action, in the moral sense, takes place, and the character, in that sense in which it is the basis of moral goodness or badness, is not affected; though probably even from such 'unconscious'[1] experiences there remain consequences affecting the conditions with which the character afterwards

[1] I use the word 'unconscious' here advisedly, in order to call attention to an ambiguity in the use of the term; which is sometimes applied in a strict sense to a process which is not one of consciousness at all, but merely nervous or automatic, sometimes in a less strict sense to a process of consciousness not attended to or reflected upon.

has to deal.   In other cases the Ego does react upon the experience of the moment.   Through this reaction, in the region of knowledge as distinct from practice, an image recurring becomes an object to be thought about, a feeling becomes a fact to be known ; other facts and objects are recalled from past experience, to be brought into relation with the given fact or given object, and there is thus constituted an act of speculative thought or knowledge, an act in which the man sets himself to understand something. Or, through another form of the same reaction, the Ego identifies itself with some desire, and sets itself to bring into real existence the ideal object, of which the consciousness is involved in the desire.   This constitutes an act of will; which is thus always free, not in the sense of being undetermined by a motive, but in the sense that the motive lies in the man himself, that he makes it and is aware of doing so, and hence, however he may excuse himself, imputes to himself the act which is nothing else than the expression of the motive.

103. An ambiguity in the use of this term motive has caused much ambiguity in the controversy that has raged over 'free-will.'   The champions of free-will commonly suppose that, before the act, a man is affected by various motives, none of which necessarily determines his act; and that between these he makes a choice which is not itself determined by any motive.   Their opponents, on the other hand, argue that there is no such thing as this unmotived choice, but that the motive which, possibly after a period of conflict with other motives, ultimately proves the strongest, necessarily determines the act.   They have to admit, indeed, that the prevalence of this or that motive depends on the man's character ; but the character, they say, itself results from the previous operation of motives, by which they understand simply desires and aversions.

As against the former view it must be urged that, however we may try to give meaning to the assertion that an act of will is a choice without a motive, we cannot do so. Unless there is an object which a man seeks or avoids in doing an act, there is no act of will. Thus a motive is necessary to make such an act. It is involved in it, is part of it ; or rather it *is* the act of will, in its relation to the agent as distinct from its relation to external consequences. On the other hand, the motive which is thus necessarily involved in the act of will, is not a motive in the same sense in which each of the parties to the controversy constantly uses the term. It is not one of the mere desires or aversions, between which the advocate of 'free-will' supposes a man to exercise an arbitrary choice, and of which the strongest, according to the opposite view, necessarily prevails. It is constituted by the reaction of the man's self upon these, and its identification of itself with one of them, as that of which the satisfaction forms for the time its object.

104. We may say, for instance, that there are various 'motives,' *i.e.* desires and aversions, which tend to make *A. B.* pay a debt, others which tend to prevent him from paying it. He wishes for the good opinion of others, for the approval of his conscience, for the sense of relief which he would obtain by paying it. On the other hand, he wishes for sundry pleasures which he would have to forego in paying it. Let us suppose that finally the debt is paid. The act of payment represents, expresses, is made what it is by a motive ; by the consciousness of an object which the man seeks in doing the act. This object, however, as an object *of will*, is not merely one of the objects of desire or aversion, of which the man was conscious before he willed. It is a particular self-satisfaction to be gained in attaining one of these objects or a combination of them. The 'motive' which the act of will expresses is the desire for this self-satisfaction. It is not one of the 'motives,' the desires or aversions, of which the man was conscious previously to the act, as disposing him to it ; at any rate, not one of these or a combination of them, as they were before the determination of the will, before the man 'made up his mind.' It is only as they become through the reaction of the self-seeking self upon them, and through its formation to itself of an object out of them—only as they merge in an effort after a self-satisfaction to be found in this object,—that they yield the motive of the act of will, properly so called.

105. This motive does indeed necessarily determine the act; it *is* the act on its inner side. But it is misleading to call it the *strongest* motive; for this implies a certain parity between it and the impulses which have been previously soliciting the will. The distinction of greater or less strength properly applies only to 'motives' in that sense in which they do *not* determine the will—to desires and aversions, as they are without that reaction of the self upon them which yields the final motive expressed by the action. It may very well happen that the desire which *affects* a man most strongly is one which he decides on resisting. In spite of its strength, he cannot make its object *his* object, the object with which he seeks to satisfy himself. His character prevents this. In other words, it is incompatible with his steady direction of himself towards certain objects in which he habitually seeks satisfaction.

If we like, we may express the state of the case by saying that his strength of character overcomes the strength of the desire. There is no intrinsic objection to this metaphorical application of the term 'strength'; all our terms for what is spiritual being metaphors from what is physical. But, if we would save ourselves from being misled by our metaphor, we must bear two things in mind. In the first place the power by which the 'strong' desire or motive is overcome, is not that of a *co-ordinate* desire or motive—not that of a desire or motive in the same sense of the words—but the power of a desire with the satisfaction of which (as explained) the man has identified his good, as he had not identified it with the satisfaction of the desire overcome. In the second place, the term 'strength' is not applied in the same sense to the desire which *affects* a man, and to the character which *is* the man. A 'strong' desire means generally a desire which causes much disturbance in the tenour of a man's conscious life : a strong character means that habitual concentration of a man's faculties towards the fulfilment of certain purposes, good or bad, which commonly prevents the disturbance caused by strong desire from making its outward sign, from appearing in the man's behaviour. If we are sometimes tempted to say that the weakest men have the strongest desires, the plausibility of such a statement is due to the fact that the strength of the stronger man's character makes us ignore the strength of his desires.

What we call a strong character we also call a strong 'will.' This is not to be regarded as a particular endowment or faculty, like a retentive memory, or a lively imagination, or an even temper, or a great passion for society. A strong will means a strong man. It expresses a certain quality of the man himself, as distinguishable from all his faculties and tendencies, a quality which he has in relation to all of them alike. It means that it is the man's habit to set clearly before himself certain objects in which he seeks self-satisfaction, and that he does not allow himself to be drawn aside from these by the suggestions of chance desires. He need not therefore be a good man ; for the objects upon which he concentrates himself may be morally bad, according to the criteria of badness which we have yet to consider. But, on the other hand, the weak man, taking his object at any time from the desire which happens to affect him most strongly, cannot be a good man. Concentration of will does not necessarily mean goodness, but it is a necessary condition of goodness.

106. According to what has been said, the proposition, current among 'determinists,' that a man's action is the joint result of his character and circumstances, is true enough in a certain sense, and, in that sense, is quite compatible with an assertion of human freedom. It is *not* so compatible, if character and circumstances are considered reducible, directly or indirectly, to combinations and sequences of natural events. It *is* so compatible, if a 'free cause,' consisting in a subject which is its own object, a self-distinguishing and self-seeking subject, is recognised as making both character and circumstances what they are. It is not necessary to moral freedom that, on the part of the person to whom it belongs, there should be an indeterminate possibility of becoming and doing anything and everything. A man's possibilities of doing and becoming at any moment of his life are as thoroughly conditioned as those of an animal or a plant; but the conditions are different. The conditions that determine what a plant or animal or any natural agent shall do or become, are not objects that it presents to itself; not objects in which it seeks self-satisfaction. On the other hand, whatever conditions the man's possibilities does so through his self-consciousness. The climate in which he lives, the food and drink accessible to him, and other strictly physical circumstances, no doubt make a difference to him ; but it is only through the medium of a conception of personal good, only so far as the man out of his relations to them makes to himself certain objects in which he seeks self-satisfaction, that they make a difference to him as a man or moral being. It is only thus that they affect his character and those moral actions which are properly so called as representing a character. Any difference which circumstances make to a man, except as affecting the nature of the personal good for which he lives, of the objects which he makes his own, is of a kind with the difference they make to the colour of his skin or the quality of his secretions. He is concerned with it, he cannot live as if it were not, but it is still not part of himself. It is still so far aloof from him that it rests with him, with his character, to determine what its moral bearing on him shall be. For that moral bearing depends not directly on the physical circumstances, but on the object which, upon occasion or in view of the circumstances, he presents to himself. The imminence of the same dangers will make a hero of one man, a rake of another, a miser of a third. The character which makes circumstances, physically the same, so diverse in their moral influence, has doubtless had its history ; but the history which thus determines moral action has been a history *of* moral action, *i.e.* of action in which the agent has been an object to himself, seeking to realise an idea of his own good which he is conscious of presenting to himself.

107. The less patient reader may here be inclined to object that, in professing to oppose the naturalistic view of human action, we have given up the only position that was worth defending. 'Does not this account of moral action,' he will ask, 'though you call it a vindication of freedom, lead to all the practical ill consequences to which the strictly physical theory of the matter is said to lead?' If a man's character and circumstances together necessarily determine his action, is he not entitled to say, "I have got my character, it matters not how; my circumstances are given; therefore I cannot help acting as I do"? And when once he has learnt to use this language, will there not be an end to shame and remorse, and to all effort after self-reformation?' Such an objection implies a misconception of the real meaning of the doctrine objected to, which may be partly due to the form in which it is commonly stated. That moral action is a joint result of character and circumstances is not altogether an appropriate statement of it. It would be better to say that moral action is the expression of a man's character, as it reacts upon and responds to given circumstances. We might thus prevent the impression which the ordinary statement, in default of due consideration, is apt to convey, the impression that a man's character is something other than himself; that it is an alien force, which, together with the other force called circumstances, converges upon him, moving him in a direction which is the resultant of the two forces combined, and in which accordingly he cannot help being carried.

108. It can only be by some such impression as this that the objection, just stated, is to be accounted for. It disappears upon a due consideration of what is meant by character. An action which expresses character has no *must*, in the physical sense, about it. The 'can't help it' has no application to it. Where it has any true application the action is not determined by character, any more than is a sneeze, or a twitching produced by a galvanic battery. A character is only formed through a man's conscious presentation to himself of objects as his good, as that in which his self-satisfaction is to be found. Just so far as an action is determined by character, it is determined by an object which the agent has thus consciously made his own, and has come to make his own in consequence of actions similarly determined. He is thus conscious of being the author of the act; he imputes it to himself. The very excuses that he makes for it—not less when they take the form of an appeal to some fatalistic or 'necessarian' doctrine than in a more vulgar guise—are evidence that he does so. And in such a case the evidence of consciousness, fairly interpreted, is final. The suggestion that consciousness may not correspond with reality is, here at least, unmeaning. The whole question is one of consciousness, a question of the relation in which a man consciously stands to objects (those of desire) which exist only in and for consciousness. If the man is consciously determined by himself in being determined by those objects, he is so really : or rather this statement is a mere pleonasm, for the only reality in question is consciousness.

109. It is strictly a contradiction, then, to say that an action which a man's character determines, or which expresses his character, is one that he cannot help doing. It represents him as standing in a relation to external agency, while doing the act, in which he does not stand if his character determines it. We may say, if we like, without any greater error than that of inappropriate phraseology, that, given the agent's character and circumstances as they at any time are, the action 'cannot help being done,' if by that we merely mean that the action is as necessarily related to the character and circumstances as any event to the sum of its conditions. The meaning in that case is not untrue ; but the expression is inappropriate, for it implies a kind of personification of the action. It speaks of the action, as abstracted from the agent, in terms only appropriate to an agent whose powers are directed by a force not his own.

It is probably a sort of confusion between the improper sense in which it may be said that a moral action cannot help being done, because the outcome of character in contact with certain circumstances, and the proper sense in which it is said that a man under compulsion cannot help doing something, which generates the notion that, if an action is the result of character and circumstances, the agent cannot help doing it and is a necessary agent. All results are *necessary* results. If a man's action is the result of his character and circumstances, we in effect add nothing by saying that it is their necessary result. If it is not the result of character or circumstances, or (as we prefer to say) if it is not the expression of a character in contact with certain circumstances, there must be some further element that contributes to its determination. What is that further element? 'Free-will,' some one may say. Very well; but 'free-will' is either a name for you know not what, or it is included, is the essential factor, in character. Rightly understood, the ascription of an action to character as, in respect to circumstances, its cause, is just that which effectually distinguishes it as free or moral from any compulsory or merely natural action. It is simply a confusion to suppose that, because an action is a result—and if a result, a *necessary* result—of character and circumstance, the agent is therefore a 'necessary' agent, in the sense of being an instrument of external force or a result of natural events and agencies; in other words, that 'he cannot help' acting as he does. Nay, it is more than a confusion: it is an inference positively forbidden by the proposition from which it is inferred. For to say that character is a determinant of the act, is, as we have seen, to deny that it proceeds from an agent in this sense 'necessary.'

110. The view, then, that action is the joint result of character and circumstances, if we know what we are about

when we speak of character, does not render shame and remorse unaccountable and unjustifiable, any more than, in those by whom it is most thoroughly accepted, it actually gets rid of them. On the contrary, rightly understood, it alone justifies them. If a man's action did not represent his character but an arbitrary freak of some unaccountable power of unmotived willing, why should he be ashamed of it or reproach himself with it? As little does such a view render the impulse after self-reform unaccountable, or, with those who accept it *bona fide* and not as an excuse for the 'sins they have a mind to,' actually tend to weaken the impulse. There is nothing in the fact that what a man now is and does is the result (to speak pleonastically, the *necessary* result) of what he has been and has done, to prevent him from seeking to become, or from being able to become, in the future other and better than he now is, unless the capacity for conceiving a better state of himself has been lacking to him in the past or has become lost to him at present: and that this is not so is shown by the fact that he does ask the question whether and how he can become better, even though he answer the question in the negative. The dependence of a man's present and future on his past would indeed be fatal to the possibility of that self-reform which is conditional upon the wish for it, if his past had not been one in which his conduct was determined by a conception of personal good. But because his past has been of such a kind, there has been in it, and has been continued out of it into his present, a perpetual potentiality of self-reform, consisting in the perpetual discovery by the man that he is not satisfied; that he has not found the personal good which he sought; that, however many pleasures he has enjoyed, he is none the better off in himself, none the nearer to that which he would wish to be.

The capacity for the conception of being better, which such an experience at once evinces and maintains, forms in itself both the inchoate impulse to realise the conception, and the possibility of its realisation. The possibility is no doubt very different from the realisation. The inchoate impulse may be constantly overborne by other impulses, with the gratification of which the man for the time, from habit or strength of passion, identifies his personal good. Its actualisation, however, depends simply on its own relative strength, not on any accessories or command of means. The *prevalent* wish to be better constitutes the being better. Whether or no in any individual case it shall obtain that prevalence, depends (to use the most general expression) on the social influences brought to bear on the man ; but the influences effective for the purpose all have their origin, ultimately, in the desire to be better on the part of other men, as carrying with it a desire for the bettering of those in whom they are interested. The 'Grace of God' works through no other channels but such as fall under this general description. If, and so far as, in the past and present of individual men and of the society which is at once constituted by them and makes them what they are, this desire is operative, the dependence of the individual's present on his past, so far from being incompatible with his seeking or being able to become better than he is, is just what constitutes the definite possibility of this self-improvement being sought and attained. If there were no such dependence, if I could be something to-day irrespectively of what I was yesterday, or something to-morrow irrespectively of what I am to-day, the motive to the self-reforming effort furnished by regrets for a past of which I reap the fruit, that growing success of the effort that comes with habituation, and the assurance of a better future which animates it, would alike be impossible.

111. That denial, then, of the possibility of a moral new birth, which is sometimes supposed to follow logically from the admission of a necessary connexion between present and past in human conduct, is in truth no consequence of this admission, but of the view which ignores the action of the self-presenting Ego in present and past alike. Once recognise this action, and it is seen that the necessary relation in which a man stands to his own past may be one of such conscious revulsion from it, on account of its failure to yield the self-satisfaction which he seeks, as amounts to what is called a conversion.   But, though there is no valid reason why the acceptance of 'determinism,' in the sense explained, should debar us from looking for 'changes of heart and life' in the individual, it may yet be that a misunderstanding of the doctrine does sometimes in some degree tend to paralyse the moral initiative and weaken the power of self-reform.   It is probably never fair to lay the blame of a moral deterioration or enfeeblement primarily on intellectual misapprehension ; but in a speculative age even misapprehension may tend to promote vicious tendencies, by interfering with the convic tion which would otherwise be the beginning of their cure The form of misunderstanding on the subject now before us, most likely to be practically mischievous, will be the confusion, already noticed, between the true proposition that there is a necessary connexion between character and motive, and between motive and act, and the false proposition that man is a necessary agent, in the sense of not being his own master but an instrument of natural forces.   Men may be found to argue, more or less explicitly, that, if that which he is depends on what he has been and has done, and if, further, whatever he may become in the future will depend on what he now is—that if this is so, as it cannot be denied that it is, there is no good in his trying painfully to become better ; that he may as well live for the pleasure of the hour as it comes.   How may such self-sophistication most compendiously be met?

112.   In the first place, it should be pointed out that such language implies in the highest degree, on the part of any one who uses it, a self-distinguishing and self-seeking consciousness.   But for this he could not thus present to himself his own condition, as determined by what he has been in the past and determining what he will be in the future. Nor unless there were something which he sought to become, a good of himself *as himself* which he sought to attain— unless he were thus determined by himself as an object to himself—could the question, whether there was any use in trying to improve himself instead of letting things take their course, have any meaning for him.

It should be shown, secondly, that this self-distinguishing and self-seeking consciousness, with the yearning for a better state of himself, as yet unattained, which it carries with it, in a special sense makes him what he is, and has made that past history of himself, on which his present state depends, what it has been ; that therefore, just so far as his future depends on his present and his past, it depends on this consciousness, depends on a direction of his inner life in which he is self-determined and his own master, because his own object.

Further, it should be shown that, so far from the dependence of his future upon what he now is and does being a reason for passivity, for letting things take their course (which means, practically, for following the desire or aversion of which the indulgence gives him most present pleasure or saves him most present pain), it would only be the absence of this dependence that could afford a reason for such passivity.   If I could 'trammel up the consequence' of that which at any time I am and do ; if there could be any break of continuity between what I shall be and what I am ; then indeed I might be reckless of what I do, so long as it is pleasant, and, in what I allow myself to be, might take no thought of what it is desirable that I should become.   It is the unthinkableness of any such break of continuity which, in the presence of the self-distinguishing and self-seeking consciousness of man, makes it impossible for the most reckless sensualist to live absolutely for the moment, and forms the standing possibility of self-improvement even in him.   So long as a man presents himself to himself as possibly existing in some better state than that in which he actually is—and that he does so is implied even in his denial that the possibility can be realised—there is something in him to respond to whatever moralising influences society in any of its forms or institutions, themselves the gradual outcome through the ages of man's free effort to better himself, may bring to bear on him. The claims of the family, the call of country, the pleading of the preacher, the appeal of the Church through eye and ear, may at any time awaken in him that which we call (in one sense, truly) a new life, but which is yet the continued working of the spirit which has never ceased to work in, upon, and about him.

113. 'But what becomes of this theory,' the enlightened man of pleasure may reply, 'if it can be shown that the human agent, in that earliest stage of conscious personal being between which and all the following stages you admit that there is a necessary connexion, is a result of strictly physical forces and processes? Will it not then follow that the man's life is throughout determined in the same strictly physical way as is its earliest stage of personal consciousness; and, this being so, that it is as much a delusion for him to suppose that he can alter himself for better or for worse, as it would be for a plant or an animal to suppose so? Neither plant nor animal, indeed, is unimprovable. The produce of the plant can be modified by grafting, and improved by tillage. Animals can be trained to behave in a way in which, to begin with, they are incapable of behaving. So man, the highest of animals, is capable of improvement; but it must be by circumstance, it must be initiated from without. The improvement, the development, will not come for the wishing. It will come, for some, in the struggle for existence. To those for whom it does not so come it will not come at all, and they might as well not bother themselves about it.'

[margin note: Argument for external (of any) improvement.]

114. We answer that the improvement determined by the wish to be better on the part of the improving subject— more properly, the improvement which that wish, so far as prevalent, itself constitutes—has nothing in common with an improvement of plants or animals such as that referred to, which is related to no such wish, and, if related to any wish at all, not to one on the part of the animal or plant improved. That there is such a wish, at any rate in the developed man, cannot be denied even by those who may

[margin note: Answer.]

profess to regard it as ineffectual. We meet them, then, by saying that the child which is to be father of the man capable of such a wish, cannot be the mere child of nature; or, conversely, that the mere child of nature cannot be father of the man, as in our own persons we know the man to be. More fully: when we say that the character of a man, and his consequent action, as it at any time stands, is the result of what his character has previously been, as gradually modified through the varying response of the character to varying circumstances, and the registration in the character of *residua* from these responses, we must assume, as the basis of the character throughout, a self-distinguishing and self-seeking consciousness.

Unless we do so, the proposition stated will not hold good. No response to circumstances of a being which has not, or is not, this consciousness, will account for its coming to have or to be it. Such a being could not be father of the moral man affiliated to it. It will have to be admitted that the consciousness necessary to a character and exhibited in moral action has supervened from without upon the supposed primitive being. No true development will be possible of the moral man from the state of being from which he is said to have been developed, because no true thread of identity can be traced between the two states. If, recognising this, we ascribe to the man or child of the past, whose character and action we suppose to have made the man of the present what he is, that self-determining consciousness which distinguishes the man as he is, the same impossibility meets us again as soon as we try to affiliate this man or child of the past to mere nature—to treat him as the outcome of natural forces and processes. It is difficult, no doubt, to understand the relation to man's self-determining consciousness of that in him which is merely natural (or, to speak more properly, of that in him which would be merely natural, if it were not related to such a consciousness); but we do not overcome the difficulty by ignoring the absolute difference between such a consciousness and everything else in the world, a difference which remains the same, whether we do or do not extend the meaning of 'nature' so as to include modes of being thus absolutely different. In its primitive, no less than in its most developed form, the self-determining consciousness as little admits of derivation from that which has or is it not, as life from that which has or is it not.

The statement then, that the human being, in the earliest stage of his conscious existence, between which and all the following stages there is a necessary connexion, is a result of forces and processes which exclude a self-determining consciousness,—though if it were admitted, it would be fatal to any doctrine of human freedom,—cannot be admitted without self-contradiction. The earlier stage will not, under any modification by circumstances, account for the latter, *if* it is the result of the processes described, or *unless* it already involves the self-determining consciousness which carries freedom with it in all modes of its existence. Should the question be asked, If this self-consciousness is not derived from nature, what then is its origin? the answer is that it has no origin. It never began, because it never was not. It is the condition of there being such a thing as beginning or end. Whatever begins or ends does so for it or in relation to it.

CHAPTER II

DESIRE, INTELLECT, AND WILL

115. THE ground upon which, rightly or wrongly, the reducibility of moral conduct to a series of natural phenomena, and with it the possibility of a physical science of ethics, is here denied, should by this time be sufficiently plain. It lies in the view that in all conduct to which moral predicates are applicable a man is an object to himself; that such conduct, equally whether virtuous or vicious, expresses a motive consisting in an idea of personal good, which the man seeks to realise by action; and that the presentation of such an idea is not explicable by any series of events in time, but implies the action of an eternal consciousness which makes the processes of animal life organic to a particular reproduction of itself in man. The first impression of any one reading this statement may probably be that in our zeal to maintain a distinction of ethics from natural science we have adopted a view which, if significant and true, would take away the only intelligible foundation of ethics by reducing virtuous and vicious action to the same motive; a motive the rejection of which by the will we virtually declare to be impossible, by treating it as itself the act or expression of will. In order to avoid misapprehension on this point, and to explain how we understand that distinction between the good and the bad will which undoubtedly forms the true basis of ethics, it will be necessary to enter on a fuller discussion of the nature of Will, in its relation to Desire and Reason.

116. We are all familiar with the quasi-personifications of Desire, Reason, and Will, which in one form or another have governed the language of moral philosophy in all ages in which such philosophy has existed. Sometimes desire and reason have been represented as inviting the man in different directions, while the will has been supposed to decide which of the two directions shall be followed. Sometimes the opposition has been represented as lying rather between different desires, of which reason however (according to the supposition) supplies the object to the one, while some irrational appetite is the source of the other; the will being the arbiter which determines the action according to the rational or irrational desire. Meanwhile criticism has been always ready to suggest that the only possible conflict is between desires, to which reason is related only as the minister who counts the cost and calculates means, without having anything to do with their initiation or their direction to an end; that the only tenable distinction between irrational and rational desires is really one between desire for the nearer pleasure and desire for the more remote, or between desire for a pleasure which a just calculation would pronounce to be overbalanced by the pains incidental to or consequent upon its attainment, and desire for one not liable to be thus cancelled in the total result[1].

When this view is accepted, the will is naturally taken to be merely a designation for any desire that happens for the time to be strong enough to determine action. ' No doubt,' it will be said, ' there is a particular class of the phenomena observable by the inner sense—a class called acts of will— which are distinguished from other events that take place in nature as being directed by our feeling. But we are not entitled to suppose that in the case of each man there is really a single agent or power exerted in his acts of willing, a single basis of these phenomena. To do so would be of a piece with the logical fiction of "things" underlying the several groups of phenomena which we connect by a common name. Any act of willing is the result of the manifold conditions which go to constitute the feeling by which it is directed—conditions most various in the various cases of willing.'

[1] Cf. Hume, *Treatise on Human Nature*, Book II. Part III. §§ 3, 4.

The same criticism may be applied to our usual assumptions in regard to 'desire,' and 'intelligence' or 'reason,' which we are apt to distinguish from will, as faculties having something in common with it and yet different from it. 'No doubt,' it may be said, 'there are certain inner acts or phenomena which in virtue of certain resemblances we describe by the common name "desire;" others which on a similar ground we designate "perceptions," "conceptions" and "inferences," and afterwards reduce to the higher genus of intellectual acts. But we are deceived by a process of language if, having arrived at an abstract term to indicate the elements of likeness in these several groups of phenomena, we allow ourselves to believe in the existence of a single agent or faculty—desire as such—underlying the manifold desires of this or that man, and of another such faculty—intelligence or reason as such—underlying his manifold perceptions, conceptions and inferences.'

117. We have then first to enquire whether there is any real unity corresponding to the several terms, desire, intelligence, will, on the part of spiritual principles to which these terms are appropriate. Do they merely indicate each certain resemblances between certain sets of inner phenomena, a single point of view from which these several sets of phenomena may be regarded, and thus a unity not in the phenomena themselves but on the part of the person contemplating them? Or is there, on the other hand, a single principle which manifests itself under endless diversity of circumstance and relation in all the particular desires of a man, and is thus in virtue of its own nature designated by a single name? And, in like manner, are our acts of intelligence and will severally the expression of a single principle, which renders each group of acts possible and is entitled in its own right to the single name it bears? We shall find reason to adopt this latter view. The meaning we attach to it, however, is not that in one man there are three separate or separable principles or agents severally underlying his acts of desire, understanding, and will. We adopt it in the sense that there is one subject or spirit, which desires in all a man's experiences of desire, understands in all operations of his intelligence, wills in all his acts of willing; and that the essential character of his desires depends on their all being desires of one and the same subject which also understands, the essential character of his intelligence on its being an activity of one and the same subject which also desires, the essential character of his acts of will on their proceeding from one and the same subject which also desires and understands.

118. Let us begin with the further consideration of *desire*. The distinction has already been pointed out between instinctive impulse and desire of that kind which is a factor in our human experience. The latter involves a consciousness of its object, which in turn implies a consciousness of self. In this consciousness of objects which is also that of self, or of self which is also a consciousness of objects, we have the distinguishing characteristic of desire (as we know it), of understanding and of will, as compared with those processes of the animal soul with which they are apt to be confused. And this consciousness is also the common basis which unites desire, understanding, and will with each other. Our habitual language for expressing the life of the soul naturally lends itself to obscure the distinction upon which it is important here to insist. We constantly speak of sensation as if it were in itself a consciousness of an object by which it is excited. We speak of feeling this thing and that, which we no doubt do feel, but which we only feel because we are self-conscious; because in feeling we distinguish ourselves from the feelings as their subject. The confusion is complicated by the common usage of feeling and consciousness as equivalent terms; which makes it difficult to mark the difference between the *feeling* of self, implied in all pleasure and pain, and that distinguishing presentation of self, as at once the subject of feelings and other than them, which properly constitutes self-consciousness. Nor when we have recognised the distinction between mere feeling and feeling as it is in the self-conscious man, is it easy to express it. If we use one set of terms, we fail to convey the difference between sensation, as the affection of a soul or of an individual subject properly so called, and any affection of one material thing by another. Adopting another set of terms, we seem to fall into the error just noticed, of identifying mere sensation with the consciousness of self and object.

119. The unity of an individual soul is implied in all feeling; or perhaps we should rather say that feeling constitutes the unity of the individual soul. The individual animal is not merely one for us, who contemplate the connexion between the members organic to its life. It is one in itself, as no material atom or material compound is, in virtue of the common feeling through which, if one member suffer, all the members suffer with it. It is not one, as the atom is supposed to be, in the sense of being absolutely simple and excluding everything else from itself. Nor is it one, like the material universe, merely in respect of unity of relation between manifold elements. It is one in the sense that upon certain occurrences in the parts of a peculiarly constituted body there supervenes feeling, which is not any one or number of the occurrences, nor a result of their combination, in the sense of being analysable into them; which does not admit of being analysed into or explained by anything else, and would therefore be unknown but for our immediate experience of it; which, while it is not the attribute of any or all of the elements organic to it, is incommunicably private to a subject experiencing it, affected by the past and affecting the future of that particular subject, his own and not another's.

The question of the distinction between animals and plants, the question whether all 'animals' feel, whether any 'plants' do, is one of classification with which we are not here concerned. However such a question may be answered, it does not affect the importance of noticing the distinctive nature of the individuality which feeling constitutes. It is only indeed from experience of ourselves, not from observation of the animals, that we know what this individuality is; but according to all indications we are justified in ascribing it at any rate to all vertebrate animals. To say that they feel *as* men do, or that they are individual in the same sense as men, is misleading, because it is to ignore the distinctive character given to human feeling and human individuality by a self-consciousness which we have no reason to ascribe to the animals. But the assertion that they feel no less, and are no less individual, than ourselves seems to be within the mark. And if by desire we mean no more than that felt impulse after riddance from pain which pain carries with it to the individual, or that felt want which survives a feeling of pleasure; if by will we mean no more than 'activity determined by feeling;' then we cannot do otherwise than ascribe desire and will to the animals.

120. But though feeling, in the sense explained, constitutes individuality, it does not in that sense amount to the full individuality of man. It does not make the human self what it is. Each of us is one or individual, not merely in the sense that he feels and is *so far* conscious, but in the sense that he presents his feelings to himself, that he distinguishes himself from them, and is conscious of them as manifold relations in which he, the single self, stands to the world,—in short, as manifold facts. It is thus only as self-conscious that we are capable of knowledge, because only as self-conscious that we are aware of being in the presence of facts. Only in virtue of self-consciousness is there for us a world to be known. In that sense man's self-consciousness is his understanding. This does not of course mean that the abstract form of self-consciousness is an intelligence of facts. We know nothing of self-consciousness apart from feeling, and are probably entitled to assume that there is no such thing. The self-consciousness therefore of which we speak includes feeling; not indeed feeling as it is before the stage of self-consciousness is reached, but feeling as it is for the self-conscious soul, or feeling as manifold recognised relation to an objective world. In this reality of its existence, in this actual co-operation with the senses, self-consciousness is the *faculty* of understanding, which in its full activity, with the progressive analysis of that which the senses contain or reveal, becomes knowledge, or the actual understanding of a world. In the same way self-consciousness is the faculty or possibility of desire, in so far as it is the characteristic of desire to be directed to objects present to the mind of the person desiring them.

If this statement seems strange, it is because we are misled by our habit of abstraction. Regarding self-consciousness in unreal detachment from the sensations which to the self-conscious soul become intelligible facts, we find a paradox in the statement that it is the basis of understanding. For a like reason, because we are habituated to abstract self-consciousness from the wants and impulses which are the *sequelæ* of sensation, we stumble at the notion of our desires being founded on self-consciousness. We suppose self-consciousness, in short, apart from a soul and from the activities of sense and appetite which belong to a soul before self-consciousness supervenes. We then oppose it to those very faculties and acts of desire and understanding which are really its expression, in the sense that it is only as self-conscious that the soul exhibits them. No doubt, if self-consciousness were not the self-consciousness of a soul, if it did not supervene upon a sentient and appetitive life, it would not exhibit itself as understanding and desire ; but neither would it be what it is at all. The forms of psychical activity on which it supervenes are carried on into it, though with a character altered by its supervention. They form its content, its filling ; not one, however, which remains what it was upon the first manifestation of self-consciousness in the soul, but one which is constantly taking new determinations to itself through the activity of which self-consciousness is the distinguishing form.

121. Just as the action of self-consciousness in understanding becomes apparent as soon as we ask ourselves how the facts with which our intelligence deals come to be there *for us*—how occurrences of sensation come to be apprehended by us as facts—so its action in desire becomes apparent as soon as we ask ourselves how the objects to which our desires are directed, and which make them what they are, come to arise in our minds. To take an elementary instance, how do we come to desire food? Because we are hungry, is the answer that first suggests itself. But, before we accept the answer, we must enquire more carefully what we mean by the desire. Do we mean by it (1) hunger itself, as a particular sort of painful feeling; or (2) an instinctive impulse to obtain food, excited by this painful feeling but without consciousness of an object to which the impulse is directed; or (3) an impulse excited by the image of a pleasure previously experienced in eating, such as we seem to notice in a well-fed dog or cat when the dinner-bell rings; or (4) desire for an object in the proper sense; *i. e.* for something which the desiring subject presents to itself as distinct at once from itself, the subject that desires, and from other objects which might be desired but for the time are not?

It is only if we understand 'desire for food' in the second of these senses that any one can be said to desire food merely because he is hungry. In the first sense the desire, being the same thing as hunger, obviously cannot be explained by it, but only by a physiological account of the way in which hunger arises. In the two latter senses of the 'desire for food' hunger does not account for it. Hunger, whether considered simply as a painful feeling or as involving an instinctive impulse to remove that feeling, may exist without the desire for food in either of these senses. The quest and taking of food do not necessarily imply more than hunger and an instinctive impulse to remove it. They do not necessarily imply even the revival of an image of pleasure previously associated with eating some sort of food; much less desire for an object, presented as such. To begin with, even by the human infant, food must be sought and obtained instinctively, without any previous experience of it as something that will remove the pain of hunger, without any presentation to the mind of the removal of pain as an end to which means are to be sought. If the quest of food must thus in some cases be instinctive, *i.e.* carried on without consciousness of an object to which it is directed, there is nothing to show that it is not so in all, except where an experience of our own, or an experience which admits of communication to us, testifies to the contrary.

122. Now that which takes place in the soul of an animal when hungry and seeking food is not an experience of this kind. The reason, therefore, which we have for saying of ourselves or our fellow-men that we desire food as an object of which we are conscious, does not apply to animals. Those animals indeed with which we chiefly associate, exhibit all the signs of impulses to action excited by recurrent images of pleasure previously experienced, but this recurrence of the image of a past pleasure does not in itself amount to the consciousness of a desired object consisting in a particular pleasure. Self-consciousness is implied in the one as it is not in the other. The mere revival in a sentient subject of the image of a past pleasure, with the consequent impulse after the renewal of the pleasure, does not imply any consciousness by the subject of itself in distinction from the pleasure, as the subject which has enjoyed it, and may enjoy it again, and which has also enjoyed other pleasures comparable with it ; nor any consciousness of an objective world to which belong the conditions of the pleasure—the means to it, and its consequences.

123. As our principal concern is to ascertain what desire in ourselves is, not what desire in the animals is not, we need not dwell on the objections which naturally suggest themselves to the view that the actions of animals in all cases admit of being explained without the ascription to them of self-consciousness. They are objections which would probably disappear when once the difference was realised between the existence of an individual soul and the individual's presentation of his individuality to himself—his distinction of himself from relations in which he stands to a world. Even when the difference has been apprehended, the affectionate observer of the dog and the horse may be slow to admit that their behaviour represents merely the sequence of impulses upon images of pain and pleasure, without conscious reference to self or to a world; which means without either such memory or such perception, such fear or such hope, as ours. We cannot deny, at any rate of the beasts friendly to man, that in a certain sense they learn by experience; that the processes by which the trained or practised animal seeks to obtain the pleasure or avoid the pain, of which the imagination excites its impulse, imply the association with the imagined pleasure or pain of the images of many sensations which have been found to be connected with that pleasure or pain. It is readily assumed that such habitual sequence of images amounts to an experience of facts like our own; to an apprehension of an objective world, of which the necessary correlative is consciousness of self. The assumption becomes inveterate through the practice of describing the behaviour of animals in terms derived from our own experience,—a practice constantly becoming more prevalent, as the description of animal life becomes a more favourite subject of literary art. It is not to the purpose here to criticise the assumption in detail. It is enough to point out that it *is* an assumption; that the consciousness of objects as such, whether objects of knowledge or objects of desire, is more and other than any established sequence of images or any direction of desire by such sequent images; and that this consciousness of objects, whether any animals partake of it or no, is the characteristic thing in human experience, both in the experience through which we become acquainted with nature and in that through which morality arises.

124. The desire for food—to return to that primary instance—though there are senses in which it is independent of self-consciousness, is not in those senses an element in

our moral experience.   As a determinant of our action as
men, it is a desire for an object, of the presentation of which
self-consciousness is the condition.   Whether we take the
object desired to be the removal of a particular pain or
enjoyment of a particular pleasure, or the maintenance of
life and strength, or some further object for the sake of which
life and strength are sought; or whether we suppose a wish
for each of these ends to be included in the unity of a will
directed to the taking of food; in any case the object is
rendered an object to us by a self which distinguishes itself
from its experience.   The pain of hunger, the pleasure of
eating, are alike presented as constituents in a universe of
pains and pleasures, which the subject contemplates himself
as possibly suffering and enjoying, and in relation to which
he places the pain or pleasure that for the time predominates
in his imagination.   There is for him a world of feeling, however limited in its actual range yet boundless in capacity, of
which he presents himself as the centre.   It is by its relation
to this world that any particular pleasure is defined for him
as an object of desire, and thus, however animal in its origin,
becomes to him, through such reference to a 'before and
after' of experience, what it is not to the animal that feels
but does not distinguish itself from its immediate feeling.
This being true even of animal pleasure, if desired as an
object or as we desire it, it is more plainly true of such an
object as the maintenance of life and strength, and of any
end for the sake of which life and strength are desired.   To
conceive his life as an end, to conceive ends for which he
seeks to live, are clearly the functions only of a being who
can distinguish the manifold of his experience actual and
possible from himself, and at the same time gather it together as related to his single self.

125.   Even those desires of a man, then, which originate in
animal want or susceptibility to animal pleasure, in the sense
that without such want or susceptibility they would not be,
yet become what they are in man, as desires consciously
directed to objects, through the self-consciousness which is

the condition of those objects or any objects being presented. And it is only as consciously directed to objects that they have a moral quality or contribute to make us what we are as moral agents.   To desire food, in the sense either of being hungry or of having an impulse excited by an imagination of some pleasure of eating, without reference to a self which presents the pleasure to itself as a good among other possible good things, is not a function of our moral nature.   If in our waking and sane life we are capable of such a merely animal experience at all, it at any rate does not affect us for the better or worse as men.   It has no bearing on the state of soul or character to which the terms good or bad in the moral sense are applied.   In order to have such a bearing, however dependent on susceptibilities of the animal soul, it must take its essential character from that supervention of self-consciousness upon these susceptibilities through which a man becomes aware of the pleasure derived from them as an end which he makes his own.

126. Nor can it be admitted that those desired objects which are of most concern in the moral life of the civilised and educated man, who has outgrown mere sensuality, are directly dependent on animal susceptibilities at all. . It is not merely their character as objects which the man makes his good that they owe to self-consciousness.   The susceptibilities in which the desires themselves originate, unlike the susceptibilities to the pain of hunger or pleasure of eating, do not arise out of the animal system, but out of a state of things which only self-conscious agents can bring about. The conflict of the moral life would be a much simpler affair than it is if it were mainly fought over those 'bodily pleasures,' in dealing with which, according to Aristotle, the qualities of 'continence and incontinence' are exhibited. The most formidable forces which 'right reason' has to subdue or render contributory to some 'true good' of man, are passions of which reason is in a certain sense itself the parent.   They are passions which the animals know not, because they are excited by the conditions of distinctively human society. They relate to objects which only the intercourse of self-conscious agents can bring into existence.

This is often true of passions which on first thoughts we might be inclined to reckon merely animal appetites. The drunkard probably drinks, as a rule, not for the pleasure of drinking, but to drown pains or win pleasures—pains for instance of self-reproach, pleasures of a quickened fancy or of a sense of good fellowship—of which only the thinking man is capable. The love which is apt to be most danger-ously at war with duty is not a mere sexual impulse, but the passion for a person, in which the consciousness on the lover's part both of his own individuality and of that of the beloved person is at the utmost intensity. Our envies, jealousies, and ambitions—whatever the resemblance between their outward signs and certain expressions of emotion in animals—are all in their proper nature distinctively human, because all founded on interests possible only to self-con-scious beings. We cannot separate such passions from their exciting causes. Take away those occasions of them which arise out of our intercourse as persons with persons, and the passions themselves as we know them disappear. The advantages which I envy in my neighbour, the favour of society or of a particular person which I lose and he wins and which makes me jealous of him, the superiority in form or power or place of which the imagination excites my ambition—these would have no more existence for an agent not self-conscious, or not dealing with other self-conscious agents, than colour has for the blind.

127. It should further be noticed that not only do those desires and passions which form part of our moral experience depend on the action of a self-conscious soul in respect of the presentation of their objects, many of them also in respect of the conditions under which the susceptibility to them arises, but that the same action is implied in the manner in which they qualify each other. We are apt to speak of our desires for this object and that as if each operated on us singly, or as if each had its effect on us

independently of the others, though our conduct may represent their combined result.   But such language is not a true
expression of our experience.   We are never so exclusively
possessed by the desire for any object as to be quite unaffected by the thought of other desired objects, of which
we are conscious that the loss or gain would have a bearing
on our happiness.   In reflection upon our motives we
abstract the predominant desire from that qualification,
whether in the way of added strength or of abatement,
which it derives from the belief on the part of the desiring
subject that its satisfaction involves the satisfaction or
frustration of other desires.   But it is in fact always so
qualified.   Our absorption in it is never so complete but
that the consideration of a possible happiness conditional
upon the satisfaction of other desires makes a difference to
it, though it may not be such a difference as makes its sign
in outward conduct.   We do not indeed desire the objects
of our ordinary interests for the sake of our general happiness, any more than for the sake of the pleasure which the
satisfaction of desire constitutes.   As has often been pointed
out, if there were not desires for particular objects other
than the desire for happiness, there could be no such thing
as the desire for happiness ; for there would be nothing to
constitute the happiness desired.   But in every desire I so
far detach myself from the desire as to conceive myself in
possible enjoyment of the satisfaction of other desires, in
other words, as a subject of happiness ; and the desire itself
is more or less stimulated or checked, according as its
gratification in this involuntary forecast appears conducive
to happiness or otherwise.

128. Even with the man of most concentrated purpose,
the object on which his heart is set—*e.g.* the acquisition of
an estate, election to Parliament, the execution of some
design in literature or art—though it may admit of description by a single phrase, really involves the satisfaction of
many different desires.   The several objects of these admit
of distinction, but they are not to be considered so many

separate forces combining to make up the actual resultant motive. No one of them apart from the rest would be what it is, because each, as it really actuates the man, is affected by the desire for personal well-being; and that well-being presents itself to him as involving the satisfaction of them all. In the cases of concentrated purpose supposed, the man has come to identify his well-being with his success in bringing about a certain event or series of events. To him, as he forecasts his future, the possibility of that success being attained (his acquisition of the estate, his election to Parliament) presents itself as the possibility of his greatest good. It would not seem so, indeed, unless he had (or had once had) various desires, each directed to its specific object other than his well-being, and unless he contemplated the satisfaction of these desires as involved in this particular success; but on the other hand no one of these desires would actuate him as it does, in the way of directing all his effort to the single end for which he lives, unless it were strengthened and sustained by the anticipation of a well-being, in which he conceives the satisfaction of the other desires to be as much involved as the satisfaction of this particular one. The conception of this well-being is the medium through which each desire is at once qualified and reinforced by all the rest, in directing the man's effort to that end in which he presents to himself the satisfaction of them all. In the case of men whose effort is less concentrated in its direction, who live with more divided aims, though 'chance desires' have greater weight, yet none of these is unaffected by the idea of a happiness not to be identified with the satisfaction of any single desire.

Now it is only to the self-conscious soul, which distinguishes itself from all desires in turn, that such an idea is possible. In this further sense, then—not only as the condition (1) of the presentation of *objects*, whether desired or perceived, and (2) of the susceptibilities in which those of our desires which are of most moral importance for good or evil originate, but (3) as the source of the idea of happiness—

it is self-consciousness that makes the action of desire what it really is in the life of moral beings. If it is true that no desire actuates us without qualification by the consciousness of our capacity for other experience than that which this particular desire constitutes, then, in that sense, as well as in the other senses indicated, it is true that every desire which actuates us has a character that self-consciousness gives it. The objects of a man's various desires form a system, connected by memory and anticipation, in which each is qualified by the rest; and just as the object of what we reckon a single desire derives its unity from the unity of the self-presenting consciousness in and for which alone it exists, so the system of a man's desires has its bond of union in the single subject, which always carries with it the consciousness of objects that have been and may be desired into the consciousness of the object which at present is being desired.

129. To revert then to the question from which this part of our discussion started, we shall be right in refusing to admit that particular desires are the only realities and that 'Desire' is a logical fiction; right in asserting a real existence of Desire as such, if by this we understand the one soul or subject, and that a self-conscious soul or subject, which desires in all the desires of each of us, and as belonging to which alone, as related to each other through relation to it, our several desires are what they are. But if we mean anything else than this when we hypostatise desire—as we do when we talk of Desire moving us to act in such or such a way, misleading us, overcoming us, conflicting with Reason, &c.—then 'Desire' is a logical abstraction which we are mistaking for reality. It is thus equally important to bear in mind that there is a real unity in all a man's desires, a common ground of them all, and that this real unity or common ground is simply the man's self, as conscious of itself and consciously seeking in the satisfaction of desires the satisfaction of itself.

But the real unity underlying the operations of intelligence is also the man's self-conscious self. It is only in virtue of his self-consciousness, as has previously been pointed out, that he is aware of facts as facts, or that his experience reveals to him a world of related objects. It is clear then that we must not imagine Desire and Intellect, as our phraseology sometimes misleads us into doing, to be separate agents or influences, always independent of each other, and in the moral life often conflicting. The real agent called Desire is the man or self or subject as desiring ; the real agent called intellect is the man as understanding, as perceiving and conceiving ; and the man that desires is identical with the man that understands. Yet, on the other hand, to desire is clearly not the same thing as to understand. How then is the state of the case to be truly represented ?

130. We commonly content ourselves with saying that the same person has distinct faculties of desire and understanding ; and to this statement, so far as it goes, no objection can fairly be made. It is equally impossible to derive desire from intellect and intellect from desire ; impossible to treat any desire as a mode of understanding, or any act of understanding as a mode of desire. No reason can be given why any perception or conception should lead to desire, unless the soul has to begin with some possibility called into activity by the idea, but other than that of which the activity constitutes the idea – the perception or conception. And, conversely, we cannot explain how a desire should set intellectual activities in motion except on a corresponding supposition. This being so, we must ascribe to the self-conscious soul or man two equally primitive, co-ordinate, possibilities of desiring and understanding. But we may not regard these as independent of each other, or suppose that one can really exist without the other, since they have a common source in one and the same self-consciousness. The man carries with him into his desires the same single self-consciousness which makes his acts of understanding what they are, and into his acts of understanding the same single self-consciousness which makes his

desires what they are. No desire which forms part of our
moral experience would be what it is, if it were not the
desire of a subject which also understands : no act of our
intelligence would be what it is, if it were not the act of
a subject which also desires.

This point would not be worth insisting on, if it meant
merely that desires and operations of the intellect mutually
succeed each other; that in order to the excitement of
desire for an object, as distinct from appetite or instinctive
impulse, there must have been a perception, involving at
least some elementary acts of memory and inference; and
that a desire, again, commonly sets in motion an intellectual
consideration of consequences and ways and means.   The
meaning is that every desire which is within the experience
of a moral agent, involves a mode of consciousness the same
as that which is involved in acts of understanding ; every act
of understanding a mode of self-consciousness the same as
that which is involved in desire.   The element common to
both lies in the consciousness of self and a world as in
a sense opposed to each other, and in the conscious effort
to overcome this opposition.   This, however, will seem one
of those dark and lofty statements which excite the
suspicion of common sense.   The reader's patience is therefore requested during one or two paragraphs of explanation.

131. Desire for an object may be said generally to be a
consciousness of an object as already existing in and for
the consciousness itself, which at the same time strives to
give the object another existence than that which it thus
has—to make it exist really and not merely in the desiring
consciousness.   A man desires, let us suppose, to taste a
bottle of fine wine, to hear a certain piece of music, to see
Athens, to do a service to a friend, to finish a book that
he has in hand.   In each case the desired object, as such,
exists merely in his consciousness, and the desire for it
involves the consciousness of the difference between such
existence of the desired object and that realisation of it
towards which the desire strives, and which, when attained,

is the satisfaction or extinction of the desire. In that sense the desire is at once a consciousness of opposition between a man's self and the real world, and an effort to overcome it by giving a reality in the world, a reality under the conditions of fact, to the object which, as desired, exists merely in his consciousness. It is true of course that the bottle of wine, the piece of music, the city of Athens, exist quite independently of the consciousness of any desiring subject; but these are not the desired objects. The experience of tasting the wine or hearing the music is the desired object; and this does not, any more than the anticipated service to the friend or the achievement of writing the book, exist while desired except in and for the consciousness of the person desiring it. So soon as it existed otherwise the desire would cease. It is true also that, though the desired object is one which for the person desiring it remains to be realised—to have reality given it—yet his desire for it is a real and definitely conditioned fact. To a superior intelligence contemplating the state of the case, the man's desire, with the unattained object which it implies, would be as real as anything else in the world. And further, while it would be apparent to such an intelligence that it was only in virtue of the man's self-consciousness that the desired object existed for him, as such; only through it that he was capable of such an experience as that of which, if the desire be not simply sensual, the forecast moves him; on the other hand it would be no less apparent that the desire, however distinctively human, presupposes and entails some modification of the animal system. We are here considering, however, what desire for an object is to the person experiencing the desire, while experiencing it, not what it might be to another regarding it speculatively as a fact. As so experienced, the common characteristic of every such desire is its direction to an object consciously presented as not yet real, and of which the realisation would satisfy, *i.e.* extinguish, the desire. Towards this extinction of itself in the realisation of its object **every** desire is in itself an effort, however the effort may be prevented from making its outward sign by the interference of other desires or by the circumstances of the case.

132. Such desire, then, implies on the part of the desiring subject (*a*) a distinction of itself at once from its desire and from the real world ; (*b*) a consciousness that the conditions of the real world are at present not in harmony with it, the subject of the desire ; (*c*) an effort, however undeveloped or misdirected, so to adjust the conditions of the real world as to procure satisfaction of the desire.   Let us now turn for a moment to consider the generic nature of our thought. Here too we find the same general characteristic, a relation between a subject and a world of manifold facts, of which at first it is conscious simply as alien to itself, but which it is in constant process of adjusting to itself or making its own.   This is no less true of thought in the form of speculative understanding, the process of learning to know facts and their relations, than it is true of it in the practical form of giving effect and reality to ideas.   We have already seen how it is only for a self-conscious soul that the senses reveal facts or objects at all.   The same self-consciousness which arrests successive sensations as facts to be attended to, finds itself baffled and thwarted so long as the facts remain an unconnected manifold.   That it should bring them into relation to each other is the condition of its finding itself at home in them, of its making them its own.   This establishment or discovery of relations— we naturally call it *establishment* when we think of it as a function of our own minds, *discovery* when we think of it as a function determined for us by the mind that is in the world—is the essential thing in all understanding.   It is involved in those perceptions of objects which we are apt improperly to oppose to acts of understanding, but which all imply the discursive process of consciousness, bringing different sensuous presentations into relation to each other as equally related to the single conscious subject ; and it is involved in those inferences and theories of relations between relations which we commonly treat as the work of understanding *par excellence.*

Whatever the object which we set ourselves to understand, the process begins with our attention being challenged by some fact as simply alien and external to us, as no otherwise related to us than is implied in its being there to be known; and it ends, or rather is constantly approaching an end never reached, in the mental appropriation of the fact, through its being brought under definite relations with the cosmos of facts in which we are already at home.

133. Now if this is a true account of speculative thinking, which it is our natural habit to put in stronger contrast with desire than we do practical thinking, it is clear that between the action of the self-conscious soul in desiring and its action in learning to know there is a real unity. Each implies on the part of the soul the consciousness of a world not itself or its own. Each implies the effort of the soul in different ways to overcome this negation or opposition—the one in the way of gathering the objects presented through the senses into the unity of an intelligible order; the other in the way of giving to, or obtaining for, objects, which various susceptibilities of the self-conscious soul suggest to it and which so far exist for it only in idea, a reality among sensible matters of fact. The unity of the self-conscious soul thus exhibits itself in these its seemingly most different activities.

Accordingly, if we understand by thought, as exercised *ex parte nostra*, the consciousness in a soul of a world of manifold facts, related to each other through relation to itself but at the same time other than itself, and its operation in appropriating that world or making itself at home in it, it will follow from what has been said that thought in this sense is equally involved in the exercise of desire for objects and in the employment of understanding about facts. In the one case it appears in the formation of ideal objects and the quest of means to their realisation; in the other, it appears in the cognisance of a manifold reality which it is sought to unite in a connected whole. This community of principle in the two cases we may properly indicate by calling our inner life, as determined by desires for objects, practical thought, while we call the activity of understanding speculative thought.

134. Nor is this all. The exercise of the one activity is always a necessary accompaniment of the other. In all exercise of the understanding desire is at work. The result of any process of cognition is desired throughout it. No man learns to know anything without desiring to know it. The presentation of a fact which does not on the first view fit itself into any of our established theories of the world, awakens a desire for such adjustment, which may be effected either by further acquaintance with the relations of the fact, or by a modification of our previous theories, or by a combination of both processes. All acquisition of knowledge takes place in this way, and in every stage of the process we are moved by a forecast, however vague, of its result. The learner of course knows not how he will assimilate the strange fact till he has done so, but the idea of its assimilation as possible evokes his effort, precisely as, in a case naturally described as one of desire, the idea, let us say, of winning the love of a woman evokes the effort of the lover to realise the idea.

Thus the process of our understanding in its most distinctive sense is necessarily accompanied by desire. But can it conversely be maintained of desire, as we experience it, not only that it has in common with understanding the essential characteristics of conscious relation between self and a world, and of conscious effort to overcome the opposition between the two, but that it necessarily carries with it an exercise of understanding in the distinctive sense, as we have just seen that our exercise of understanding necessarily carries with it desire? On reflection it will appear to be only some arbitrary abridgment of our conception of desire which makes us hesitate to admit that it is so. So soon as any desire has become more than an indefinite yearning for we know not what, so soon as it is really desire *for some object of which we are conscious*, it necessarily involves an employment of the understanding upon those conditions of the real world which make the difference, so to speak, between the object as desired and its realisation. In the primary stages of desire for an object, when it is either a desire on the part of a child still feeling its way in the world, or desire for some object that has newly suggested itself, the apprehension of the conditions of its realisation may be of the most elementary kind; or, again, the person desiring may be so familiar with those conditions that he is scarcely aware of his mind dwelling on them. But in every case, if desire is consciously directed to an object, and if that object is presented as still unrealised and as dependent for its realisation upon the fulfilment of certain conditions not yet fulfilled—and otherwise it would be an object already attained, not *desired*—then a discursive action of understanding among those conditions, essentially the same as that by which we learn the nature of a matter of fact, is the necessary accompaniment of the desire. To the extent at least of an apprehension that there are conditions of which the fulfilment is necessary to the attainment of the object, it is implied in that merely inchoate desire (if it is consciously directed to an object at all) which stops short of initiating any actual exertion for the fulfilment of the conditions. Without it the consciousness of distinction between the object as desired, and those conditions of reality that would satisfy the desire, could not exist.

135. Thus these two modes of our soul's action, desire and intellect, or practical thought and speculative thought, have not merely the element in common which is expressed by the designation of each as thought, but, as has just been shown, neither action can really be exerted without calling the other into play. This is so even when the matters of fact upon which the understanding is employed are such as neither have any bearing, or are not conceived as having any, upon the improvement of man's estate, nor make any appeal to the artistic interest. It is so, again, when the object, of which the realisation is desired, is merely the enjoyment of a sensual pleasure. But in other cases the mutual involution of desire and understanding, of practical and speculative thought, is even more complete.   There are processes, naturally described as intellectual, in which desire is not merely involved in the sense that the completion of the intellectual task is presented as an object which stimulates effort; while on the other hand there are processes which we naturally ascribe to desire, but in which the intellect is not merely involved as the apprehension of that reality which the desired object, as desired, lacks, or as the quest of means to its realisation.   The activity of the artist, not merely in the region which we call that of the fine arts, but in any form affected by an ideal of perfect work, from that of the writer of books to that of the craftsman, we naturally and properly count intellectual.   Yet it is throughout a realisation of desire.   Of the mathematician or man of science it may possibly be held that he first thinks of his problem, or of facts not yet intelligible, and that the desire to solve the problem or to understand the facts is a subsequent and distinguishable activity.   But with the artist, of whatever kind, the intellectual consciousness of the ideal, which initiates and directs his work, is itself a desire to realise it.   An intellectual passion is our natural designation for his state of mind.

Again, if we consider any of the more worthy practical pursuits of men, which, as is implied in calling them pursuits, are an expression of desire, we shall find not merely that implication of self-consciousness in the presentation of the object, which may not be ignored even when the object is the enjoyment of some animal pleasure, nor a mere sequence of intellectual action upon previous desire for an end; we shall find that the end itself is an object of understanding no less than of desire.   It is only the fallacy of taking the pleasure that ensues on satisfaction of a desire to be the object of the desire, which blinds us to this.   If the end of a man whose chief interest is in the better management of an estate, or the better drainage of the town where he lives, or the better education of his family, or the better administration of justice, were indeed the pleasure which he anticipates in the success of his pursuit, it might be held that, since pleasure (in distinction from the facts conditioning it) is not an object of the understanding, the understanding was not co-operant with desire in the initiation of his pursuit. But, as has often been pointed out, the possibility of pleasure in the attainment of an object presupposes a desire directed not to that pleasure but to the object; and the object in the cases supposed is plainly one that originates in intellectual conception—not indeed in a passionless intellect, if there is such a thing, but in a soul which desires in understanding and in desiring understands. The same is true in regard to objects of less worthy, more selfish, ambition. The applause of a senate or a town-council, the government of an empire or a borough, are objects pursued for their own sake, not for the sake either of the pleasure of attaining them, or of ulterior pleasures to which they may be the means; and in order to the presentation of such objects the soul must understand, in the proper and distinctive sense, no less than desire.

136. On the whole matter, then, our conclusion must be that there is really a single subject or agent, which desires in all the desires of a man, and thinks in all his thoughts, but that the action of this subject as thinking—thinking speculatively or understanding, as well as thinking practically —is involved in all its desires, and that its action as desiring is involved in all its thoughts. Thus thought and desire are not to be regarded as separate powers, of which one can be exercised by us without, or in conflict with, the other. They are rather different ways in which the consciousness of self, which is also necessarily consciousness of a manifold world other than self, expresses itself. One is the effort of such consciousness to take the world into itself, the other its effort to carry itself out into the world; and each effort is involved in every complete spiritual act— every such act as we can impute to ourselves or count our own, whether on reflection we ascribe the act rather to

intellect or rather to desire.   If the 'intellectual' act implies
attention —and otherwise we cannot ascribe it to ourselves
—it implies desire for the attainment of an intellectual
result, though the result be attained as quickly as, for
instance, the meaning of a sentence in a familiar language
is arrived at upon attention being drawn to it.   If the desire
is consciously for an object—and this again is the condition
of its being imputable to ourselves—it implies, as we have
seen, an intellectual apprehension at least of the difference
between the object as desired and its realisation.   In all the
more important processes of desire the exertion of understanding is implied to a much more considerable extent,
just as in every intellectual achievement of importance
the action of desire is much more noticeable and protracted
than in the case just instanced of intelligent attention to the
import of a proposition, heard or read.

137. But if it be true that all desire is the act of a subject
which thinks in desiring, all thought the act of a subject
which desires in thinking, what is to be said of willing?
Any identification of the will with any form of desire seems
inconsistent with the apparent fact that a man has the
power, however seldom he may exercise it, of willing to
resist all his desires, even the strongest, and of acting
accordingly.   The existence of such a power has often been
supposed to be the condition of any disinterested performance of duty ;   and the supposition is not one to be lightly
set aside.   Apart from any such 'transcendental' doctrine,
the difference between desire and will, it may be said, is too
firmly established in the experience of men, as expressed in
our habitual language (*i.e.* in such phrases as 'I should like
to, but I won't'), for all the psychologists to get over it.   To
identify the will, again, with thought or judgment seems to
imply forgetfulness of the familiar fact that a man may 'know
the better and prefer the worse.'   Even when it is our own
action that is the object of thought, our will as evinced by
action is apt not to correspond with our thought, with our

judgment of what is best; while our merely speculative thoughts seem to have as little connexion with the will as a proposition of pure mathematics has to do with the happiness or goodness of man. Our doctrine that the entire self-conscious subject, desiring as well as thinking, is concerned in every complete intellectual act, and in every desire for an object, may seem to increase the difficulty. If this is so, what are we to make of the man who is 'torn by conflicting desires'; who under the influence of one desire wills to do what he knows to be inconsistent with the satisfaction of another desire, which yet he strongly feels? What of the man who has the truest thoughts, not merely on scientific matters, but about the ideal of virtuous conduct—thoughts which on our doctrine should involve desires—and who yet is led by desire to act viciously?

138. Let us first be sure what we mean by a conflict of desires, and by the resistance of the will to desire. Does a man ever really desire, at the same time and *in the same sense,* objects which he recognises as incompatible with each other? Our first answer will probably be: 'Yes; we are constantly divided between conflicting desires. This is the explanation of our irresolution before action, and of our regrets in action. We are irresolute so long as the strength of competing desires is evenly matched: we act with regret when, in following the desire which prevails, we are conscious of foregoing the gratification of another, only less strong.' But the question is whether, when a man is in that state in which it can truly be said that conflicting passions are striving for the mastery in him, he actually desires an object at all; and whether, conversely, when his desire is consciously directed to a certain object, he at the same time and in the same sense desires another object, which is neither included in it nor a means to it, but recognised as incompatible with it. At any rate, if we are to allow that in the divided state of mind supposed he desires an object at all, it is in quite a different sense that he desires the object which, when the scale is finally turned, he 'makes up his mind' to pursue. And, again, he desires this object for the time in quite a different sense from that in which he can be supposed at the same time to desire the object which has come off second best in his choice. The object of his final pursuit is one which he desires in the sense that for the time he identifies himself with it. Living for himself (as he necessarily does) he lives for it. The single self of which he is conscious, the unit in which all the influences of his life centre, but which distinguishes itself from them all, is for the time directed to making it real. It is not in this sense that any of the objects are desired, between which his interests are divided while he is in the state of irresolution. If it were, there would be no suspense of action. Nor is it thus that the objects are desired of which he is still aware as having attractions for him after he has made up his mind to pursue another incompatible object. If it were, he would not be pursuing the other.

139. There are two familiar ways of dealing with the distinction here pointed out. It may be said (*a*) that the difference between the sense in which a man desires sundry incompatible objects, when he cannot make up his mind between them, and the sense in which he finally desires the object of his ultimate preference, is merely that in the latter case one of the competing desires has become stronger than all the rest. The man may be supposed still to continue to desire any of the objects which he does not pursue, just in the same way as he desires the object which he does prefer and pursue at the very time that he prefers the latter. The difference may be held to lie merely in the strength of the several desires; the satisfaction of the strongest, when the incompatibility of their several objects has become apparent, being that which is finally pursued. It may be said (*b*) that the difference pointed out is just that between desire and will. The desires between which we have supposed a man to be suspended, it may be argued, are desires properly so called, while the 'desire' with which he pursues the object to which his preference is finally given, is not properly desire but will. Thus any of the objects which he *desired* in the state of irresolution he may continue to *desire* when his mind is made up, though his *will* is otherwise directed.

140. Neither of these views can be quite accepted. If we are to admit that the man, suspended for the time between desires of which he knows the several satisfactions to be incompatible, desires incompatible objects, instead of rather saying that for the time he desires no object at all, since he does not seek to realise the idea of any object; at any rate the inward relation of the man towards the incompatible objects, between which his desires are divided, is wholly different from his relation towards that which he finally prefers. His relation towards the latter, again, is wholly different from his relation towards that which he is supposed still to desire though not to pursue. And this difference is not appropriately described as one between different degrees of strength of desire.

We will suppose a man divided between hatred of a rival whom he has opportunity of injuring, and some sense of duty (however that is to be explained), or fear of consequences, which inclines him to do to his rival as he would be done by. Here is a conflict of passions or emotions by which the man, so far as any action towards his rival goes, is for the time paralysed. Hatred of his rival stirs him, the idea of doing the magnanimous thing attracts him, fear of discredit deters him, but the total effect of these influences is not such that any definite object of desire presents itself to him of which he seeks the realisation. We will suppose that some fresh provocation intensifies the hatred, that he finally gives way to it and does the wrong from which he had previously abstained; or, on the other hand, that by some bright example or some warning voice the counter influences are strengthened, and that he does a service, or at least an act of justice, to the rival. In neither case is the result truly described by saying that the desire which the action represents is simply the continuation, in greater relative strength, of one among several which were previously competing in the man. It differs in kind from the competing influences. It is what none of them were while competing, what none of them are, so far as any of them survive along with it. It implies, as did none of them, the presentation of an object with which the man for the time identifies himself or his good, and a consequent effort to realise this object. However connected with an intensification of one of the previously competing passions, it is a distinctly new motive, arising out of a changed relation of the man himself to the competing passions. He now, as he did not before, consciously directs himself to the realisation of a desired object. If he desired before, it is at any rate in another way that he desires now.

141. This is equally the case, whether the object for which he acts is that suggested by his hatred or that suggested by his conscience. When it is the pure desire to do the nobler thing, or this as reinforced by fear of discredit, that governs the man's final conduct, the impropriety of treating it as a continuation of one of the previously competing passions, which has finally gained superior strength, is most apparent. The disturbance of the inner life, caused by such passion as hatred or love, is so marked in comparison with such an emotion as a sense of duty or fear of discredit, that to speak of the latter as prevalent in virtue of its superior strength as a passion strikes us at once as unreal. It is accordingly to the example of virtuous resolution, maintained in spite of some violent passion, that the appeal is commonly made by those who would distinguish will from strongest desire. And the distinction is a true one, if it means that the motive expressed in a man's action differs in kind, and not merely in degree of strength, from passions of which the competition suspends his action or with which he has to struggle when he finally acts. But the distinction holds good just as much if, in the case supposed, the man finally acts to gratify his hatred, to realise the idea of crushing his rival, as if he takes the opposite course. Between the man's state of mind while his hatred is merely a competing passion, and his state of mind when acting for the gratification of his hatred, the

difference does not lie in the degree of strength attained by
the hatred, but in the fact that in the latter state the gratification of the hatred has become what it was not in the
former, an object which the man seeks to realise, one which
for the time he has made his good.

142. The distinction, then, between 'desires' of which
the competition suspends action, and the 'desire' which
expresses itself in a morally imputable action—visible or
invisible, overt or only intended—is not to be understood
as lying in the greater relative strength of the latter. Rather,
if the term 'desire' is to be employed in both cases, it should
be understood that it is used in different senses, for in the
one case the man consciously directs himself to the realisation of an ideal object (though perhaps not so as to commit
an 'overt act'), in the other he does not so direct himself.
On the other hand, if we say, according to the second view
(*b*) mentioned above, that the final preference, represented
by the actual pursuit of an object after an interval of suspense between competing passions, is not a desire but an
act of will, we must say the same of the actual pursuit of an
object, even though there has been no previous suspense or
conflict of desires. There is nothing in the fact that the
direction of the man's powers to the realisation of an object
in one case supervenes upon a period of divided mind, and
in another case does not, to justify us in ascribing it to
desire in the latter case if we do not in the former. Yet
when a man sets himself to gain the love of a woman or to
save a friend's life, without another course of action suggesting itself to him as possible, who would question that
he desired the object or that his action was an expression
of desire? But if the principle of action is desire in such
cases, why should the fact of its being accompanied by the
consciousness of a gratification, otherwise possible, having
been forgone, or the fact that, before it was in operation as
a principle of action, the man was for a time divided
between the attractions of different objects, make it any the
less desire in those cases where it is supposed to be dis-

tinctively 'will'?   If, however, it is thus difficult to suppose the principle of action to be a will which is not desire, in the case of an action which follows upon an interval of divided mind, it is equally difficult to regard it as a desire which is not a will in the contrasted case, that of the man who is said to act upon impulse.   If in such a case, being constrained to admit that the action proceeds from desire, we persist in our opposition between desire and will, we shall have to say that it is not willed.   And it will follow that, just so far as a man is 'single-minded,' he has no will; that the voluptuary who has no scruples, the saint who has no temptations, the enthusiast who never hesitates, are so far involuntary agents.

143. The reader may here fairly object, with some impatience, that we have had enough of disputation about the mere usage of the terms desire and will.   We no doubt often use the term 'desire' for impulses or inward solicitations of which the man is conscious, but which do not amount to a conscious direction of himself to the realisation of an object imagined or conceived.   We say that a man desires what his will rejects.   But we represent such a state of the case quite as naturally by saying that, although such and such objects have attractions for the man, yet *on the whole* he does not desire them but only the object for which he acts.   On the other hand, though we now most commonly apply the term 'will' to the direction of the conscious self to action, as opposed to a mere wish not amounting to such direction, yet the usage has been by no means uniform. 'My poverty but not my will consents,' says the seller of poisons in 'Romeo and Juliet.'   Here the consent, though said not to be of the will, might have been enough to hang for.   The will is only the strong competing wish which does not suffice to determine action.   Compare the outburst of St. Paul, as rendered in our authorised translation,—'To will is present with me, but how to perform that which is good I find not.'   But though we cannot fix the usage of words, it is clear that the important real distinction is that

M

between the direction of the self-conscious self to the real-isation of an object, its identification of itself with that object, on the one side (whether that direction and identifi-cation does or does not supervene upon a previous period of indecision, is or is not accompanied by the consciousness of attraction in an object other than that pursued), and, on the other side, the mere solicitations of which a man is conscious, but with none of which he so identifies himself as to make the soliciting object his object—the object of his self-seeking—or to direct himself to its realisation.

144. When it is urged, therefore, that the will often con-flicts with and overcomes a man's desires—even if it be not necessary in order to constitute a will, as sometimes seems to be supposed, that there should be such a conflict with desire—and that an act of will therefore must be other than a desire, we answer, Certainly it is other than any such desire as those which it is said to overcome. But it is not other than desire in that sense in which desire is ever the principle or motive of an imputable human action, of an action that has any moral quality, good or bad, that can properly be rewarded or punished, or is fit matter for praise or blame. It is not necessary to such an action that there should be any overt effect, of which other men can take note. Morally the action of a man who has made up his mind to sacrifice himself for his friend or to commit a murder is the same though he be accidentally disabled before either the good resolution or the bad one, as the case may be, has taken effect. The essential thing morally is the man's direction of himself to the realisation of a con-ceived or imagined object, whether circumstances allow of its issuing in *outward* action, action that affects the senses of other people, or no.

It would be a forced restriction of the term desire to refuse to apply it to such direction of the self; but unless we so restrict it, there is no ground for holding that will is other than desire. The 'desire' which is motive to the man who barters his heritage for a mess of pottage, differs no doubt *in its object* from the 'will' of the man who sacrifices his inclinations in adhering to a rule of abstinence which he has imposed on himself; but *in the same respect* it differs from the 'desire' or 'impulse' of a man who swims the Hellespont to see his mistress; just as, again, the 'will' described in the above instance differs in object from the 'will' of the man who, upon cool calculation, sacrifices natural affection in order to get a better position in the world. In each of these cases the principle of action is different in respect of its object, but this is a difference to which, as we see, the distinction in the usage of the terms 'desire' and 'will' does not correspond; and, apart from the difference of object, there is no difference between the principles of action in the several cases. Where it is described as will it is equally desire; where it is described as desire or impulse it is equally will. But whether described as desire or as will, it is wholly different in its relation to the subject—to the man willing or desiring—from such desires as are said to compete for mastery in the man, or from any desire that he retains when consciously acting in a way incompatible with its gratification. It is an expression or utterance of the man, as he for the time is. It begins from him, from his self-conscious self. These other 'desires' end where it begins, *viz.* in this self. They are influences or tendencies by which the man, the self, is affected, not a motion proceeding from him. They tend to move him, but *he* does not move in them; and none of them actually moves him unless the man takes it into himself, identifies himself with it, in a way which wholly alters it from what it was as a mere influence affecting him.

145. The objection to saying that will is merely a strongest desire is that, as it is apt to be understood, it leads to this difference being ignored. It is taken to imply that the principle of a man's action is no more than one of the influences to which the man in his inner life is susceptible — that one which, under the conditions of the moment, or upon consideration of the circumstances, becomes the strongest. In truth it is never any or all of these, however much it may be affected by them, but a self-distinguishing and self-realising consciousness, through which, as a transforming medium, these influences must pass before they can take effect in a moral action at all. Just as each of us is constantly having sensations which do not amount to perceptions, make no lodgment in the cosmos of our experience, add nothing to our knowledge, because not gathered into the focus of self-consciousness and through it referred to objects or determined by relation to each other; so there are impulses constantly at work in a man—the result of his organisation, of habits (his own or his ancestors'), of external excitement, &c.—of which he is more or less aware according to the degree to which their antagonism to each other calls attention to them, but which yet do not amount to principles of imputable action, or to desires of which it is sought to realise the objects, because the self-seeking, self-determining person has not identified himself with any of them. It is such impulses alone that are properly said to compete for mastery in a man before his determination to act, and that may survive along with an enacted desire that represents none of them. The 'strongest desire' or will which is realised in act is not one of them nor co-ordinate with them, though apart from them it would not be. It is a new principle that supervenes upon them through the self-conscious subject's identification of itself with one of them, just as a perception is not a sensation or congeries of sensations, but supervenes upon certain sensations through a man's attending to them, *i. e.* through his taking them into self-consciousness and determining them, as in it, by relation to others of its contents.

146. A man, we will suppose, is acted on at once by an impulse to avenge an affront, by a bodily want, by a call of duty, and by fear of certain results incidental to his avenging the affront or obeying the call of duty. We will suppose further that each passion (to use the most general term) suggests a different line of action. So long as he is undecided how to act, all are, in a way, external to him. He presents them to himself as influences by which he is consciously affected but which are not he, and with none of which he yet identifies himself; or, to vary the expression, as tendencies to different objects, none of which is yet *his* object. So long as this state of things continues, no moral effect ensues. It ensues when the man's relation to these influences is altered by his identifying himself with one of them, by his taking the object of one of the tendencies as for the time his good. This is to *will*, and is in itself moral action, though circumstances may prevent its issuing in that sensible effect which we call an overt act. But in the act of will the man does not cease to desire. Rather he, the man, for the first time desires, having not done so while divided between the conflicting influences. His willing is not a continuation of any of those desires, if they are to be so called, that were previously acting upon him. It is that which none of these had yet become; a desire in which the man enacts himself, as distinct from one which acts upon him. Whether its object — the object to which the moral action is directed—be the attainment of revenge, or the satisfaction of a bodily want, or the fulfilment of a call of duty, it has equally this characteristic. The object is one which for the time the man identifies with himself, so that in being determined by it he is consciously determined by himself.

147. It is not necessary, however, to that putting forth of the man or self in desire which constitutes an act of will, that there should have been beforehand any conscious presentation of competing objects of desire, with consequent deliberation as to which should be pursued. When a man acts 'impulsively' or according to a settled habit, without contemplating the possibility of a motive that might lead him to another sort of action, it is still only through the self-seeking and self-distinguishing self that the inducement, or influence, or tendency, becomes a principle of action. In such a case the man makes the object, which the passion or habit suggests, his own, and sets himself to realise it, just as much as in the case where he contemplates alternatives. The evidence of this is his self-imputation of the act upon reflection. He may make excuses for it, should there be occasion to do so, on the ground of the strength of the inducement, but these very excuses witness that he is conscious of himself as other than the inducements and influences of which he pleads the strength, and conscious that it is not from them, but from himself as affected by them, that the action proceeds. When the case is otherwise, when he is conscious of having really been but an instrument in doing what he did, he does not make excuses but explains the fact.

So much for the opposition, sometimes alleged, between will and desire. It must be admitted that an act of will is never *mere* desire, never a desire which has been in conflict with other co-ordinate desires and has come out the strongest, if in speaking of such desire we suppose abstraction to be made of the action of a self-determining self upon and within it. But in this there lies no difference between will and any other principle of moral or human or imputable, as distinct from merely animal, action ; for mere desire, of that kind to which will can properly be opposed, never amounts to such a principle. The true distinction lies between passions as influences affecting a man—among which we may include ' mere desires,' if we please—and the man as desiring, or putting himself forth in desire for the realisation of some object present to him in idea, which is the same thing as willing.

148. The recognised opposition between Will and Intellect stands on a different footing. We have already pointed out that, though a man in desiring (in the sense of consciously directing himself to the realisation of objects) necessarily exercises intellect, and in exercising intellect desires, yet such desire and such speculative thought are differently directed activities of the self-conscious subject. It is to be remembered further that the understanding employed in the exercise of desire relates to the desired object and to the conditions of its realisation, while the desire involved in a process of thinking has for its object the completion of that process.   It is therefore not to the purpose to insist on the obvious fact that a man morally excellent, in the sense that his desires are habitually directed to good practical objects, may be 'stupid,' unskilled, and uninterested in the exercise of intellect on all matters of literature, science, and art, as well as lacking in power of expression upon the matters in which he is interested ; or conversely, that a man whose thoughts are habitually occupied, and occupied to great effect, in the region of literature, science, and art, may be deficient in moral interests.   From a certain point of view, no doubt, this apparent discrepancy between moral interests or objects, and those of the artist and the man of science or letters, presents a serious difficulty.   If we were forming a theory of the universe, or trying to regard the facts of human nature and history as the realisation of one idea (and the effort thoroughly to understand them doubtless implies such an attempt), then it would be a necessary problem to show that these seemingly discrepant interests and objects have some ultimate point of meeting.   Our present concern, however, is with the individual conscious-ness and its objects—the objects of this or that man, as he is actually conscious of them, not as they may be combined with other objects in an idea which is not consciously his though it may be operative in him.

For the consciousness of the individual the direction of himself to such objects as, *e.g.*, the settlement of a vexed question in philology, or the perfect rendering of certain atmospheric effects in landscape painting, has nothing in common with the direction of himself to such objects as, *e.g.*, the discipline of his own tongue, or the promotion of sobriety among his neighbours.   It is easy indeed to see that, even within the experience and sphere of action of the individual, interests of the one kind are not without a bearing—at any rate in the result—on interests of the other kind.   The effect of 'moral' interests appears in habits without which the scholar or artist is not properly free for his work, nor exempt from the temptation to be showy instead of thorough in it. Conversely, the effect of scientific and artistic interests may be to neutralise to some extent the attractions which compete most actively with reverence for moral law and devotion to the service of men. There is also such a thing as a consciousness of the ultimate unity of all pursuits that contribute to the perfection of man, which may import a certain enthusiasm of humanity into the devotion with which the scholar or artist applies himself to his immediate object, and which may keep the practical mind open to interests in literature and art. Still the immediate difference, for the consciousness of the individual, between the kinds of object distintinguished is such that the employment of thought upon objects of a non-practical kind, though it necessarily carries with it a direction of desire to the realisation of the intellectual ideal, may very well go along with an absence of desire for the realisation of any moral ideal; while, on the other hand, the direction of desire to the latter object, though it necessarily implies an exercise of intellect in the conception of the moral object and of the conditions of its attainment, may very well go along with a want of inclination to think, and of ability to think well, about other things.

149. It is clear then that a particular act of will does not, on the part of the person willing, involve thought except about the object of the act of will—such thought as is implied in the conception of self, of an object present to the self in idea as desired, of a world in which that object awaits realisation, of conditions under which it is to be realised. Now when we oppose thinking and willing, we may have in view the distinction between the speculative and the practical employment of the human spirit, the distinction between its work as directed to that discovery of relations between existing things which enables it to regard them as one, and its work as bringing conceived or imagined objects into real existence. This is a valid distinction, though it must be borne in mind, as previously pointed out, that the *speculative* employment is necessarily accompanied by willing

—for we only find unity in the world because we have an idea that it is there, an idea which we direct our powers to realise—and that throughout any *practical* process ideas operate and are operated upon (to use the most general expression) in a manner which we should describe as thought, if the term had not come to be specially associated with the *speculative* exercise of thought.   But if this is the distinction that we have in view when we oppose thinking and willing, it is improper to say that *mere* thinking is not willing, or that willing is *more* than thinking.   Speculation and moral action are co-ordinate employments of the same self-conscious soul, and of the same powers of that soul, only differently directed. Speculative thinking is not an element of moral action, requiring the addition of something else to constitute moral action.   But when we say that *mere* thinking is not willing, we imply that the thinking of which we speak does stand in this relation to moral action—that some complementary element needs to be added to it in order to constitute moral action.   And of the speculative exercise of thought this is not true.

150. If then the proposition in question is to be to the purpose at all, it must relate to such thinking as is involved in or presupposed by an act of will.   If we say, *e.g.*, that the act of willing to pay a debt is more than mere thinking, what we wish to point out is certainly not that thinking about a mathematical theorem is not equivalent to willing to pay the debt.   We probably mean to say that the mere thinking about paying the debt falls short of willing to pay it.   But here our rejoinder will be that this depends on what we mean by the thinking.   If thinking about payment of the debt means merely an otiose contemplation of a possible event, the proposition may be true but is little to the purpose.   Such thought does not amount to either of those activities of the thinking self which have been described above.   Just as sensuous impressions are constantly occurring to us which tell us nothing, suggest nothing, because they do not fit into any context of ideas,

so ideas are constantly, as we say, passing through our minds without forming part of any process of thought speculative or practical, as defined by reference to an end. The possibility of paying his debts may thus pass through the mind of the debtor without really amounting to an object of thought at all, either in the sense in which a fact that I am trying to understand, or that I am applying to other facts in order to understand them, is an object of thought, or in the sense in which an understanding that interests me is so. At any rate the object thought of in such thinking, such otiose contemplation, is not the object willed in the will to pay the debt. The object thought of is a possible occurrence—an object of speculative thought, if of thought at all. The man presents to himself the payment of his debt as an event that may happen, with its various incidents. But it is not such a possible event that a man *wills* in willing to pay the debt. To will an event, as distinguished from an act, is a contradiction. The object willed is the realisation of an idea—an idea of relief from annoyance, of satisfying one's neighbours' expectations, of what self-respect requires, or of a good in which all these ends are included.

151. Thus, though such an object of thought as the possible event of the debt being paid is not the object willed, the object willed is yet an object of thought. There is always thinking in willing. A thoughtless will would be no will. Without the thought of self and a world as mutually determined, of an object present to the self in a desire felt by it, but awaiting realisation in the world, there would be no will but only blind impulse. Even in cases where the will is said to be governed by animal appetite, it is still the realisation of an idea that is the object willed. The pleasure incidental to the gratification of the appetite exists ideally or in anticipation for me, and what I will is the realisation of this idea. Otherwise it would be no longer *I* that did the act, but an appetite dwelling in me. The act would not be mine; I should not impute it to myself, any more than, *e.g.*, an operation which I find the animal system has performed while I have been asleep. But if in all cases of willing the object willed is the realisation of an idea, the object of will is also an object of thought. It is only for a subject which thinks, and so far as thinking, that it can exist.

The question accordingly arises whether thinking, of the kind which is thus essential to willing, can properly be regarded as merely a *part* of, or an *element* in, willing, to which something must be added in order to constitute an act of will. Unless this is so, the proposition that *mere* thinking is not willing, that willing is *more* than thinking, conveys a false impression. And it would seem not to be so. The act of willing is not *in part* one of thinking. It is an act of thought, though not of thought speculatively directed, wholly and throughout. There is no factor or element in it separable (except verbally) from thought, and of which the addition to thought makes up the whole called an act of will. Is it not, we may perhaps ask, the addition of desire to thought that constitutes will? But the answer must be, No, will is not thought *plus* desire. Desire of the kind which enters into willing involves thought; thought of the kind which enters into willing involves desire; for the desire is the direction of a self-conscious subject to the realisation of an idea, while the thought is the presence of an idea in such a subject impelling to its own realisation. We cannot say that the thought is separate from the desire and supervenes upon it, or that the desire is so related to the thought.

152. The notion of their being separate elements which together make up an act of will arises from thought and desire being severally supposed to be something which, *as in will*, they are not. We have already seen that when, on the one hand, different *desires* are said to compete for mastery in a man, or when it is said that one object is *desired* but another willed, and when, on the other hand, a moral action is said to proceed from or represent some *desire*, 'desire' is being used in different senses. In one sense it means desire as it affects a man, in the other the desire which proceeds from a man or in which he expresses himself. Desire of the one sort ends where the other begins, *viz.* in the direction of the man's self to an object. In the one case he does, in the other he does not, put himself forth to the realisation of the desired object, as one in the realisation of which he seeks self-satisfaction. In like manner our thoughts may mean either thoughts that, as we say, occur to us, or thoughts to the realisation of which we direct ourselves. It is thought only in the latter of the two senses distinguished, desire likewise in the latter of its two senses, that enters into willing.

No doubt, both thought in the other sense and desire in the other sense are presupposed by willing, as *conditions antecedent ;* and in the sense in which they are severally conditions antecedent of the act of willing but do not enter into it, they are clearly separable. There may very well be one without the other. I may, *e.g.*, contemplate payment of a debt as a possible event, consider how much money would be required for the purpose, how the creditor would behave when he got his money, and so on, without being affected by any desire to pay ; and conversely I may feel that I should be more at ease if I paid, without my thoughts running further on the event. But in the sense in which thought and desire enter into an act of will, each is the whole act ; and we can only distinguish them by describing one and the same act of the inner man, which thought and desire equally constitute, as in respect of desire the direction of a self-conscious subject to the realisation of an idea, in respect of thought the action of an idea in such a subject impelling to its realisation.

153. Will then is equally and indistinguishably desire and thought—not however *mere* desire or *mere* thought, if by that is meant desire or thought as they might exist in a being that was not self-distinguishing and self-seeking, or as they may occur to a man independently of any action of himself ;

but desire and thought as they are involved in the direction of a self-distinguishing and self-seeking subject to the realisation of an idea [1]. If so, it must be a mistake to regard the will as a faculty which a man possesses along with other faculties—those of desire, emotion, thought, &c.—and which has the singular privilege of acting independently of other faculties, so that, given a man's character as it at any time results from the direction taken by those other faculties, the will remains something apart which may issue in action different from that prompted by the character. The will is simply the man. Any act of will is the expression of the man as he at the time is. The motive issuing in his act, the object of his will, the idea which for the time he sets himself to realise, are but the same thing in different words. Each is the reflex of what for the time, as at once feeling, desiring, and thinking, the man is. In willing he carries with him, so to speak, his whole self to the realisation of the given idea. All the time that he so wills, he may feel the pangs of conscience, or (on the other hand) the annoyance, the sacrifice, implied in acting conscientiously. He may think that he is doing wrong, or that it is doubtful whether after all there is really an objection to his acting as he has resolved to do. He may desire some one's good opinion which he is throwing away, or some pleasure which he is sacrificing. But for all that it is only the feeling, thought, and desire represented by the act of will, that the man recognises as for the time himself. The feeling, thought, and desire with which the act conflicts are influences that he is aware of, influences to which he is susceptible, but they are not *he*.

[1] It may prevent possible misapprehension, if I say that the term idea is here and in all similar passages used in the wide sense generally attached to it by English writers, who have followed the definition of it by Locke as 'the immediate object of the mind in thinking.' In this sense it seems pretty much equivalent to the German 'Vorstellung.'

BOOK III

THE MORAL IDEAL AND MORAL PROGRESS

CHAPTER I

GOOD AND MORAL GOOD

154. WE are now in a position to return to the difficulty which was raised at the beginning of the last chapter, and which led to our attempt to ascertain the nature of Will, in its relation to desire and thought. That difficulty was as to the ground of distinction between the good and the bad will; a distinction which in some form or other—whether we consider the goodness of a will to be an attribute which it possesses on its own account, or to be relative to some result to which it contributes beyond the will itself—must lie at the root of every system of Ethics. What becomes of this distinction, we supposed an objector to ask, if the doctrine previously stated is admitted, 'that in all conduct to which moral predicates are applicable a man is an object to himself; that such conduct, equally whether virtuous or vicious, expresses a motive consisting in an idea of personal good which the man seeks to realise by action' (§ 115)? Further consideration has confirmed this statement. If it is a genuine definition that we want of what is common to all acts of willing, we must say that such an act is one in which a self-conscious individual directs himself to the realisation of some idea, as to an object in which for the time he seeks self-satisfaction. Such being an act of willing, the will in actuality must be the self-conscious individual as so directing himself, while the will in possibility, or as a faculty, will be the self-conscious individual as capable of so directing himself.

The above, however, is merely a *formal* account of willing and the will. It does not tell us the real nature of any act

of will, or of any man as willing, or of any national will—
if there be such a thing as one will operating in or upon the
several members of a nation—or of the human will, if again
there be such a thing as one will operating throughout the
history of mankind. For the real nature of any act of will
depends on the particular nature of the object in which the
person willing for the time seeks self-satisfaction ; and the
real nature of any man as the subject of will—his character
—depends on the nature of the objects in which he mainly
tends to seek self-satisfaction. Self-satisfaction is the form
of every object willed ; but the filling of that form, the
character of that in which self-satisfaction is sought, ranging
from sensual pleasure to the fulfilment of a vocation conceived as given by God, makes the object what it really is.
It is on the specific difference of the objects willed under the
general form of self-satisfaction that the quality of the will
must depend. It is here therefore that we must seek for the
basis of distinction between goodness and badness of will.

155. The statement that the distinction between the good
and bad will must lie at the basis of any system of Ethics,
and the further statement that this distinction itself must
depend on the nature of the objects willed, would in some
sense or other be accepted by all recognised 'schools' of
moralists, but they would be accepted in very different
senses. On the one side the modern Utilitarian would only
accept the former statement in the sense that, unless an
action is done *intentionally*, it is not the subject of moral
predicates. The action, in his view, derives its moral quality
not from the motive or character which it expresses, but
from the effects which it produces. Those effects, indeed,
do not entitle the act to be reckoned morally good or bad,
unless it is one which the agent intends or wills to do ; but,
given the intentional act, it is not on the motive which leads
to its being intended, but on its effects in the way of pleasure
or pain, that its morality depends. This is very plainly put
by J. S. Mill : 'The morality of the action depends entirely
upon the intention—that is, upon what the agent *wills to do*.

But the motive, that is, the feeling which makes him will so to do, when it makes no difference in the act, makes none in the morality : though it makes a great difference in our moral estimation of the agent, especially if it indicates a good or a bad habitual *disposition*—a bent of character from which useful or from which hurtful actions are likely to arise [1].' In other words, while there are two distinct objects of moral approbation or disapprobation, or two objects which admit of the designation morally good or bad, (*a*) intentional action, (*b*) the motive or character of an agent, the latter is only to be judged relatively to the former, just as the former is only to be judged relatively to its effects as producing pleasure or pain. The motive or character is morally good, if likely on the whole to issue in intentional actions which are good in the sense of producing on the whole, one person taken with another and one time with another, an excess of pleasure over pain.

Clearly, upon this view, our statement that Ethics is founded on the distinction between the good and bad will could only be accepted under the proviso that by good and bad will is understood good and bad intentional action, and further that intentional action is understood to be good or bad according to its relation to an ultimate good and evil, which are constituted not by any kind of action, intention, or character, but by pleasure and pain. The other statement that 'the distinction between the good and bad will must depend on the nature of the objects willed' would be subjected by the Utilitarian to a similar qualification. He could accept it if by 'will' is understood intention, and if by 'the objects willed' are understood the effects of the intentional act in the way of producing pleasure and pain. If by 'will' is meant 'habitual disposition,' and by 'objects willed' motives, he could only accept the statement on the understanding that the 'nature of the objects willed' is itself taken to depend on the tendency of the motives to issue in actions productive of a preponderance of pleasure or pain as the case may be.

[1] *Utilitarianism*, p. 27, note.

It is in a precisely opposite sense that the propositions in question would have to be understood, in order to be approved by a strict follower of Kant. With him an act of will would never be understood merely of an intention to do a certain deed, in abstraction from the motive or object for the sake of which the deed is done; and with him again the good will is good, not in virtue of any effects extrinsic to it, but in virtue of what it is in itself, not as a means, but as an absolute end. The first of the above statements, therefore, he would accept in the sense which it naturally bears. In the second he might see a loophole for error. To say that a will is good in virtue of the nature of the objects willed, does not exclude the notion that it may be good in virtue of desired effects other than its own goodness, or as directed to objects which are willed otherwise than for the reason of their being prescribed by a universal practical law. So far as the statement in question is understood according to any such notion as this, Kant—at any rate if interpreted according to the reiterated letter of his doctrine—would reckon it fundamentally erroneous.

156. It is not according to the plan of the present treatise to examine critically either the moral doctrine of Kant as stated by himself, or that of Utilitarianism as stated by leading authorities, until it has been attempted to give the outline of a positive doctrine in regard to the nature of goodness and of our moral progress[1]. This done, the criticism may be undertaken with less liability to its drift being misunderstood, and without conveying the impression that no truth is thought to remain where some error has been detected. What then are the questions naturally raised for us by the considerations which we have so far pursued, and which a positive ethical doctrine should begin by attempting to answer? The first of them may perhaps be stated thus. Granted that, according to our doctrine, in all willing a self-conscious subject seeks to satisfy itself—

[1] [See Preface.]

N

seeks that which for the time it presents to itself as its good—how can there be any such intrinsic difference between the objects willed as justifies the distinction which 'moral sense' seems to draw between good and bad action, between virtue and vice? And if there is such a difference, in what does it consist?

A possible answer to the question would of course be a denial that there is any such difference at all. By an *intrinsic* difference between the objects willed we mean a difference between them in respect of that which is the motive to the person willing them, as distinct from a difference constituted by any effects which the realisation of the objects may bring about, but of which the anticipation does not form the motive. Now according to all strictly Hedonistic theories the difference between objects willed is, according to this sense of the terms, extrinsic, not intrinsic. The motive to the persons willing is supposed to be in all cases the same, *viz.* desire for some pleasure or aversion from some pain. The conditions of the pleasures which different men desire, or which the same man desires at different times, are of course most various; but it is not the conditions of any pleasure but the pleasure itself that a man desires, if pleasure is really his object at all. On the Hedonistic supposition, therefore, every object willed is on its inner side, or in respect of that which moves the person willing, the same. It moves him as anticipated pleasure, or anticipated escape from pain. The difference between objects willed lies on their outer side, in effects which follow from them but are not included in them as motives to the persons willing. Two objects having been equally willed as so much anticipated pleasure, the realisation of the one does in the event produce a preponderance of pleasure over pain to the agent himself or to others, while the realisation of the other produces a preponderance of pain over pleasure. Thus and thus only, according to this theory—extrinsically not intrinsically—is the difference constituted between a good object of will and a bad one.

157. A detailed criticism of this doctrine would be out of place till we come to the examination of Utilitarianism. If the αἴτιον τοῦ ψευδοῦς can be explained, it will not stand seriously in our way ; for though excellent men have argued themselves into it, it is a doctrine which, nakedly put, offends the unsophisticated conscience. Whatever the process may have been, we have reached a state in which we seem to know that the desires we think well of in ourselves differ absolutely as desires, or in respect of the objects desired in them, from those which we despise or condemn. If asked straight out to admit that all objects of desire, as desired, are alike, since it is pleasure that is equally the desired thing in them all ; that it is only in the effects of the actions arising out of them, not in what they are for the desiring consciousness, that good desires differ from bad ones ; upon first thoughts we should certainly refuse to do so. Hesitation would only ensue if the enlightened enquirer asked us to reflect, whether we ever find ourselves desiring any thing from which we do not anticipate pleasure of some sort, and whether it is not this anticipation that makes us desire it. Thus challenged, we feel ourselves in a difficulty. This account of desire has a plausibility which we do not at once see our way to explaining. Yet to accept it seems to involve us logically[1] in an admission of the intrinsic identity of all desires, good and bad, which offends our moral conviction. If we could explain away the apparent cogency of the plea that it is some anticipated pleasure, as such, which we always find ourselves desiring, the conviction of the difference between good and bad desires, as states of consciousness on the part of the persons desiring, would hold its own undisturbed.

158. Now, according to the account previously given of desire, it is not difficult to explain the confusion which

---

[1] The attempt to combine the doctrine that pleasure as such is the sole object of desire, with the assertion of an *intrinsic* difference between good and bad desires, on the ground that pleasures differ in quality, will be considered below.

makes pleasure seem to be its only object. We saw that, in all such desire as can form the motive to an imputable act, the individual directs himself to the realisation of some idea, as to an object in which he seeks self-satisfaction. It is the consciousness that self-satisfaction is thus sought in all enacted desire, in all desire that amounts to will, combined with the consciousness that in all self-satisfaction, if attained, there is pleasure, which leads to the false notion that pleasure is always the object of desire. Whether in any case it really is so, or no, depends on whether pleasure is the object with which a man is seeking to satisfy himself. If it is not, pleasure is not the object of his dominant desire. However much pleasure there may prove to be in the self-satisfaction, if any, which the attainment of his object brings with it—and our common experience is that the objects with which we seek to satisfy ourselves do not turn out capable of satisfying us—it cannot be *this* pleasure that is the object which he desires. Its possibility presupposes the desire and its fulfilment. It cannot therefore be the exciting cause of the desire, any more than the pleasure of satisfying hunger can be the exciting cause of hunger. Only if the idea which in his desire the man seeks to realise is the idea of enjoying some pleasure—whether a pleasure of the kind which we commonly call sensual in a special sense, *i.e.* one incidental to the satisfaction of animal appetite, or a pleasure of pure emotion—can we truly say that pleasure is the object of his desire.

159. When the idea of which the realisation is sought is not that of enjoying any pleasure, the fact that self-satisfaction is sought in the effort to realise the idea of the desired object does not make pleasure the object of the desire. It may very well be that a man pursues an object in which he seeks self-satisfaction with the clear consciousness that no enjoyment of pleasure can yield him satisfaction, and that there must be such pain in the realisation of the idea to which he devotes himself as cannot be compensated, in any scale where pleasure and pain alone are weighed, by any

enjoyment of an end achieved [1].   So it is in the more heroic
forms of self-sacrifice.   Self-satisfaction is doubtless sought
in such sacrifice.   The man who calmly faces a life of suffering in the fulfilment of what he conceives to be his mission
could not bear to do otherwise.   So to live is his good.
If he could attain the consciousness of having accomplished
his work, if he could 'count himself to have apprehended'
—and probably just in proportion to the elevation of his
character he is unable to do so—he would find satisfaction
in the consciousness, and with it a certain pleasure.   But
supposing this pleasure to be attained, only the exigencies of
a theory could suggest the notion that, as so much pleasure,
it makes up for the pleasures forgone and the pains endured
in the life through which it has been reached.   Such a
notion can only be founded on the see-saw process which
first assumes that preference in every case is determined by
amount of anticipated pleasure, and then professes to ascertain
the relative amount of pleasure which a given line of action
affords a man by the fact that he prefers so to act.

160.   Even if it were the case, however, that self-satisfaction was more attainable than it is, and that the pleasure of
success to the man who has 'spurned delights and lived
laborious days' really admitted of being set against the
pleasure missed in the process, it would none the less be
a mere confusion to treat this pleasure of success as the
desired object, in the realisation of which the man seeks
to satisfy himself.   A man may seek to satisfy himself with
pleasure, but the pleasure of self-satisfaction can never be
that with which he seeks to satisfy himself.   This is equally
true of the voluptuary and of the saint.   The voluptuary
must have his ideas of pleasures, unconnected with self-
satisfaction, before he can seek self-satisfaction (where it is
not to be found) in the realisation of those ideas; just as

---

[1] Cf. Arist. Eth. Nic. III. ix. 5.   Οὐ δὴ ἐν ἁπάσαις ταῖς ἀρεταῖς τὸ
ἡδέως ἐνεργεῖν ὑπάρχει, πλὴν ἐφ' ὅσον τοῦ τέλους ἐφάπτεται.   'Thus the
rule that the exercise of virtue is pleasant does not hold of all the virtues,
except in so far as the end is attained'

much as the saint must have ideas, not of pleasures but of services due to God and man, before he can seek self-satisfaction in their fulfilment. Most men, however, at least in their ordinary conduct, are neither voluptuaries nor saints; and we are falling into a false antithesis if, having admitted (as is true) that the quest of self-satisfaction is the form of all moral activity, we allow no alternative (as Kant in effect seems to allow none) between the quest for self-satisfaction in the enjoyment of pleasure, and the quest for it in the fulfilment of a universal practical law. Ordinary motives fall neither under the one head nor the other. They are interests in the attainment of objects, without which it seems to the man in his actual state that he cannot satisfy himself, and in attaining which, because he has desired them, he will find a certain pleasure, but only because he has previously desired them, not because pleasures are the objects desired.

161. Such interests, though not mere appetites because conditioned by self-consciousness, correspond to them as not having pleasure for their object. This point was sufficiently made out in the controversy as to the 'disinterestedness' of benevolence, carried on during the first part of the eighteenth century. When philosophers of the 'selfish school' represented benevolence as ultimately desire for some pleasure to oneself, Butler and others met them by showing that this was the same mistake as to reckon hunger a desire for the pleasure of eating. The appetite of hunger must precede and condition the pleasure which consists in its satisfaction. It cannot therefore have that pleasure for its exciting object. 'It terminates upon its object,' and is not relative to anything beyond the taking of food; and in the same way benevolent desires terminate upon their objects, upon the benefits done to others. In the 'termination' in each case there is pleasure, but it is a confusion to represent this as an object beyond the obtaining of food or the doing a kindness, to which the appetite or benevolent desire is really directed. What is true of benevolence is true of motives which we oppose to it, as the vicious to the virtuous, *e.g.* of jealousy or the desire for revenge. Iago does not work upon Othello for the sake of any pleasure that he expects to experience when his envy is gratified, but because in his envious state an object of which the realisation seems necessary to the satisfaction of himself is Othello's ruin, just as the consumption of food is necessary to the satisfaction of hunger. What he desires is to see Othello down, not the pleasure he will feel when he sees him so—a pleasure which he could not feel unless he had desired the object independently of such anticipation.

It is true that any interest or desire for an object may come to be reinforced by desire for the pleasure which, reflecting upon past analogous experience, the subject of the interest may expect as incidental to its satisfaction. In this way 'cool self-love,' according to the terminology of the last century, may combine with 'particular desires or propensions.' If there is to be any chance, however, of the expected pleasure being really enjoyed, the 'self-love' of which pleasure is the object must not supersede the 'particular propension' of which pleasure, in the case of ordinary healthy interests, is *not* the object. The pleasure incidental to the satisfaction of an interest cannot be attained after loss of the interest itself, nor can the interest be revived by wishing for a renewal of the pleasure incidental to its satisfaction. Hence just so far as 'cool self-love,' in the sense of a calculating pursuit of pleasure, becomes dominant and supersedes particular interests, the chances of pleasure are really lost; which accounts for the restlessness of the pleasure-seeker, and for the common remark that the right way to get pleasure is not to seek it.

162. It may seem presumptuous to charge clear-headed moralists with the mistake of supposing that a desire can be excited by the anticipation of its own satisfaction. But such a mistake certainly seems to be accountable for the acceptance of the doctrine that pleasure is the sole object of desire by so powerful a writer as J. S. Mill. He, as is well known, differs from the older Utilitarians in holding that, although pleasure and freedom from pain are the only things desirable as ends, some *kinds* of pleasure are more desirable and valuable than others, not as involving a greater amount of pleasure, but in their intrinsic nature [1]. Every one must feel that the Utilitarian theory receives a certain exaltation from his treatment of it, and especially from his assertion of this point. But the question is, whether the admissions which he has to make in order to establish it do not virtually amount to a departure from the doctrine that pleasure or freedom from pain is the only object of desire ; a departure which he only disguises from himself and his reader by virtually assuming that a desire may have for its object the pleasure, or deliverance from pain, involved in its satisfaction. It will be useful to dwell a little longer on this question, not for the sake of picking holes in a writer from whom we have all learnt much, but in order to bring out more clearly the distinction between the quest for self-satisfaction which all moral activity is rightly held to be, and the quest for pleasure which morally *good* activity is not.

163. No one of course can doubt that pleasures admit of distinction in quality according to the conditions under which they arise. So Plato and Aristotle distinguished pleasures incidental to the satisfaction of bodily wants from pleasures of sight and hearing, and these again from the pleasures of pure intellect. So too we might distinguish pleasures of satisfied desire from pleasures of pure emotion, and subdivide each sort according to the various conditions under which desire or emotion is excited. No one pretends that the pleasures of a sot are not really different from those of a man of refined taste. The question is in what sense, upon the principle that pleasure is the ultimate good by relation to which all other good is to be tested, these differences of kind between pleasures may be taken to constitute any difference in the degree of their goodness or desirability. All Utilitarians would hold that on one ground or another

[1] Utilitarianism, pp. 10–12.

they might be so taken, but they would not all agree upon the ground. The strict Benthamites hold that such differences of kind between pleasures as arise from differences in their exciting causes only affect their value or the degree of their goodness, in so far as they affect the amount of pleasure enjoyed on the whole; while Mill holds that these differences affect the value of pleasures independently of the effect they have on their amount. The estimation of pleasures should not depend on quantity alone: quality is to be considered as well as quantity [1].

164. For an explanation and defence of this variation from the doctrine of his master, Mill appeals to the 'unquestionable fact that those who are equally acquainted with, and equally capable of appreciating and enjoying, both, do give a most marked preference to the manner of existence which employs their higher faculties,' as compared with one involving more sensual pleasures. They do this, 'even though knowing it to be attended with a greater amount of discontent.' We naturally accept such an appeal because we cannot help thinking of the man whose preference Mill describes, as *better in himself* than one more 'sensual,' and of the 'higher faculties' as intrinsically of more value; in other words, because we regard the attainment of a certain type of character or some realisation of the possibilities of man, not pleasure, as the end by relation to which goodness or value is to be measured. But, on the principle that pleasure is the only thing good ultimately or in its own right, we are not justified in so doing. On this principle one man can be better, one faculty higher than another, only as a more serviceable instrument for the production of pleasure. On this ground it is open to the Utilitarian to argue that a man who devotes himself to the exercise of such 'higher faculties' as Mill is here thinking of, produces a greater amount of pleasure on the whole, all circumstances affecting that amount being taken into account, than does the man who does not trouble himself about his 'higher faculties.'

[1] *Utilitarianism*, pp. 10-12.

But it is altogether against Utilitarian principles that a pleasure should be of more value because the man who pursues it is better. They only entitle us to argue back from the amount of pleasure to the worth of the man who acts so as to produce it.

If we rid ourselves then of all presuppositions, illegitimate on Utilitarian principles, in regard to the superiority of the man or the faculties exercised in what we call the highest pursuits, and if we admit that all desire is for pleasure, the strongest desire for the greatest pleasure, what is proved by the example of the man who, being 'competently acquainted with both,' prefers the life of moral and intellectual effort to one of healthy animal enjoyment? Simply this, that the life of effort brings more pleasure to the man in question than *he* would derive from the other sort of life. It outweighs for him any quantity of other pleasure *of which his nature is capable*. The fact that he is 'competently acquainted with both' sorts of pleasure can give no significance beyond this to his preference of one above the other. He may be 'competently acquainted' with animal enjoyments; but it does not follow that the pleasure they afford him is as intense and unmixed as that which they afford to the man who makes them his principal pursuit. The question of value then between the two sorts will have to be settled by a calculation of amount, the intensity of each kind, as experienced by those to whom it is most intense, being weighed against its duration and its degree of purity, productiveness, and extent[1]. The calculation is certainly very hard to make —whether it can be made at all is a question to be touched on when we come to a more detailed examination of Utilitarianism[2]—but it is the only possible way, if pleasure is the sole and ultimate good, of measuring the comparative worth of pleasures. The example of a certain man's preference, unless we have some other standard of his excellence than

---

[1] Cf. Dumont's version of the Principles of Morals and Legislation (Hildreth's translation), p. 31.

[2] [See Book IV. chap. iii.]

such as is relative to pleasure as the ultimate good, proves nothing as to the superiority of the pleasure which he chooses to another sort of pleasure preferred by some one else.   It only proves that it is more of a pleasure *to him* than is that to which he prefers it ; and this it only proves on supposition that the stronger desire is always for the greater pleasure.

165. Now it will be found, we think, that with Mill this supposition really rests on a confusion between the pleasure or removal of pain which ensues upon the satisfaction of any desire and the object of that desire.   In an eloquent passage he illustrates the unwillingness of any one acquainted with the 'higher' pleasures to exchange them for any quantity of the lower :—

'Now it is an unquestionable fact that those who are equally acquainted with, and equally capable of appreciating and enjoying, both, do give a most marked preference to the manner of existence which employs their higher faculties. Few human creatures would consent to be changed into any of the lower animals, for a promise of the fullest allowance of a beast's pleasures ; no intelligent human being would consent to be a fool, no instructed person would be an ignoramus, no person of feeling and conscience would consent to be selfish and base, even though they should be persuaded that the fool, the dunce, or the rascal is better satisfied with his lot than they are with theirs.   They would not resign what they possess more than he, for the most complete satisfaction of all the desires which they have in common with him.   If they ever fancy they would, it is only in cases of unhappiness so extreme, that to escape from it they would exchange their lot for almost any other, however undesirable in their own eyes.   A being of high faculties requires more to make him happy, is capable probably of more acute suffering, and is certainly accessible to it at more points, than one of an inferior type ; but in spite of these liabilities, he can never really wish to sink into what he feels to be a lower grade of existence.   We may give what explanation we please of this unwillingness ; we may attribute it to pride, a name which is given indiscriminately to some of the most and to some of the least estimable feelings of which mankind are capable ; we may refer it to the love of liberty and personal independence, an appeal to which was with the Stoics one of the most effectual means for the inculcation of it ; to the love of power, or to the love of excitement, both of which do really enter into and contribute to it : but its most appropriate appellation is a sense of dignity, which all human beings possess in one form or other, and in some, though by no means in exact, proportion to their higher faculties ; and which is so essential a part of the happiness of those in whom it is strong, that nothing which conflicts with it could be, otherwise than momentarily, an object of desire to them[1].'

It appears from this passage that there is a motive, which has been variously described as 'pride,' 'love of liberty,' 'love of power,' 'love of excitement,' but of which the most appropriate designation is 'sense of dignity,' that makes a man of a certain sort refuse to accept any amount of such pleasure as a fool, or a dunce, or a rascal might share, in lieu of the exercise of the higher faculties, however much suffering this may entail. This refusal is appealed to as showing that the pleasure attending this exercise is intrinsically preferable to such as may be shared with a dunce or a rascal. That it is intrinsically preferable those who are not Utilitarians will readily agree. But unless it is a greater pleasure on the whole, it is not on Utilitarian principles more really desirable or the greater good, and the fact that by the sort of person in contemplation it is preferred does not show that it is even for him, much less that it is on the whole, the greater pleasure, unless his preference is necessarily for what is to him the greater pleasure.

166. But with what plausibility can the motive described as a sense of dignity be reckoned a desire for pleasure at all? Mill indeed calls it 'an essential part of the happiness of those in whom it is strong'; but no desire as such, since it must rather be painful than pleasant, can properly be called a 'part of happiness.' It may be suggested therefore that by the 'sense of dignity' spoken of Mill understands an emotion, as distinct from desire, which he would no doubt be justified in calling a part of happiness, an ingredient in the sum of a man's pleasures. In that case we must suppose that it is desire for the pleasure of this emotion which makes the man, who is capable of the pleasure attending the exercise of the higher faculties, prefer this to the pleasure which he might share with the dunce. If this indeed were the true account

[1] Utilitarianism, pp. 12-13.

of the matter, the strict Benthamite who will recognise no distinction in quality as distinct from quantity of pleasure, might say that it was simply a case of the pleasure preferred being more 'productive.' The intellectual pleasure brings the additional pleasure, consisting in the emotion called sense of dignity, which the animal pleasure does not. It is scarcely however a plausible account of the motive which makes an intelligent person unwilling to be a fool, a person of feeling and conscience unwilling to be selfish or base, though persuaded that the change would save him much discontent, to say that it is desire for the preponderating pleasure involved in the sense of being a superior person. Nor, if it were, would there be any ground for holding the man so actuated to be really happier than the fool or the selfish man, who, according to his standard of measurement, has as good a chance of feeling the pleasure of superiority without corresponding discontent. The truth is that Mill does not really regard this 'sense of dignity' as an emotion in distinction from desire. He regards it as a counter motive to desires for animal pleasure, which mere emotion could not be. Nor does he mean that the preference determined by it is preference for the pleasure of feeling superior to the pleasures shared with average men. The motive which he has in view is a desire to be worthy, not a desire to feel the pleasure of being worth more than others; and he only regards it as desire for pleasure at all, because he fancies that a desire, of which the disappointment makes *me* unhappy, is therefore a desire for happiness—that a desire is for the pleasure which ensues upon its satisfaction.

167. The real ground then of Mill's departure from the stricter Utilitarian doctrine, that the worth of pleasure depends simply on its amount, is his virtual surrender of the doctrine that all desire is for pleasure; but he does not recognise this surrender, because he thinks that to call a desired object part of the happiness of the person desiring it is equivalent to saying that the desire for the object is a desire for pleasure. Yet little reflection is needed to show that it is not so. The latter proposition can only mean that a possible action or experience is contemplated as likely to be pleasant, and is then desired for the sake of the pleasure. It means that the anticipation of pleasure determines desire. But the other proposition, that a desired object is part of the happiness of the person desiring it, rather means that desire determines the anticipation of pleasure ; that, given desire for an object, however different from pleasure that object may be, there results pleasure, or at least a removal of pain, in the satisfaction of the desire ; that the man feeling the desire necessarily looks forward to this result as part of a possible happiness to come, and cannot be completely happy till the object is attained. This is equivalent to saying, as has been so often mentioned above, that to desire an object is to seek self-satisfaction in its attainment, but it does not in the least imply that pleasure is the object in which self-satisfaction is sought.

168. The same is true of the other forms in which Mill expresses the conception on which he considers the proof of Utilitarianism to rest. ' Desiring a thing and finding it pleasant . . . are two parts of the same phenomenon.' ' To think of an object as desirable . . . and to think of it as pleasant are one and the same thing [1].' Both statements are ambiguous. Each is in a sense true, but not in the sense which would imply that a pleasure is the only possible object of desire. In the latter statement, what is meant by ' thinking of an object as desirable ' ? Does it mean thinking of it as one that *should be* desired ? Thus understood, the statement would lose all plausibility. No one would pretend that to think of an object as one which he *should* desire is the same thing as thinking of it as pleasant. Rather, so long as he thinks of it as one in which he finds pleasure, it is impossible for him to place it in any such relation to himself as could be represented by saying that he thinks of it as an object which he should desire. Nor is there any sign that Mill uses the terms ' desired ' and

[1] *Utilitarianism*, p. 58.

'desirable' except as pretty much equivalent. To 'think of an object as desirable' means with him to reflect on it as one that is desired. Now it is quite true that I cannot reflect on an object as one that I desire without thinking of it as pleasant, in the sense that I cannot reflect on my desire for it without thinking of the pleasure there would be in the satisfaction of the desire. But this in no way implies that the desire is a desire for that or any other pleasure.

As regards the other statement, if the 'phenomenon' under consideration is taken to include both the desire for an object and the satisfaction of that desire in the attainment of its object, then to desire the object and to find its *attainment* pleasant are doubtless parts of that one phenomenon. If, on the other hand, the phenomenon is held to be confined to the desire, and not to include its satisfaction, then 'to find a thing pleasant' is no part of the phenomenon; for unsatisfied desire involves no pleasure. We may suppose, however, that 'to find it pleasant' is here hastily written for 'to anticipate pleasure from it.' Thus interpreted, the statement is indisputable so far as it goes. To desire an object, and to anticipate pleasure from its attainment, are certainly parts of one and the same phenomenon. But the question remains of the relation in which the two parts of the phenomenon stand to each other. Is it always the anticipation of pleasure from an object that excites the desire for it, or are there cases in which the anticipation of pleasure in the satisfaction of desire arises out of an independent desire for an object which is not pleasure at all? The former is the view which Mill believed himself to hold, and which his 'Proof of Utilitarianism' requires; but the proposition under consideration is equally compatible with the latter view, and it may be doubted whether it would have seemed so self-evident to most readers, or even to Mill himself, if it were not so.

169. The reason for this doubt as regards Mill himself is that he insists upon the reality of desires which, as he

describes them, are only desires for *pleasure* in the improper and illogical sense; which are not determined by an antecedent imagination of pleasure; but from which there results pleasure in the attainment of the desired object, pain in its absence.   Thus, having pointed out that the Utilitarian doctrine requires us to consider happiness, or pleasure, the only thing desirable as an end, he goes on to say[1] that 'it maintains not only that virtue is to be desired, but that it is to be desired disinterestedly,' *i.e.*, as he explains, not as a means to 'any end beyond it.'   The mind, he tells us, is 'not in a right state, not in a state conformable to Utility,' unless it so desires virtue.   But such desire for virtue is clearly not determined by any antecedent imagination of pleasure.   It is of course open to any one to argue that what is called desire for virtue is really desire for pleasures that are to be obtained in a certain way; but in that case virtue is not an ultimate object of desire, the desire for it is not disinterested.   That presentation of virtue which determines any disinterested desire for it, can only be a presentation of a possible state of character or mode of action as an ideal object which we seek to realise; and the object thus presented cannot be identified with any pleasant feeling or series of feelings, which, having experienced it, we imagine and desire to experience again.   If, then, the presentation of virtue as an ultimate object, and not merely as a means, does determine desire, there are desires which are not excited by the anticipation of pleasure, though in such cases as much as in any other the desired object, just so far as desired, is 'part of the happiness' of the person desiring it, in the sense that, having desired it, he cannot be happy without it.

There are other objects of desire recognised by Mill— money, power, fame—which he admits are not pleasures (though to power and fame, he thinks, 'there is a certain amount of immediate pleasure annexed[2]'), but which have yet come to be desired for their own sake.   In regard to them, as in regard to virtue, he suggests that they were ori-

[1] *Utilitarianism*, p. 54.   [2] *Ibid.*, p. 55.

ginally desired as means, as conducive to pleasure or to protection from pain, but he does not pretend that, by those who desire them most strongly, they are so desired any longer. 'What was once desired as an instrument for the attainment of happiness has come to be desired for its own sake.' That the desire for them originated in a desire *for pleasure* is, indeed, a view founded on the assumption that pleasures alone are wished for. ' To aid in the attainment of our wishes, as these things do, is with Mill the same thing as to aid in the attainment of pleasure. But we may waive this point, for questions as to the history of any desire do not affect its present relation to its object. If money, fame, and power are desired not as a means to pleasure but for their own sake—and this Mill admits—then there are desires, whatever their history, which are not desires for pleasure, however essential their gratification may be to the happiness of those who so desire.

170. As against the view, therefore, that all desire is for some pleasure or other, from which it would seem to follow that the good will cannot differ intrinsically, or as desire, from the bad, but only in virtue of effects in the way of pleasure and pain, we may adduce the involuntary evidence of the most eminent modern advocate of that view. We find him explicitly recognising desires which, as they exist, however they may have originated, are not desires for pleasure, and which he only brings under his general theory of desire on the ground that the objects of such desires are desired by us as part of our happiness. But this, as we have seen, is no more than saying that they are desired by a self-conscious subject, who in all desire, or at any rate in all that amounts to will, is seeking self-satisfaction, and who, so far as he reflects on any desire, reflects also on the pleasure of its possible fulfilment. It leaves the question open what the ideal object is, in the realisation of which self-satisfaction is sought. It does not exclude the possibility of its being even the endurance of pain, as perhaps, under sterner conditions of society than ours, or under the

O

influence of fanatical belief, it not unfrequently has been. The formula is at any rate elastic enough to allow of the strong assertion by Mill himself, that the attainment of a certain disposition may be an object of desire in itself, irrespectively of any pleasures that flow from it. We may return then to examine the question whether there is any *intrinsic* distinction between objects willed, on which the difference between a good and a bad will may rest, without allowing ourselves to be stopped *in limine* by a denial of the possibility of such distinction and a reduction of all motives, however various in their effects, to desire for some pleasure or other on the part of the person desiring.

171. It will have appeared from the foregoing discussion that the primary difference between the view here advanced and that of ' Hedonistic' philosophers relates to the generic definition of the good—not only of the morally good, but of good in the wider sense. Whereas with them the good generically is the pleasant, in this treatise the common characteristic of the good is that it satisfies some desire. In all satisfaction of desire there is pleasure, and thus pleasantness in an object is a necessary incident of its being good. We cannot think of an object as good, *i.e.* such as will satisfy desire, without thinking of it as in consequence such as will yield pleasure ; but its pleasantness depends on its goodness, not its goodness upon the pleasure it conveys. This pleasure, according to our view, so far as it is a necessary incident of any good, presupposes desire and results from its satisfaction, while according to the Hedonistic view desire presupposes an imagination of pleasure. The importance of this distinction, which may at first sight seem somewhat finely drawn, will appear as soon as we consider its bearing on the question of the distinguishing nature of the moral good, or on that other form of the same question—the form in which it seems to have been first raised by philosophy—in which it is enquired, how the true good differs from the merely apparent.

If the generic definition of good is that it is pleasure, the moral good as distinct from the natural can only be pleasure obtained in a particular way; either simply pleasure experienced as a result of intentional action, in distinction from such pleasure as comes to us in a natural course of events which we have not contributed to bring about, or such pleasure as, in Locke's language, 'is not the natural product and consequence of the action itself,' but is attached to it by some positive law, either the law of God, or civil law, or the law of opinion[1]. This at any rate is what 'moral good' according to this view must mean, so long as it is understood to be the designation of an end. As a designation of means, it will be applicable to actions which tend to produce the pleasure obtainable in the particular manner described. From the same point of view the apparent good can only be distinguished from the true as a pleasure of which the enjoyment in its consequences yields a preponderance of pain over pleasure, whether to the individual enjoying it or (according to the Utilitarian view) to the majority of persons or of sentient beings. On the other hand, regarding the good generically as that which satisfies desire, but considering the objects we desire to be by no means necessarily pleasures, we shall naturally distinguish the moral good as that which satisfies the desire of a moral agent, or that in which a moral agent can find the satisfaction of himself which he necessarily seeks. The true good we shall understand in the same way. It is an

[1] See Locke's Essay, Book II. ch. xxviii. § 5 : 'Good and evil are nothing but pleasure or pain, or that which occasions or procures pleasure or pain to us. Moral good and evil, then, is only the conformity or disagreement of our voluntary actions to some law, whereby good or evil [*i. e.* pleasure or pain] is drawn on us by the will and power of the law-maker.' Here it will be seen that the terms 'good and evil,' when qualified as 'moral,' are transferred from end to means. But, according to the general definition of 'good and evil' as equivalent to pleasure and pain, we must suppose that Locke considered the 'conformity of our voluntary actions to some law' to constitute 'moral good' only because it brings about the pleasure which, by one or other of the laws which he recognises, is attached to such conformity.

end in which the effort of a moral agent can really find rest.

172. It will at once be objected that this account of moral good either tells us nothing at all about it, or only tells us anything in virtue of some assumption in regard to moral good involved in our notion of a moral agent. The objection is in a certain sense a valid one. The question, What is our moral nature or capability?—in other words, What do we mean by calling ourselves moral agents?—is one to which a final answer cannot be given without an answer to the question, What is moral good? For the moral good is the realisation of the moral capability, and we cannot fully know what any capability is till we know its ultimate realisation. It may be argued therefore that we either know what the moral good in this sense is, and accordingly have no need to infer what it is from our moral nature, or else we do not know what it is, in which case neither can we know what the moral nature is from which we profess to infer what the moral good is.

The answer is that from a moral capability which had not realised itself at all nothing could indeed be inferred as to the moral good which can only consist in its full realisation; but that the moral capability of man is not in this wholly undeveloped state. To a certain extent it has shown by actual achievement what it has in it to become, and by reflection on the so far developed activity we can form at least some negative conclusion in regard to its complete realisation. We may convince ourselves that this realisation can only be attained in certain directions of our activity, not in others. We cannot indeed describe any state in which man, having become all that he is capable of becoming—all that, according to the divine plan of the world, he is destined to become—would find rest for his soul. We cannot conceive it under any forms borrowed from our actual experience, for our only experience of activity is of such as implies incompleteness. Of a life of completed development, of activity with the end attained, we can only speak or think in negatives, and thus only can we speak or think of that state of being in which, according to our theory, the ultimate moral good must consist. Yet the conviction that there must be such a state of being, merely negative as is our theoretical apprehension of it, may have supreme influence over conduct, in moving us to that effort after the Better which, at least as a conscious effort, implies the conviction of there being a Best.

And when the speculative question is raised as to what this Best can be, we find that it has not left itself without witness. The practical struggle after the Better, of which the idea of there being a Best has been the spring, has taken such effect in the world of man's affairs as makes the way by which the Best is to be more nearly approached plain enough to him that will see. In the broad result it is not hard to understand how man has bettered himself through institutions and habits which tend to make the welfare of all the welfare of each, and through the arts which make nature, both as used and as contemplated, the friend of man. And just so far as this is plain, we know enough of ultimate moral good to guide our conduct ; enough to judge whether the prevailing interests which make our character are or are not in the direction which tends further to realise the capabilities of the human spirit.

173. But here again it may be urged that we are going too fast, that we are making huge assumptions. We seem to be taking for granted that there is some best state of being for man—best in the sense that in it lies the full realisation of his capabilities, and that in it therefore alone he can satisfy himself, though as a matter of fact in his efforts after self-satisfaction he constantly acts in a manner inconsistent with his attaining it. We seem to be taking for granted, further, that this best state of man is already present to some divine consciousness, so that it may properly be said to be the vocation of man to attain it ; that some unfulfilled and unrealised, but still operative, idea of there being such a state has been the essential influence in the process by which man has so far bettered himself; and that a continued operation of the same idea in us, with that growing definiteness which is gathered from reflection on the actions and institutions in which it has so far manifested itself, is the condition of character and conduct being morally good in the proper sense of the words.   How are such assumptions to be justified?

174. In order to justify them, we must in the first place recall the conclusions arrived at in an earlier stage of this treatise.   We saw reason to hold that the existence of one connected world, which is the presupposition of knowledge, implies the action of one self-conditioning and self-determining mind; and that, as our knowledge, so our moral activity was only explicable on supposition of a certain reproduction of itself, on the part of this eternal mind, as the self of man—'a reproduction of itself to which it makes the processes of animal life organic, and which is qualified and limited by the nature of those processes, but which is so far essentially a reproduction of the one supreme subject, implied in the existence of the world, that the product carries with it under all its limitations and qualifications the characteristic of being an object to itself' (§ 99).   Proof of such a doctrine, in the ordinary sense of the word, from the nature of the case there cannot be.   It is not a truth deducible from other established or conceded truths.   It is not a statement of an event or matter of fact that can be the object of experiment or observation.   It represents a conception to which no perceivable or imaginable object can possibly correspond, but one that affords the only means by which, reflecting on our moral and intellectual experience conjointly, taking the world and ourselves into account, we can put the whole thing together and understand how (not *why*, but *how*) we are and do what we consciously are and do.   Given this conception, and not without it, we can at any rate express that which it cannot be denied demands expression, the nature of man's reason and man's will, of human progress and human short-coming, of the effort after good and the failure to gain it, of virtue and vice, in their connection and in their distinction, in their essential opposition and in their no less essential unity.

175. The reason and will of man have their common ground in that characteristic of being an object to himself which, as we have said, belongs to him in so far as the eternal mind, through the medium of an animal organism and under limitations arising from the employment of such a medium, reproduces itself in him. It is in virtue of this self-objectifying principle that he is determined, not simply by natural wants according to natural laws, but by the thought of himself as existing under certain conditions, and as having ends that may be attained and capabilities that may be realised under those conditions. It is thus that he not merely desires but seeks to satisfy himself in gaining the objects of his desire ; presents to himself a certain possible state of himself, which in the gratification of the desire he seeks to reach ; in short, wills. It is thus, again, that he has the impulse to make himself what he has the possibility of becoming but actually is not, and hence not merely, like the plant or animal, undergoes a process of development, but seeks to, and does, develop himself. The conditions of the animal soul, 'servile to every skiey influence,' no sooner sated than wanting, are such that the self-determining spirit cannot be conscious of them as conditions to which it is subject—and it is so subject and so conscious of its subjection in the human person—without seeking some satisfaction of itself, some realisation of its capabilities, that shall be independent of those conditions.

176. Hence arises the impulse which becomes the source, according to the direction it takes, both of vice and of virtue. It* is the source of vicious self-seeking and self-assertion, so far as the spirit which is in man seeks to satisfy itself or to realise its capabilities in modes in which, according to the law which its divine origin imposes on it and which is equally the law of the universe and of human society, its self-satisfaction or self-realisation is not to be

found. Such, for instance—so self-defeating—is the quest
for self-satisfaction in the life of the voluptuary.   Animals
are not voluptuaries ; for, if they seek pleasure at all, they
do so in the sense that they are stimulated to action by the
images of this pleasure and that, as those images recur.
They are not objects to themselves, as men are, and therefore cannot set themselves, as the voluptuary does, to seek
self-satisfaction in the enjoyment of all the pleasures that are
to be had.   It is one and the same principle of his nature—
his divine origin, in the sense explained—which makes it
possible for the voluptuary to seek self-satisfaction, and thus
to live for pleasure, at all, and which according to the law
of its being, according to its inherent capability, makes it
impossible that the self-satisfaction should be found in any
succession of pleasures.   So it is again with the man who
seeks to assert himself, to realise himself, to show what he
has in him to be, in achievements which may make the
world wonder, but which in their social effects are such that
the human spirit, according to the law of its being, which
is a law of development in society, is not advanced but
hindered by them in the realisation of its capabilities.   He
is living for ends of which the divine principle that forms
his self alone renders him capable, but these ends, because
in their attainment one is exalted by the depression of
others, are not in the direction in which that principle can
really fulfil the promise and potency which it contains.

How in particular and in detail that fulfilment is to be
attained, we can only tell in so far as some progress has
actually been made towards its attainment in the knowledge,
arts, habits, and institutions through which man has so far
become more at home in nature, and through which one
member of the human family has become more able and
more wishful to help another.   But the condition of its further fulfilment is the will in some form or other to contribute
to its fulfilment.   And hence the differentia of the virtuous
life, proceeding as it does from the same self-objectifying
principle which we have just characterised as the source of

the vicious life, is that it is governed by the consciousness of there being some perfection which has to be attained, some vocation which has to be fulfilled, some law which has to be obeyed, something absolutely desirable, whatever the individual may for the time desire; that it is in ministering to such an end that the agent seeks to satisfy himself. However meagrely the perfection, the vocation, the law may be conceived, the consciousness that there is such a thing, so far as it directs the will, must at least keep the man to the path in which human progress has so far been made. It must keep him loyal in the spirit to established morality, industrious in some work of recognised utility.   What further result it will yield, whether it will lead to a man's making any original contribution to the perfecting of life, will depend on his special gifts and circumstances.   Though these are such, as is the case with most of us, that he has no chance of leaving the world or even the society immediately about him observably better than he found it, yet in 'the root of the matter'—as having done loyally, or 'from love of his work' (which means under consciousness of an ideal), or in religious language 'as unto the Lord,' the work that lay nearest him—he shares the goodness of the man who devotes a genius to the bettering of human life.

177. It may seem that in the preceding section we have gone off prematurely into an account of virtue and vice, in respect at once of the common ground of their possibility and of their essential difference, without the due preliminary explanation of the relation between reason and will.   A very little reflection, however, on what has been said will show the way in which this relation is conceived.   By will is understood, as has been explained, an effort (or capacity for such effort) on the part of a self-conscious subject to satisfy itself: by reason, in the practical sense, the capacity on the part of such a subject to conceive a better state of itself as an end to be attained by action.   This is what will and reason are severally taken to imply in the most primitive form in which they appear in us.   A being without capacity for such effort or such conception would not, upon our theory, be considered to have will or reason. In this most primitive form they are alike modes of that eternal principle of self-objectification which we hold to be reproducing itself in man through the medium of an animal organism, and of which the action is equally necessary to knowledge and to morality. There is thus essentially or in principle an identity between reason and will; and widely as they become divergent in the actual history of men (in the sense that the objects where good is actually sought are often not those where reason, even as in the person seeking them, pronounces that it is to be found), still the true development of man, the only development in which the capabilities of his 'heaven-born' nature can be actualised, lies in the direction of union between the developed will and the developed reason. It consists in so living that the objects in which self-satisfaction is habitually sought contribute to the realisation of a true idea of what is best for man—such an idea as our reason would have when it had come to be all which it has the possibility of becoming, and which, as in God, it is.

178. Such a life, as in vague forecast conceived, has always been called, according to a usage inherited from the Greek fathers of moral philosophy, a life according to reason. And this usage is in harmony with the definition just given of reason at its lowest potency in us. For any truest idea of what is best for man that can guide our action is still a realisation of that capacity for conceiving a better state of himself, which we must ascribe to every child whom we can regard as 'father of the man' capable of morality, to any savage to whom we would affiliate the moral life that we inherit. Nay, even if we mean by a 'true idea of what is best for man' such an adequate and detailed idea of our perfection as we cannot conceive ourselves to have—since to have it would imply that the perfection was already attained, and the conception of ourselves in perfection is one that we cannot form—still such an idea would be but the completed expression of that self-realising principle of which the primary expression is the capacity, distinctive of the 'animal rationale' in all its forms, of conceiving itself in a better state than it is.

On the other hand it must be borne in mind that this same capacity is the condition, as has been pointed out, no less of the vicious life than of the virtuous. The self-objectifying principle cannot exert itself as will without also exerting itself as reason, though neither as will nor as reason does it, in the vicious life, exert itself in a direction that leads to the true development of its capacity. That a man should seek an object as 'part of his happiness,' or as one without which in his then state he cannot satisfy himself,— and this is to will—implies that he presents himself to himself as in a better state with the object attained than he is without it; and this is to exercise reason. Every form of vicious self-seeking is conditioned by such presentation and, in that sense, by reason. Why then, it may be asked, should the moralising influence in man, the faculty through which the paths of virtue are marked out, whether followed or no, be specially called reason? We answer: because it is through the operative consciousness in man of a possible state of himself better than the actual, though that consciousness is the condition of the possibility of all that is morally wrong, that the divine self-realising principle in him gradually fulfils its capability in the production of a higher life. With this consciousness, directed in the right path, *i.e.* the path in which it tends to become what according to the immanent divine law of its being it has in it to be—and it is as so directed that we call it 'practical reason'—rests the initiative of all virtuous habit and action.

179. It is true that, just so far as this consciousness is operative in the direction supposed, it carries an improvement of the will with it. Men come to seek their satisfaction, their good, in objects conceived as desirable because contributing to the best state or perfection of man; and this change we describe by saying that their will becomes conformable to their reason. For the self-realisation of the divine principle in man this change of will is just as necessary as the development of practical reason, and to an intelligence which could view the process as a whole would appear inseparable from it.   But to us who view the process piece-meal, ourselves representing certain stages in it, it is natural to treat the development of practical reason, *i.e.* the gradual filling up and definition of the idea of human perfection, as a separate process, upon which the corresponding con-formation of will may or may not ensue.   We see that in the individual the idea of what is good for him in his actual state of passion and desire—the idea which in fact he seeks to realise in action—is apt not to correspond to his convic-tion of what is truly good.   That conviction is the echo in him of the expression which practical reason has so far given to itself in those institutions, usages, and judgments of society, which contribute to the perfection of life, but his desires and habits are not yet so far conformed to it that he can seek his good in obeying it, that he can will as it directs. He knows the better—knows it, in a sense, even as better for himself, for he can think of himself as desiring what he *does not*, but feels that he *should*, desire—but he prefers the worse.   His will, we say, does not answer to his reason.

It is thus natural for us to treat will and reason as separate and even as conflicting faculties, though when we reflect on moral action in its real integrity we see that it involves each alike, and that it is only some *better* reason with which in vicious action a man's will conflicts, while there is an exercise of reason by him which is the very condition of his vicious-ness.   The 'better' reason is his capacity for conceiving a good of his own, so far as that capacity is informed by those true judgments in regard to human good which the action of the eternal spirit in man has hitherto yielded; while the reason which shows itself in his actual vice is the same capacity, as taking its object and content from desires of which the satisfaction is inconsistent with the real better-ing of man.   But just because it is this capacity in a man which, while it alone renders selfishness in all its forms possible, is the medium through which alone ideas of a better life than he is living are brought home to him— ideas themselves arising from the development of this capacity as it has so far gone in men—we are right, when once we have allowed ourselves to treat reason and will as separate faculties, in regarding reason as the one which has the initiative in the bettering of life. In the same way of thinking we may properly ascribe to reason—not as gradually unfolding itself in us, but as in the perfection to which that process tends, and which we must suppose to be actually attained in the eternal mind—a fully articulated idea of the best life for man, and accordingly speak of life according to reason as the goal of our moral effort. Meanwhile the error which lies in the treatment of reason and will as separate faculties we may correct by bearing in mind that it is one and the same self of which reason and will are alike capacities; that in every moral action, good or bad, each capacity is exerted as much as the other; and that every step forward in the self-realisation of the divine principle in man involves a determination of will no less than of reason, not merely a conception of a possible good for man, but the adoption by some man or men of that good as his or theirs.

CHAPTER II

CHARACTERISTICS OF THE MORAL IDEAL

A. *The Personal Character of the Moral Ideal*

180. LET us pause here to take stock of the conclusions so far arrived at. It will be convenient to state them in dogmatic form, begging the reader to understand that this form is adopted to save time, and does not betoken undue assurance on the part of the writer. Through certain *media*, and under certain consequent limitations, but with the constant characteristic of self-consciousness and self-objectification, the one divine mind gradually reproduces itself in the human soul. In virtue of this principle in him man has definite capabilities, the realisation of which, since in it alone he can satisfy himself, forms his true good. They are not realised, however, in any life that can be observed, in any life that has been, or is, or (as it would seem) that can be lived by man as we know him ; and for this reason we cannot say with any adequacy what the capabilities are. Yet, because the essence of man's spiritual endowment is the consciousness of having it, the idea of his having such capabilities, and of a possible better state of himself consisting in their further realisation, is a moving influence in him. It has been the parent of the institutions and usages, of the social judgments and aspirations, through which human life has been so far bettered ; through which man has so far realised his capabilities and marked out the path that he must follow in their further realisation. As his true good is or would be [1] their complete realisation, so his good-

---

[1] We say that his true good *is* this complete realisation when we think of the realisation as already attained in the eternal mind. We say that it *would be* such realisation when we think of the realisation as for ever problematic to man in the state of which we have experience.

ness is proportionate to his habitual responsiveness to the idea of there being such a true good, in the various forms of recognised duty and beneficent work in which that idea has so far taken shape among men. In other words, it consists in the direction of the will to objects determined for it by this idea, as operative in the person willing; which direction of the will we may, upon the ground stated, fitly call its determination by reason.

181. Our next step should be to explain further how it is that the idea in man of a possible better state of himself, consisting in a further realisation of his capabilities, has been the moralising agent in human life; how it has yielded our moral standards, loyalty to which—itself the product of the same idea—is the condition of goodness in the individual. Before we attempt this explanation, however, it will be well to clear up an ambiguity which will probably be thought to lurk in the doctrine already advanced. We have spoken of a certain 'divine principle' as the ground of human will and reason; as realising itself in man; as having capabilities of which the full development would constitute the perfection of human life; of direction to objects contributory to this perfection as characteristic of a good will. But what, it will be asked, is to be understood in regard to the relation of this 'divine principle' to the will and reason of individuals? Does it realise itself in persons, in you and me, or in some impersonal Humanity? Do the capabilities spoken of admit of fulfilment in individuals, or is the perfection of human life some organisation of society in which the individual is a perfectly adjusted means to an end which he is not in himself? Until these questions have been dealt with, a suspicion may fairly be entertained that we have been playing fast and loose with the conception of man as in himself an end to himself. We have been taking advantage, it may be said, of a speculation in regard to the development of the human race, which is quite a different thing from what is naturally understood by a moral progress of the individual, to justify a theory which that speculation.

fairly interpreted, tends rather to invalidate.   The theory we want to maintain is one that would found a supposed duty, and a supposed possible effort, on the part of the individual to make himself better, upon an ideal in him of a possible moral perfection, upon a conception actuating him of something that he may possibly become as an absolute end in himself.   Does not the belief in a development of the human race, which individuals indeed unwittingly promote but perish in promoting, logically involve the complete negation of such a theory?

182.   It is clearly of the very essence of the doctrine above advanced that the divine principle, which we suppose to be realising itself in man, should be supposed to realise itself in persons, as such.   But for reflection on our personality, on our consciousness of ourselves as objects to ourselves, we could never dream of there being such a self-realising principle at all, whether as implied in the world or in ourselves. It is only because we are consciously objects to ourselves, that we can conceive a world as an object to a single mind, and thus as a connected whole.   It is the irreducibility of this self-objectifying consciousness to anything else, the impossibility of accounting for it as an effect, that compels us to regard it as the presence in us of the mind for which the world exists.   To admit therefore that the self-realisation of the divine principle can take place otherwise than in a consciousness which is an object to itself, would be in contradiction of the very ground upon which we believe that a divine principle does so realise itself in man.   Personality, no doubt, is a term that has often been fought over without any very precise meaning being attached to it.   If we mean anything else by it than the quality in a subject of being consciously an object to itself, we are not justified in saying that it necessarily belongs to God and to any being in whom God in any measure reproduces or realises himself.   But whatever we mean by personality, and whatever difficulties may attach to the notion that a divine principle realises itself through a qualifying medium in the persons of men, it is certain that we shall only fall into contradictions by substituting for persons, as the subject in which the divine self-realisation takes place, any entity to which self-consciousness cannot intelligibly be ascribed. If it is impossible that the divine self-realisation should be complete in such persons as we are or can conceive ourselves coming to be, on the other hand in the absence of self-objectification, which is at least the essential thing in personality, it cannot even be inchoate.

183. This consideration has an important bearing upon certain ways of thinking or speaking in which we are apt to take refuge when, having adopted a theory of the moral life as the fulfilment in the human spirit of some divine idea, we are called upon to face the difficulty of stating whether and how the fulfilment is really achieved. Any life which the individual can possibly live is at best so limited by the necessities of his position, that it seems impossible, on supposition that a divine self-realising principle is at work in it, that it should be an adequate expression of such a principle. Granted the most entire devotion of a man to the attainment of objects contributory to human perfection, the very condition of his effectually promoting that end is that the objects in which he is actually interested, and upon which he really exercises himself, should be of limited range. The idea, unexpressed and inexpressible, of some absolute and all-embracing end is, no doubt, the source of such devotion, but it can only take effect in the fulfilment of some particular function in which it finds but restricted utterance. It is in fact only so far as we are members of a society, of which we can conceive the common good as our own, that the idea has any practical hold on us at all, and this very membership implies confinement in our individual realisation of the idea. Each has primarily to fulfil the duties of his station. His capacity for action beyond the range of those duties is definitely bounded, and with it is definitely bounded also his sphere of personal interests, his character, his *realised* possibility. No one so confined, it would seem, can exhibit all that the Spirit, working through and in him, properly

P

and potentially is. Yet is not such confinement the condition of the only personality that we know? It is the condition of social life, and social life is to personality what language is to thought. Language presupposes thought as a capacity, but in us the capacity of thought is only actualised in language. So human society presupposes persons in capacity—subjects capable each of conceiving himself and the bettering of his life as an end to himself—but it is only in the intercourse of men, each recognised by each as an end, not merely a means, and thus as having reciprocal claims, that the capacity is actualised and that we really live as persons. If society then (as thus appears) is the condition of all development of our personality, and if the necessities of social life, as alone we know or can conceive it, put limits to our personal development, can we suppose it to be in persons that the spirit operative in men finds its full expression and realisation?

184. It is from this difficulty that we are apt to seek an escape by speaking as if the human spirit fulfilled its idea in the history or development of mankind, as distinct from the persons whose experiences constitute that history, or who are developed in that development; whether in the achievements of great nations at special epochs of their history, or in some progress towards a perfect organisation of society, of which the windings and back-currents are too complex for it to be surveyed by us as a whole. But that we are only disguising the difficulty, not escaping it, by this manner of speech, we shall see upon reflecting that there can be nothing in a nation however exalted its mission, or in a society however perfectly organised, which is not in the persons composing the nation or the society. Our ultimate standard of worth is an ideal of *personal* worth. All other values are relative to value for, of, or in a person. To speak of any progress or improvement or development of a nation or society or mankind, except as relative to some greater worth of persons, is to use words without meaning. The saying that 'a nation is merely an aggregate of individuals' is indeed fallacious, but mainly on account of the introduction of the emphatic 'merely.' The fallacy lies in the implication that the individuals could be what they are, could have their moral and spiritual qualities, independently of their existence in a nation. The notion is conveyed that they bring those qualities with them ready-made into the national existence, which thereupon results from their combination; while the truth is that, whatever moral capacity must be presupposed, it is only actualised through the habits, institutions, and laws, in virtue of which the individuals form a nation. But it is none the less true that the life of the nation has no real existence except as the life of the individuals composing the nation, a life determined by their intercourse with each other, and deriving its peculiar features from the conditions of that intercourse.

Nor, unless we allow ourselves to play fast and loose with the terms 'spirit' and 'will,' can we suppose a national spirit and will to exist except as the spirit and will of individuals, affected in a certain way by intercourse with each other and by the history of the nation. Since it is only through its existence as our self-consciousness that we know anything of spirit at all, to hold that a spirit can exist except as a self-conscious subject is self-contradictory. A 'national spirit' is not something in the air; nor is it a series of phenomena of a particular kind; nor yet is it God—the eternal Spirit or self-conscious subject which communicates itself, in measure and under conditions, to beings which through that communication become spiritual. It would seem that it could only mean one of two things; either (*a*) some type of personal character, as at any time exhibited by individuals who are held together and personally modified by national ties and interests which they recognise as such; or (*b*) such a type of personal character as we may suppose *should* result, according to the divine idea of the world, from the intercourse of individuals with each other under the influence of the common institutions which make a particular nation, whether that type of character is actually attained or no. At any rate, if a 'national spirit' is held to be a form in which an eternal Spirit, in the only sense in which we have reason to think there is such a thing, realises itself, then it can only have its being in persons, though in persons, of course, specially modified by the special conditions of their intercourse with each other. The degree of perfection, of realisation of their possibilities, attained by these persons is the measure of the fulfilment which the idea of the human spirit attains in the particular national spirit. If the fulfilment of the idea is necessarily incomplete in them, it can be no more complete in the national spirit, which has no other existence, as national, than that which it has in them.

185. A like criticism must apply to any supposition that the spirit which is in man could fulfil its capability—the capability which belongs to it as a self-realisation of the eternal mind through the medium of an animal soul—in some history of mankind or some organisation of society, except in respect of a state of personal being attained by the individuals who are subjects of the history or members of the society. It does not appear how any idea should express or realise itself in an endless series of events, unless the series is relative to something beyond itself, which abides while it passes; and such a mere endless series the history of mankind must be, except so far as its results are gathered into the formation of the character of abiding persons. At any rate the idea of a spirit cannot realise itself except in spirits. The human spirit cannot develope itself according to its idea except in self-conscious subjects, whose possession of the qualities—all implying self-consciousness—that are proper to such a spirit, in measures gradually approximating to the realisation of the idea, forms its development. The spiritual progress of mankind is thus an unmeaning phrase, unless it means a progress *of* personal character and *to* personal character—a progress of which feeling, thinking, and willing subjects are the agents and sustainers, and of which each step is a fuller realisation of the capacities of such subjects. It is simply unintelligible unless understood to be in the direction of more perfect forms of personal life.

There may be reason to hold that there are capacities of the human spirit not realisable in persons under the conditions of any society that we know, or can positively conceive, or that may be capable of existing on the earth. Such a belief may be warranted by the consideration on the one hand of the promise which the spirit gives of itself, both in its actual occasional achievement and in the aspirations of which we are individually conscious, on the other hand of the limitations which the necessity of confinement to a particular social function seems to impose on individual attainment. We may in consequence justify the supposition that the personal life, which historically or on earth is lived under conditions which thwart its development, is continued in a society, with which we have no means of communication through the senses, but which shares in and carries further every measure of perfection attained by men under the conditions of life that we know. Or we may content ourselves with saying that the personal self-conscious being, which comes from God, is for ever continued in God. Or we may pronounce the problem suggested by the constant spectacle of unfulfilled human promise to be simply insoluble. But meanwhile the negative assurance at any rate must remain, that a capacity, which is nothing except as personal, cannot be realised in any impersonal modes of being.

186. It is not, of course, to be denied that the facts of human life and history put abundant difficulties in the way of any theory whatever of human development, as from the less to the more perfect kind of life, in distinction from mere generalisations as to the nature of the changes which society has undergone. If it were not for certain demands of the spirit which is ourself, the notion of human progress could never occur to us. But these demands, having a common ground with the apprehension of facts, are not to be suppressed by it. They are an expression of the same

principle of self-objectification without which, as we have seen, there could be no such thing as facts for us, for our consciousness, at all. Their strength is illustrated by the persistency with which, in spite of the rebuff they for ever seem to be receiving from observations of nature and history, they for ever reassert themselves. It is the consciousness of possibilities in ourselves, unrealised but constantly in process of realisation, that alone enables us to read the idea of development into what we observe of natural life, and to conceive that there must be such a thing as a plan of the world. That we can adjust all that we observe to this idea is plainly not the case. When we have traced processes of development in particular regions of organic life, we are scarcely nearer the goal. For, in order to satisfy the idea which sets us upon the search for development, we should be able to connect all particular processes of development with each other, the lower as subservient to the higher, and to view the world, including human history, as a whole throughout which there is a concerted fulfilment of capabilities. This we cannot do; but neither our inability to do it, nor the appearance of positive inconsistency between much that we observe and any scheme of universal development, can weaken the authority of the idea, which does not rest on the evidence of observation but expresses an inward demand for the recognition of a unity in the world answering to the unity of ourselves—a demand involved in that self-consciousness which, as we have seen, alone enables us to observe facts as such. The important thing is that we should not, in eagerness to reconcile the idea of development with facts known only bit by bit and not in their real integrity, lose sight of the essential implications of the idea itself.

187. Of these implications one is the eternal realisation for, or in, the eternal mind of the capacities gradually realised in time. Another is that the end of the process of development should be a real fulfilment of the capacities presupposed by the process. When we speak of any subject as in process of development according to some law, we must mean, if we

so speak advisedly, that that into which the subject is being developed already exists for some consciousness. We express the same thing by saying that the subject is something, in itself or potentially, which it has not yet in time actually become; and this again implies that in relation to some conscious being it is eternally that which in some other relation it is in time coming to be. A state of life or consciousness not yet attained by a subject capable of it, *in relation to that subject* we say *actually is not;* but if there were no consciousness for which it existed, there would be no sense in saying that *in possibility it is,* for it would simply be nothing at all. Thus, when we speak of the human spirit being in itself, or in possibility, something which is not yet realised in human experience, we mean that there is a consciousness for and in which this something really exists, though, on the other hand, for the consciousness which constitutes human experience it exists only in possibility.

It would not be enough to say 'a consciousness *for* which it really exists.' That might merely mean that this undeveloped capability of the human spirit existed as an object of consciousness to the eternal mind, in the same way in which facts that I contemplate exist for me. Such a statement would suffice, were the subject of development merely a natural organism. But when that which is being developed is itself a self-conscious subject, the end of its becoming must really exist not merely *for,* but *in* or *as,* a self-conscious subject. There must be eternally such a subject which is all that the self-conscious subject, as developed in time, has the possibility of becoming; in which the idea of the human spirit, or all that it has in itself to become, is completely realised. This consideration may suggest the true notion of the spiritual relation in which we stand to God; that He is not merely a Being who has made us, in the sense that we exist as an object of the divine consciousness in the same way in which we must suppose the system of nature so to exist, but that He is a Being in whom we exist; with whom we are in principle one; with whom the human spirit is identical, in the sense that He *is* all which the human spirit is capable of becoming.

188. In regard to the other principle which we have noticed as implied in the idea of development—that the end of the process of development should be a real fulfilment of the capacities pre-supposed by the process—it may be argued that, however indisputable, it can afford us little guidance in judging of the ultimate end to which any process of development is tending.   In cases where end or function are matter of observation, and capacity or faculty are inferred from them, it has no application ; and if it is to be available in other cases, we must have some means of ascertaining the nature of capacities, independently of observation of the ends to which they are relative.   But have we any such means ?   And in their absence, since the ultimate end of human progress must be beyond the reach of observation, are not our conclusions as to capacities of men which must be fulfilled in the course of human development mere arbitrary guess-work ?   May it not turn out that what we have been regarding as permanent capacities of men, from which something might be inferred as to the end of human development, on the ground that this end must be such as really to fulfil them, are temporary phases of some unknown force, working in we know not what direction, and that their end may be simply to disappear, having borne their part in the generation of an unknowable future ?

189. To such questions we should reply as follows.   We must be on our guard against lapsing into the notion that a process *ad infinitum*, a process not relative to an end, can be a process of development at all.   If the history of mankind were simply a history of events, of which each determines the next following, and so on in endless series, there would be no progress or development in it.   As we cannot sum an infinite series, there would be nothing in the history of mankind, so conceived, to satisfy that demand for unity of the manifold in relation to an end, which alone leads us to read the idea of development into the course of human affairs. If there is a progress in the history of men it must be towards an end consisting in a state of being which is not itself a series in time, but is both comprehended eternally in the eternal mind and is intrinsically, or in itself, eternal. Further: although any other capacity may be of a kind which, having done its work in contributing to the attainment of such a state of being, passes away in the process of its attainment—as the particular capacities of myriads of animals, their function fulfilled, pass away every hour—yet a capacity consisting in a self-conscious personality cannot be supposed so to pass away. It partakes of the nature of the eternal. It is not itself a series in time; for the series of time exists for it. We cannot believe in there being a real fulfilment of such a capacity in an end which should involve its extinction, because the conviction of there being an end in which our capacities are fulfilled is founded on our self-conscious personality—on the idea of an absolute value in a spirit which we ourselves are. And for the same reason we cannot believe that the capacities of men—capacities illustrated to us by the actual institutions of society, though they could not be so illustrated if we had not an independent idea of them—can be really fulfilled in a state of things in which any rational man should be treated merely as a means, and not as in himself an end. On the whole, our conclusion must be that, great as are the difficulties which beset the idea of human development when applied to the facts of life, we do not escape them but empty the idea of any real meaning, if we suppose the end of the development to be one in the attainment of which persons—agents who are ends to themselves—are extinguished, or one which is other than a state of self-conscious being, or one in which that reconciliation of the claims of persons, as each at once a means to the good of the other and an end to himself, already partially achieved in the higher forms of human society, is otherwise than completed.

190. Meanwhile, as must constantly be borne in mind,

in saying that the human spirit can only realise itself, that the divine idea of man can only be fulfilled, in and through persons, we are not denying but affirming that the realisation and fulfilment can only take place in and through society. Without society, no persons : this is as true as that without persons, without self-objectifying agents, there could be no such society as we know.   Such society is founded on the recognition by persons of each other, and their interest in each other, *as persons, i.e.* as beings who are ends to themselves, who are consciously determined to action by the conception of themselves, as that for the sake of which they act.   They are interested in each other *as persons* in so far as each, being aware that another presents his own self-satisfaction to himself as an object, finds satisfaction for himself in procuring or witnessing the self-satisfaction of the other. Society is founded on such mutual interest, in the sense that unless it were operative, however incapable of expressing itself in abstract formulae, there would be nothing to lead to that treatment by one human being of another as an end, not merely a means, on which society even in its narrowest and most primitive forms must rest.   There would be nothing to countervail the tendency, inherent in the self-asserting and self-seeking subject, to make every object he deals with, even an object of natural affection, a means to his own gratification.   The combination of men as ἴσοι καὶ ὅμοιοι for common ends would be impossible.   Thus except as between persons, each recognising the other as an end in himself and having the will to treat him as such, there can be no society.

But the converse is equally true, that only through society, in the sense explained, is personality actualised.   Only through society is any one enabled to give that effect to the idea of himself as the object of his actions, to the idea of a possible better state of himself, without which the idea would remain like that of space to a man who had not the senses either of sight or touch.   Some practical recognition of personality by another, of an 'I' by a 'Thou' and a

'Thou' by an 'I,' is necessary to any practical consciousness of it, to any such consciousness of it as can express itself in act. On the origin of such recognition in the past we speculate in vain. To whatever primitive groupings, as a matter of history or of imagination, we can trace our actual society, these must already imply it. But we know that we, who are born under an established system of family ties, and of reciprocal rights and obligations sanctioned by the state, learn to regard ourselves as persons among other persons because we are treated as such. From the dawn of intelligence we are treated, in one way or another, as entitled to have a will of our own, to make ourselves the objects of our actions, on condition of our practically recognising the same title in others. All education goes on the principle that we are, or are to become, persons in this sense. And just as it is through the action of society that the individual comes at once practically to conceive his personality—his nature as an object to himself—and to conceive the same personality as belonging to others, so it is society that supplies all the higher content to this conception, all those objects of a man's personal interest, in living for which he lives for his own satisfaction, except such as are derived from the merely animal nature.

191. Thus it is equally true that the human spirit can only realise itself, or fulfil its idea, in persons, and that it can only do so through society, since society is the condition of the development of a personality. But the function of society being the development of persons, the realisation of the human spirit in society can only be attained according to the measure in which that function is fulfilled. It does not follow from this that all persons must be developed in the same way. The very existence of mankind presupposes the distinction between the sexes ; and as there is a necessary difference between their functions, there must be a corresponding difference between the modes in which the personality of men and women is developed. Again, though we must avoid following the example of philosophers who have

shown an *a priori* necessity for those class-distinctions of their time which after ages have dispensed with, it would certainly seem as if distinctions of social position and power were necessarily incidental to the development of human personality. There cannot be this development without a recognised power of appropriating material things. This appropriation must vary in its effects according to talent and opportunity, and from that variation again must result differences in the form which personality takes in different men. Nor does it appear how those reciprocal services which elicit the feeling of mutual dependence, and thus promote the recognition by one man of another as an 'alter ego,' would be possible without different limitations of function and ability, which determine the range within which each man's personality developes, in other words, the scope of his personal interests.

Thus, under any conditions possible, so far as can be seen, for human society, one man who was the best that his position allowed, would be very different from another who was the best that *his* position allowed. But, in order that either may be good at all in the moral sense, *i. e.* intrinsically and not merely as a means—in order that the idea of the human spirit may be in any sense fulfilled in him—the fulfilment of that idea in some form or other, the contribution to human perfection in some way or other, must be the object in which he seeks self-satisfaction, the object for which he lives in living for himself. And it is only so far as this development and direction of personality is obtained for all who are capable of it (as presumably every one who says 'I' is capable), that human society, either in its widest comprehension or in any of its particular groups, can be held to fulfil its function, to realise its idea as it is in God.

B. *The Formal Character of the Moral Ideal or Law.*

192. Having thus endeavoured to explain the relation in which the development of the human race must stand to the personal perfection of individuals, we return to the problem

which was postponed to make way for that explanation. We have seen how there is a real identity between the end for which the good man consciously lives—the end of fulfilling in some way his rational capacity, or the idea of a best that is in him—and the end to which human development, if there is such a thing, must be eternally relative in the eternal mind. It may be no more than such an identity as there is between the mere consciousness *that* there is an object and the consciousness *what* the object is. More precisely, it may be no more than the identity between the idea that a man has, in virtue of his rational capacity, of something, he knows not what, which he may and should become, and the idea, perfectly articulated and defined in the divine consciousness, of a state of being in which the capacities of all men are fully realised. But the idea as it is in the individual man, however indefinite and unfilled,. is a communication in germ or principle of the idea as it is in God, and the communication is the medium through which the idea as in God determines the progressive development of human capacities in time. Alike as in God, as communicated in principle to men, and as realising itself by means of that communication in a certain development of human capacities, the idea can have its being only in a personal, *i. e.* a self-objectifying, consciousness. From the mere idea in a man, however, 'of something, he knows not what, which he may and should become,' to the actual practice which is counted morally good, it may naturally seem a long step. We have therefore to explain in further detail how such an idea, gradually taking form and definiteness, has been the moralising agent in human life, yielding our moral standards and inducing obedience to them.

193. Supposing such an idea to be operative in man, what must be the manner of its operation? It will keep before him an object, which he presents to himself as absolutely desirable, but which is other than any particular object of desire. Of this object it can never be possible for him to give a sufficient account, because it consists in the realisation of capabilities which can only be fully known in their ultimate realisation. At the same time, because it is the fulfilment of himself, of that which he has in him to be, it will excite an interest in him like no other interest, different in kind from any of his desires and aversions except such as are derived from it. It will be an interest as in an object conceived to be of unconditional value; one of which the value does not depend on any desire that the individual may at any time feel for it or for anything else, or on any pleasure that, either in its pursuit or in its attainment or as its result, he may experience. The conception of its desirableness will not arise, like the conception of the desirableness of any pleasure, from previous enjoyment of it or from reflection on the desire for it. On the contrary, the desire for the object will be founded on a conception of its desirableness as a fulfilment of the capabilities of which a man is conscious in being conscious of himself.

In such men and at such times as a desire for it does actually arise—a desire in that sense which implies that the man puts himself forth for the realisation of the desired object—it will express itself in their imposition on themselves of rules requiring something to be done irrespectively of any inclination to do it, irrespectively of any desired end to which it is a means, *other than this end, which is desired because conceived as absolutely desirable.* With the men in whom, and at the times when, there is no such desire, the consciousness of there being something absolutely desirable will still be a qualifying element in life. It will yield a recognition of those unconditional rules of conduct to which, from the prevalence of unconformable passions, it fails to produce actual obedience. It will give meaning to the demand, without which there is no morality and in which all morality is virtually involved, that 'something be done merely for the sake of its being done [1],' because it is a con-

---

[1] 'So gewiss der Mensch ein Mensch ist, so gewiss äussert sich in ihm eine Zunöthigung, einiges ganz unabhängig von äusseren Zwecken zu thun, lediglich damit es geschehe, und andres eben so zu unterlassen, lediglich damit es unterbleibe.'—J. G. FICHTE.

sciousness of the possibility of an action in which no desire shall be gratified but the desire excited by the idea of the act itself, as of something absolutely desirable in the sense that in it the man does the best that he has in him to do.

194. But, granted the conception of an unconditional good for man, with unconditional rules of conduct which it suggests, what in particular will those rules enjoin? We have said that man can never give a sufficient account of what his unconditional good is, because he cannot know what his capabilities are till they are realised. This is the explanation of the infirmity that has always been found to attach to attempted definitions of the moral ideal. They are always open to the charge that there is employed in the definition, openly or disguisedly, the very notion which profession is made of defining. If, on being asked for an account of the unconditional good, we answer either that it is the good will or that to which the good will is directed, we are naturally asked further, what then is the good will? And if in answer to this question we can only say that it is the will for the unconditional good, we are no less naturally charged with 'moving in a circle.' We do but slightly disguise the circular process without escaping from it if, instead of saying directly that the good will is the will for the unconditional good, we say that it is the will to conform to a universal law for its own sake or because it is conceived as a universal law; for the recognition of the authority of such a universal law must be founded on the conception of its relation to an unconditional good.

It is one of the attractions of Hedonistic Utilitarianism that it seems to avoid this logical embarrassment. If we say that the unconditional good is pleasure, and that the good will is that which in its effects turns out to produce most pleasure on the whole, we are certainly not chargeable with assuming in either definition the idea to be defined. We are not at once explaining the unconditional good by reference to the good will, and the good will by reference to the unconditional good. But we only avoid doing so by taking the good will to be relative to something external to itself; to have its value only as a means to an end wholly alien to, and different from, goodness itself. Upon this view the perfect man would not be an end in himself; a perfect society of men would not be an end in itself. Man or society would alike be only perfect in relation to the production of feelings which are felt, with whatever differences of quantity, by good men and bad, by man and brute, indifferently. By such a theory we do not avoid the logical embarrassment *attending the definition of a moral ideal;* for it is not a moral ideal, in the sense naturally attached to that phrase, that we are defining at all. By a moral ideal we mean some type of man or character or personal activity, considered as an end in itself. But, according to the theory of Hedonistic Utilitarianism, no such type of man or character or personal activity is an end in itself at all.

195. It may not follow that the theory is false on this account. That is a point which would have to be considered in a full critical discussion of Hedonism. What has to be noticed here is that such a theory is not available for our purpose. It affords no help when once we have convinced ourselves that man can only be an end to himself; that consequently it is only in himself as he may become, in a complete realisation of what he has it in him to be, in his perfect character, that he can find satisfaction; that in this therefore alone can lie his unconditional good. When we are seeking for a definition of the moral ideal in accordance with this view, we should be aware what we are about. It is as well to confess at once that, when we are giving an account of an agent whose development is governed by an ideal of his own perfection, we cannot avoid speaking of one and the same condition of will alternately as means and as end. The goodness of the will or man as a means must be described as lying in direction to that same goodness as an end. For the end is that full self-conscious realisation of capabilities to which the means lies in the self-conscious exercise of the same capabilities—an exercise of them in imperfect realisation, but under the governing idea of the desirability of their fuller realisation. If we had know-ledge of what their fuller realisation would be, we might so describe it as to distinguish it from that exercise of them in less complete development which is the means to that full realisation. We might thus distinguish the perfection of man as end from his goodness as means to the end, though the perfection would be in principle identical with the good-ness, differing from it only as the complete from the incom-plete. But we have no such knowledge of the full realisation. We know it only according to the measure of what we have so far done or are doing for its attainment. And this is to say that we have no knowledge of the perfection of man as the unconditional good, but that which we have of his good-ness or the good will, in the form which it has assumed as a means to, or in the effort after, the unconditional good; a good which is not an object of speculative knowledge to man, but of which the idea—the conviction of there being such a thing—is the influence through which his life is directed to its attainment.

196. It is therefore not an illogical procedure, because it is the only procedure suited to the matter in hand, to say that the goodness of man lies in devotion to the ideal of humanity, and then that the ideal of humanity consists in the goodness of man. It means that such an ideal, not yet realised but operating as a motive, already constitutes in man an inchoate form of that life, that perfect development of himself, of which the completion would be the realised ideal itself. Now in relation to a nature such as ours, having other impulses than those which draw to the ideal, this ideal becomes, in Kant's language, an imperative, and a categorical imperative. It will command something to be done univer-sally and unconditionally, irrespectively of whether there is in any one, at any time, an inclination to do it. But when we ask ourselves what it is that this imperative commands to be done, we are met with just the same difficulty as when asked to define the moral ideal or the unconditional good. We can only say that the categorical imperative commands us to obey the categorical imperative, and to obey it for its own sake. If—not merely for practical purposes but as a matter of speculative certainty—we identify its injunction with any particular duty, circumstances will be found upon which the bindingness of that duty is contingent, and the too hasty identification of the categorical imperative with it will issue in a suspicion that, after all, there is no categorical imperative, no absolute duty, at all. After the explanations just given, however, we need not shrink from asserting as the basis of morality an unconditional duty, which yet is not a duty to do anything unconditionally except to fulfil that unconditional duty. It is the duty of realising an ideal which cannot be adequately defined till it is realised, and which, when realised, would no longer present itself as a source of duties, because the *should be* would be exchanged for the *is*. This is the unconditional ground of those particular duties to do or to forbear doing, which in the effort of the social man to realise his ideal have so far come to be recognised as binding, but which are each in some way or other conditional, because relative to particular circumstances, however wide the range of circumstances may be to which they are relative.

197. At the same time, then, that the categorical imperative can enjoin nothing *without liability to exception* but disinterested obedience to itself, it will have no lack of definite content. The particular duties which it enjoins will *at least* be all those in the practice of which, according to the hitherto experience of men, some progress is made towards the fulfilment of man's capabilities, or some condition necessary to that progress is satisfied. We say it will enjoin these *at least*, because particular duties must be constantly arising out of it for the individual, for which no formula can be found before they arise, and which are thus extraneous to the recognised code. Every one, however, of the duties which the law of the state or the law of opinion recognises must in some way be relative to circumstances. The rule therefore in which it is conveyed, though stated in the most general terms compatible with real significance, must still admit of exceptions. Yet is there a true sense in which the whole system of such duties is unconditionally binding. It is so as an expression of the absolute imperative to seek the absolutely desirable, the ideal of humanity, the fulfilment of man's vocation. Because an expression (though an incomplete one) of this absolute imperative, because a product of the effort after such an unconditional good, the requirements of conventional morality, however liable they may be to exceptions, arising out of circumstances other than those to which they are properly applicable, are at least liable to no exception for the sake of the individual's plea-sure. As against any desire but some form or other of that desire for the best in conduct, which will, no doubt, from time to time suggest new duties in seeming conflict with the old—against any desire for this or that pleasure, or any aversion from this or that pain—they are unconditionally binding.

198. Upon this view, so far from the Categorical Impera-tive having no particular content, it may rather seem to have too much. It enjoins observance of the whole complex of established duties, as a means to that perfection of man of which it unconditionally enjoins the pursuit. And it enjoins this observance as unconditionally as it enjoins the pursuit of the end to which this observance is a means, *so long as it is such a means.* It will only allow such a departure from it in the interest of a fuller attainment of the unconditional end, not in the interest of any one's pleasure. The ques-tion indeed is sure to suggest itself, what available criterion such a doctrine affords us, either for distinguishing the es-sential from the unessential in the requirements of law and custom, or for the discernment of duty in cases to which no recognised rule is applicable. So far as it can be translated into practice at all, must not its effect be either a dead con-formity to the code of customary morality, anywhere and at any time established, without effort to reform or expand it, or else unlimited license in departing from it at the prompting of any impulse which the individual may be pleased to consider a higher law? These questions shall be considered in due course[1]; but before we enquire into the practical bearings of our doctrine as to the relation between the system of duties anywhere recognised and the unconditional ground of all duties—before we ask how it affects our criteria of what in particular we should do or not do—we have further to make good the doctrine itself. We have to revert to the question, still left unanswered, how the mere idea of something absolutely desirable—an idea which, we confess, does not primarily enable us to say anything of its object but that there must be such a thing—should have gradually defined itself, should have taken body and content, in the establishment of recognised duties, in the formation of actual virtues, among men.

[1] [See Book IV.]

CHAPTER III

A. *Reason as Source of the Idea of a Common Good.*

199. THAT an idea of something absolutely desirable, which we cannot identify with any particular object of desire without soon discovering our mistake in the dissatisfaction which ensues upon the attainment of the particular object—that such an idea of a supreme good, which is no good thing in particular, should express itself in a system of social requirements and expectations, of which each would seem to have reference to a definite social need, may naturally at first be thought an extravagant supposition. Further consideration, however, may change our view. The idea of the absolutely desirable, as we have seen, arises out of, or rather is identical with, man's consciousness of himself as an end to himself. It is the forecast, proper to a subject conscious at once of himself as an absolute end, and of a life of becoming, of constant transition from possibility to realisation, and from this again to a new possibility—a forecast of a well-being that shall consist in the complete fulfilment of himself. Now the self of which a man thus forecasts the fulfilment, is not an abstract or empty self. It is a self already affected in the most primitive forms of human life by manifold interests, among which are interests in other persons. These are not merely interests dependent on other persons for the means to their gratification, but interests in the good of those other persons, interests which cannot be satisfied without the consciousness that those other persons are satisfied. The man cannot contemplate himself as in a better state, or on the way to the best, without contemplating others, not merely as a means to that better state, but as sharing it with him.

200. It may seem unphilosophical now-a-days to accept

this distinctive social interest on our part as a primary fact, without attempting to account for it by any process of evolution. Any history indeed that might be offered of it, which should enable us to connect its more complex with its simpler forms, would be much to be welcomed. But the same could not be said for a history which should seem to account for it by ignoring its distinctive character, and by deriving it from forms of animal sympathy from which, because they have no element of identity with it, it cannot in the proper sense have been developed. What the real nature may be of the sympathy of the higher animals with each other, we have probably no means of knowing. *If* it is merely an excitement of pleasure or pain in one animal, upon sign of pleasure or pain being given by another; *if* it is merely an impulse on the part of one animal to act so as to give pleasure to another, with whose pleasure its own is thus associated; then what we know as the social interest of men is more and other than a development of it. For it is characteristic of this interest that, to the man who is the subject of it, those who are its objects are ends, in the same sense in which he is an end to himself. Or, more properly, they are included in the end for which he lives in living for himself. The feeling of pleasure or pain in response to manifested pleasure or pain on the part of another sentient being does not contain the germ of such an interest, unless the subject of the feeling is conscious of himself as other than the feeling which he experiences, and of the agent occasioning it as an 'alter ego.' Only on that condition can desire for a renewal of the pleasure become, or give place to, desire for a good, to be shared by the person desiring it with another whose good is as his own.

However dependent therefore the social interest, as we know it, may be upon feelings of animal origin, such as sexual feelings, or feelings of want in the offspring which only the parent can supply, it is not a product of those feelings, not evolved from them. In order to issue in it they must have taken a new character, as feelings of one who can and does present to himself a good of himself as an end in distinction from any particular pleasure, and a like good of another or others as included in that end.   To ignore the distinctive character which our sympathies thus derive, and must have derived in any being to whom we can reasonably affiliate ourselves, from the action of a self-objectifying consciousness, is as misleading an abstraction from the reality of human nature as it would be, on the other hand, to separate that consciousness from those sympathies and interests, without which the formal idea in a man of a possible better state of himself would have no actual filling.

201. We may take it, then, as an ultimate fact of human history—a fact without which there would not be such a history, and which is not in turn deducible from any other history—that out of sympathies of animal origin, through their presence in a self-conscious soul, there arise interests as of a person in persons.   Out of processes common to man's life with the life of animals there arise for man, as there do not apparently arise for animals,

> Relations dear and all the charities
> Of father, son, and brother :

and of those relations and charities self-consciousness on the part of all concerned in them is the condition.   At the risk of provoking a charge of pedantry, this point must be insisted on.   It is not any mere sympathy with pleasure and pain that can by itself yield the affections and recognised obligations of the family.   The man for whom they are to be possible must be able, through consciousness of himself as an end to himself, to enter into a like consciousness as belonging to others, whose expression of it corresponds to his own. He must have practical understanding of what is meant for them, as for himself, by saying 'I.'   Having found his pleasures and pains dependent on the pleasures and pains of others, he must be able in the contemplation of a possidle satisfaction of himself to include the satisfaction of those others, and that a satisfaction of them as ends to themselves and not as means to his pleasure.   He must, in short, be capable of conceiving and seeking a permanent well-being in which the permanent well-being of others is included.

202. Some sort of community, founded on such unity of self-consciousness, on such capacity for a common idea of permanent good, must be presupposed in any groupings of men from which the society that we know can have been developed.   To the man living under its influence the idea of the absolutely desirable, the effort to better himself, must from the first express itself in some form of social require-ment.   So far as he is set on making his way to some further fulfilment of himself, he must seek to carry those in whom he is interested with him in the process.   That 'better reason'[1] which, in antagonism to the inclinations of the moment, presents itself to him as a law for himself, will present itself to him as equally a law for them ; and as a law for them on the same ground and in the same sense as it is a law for him, *viz.* as prescribing means to the fulfilment of an idea of absolute good, common to him with them—an idea indefinable indeed in imagination, but gradually defin-ing itself in act.

The conception of a moral law, in its strict philosophical form, is no doubt an analogical adaptation of the notion of law in the more primary sense—the notion of it as a com-mand enforced by a political superior, or by some power to which obedience is habitually rendered by those to whom the command is addressed.   But there is an idea which equally underlies the conception both of moral duty and of legal right; which is prior, so to speak, to the distinction between them ; which must have been at work in the minds of men before they could be capable of recognising any kind of action as one that *ought* to be done, whether because it is enjoined by law or authoritative custom, or because, though not thus enjoined, a man owes it to himself or to his neighbour or to God.   This is the idea of an absolute and a common good ; a good common to the person conceiving it with others, and good for him and them, whether at any

[1] See above, § 179.

moment it answers their likings or no. As affected by such an idea, a man's attitude to his likes and dislikes will be one of which, in his inward converse, the 'Thou shalt' or 'Thou must' of command is the natural expression, though of law, in the sense either of the command of a political superior or of a self-imposed rule of life, he may as yet have no definite conception.

And so affected by it he must be, before the authority either of custom or of law can have any meaning for him. Simple fear cannot constitute the sense of such authority nor by any process of development, properly so called, become it. It can only spring from a conviction, on the part of those recognising the authority, that a good which is really their good, though in constant conflict with their inclinations, is really served by the power in which they recognise authority. Whatever force may be employed in maintaining custom or law, however 'the interest of the stronger,' whether an individual or the few or the majority of some group of people, may be concerned in maintaining it, only some persuasion of its contribution to a recognised common good can yield that sort of obedience to it which, equally in the simpler and the more complex stages of society, forms the social bond.

203. The idea, then, of a possible well-being of himself, that shall not pass away with this, that, or the other pleasure; and relation to some group of persons whose well-being he takes to be as his own, and in whom he is interested in being interested in himself—these two things must condition the life of any one who is to be a creator or sustainer either of law or of that prior authoritative custom out of which law arises. Without them there might be instruments of law and custom; intelligent co-operating subjects of law and custom there could not be. They are conditions at once of might being so exercised that it can be recognised as having right, and of that recognition itself. It is in this sense that the old language is justified, which speaks of Reason as the parent of Law. Reason is the self-objectifying consciousness. It constitutes, as we have seen, the capability in man of seeking an absolute good and of conceiving this good as common to others with himself: and it is this capability which alone renders him a possible author and a self-submitting subject of law.

In saying this we are saying nothing for or against any theory of the conditions under which, as a matter of history, laws may have been first established. It is easy, and for certain purposes may be advisable, to define a sense of the term in which 'laws' do not exist till an advanced stage of civilisation, when sovereignties of ascertained range and scope have been established, and when the will of the sovereign has come to be expressed in general and permanent forms. In proportion as we thus restrict our usage of the term 'law' we shall have to extend our view of the effect upon human life of social requirements, which are not 'laws,' but to which the good citizen renders an obedience the same in principle as that which he renders to 'laws'; an obedience at once willing and constrained— willing, because recognised as the condition of a social good, which is his own highest good; constrained, in so far as it prevents him from doing what he would otherwise like to do. It is with the ground of this obedience that the moralist is concerned, as having been rendered when as yet 'law' in the restricted sense was not, and as still rendered equally by the good citizen to the law which the state enforces, and to that of which the sanction is a social sentiment shared by him.

204. This ground the moralist finds in Reason, according to the sense explained. He will listen respectfully to any account, for which historians can claim probability, of the courses of events by which powers, strong enough to enforce general obedience, have been gathered into the hands of individuals or groups of men; but he will reflect that, though the exercise of force may be a necessary incident in the maintenance of government, it cannot of itself produce the state of mind on which social union in any of its forms depends. He will listen, further, to all that the anthro-

pologist can tell him of the earliest forms in which such
union can be traced; but here again he will reflect that,
when the phenomena of some primitive usage have been
duly established, the interpretation of the state of mind
which they represent is a further question, and one that
cannot be answered without reference to the developed
consciousness which is ours.   When the anthropologist has
gathered all the results he can from a collation of the sayings
and doings of such uncivilised people as can now be observed, with records and survivals from the lives of our ancestors,
his clue for the interpretation of his material will depend in
the last resort on his analysis of that world of feeling, thought,
and desire, in which he himself lives.   Unless the fragmentary
indications obtainable of the life of primitive humanity can
be interpreted as expressing a consciousness in germ or principle the same as ours, we have no clue to their inner significance at all.   They are at best no more to us than the
gestures of animals, from which we may conjecture that the
animal is pleased or pained, but by which no consciousness
in its intrinsic nature is conveyed to us, as it is conveyed in
the speech of another man.   We may, of course, take this
view of them.   We may hold that no inference is possible
from them to any state of mind on the part of primitive man.
But we cannot interpret them as expressing a state of mind
without founding our conception of the state of mind on our
own consciousness.   Even if it were possible on any other
plan to read a state of mind in them at all, we certainly could
not read in them a consciousness from which our own has
been developed, without assuming an identity, under whatever variety of modification, between the less and the more
developed consciousness.

Thus, though our information about primitive man were
very different from what it is, it could never be other than
a contradiction to found upon it a theory of the state of mind
underlying the earliest forms of social union, which should
represent this state of mind as different in kind from that
which, upon fair analysis of the spiritual life now shared by

us, we find to be the condition of such social union as actually exists. If we are right in ascribing to Reason a function of union in the life that we know; if we are right in holding that through it we are conscious of ourselves, and of others as ourselves,—through it accordingly that we can seek to make the best of ourselves and of others with ourselves, and that in this sense Reason is the basis of society, because the source at once of the establishment of equal practical rules in a common interest, and of self-imposed subjection to those rules; then we are entitled to hold that Reason fulfilled a function intrinsically the same in the most primitive associations of man with man, between which and the actual institutions of family and commune, of state and nation, there has been any continuity of development.

205. The foundation of morality, then, in the reason or self-objectifying consciousness of man, is the same thing as its foundation in the institutions of a common life—in these as directed to a common good, and so directed not mechanically but with consciousness of the good on the part of those subject to the institutions. Such institutions are, so to speak, the form and body of reason, as practical in men. Without them the rational or self-conscious or moral man does not exist, nor without them can any being have existed from whom such a man could be developed, if any continuity of nature is implied in development. No development of morality can be conceived, nor can any history of it be traced (for that would imply such a conception), which does not presuppose some idea of a common good, expressing itself in some elementary effort after a regulation of life. Without such an idea the development would be as impossible as it is impossible that sight should be generated when there is no optic nerve. With it, however restricted in range the idea may be, there is given 'in promise and potency' the ideal of which the realisation would be perfect morality, the ideal of a society in which every one shall treat every one else as his neighbour, in which to every rational agent the well-being or perfection of every other such agent shall be included in that perfection of himself for which he lives. And as the most elementary notion in a rational being of a personal good, common to himself with another who is as himself, is in possibility such an ideal, so the most primitive institutions for the regulation of a society with reference to a common good are already a school for the character which shall be responsive to the moral ideal.

It has become a common-place among us that the moral susceptibilities which we find in ourselves, would not exist but for the action of law and authoritative custom on many generations of our ancestors. The common-place is doubtless perfectly true. It is only misleading when we overlook the rational capacities implied in the origin and maintenance of such law and custom. The most elementary moralisation of the individual must always have arisen from his finding himself in the presence of a requirement, enforced against his inclinations to pleasure, but in an interest which he can recognise as being his own, no less than the interest of those by whom the requirement is enforced. The recognition of such an interest by the individual is an outcome of the same reason as that which has led to the maintenance of the requirement by the society he belongs to. All further development of morality—all articulation of duties, all education of conscience in response to them—presupposes this primary recognition. Of the principal movements into which the development may be analysed we shall now go on to speak in more detail, only premising that the necessity of describing them separately should not lead us to forget that they are mutually involved.

B. *The Extension of the Area of Common Good.*

206. The first of the movements into which the development of morality may be analysed consists in a gradual extension, for the mental eye of the moral subject, of the range of persons to whom the common good is conceived as common ; towards whom and between whom accordingly obligations are understood to exist. What may have been the narrowest restrictions on this range within which the process of moralisation has gone on, we have no means of saying. We only know that the earliest ascertainable history exhibits to us communities, relatively very confined, within any one of which a common good, and in consequence a common duty, is recognised as between the members of the community, while beyond the particular community the range of mutual obligation is not understood to extend. Among ourselves, on the contrary, it is almost an axiom of popular Ethics that there is at least a potential duty of every man to every man—a duty which becomes actual so soon as one comes to have any dealing with the other. It is true that plenty of pretexts, some under very philosophical disguise, are always forthcoming when it is wished to evade the duty ; but, when we are free from private bias, we do not seriously dispute its validity. Conscience is uneasy at its violation, as it would not have been, according to all indications, in the case, let us say, of a Greek who used his slave as a chattel, though according to his lights the Greek might be as conscientious as any of us. Yet the language in which we most naturally express our conception of the duty of all men to all men indicates the school—that of tribal, or civil, or family obligation—in which we have been trained to the conception. We convey it in the concrete by speaking of a human family, of a fraternity of all men, of the common fatherhood of God ; or we suppose a universal Christian citizenship, as wide as the Humanity for which Christ died, and in thought we transfer to this, under certain analogical adaptations, those claims of one citizen upon another which have been actually enforced in societies united under a single sovereignty.

207. It is not uncommon indeed with men to whom a little philosophy has proved a dangerous thing, to make much of the distinction between an obligation that admits of being enforced between persons subject to a common sovereign, and what is alleged to be due from man to man, as such ; to extenuate the claims of humanity, and even to make merry over the fraternity of men and nations. The distinction is easily drawn, and, so long as there continue to be men who will not observe obligations unless enforced, it cannot be considered practically unimportant. But for the moralist it is more important to observe the real fusion, in the conscience of those citizens of the modern world who are most responsive to the higher influences of their time, of duties enforced by legal penalties and those of which the fulfilment cannot be exacted by citizen of citizen, or by sovereign of subjects, but is felt to be due from man to man. It is not more certain that a man would not recognise a duty, *e. g.* of educating his poor neighbours or helping to liberate a slave, unless, generations before him, equal rights had been enforced among men who could not have understood the wrong of slavery or the claim of the labourer to a chance of raising himself, than that there are men now to whom such duties present themselves with just the same cogency as legal obligations ; men to whom the motive for fulfilling the latter has been so entirely purged from any fear of penalties, that the absence of such fear, as a motive to the fulfilment of humanitarian duties, makes no difference to the felt necessity of fulfilling them.

No gradual modification of selfish fear or hope could yield a disposition of this kind ; and if these were the sole original motives to civil or tribal or family obedience, it would be unintelligible that a state of mind should result, in which a man imposes duties on himself quite beyond the range of such obedience. But if at the root of such obedience, as well as of the institutions to which it has been rendered, there has been an idea of good, suggested by the consciousness of unfulfilled possibilities of the rational nature common to all men, then it is intelligible that, as the range of this idea extends itself—as it comes to be understood that no race or religion or status is a bar to self-determined co-operation in its fulfilment—the sense of duty which it yields, and which has gained its power over natural desires and aversions through generations of discipline in the family and the state, should become a sense of what is due to man as such, and not merely to the members of a particular community. The change is not necessarily in the strength, in the constraining power, of the feeling of duty—perhaps it is never stronger now than it may have been in an Israelite who would have yet recognised no claim in a Philistine, or in a Greek who would yet have seen no harm in exposing a sickly child—but in the conceived range of claims to which the duty is relative. Persons come to be recognised as having claims who would once not have been recognised as having any claim, and the claim of the ἴσοι καὶ ὅμοιοι comes to be admitted where only the claim of indulged inferiors would have been allowed before. It is not the sense of duty to a neighbour, but the practical answer to the question Who is my neighbour? that has varied.

208. The extension of this process has indeed often been looked on with suspicion by practical men. It has been suggested that the friend of man is apt to be the friend of no one in particular. 'Enthusiasm for humanity' is thought to interfere with the ties of country and fellow-citizenship, without putting any influence in their place which can be relied on for controlling the selfish inclinations of the individual. The suspicion is probably groundless. The excuses which selfishness makes for itself in the mouths of cultivated men will, no doubt, vary according to the philosophical tendencies of the time; and it would be hard to deny that it may take advantage of a cant of Humanitarianism, as of any other cant that may be in vogue. But if this illustrates the old lesson—too familiar to need illustration—that there are no intellectual formulae of which the adoption will serve as a substitute for discipline of character, it argues nothing against the view that, given the discipline of character by which alone our selfish or pleasure-seeking tendencies can be controlled or superseded, the practical value of a man's morality increases with the removal of limitations upon his view of the kind of humanity which constitutes a claim equal with his own. If the fundamental readiness to forgo pleasure for duty cannot be produced merely by a wider view of the claims which others have on us, it can scarcely suffer from such a view. Indeed, if habit is strengthened by exercise, it would seem that the habit on which the fulfilment of known duties depends, once partially formed, must be strengthened rather than otherwise by that more constant call for the practice of duty which naturally arises from recognition of a wider range of persons to whom duties are due. Self-indulgent tendencies which often tend to revive, as life goes on, in those who have mastered themselves enough for 'respectability,' but to whom the range of duties implied in respectability is a narrow one, will be more constantly challenged by situations in which unfamiliar duties have to be met. And if the dutiful disposition must thus gain rather than lose in strength from the enlightenment before which the exclusive dependence of moral claims on relations of family, status, or citizenship disappears, it would seem that with this disappearance its effect in furthering the social realisation of human capabilities must greatly increase. Faculties which social repression and separation prevent from development, take new life from the enlarged co-operation which the recognition of equal claims in all men brings with it. Nor is it the case, as we are apt to suppose, that the gain in this respect is confined merely to the majority, while the few favoured by the system of privileged status and national antagonism proportionately lose. We only imagine this to be the case from a misleading association of greater capability with more distinctive supremacy. The special qualities of command are, no doubt, less highly developed as the idea of the brotherhood of men comes to be more fully carried out in the institutions of the world, but meanwhile the capabilities implied in social self-adjustment become what they could not be before. If we admire these capabilities less than the qualities of command, it is perhaps because we have not adjusted our admirations to what we must yet admit to be the divine plan of man's development.

209. The very possibility, however, of raising the question whether men are really the better for the acceptance of humanitarian ideas, indicates the extent of their actual currency. Their influence may be traced alike in the positive laws, and institutions maintained by law, of civilised nations; in the law of opinion, the social sentiments and expectations, prevalent among them ; and in the formulae by which philosophers have sought to methodise this law of opinion. It would be superfluous here to follow in detail the process by which the law of Christendom has gradually come to conform to the 'Jus naturale' already recognised by Ulpian and the Institutes, according to which 'omnes homines aequales sunt.' Nor is it to the purpose to discuss the share which Stoic philosophers, Roman jurists, and Christian teachers may severally have had in gaining acceptance for the idea of human equality. It is only some spirit of partisanship that can lead us to put one set of teachers or institutions into competition with another for the credit of having contributed most to what, after all, is but the natural fulfilment of a capability given in reason itself—a fulfilment which only special selfish interests can withstand. Given the idea of a common good and of self-determined participators in it—the idea implied, as we have seen, in the most primitive human society—the tendency of the idea in the minds of all capable of it must be to include, as participators of the good, all who have dealings with each other and who can communicate as 'I' and 'Thou.' With growing means of intercourse and the progress of reflection the theory of a universal human fellowship is its natural outcome. It is rather the retardation of the acceptance of the theory that the historian has to explain ; its retardation by those private interests which have made it inconvenient for powerful men and classes to act upon it, and have led them to welcome any counter-theory which might justify their practice ; such, *e.g.*, as the interests which led some of the American communities, after claiming their own independence on the ground that 'all men are born free and equal,' to vindicate negro slavery for nearly

a hundred years and only to relinquish it after a tremendous
war in its defence.

210. However retarded, equality before the law has at
length been secured, at least ostensibly, for all full-grown
and sane human beings throughout Christendom.   Under
ordinary circumstances the right to free movement, and to
the free enjoyment and disposal of the fruits of his labour,
is guaranteed to every one, on condition of his respecting
the like freedom in others.   Social sentiment not merely
responds to the requirements of law in this respect and
secures their general observance, but often demands, on the
ground of a common humanity, some positive contribution
to the service of others where law can merely prevent a violation of rights, and some abatement from the strict exaction
of a claim which law sanctions.   It would almost everywhere condemn the refusal of help to a man, however alien
in blood, language and religion, whose life depended on the
help being given him, or the exaction of a debt legally due
at the cost of the debtor's starvation.   The necessities of
war indeed are treated as practically suspending the claims
of a common humanity.   The processes by which the general
conscience reconciles itself to their so doing cannot be considered here ; but the fact that it is only when in conflict
with the apparent claims of a common country that the
claims of a common humanity are thought to be superseded,
shows what a strong hold the latter have obtained on social
sentiment.

211. For an abstract expression of the notion that there
is something due from every man to every man, simply as
men, we may avail ourselves of the phrase employed in the
famous definition of Justice in the Institutes :—' Justitia est
constans et perpetua voluntas suum cuique tribuendi.'
Every man both by law and common sentiment is recognised as having a ' suum,' whatever the ' suum' may be, and
is thus effectually distinguished from the animals (at any
rate according to our treatment of them) and from things.
He is deemed capable of having something of his own, as

animals and things are not. He is treated as an end, not merely as a means. It is obvious indeed that the notion expressed by the 'suum cuique,' even when it carries with it the admission that every man, as such, has a 'suum,' is a most insufficient guide to conduct till we can answer the question what the 'suum' in each case is, and that no such answer is deducible from the mere principle that every one has a 'suum.' In fact, of course, this principle is never wrought into law or general sentiment without very precise, though perhaps insufficient and ultimately untenable, determinations of what is due from one to another in the ordinary intercourse of those habitually associated. Particular duties to this man and that have been recognised long before reflection has reached the stage in which a duty to man as such can be recognised. How far upon reflection we can find in these particular duties—in the detail of conventional morality—a permanent and universal basis for right conduct, is a separate question. For the present we wish to follow out the effect exerted upon the responsive conscience by life in a society where a capacity for rights, some claim on his fellow-men, has come to be ascribed to every man. Given that readiness to recognise a duty and to act upon the recognition, which is the proper outcome in the individual of family and civil discipline as governed by an idea of common good, what sort of rule of conduct will the individual, upon unbiassed reflection, obtain for himself from the establishment in law and general sentiment of the principle that every man can claim something as his due? How will it tend to define for him the absolutely desirable, and the ideal of conduct as directed thereto?

212. The great result will be to fix it in his mind, as a condition of such conduct, that it should be *alike* for the real good of all men concerned in or affected by it, as estimated on the same principle. This rule has indeed become so familiarised to our consciences, however frequently we violate it, that at first sight it may seem to some too trivial to be worthy a philosopher's attention,

while by others it may be remarked that, till we have
decided what the real good of all men is, and have at least
some general knowledge of the effect upon it, under certain
conditions, of certain lines of conduct, the rule will not tell
us how we ought to act in particular cases. Such a remark
would be plainly true. For the present, however, we are
considering the importance to the conscientious man of
this recognition of a like claim in all men, taken simply by
itself, irrespectively of those criteria of the good and of those
convictions as to the means of arriving at it by which the
recognition is in fact always accompanied. It is the source
of the refinement in his sense of justice. It is that which
makes him so over-curious, as it seems to the ordinary man
of the world, in enquiring, as to any action that may suggest
itself to him, whether the benefit which he might gain by it
for himself or for some one in whom he is interested, would
be gained at the expense of any one else, however indiffer-
ent to him personally, however separated from him in family,
status, or nation. It makes the man, in short, who will be
just before he is generous ; who will not merely postpone his
own interest to his friend's, but who, before he gratifies an
'altruistic' inclination, will be careful to enquire how in
doing so he would affect others who are not the object of
the inclination. This characteristic of the man who is just
in the full light of the idea of human equality is independent of any theory of well-being on his part. Whether he
has any theory on the matter at all, whether he is theo-
retically an 'Ascetic' or a 'Hedonist,' makes little practical
difference. The essential thing is that he applies no other
standard in judging of the well-being of others than in
judging of his own, and that he will not promote his own
well-being or that of one whom he loves or likes, from whom
he has received service or expects it, at the cost of impeding
in any way the well-being of one who is nothing to him but
a man, or whom he involuntarily dislikes ; that he will not do
this knowingly, and that he is habitually on the look-out to
know whether his actions will have this effect or not.

On supposition that a man has really attained this habit of practical justice, that it is his constant and uniform state, he has in him at least the negative principle of all virtue; a principle that will effectually restrain him from doing all that he ought not, if it does not move him to do all that he ought. We cannot indeed be sure that it will prevent the possibility of his doing acts which in the general result yield more pain than pleasure. The most equitable intentions, most carefully carried out, will not, for instance, save a man from liability to do something, in ignorance of its consequences, which will in fact promote a dangerous disease. If however we do not speak of a man doing an action which he ought not except in contemplation of his state of mind, as at any rate intending consequences which he might have known to be mischievous, then the man who is just in the sense described will be safe from doing what he ought not.

213. Such a man perhaps would not, even at this day and in the most Christianised and civilised society, command universal or very hearty admiration. Moral emotions have not been so far wrought into accord with that principle of right in man as man, which has been established in law and recognised (though by no means in its full application) by social opinion. There may indeed be a well-founded suspicion that the plea of justice before generosity is often rather made an excuse for deficient generosity than a ground for scrupulosity of justice. But, more than this, the duty of treating all men equally, even to the extent of not serving a friend or kinsman or countryman in a manner prejudicial to any one else, though it would no longer be in words denied, has yet little hold on the 'hearts' even of educated and respectable men. It has been for this reason, far more than from its being founded on a Hedonistic psychology, which in fact was common to it with nearly all the Moral Philosophy of England, that Utilitarianism has encountered so much popular dislike. The principle embodied in the formula, that 'every one should count for one and no one for more than one' in the calculation of felicific consequences,

has been the source at once of its real beneficence in the life
of modern society and of the resistance, far more formidable
than that of 'Ascetic' philosophy, which it has met with.
It has been the source of its beneficence because, quite
independently of the identification of the highest good
with a greatest possible sum of pleasures—perhaps indeed,
as we shall see later on, inconsistently with that identification—it has practically meant for Utilitarians that every
human person was to be deemed an end of absolute value,
as much entitled as any one else to have his well-being
taken account of in considering the justifiableness of an
action by which that well-being could be affected.   And it
is precisely this that has brought the Utilitarian into conflict
with every class-prejudice, with every form of family or
national pride, with the inveterate and well-reputed habit of
investing with a divine right the cause of the friend or the
party or the institution which happens to interest us most,
without reference to its bearings on the welfare of others
more remote from our sympathies.

214. For practical purposes the principle that, in the estimate of the resulting happiness by which the value of an
action is to be judged, 'every one should count for one and
no one for more than one,' yields very much the same
direction as that one of the formulae employed by Kant for
the statement of the Categorical Imperative, which has
probably always commended itself most to readers alive to
the best spirit of their time :—' Act so as to treat humanity,
whether in your own person or in that of others, always as
an end, never merely as a means.'   We say *for practical
purposes*, because, as strictly interpreted, the one by a Benthamite, the other by a Kantist, the significance of the two
formulae is wholly different.   The Benthamite would repu-
diate or pronounce unintelligible the notion of an absolute
value in the individual person.   It is not every person, according to him, but every pleasure, that is of value in itself ;
and in accordance with this view he has to qualify the formula
we have been dwelling on, so as to empty it, if not of all

practical significance, at any rate of the significance which we have ascribed to it, and which has been the real guide to the reforming Utilitarian.

Upon Hedonistic principles it will only be as 'supposed equal in degree'[1] that one person's happiness, *i.e.* his experience of pleasure, is to count for as much as another's. Now as the ascertainment of this equality in degree between the happiness of one man and that of another is practically impossible, and as there is every reason to think that different men are susceptible of pleasure in most different degrees, it is hard to see how the formula, thus interpreted, can afford any positive ground for that treatment of all men's happiness as entitled to equal consideration, for which Utilitarians have in practice been so laudably zealous. The most that could be deduced from it would be some very general condemnation of those fixed class-distinctions which, by interfering with the free pursuit of pleasure on the part of unprivileged persons, would seem to lessen the aggregate of pleasure resulting on the whole. Under it a superior race or order could plead strong justification, not indeed for causing useless pain to the inferior, but for systematically postponing the inferior's claims to happiness to its own. Certainly no absolute rule could be founded on it, prohibiting all pursuit of happiness by one man which interferes with the happiness of another, or what we commonly call the oppression of the weaker by the stronger ; for, the stronger being presumably capable of pleasure in higher degree, there could be nothing to show that the quantity of pleasure resulting from the gain to the stronger through the loss to the weaker was not greater than would have been the quantity resulting if the claims of each had been treated as equal. Instead of such a rule as that on which Utilitarians have been among the forwardest to act— 'We that are strong ought to bear the infirmities of the weak, and not to please ourselves '—we should be logically entitled at most to a counsel of prudence, advising much circumspection on the part of the strong before he assumes that an

[1] See Mill's Utilitarianism, p. 93.

addition to his pleasure, which involves a subtraction from the pleasure of the weak, would neutralise the subtraction in the hedonistic calculus.

215. There is reason to hold, then, that Kant's formula affords a better expression than does Bentham's, as interpreted according to Bentham's notion of the good, for the rule on which the ideally just man seeks to act. That rule, as we have seen, is one that such a man gathers for himself from the lessons which law and conventional morality have taught him. It is his ἐπανόρθωμα νόμου, ᾗ ἐλλείπει διὰ τὸ καθόλου[1], his articulation, and application to the particulars of life, of that principle of an absolute value in the human person as such, of a like claim to consideration in all men, which is implied in the law and conventional morality of Christendom, but of which the application in law is from the nature of the case merely general and prohibitory, while its application in conventional morality is in fact partial and inconsistent. 'The recognition of the claims of a common humanity' is a phrase that has become so familiar in modern ears that we are apt to suspect it of being cant. Yet this very familiarity is proof of the extent to which the idea represented by it has affected law and institutions. The phrase is indeed cant in the mouth of any one in whom there is no conscientious will giving vitality and application to the idea which, as merely embodied in laws and institutions, would be abortive and dead. But if it is only the conscience of the individual that brings the principle of human equality into productive contact with the particular facts of human life, on the other hand it is from the embodiment of the principle in laws and institutions and social requirements that the conscience itself appropriates it. The mistake of those who deny the *a priori* character of such 'intuitions'[2] of the conscience as that

---

[1] I.e. his 'rectification of law, where law fails through being general.' Arist. Eth. Nic. V. x. 6.

[2] I use the term 'intuition' here, in the sense commonly attached to it by recent English writers on Morals, for a judgment not derived deductively or inductively from other judgments. The reader should be on his guard against confusing this sense of the term with that in

represented by Kant's formula, does not lie in tracing a history of the intuitions, but in ignoring the immanent operation of ideas of the reason in the process of social organisation, upon which the intuitions as in the individual depend.   A short summary of the view which we have been seeking to oppose to theirs will make this view clearer, as it affects the intuition on which the practice of justice is founded.

216. The individual's conscience is reason in him as informed by the work of reason without him in the structure and controlling sentiments of society.   The basis of that structure, the source of those sentiments, can only be a self-objectifying spirit; a spirit through the action of which beings such as we are, endowed with certain animal susceptibilities and affected by certain natural sympathies, become capable of striving after some bettering or fulfilment of themselves, which they conceive as an absolute good, and in which they include a like bettering or fulfilment of others.   Without such spiritual action, in however elementary a form, there can be no society, in the proper human sense, at all ; no community of persons, however small, to whom the treatment in any respect by each of the other as himself would be intelligible.

On the other hand, given any community of persons rendered possible by such a spiritual principle, it is *potentially* a community of all men of whom one can communicate with the other as ' I ' with ' Thou.'   The recognition of reciprocal claims, established as between its own members within each of a multitude of social groups, admits of establishment between members of all the groups taken together.   There is no necessary limit of numbers or space beyond which the spiritual principle of social relation becomes ineffective.   The impediments to its action in bringing about a practical recognition of universal human fellowship, though greater in degree, are the same in kind as those which interfere with the maintenance of unity in the family, the tribe, or the urban commonwealth.   They are all reducible to what we may con-

which it is used as an equivalent for the German 'Anschauung,' or apprehension of an object.

veniently call the antagonism of the natural to the spiritual man. The prime impediment, alike to the maintenance of the narrower and to the formation of wider fellowships, is selfishness : which we may describe provisionally (pending a more thorough enquiry into the relation between pleasure and the good) as a preference of private pleasure to common good. But the wider, the more universal the fellowship that is in question, the more serious become those impediments to it, of which selfishness may and does take advantage, but which are so far independent of it that they bring the most self-devoted members of one tribe or state into what seems on both sides inevitable hostility with those of another. Such are ignorance, with the fear that springs from ignorance; misapprehension of the physical conditions of well-being, and consequent suspicion that the gain of one community must be the loss of another ; geographical separations and demarcations, with the misunderstandings that arise from them. The effect of these has often been to make it seem a necessary incident of a man's obligation to his own tribe or nation that he should deny obligations towards men of another tribe or nation. And while higher motives have thus co-operated with mere selfishness in strengthening national separation and antagonism, it would be idle to deny a large share, in the process by which such influences have been partially overcome, to forces— *e.g.* the force of conquest and, in particular, of Roman conquest—which, though they have been applied and guided in a manner only possible to distinctively rational agents, have been very slightly under the control of any desire for social good on the part of the persons wielding them.

But where the selfishness of man has proposed, his better reason has disposed. Whatever the means, the result has been a gradual removal of obstacles to that recognition of a universal fellowship which the action of reason in men potentially constitutes. Large masses of men have been brought under the control each of a single system of law ; and while each system has carried with it manifold results of selfish violence and seeming accident, each has been essentially an expression of reason, as embodying an idea of permanent well-being which the individual conceives to be common to his nation with himself. Each has maintained alike, under whatever differences of form, the institutions of the family and of property ; and there has thus arisen, along with an order of life which habituates the individual to the subordination of his likes and dislikes to social requirements, a sort of common language of right, in which the idea of universal human fellowship, of claims in man as man—itself the outcome of the same reason which has yielded the laws of particular communities—can find the expression necessary to its taking hold on the minds of men.

217. In the light of these considerations we may trace a history, if we like to call it so, of the just man's conscience —of the conscience which dictates to him an equal regard to the well-being, estimated on the same principle as his own, of all whom his actions may affect. It is a history, however, which does not carry us back to anything beyond reason. It is a history of which reason is the beginning and the end. It is reason which renders the individual capable of self-imposed obedience to the law of his family and of his state, while it is to reason that this law itself owes its existence. It is thus both teacher and learner of the lesson through which a conscience of any kind, with the habit of conformity to conscience, is first acquired, and the individual becomes capable of a reverence which can control inclinations to pleasure. Reason is equally the medium of that extension of one system of law over many communities, of like systems over a still wider range, which, in prophetic souls reflecting on it, first elicits the latent idea of a fellowship of all, and furnishes them with a mode of expression through which the idea may be brought home to ordinary men. When it is so brought home, the personal habits which are needed to give practical effect to it, and which on their part only needed the leaven of this idea to expand into a wider beneficence, are already there. But they are there through the action

of the same reason, as already yielding social order and obedience within narrower forms of community.

Thus in the conscientious citizen of modern Christendom reason without and reason within, reason as objective and reason as subjective, reason as the better spirit of the social order in which he lives, and reason as his loyal recognition and interpretation of that spirit—these being but different aspects of one and the same reality, which is the operation of the divine mind in man—combine to yield both the judgment, and obedience to the judgment, which we variously express by saying that every human person has an absolute value; that humanity in the person of every one is always to be treated as an end, never merely as a means ; that in the estimate of that well-being which forms the true good every one is to count for one and no one for more than one; that every one has a 'suum' which every one else is bound to render him.

CHAPTER IV

C. *The Determination of the Idea of Common Good*

218. THE development of morality, which we have been considering, has been a development from the primary recognition of an absolute and common good—a good common as between some group of persons interested in each other, absolute as that of which the goodness is conceived to be independent of the likes and dislikes of individuals; but we have so far considered the development only with reference to the extension of the range of persons between whom the good is conceived to be common, and who on this ground come to recognise equivalent duties to each other. The outcome of the process, when treated in this one-sided way, exhibits itself merely as the intuition of the educated conscience that the true good must be good for all men, so that no one should seek to gain by another's loss, gain and loss being estimated on the same principle for each. It has not appeared so far how the conscience is trained in the apprehension of what in particular the good is, and in the consequent imposition on itself of particular duties. We have treated the precept 'suum cuique' as if the just man arrived at the idea of its applicability to all men, and at the corresponding disposition to apply it, without any such definite enlightenment in regard to the good proper to every one with whom he may have to do, as is necessary for his practical guidance. Some such defect of treatment is unavoidable so long as abstraction of some kind is the condition of all exposition; so long as we can only attend to one aspect of any reality at a time, though quite aware that it is only one aspect. We have now to make up for the defect by considering the gradual determination of the idea of good, which goes along with the growth of the conviction that it is good for all men alike, and of the disposition to act accordingly.

219. In doing so we must first recall some conclusions previously arrived at. The idea of a good, we saw, is the idea of something that will satisfy a desire. In no case is to think of a pleasure the same thing as to think of a good. Only if some pleasure is the object of desire does the anticipation of the satisfaction of the desire yield the idea of the pleasure as a good. When, as is constantly the case, the object of strongest desire to a man—the object to which he is actually directing himself—is not any pleasure, then it is not any pleasure that is thought of as a good, for it is not any pleasure that is the object with which the man thinks of satisfying himself. In that case it is only so far as the man in desiring contemplates the pleasure, or relief from pain, that will be constituted by satisfaction of the desire—a pleasure of which the imagination cannot from the nature of the case have excited the desire—that any idea of pleasantness enters into the idea of the object as good at all. Taken by itself, then, if it could be taken by itself, the mere succession of desires in a man, as reflected on, would yield the presentation of many different good things, in which the satisfaction of those desires had been found and was expected to recur. Many of these would be pleasures, because many objects of desire are pleasures (though the thought even of these as pleasures is different from the thought of them as good) ; but many would not be pleasures, because there are many objects of desire which are not imagined pleasures, and which, though pleasure may be anticipated in their attainment, cannot be desired on account of that pleasure. That very reflection on desires, however, which is necessary to the idea of the several objects satisfying them as good, implies that the subject of the desires distinguishes himself from them. Hence there necessarily accompanies or supervenes upon the idea of manifold good things, in which manifold satisfactions have been or may be found, the idea of a possible object which may yield satisfaction of the desiring man or self, as such, who, as satisfaction of each particular desire is attained, still finds himself anew dissatisfied and wanting.

220. Such an idea is implied in the most elementary moral judgments. It must be operative in every one who judges of actions or dispositions as virtuous or vicious, and must be supposed by him to be operative in every one to whom he ascribes virtue or vice. For an agent merely capable of seeking the satisfaction of successive desires, without capacity for conceiving a satisfaction of himself as other than the satisfaction of any particular desire, and in consequence without capacity for conceiving anything as good permanently or on the whole, there could be no possibility of judging that any desire should or should not be gratified. No such judgment can be formed of any desire, unless the desire is considered with reference to a good other than such as passes with the satisfaction of a desire. Even if the judgment involved no more than a comparison of the pleasures that had been experienced in the gratification of different desires, and a decision that one should not be gratified because interfering with the gratification of another from which more pleasure was expected, this very comparison would imply that the person making it distinguished himself from his desires and was cognisant of something good for himself on the whole—though for himself only in respect of his capacity for pleasure—to which good he expects the gratification of one desire to contribute more than that of another. Now the capacity for regarding certain desires as desires which should not be gratified, must be supposed in any one who is either to form moral judgments or to have them applied to him. This must be equally admitted whether we consider action or disposition to be the proper object of moral judgment; whether we hold it to be by effects or by motives that actions are rendered morally good or bad. Unless a man could think of himself as capable of governing his actions by the consideration that of his desires some should, while others should not, be gratified, the distinction of praise-worthy and blame-worthy actions would be unmeaning to him. He could not apprehend the distinction, nor could it with any significance be applied to his actions.

221. It will scarcely be disputed, then, that the possibility of moral judgments implies some idea of a good, other than any particular pleasure or satisfaction of passing desire, with the superior value of which the value of any such pleasure or satisfaction may be compared. But we are apt to look upon the idea of superior good as formed merely by the combination in thought of the many particular pleasures and satisfactions, as an imagined sum of them. Every one has experience of certain pleasures, of which he retains the memory and desires the recurrence. Their recurrence in the largest quantity and with the greatest intensity that he can imagine, forms for him, it is supposed, when he thinks calmly of the matter, that greatest good by reference to which he can estimate the value of the pleasures which from time to time he desires, counting them objects of which the desire should or should not be gratified, according as their enjoyment is found upon experience to be compatible or otherwise with the enjoyment of that greatest sum of imaginable pleasures.

Now the question is whether the practical idea of something good on the whole, of a true or chief or highest or ultimate good—the idea implied in the capacity for moral judgment—could even in its earliest stages be formed in this way. The process by which on first thoughts we are led to suppose that it can be and is so formed, would seem to be as follows. The good we rightly identify with the desired. We at the same time accept the notion that the object of desire is always some imagined pleasure—a notion which would not commend itself as it does, but for the confusion into which we readily fall between the pleasure, or relief from pain, constituted by the satisfaction of any desire, and the object exciting the desire. Every particular good being thus supposed to be some pleasure, we infer that the greatest good for any individual must be the greatest quantity of pleasure possible for him, and that the greatest good of which the idea can affect him must be the greatest sum of pleasures that he can imagine.

It is the latter part of the inference that is here specially in question. Upon reflection it will appear that, from the supposition that every desire has some imagined pleasure for its object, it not only is no legitimate inference that a greatest sum of imaginable pleasures is most desired and therefore presents itself to the individual as his greatest good ; it rather follows that no such sum of pleasures can be desired at all. If the supposition is admitted, we are justified indeed in arguing that, in one sense of the term, the greatest pleasure is most desired, but only in the sense in which the greatest pleasure means the most intense particular pleasure that can be remembered or imagined. To argue from it that a greatest sum of imaginable pleasures is the object most desired, or one that can be desired at all, is to argue from desire for a state of feeling to desire for something which is not a possible state of feeling. There can be no such thing as a state of feeling made up of a sum of pleasures ; and if the only possible object of desire is a state of pleasant feeling, as remembered or imagined, there can be no such thing as desire for a sum of pleasures. A sum of pleasures is not a pleasure, nor is the thought of it a remembrance or imagination of pleasure, such as on the supposition excites desire. It can only exist for the thought of a person considering certain pleasures as addible quantities, but neither enjoying them nor imagining their enjoyment. For the feeling of a pleased person, or in relation to his sense of enjoyment, pleasures cannot form a sum. However numerous the sources of a state of pleasant feeling, it is one, and is over before another can be enjoyed. It and its successors can be added together in thought, but not in enjoyment or in imagination of enjoyment. If then desire is only for pleasure, *i.e.* for an enjoyment or feeling of pleasure, we are simply the victims of words when we talk of desire for a sum of pleasures, much more when we take the greatest imaginable sum to be the most desired. We are confusing a sum of pleasures as counted or combined in thought, with a sum of pleasures as felt or enjoyed, which is a nonentity.

222. In the above it is not intended to deny that there may be in fact such a thing as desire for a sum or contemplated series of pleasures, or that a man may be so affected by it as to judge that some particular desire should not be gratified, if its gratification would interfere with the attainment of that more desirable object. The contention is merely that there could not be such a desire if desire were solely for pleasure, in the sense of being always excited by an imagination of some feeling of pleasure. As there cannot be a feeling of a sum of pleasures, neither can there be an imagination of such a feeling. Desire for a sum or series of pleasures is only possible so far as upon sundry desires, each excited by imagination of a particular pleasure, there supervenes in a man a desire not excited by any such imagination; a desire for self-satisfaction. The man thinks of himself—he cannot be properly said to imagine himself—as the permanent subject of these successive desires and of the successive pleasures by imagination of which they have been excited; and a desire to satisfy himself in their successive enjoyment, unless counteracted by a desire to satisfy himself in some other way (whether with some particular pleasure imagined, or with some object that is not pleasure at all), may arise in consequence. Thus, in order to account for the transition from desire for imagined pleasures to desire for a sum or series of pleasures, we must suppose the action of a principle wholly different from desire for imagined pleasures. We must suppose a determination of desire by the conception of self, its direction to self-satisfaction. The idea of something good on the whole, even if nothing but a sum of pleasures entered into the idea as present to the mind of one whom it renders capable of moral judgment, could yet not result from the recurrence of images of pleasure or from a combination of desires each excited by such an image. A desire to satisfy oneself, then, as distinct from desire for a feeling of pleasure, being necessary even to desire for a sum of pleasures, the question is whether it can be a contemplated possibility of satisfying oneself *with pleasures* that yields the idea of a true or highest good, with which particular gratifications of desire may be contrasted.

223. Now it is not in dispute that we may and constantly do seek self-satisfaction for the moment in some imagined pleasure, though in our calmer mind we know that the pleasure cannot afford the self-satisfaction sought. We could not deny this, according to the account previously given of the will, without denying that the will is often directed to the attainment of pleasure. To deny it would be as untrue as to say of any one that his object is always a pleasure, even the habitual 'pleasure-seeker' being liable to particular propensions excited quite otherwise than by imaginations of pleasure. But, though self-satisfaction is constantly being sought in some pleasure or another, without reflection on the impossibility of its being found there, it is clear that interest in the attainment of a pleasure cannot suggest an idea, such as can control action, of something truly good or good on the whole—an idea of which the import lies in contrast with the pleasure of which the attraction is for the moment most strongly felt, and which presupposes some consideration of the question where self-satisfaction is really to be found. Reflecting on his desires for certain pleasures, a man may, no doubt, judge one of them to be more of a good than another, on the ground of its greater present attraction for him ; but such a judgment neither implies nor could yield the contrast of the desired with the desirable, of good for the moment with good on the whole. It does indeed imply in any one so judging a distinction of himself from his feelings, which, at a further stage of its action, yields the idea of something good on the whole. This idea arises from a man's thought of himself as there to be satisfied when any feeling, in the enjoyment of which he may have sought satisfaction, is over. It is the idea of something in which he may be satisfied, not for this time and turn merely, but at least *more* permanently. Could a contemplated succession of pleasures, then, seem to him to offer this relatively permanent satisfaction? Could he, while reflecting on himself so far as to conceive the need of a lasting good, fail to reflect also on the fleeting nature of the pleasures of which he contemplates the succession? Could he be deluded by his own faculty of summing the stages of a succession into supposing that a series of pleasures, of which only one will be in enjoyment at each stage of the series, and none at all at the end, is the more lasting good of which he is in search, and for the sake of which he calls in question the value of the pleasure for the time most attractive in imagination?

224. To answer these questions in the negative may seem unwarrantable, if for no other reason, in presence of the deliberate judgment of so many enlightened persons who tell us that their only conception—the only conception which seems to them possible—of a true good is just that of a greatest sum of pleasures; that when they decide against the pursuit of a particular pleasure as not good on the whole, they simply mean that its enjoyment would be incompatible with the attainment of a larger sum of pleasures which it is open to them to enjoy. Can we doubt that such persons really form their judgments of the good as they suppose themselves to do; and is it not absurd to deny that those conceptions of the true good, which we inherit and which affect our consciences, *may* at any rate have been formed in the same way?

Now undoubtedly, if we must accept as true the account which most persons, under the influence of the current philosophy, give of the ultimate moral idea which actuates them; if we are to admit that well-being means for them a sum of pleasures, the highest well-being the largest possible sum of pleasures; it is useless further to argue the question before us. But there are reasons for not accepting that account. It rests on a supposition that all desire is for pleasure. This supposition chiefly commends itself, as has been previously pointed out, through the confusion into which we readily fall, in reflecting on any desire, between the object of which the idea excites the desire, and the pleasure we anticipate in the fulfilment of the desire—the pleasure, as it is sometimes called, of success. If an ordinarily unselfish man, unaccustomed to precise analysis of mental experiences, is appealed to by a Hedonistic philosopher to say whether in calm moments of reflection, when exempt from the pressure of appetite or of any particular passion, the good for which he finds himself wishing is not always pleasure— not any single pleasure, but a quantity of pleasures more or less distinctly articulated in thought, or perhaps simply pleasurable existence—he is apt to assent. He does so because, being interested in certain objects, and being aware that, when he reflects on his interests, he often says to himself 'how pleasant it will be when such or such an object is attained,' he mistakes the desire to satisfy himself in the attainment of the objects for a desire to satisfy himself with the pleasure of the attainment.

No doubt this pleasure of attainment is one which, upon self-reflection, the man really contemplates himself as enjoying; there is really a desire for it which co-operates with his various interests; but it could not take the place of the objects of these various interests without destroying the interests and with them its own possibility. This however does not prevent men who are in fact deeply absorbed in the pursuit of objects other than pleasures from being argued into the belief that, because they are conscious of anticipating pleasures of attainment, pleasure is the object of their pursuit. The further step is then easily taken of interpreting this pleasure as made up of those several pleasures to which, through the confusion above noticed, it has come to be supposed that all desires are directed. Thus we settle down into the notion that our motive principles are on the one hand particular passions, each excited by imagination of some pleasure or some pain, and on the other a deliberate desire for a good made up of as many particular desired pleasures as, after deduction for incidental pains, we deem ourselves capable of obtaining. This deliberate desire is taken to be the source of our disapproval of certain pleasures as not good on the whole, because not compatible with the acquisition of that larger sum of pleasures which is more deliberately desired.

225. As to the mistake of supposing all desires to have some pleasure or other for their object, enough has perhaps been said. But writers who have fully recognised this mistake, who have most strenuously asserted that particular desires terminate upon their objects, and that those objects in many cases are not pleasures, have adhered to the notion that the deliberate desire for what is good on the whole is equivalent to desire for a greatest possible quantity of pleasure. They have indeed generally expressed this as a desire for happiness, but they have also been generally ready to accept the identification of happiness with a sum of pleasures, of greatest happiness with a greatest sum of pleasures. It might perhaps have been otherwise if the convenient ambiguity attaching to the term 'happiness' did not tend to hide from us the difficulty of dealing upon this theory with that desire for the good of others, the genuineness of which we should be slow to dispute. Clearly a desire for the good of others, though that greatest good be understood to consist for them in pleasures, is not a desire for pleasure on the part of the person who entertains it, unless he desires the production of pleasure to others, not as an end, but as a means to his own. Now that benevolence is not to be considered as a desire for any pleasure to oneself, other than that of doing the benevolent act, is one of the few points—and it speaks well for the improvement of our time that it should be so—on which moralists seem to have come almost to an agreement. But to consider it a desire for the pleasure of doing the benevolent act is to fall into the fallacy of supposing a desire to be excited by imagination of its own satisfaction—a fallacy from which such writers as Butler and Hutcheson, and in recent years Mr. H. Sidgwick[1], have kept themselves clear.

226. A desire for the good of others, then, though it be

[1] Methods of Ethics, Book I. chap. iv.

a desire to produce pleasure in them, is not a desire for pleasure. We may, if we like, apply both to it and to the desire for our own true well-being the common designation 'desire for happiness;' but, if the desire for our own well-being consists in a desire for a sum of pleasures, we are applying the common designation to the two kinds of desire in absolutely different senses. We shall have to take it that there are two co-ordinate principles, 'Benevolence' and 'Reasonable Self-Love,' alike, according to the phraseology of the last century, in being calm or settled or deliberate principles, but wholly different as desires in respect of the objects to which they are directed, since one is, while the other is not, a desire for pleasure ; and we shall have to suppose that these serve indifferently as grounds for moral approbation and disapprobation, the reason for rejecting desired pleasures as not good on the whole being sometimes that they are incompatible with the object sought by Benevolence, sometimes that they are incompatible with that sought by Reasonable Self-Love.

That our practical judgments as to the true good rest on two such different principles is a conclusion which, once clearly faced, every enquirer would gladly escape, as repugnant both to the philosophic craving for unity, and to that ideal of 'singleness of heart' which we have been accustomed to associate with the highest virtue. The method of escaping it generally favoured by Utilitarians involves the fallacy, already sufficiently noticed, of supposing benevolent desires to have for their object the pleasure of their own satisfaction. This fallacy once discerned, the conclusion can only be avoided either by a bolder denial of the existence of a deliberate and disinterested benevolence than we are generally prepared for—by a return, in short, to the position of Hobbes—or by reconsideration of the view that 'Reasonable Self-Love,' desire for one's own true good, is equivalent to desire for a sum of pleasures.

227. Such a reconsideration is forced upon us from a different quarter so soon as we take account of the fact, already noticed, that pleasures do not admit of being accumulated in enjoyment. A man who is enjoying a pleasure for the thousandth time *has* no more pleasure, however much more an enumerator might reckon him to have *had*—nay, if novelty adds a charm to pleasure, he has less — than the man who is enjoying it for the first time. We may talk, if we like, of a larger sum of pleasures as more of a good than a less sum, of a largest possible sum as the greatest or highest good, but in doing so we are bound to remember, if we would not be misled by words, that we are talking of 'goods' of which, from the nature of the case, there can be neither possession nor any approach to possession. Now when any one is deliberately judging what is for his good on the whole, in the light of the experience presupposed by such a judgment, it would seem that he can scarcely help being alive to this state of the case and being affected by it in his judgment. Reflection upon the perishing nature of pleasures suggests itself to every one unsophisticated in his 'moralising' and unbiassed by philosophical systems. It is traceable in literature as far back as the literature of reflection extends. It would be far more reasonable to suppose that it was the source of the deliberate quest for something good on the whole, than that it could be set aside in such a quest. And if it cannot be set aside, it must effectually prevent the man who has practically asked himself what it is that can satisfy him, from seeking a sum of pleasures, even 'the greatest possible,' in expectation that it can satisfy or tend to satisfy him ; in other words, under the persuasion that it is that truly or ultimately desirable object for the sake of which a particular desired pleasure should be rejected. He cannot really look forward to any millionth repetition of a pleasant feeling as bringing him nearer to the satisfaction of himself than he was the first time the pleasure was felt. It will not at all follow that such a person, if challenged by a philosopher to say what the ultimate good is, of which the idea actuates him, might not, under pressure of the impossibility of adequately defining it, be drawn into accepting an account of it as.

a greatest sum of pleasures.   The action of the idea in him,
however, is not dependent on the account he may give of it.
The question is whether the idea, as it really actuates him,
can be the idea of a sum of pleasures, of which he must be
aware—and have become aware before the idea could consciously actuate him—that each perishes in the enjoyment.
To the present writer it seems that this question, once
plainly put, carries a negative answer with it.

228. ' But why,' it may be objected, ' should the fact that
a greatest sum of pleasures cannot be enjoyed as a sum, *i.e.*
all at once, prevent a man from wishing to enjoy this greatest
sum, as it may be enjoyed, successively, and from regarding
this successive enjoyment as the object supremely desirable?'
Now undoubtedly, as already admitted, a man may think of
himself as enjoying many pleasures in succession, may desire
their successive enjoyment and, reflecting on his desire,
esteem the enjoyment a good.   But it is not the pleasures
as a sum that attract him.   He cannot imagine them as
a sum, for the imagination of pleasure must always be of
some specific feeling of pleasure, which must have ceased to
possess the imagination before another can possess it.   What
affects him is the thought of himself as capable of a state of
continuous enjoyable existence, and on the contrary as liable
to a like continuity of pain.   The consideration how many
pleasures there will be in the course of the enjoyable existence, what their sum will amount to, does not at all enter
into or affect the thought of it as desirable.   If he judges
a pleasure, which now attracts him, to be not truly a good
on the ground of its incompatibility with ulterior pleasure, it
is not because he presents to himself two possible sums of
pleasure—one as the result would be if the pleasure now
attracting him were enjoyed, the other as it would be if that
pleasure were forgone—and pronounces the latter the larger.
It is because he believes the pleasure which he disapproves
to entail an unnecessary breach in the enjoyable existence,
which he wishes for without reference to any sum of pleasures
that an enumerator might find it to contain.

This, we say, is the case *if* a particular imagined pleasure is 'in a calm hour' condemned on account of its known incompatibility with ulterior pleasure, which must mean not any imagined pleasure but a conceived succession of pleasures. But while not denying that an attractive pleasure *may* be disapproved on this account, we could not admit that the ordinary reference of a healthy moral man to his own true happiness, as a reason for rejecting present pleasure, was to be thus explained. If it were, it would not have much effect upon conduct. The thought of oneself as in a state of enjoyable existence, if it were not a thought of anything else than this, could scarcely countervail the attraction of an imagined pleasure, here and now intensely desired. An imagination of pain might be effectual for the purpose, but hardly a thought of pleasure, which is not an imagination of any pleasure in particular. In truth a man's reference to his own true happiness is a reference to the objects which chiefly interest him, and has its controlling power on that account. More strictly, it is a reference to an ideal state of well-being, a state in which he shall be satisfied; but the objects of the man's chief interests supply the filling of that ideal state. The idea of such a state, indeed, neither is, nor is conceived as being, fully realisable by us. The objects of which we contemplate the attainment as necessary to its fulfilment are not contemplated as completely fulfilling it. In our contemplation of them as truly good the forecast of an indefinable Better is always present. But in any consideration of true happiness which is other than the vague discontent of the sated or baffled voluptuary, the consciousness of objects which we are seeking to realise, of ideas to which we are trying to give effect, holds the first place. Just because we wish for the attainment of such objects, we are unhappy till we attain them; and thus, owing to the difficulty of mentally articulating them, we are apt to lump them in our thoughts as happiness. But they do not consist in pleasures. The ideas of them, which we are seeking to realise, are not ideas of pleasures. Though we may look forward to our life in attaining them, or when they are attained, as a pleasant one—and certainly we cannot look forward to it as otherwise — this anticipation is quite secondary. It is only brought into distinct consciousness. if at all, during intervals of relaxed energy or under the pressure of an argumentative Hedonist. In short, it is the realisation of those objects in which we are mainly interested, not the succession of enjoyments which we shall experience in realising them, that forms the definite content of our idea of true happiness, so far as it has such content at all.

229. Our conclusion then is that it is a misinterpretation of consciousness, arising in a manner not inexplicable, to regard the idea of a truer or higher good, with which the good of any particular pleasure or the gratification of any particular passion may be contrasted—an idea necessary to the capacity for moral judgment—as equivalent or reducible to the idea of a larger sum of pleasures enjoyable by the person entertaining the idea. In the mind at least of those persons over whom the idea has any controlling power, its filling is supplied by ideal objects to which they are seeking to give reality, and of which the realisation forms their prevailing interest. Such an ideal object [1], for example, is the welfare of a family. In those forms of human life which we can know, either from the intercourse of present society or from the record of the past, this object has probably had the largest share in filling up the idea of true or permanent good. As a man reflects—perhaps quite inarticulately—on the transitoriness of the pleasures by imagination of which his desires are from hour to hour excited ; as he asks (practically, if without formal expression) what can satisfy the self which abides throughout and survives those desires ; the thought of the well-being of a family, with which he identifies himself and of which the continuity is as his own, possesses his mind. It is interest in this well-being which forms the most primitive and universal counter-

---

[1] It will be understood that by an ideal object is meant an object present in idea but not yet given in reality.

vailing influence, apart from imagination of pain, to the attraction of imagined pleasures. If not strong enough to prevent such pursuit of pleasures as has been found incompatible with the well-being of a family, it at least awakens self-reproach in the pursuit, a consciousness that it should not be.

Now whatever difficulty there may be in adequately defining this interest—as there must be, for it is an interest which, though fundamentally always the same, is constantly actualising itself in new ways—there is one thing which it clearly is not. It is not, directly or indirectly, an interest, on the part of the person influenced by it, either in winning any particular pleasure, or in securing an enjoyable existence, or in getting as much pleasure as he can. Doubtless in looking forward to a well-being of his family, he thinks of himself as conscious of it and sharing in it, even though he may expect to be 'laid in the grave' before his idea of the family well-being is realised. Every one thus immortalises himself, who looks forward to the realisation of ideal objects, with which on the one hand he identifies himself, and which on the other hand he cannot think of as bounded by his earthly life,—objects in which he thinks of himself as still living when dead. But to suppose, because a man looks forward to a satisfaction of his interest in the well-being of his family and contemplates enjoyment in that satisfaction, that therefore such enjoyment is the object of the interest, would be to repeat the mistake of supposing a desire to be excitable by the idea of its own satisfaction. The fact, if it be a fact, that the man's conception of the well-being of his family is nothing but a conception of it as possessing the means to a sustained succession of pleasures, does not affect the case in this respect. It remains equally true that his desire for the family well-being is absolutely different from a desire for pleasure.

230. There may not be the means of proving that, as a matter of fact, the form in which true good, or good on the whole, was first conceived was that of family well-being. The earliest forms in which the most essential practical ideas have taken effect must always, from the nature of the case, remain beyond the reach of historical investigation. We are warranted however by simple consideration of its nature, in holding that the idea of true good could only become matter of definite consciousness in view of its possible realisation in an object which at once excites a strong interest, and can at the same time be regarded as having the permanence necessary to satisfy the demand arising from a man's involuntary contemplation of his own permanence. The idea of the good, it must be remembered, like all practical ideas, is primarily a demand. It is not derived from observation of what exists but from an inward requirement that something should be ; something that will yield self-satisfaction of the kind that is sought when we think of ourselves as surviving each particular desire and its gratification. It is this requirement or demand that first sets us upon seeking to bring objects into existence, in which some sort of abiding satisfaction may be found ; but it is only in contemplation of these objects as in some measure realised or in process of realisation, that the demand arrives at any clear consciousness of itself, or that it can yield the idea of something as truly good, in contrast with something else that is not so.

231. Now among the objects thus brought into existence by demand for the satisfaction of an abiding self, and of which the contemplation first supplied some definite content to the idea of a true good, it would seem that the most primitive and elementary must have been those that contribute to supply the wants of a family—to keep its members alive and comfortably alive. If it is asked by what warrant we carry back the institution of the family into the life of the most primitive men, we answer that we carry it back no further than the interest in permanent good. From beings incapable of such an interest, even though connected by acts of generation with ourselves, we cannot in any intelligible sense have been developed. They cannot have had any such essential community with ourselves as would be implied in calling them men. But the capacity for such an interest is also the capacity which renders possible the family bond. That determination of an animal organism by a self-conscious principle, which makes a man and is presupposed by the interest in permanent good, carries with it a certain appropriation by the man to himself of the beings with whom he is connected by natural ties, so that they become to him as himself and in providing for himself he provides for them. Projecting himself into the future as a permanent subject of possible well-being or ill-being—and he must so project himself in seeking for a permanent good—he associates his kindred with himself. It is this association that neutralises the effect which the anticipation of death must otherwise have on the demand for permanent good. At a stage of intellectual development when any theories of immortality would be unmeaning to them, men have already, in the thought of a society of which the life is their own life but which survives them, a medium in which they carry themselves forward beyond the limits of animal existence.

232. Thus we conclude that, in the earliest stages of human consciousness in which the idea of a true or permanent good could lead any one to call in question the good of an immediately attractive pleasure, it was already an idea of a social good—of a good not private to the man himself, but good for him as a member of a community. We conclude that it must have been so, because it is a man's thought of himself as permanent that gives rise to the idea of such a good, and because the thought of himself as permanent is inseparable from an identification of himself with others, in whose continued life he contemplates himself as living; and because further, as a consequence of this, the objects which the effort to realise this thought brings into being, and in contemplation of which the idea of permanent good passes from the more blindly operative to the more clearly conscious stage, are arrangements of life, or habits of action, or applications of the forces and products of nature, calculated to contribute to a common well-being. Hence the distinction commonly supposed to exist between considerate Benevolence and reasonable Self-Love, as co-ordinate principles on which moral approbation is founded, is a fiction of philosophers.

In saying this we must not be understood either to be denying that reasonable Self-Love is a source of moral approbation, or to be seeking to reduce Benevolence in any way to desire for pleasure to oneself. The meaning is that the distinction of good for self and good for others has never entered into that idea of a true good on which moral judgments are founded. It must have been held to do so, no doubt (except upon the selfish hypothesis), if the actuating idea of a true good, as for oneself, had been founded on desire for a sum of pleasures ; since a desire for pleasure, though it may be balanced by a desire to produce pleasure, and though the two desires may suggest in certain cases the same course of outward action, must always be absolutely different from it as a motive. But in fact the idea of a true good as for oneself is not an idea of a series of pleasures to be enjoyed by oneself. It is ultimately or in principle an idea of satisfaction for a self that abides and contemplates itself as abiding, but which can only so contemplate itself in identification with some sort of society ; which can only look forward to a satisfaction of itself as permanent, on condition that it shall also be a satisfaction of those in community with whom alone it can think of itself as continuing to live. For practical purposes, or as it ordinarily affects a man, it is an idea of an order of life, more or less established, but liable to constant interference from actions prompted by passion or desire for pleasure ; an order in the maintenance and advancement of which he conceives his permanent well-being to consist. This well-being he doubtless conceives as his own, but that he should conceive it as exclusively his own—his own in any sense in which it is not equally and coincidentally a well-being of others—would be incompatible with the fact that it is only as living in community, as sharing the life of others, as incorporated in the continuous being of a family or nation, of a state or a church, that he can sustain himself in that thought of his own permanence to which the thought of permanent well-being is correlative. His own permanent well-being he thus necessarily presents to himself as a social well-being. The rule of action, which a consideration of this well-being suggests, may sometimes forbid the indulgence of generous impulses, as it will constantly forbid the pursuit of an attractive pleasure ; but between it and the rule of considerate Benevolence there can never be a conflict, for they are one and the same rule, founded on one and the same quest for a self-satisfaction which shall abide, but which no man can contemplate as abiding except so far as he identifies himself with a society whose well-being is to him as his own.

233. After all this argumentation, however, which may already seem too prolix, we may be sure that the old objection will here return. This permanent well-being, what is it—what is it conceived as being by the person who desires it—but a succession of pleasures, or of states in which pleasure predominates over pain, whether it is of himself or of others that the man thinks as enjoying this succession ? We can best finally answer this question by gathering into a summary form the view which it is sought to oppose to that suggested by the question. But before doing so it will be well also to put in a final 'caveat' against two misapprehensions, which may be lurking in our minds when we put the question. Though we answered it in the affirmative, we should be none the nearer to a reduction of the moral life to an origin in mere succession of feelings. As has already been pointed out [§ 222], a desire for one's own permanent well-being, though the well-being looked forward to consisted merely in a succession of pleasures, would still be quite a different thing, would imply a consciousness of quite a different nature, from desire excited by an imagined pleasure. Nor, if we answer it in the affirmative, will any recognition of sympathy bring us nearer to an identification of self-regarding and 'altruistic' motives. It is clear that desire for a well-being as consisting in a succession of pleasures to oneself, is quite different from desire for a well-being that consists in a succession of pleasures to others. The fact that one man may be pleased or pained by the knowledge of another's pleasure or pain does not alter the fact that each man's pleasure or pain is private to himself. Desires are determined by their objects; and desire for pleasure, having an absolutely different object, is an absolutely different desire from desire for the production of pleasure to others. If therefore a man's desire for his own true well-being is essentially a desire that he may enjoy a succession of pleasures, and that for the well-being of others a desire to convey to them a succession of pleasures, the two desires are opposite, though perhaps reconcilable principles of action, and we must fall back on the view, which we have been seeking to set aside, of the co-ordination, as distinct from the identity, of Benevolence and Reasonable Self-Love.

234. This premised, to the question, What is the well-being which in a calm hour we desire but a succession of pleasures? we reply as follows. The ground of this desire is a demand for an abiding satisfaction of an abiding self. In a succession of pleasures there can be no such satisfaction, nor in the longest prolongation of the succession any nearer approach to it than in the first pleasure enjoyed. If a man, therefore, under the influence of the spiritual demand described, were to seek any succession of pleasures as that which would satisfy the demand, he would be under a delusion. Such a delusion may be possible, but we are not to suppose that it takes place because many persons, through a mistaken analysis of their inner experience, affirm that they have no idea of well-being but as a succession of pleasures. The demand for an abiding self-satisfaction has led to an ordering of life in which some permanent provision is made, better or worse, for the satisfaction of those interests which are not interests in the procuring of pleasure, but which may be described most generally as interests in the development of our faculties, and in the like development of those for whom we care.

When a man 'sits down in a calm hour' to consider what his permanent well-being consists in, what it is that in desiring it he really desires, it is not indeed to be supposed that he traces the desire back to its ultimate source in his self-objectifying personality, or that he thinks of its object in the abstract form of that which will satisfy the demand arising from such a personality. But, if unbiassed either by particular passions or by philosophical prepossessions, he will identify his well-being with an order of life which that demand has brought into existence. The thought of his well-being will be to him the thought of himself as living in the successful pursuit of various interests which the order of society – taking the term in its widest sense—has determined for him ; interests ranging, perhaps, from provision for his family to the improvement of the public health or to the production of a system of philosophy. The constituents of the contemplated well-being will be the objects of those various interests, objects (*e. g.* the provision for a family or the sanitation of a town) in process of realisation, which, when realised, take their place as permanent contributions to an abiding social good. In them therefore the man who carries himself forward in thought along the continued life of a family or a nation, a state or a church, anticipates a lasting and accumulating possession, as he cannot do in successive enjoyments. In them he can think of himself as really coming nearer to an absolute good. Just so far as he is interested in such objects, he must indeed anticipate pleasure in their realisation, but the objects, not the pleasure, form the actuating content of his idea of true well-being. A transfer of his interest from the objects to the pleasure would be its destruction.

235. If this answer is accepted to the question, what it is that we desire in desiring our own true or permanent well-being, it would seem that we have already answered the question, what it is that we desire in desiring the true well-being of others. It is the same common well-being, the same good of a society which we also desire as our own. No doubt, there are generous impulses consisting in desires to convey pleasures, simply as such, to others, or to lessen their pains. These are as little to be ignored as they are to be identified with desires for pleasures to oneself. But the desire for the well-being, whether as of others or as of oneself, is no more to be identified with such generous impulses, with which it may very well conflict, than those impulses that are excited by the imagination of pleasure. The objects of which a man anticipates the realisation in looking forward to such well-being, are objects, as we have seen, which he necessarily thinks of as realised for a society no less than for himself, for himself only as a member of a society. The opposition of self and others does not enter into the consideration of a well-being so constituted. Generous impulses and desires for pleasures may indeed co-operate with the desire for it, though never equivalent to that desire, and may do so in different degrees in different cases. The objects most prominent in a man's working idea of true well-being will vary, no doubt, according to circumstances and his idiosyncrasy. To revert to instances previously given, in one case the sanitation of a town, in another the composition of a book on an abstruse subject, may hold the largest place in a man's mind when he sets himself to enquire what in particular forms the content of the idea of true well-being, as he individually is actuated by it. In the former case it can be understood that the impulse to convey pleasures to particular persons, or to relieve their pains, might effectually co-operate with the idea as it actuates the individual, while it scarcely could do so in the latter case. In both cases, again, anticipated pleasures of achievement might stimulate the work which interest in a well-being not constituted by pleasures initiates and directs, though that they should become the main objects of interest would be fatal to the work. But however the idea of a true good may vary in the particular aspect which it presents to the individual according to the special nature of his higher interests, and in whatever measures impulsive benevolence or any desire for pleasure may respectively further its operation in him, it remains true that, in its actuation of the individual, no less than in that ordering of society which at once is effected through that actuation of individuals and in turn conditions it, the idea does not admit of the distinction between good for self and good for others. As the source of moral action and of moral judgment, it has equally to control, and in controlling must be equally independent of, the desire for pleasure and the desire to please.

236. But granting that in a man's idea of well-being as true or permanent there is such an identification of his own and others' well-being, he must still think of it as standing in some definite relation to others as to himself. He may think of their true good as also his and of his as also theirs, but how, it will be asked, does he conceive of the true good for others, if not as their happiness, *i.e.* as the most unbroken succession of pleasures possible for them? We answer that the happiness which, under influence of the idea of permanent good, a man seeks for others is of the same kind as the happiness which, under influence of the same idea, he seeks for himself. We have seen that true happiness, as he conceives it for himself, consists in the realisation of the objects of various interests by which he is possessed— interests of which he is only capable through self-identification with a society. True happiness, as he conceives it for others, consists in the realisation for them of the same objects. His own interest in these objects carries with it an ascription of a like interest to others, and in the realisation of the objects he anticipates a happiness to them, just as he anticipates it to himself. Now the interest, as he experiences it in himself, is an interest, not in pleasure, but in the objects—these not being pleasures; and what he seeks to procure for others is a satisfaction of a like interest, which is not an interest in pleasures. He seeks to help them in attaining objects which he supposes to be common to them with him, and these objects, not being pleasures in his case, cannot be pleasures in theirs. In the realisation of the objects there must be pleasure for the others, on supposition of their interest in the objects, as for himself, and in anticipating their realisation of the objects he will doubtless also anticipate the pleasure incidental to it; but it is primarily the objects which he seeks to help them in gaining, the pleasure only as incidental to the attainment of those particular objects. Pleasures incidental to the attainment of other objects, though equally pleasures, he would have no interest in conveying to them. It is a *true* happiness which he seeks for them, and the truth of their happiness depends on the nature of the desired objects, not themselves pleasures, to the realisation of which it is incidental.

237. By way of illustration, we may again revert to the instance of a man supremely interested in the sanitation of a town. Such a man would naturally be described as devoted to the true happiness of his fellow-creatures. No doubt his great object is to help the men whom he sees about him to live more happily, and, absorbed in his work, he is not likely to analyse very accurately what it is that he presents to himself when he thinks of their living more happily. It is not at all essential that he should do so. If in confusion or haste he pronounces that the happiness he is seeking for them consists merely in a succession of pleasures, the mistake is probably of little practical importance. It matters less than if he made the same speculative mistake in regard to the end which he seeks for himself. A theory that his object for himself was pleasure—the pleasure, as perhaps he might say, of successful work—might strengthen the pleasure-seeking tendency, by which such a man, like all the rest of us, must really be affected, till there might be danger of its weakening or supplanting the interest which is, in fact, the condition of his pleasure in his work. A misinterpretation of the happiness which he seeks for others can have no such mischievous effect. Even if, through the notion that his motive was desire for the mere pleasure of others, it really became so, he would not have become a pleasure-seeker. He would have become a practically less wise and useful, but not a selfish man.

None the less, however, such a beneficent person would be really misinterpreting the object which mainly moves him in so describing it. It is not pleasure, as such, to be enjoyed by other persons, that he seeks to bring about, but an improvement of the persons, of which pleasure is the incident and the sign. He conceives them, like himself, as having objects which it is their vocation to realise, which health is the condition of their realising, and which form part of one great social end, the same for himself as for them. What this end is he conceives, like the rest of us, very dimly, though, but for the power which the idea of there being such an end exercises over him, not only directly but indirectly through those institutions of society which are its product, he would not live the life which he does. Pressed to give an account of it, he readily in his description puts the pleasure, which is the incident of realisation, in place of that realisation of worthy objects to which he is in fact seeking to help his neighbours. He speaks as if that 'happiness' of others which he is seeking to promote were merely pleasure irrespectively of the conditions of the pleasure, whereas in truth it is a fulfilment of capabilities which, without clear analysis of what they are, but on the strength of his own experience, he assigns to the others.

238. There are two questions, however, of which the consideration might make him more clearly aware what his mind on the matter really is; might convince him that, not pleasure as such, but the attainment of objects other than pleasures though involving pleasure in their attainment, is the end to which he seeks to help other men. Let him ask himself whether he can look upon the value of the pleasure, which he supposes himself to be labouring to produce, as depending simply on its amount; whether he does not, for others as for himself, distinguish between higher and lower

pleasures according to the nature of the pursuit out of which
they arise, or according to the state of mind to which they
are relative. If he does, it must follow that it is not pleasure
as such, or by itself, that he is seeking to produce, but
pleasure as an incident of a life of which the value or
desirability does not consist in its pleasantness. Let him
ask himself, further, whether the ideal end which he seeks
for others as for himself, though it be an end never realised,
is not something in which a permanent satisfaction can be
found ; whether he himself could find true happiness in a
succession of pleasures of which each, having been enjoyed,
leaves him with the consciousness of being no nearer satisfaction than he was before ; whether on the contrary he does
not count it an essential condition of every contribution to
his own true happiness that it should bring him nearer to
the fulfilment of his mission, to a completion of his capacities, as no enjoyment of pleasure can be held to do ; and
whether his final object in working for the true happiness of
others can be to help them to a succession of pleasures,
which would be no contribution to a true happiness as he
seeks it for himself.

239. These considerations might make such a man aware
that his interest in true happiness as for himself, and his
interest in it as for others, are not two interests but one in·
terest, of which the object is not a succession of pleasures
but a fulfilment of itself, a bettering of itself, a realisation of
its capabilities, on the part of the human soul. These
capabilities are not distinctively capabilities of pleasure.
The pleasure of their realisation does not differ as pleasure,
except perhaps in respect of its less intensity, from any
animal enjoyment. They are capabilities of certain kinds
of life and action, of which (as previously explained) no
adequate account can be given till they are attained. Of
what ultimate well-being may be, therefore, we are unable
to say anything but that it must be the complete fulfilment
of our capabilities, even while the idea that there is such an
ultimate well-being may be the guiding idea of our lives.

But of particular forms of life and action we can say that they are better, or contribute more to true well-being than others, because in them there is a further fulfilment of man's capabilities, and therefore a nearer approach to the end in which alone he can find satisfaction for himself.

That interest in a true good which leads us to reject attractive pleasures as pleasures which should not be enjoyed, and to endure repellent pains as pains which should be undergone, is interest in the furtherance of such better forms of life and action—in their furtherance because they are better. The special features of the object in which the true good is sought will vary in different ages and with different persons, according to circumstances and idiosyncrasy. There are circumstances in which it cannot present itself to the individual as anything else than the work of keeping a family comfortably alive, without reference to the well-being of any wider society in which the family is included, or to any other form of family well-being than such as consists in the decent satisfaction of animal wants. From such a form of the interest in true good to one in which it mainly expresses itself in the advancement of some branch of knowledge, or the improvement of the public health, or the endeavour after 'personal holiness,' there may seem to be a great step. But in all its forms the interest has the common characteristic of being directed to an object which is an object for the individual only so far as he identifies himself with a society, and seeks neither an imagined pleasure nor a succession of pleasures, but a bettering of the life which is at once his and the society's.

240. We have dwelt thus at length on the difference between the interest in a true good or permanent well-being in all its forms, and the desire to experience any succession of pleasures, even such a succession as an imaginary enumerator might find to make up the largest possible sum, in order to avoid misapprehension in consideration of the process by which the idea of a true good defines itself and, in defining itself, gives rise to the conception of particular duties. This process, we saw, was really inseparable from that of which the main features have already been considered ; the extension, namely, of the range of persons between whom the good is conceived to be common, and who on this ground recognise equivalent duties to each other. Following out that extension as if it were a separate process, we found that its outcome was the intuition of the educated conscience that the true good must be good for all men, so that no one should seek to gain by another's loss, gain and loss being estimated on the same principle for each. But it had not so far appeared how the conscience is trained in the apprehension of what in particular the good is, and in the consequent imposition on itself of particular duties. This defect was to be made up by considering the gradual determination of the idea of good, which goes along with the growth of the conviction that it is good for all men alike.

We committed ourselves a little way back to the familiar opinion—more likely to find acceptance than many here advanced—that the idea of a true good first took hold of men in the form of a consideration of what was needed to keep the members of a family alive and comfortably alive. Now between a state of mind in which the idea of good is only operative in this form, and one which can at least naturally express itself in the proposition that the only true good is the good will, can there be anything in common ? Is it not idle to attempt to connect them as phases in the operation of a single spiritual principle ? It would be so, no doubt, if interest in provision for the necessities of a family really exhausted the spiritual demand from which it arises. But this is not the case. It must be remembered that provision for the wants of a family, of the kind we are contemplating, cannot have been a merely instinctive process. It cannot have been so, at least, on supposition that it was a ‘process of which we can understand the nature from our own experience, or that it was a stage in the development of the men that we are and know. It would not have had anything in common with the family interests by which we are ourselves influenced, unless it rested not on instinct but on self-consciousness— on a man's projection of himself in thought into a future, as a subject of a possibly permanent satisfaction, to be found in the satisfaction of the wants of the family with which he identifies himself.   Now this power of contemplating himself as possibly coming to be that which he is not, and as so coming to be in and through a society in which he lives a permanent life, is in promise and potency an interest in the bettering of mankind, in the realisation of its capabilities or the fulfilment of its vocation, conceived as an absolutely desirable end.

Between the most primitive and limited form of the interest, as represented by the effort to provide for the future wants of a family, and its most highly generalised form, lie the interests of ordinary good citizens in various elements of a social well-being.   All have a common basis in the demand for abiding self-satisfaction which, according to the theory we have sought to maintain, is yielded by the action of an eternal self-conscious principle in and upon an animal nature. That demand however only gradually exhibits what it has in it to require.   Until life has been so organised as to afford some regular relief from the pressure of animal wants, an interest in what Aristotle calls τὸ εὖ ζῆν, as distinct from τὸ ζῆν[1], cannot emerge.   Yet that primitive organisation of life through which some such relief is afforded, being rational not instinctive, would be impossible without the action of the same self-objectifying principle which in a later stage exhibits itself in the pursuit of ends to which life is a means, as distinct from the pursuit of means of living.   The higher interest is latent in the lower, nor would it be possible to draw a line at which the mere living of the family ceases to be the sole object and its well-being begins to be cared for.

241. But, when a supply of the means of living has been sufficiently secured to allow room for a consideration of the ends of living, what are those ends taken to be?   Can any

---

[1] ' Living well,' or ' well-being,' as distinct from merely ' living.'

such progress be noted in men's conception of them as could justify us in speaking of a development of the idea of duty? If the idea of good were simply equivalent to the idea of a maximum of pleasure, a growth of moral ideas would simply mean a progressive discovery of means to pleasure. A development of the idea of duty, in the sense of a process affecting our conception of the ends of action, there could not be. If on this hypothesis we are to speak of a moral development at all, it can only be in the sense of an increasing enlightenment as to what should be done, in order to an end of which itself the idea undergoes no modification. It is otherwise if the idea of the good is an idea of something which man should become for the sake of becoming it, or in order to fulfil his capabilities and in so doing to satisfy himself. The idea of the good, according to this view, is an idea, if the expression may be allowed, which gradually creates its own filling. It is not an idea like that of any pleasure, which a man retains from an experience that he has had and would like to have again. It is an idea to which nothing that has happened to us or that we can find in existence corresponds, but which sets us upon causing certain things to happen, upon bringing certain things into existence. Acting in us, to begin with, as a demand which is ignorant of what will satisfy itself, it only arrives at a more definite consciousness of its own nature and tendency through reflection on its own creations — on habits and institutions and modes of life which, as a demand not reflected upon, it has brought into being. Moral development then will not be merely progress in the discovery and practice of means to an end which throughout remains the same for the subject of the development. It will imply a progressive determination of the idea of the end itself, as the subject of it, through reflection on that which, under influence of the idea but without adequate reflection upon it, he has done and has become, comes to be more fully aware of what he has it in him to do and to become.

242. Of a moral development in this sense we have

evidence in the result; and we can understand the principle of it; but the stages in the process by which the principle thus unfolds itself remain obscure. As has been already pointed out, such an end as provision for the maintenance of a family, if pursued not instinctively but with consciousness of the end pursued, implies in the person pursuing it a motive quite different from desire either for an imagined pleasure or for relief from want. It implies the thought of a possibly permanent satisfaction, and an effort to attain that satisfaction in the satisfaction of others. Here is already a moral and spiritual, as distinct from an animal or merely natural, interest—an interest in an object which only thought constitutes, an interest in bringing about something that should be, as distinct from desire to feel again a pleasure already felt. But to be actuated by such an interest does not necessarily imply any reflection on its nature; and hence in men under its influence there need not be any conception of a moral as other than a material good. Food and drink, warmth and clothing, may still seem to them to be the only good things which they desire for themselves or for others.

This may probably still be the case with some wholly savage tribes; it may have once been the case with our own ancestors. If it was, of the process by which they emerged from it we know nothing, for they have already emerged from it in the earliest state of mind which has left any record of itself. All that we can say is that an interest moral and spiritual in the sense explained—however unaware of its own nature, however unable to describe itself as directed to other than material objects—must have been at work to bring about the habits and institutions, the standards of praise and blame, which we inherit, even the remotest and most elementary which our investigations can reach. We know further that *if* that interest, even in the form of interest in the mere provision for the material support of a family, were duly reflected upon, those who were influenced by it must have become aware that they had objects independent of the gratification of their animal nature; and, having become aware of this, they could not fail with more or less distinctness to conceive that permanent welfare of the family, which it was their great object to promote, as consisting, at any rate among other things, in the continuance in others of an interest like their own ; in other words, as consisting in the propagation of virtue.

243. When and how and by what degrees this process of reflection may have taken place, we cannot say. It is reasonable to suppose that till a certain amount of shelter had been secured from the pressure of natural wants, it would be impossible. The work of making provision for the family would be too absorbing for a man to ask himself what was implied in his interest in making it, and thus to become aware of there being such a thing as a moral nature in himself and others, or of a moral value as distinct from the value of that which can be seen and touched and tasted. However strong in him the interest in the welfare of his society—which, as we have seen, is essentially a moral interest—until some relief had been won from the constant care of providing for that welfare in material forms, he would have no time to think of any intrinsic value in the persons for whom the provision was made, or in the qualities which enabled it to be made. Somehow or other, however—by what steps we know not— with all peoples that have a history the time of reflection has come, and with it the supervention upon those moral interests that are unconscious of their morality, of an interest in moral qualities as such. An interest has arisen, over and above that in keeping the members of a family or tribe alive, in rendering them persons of a certain kind ; in forming in them certain qualities, not as a means to anything ulterior which the possession of these qualities might bring about, but simply for the sake of that possession ; in inducing in them habits of action on account of the intrinsic value of those habits, as forms of activity in which man achieves what he has it in him to achieve, and so far satisfies himself. There has arisen, in short, a conception of good things of the soul, as having a value distinct from and independent of the good things of the body, if not as the only things truly good, to which all other goodness is merely relative.

Already in the earliest stages of the development of the human soul, of which we have any recorded expression, this distinction is virtually recognised. Such a formal classification as that which Aristotle assumes to be familiar, between τὰ ἐκτὸς ἀγαθά, τὰ περὶ ψυχήν, and τὰ περὶ σῶμα[1], is, of course, only the product of what may be called reflection upon reflection. It is the achievement of men who have not only learnt to recognise and value the spiritual qualities to which material things serve as instruments or means of expression, but have formed the abstract conception of a universe of values which may be exhaustively classified. But independently of such abstract conceptions, we have evidence in the earliest literature accessible to us of the conception and appreciation of impalpable virtues of the character and disposition, standing in no direct relation to the senses or to animal wants— courage, wisdom, fidelity, and the like. The distinction is at least apprehended between the sensible good things that come to a man, or belong or attach to him as from without, and the good qualities of the man. It may be that the latter are chiefly considered in relation to the former, as qualities contributing to the material welfare of a society ; but, though there may be as yet no clear notion of virtue as a pure good in itself independently of anything extraneous that it may obtain, it is understood that prosperity and the desert of prosperity are different things. And the recognition of desert is in itself a recognition of a moral or spiritual good, as distinct from one sensible or material. It is evidence that the moral nature, implied in the interest in a social well-being, has so far reflected on itself as to arrive at moral conceptions.

244. Whenever and wherever, then, the interest in a social good has come to carry with it any distinct idea of social merit—of qualities that make the good member of a family,

[1] External goods, goods of the soul, and goods of the body. *Eth. Nic.* I. viii. 2.

or good tribesman, or good citizen—we have the beginning
of that education of the conscience of which the end is the
conviction that the only true good is to be good.   This
process is properly complementary to that previously analysed,
of which the end was described as the conviction that the true
good is good for all men, and good for them all in virtue of
the same nature and capacity.   The one process is complementary to the other, because the only good in the pursuit
of which there can be no competition of interests, the only
good which is really common to all who may pursue it, is
that which consists in the universal will to be good—in the
settled disposition on each man's part to make the most and
best of humanity in his own person and in the persons of
others.   The conviction of a community of good for all men
can never be really harmonised with our notions of what is
good, so long as anything else than self-devotion to an ideal
of mutual service is the end by reference to which those
notions are formed.

245. In fact we are very far, in our ordinary estimates of
good, whether for ourselves or for others, from keeping such
a standard before us, and just for that reason the conviction
of the community of good for all men, while retaining its
hold on us as an abstract principle, has little positive influence
over our practical judgments.   It is a source of counsels of
perfection which we do not 'see our way' to carrying out.
It makes itself felt in certain prohibitions, *e.g.* of slavery, but
it has no such effect on the ordering of life as to secure for
those whom we admit that it is wrong to use as chattels much
real opportunity of self-development.   They are left to sink
or swim in the stream of unrelenting competition, in which
we admit that the weaker has not a chance.   So far as negative
rights go—rights to be let alone—they are admitted to membership of civil society, but the good things to which the pursuits
of society are in fact directed turn out to be no good things
for them.   Civil society may be, and is, founded on the idea
of there being a common good, but that idea in relation to
the less favoured members of society is in effect unrealised,

and it is unrealised because the good is being sought in objects which admit of being competed for. They are of such a kind that they cannot be equally attained by all. The success of some in obtaining them is incompatible with the success of others.   Until the object generally sought as good comes to be a state of mind or character of which the attainment, or approach to attainment, by each is itself a contribution to its attainment by every one else, social life must continue to be one of war—a war, indeed, in which the neutral ground is constantly being extended and which is itself constantly yielding new tendencies to peace, but in which at the same time new vistas of hostile interests, with new prospects of failure for the weaker, are as constantly opening.

CHAPTER V.

D. *The Greek and the Modern Conceptions of Virtue.*

246. OUR next business will be to consider more in detail how that gradual spiritualisation or dematerialisation (in the sense explained) of the idea of true good, through which alone it can come to answer the inward demand which is its source, exhibits itself in the accepted standards of virtue and in the duties which the candid conscience recognises.   The conception of virtue is the conception of social merit as founded on a certain sort of character or habit of will.   Every form of virtue arises from the effort of the individual to satisfy himself with some good conceived as true or permanent, and it is only as common to himself with a society that the individual can so conceive of a good.   He must in some way identify himself with others in order to conceive himself as the subject of a good which can be opposed to such as passes with his own gratification.   Thus both the practice of virtue and the current standard of virtue, which on the one hand presupposes the practice and on the other reacts upon and sustains it, have a history corresponding to the gradual development and deter- mination of the idea of what social good consists in.

The virtue which is practised and esteemed with reference to a common well-being, constituted by such good things as, according to the distinction above noticed, would fall under the head of ' external ' or ' bodily goods,' has indeed an ele- ment of identity with the virtue practised or esteemed with reference to a well-being of which the virtue itself is an integral element, but has also an important difference from it.   The identity between the two kinds of virtue consists in the fact that the good to which each is relative is a *common* good and is desired as such.   In both cases the virtue rests upon an interest which is effectually distinguished from any desire for pleasure, from any egoistic passion, by being directed to an object which the individual presents to himself as common to him with others and as desirable on that account. The difference lies in the degree of truth and adequacy with which the common good is conceived in one case as compared with the other.

When the end with reference to which social merit is judged of is merely some form of material well-being, the moral effort is being directed to an end of merely relative value as if it were of absolute value. That effort rests, as we have seen, on the inward demand for a true or abiding self-satisfaction, and this is not to be found in the possession of means to a succession of pleasures any more than in the succession itself, not in the possession of anything which one man or group of men can possess to the exclusion of another. A common good conceived as consisting in such possession is inadequately conceived—conceived in a manner which must ultimately lead to the self-defeat of the moral effort— and the virtue directed by the conception, though it has the root of identity, just pointed out, with a higher virtue, is so far inferior. Considered merely as 'self-devotion' it may be on a level with the highest virtue. There may be as genuine self-devotion in the act of the barbarian warrior who gives up his life that his tribe may win a piece of land from its neighbours, as in that of the missionary who dies in carrying the gospel to the heathen. But it is a falsely abstract view of virtue to take no account of the end in pursuit of which the self is devoted. The real value of the virtue rises with the more full and clear conception of the end to which it is directed, as a character not a good fortune, as a fulfilment of human capabilities from within not an accession of good things from without, as a function not a possession. The progress of mankind in respect of the standard and practice of virtue has lain in such a development of the conception of its end.

247. We cannot so write without being reminded of the

famous opening of Kant's ' Foundation of the Metaphysic of
Morals,'—' Nothing can be conceived in the world, or even
out of it, which can be called good without qualification, but
a Good Will.' In describing the development in question,
however, as a growth of the conviction that the only unconditional good is a good will, and a consequent more definite
reference of virtue to this unconditional good as its end, we
run a risk of misapprehension. Can it be intended, the
reader may ask, that no action is morally good, or directed
as it should be, unless the object of the doer is to promote
goodness or to become good? Has this been the object with
reference to which, as a matter of fact, the habits and dispositions ordinarily reputed virtuous have come to be so
reputed? If the ultimate dictum of the enlightened conscience is to be that, just as according to St. Paul 'whatsoever
is not of faith is sin,' so no action is morally good unless
done for the sake of its goodness, shall we not have to make
out some wholly new διαγραφή or ' table ' of the virtues, incapable of natural adjustment to the actual usage of our
terms of praise and blame? Is it not more rational to say
with Hume that 'no action can be virtuous, or morally good,
unless there be in human nature some motive to produce it,
distinct from the sense of its morality'?[1]

The formula quoted from Kant is certainly liable to be
understood in a way which challenges these objections. The
good will may be taken to mean a will possessed by some
abstract idea of goodness or of moral law ; and, if such
possession were possible at all, except perhaps during

---

[1] Treatise on Human Nature, Book III. Part II. § 1. The ground
for the proposition in the text is thus put by Hume in the sequel :
' It is a plain fallacy to say, that a virtuous motive is requisite to
render an action honest, and at the same time that a regard to the
honesty is the motive of the action. We can never have a regard to
the virtue of an action, unless the action be antecedently virtuous.
No action can be virtuous but so far as it proceeds from a virtuous
motive. A virtuous motive therefore must precede the regard to the
virtue ; and 'tis impossible that the virtuous motive and the regard to
the virtue can be the same.'

moments of special spiritual detachment from the actualities of life, it would amount to a paralysis of the will for all effectual application to great objects of human interest. It would no longer be the will of the good workman, the good father, or the good citizen. But it is not thus that we understand the good will. The principle which it is here sought to maintain is that the perfection of human character—a perfection of individuals which is also that of society, and of society which is also that of individuals—is for man the only. object of absolute or intrinsic value; that, this perfection consisting in a fulfilment of man's capabilities according to the divine idea or plan of them, we cannot know or describe in detail what it is except so far as it has been already attained; but that the supreme condition of any progress towards its attainment is the action in men, under some form or other, of an interest in its attainment as a governing interest or will; and that the same interest—not in abstraction from other interests, but as an organising influence upon and among them—must be active in every character which has any share in the perfection spoken of or makes any approach to it, since this perfection, being that of an agent who is properly an object to himself, cannot lie in any use that is made of him, but only in a use that he makes of himself.

248. We hold that in fact the estimation of virtue, the award of praise and blame, has always had reference to man himself, not to anything adventitious to man, as the object of ultimate value from which the value of any virtue was derived. In those primitive conditions of society, in which attention was so necessarily concentrated on the simple maintenance of life that there was no room for the virtues of culture and reflection to develope, we have no reason to doubt that it was a contemplation of possible persons who should exist in the family which gave the family interest its real meaning to those who were actuated by it; just as now, to the poor person whose waking hours are spent in the struggle to keep his family respectable, it is not any abstraction of the family, but the contemplation of sons and daughters, as persons living decent lives in the future, that is the moving influence. The primitive virtue that meant merely valour in the struggle for a life of which others were to share the benefit had yet its animating principle in the idea of something which the valorous man and the others, in and for themselves, were to become. As the horizon of man's possibilities expands upon the view, as new forms of social merit relative to the fulfilment of those capabilities come to be recognised, the conception of virtue becomes proportionately complex. With an Athenian in the period of the bloom of Hellas, the term which we can only render 'virtue' was apparently used for any eminent faculty exercised in any of the regions of human achievement[1]—regions scarcely less wide and various then than now—so that Aristotle found it necessary to distinguish 'intellectual virtues' from those of habit and character. But however discrepant may seem to us to have been the kinds of excellence or ability that were alike spoken of as the 'virtue' of men, however little they may have been affected by any conception of moral law, of any duty owed by man to God or his neighbour, as such, they were still dependent both for their estimation and for their practice on the conception of intrinsic value, as lying not in anything that might happen to a man, in his pleasure or his good fortune, but in what he might do and might become. Virtue was a δύναμις εὐεργετική, a faculty of beneficence[2]. The range of recognised beneficence was wide, as the range of capabilities of which men were becoming conscious was wide. There was a 'virtue' to be exhibited in handicraft no less than in the functions of a magistrate or citizen-soldier or head of a family; but it was some interest in the achievement by men of what they had it in them to do, in their becoming the best they had it in them to become, that at once governed the estimation of virtue in all these cases and inspired or sustained the practice.

249. There were ages, no doubt, in which this interest,

---

[1] Thuc. I. xxxiii. 2 ; II. xl. 6 (Arnold's note); Arist. Rhet. I. ix. 2.
[2] Arist. *loc. cit.*

though active enough, took little account of itself ; ages in which the question was never raised how far the forms of action which commonly excited praise were really co-operative with each other, or really contributory to the end which was being pursued with little reflection on its nature.   When and how the period of reflection is reached, what are the conditions which enable some nations to reach it while others apparently do not, we do not know ; but when it is reached, there arises a quest for some definite and consistent conception of the main ends of human achievement.   Is there some one direction, common to all the forms of activity esteemed as virtuous, which explains and justifies that estimation ?   This question, it is to be observed, is in its effect by no means merely a speculative one.   In the process of bringing into clear and harmonious consciousness the nature of ends previously pursued under the influence of some idea of value which could give no account of itself, the incompatibility of some of these ends with others becomes apparent, and the possibility suggests itself of so methodising life as to avoid the misdirection of activity and keep it to channels in which it may really contribute to the one end of supreme value, however that may be conceived.   Hence along with the conviction of the unity of virtue, which finds so clear and strong an expression in the Greek philosophers, we find an attempt both to reform the current estimation of the several practices and dispositions counted virtuous, and to introduce a systematic order of living for individuals and communities, corresponding to the idea of the unity of the end.

The habit of derogation from the uses of 'mere philosophy,' common alike to Christian advocates and the professors of natural science, has led us too much to ignore the immense practical service which Socrates and his followers rendered to mankind.   From them in effect comes the connected scheme of virtues and duties within which the educated conscience of Christendom still moves, when it is impartially reflecting on what ought to be done.   Religious teachers have no doubt affected the hopes and fears which actuate us in the pursuit of virtue or rouse us from its neglect. Religious societies have both strengthened men in the performance of recognised duties, and taught them to recognise relations of duty towards those whom they might otherwise have been content to treat as beyond the pale of such duties; but the articulated scheme of what the virtues and duties are, in their difference and in their unity, remains for us now in its main outlines what the Greek philosophers left it.

250. In their Ethical teaching, however, the greatest of the Greek philosophers—those to whom Christendom owes, not indeed its highest moral inspiration, but its moral categories, its forms of practical judgment—never professed to be inventors. They did not claim to be prophets of new truth, but exponents of principles on which the good citizen, if he thought the matter out, would find that he had already been acting. They were seeking a clearer view of the end or good towards which the βίος πολιτικὸς, the citizen-life, was actually directed. And this conception of their vocation was not less true than, in its superiority to personal self-assertion, it was noble. They were really organs through which reason, as operative in men, became more clearly aware of the work it had been doing in the creation and maintenance of free social life, and in the activities of which that life is at once the source and the result. In thus becoming aware of its work the same reason through them gave a further reality to itself in human life. The demand for an abiding satisfaction, for a true or permanent good, in action upon the wants and fears and social impulses of men, had yielded the institutions of the family and the state. These again had brought into play certain spiritual dispositions and energies, recognised as beneficent and stimulated by the effect of that recognition on the social man, but not yet guided by any clear consciousness of the end which gave them their value. In arriving at that consciousness of itself, as it did specially through the Greek philosophers, the same spiritual demand which had given rise to the old virtue yielded a virtue which was in a certain important sense new; a character which

would not be satisfied without understanding the law which it obeyed, without knowing what the true good was, for which the demand had hitherto been more blindly at work.

251. We speak of the change advisedly as consisting not merely in a new theory about virtue, but in a higher order of virtue itself. Socrates and his followers are not rightly regarded as the originators of an interesting moral speculation, such, for instance, as Hume may have started as to the nature of 'moral sense,' or the evolutionists as to its hereditary development. They represent, though it might be too much to say that they introduced, a new demand, or at least a fuller expression of an old demand, of the moral nature. Now though our actual moral attainment may always be far below what our conscience requires of us, it does tend to rise in response to a heightened requirement of conscience, and will not rise without it. Such a requirement is implied in the conception of the unity of virtue, as determined by one idea of practical good which was to be the conscious spring of the perfectly virtuous life—an idea of it as consisting in some intrinsic excellence, some full realisation of the capabilities, of the thinking and willing soul. Here we have— not indeed in its source, but in that first clear expression through which it manifests its life—the conviction that every form of real goodness must rest on a will to be good, which has no object but its own fulfilment. When the same conviction came before the world, not in the form of a philosophy but in the language of religious aspiration—'Blessed are the pure in heart, for they shall see God'—and when there seemed to be a personal human life which could be contemplated as one in which it had been realised, it appealed to a much wider range of persons than it had done in the schools of Greece, and moved the heart with a new power. But if those affected by it came to ask themselves what it meant for them—in what the morality resting on purity of heart consisted—it was mainly in forms derived, knowingly or unknowingly, from the Greek philosophers that the answer had to be given.

252. The purity of the heart can only consist in the nature

of its motives or governing interests.   Actions, the same outwardly, represent a heart more or less pure, according as the
motive which prompts them is more or less singly or predominantly an interest in some form or other of that which
is truly good ; or—to say the same thing in a manner less
liable to be misunderstood, since motives do not admit of
isolation—according as the motive belongs to a character
more or less thoroughly governed by such an interest.   This
distinction of true from seeming virtue, as dependent on the
motive of each, was brought out by Plato and Aristotle with
a clearness which was in fact final.   Their account of the
true good itself was indeed but formal and provisional, as,
for reasons already indicated, every such account must be ;
though, unless mankind has lived its last two thousand years
in vain, the formal and provisional account of the good should
mean more for us than it could mean for the Greeks.   But
that a conscious direction to this good—a ' purity of heart ' in
this sense—was the condition of all true virtue and constituted
the essential unity between one form of virtue and another,
this they taught with all the consistency and directness which
a Christian teacher could desire, which indeed stands in strong
contrast with the appeal to semi-sensual motives that has been
common, and perhaps necessary for popular practical effect,
in the Christian Church.   Τοῦ καλοῦ ἕνεκα· κοινὸν γὰρ τοῦτο ταῖς
ἀρεταῖς [1], is the formula in which Aristotle sums up the teaching of himself and his master as to the basis of goodness.
Like every formula, it may have come to be used as cant,
but in its original significance it conveyed the great principle
that a direction of a man's will to the highest possible realisation of his faculties is the common ground of every form of
true virtue.   This direction of the will, according to both
Aristotle and Plato, was to be founded on habit ; but the
habit even in its earliest and least reflective stage was to be
under the direction of reason, as embodied in law or acting
through a personal educator, and through appropriate teach-

---

[1] ' Desire for what is beautiful or noble ; this is the common
characteristic of all the virtues.'   Arist. Eth. Nic. IV. ii. 7.

ing was in due time to pass into a fully intelligent and appreciative conformity to the reason which was its source. Given this direction of the will, uniting intellectual apprehension with strongest desire, all virtue was given[1]: without it there was, in the proper sense, none, but at best only such a possibility of virtue as may be afforded by tendencies and habits, directed from without to higher ends than the subject has intelligently made his own.

253. This view of the essential principle of all virtue at once distinguishes the doctrine of Plato and Aristotle from any form of Hedonism, or of Utilitarianism so far as Hedonistic. The condition of virtuous action according to them did not lie in its production of a certain effect, but in its relation to a certain object, as rationally desired by the agent; and this was an object of which the nature, as desired, was not that which according to the Hedonist alone excites desire. It was not an imagined pleasure. But a student of these philosophers will be apt to remark that, although clearly the quality which, according to them, makes an action good is not that which makes it good according to the Utilitarian, and is relative to some other end than the pleasure which the Utilitarian deems alone either desired or desirable, it is not so clear what this other end is. And this indefiniteness, he will argue, in the conception of the end, on conscious direction to which virtue is made to depend, must be just so far an indefiniteness in the conception of virtue itself. An end, which is not pleasure, is to be desired for its own sake; so far 'purity of heart' is insisted on; but, unless we know what the end is, we are still in the dark as to the real characteristics of the heart purely devoted to it. If from the Hedonistic point of view 'purity of heart' can have no meaning at all, can the Greek philosophers on the other hand, it may be asked, do more than assure us that there must be such a thing and that it

---

[1] Cf. Arist. Eth. Nic. VI. xiii. 6. Ἅμα τῇ φρονήσει μιᾷ οὔσῃ πᾶσαι ὑπάρξουσιν (sc. αἱ ἀρεταί). 'The single virtue of practical wisdom implies the presence of all the moral virtues.'

is morally all-important, without being able to point to any real interest corresponding to this formal idea? Did not 'purity of heart' acquire a meaning in the Christian Church, other than it could have borne in the schools of philosophy, because the Christian revelation supplied this interest?

Now that there are senses in which a higher moral standard is possible for the Christian citizen than was possible for the Greek of Aristotle's age, will not be disputed. We have already dwelt on an important difference, arising out of the fact that a practical conviction of the brotherhood of all men, such as was impossible to the Greek, brings with it for us a new standard of justice—not indeed a new conception of what is due towards those who have claims of right upon us, but a new view of the range of persons who have such claims. As we proceed we shall see how the interests of the 'pure heart' have become really more determinate, its demands upon itself fuller, in the Christian society than they were to the most enlightened and conscientious Greek. But for the present our concern is rather to point out the greatness—in a certain sense the completeness and finality —of the advance in spiritual development which the Greek philosophers represent. Once for all they conceived and expressed the conception of a free or pure morality, as resting on what we may venture to call a disinterested interest in the good; of the several virtues as so many applications of that interest to the main relations of social life; of the good itself not as anything external to the capacities virtuously exercised in its pursuit, but as their full realisation. This idea was one which was to govern the growth of all the true and vital moral conviction which has descended to us. It had indeed still to acquire fulness and determinateness with the formation of habits and institutions corresponding to it, but it was itself the source of that formation. It was not indeed ever to become such a definitely presentable rule of life as we often sigh for, but we must bear in mind that, so far as the shortcomings which we are apt to complain of in it arise from the impossibility either of envisaging or of exhaustively defining the good which it presupposes, they are inseparable from the very nature of morality, as an effort not an attainment, a progressive construction of what should be, not an enjoyment of what is, governed not by sight but by faith. They are shortcomings, in fact, to which it is only through illusions that we can claim superiority.

254. Aristotle, as we know, with all the wisdom of Plato before him, which he was well able to appropriate, could find no better definition of the true good for man than the full exercise or realisation of the soul's faculties in accordance with its proper excellence, which was an excellence of thought, speculative and practical. The pure morality then, which we credit him with having so well conceived, must have meant morality determined by interest in such a good. But what real import or filling, it will be asked, can such an interest have? Is not the conception of morality, as determined by this interest, if it is really no more than it professes to be, essentially an empty conception? To this we answer that it would have been an empty conception, if there had not already taken place such a realisation of the soul's faculties as gave a meaning, though not its full and final meaning, to the definition of the good. In fact, however, as we have already seen, the same spiritual principle which yielded the demand for an account of what was good in itself, and the conception of true goodness as determined by interest in that good, had also yielded a realisation of the soul's faculties in certain pursuits and achievements, and in a certain organisation of life. Already there were arts and sciences, already families and states, with established rules of what was necessary for their maintenance and furtherance. Thus such a definition of the good as Aristotle gives us was more than explanatory of the meaning of a name. It was rather the indication of a spiritual problem, of which some progress had been made in the solution. The realisation of the soul's faculties had not to wait to begin; the desire for, the interest in, such a good had not

still to be initiated.   The philosopher had not to bring
before men an absolutely new object of pursuit, but to bring
them to consider what gave its value to an object already
pursued.

255. From that very consideration, it is true, the object
took a new character for the consciousness of the person
pursuing it.   It began to be for him what it had previously
been only in itself, or in idea, or for some divine spirit
working through him but without his knowledge.   The
realisation of the soul's faculties in the state, for instance,
though in one sense it has already been an object to every
one who duly performs his functions as a citizen, becomes
an object in a new sense to one who is conscious of his
citizen's work as contributing in some humble way to an
end which is the bettering of the citizens, and who does it
or seeks to do it, not for incidental pleasure or reward, but
for the sake of that end.   To awaken such a consciousness
in men, and thus to enable them to do old work in a spirit
that made it new, was the function of the Socratic philosophers.   They had not to create wisdom, or fortitude, or
temperance, or justice.   They had not to direct the habits
of action, recognised as laudable under those names, to any
other object than that in relation to which they had always
had their value; but they had to make it clear that this
object, being a perfection of the rational man, an unfolding
of his capacities in full harmonious activity, was not one to
which the virtuous practices were related as means to an
external end, but itself included their exercise.   To do so
was to establish the principle of the conviction that goodness
is to be sought for its own sake and, as so sought, is itself
and alone the good; but it was not to leave the conception
of goodness without definite content.   On the contrary it
was to determine it further, as a conception of the modes of
action hitherto counted virtuous, with the added qualification that, in order to be truly virtuous, they must be brought
into harmony with each other as jointly contributing to a
perfection of life, and must each have their root in a char-

acter of which the governing interest was an interest in that
perfection.

256. In the development of that reflective morality which
our own consciences inherit, both the fundamental principle
and the mode of its articulation have retained the form
which they first took in the minds of the Greek philosophers. To whatever alien speculative influences we may
have been subject—and of late no doubt the influences of
evolutionary Hedonism have been strongly alien—we do
not get rid of the conviction that to be good in one of the
many forms of goodness is for the individual the good ; that,
inexhaustibly various as those forms may be, each of them
must be founded on a will, of which the good in one or
other of these forms is the object ; and that the good for
man, in that universal sense in which it is beyond the
reach of the individual's realisation, must yet be of a kind
which is related to all forms of individual goodness as the
life of a body to the various vital functions, at once resulting from them and rendering them possible. And when
we come to ask ourselves what are the essential forms in
which, however otherwise modified, the will for true good
(which is the will to be good) must appear, our answer
follows the outlines of the Greek classification of the virtues.
It is the will to know what is true, to make what is beautiful ; to endure pain and fear, to resist the allurements of
pleasure (*i.e.* to be brave and temperate), if not, as the
Greek would have said, in the service of the state, yet in the
interest of some form of human society ; to take for oneself,
to give to others, of those things which admit of being given
and taken, not what one is inclined to but what is due.

257. It was not, of course, by accident that, when reflective morality first took shape among the Greeks, it became
aware of these main lines through which the good was to be
pursued. As was said above, the effort after a true good
had already worked in these lines and was to continue to
work in them, and it is the continuity of that work as carried
on by us—the actual progressive realisation of human capaci-

ties in knowledge, in art, and in social life—that has been the ground of identity between the first systematic reflection on the goodness exhibited in those lines, and all reflection on the same subject that has followed. And just as it has been the continuity in the actual pursuit of the true good that has kept those standards of virtue, which arise in reflection upon the pursuit, the same through succeeding ages, so it has been in sequence upon variations in the actual pursuit, which have taken place independently of reflection, that variations in the standards implying reflection have arisen.

On the whole the variations in the object pursued as good, though there have been periods apparently of mere loss and shrinkage, have consisted in its acquisition of greater fulness and determinateness. In like manner the differences between our standards of virtue and those recognised by the Greek philosophers arise from the greater fulness of conditions which we include in our conception of the perfecting of human life. The realisation of human capacities has, in fact, taken a far wider range with us than in the most advanced of ancient states. As actually achieved, it is a much more complete thing than it was two thousand years ago, and every progress achieved opens up a further vista of possibilities still unrealised. In consequence the attainment of true good presents itself to men under new forms. The bettering of human life, though the principle of it is the same now as in the Socratic age, has to be carried on in new ways; and the actual pursuit of true good being thus complicated, reflection on what is implied in the pursuit yields standards of virtue which, though identical in principle with those recognised by Aristotle, are far more comprehensive and wide-reaching in their demands. This will appear more clearly if we consider how Aristotle's account of fortitude and temperance would have to be modified in order to answer the requirements of the Christian conscience.

258. If a 'Christian worker' who devotes himself, unnoticed and unrewarded, at the risk of life and at the

sacrifice of every pleasure but that of his work, to the service
of the sick, the ignorant and the debased, were told that his
ideal of virtue was in principle the same as that of the ἀνδρεῖος,
'the brave man,' described by Aristotle, and if he were in-
duced to read the description, he would probably seem to
himself to find nothing of his ideal in it.   Yet the statement
would be true.   The principle of self-devotion for a worthy
end in resistance to pain and fear is the same in both cases.
But Aristotle could only conceive the self-devotion in some
form in which it had actually appeared.   He knew it in no
higher form than as it appeared in the citizen-soldier, who
faced death calmly in battle for his State.   In that further
realisation of the soul's capacities which has taken place in
the history of Christendom, it has appeared in a far greater
wealth of forms.   In Aristotle's view the βίος πρακτικὸς—the
life of rational self-determined activity—was only possible
for a few among the few.   It presupposed active participation in a civil community.   Such communities could only
exist in certain select nations, and, where they existed, only
a few of the people contributing to their maintenance and
living under their direction were fit to share in civil functions.   These alone had moral claims or capabilities.   The rest
were instruments of their convenience.   In modern Christendom it is not merely our theories of life but the facts of life
that have changed.   'Weak things of the world and things
that are despised hath God called.'   With the recognition of
rights in human beings as such, on which we have previously
dwelt (§ **201** and foll.), there comes a new realisation of
human capacities, not only for the emancipated multitude,
but for those whom Aristotle would have allowed to be
previously sharers in the βίος πρακτικός.   The problems of life
become for them far more difficult indeed, but, just on
account of their greater range and complication, they become of such a kind as to elicit powers previously unused.

   We are apt to speak as if the life of the Greek or Roman
citizen, in the full bloom of municipal civilisation, was much
fuller and richer than that of the modern citizen under a

régime of universal freedom and equal rights. For the
many we admit the modern system may be a gain, but for
the few we take it to be a corresponding loss. Yet this is
surely a very superficial view. The range of faculties called
into play in any work of social direction or improvement
must be much wider, when the material to be dealt with
consists no longer of supposed chattels but of persons asserting recognised rights, whose welfare forms an integral
element in the social good which the directing citizen has
to keep in view. Only if we leave long-suffering, consider-
ateness, the charity which ‘ beareth all things, believeth all
things, hopeth all things,’ with all the art of the moral
physician, out of account in our estimate of the realisation
of the soul's powers, can we question the greater fulness of
the realisation in the present life of Christendom, as compared with the highest life of the ancient world.

259. It is a consequence of this change in the realities
of social life that the conception of moral heroism has
greatly widened—widened not in the sense of more attenu-
ated abstraction but of more concrete filling—so that it
requires some patience of reflection to trace the identity of
principle through all its forms. The Quaker philanthropist
can scarcely recognise a brother in the citizen-soldier, or the
soldier a brother in the philanthropist. It is indeed in one
sense a new type of virtue that has come into being with the
recognition of the divine image, of spiritual functions and
possibilities, in all forms of weak and suffering humanity.
The secondary motives, which assist self-devotion in war or
in the performance of functions of recognised utility before the eyes of fellow-citizens, are absent when neither from
the recipients of the service done nor from any spectators of
it can any such praise be forthcoming as might confirm in
the agent the consciousness of doing nobly. Yet every day
and all about us pain is being endured and fear resisted
in rendering such service. The hopelessly sick are being
tended ; the foolish and ignorant are being treated as rational
persons ; human beings whom a Greek would have looked

on as chattels, or as a social encumbrance to be got rid of,
are having pains bestowed on them which only a faith in
unapparent possibilities of their nature could justify.   In
the whole view of life which this work implies, in the objects
which inspire it, as those whom they influence would describe them, in the qualities of temper and behaviour which
it calls into play, it seems to present a strong contrast to
that which the Greek philosopher would have looked for
from his ideally brave man.   It implies a view of life in which
the maintenance of any form of political society scarcely
holds a place ; in which lives that would be contemptible
and valueless, if estimated with reference to the purposes of
the state, are invested with a value of their own in virtue of
capabilities for some society not seen as yet.   Its object,
whether described simply as the service of the suffering and
ignoble, or as the service of God manifested in suffering and
ignobility, is one which the philosophic Greek would scarcely
have recognised as a form of the καλόν.   The qualities of
self-adjustment, of sympathy with inferiors, of tolerance for
the weak and foolish, which are exercised in it, are very
different from the pride of self-sufficing strength which with
Aristotle was inseparable from heroic endurance.

260.   Yet beneath these differences lies a substantial
identity.   The willingness to endure even unto complete self-
renunciation, even to the point of forsaking all possibility of
pleasure, or, as Aristotle puts it, of passing the point beyond
which there seems no longer to be either good or evil[1]; the
willingness to do this in the service of the highest public
cause which the agent can conceive— whether the cause of
the state or the cause of the kingdom of Christ—because it
is part of the noble life, of the 'more excellent way,' so to
do ; this is common to the ideal of fortitude equally as
conceived by Aristotle and as it has been pursued in the
Christian Church.   If we cannot ignore, on the one hand,
the limitations in Aristotle's view of the conditions under
which his ideal could be realised[2]—conditions which would

---

[1] Eth. Nic. III. vi. 6 ; ix. 4, 5.   [2] Ib. III. vi. 7, and foll.

have rendered it wholly unrealisable in the chief occupations of Christian charity—on the other hand it is only fair to notice how free it is from debasement by any notion of a compensation which the brave man is to find in pleasures of another world for present endurance. The fact, indeed, that Christian preachers have not been ashamed to dwell upon such compensation as a motive to self-renunciation, ought not to be taken to imply that the heroism of charity exhibited in the Christian Church has really been vitiated by pleasure-seeking motives. Religious rhetoric is apt to be far in arrear of the motives which it seeks to express, and to strengthen by expression. 'Unspeakable joys' has been but a phrase to convey the yearning of the soul for that perfection which is indescribable except so far as attained. Joys that are unspeakable are unimaginable, and the desire which really has such joys for its object is quite different from a desire excited by an imagination of pleasure.

In short, we are not entitled to say that the Aristotelian ideal of fortitude has been either more or less *pure* than that which has been operative in Christendom; but there is no doubt that the latter has become far more comprehensive, and it has become so in correspondence with an enhanced fulness in our conception of the ends of living. Faculties, dispositions, occupations, persons, of which a Greek citizen would have taken no account, or taken account only to despise, are now recognised as having their place in the realisation of the powers of the human soul, in the due evolution of the spiritual from the animal man. It is in consequence of this recognition that the will to endure even unto death for a worthy end has come to find worthy ends where the Greek saw nothing but ugliness and meanness, and to express itself in obscure labours of love as well as in the splendid heroism at which a world might wonder.

261. Alongside of 'fortitude' in the reflective morality of Greece was placed 'temperance,' as that habit of will which stands to the allurements of pleasure in the same relation as 'fortitude' to pain and fear. If we wish to compare the

standard of self-denial in respect of pleasures, which the
conscience of Christendom in its highest forms has come to
prescribe, with the standard recognised by the Greek philosophers, it is to the account which the latter give of
σωφροσύνη that we must turn.   The first impression of any
one who came to this account, having his mind charged
with the highest lessons of Christian self-denial, would be of
its great poverty—a poverty more striking, as it will probably
appear, in the case of 'temperance' than in the case of
'courage.'   He finds 'temperance' restricted by Aristotle to
control over the mere animal appetites ; or, more exactly, to
control over desire for the pleasures incidental to the satisfaction of those appetites.   The particular usage of a name,
indeed, is of slight importance.   If Aristotle had reasons for
limiting σωφροσύνη to a certain meaning, and made up
elsewhere for what is lacking in his account of the virtue
described under that name, no fault could be found.   But
σωφροσύνη and ἀνδρεία between them have to do duty for the
whole of what we understand by self-denial.   However little
we may have cleared up the moral demand which we express
to ourselves as the duty of self-denial, we cannot get rid of
the conviction that it is a demand at any rate of much wider
significance in regard to indulgence in pleasures than that
which Aristotle describes as actuating the 'temperate' man,
nor do we find the deficiency made good in any account
which he gives of other forms of virtue.

262. If we look a little closer, however, we shall notice
the identity between the habit of will of which 'temperance,'
as conceived by Aristotle, is an expression, and that on
which every renunciation of pleasures, even the widest and
completest, if it is to be of moral value, must rest.   No
'ascetic' moralist, so far as known, has supposed such
renunciation to be possible, or, if possible, to be of value
merely on its own account.   It becomes possible only
through the prevalence of desire for some object other than
the enjoyment of pleasure.   It is this desire alone, not the
renunciation of pleasures except as an incident or sign of

such desire, that can be of moral value; just as, on the other side, it is not desires for pleasures that are in themselves morally evil, but the occupation of the will by them—the direction of a man's self to this or that pleasure as his good—to the exclusion of those higher interests which cannot possess the man along with them, and which can only themselves be accounted desires for pleasure through the fallacy, previously dwelt upon, of supposing a desire to have for its object the pleasure of its own satisfaction. Perhaps, under a true conviction of the essential immorality of the pleasure-seeking character, certain moralists may have sometimes spoken as if there were intrinsic evil in desires for pleasure apart from their competition with other desires, and again some intrinsic good in the renunciation of pleasures apart from interest in the higher object for the sake of which they are renounced; but this has only been through unguardedness in expression.   With Kant, for instance, whatever his rigour in identifying moral badness with selfishness and this with pleasure-seeking, it was never doubtful that the goodness of the good will lay in the prevalence of interest in a worthy object, badness in such a failure of the worthy interest as enables the desire for pleasure to prevail. His error consisted in his too abstract view of the interest on which he held that true goodness must depend, and which he seems to reduce to interest in the fulfilment of moral law according to the most abstract possible conception of it.   Of this no more can be said here.   For the present our concern is to point out the agreement between the motive which the reflective Greek regarded as the basis of the virtue manifested in control over certain desires for pleasure, and the source of that self-denial which our own consciences require of us.

263. It must be admitted that, when Aristotle treats most methodically of σωφροσύνη, he does little to specify the particular form of that interest in the καλὸν which he considered to be the basis of the virtue.   He seems more intent on specifying the psychological nature of the pleasures, over desire for which the term σωφροσύνη, as strictly applied, implies due control. But to a Greek who was told that the virtue of temperance was a mastery over certain desires, exercised τοῦ καλοῦ ἕνεκα, there would be no practical doubt what the motive was to be, what was to be the object in which a prevailing interest was to enable him to exercise this mastery. In his view it could only be reverence for the divine order of the state, such a desire to fulfil his proper function in the community as might keep under the body and control the insolence of overweening lust. The régime of equal law, the free combination of mutually respecting citizens in the enactment of a common good, was the 'beautiful thing' of which the attraction might, through a fitting education, become so strong as to neutralise every lust that tended to disqualify a man for the effectual rendering of service to his state, or tempted him to deal wantonly with his neighbour. It was this character of the motive or interest on which it was understood to rest, that gave to σωφροσύνη an importance in the eyes of the Greek moralist which, if we looked simply to the very limited range of pleasures—pleasures of the merely animal nature—in regard to which Aristotle supposes the 'temperate man' to exercise self-restraint, would scarcely be intelligible. Not the mere sobriety of the appetites, but the foundation of that sobriety in a truly civil spirit, in the highest kind of rational loyalty, gave the virtue its value. And hence it was—because it was associated with such a basis—that σωφροσύνη came to be regarded as carrying with it a group of virtues with which control of the animal impulses might seem to us to have little to do. As it is put by a writer of the Aristotelian school, παρέπεται τῇ σωφροσύνῃ εὐταξία, κοσμιότης, αἰδώς, εὐλάβεια[1].

264. When we compare this conception of 'temperance' with the demand for self-denial which the enlightened Christian conscience makes on itself, we are struck alike

---

[1] De virt. et vit. 1250 b. 12.   'With temperance go orderliness, regularity, the feeling of shame, discreetness.'

with the unity of principle and the difference of range or comprehension in the application of the principle. The idea of the subjection in us of a lower or animal man to a higher appeals to us as it did to the Greek. We too think of the higher man as the law-abiding, law-reverencing man. An abstinence or temperance dictated merely by fear of some painful result of indulgence we do not count a virtue. The true virtue of self-denial we deem to be only reached when it is through interest in the performance of some public duty or other, in the fulfilment of some function or other which falls to us as members of a community, that we come practically to forbid ourselves the pursuit of certain · pleasures, or to reach a state in which the prohibition is unnecessary because the inclination to them is neutralised by higher interests. On the other hand, we present to ourselves the objects of moral loyalty which we should be ashamed to forsake for our pleasures, in a far greater variety of forms than did the Greek, and it is a much larger self-denial which loyalty to these objects demands of us. It is no longer the state alone that represents to us the 'melior natura' before whose claims our animal inclinations sink abashed. Other forms of association put restraints and make demands on us which the Greek knew not. An indulgence, which a man would otherwise allow himself, he forgoes in consideration of claims on the part of wife or children, of men as such or women as such, of fellow-Christians or fellow-workmen, which could not have been made intelligible in the ancient world. It is easy, no doubt, in making such comparisons to be misled by names. We must not conclude, because to a Greek all duty was summed up in what he owed to his πόλις, that he recognised no duties but such as we should naturally call duties to the state. The term 'state' is generally used by us with a restricted meaning which prevents it from being a proper equivalent for πόλις. But, apart from any question of names, it is certain that the requirements founded on ideas of common good, which in our consciences we recognise as calling for the surrender of our inclinations to pleasure, are more far-reaching and penetrate life more deeply than did such requirements in the ancient world, and that in consequence a more complete self-denial is demanded of us.

265. Even if we confine our view to 'temperance' as Aristotle conceived it, *i.e.* as a virtue exhibited only in dealing with the pleasure ἢ γίνεται ἐν σιτίοις καὶ ἐν ποτοῖς καὶ τοῖς ἀφροδισίοις λεγομένοις [1]—waiving the consideration of other forms of self-denial—we shall find that the highest Greek standard, as represented by the philosophers, falls short of that which a conscience, duly responsive to the highest claims, would now require of us. The principles from which it was derived, so far as they were practically available and tenable, seem to have been twofold. One was that all indulgence should be avoided which unfitted a man for the discharge of his duties in peace or war; the other, that such a check should be kept on the lusts of the flesh as might prevent them from issuing in what a Greek knew as ὕβρις—a kind of self-assertion, and aggression upon the rights of others in respect of person and property, for which we have not an equivalent name, but which was looked upon as the antithesis of the civil spirit.

We speak of these as the only practically available and tenable principles that were recognised for the regulation of 'temperance.' There is indeed another notion which is perhaps the one most constantly and distinctly alleged by the philosophers as a reason for being 'temperate.' This is the notion that the kind of pleasure with which temperance has to do is in some way unworthy of man, because one of which the other animals are susceptible. It is not very likely, however, to have represented a conviction of the general conscience, nor does it appear how any practical standard of temperance could have been derived from such a notion. The conviction that there is a lower and a higher—that there are objects less and more worthy of man—is no doubt one

[1] 'The pleasures of eating, drinking, and sexual intercourse.' Eth. Nic. III. x. 10.

of the most fundamental of our moral nature ; or rather it is one of the simplest expressions for the demand which is that nature. This conviction must carry with it a disapproval of indulgences which interfere with the pursuit of the more worthy objects—such, *e. g.*, as disqualify for efficient citizenship—but it is a false philosophical gloss on this disapproval to treat it as grounded on the fact that these indulgences are of a kind which are not distinctive of man, but are shared by the 'lower animals.' Just in that respect in which they are matter of disapproval, in so far, that is to say, as they interfere with the fulfilment of some higher human function, they are not indulgences of a kind in which the animals are found to partake. The animals do not, so far as we know, gratify their appetites in a way that interferes with the attainment of any object that they are capable of presenting to themselves[1]. If the gratification of appetites, therefore, called for our disapproval on the ground of its being common to us with them, it should be disapproved in itself and altogether, not on account of any obstruction which it offers to other and higher ends (for in the case of the animals there is no such obstruction), but on account of some intrinsic quality belonging to it. The conclusion would be that we should aim at an entire suppression of animal gratification, which would entail the extinction of the human race. We should have no measure of excess in such gratification—for one degree of it is no more 'brutal' than another—but a reason, practically inoperative, for rejecting it altogether.

On the other hand, a little consideration would show that the attraction of pleasures, 'of which the other animals partake,' has really little to do with the practices condemned by the philosophers and by our conscience as 'intemperate.' It is probably never the pleasure of drinking, strictly so called, that leads a man to get drunk. The mere pleasures of eating, apart from the gratification of vanity and undefinable social enjoyments, have but a slight share in promoting

---

[1] So Aristotle remarks that temperance and its opposite are not predicable of brutes. Eth. Nic. VII. vi. 6.

the 'excesses of the table.' The temptations to sexual immorality would be much less formidable than they are, if the attractive pleasure consisted merely in the satisfaction of sexual appetite. Thus, without including in our conception of intemperance any other vices than Aristotle had in view when applying the name, we must still maintain (1) that these vices are not in fact mainly due to the attraction of pleasures of which other animals, so far as we know, are susceptible, and (2) that, if they were, this would afford no intelligible ground for treating such practices as vices, which might not equally be urged as a reason for an abstinence incompatible with the continuance of our race.

266. Returning, then, to those really tenable principles of temperance, περὶ σιτίων καὶ ποτῶν καὶ τῶν ἀφροδισίων, specified above, with which the Greek philosophers supply us, do we find that, as applied by the philosophers, they afford a standard of temperance adequate either to the recognised ideal, or to the highest practice, of the modern world? The answer must be that on the most important point, περὶ τῶν ἀφροδισίων, they do not. The limit which, on the strength of them, the philosophers would have drawn between lawful and lawless love, would not have been that which our consciences would call on us to observe. It would not have excluded all indulgence of the sexual passion except as between man and woman in monogamous married life. The failure, however, was not in the intrinsic nature of the principles recognised by the philosophers, for there is no true foundation for the strictest sexual morality other than that social duty which they asserted. The failure arose from the structure of existing society, which determined their application of their principles. As we have more than once pointed out, while there is one sense in which moral ideas must precede practice, there is another in which they follow and depend upon it. The moral judgment at its best in any age or country—*i.e.* in those persons who are as purely interested in the perfection of mankind and as keenly alive to the conditions of that perfection as is then possible—is still limited in many ways

by the degree of progress actually made towards the attainment of that perfection.   It was thus the actual condition of women, the actual existence of slavery, the fact that as yet there had been no realisation, even the most elementary, of the idea of there being a single human family with equal rights throughout—it was this that rendered the Greek philosophers incapable of such an idea of chastity as any unbrutalised English citizen, whatever his practice, if he were honest with himself would acknowledge.   To outrage the person of a fellow-citizen, to violate the sanctity of his family rights, was for the Greek as much as for us a blamable intemperance.   In the eye of the philosophers it meant a subjection of the higher, or civil, or law-reverencing, man to that lower man in us which knows not law ; and they were quite aware that not merely the abstinence from such acts, but the conquest of the lusts which lead to them by a higher interest, was the condition of true virtue.   To the spirit of our Lord's re-enactment of the seventh commandment in the sermon on the Mount, to the substitution of the rule of the pure heart for that of mere outward observance, they were no strangers. What they had still to learn was not that the duty of chastity, like any other, was to be fulfilled from the heart and with a pure will, but the full extent of that duty.

267. And this they failed to appreciate because the practical realisation of the possibilities of mankind in society had not then reached a stage in which the proper and equal sacredness of all women, as self-determining and self-respecting persons, could be understood.   Society was not in a state in which the principle that humanity in the person of every one is to be treated always as an end, never merely as a means, could be apprehended in its full universality ; and it is this principle alone, however it may be stated, which affords a rational ground for the obligation to chastity as we understand it.   The society of modern Christendom, it is needless to say, is far enough from acting upon it, but in its conscience it recognises the principle as it was not recognised in the ancient world.   The legal investment of every one with personal rights makes it impossible for one whose mind is open to the claims of others to ignore the wrong of treating a woman as the servant of his pleasures at the cost of her own degradation.   Though the wrong is still habitually done, it is done under a rebuke of conscience of which a Greek of Aristotle's time, with most women about him in slavery, and without even the capacity (to judge from the writings of the philosophers) for an ideal of society in which this should be otherwise, could not have been sensible. The sensibility could only arise in sequence upon that change in the actual structure of society through which the human person, as such, without distinction of sex, became the subject of rights.   That change was itself, indeed, as has been previously pointed out in this treatise, the embodiment of a demand which forms the basis of our moral nature—the demand on the part of the individual for a good which shall be at once his own and the good of others.   But this demand needed to take effect in laws and institutions which give every one rights against every one, before the general conscience could prescribe such a rule of chastity, founded on the sacredness of the persons of women, as we acknowledge.   And just as it is through an actual change in the structure of society that our ideal in this matter has come to be more exacting than that of the Greek philosophers, so it is only through a further social change that we can expect a more general conformity to the ideal to be arrived at.   Only as the negative equality before the law, which is already established in Christendom, comes to be supplemented by a more positive equality of conditions and a more real possibility for women to make their own career in life, will the rule of chastity, which our consciences acknowledge, become generally enforced in practice through the more universal refusal of women to be parties to its violation.

268. In this matter of chastity, then, there is a serious inferiority of the highest Greek ideal to the highest ideal of Christendom, but it is important to notice where the inferiority lies.   We have no right to disparage the Greek ideal on the ground of any inferiority in the motive which the Greek philosophers would have considered the true basis of this, as of every, form of temperance.   There can be no higher motive to it than that civil spirit, in the fullest and truest sense, on which they conceived it to rest.   But we may fairly disparage their ideal in respect of the kind of life which the realisation of this motive was considered to require.   The sexual temperance which they demanded, they demanded on the true ground, but not in full enough measure.   In that respect their ideal had certain inevitable shortcomings—inevitable, because no ideal can go more than a certain distance, in the detail of conduct which it requires, beyond the conditions of the given age.

And this comparative poverty of the Greek ideal becomes more apparent when we reflect that, as has been pointed out above, the only form in which the virtuous renunciation of pleasures presents itself to the philosophers is that of temperance περὶ σιτίων καὶ ποτῶν καὶ τῶν ἀφροδισίων.   Temperance, thus limited, has in their systems to do duty for the whole of what we should call self-denial.   Under no other title than that of the σώφρων is the self-denying man described by the philosophers.   And it may fairly be argued that, in respect of the governing principle of the will, the σώφρων, as they conceive him, does not differ from the highest type of self-denial known to Christian society.   But the range of action which they looked for from him, as the expression of this principle, was very limited in comparison with the forms of self-denial with which we are practically familiar ; and it was so limited because great part of the objects, by which in the society of modern Christendom self-denial is in fact elicited, in Greek society was not there to elicit it.

269. If we consider, in regard to any person whom we credit with a high degree of habitual self-denial, what are the pleasures which we suppose him to deny himself, it will appear that those, in relation to which alone Aristotle supposed 'temperance' to be exercised, form a very small part of them.   In determining the province of 'temperance'

Aristotle, following the psychology of Plato [1], expressly excludes two kinds of pleasure: (1) 'pleasures of the soul,' as instances of which he gives the pleasures of gratified ambition and love of learning; (2) such 'pleasures of the body' as are received through the senses of hearing, sight, or smell. It is not such pleasures as these that the temperate man forgoes. Now, as has been already said, this exclusion would be a very small matter if it merely concerned the usage of the name 'temperance.' The important point is that the ancient philosophers seemingly give no place to that type of virtuous character in which devotion to some form of true good leads to a renunciation of such pleasures as those included in the above classes. Yet it is just such pleasures as these of which the renunciation is involved in that self-denial which in our impartial and unsophisticated judgment we most admire—that which in our consciences we set before ourselves as the highest ideal. It would seem no great thing to us that in the service of mankind one should confine himself to necessary food and drink, and should observe the strictest limitations of Christian morality in the matter of sexual indulgence; and it is such indulgence alone, we must remember, not the enjoyments of family life, that would fall within the class of pleasures in which, according to the Greek philosophers, temperance is exercised. We have examples about us of much severer sacrifice. There are men, we know, who with the keenest sensibility to such pleasures as those of 'gratified ambition and love of learning,' yet deliberately forgo them; who shut themselves out from an abundance of æsthetic enjoyments which would be open to them, as well as from those of family life; and who do this in order to meet the claims which the work of realising the possibilities of the human soul in society—a work a hundred-fold more complex as it presents itself to us than as it presented itself to Aristotle—seems to make upon them. Such sacrifices are made now, as they were not made in the days of the Greek

[1] Eth. Nic. III. x. 2, 3; Plato, Philebus, 51.

philosophers, and in that sense a higher type of living is known among us; not because there are men now more ready to fulfil recognised duties than there were then, but because with the altered structure of society men have become alive to claims to which, with the most open eye and heart, they could not be alive then.

270. To an ancient Greek a society composed of a small group of freemen, having recognised claims upon each other and using a much larger body of men with no such recognised claims as instruments in their service, seemed the only possible society. In such an order of things those calls could not be heard which evoke the sacrifices constantly witnessed in the nobler lives of Christendom, sacrifices which would be quite other than they are, if they did not involve the renunciation of those 'pleasures of the soul' and 'unmixed pleasures,' as they were reckoned in the Platonic psychology, which it did not occur to the philosophers that there could be any occasion in the exercise of the highest virtue to forgo. The calls for such sacrifice arise from that enfranchisement of all men which, though in itself but negative[1] in its nature, carries with it for the responsive conscience a claim on the part of all men to such positive help from all men as is needed to make their freedom real. Where the Greek saw a supply of possibly serviceable labour, having no end or function but to be made really serviceable to the privileged few, the Christian citizen sees a multitude of persons, who in their actual present condition may have no advantage over the slaves of an ancient state, but who in undeveloped possibility, and in the claims which arise out of that possibility, are all that he himself is. Seeing this, he finds a necessity laid upon him. It is no time to enjoy the pleasures of eye and ear, of search for knowledge, of friendly intercourse, of applauded speech or writing, while the mass of men whom we call our brethren, and whom we declare to be meant with us for eternal destinies, are left without

---

[1] Negative, because amounting merely to the denial to any one of a right to use others as his instruments or property.

the chance, which only the help of others can gain for them, of making themselves in act what in possibility we believe them to be.   Interest in the problem of social deliverance, in one or other of the innumerable forms in which it presents itself to us, but in which it could not present itself under such a state of society as that contemplated by the Greek, forbids a surrender to enjoyments which are not incidental to that work of deliverance, whatever the value which they, or the activities to which they belong, might otherwise have.

271. There thus arise those forms of self-denial which did not enter within the horizon of the ancient moralists, and in which, if anywhere, we are entitled to trace the ethical progress of our own age.   Questions whether we are better than our fathers are idle enough, but it is not so idle—indeed it is a necessity of our moral nature—to endeavour, through whatever darkness and discouragement, to trace 'some increasing purpose through the ages,' of which the gradual fulfilment elicits a fuller exertion of the moral capabilities of individuals. Such a purpose we may not unreasonably hold to be directed to the development of society into a state in which all human beings shall be treated as, actually or in promise, persons— as agents of whom each is an end equally to himself and to others.   The idea of a society of free and law-abiding persons, each his own master yet each his brother's keeper, was first definitely formed among the Greeks, and its formation was the condition of all subsequent progress in the direction described; but with them, as has been often enough remarked, it was limited in its application to select groups of men surrounded by populations of aliens and slaves.   In its universality, as capable of application to the whole human race, an attempt has first been made to act upon it in modern Christendom.   With every advance towards its universal application comes a complication of the necessity, under which the conscientious man feels himself placed, of sacrificing personal pleasure in satisfaction of the claims of human brotherhood.   On the one side the freedom of every one to

shift for himself—a freedom to a great extent really secured
—on the other, the responsibility of every one for every one,
acknowledged by the awakened conscience ; these together
form a moral situation in which the good citizen has no leisure
to think of developing in due proportion his own faculties of
enjoyment.   The will to be good is not purer or stronger in
him than it must have been in any Greek who came near to
the philosopher's ideal, but the recognition of new social
claims compels its exercise in a new and larger self-denial.

272. An objection, indeed, is pretty sure to be made to
the whole principle upon which we reckon such self-denial
as is here contemplated a higher virtue than entered into
the Greek ideal.   ' Are we entitled,' it may be asked, ' to
make a virtue out of the renunciation of anything intrinsically good, and are not the pleasures which we suppose
to be renounced by the self-denying servant of mankind
intrinsically good ?   We may indeed, upon the principles
of " universalistic Hedonism," admire the conduct of such
a person, as suited to the times of present distress.   The
general capacity for pleasure being so limited by the faulty
conditions of society, we may admit it to be the best thing
in the long run that there should be men ready to forgo the
most really desirable pleasures for the sake of rendering
others ultimately more capable of them.   The public spirit,
the altruistic enthusiasm, of such men is of great value,
as a means to the end which consists in the maximum of
pleasure obtainable by human (or perhaps all sentient)
beings, taken together ; and for that reason it is rightly
counted virtuous.   But it is not more virtuous in proportion
to the amount and desirability of the pleasure sacrificed by
those under its influence ; nor is it any inferiority of the
Greek ideal of virtue to that here put forward as characteristic of modern Christendom, that it did not imply any
sacrifice of "pure" pleasures, *i.e.* of such pleasures as carry
no pain in their train.   It would be another matter if it could
be alleged against the Greek ideal that it did not imply
public spirit ; but this is not pretended.   The fault alleged

is merely that public spirit, as the Greek conceived it, involved a less costly sacrifice on the part of the individual than do those forms of altruistic enthusiasm to which we are now taught to aspire.   But if the allegation is true, so much the better for the Greek ideal.   If the conditions of modern life are such that the completest fulfilment of social duty does often call for the renunciation of much pure pleasure on the part of the individual, this may put difficulties in the way of an optimistic view of human history, but it cannot make the ideal of virtue as more painful higher than the ideal of it as more pleasant.   The only pleasures of which a limitation is properly included in the conception of the highest virtue, are those of which the enjoyment beyond a certain point either interferes with the individual's health, and thus with his capacity for other enjoyment, or involves some aggression upon the rights of others, and thus lessens the possibility of enjoyment on their part.   It was just these pleasures of which a due limitation was taken to be implied in that constituent of the virtuous character which the ancients call temperance.   It was not their defect, but their merit, that they did not conceive the highest virtue to involve properly a rejection of normal pleasures of any other kind.'

273. From the point of view of Hedonistic Utilitarianism such an objection is inevitable and unanswerable.   It is well to allow full weight to it, were it only for the sake of forcing ourselves to consider whether the actual admiration of our consciences, which we can hardly doubt is most fully commanded by the life of the largest self-denial, is in accord with such Utilitarianism.   The answer which must be given to it, according to the theory previously set forth in this treatise, can easily be anticipated.   It is not because it involves the renunciation of so much pleasure that we deem the life of larger self-denial, which the Christian conscience calls for, a higher life than was conceived of by the Greek philosophers ; but because it implies a fuller realisation of the capacities of the human soul.   It is not the renunciation, as such, but the spiritual state which it represents, that constitutes the value of the life spent in self-devoted service to mankind; and it represents, we must remember, not merely a certain system of desires and interests, on the part of the persons who make the renunciation, but a certain social development in consequence of which those desires and interests are called into play.

As we have seen, it is the emancipation of the multitude, and the social situations arising out of it, that call forth the energies of the self-denying life as we now witness it.   When we compare the realisation of human capabilities implied in that life with the realisation of them implied in the highest type of citizenship contemplated by the ancient philosophers, we must take account not merely of some typical representative of Christian charity on the one side, and of the ideal Greek citizen on the other, each in his separate individuality, but of the moral and spiritual conditions of other men, to which these several types of character are relative.   For it is human society as a whole that we must look upon as the organism in which the capacities of the human soul are unfolded.   Human society indeed is essentially a society of self-determined persons. There can be no progress of society which is not a development of capacities on the part of persons composing it, considered as ends in themselves.   But in estimating the worth of any type of virtue, as implying or tending to bring about a realisation of man's spiritual capacities, we must not confine our view to some particular group of men exhibiting the virtue.   We must consider also those relations between them and other men, by which the particular type of virtue is determined.   We must enquire whether any apparent splendour in that virtue is due to a degradation of human society outside the particular group, or whether, on the contrary, the virtue of the few takes its character from their assistance in the struggle upward of the many.

274. Now, when we compare the life of service to mankind, involving so much sacrifice of pure pleasure, which is lived by the men whom in our consciences we think best, and which they reproach themselves for not making one of more complete self-denial, with the life of free activity in bodily and intellectual exercises, in friendly converse, in civil debate, in the enjoyment of beautiful sights and sounds, which we commonly ascribe to the Greeks, and which their philosophers certainly set before them as an ideal, we might be apt, on the first view, to think that, even though measured not merely by the quantity of pleasure incidental to it but by the fulness of the realisation of human capabilities implied in it, the latter kind of life was the higher of the two. Man for man, the Greek who at all came up to the ideal of the philosophers might seem to be intrinsically a nobler being—one of more fully developed powers—than the self-mortifying Christian, upon whom the sense of duty to a suffering world weighs too heavily to allow of his giving free play to enjoyable activities, of which he would otherwise be capable. But such a comparison of man with man, in abstraction from the rest of mankind, is not the way to ascertain the real value of the virtue of either in its relation to the possibilities of the human soul. If (as would seem to be the case) the free play of spiritual activity in the life of the Greek citizen, with its consequent bright enjoyableness, depended partly on the seclusion of the Greek communities from the mass of mankind, partly on their keeping in slavery so much of the mass as was in necessary contact with them ; if the seclusion and the slavery were incidental to a state of things in which the powers of the human soul, considered as the soul of universal human society, were still in their nonage ; then, whatever value we may ascribe to the highest type of Greek life, as suggesting an ideal of ' liberty, equality and fraternity,' afterwards to be realised on a wider scale, we cannot regard its exemption from the impeding cares, which the intercommunication of mankind on terms of recognised equality brings with it, as constituting a real superiority.

275. Though it is not to be pretended, then, that the life of the self-denying Christian citizen is morally the better on account of the burden of care and the manifold limitations, which the acknowledged claims of human brotherhood impose on it, it must be maintained on the other hand that the life of the Greek citizen was not morally the better for the freedom from such burden and limitations which he enjoyed ; because this freedom was correlative to an undeveloped condition on the part of the rest of mankind. The title of the modern or Christian type of virtue to a positive superiority is not to be found in the burden, unknown to the Greeks, which it bears, but in that which the presence of this burden implies; the new spiritual activity, namely, on the part of the multitude, now conscious of their claims and set free to assert them practically, and the wider range of interests in human good which in response to those claims are awakened in the hearts of the virtuous. That this enhanced activity, these enlarged interests, should involve for the virtuous much voluntary curtailment of the innocent pleasures which, but for such disturbing claims and interests, would be open to them, is, as regards the attainment of moral good, a matter of indifference.   For the curtailment in itself they are neither the better nor the worse ; but in the actual order of things, so far as appears, it is a necessary incident of progress towards that full development of what man has it in him to be, that satisfaction of the demand of the human soul for its own perfection, which is for us the good ; and for that reason it is the part of the highest virtue to welcome it.

276. We may speculate, indeed, on the possibility of a state of things in which the most entire devotion to the service of mankind shall be compatible with the widest experience of pleasure on the part of the devoted person. We may argue that the perfection of the human soul implies its unimpeded activity, which is pleasure ; and that therefore, though in certain stages of the progress towards such perfection there may be for certain persons an abridgment of pleasure, its attainment must be pure enjoyment.   Or again we may comfort ourselves with surmising that, though to this or that individual citizen his self-devotedness may mean a large sacrifice of pleasure, yet to others, who have the benefit of his devotion without sharing in it, there is in consequence such an accession of pleasure that the result is a large addition to the sum of enjoyment on the whole. All speculation of this kind, however, provokes much counter-speculation. By what right, it may be asked, do we assume that the more developed or perfect state of the human soul is one in which a larger aggregate of pleasure is enjoyed than in the less perfect state? There is pleasure, no doubt, in all satisfaction of desire, there is pleasure in all unimpeded activity. So far therefore as a man has desired the perfection of the human soul, there will be pleasure to him in the consciousness of contributing to that perfection, but not necessarily a greater amount than he has to forgo in order to the contribution. So far as the perfection is attained, again, there will be less impediment to the activity directed to its attainment, and therefore more pleasure in the exercise of the activity. But it would seem at least possible that, according to the plan of the world, the perfection of the human soul may involve the constant presence of a lower nature, consisting in certain tendencies, never indeed dominant, but in conflict with which alone the higher energies of man can emerge. In that case it may very well be that the desire for human perfection, which is the desire for true good, though gradually coming to taste more of the particular pleasure incidental to its satisfaction and to the free play of the action which it moves, as it more fully attains its end, may never be destined to carry men, even in its fullest satisfaction, into a state of pure enjoyment, or into one in which they will be exempt from large demands for the rejection of possible pleasure.

277. At any rate, whatever may be the future in store for it, we should scarcely question the loss of otherwise possible pleasure which the dominance of such a desire entails on those who are possessed by it, were it not for the confusion which leads us to assume that the satisfaction of a strongest desire must always convey to the subject of it a pleasure greater than any which he would otherwise have

enjoyed.   It is true, of course, that for any one in whom
the desire for goodness or the love of mankind, or however
else we may describe the impulse to a life of sacrifice, is
really the dominant motive, it would be impossible really to
enjoy those pleasures, however innocent, which interfere with
his giving effect to the desire and which he rejects for that
reason.   But it does not follow from this that he would not
have had more enjoyment on the whole if the dominant
desire had been different, and if he had been free to take
his fill of the innocent pleasures from which it has withheld
him.   According to all appearances and any fair interpretation of them, he certainly would have had more.

Whether the loss of pleasure in the life of such a man
through the disturbing action of his altruistic enthusiasm is
or is not compensated by a consequent accession of pleasure
to others, who have the benefit of the results of his enthusiasm without sharing in the disturbance or self-denial,
may be more open to doubt.   If our nature were such that
the saint or reformer could set himself to confer happiness
on others without seeking to communicate a character like
his own ; if we could take advantage of the services of such
an one without admiring and aspiring in some measure to
become like him, the gain to the general sum of pleasures
as the result of his activity would be less doubtful than it is.
But if, as we must hold to be the case, the character and
activity of the altruistic enthusiast, under ordinary conditions
of temperament and circumstance, is not preponderatingly
pleasure-giving to the enthusiast himself; and if his effect
upon others is always in greater or less degree to disturb
their acquiescence in the life of ordinary enjoyment; then
the case is at least not clear in favour of the assumption
that the effect of such a character and activity is an addition
to the aggregate of human pleasure, one man taken with
another.   He must be much stiffened in hedonistic theory
who could maintain that the life which ended on the cross
was one of more enjoyment than that which would have
been open to the Crucified but for the purpose which led

to this end ; and the Crucified himself foresaw that he came not to send peace on earth but a sword. It would be unwarrantable indeed to found a general ethical argument on this example, but it may be fairly used to bring home to our minds that question as to the sufficiency of the hedonistic justification of the self-denying life, which is all that it would be to our purpose here to suggest.

278. These considerations have arisen from our noticing that the practical attitude towards pleasures, which in our consciences we regard as belonging to the highest virtue, is one of larger renunciation than was contemplated by the Greek philosophers as entering into the ideal of virtue. In this respect we claim a superiority for the modern or Christian ideal, independently of all attempts to show that conduct in accordance with it is more productive of pleasure in the long run or to mankind on the whole. The success of such attempts we hold to be at least very questionable. It is not by their aid that we seek to show the more self-denying (or pleasure-renouncing) type of virtue to be the higher ; nor, on the other hand, is this view founded on any impression that a virtue is more of a virtue for being painful. We give the advantage to the Christian type because it implies, directly on the part of those by whom it is exhibited, a wider range of interest and activity in the work of perfecting mankind, and indirectly, on the part of the multitude by whose claims it is elicited, a liberation of their powers unknown to the ancient world.

279. This conclusion, it will be remembered, has been arrived at in the process of comparing those manifestations of the good will which the Greek philosophers presented to themselves, under the names ἀνδρεία and σωφροσύνη, as specially related to the endurance of pain and the rejection of certain pleasures for worthy objects, with the self-denying disposition which our consciences acknowledge as the best. In the root of the matter the Greek conception of these virtues is thoroughly sound. They are considered genuine

only when resting on a pure and good will, which is a will to
be good—a will directed not to anything external, or anything
in respect of which it is passive, but to its own perfection, to
the attainment of what is noblest in human character and
action.   In this respect that which we may call, after its first
clear enunciators, the Platonic or Aristotelian conception of
virtue, as has been said above, is final.   It marks the great
transition, whenever and however achieved, in the development of the idea of true good from the state of mind in which
it is conceived as a well-being more or less independent of
what a man is in himself, to that in which it is conceived as
a well-being constituted by character and action.   Its defects,
as compared with the standard which we now acknowledge,
arose from the actual shortcoming in the then achievement
of the human soul—the soul of human society—as compared
with that of which we are ourselves partakers.

As has been previously pointed out, an explicit or reflective ideal [1] of the true good, or of virtue as a habit of will
directed to it, can only follow upon a practical pursuit of the
good, arising indeed out of the same spiritual demand which
is the source of the ideal, but not yet consciously regulated
by any theoretical form of it.   In this pursuit have arisen
institutions and arrangements of life, social requirements and
expectations, conventional awards of praise and blame.   It
is in reflection upon these—in the effort to extract some
common meaning from them, to reject what is temporary
and accidental in them, while retaining what is essential —
that there is formed such an explicit ideal of the good and
of virtue as we find in the Greek philosophers.   Any one
who really conformed to their ideal of virtue would, no doubt,
have lived a better life than any one was actually living, because he would have been pursuing, sustainedly and upon
a principle of which he was aware, a line of conduct which
in fact the best men were only pursuing with frequent lapses
through defect either of will or judgment.   But in their
determinate conception or filling up of the ideal, and in

[1] *I.e.* an ideal which the persons affected by it have reflected on.

their consequent conception of the sort of behaviour in which the virtuous will was to be exhibited, they were necessarily limited by the actual state of human society. 'Human brotherhood' had no meaning for them. They had no adequate notion of the claims in response to which the good will should be exercised. In respect of the institutions and arrangements of life, of the social requirements, etc., just spoken of, a great range of new experience has come into being for us which did not exist for them. The soul of human society has realised its capacities in new ways. We know that it can achieve, because it has done so, much of which the Greek philosophers did not dream.

280. Hence has resulted a change in the ideal of what its full realisation would be, and consequently a change in the conception of what is required from the individual as a contribution to that realisation. In particular the idea has been formed of the possible inclusion of all men in one society of equals, and much has been actually done towards its realisation. For those citizens of Christendom on whom the idea of Christendom has taken hold, such a society does actually exist. For them—according to their conscientious conviction, if not according to their practice—mankind is a society of which the members owe reciprocal services to each other, simply as man to man. And the idea of this social unity has been so far realised that the modern state, unlike the ancient, secures equality before the law to all persons living within the territory over which its jurisdiction extends, and in theory at least treats aliens as no less possessed of rights. Thus when we come to interpret that formal definition of the good, as a realisation of the powers of the human soul or the perfecting of man, which is true for us as for Aristotle, into that detail in which alone it can afford guidance for the actions of individuals, the particular injunctions which we derive from it are in many ways different from any that Aristotle could have thought of. For us as for him the good for the individual is to be good, and to be good is to contribute in some way disinterestedly, or for the sake of

doing it, to the perfecting of man. But when we ask ourselves how we should thus contribute, or what are the particular forms of virtuous life to which we should aspire, our answer is determined by the consciousness of claims upon us on the part of other men which, as we now see, must be satisfied in order to any perfecting of the human soul, but which were not, and in the then state of society could not be, recognised by the Greek philosophers. It is the consciousness of such claims that makes the real difference between what our consciences require of us, or our standards of virtue, and the requirements or standards which Greek Ethics represent.

281. It must be borne in mind, however, that the social development, which has given the idea of human brotherhood a hold on our consciences such as it could not have for the Greeks, would itself have been impossible but for the action of that idea of the good and of goodness which first found formal expression in the Greek philosophers. It implies interest in an object which is common to all men in the proper sense,—in the sense, namely, that there can be no competition for its attainment between man and man; and the only interest that satisfies this condition is the interest, under some form or other, in the perfecting of man or the realisation of the powers of the human soul. It is not to be pretended, indeed, that this in its purity, or apart from other interests, has been the only influence at work in maintaining and extending social union. It is obvious, for instance, that trade has played an important part in bringing and keeping men together; and trade is the offspring of other interests than that just described. The force of conquest, again, such as that which led to the establishment for some centuries of the 'Pax Romana' round the basin of the Mediterranean, has done much to break down estranging demarcations between different groups of men; and conquest has generally originated in selfish passions. But neither trade nor conquest by themselves would have helped to widen the comprehension of political union, to extend the range within which reciprocal claims are recognised of man on man, and

ultimately to familiarise men with the idea of human brotherhood. For this there must have been another interest at
work, applying the immediate results of trade and conquest
to other ends than those which the trader and conqueror had
in view; the interest in being good and doing good. Apart
from this, other interests might tend to combine certain men
for certain purposes and for a time, but because directed to
objects which each desires for himself alone and not for
another—objects which cannot really be attained in common
—they divide in spirit, even when they combine temporarily
in outward effect; and, sooner or later, the spiritual division
must make its outward sign.

282. It is sometimes supposed, indeed, that desires of
which the object on each man's part is his own pleasure,
may gradually produce a universal harmony and adjustment
of claims, as it comes to be discovered that the means by
which each may get most pleasure for himself are also the
means which serve to yield most pleasure to every one else.
The acceptance of this view probably arises from a combination of two notions; one, the notion that in the long run,
or on the whole, the greatest amount of pleasure results to
each individual from that order of life and society which
yields most pleasure in the long run to every other individual;
the other, the notion that a man's desire for pleasure is or
may become a desire for pleasure on the whole, as distinct
from any particular pleasure. Putting these two notions
together, we conclude that men, having no other motive
than desire for pleasure, may, after sufficient experience, be
led by their several desires each to act in a way productive
of most pleasure to all the rest.

But while the first of these notions is fairly arguable, the
second is certainly false. To be actuated by a desire for
pleasure is to be actuated by a desire for some specific
pleasure to be enjoyed by oneself. No two or more persons
whose desires were only of this kind could really desire anything in common. Under the given institutions of society
one man's desire for pleasure may, no doubt, lead to a

course of action which will incidentally produce pleasure to another ; as in trade, when A's desire for the pleasure to be got by the possession of some article leads him to give B a price for it, which enables B in turn to obtain some pleasure that he desires.   But even in this case it is clear not only that the desires of A and B, as desires for pleasures, are not directed to a common object, but that, if left to their natural course, they would lead to conflict.   A desires the pleasure which he obtains by buying the article of B, but (*qua* desiring pleasure) he does not desire, he has an aversion to, the loss of means to other pleasures involved in paying a price for it.   He only pays the price, and so adjusts his desire for pleasure to B's, because under the given social order he can obtain the article in no other way. The desires, in short, of different men, so far as directed each to some pleasure, are in themselves tendencies to conflict between man and man.   In many cases, through the action of society, there has come to be some established means of compromise between them, such as that of buying and selling ; but the cases in which no such settled means of compromise is available, and in which therefore A cannot gratify his particular desire for pleasure without depriving B of the chance of gratifying his, occur constantly enough to show us what is the natural tendency of a desire for pleasure, if left to itself[1].

---

[1] Kant (Werke, ed. Rosenkranz, viii. p. 138) illustrates the fallacy, as he considers it, of supposing that a moral harmony can result from the desire on the part of each man for his own greatest pleasure, by the story of the pledge given by King Francis to the Emperor Charles, ' was mein Bruder Karl haben will (Mailand), das will ich auch haben.' It will naturally be retorted on Kant that the illustration is inapt, because, while Charles and Francis could not each possess the duchy of Milan, the pleasures desired by men of well-regulated minds are such that each can gratify his desire without interfering with the gratification of the other.   On reflection, however, it will appear that this possibility of adjusting the desires for pleasure of different men (as in buying and selling) depends on the presence of controlling agencies which are themselves not the product of desires for pleasures ; and that on the estranging tendency of these desires, if left to

283. If we are enquiring, then, for an interest adequate to account for the existence of an ever-widening social union, in which the claims of all are acknowledged by the loyal citizen as the measure of what he may claim for himself, it is not in the desire for pleasure that we can find it, or in those 'particular passions,' such as ambition, which are wrongly supposed to have pleasure for their object, but which resemble the desire for pleasure in being directed to some object private in each case to the person under the influence of the passion. Given a social authority strong enough to insist on respect for general convenience in the individual's pursuit of his ends, and minded to do so, then desire for pleasure, aversion from pain, and the various egoistic passions, may adjust themselves to its requirements and even be enlisted in its service; but they cannot be the source of such an authority. It can have its origin only in an interest of which the object is a common good; a good in the effort after which there can be no competition between man and man; of which the pursuit by any individual is an equal service to others and to himself. Such a good may be pursued in many different forms by persons quite uncon-scious of any community in their pursuits; by the craftsman or writer, set upon making his work as good as he can

---

themselves, Kant is substantially right. There are, no doubt, social pleasures, pleasures which are like all others in that each man who desires them desires them for himself alone, but which can only be enjoyed in company, and which therefore bring men together. But though desires for such pleasures might lead men to associate temporarily for the purpose of their gratification, the association would itself tend to bring them into collision with other men associated for a like pur-pose, and would be liable to perpetual disruption, as desires for plea-sures of a different kind arose in the persons so associated. There are also pleasures, such as the enjoyment of the common air and sunshine, of which the sources cannot be appropriated, and for which therefore, under the simplest conditions of life, the desire as entertained by different men cannot tend to conflict. Under any other conditions, however, the opportunity for enjoying such pleasures, though not the sources of them, would become matter of competition, and thereupon the desire even for them would become a tendency to conflict.

without reference to his own glorification ; by the father devoted to the education of his family, or the citizen devoted to the service of his state. No one probably can present to himself the manner of its pursuit, as it must have been pursued in order to the formation of the most primitive tribal or civil society. If we would find an expression applicable to it in all its forms, 'the realisation of the capacities of the human soul,' or 'the perfecting of man,' seems best suited for the purpose. To most men, indeed, engaged in the pursuit of any common good, this expression might convey no meaning. Nevertheless it is as part of, or as contributing to, such a realisation, that the object of their pursuit has its attraction for them ; and it is for the same reason that it has the characteristic described, of being an object for which there can be no competition between man and man, and of which the pursuit is of general service.

284. Of such a good there had, of course, been pursuit ages before the Greek philosophers began to reflect on it and seek to define it. A proof of this was the very existence of the communities in which the philosophers lived, and of which they themselves only professed to explain the true idea. But it is one thing for men to be actuated by an inward demand for—to make spiritual effort after—a good which in its intrinsic nature is universal or common to all men ; another thing for them to conceive it in its universality. It was because it helped men to such a conception of the good in its universality that the teaching of the philosophers was of so much practical importance in the social history of man. The Greek citizen who loyally served his state, or sought to know the truth for its own sake, was striving for a good not private to himself but in its own nature universal ; yet he had no notion of there being any identity in the ends of living, for himself on the one side, and for slaves and barbarians on the other. The philosophers themselves—such was the practical limitation of their view by the conditions of life around them—would not have told him that there was. But when they told him that the object of his life should be duly to fulfil his function as a man, or to contribute to a good consisting in a realisation of the soul's faculties, they were directing him to an object which in fact was common to him with all men, without possibility of competition for it, without distinction of Greek or barbarian, bond or free. Their teaching was thus, in its own nature, of a kind to yield a social result which they did not themselves contemplate, and which tended to make good the practical shortcomings of their teaching itself.

285. It would not be to the purpose here to enter on the complicated and probably unanswerable question of the share which different personal influences may have had in gaining acceptance for the idea of human brotherhood, and in giving it some practical effect in the organisation of society. We have no disposition to hold a brief for the Greek philosophers against the founders of the Christian Church, or for the latter against the former. All that it is sought to maintain is this ; that the society of which we are consciously members—a society founded on the self-subordination of each individual to the rational claims of others, and potentially all-inclusive—could not have come into existence except (1) through the action in men of a desire of which (unlike the desire for pleasure) the object is in its own nature common to all ; and (2) through the formation in men's minds of a conception of what this object is, sufficiently full and clear to prevent its being regarded as an object for any one set of men to the exclusion of another. It was among the followers of Socrates, so far as we know, that such a conception was for the first time formed and expressed – for the first time, at any rate, in the history of the traceable antecedents of modern Christendom. Inevitable prejudice, arising from the condition of society about them, prevented them from apprehending the social corollaries of their own conception. But the conception of the perfecting of man as the good for all, of a habit of will directed to that work in some of its forms as the good for each, had been definitely formed in certain minds, and only needed opportunity to bear its natural fruit. When through the establishment of the 'Pax Romana' round the basin of the Mediterranean, or otherwise, the external conditions had been fulfilled for the initiation of a society aiming at universality ; when a person had appeared charging himself with the work of establishing a kingdom of God among men, announcing purity of heart as the sole condition of membership of that kingdom, and able to inspire his followers with a belief in the perpetuity of his spiritual presence and work among them ; then the time came for the value of the philosopher's work to appear.

They had provided men with a definite and, in principle, true conception of what it is to be good—a conception involving no conditions but such as it belongs to man as man, without distinction of race or caste or intellectual gifts, to fulfil. When the old barriers of nations and caste were being broken down ; when a new society, all-embracing in idea and aspiration, was forming itself on the basis of the common vocation 'Be ye perfect as your Father in Heaven is perfect,' there was need of conceptions, at once definite and free from national or ceremonial limitations, as to the modes of virtuous living in which that vocation was to be fulfilled. Without them the universal society must have remained an idea and aspiration, for there would have been no intellectual medium through which its members could communicate and co-operate with each other in furtherance of the universal object. It was in consequence of Greek philosophy, or rather of that general reflection upon morality which Greek philosophy represented, that such conceptions were forthcoming. By their means men could arrive at a common understanding of the goodness which, as citizens of the kingdom of God, it was to be their common object to promote in themselves and others. The reciprocal claim of all upon all to be helped in the effort after a perfect life could thus be rendered into a language intelligible to all who had assimilated the moral culture of the Graeco-Roman world. For them conscious membership of a society founded on the acknowledgement of this claim became a definite possibility. And as the possibility was realised, as conscious membership of such a society became an accomplished spiritual fact, men became aware of manifold relations, unthought of by the philosophers, in which the virtues of courage, temperance and justice were to be exercised, and from the recognition of which it resulted that, while the principle of those virtues remained as the philosophers had conceived it, the range of action understood to be implied in being thus virtuous became (as we have seen) so much wider.

286. It will be well here to recall the main points to which our enquiry in its later stages has been directed. Our theory has been that the development of morality is founded on the action in man of an idea of true or absolute good, consisting in the full realisation of the capabilities of the human soul. This idea, however, according to our view, acts in man, to begin with, only as a demand unconscious of the full nature of its object. The demand is indeed from the outset quite different from a desire for pleasure. It is at its lowest a demand for some well-being which shall be common to the individual desiring it with others; and only as such does it yield those institutions of the family, the tribe, and the state, which further determine the morality of the individual. The formation of more adequate conceptions of the end to which the demand is directed we have traced to two influences, separable for purposes of abstract thought but not in fact: one, the natural development, under favouring conditions, of the institutions, just mentioned, to which the demand gives rise; the other, reflection alike upon these institutions and upon those well-reputed habits of action which have been formed in their maintenance and as their effect. Under these influences there has arisen, through a process of which we have endeavoured to trace the outline, on the one hand an ever-widening conception of the range of persons between whom the common good is common, on the other a conception of the nature of the common good itself, consistent with its being the object of a universal society co-extensive with mankind. The good has come to be conceived with increasing clearness, not as anything which one man or set of men can gain or enjoy to the exclusion of others, but as a spiritual activity in which all may partake, and in which all must partake, if it is to amount to a full realisation of the faculties of the human soul. And the progress of thought in individuals, by which the conception of the good has been thus freed from material limitations, has gone along with a progress in social unification which has made it possible for men practically to conceive a claim of all upon all for freedom and support in the pursuit of a common end. Thus the ideal of virtue which our consciences acknowledge has come to be the devotion of character and life, in whatever channel the idiosyncrasy and circumstances of the individual may determine, to a perfecting of man, which is itself conceived not as an external end to be attained by goodness, but as consisting in such a life of self-devoted activity on the part of all persons. From the difficulty of presenting to ourselves in any positive form what a society, perfected in this sense, would be, we may take refuge in describing the object of the devotion, which our consciences demand, as the greatest happiness of the greatest number ; and until we puzzle ourselves with analysis, such an account may be sufficient for practical purposes. But our theory becomes false to the real demand of conscience, if it interprets this happiness except as including and dependent upon the unimpeded exercise by the greatest number of a will, the same in principle with that which conscience calls upon the individual to aim at in himself.

287. No sooner, however, has such a statement been made in regard to the end of moral effort than one becomes aware how liable it is to be understood in an abstract sense, wholly inadequate to the meaning which it is intended to convey. It seems to reduce the life of thoroughly realised spiritual capacity, in which we must suppose all that is now inchoate in the way of art and knowledge, no less than of moral efforts, to have reached completion, to a level with that effort as we know it under those conditions of impeded activity which alone (as it might seem) give a meaning to such phrases as 'self-sacrifice' or a 'devoted will.' The student of Aristotle will naturally recall his saying, ἀσχολού-μεθα ἵνα σχολάζωμεν, καὶ πολεμοῦμεν ἵν᾿ εἰρήνην ἄγωμεν [1], and will object to us that, while professing to follow in principle Aristotle's conception of virtue as directed to the attainment of a good consisting in a realisation of the soul's powers, we are forgetting Aristotle's pronounced judgment that the highest form of this realisation, and with it complete 'happiness,' was to be reached not in the exercise of the 'practical virtues' with their attendant pains and unrest, but in the life of pure contemplation, which, whatever difficulty there may be in forming any positive conception of it, was certainly understood as excluding self-denial and all the qualities which we naturally take to be characteristic of moral goodness. Even those who may be disposed to think that Aristotle's language about the blessedness of the contemplative life expresses little more than a philosopher's conceit ; that, if applied to the pursuit of science and philosophy as we in fact painfully pursue them, it is quite untrue; and that, in any attempt to translate it into an account of some fruition of the Godhead higher than we can yet experience, we pass at once into a region of unreality—even such persons may be ready to accept his view in its negative application. They may think that he makes out his case unanswerably against the supposition that moral goodness in any intelligible sense can be carried on into, or be a determining element in, the life in which ultimate good is actually attained.

288. In meeting this objection it must be once more admitted that our view of what the life would be, in which ultimate good was actually attained, can never be an adequate

---

[1] *I.e.* 'We give up leisure in order to enjoy it, and we make war for the sake of having peace.' Eth. Nic. **X.** vii. **6.**

view. It consists of the idea that such a life must be possible, filled up as regards particulars, in some inadequate measure, by reflection on the habits and activities, on the modes of life and character, which through influence of that idea have been brought into being. If the idea, as it actuates us, carried with it a full consciousness of what its final realisation would be, the distinction between idea and realisation would be at an end. But while for this reason it is impossible for us to say what the perfecting of man, of which the idea actuates the moral life, in its actual attainment might be, we can discern certain conditions which, if it is to satisfy the idea, it must fulfil. It must be a perfecting of *man*— not of any human faculty in abstraction, or of any imaginary individuals in that detachment from social relations in which they would not be men at all. We are therefore justified in holding that it could not be attained in a life of mere scientific and artistic activity, any more than in one of 'practical' exertion from which those activities were absent ; in holding further that the life in which it is attained must be a social life, in which all men freely and consciously co-operate, since otherwise the possibilities of their nature, as agents who are ends to themselves, could not be realised in it ; and, as a corollary of this, that it must be a life determined by one harmonious will—a will of all which is the will of each—such as we have previously called, in treating it as the condition of individual virtue, a devoted will ; *i.e.* a will having for its object the perfection which it alone can maintain.

When we speak of the formation of such a will in all men as itself constituting that true end of moral effort, relation to which gives the virtues their value, we understand it, not as determined merely by an abstract idea of law, but as implying (what it must in fact imply) a whole world of beneficent social activities, which it shall sustain and co-ordinate. These activities, as they may become in a more perfect state of mankind, we cannot present to ourselves ; but they would not be the activities of a more perfect mankind, unless they

were the expression of a will which pursues them for their
own sake, or as its own fulfilment. Such a will therefore we
may rightly take to be *in principle* that perfect life, unknown
to us except in its principle, which is the end of morality;
a like will being the condition of those virtues, known to us
not in principle merely but in some imperfect exercise, which
form the means to that end.

289. This explanation made, we return to our statement
that 'the ideal of virtue which our consciences acknowledge
has come to be the devotion of character and life to a
perfecting of man, which is itself conceived as consisting
in a life of self-devoted activity on the part of all persons.'
This statement naturally suggests two further lines of objection and enquiry. If we are to accept it as a true account of
the ideal of virtue, what is to be said, it may be asked, of those
activities, those developed faculties, in the pursuit of knowledge and in the practice of art, which we undoubtedly value
and admire, and which the ancient philosophers for that
reason rightly reckoned virtues, but which would not commonly be thought to have anything to do with such devotion
of character and life to a perfecting of man as is here made
out to be at once the essence and the end of virtue, either
in the way of implying it on the part of the man of science
and the artist, or as tending to promote it in others? That
they tend to general pleasure may perhaps be admitted, but
can it be seriously held that they contribute to a true good
consisting in self-devoted activity on the part of all persons?
Must we not either be content to accept the account of true
good as consisting in that general pleasure to which the
practice of the moral virtues and the pursuit of science and
art may, at least with much plausibility, be alike considered
means; or, if we will not accept this account of the end of
morality, must we not admit that the value of the moral
virtues on the one side, and that of intellectual excellence,
scientific or artistic, on the other, cannot be deemed relative
to one common good?

290. To any one who has accepted the reasons given for

rejecting the notion that pleasure is the true good, and who at the same time recognises the necessity of conceiving some ultimate unity of good, to which all true values are relative, these questions present a serious difficulty. It shall be dealt with in the sequel, and is noticed here in order to record the writer's admission that it cannot be passed over [1]. But for the present, considering the readiness with which most people acquiesce in the distinction of moral from other excellence, as if it were relative to an end of its own with which science and art, as such, have nothing to do, it may be advisable to give precedence to another order of objections with which our doctrine is likely to be challenged.

Of what avail, it will be asked, is the theory of the good and of goodness here stated for the settlement of any of the questions which a moralist is expected to help us to settle? We want some available criterion of right and wrong in action. We want a theory of Duty which, as applied to the circumstances of life, can be construed into particular duties, so that we may be able to judge how far our own actions and lives (to say nothing of those of others) are what they should

---

[1] [The question is not discussed in the *Prolegomena to Ethics*, and from a mark at this point in the Author's manuscript it is almost certain that he had abandoned the idea of dealing with it in the present volume. It has however been thought best to print the section in its entirety. The reader will probably gather from Book III a general idea of the way in which the difficulty would have been met, especially if he remembers that the end has been throughout defined as the realisation of the possibilities of human nature, and that devotion to such objects as the well-being of a family, the sanitation of a town, or the composition of a book, has been described as an unconscious pursuit of this end. In other words, the pursuit of such objects for their own sakes is considered to have a latent reference to the whole of which they are parts, a reference which would become conscious if the whole and the parts were ever opposed to each other; and this point of view would no doubt have been worked out with regard to the pursuit of art and science as ends in themselves (cf. § 370 sub fin.). The question becomes more complicated when the person who devotes himself to art or science is supposed to have formed a philosophical conception of the ultimate end; and on this question the concluding pages of the volume should be consulted.]

be, and may have some general guide to the line of conduct
we should adopt in circumstances where use and wont will
either not guide us at all, or will lead us astray. But the
theory advanced above, construed in the natural way, would
seem too severe to admit of practical use, for it would offer
nothing but unrealisable counsels of perfection ; while, construed in another way, it would seem to allow of our treating
any and every action as having its measure of good. If it
is meant that, in order to be morally good—in order to satisfy
a duly exacting conscience—an action must have for its
motive a desire consciously directed to human perfection,
we shall have a standard of goodness which might indeed
serve the purpose, so far as we acknowledged it, of keeping
us in perpetual self-abasement ; but, if we were not to act
till we acted from such a motive, should we ever act at all?
If, on the other hand, our theory of the good practically
means no more than that the morality of actions represents
the operation in human society of an impulse after self-
realisation on the part of some impersonal spirit of mankind,
it will yield no criterion of the good and bad in action ; for
we must hold every distinctively human action, good and bad
alike, to be characterised by the results of such operation.
Even if our theory be correct in regard to the spiritual impulse,
other than desire for pleasure, implied in the formation of
morality and the susceptibility to moral ideals, is it not after
all by a calculation of pleasure-giving consequences that we
can alone decide whether an action which has been done
should or should not have been done, or which of the
courses of action open to us under any given complication
of circumstances should or should not be adopted?

These questions will be considered in our next Book.

BOOK IV

THE APPLICATION OF MORAL PHILOSOPHY
TO THE GUIDANCE OF CONDUCT

CHAPTER I

THE PRACTICAL VALUE OF THE MORAL IDEAL

291. IN considering whether our theory of the good and of goodness can be of use in helping us to decide what ought to be done and whether we are doing it, it is important to bear in mind the two senses—the fuller and the more restricted—in which the question, What ought to be done? may be asked. It may either mean—and this is the narrower sense in which the question may be asked—What ought an action to be as determined in its nature by its effects? or it may be asked with the fuller meaning, What ought the action to be with reference to the state of mind and character which it represents? in which case the simple τί δεῖ πράττειν; becomes equivalent to πῶς ἔχων πράττει ὁ τὸ δέον πράττων; The former is the sense in which the question is asked, when it is not one of a self-examining conscience, but of perplexity between different directions in which duty seems to call. The latter is the sense in which a man asks it when he is comparing his practice with his ideal. We reckon the latter sense the fuller, because a man cannot properly decide whether, in respect of character and motives, he is acting as he ought, without considering the effects of the course of action which he is pursuing, as compared with the effects of other courses of action which it is open to him to pursue [1]; while he can compare the value of one set of effects with another without considering the nature of the motives which might prompt him to the adoption of the several courses of

[1] [This statement should be taken in connection with § 304 and foll.]

action leading to the several effects. Thus, whereas the question in the latter sense includes the question as asked in the former sense, the question can be dealt with in the former sense without raising it in the latter.

292. It is clear, however, that in whichever of these distinguishable senses we ask the question, What ought to be done? the answer to it must be regulated by one and the same conception of the good. If we hold, according to the explanation previously given, that the one unconditional good is the good will, this must be the end by reference to which we estimate the effects of an action. The circumstances in which the question is raised, whether such or such an action ought to be done, may be of a kind, as we shall see presently, which prevent any reference to the character of an agent, and shut us up in our moral judgment of the act to a consideration of its effects; but the effects which we look to, according to our theory, must still be effects bearing on that perfection of human character which we take to be the good. In like manner the consistent Utilitarian will answer the question of 'ought or ought not' in both the distinguished senses upon one and the same principle. He decides what ought to be done under any given circumstances by considering what will be the effects, in the way of producing pleasure or pain, of the several courses of action possible under the circumstances; and for the same reasons upon which he decides what the action, as measured by its effects, should be, he will hold that it should be done—will be of more value, according to the same standard, if done—in a state of mind which itself involves pleasure; cheerfully and 'disinterestedly,' not under any kind of constraint. But it will only be indirectly, according to him, that the question of the motive—of the ultimate object which the man sets before himself in doing the act—will come into account. The act will not depend for its goodness or moral value, for being such an act as ought to be done, upon this motive or object. For this it depends simply, according to the Utilitarian view, upon its pleasure-giving effects. The question whether the motive from which the act proceeds is good or bad, a motive which a man ought or ought not to have, is a separate question, and one to which the answer depends on that given to the question whether the actions to which such a motive ordinarily incites are or are not actions which, on the ground of their pleasure-giving effects, ought to be done.   The motives which we ought to have, the dispositions which we ought to cultivate (if indeed the term 'ought,' according to the Utilitarian view, can be applied in this connection at all), will be so because they lead to actions productive of preponderating pleasure [1].

293. Upon the view of the moral end or good adopted in this treatise, the question of motive and the question of effects hold quite a different relative position to that which they hold in the Utilitarian system.   If the good is a perfection of mankind, of which the vital bond must be a will on the part of all men, having some mode of that perfection for its object, it will only be in relation to a state of will, either as expressing it or as tending to promote it, or as doing both, that an action can have moral value at all.   The actions which *ought* to be done, in the fullest sense of the word, are actions expressive of a good will, in the sense that they represent a character of which the dominant interest is in conduct contributory to the perfection of mankind, in doing that which so contributes for the sake of doing it. We cannot say with *complete* truth of any action which has

---

[1] Cf. Mill's Utilitarianism, p. 26, note.   'The morality of the action depends entirely upon the intention—that is, upon what the agent *wills to do*' (as distinct from the end which he seeks in doing it).   'But the motive, that is, the feeling which makes him will so to do, when it makes no difference in the act, makes none in the morality: though it makes a great difference in our moral estimation of the agent, especially if it indicates a good or a bad habitual *disposition*—a bent of character from which useful or from which hurtful actions are likely to arise.' 'Useful' of course here means pleasure-giving.   'When it makes no difference in the act' means, when it makes no difference in the act *as measured by its outward effects*.   That the motive should make no difference to an act, in its true or full nature, we should pronounce, according to the view stated in the text, to be an impossibility.

been done, that it has been what it ought to have been, unless it represents such a character, or of any action contemplated as possible, that it will be what it ought to be, except
on supposition that it will fulfil the same condition.

But it is clear that even among past actions it is only of
his own, if of them, that a man has really the means of judging whether they represent such a character.   Of prospective
actions for which we are not personally and immediately
responsible, we could never say that they are such as ought
to be done, if we considered them to depend for being so on
the disposition of the agent ; since we cannot foresee what
the disposition with which any agent will do them will be.
When we say that restraints ought to be put upon the liquor-
traffic, or that a mistress ought to look carefully after her
servants, or that our neighbour ought to give his children
a better education, we are not making any reference in
thought to any motive or disposition from which we suppose
that the obligatory act will proceed.   In such cases, as in all
where we apply the predicates ' ought ' and ' ought not ' otherwise than in reflection upon our own acts, or in some interpretation of the acts of others founded on an ascription to
them of motives which we think their acts evidence, we are
not contemplating the acts in their full nature.   The full
nature, for instance, of a father's act in providing for the
education of his children depends on the character or state
of will which it represents; and what this is in any particular
case no one can tell.   But the action has a nature, though
not its whole nature, in respect of its effect upon the children,
and through them upon others ; and we can abstract this
nature from its nature in relation to the will of the father,
without error resulting in our judgment as to the former,
just as we can judge correctly of the mechanical relations
of a muscular effort without taking account of the organic
processes on which the effort really depends.

It is an abstraction of this kind that we have to make in
all cases where we judge, without reference to ourselves,
that a certain sort of action, not yet done, is one that ought

to be done ; and it might be well if we could make up our minds that we are not warranted in going further when we judge the actions of others.   Histories, no doubt, would be much shortened, and would be found much duller, if speculations about the motives (as distinct from the *intentions*) of the chief historical agents were omitted ; nor shall we soon cease to criticise the actions of contemporaries on the strength of inferences from act to motive.   But in all this we are on very uncertain ground.   It is clearly quite right in judging either of historical or contemporary actions to take account, so far as possible, of all the circumstances—to appreciate the bearings of any act as presented to those who were or are concerned in doing it, to consider what the effects of it, as probably contemplated by them, were or are.   But this is a different thing from trying to ascertain the state of character on the part of the agents which the actions represent, and in ignorance of which the full moral nature of the acts is not known.   It is wiser not to make guesses where we can do no more than guess, and to confine ourselves, *where no question of self-condemnation or self-approval is involved*, to measuring the value of actions by their effects without reference to the character of the agents ; as we must do (subject to a reservation to be stated below) where the question is whether an action, not yet done, ought to be done or not.

294. After this statement we shall naturally be called on to explain in what cases and in what way, according to our theory, a man should endeavour, when it is an action which he has himself done, or thinks of doing, that is in question, to consider it in what we have called its full moral nature, *i.e.* with reference not merely to effects which it has had or is likely to have, but to the state of mind on the part of the agent which it expresses or would express.   Before doing so, however, let us make sure that the reader is under no misapprehension as to the points at issue with the Utilitarians, with whom we agree in holding that ordinary judgments upon the moral value of actions must be founded on consideration of their effects alone.   To the Utilitarian the virtuous character is good simply as a means to an end quite different from itself, namely a maximum of possible pleasure.   An action is good, or has moral value, or is one that ought to be done, upon the same ground.   If two actions, done by different men, are alike in their production of pleasure, they are alike in moral value, though the doer of one is of virtuous character and the doer of the other is not so.   In our view the virtuous character is good, not as a means to a 'summum bonum' other than itself, but as in principle identical with the 'summum bonum'; and accordingly, if two actions could be alike in their moral effects (as they very well may be in production of pleasure) which represent, the one a more virtuous, the other a less virtuous character, they would still be quite different in moral value. The one would be more, the other less, of a good, according to the kind of character which they severally represent. But it is only an action done by himself that a man has the means of estimating in relation to the character represented by it.   Actions done by others, if similar outwardly or in effect, can only be referred to similar states of character, though the states which they represent may in fact be most different; and in regard to actions simply contemplated as possible the question of the character represented by them cannot be raised at all.   When from the nature of the case, however, a consideration of effects can alone enter into the moral valuation of an act, the effects to be considered, according to our view, will be different from those of which the Utilitarian, according to his principles, would take account.   They will be effects, not in the way of producing pleasure, but in the way of contributing to that perfection of mankind, of which the essence is a good will on the part of all persons.   These are the effects which, in our view, an action must in fact tend to produce, if it is one that *ought to be done*, according to the most limited sense of that phrase; just as these are the effects *for the sake of which* it must be done, if it is done *as* it ought to be done.

295. For an omniscient being, indeed, the distinction—unavoidable for us—between the judgment that an action ought to be done, and the judgment that an action is done as it ought to be done, would not exist. It is occasioned by a separation in the moral judgment of act from motive, only possible for an imperfect intelligence. An omniscient being could not contemplate a future action as merely possible, or apart from the motive which must really cause it when it comes to be done, any more than it could fail to know the motive of every act that has been done. Knowing the state of will from which every future act will proceed, as well as that from which every past act has proceeded, it would not regard any act as being what it should be, unless the character expressed by it were what it should be. It would trace the effect of any fault on the part of the character in the actual consequences of the action. For it is only to our limited vision that there can seem to be such a thing as good effects from an action that is bad in respect of the will which it represents, and that in consequence the question becomes possible, whether the morality of an action is determined by its motive or by its consequences. There is no real reason to doubt that the good or evil in the motive of an action is exactly measured by the good or evil in its consequences, as rightly estimated—estimated, that is, in their bearing on the production of a good will or the perfecting of mankind. The contrary only appears to be the case on account of the limited view we take both of action and consequences. We notice, for instance, that selfish motives lead an able man to head a movement of political reform which has beneficent consequences. Here, we say, is an action bad in itself, according to the morality of the 'good will,' but which has good effects : is it to be judged according to its motive, or according to its effects ? But, in fact, if we look a little more closely, we shall find that the selfish political leader was himself much more of an instrument than of an originating cause, and that his action was but a trifling element in the

sum or series of actions which yielded the political movement.   The good in the effect of the movement will really
correspond to the degree of good will which has been exerted in bringing it about; and the effects of any selfishness in its promoters will appear in some limitation to the
good which it brings to society.

It is seldom indeed that the most conspicuous actors on
the world's stage are known to us enough from the inside,
or that the movements in which they take part can be contemplated with sufficient completeness, to enable us very
certainly to verify this assurance in regard to them.   But
the more we learn of such a person, for instance, as Napoleon, and of the work which seemed to be his, the more
clearly does it appear how what was evil in it arose out of
his personal selfishness and that of his contemporaries,
while what was good in it was due to higher and purer
influences of which he and they were but the medium.
And within the more limited range of affairs which each
of us can observe for himself a like lesson is being constantly learnt.   If the 'best motives' seem sometimes to
lead to actions which are mischievous in results, it is because these 'best motives' have not been good enough.
If there has been no other taint of selfishness about them,
yet they have been acted on inconsiderately; which means
that the agent has been too selfish to take the trouble duly
to think of what his action brings with it to others.   It is
only, in short, the unavoidably abstract nature of our judgments upon conduct that leads to distinction between good
in motive and good in effect.   We infer a motive from the
action of another; but, if the inference be correct so far as
it goes, we still do not know the motive in its full reality,—
in its relation, so to speak, to the universe of a character,
and to the influences which have made and are making that
character.   The effects of the action, again, we only contemplate in a like fragmentary way.   With the whole spiritual history of the action before us on the one side, with
the whole sum and series of its effects before us on the

other, we should presumably see that just so far as a good
will, *i.e.* a will determined by interest in objects contributory to human perfection, has had more or less to do with
bringing the action about, there is more or less good, *i.e.*
more or less contribution to human perfection, in its
effects.

296. Granting, then, that the moral value of an action
really depends on the motives or character which it represents, the question remains whether for us the consideration
of motives can be of any avail in deciding whether an action
ought to be done or to have been done. It must be admitted at once that, in judging of another's action, we have
not enough insight into motive (as distinct from intention)
to be warranted in founding our moral estimate on anything
but the effects of the action. At the same time we are
bound to remember that an estimate so founded is necessarily imperfect, and to be cautious in our personal criticism
accordingly. Only if the agent himself describes his motives, as interesting persons are apt to do, are we warranted
in judging them, and then *only as described by him.* Again,
when the question is whether an action ought to be done,
which we are not ourselves responsible for doing or pre-
venting, a consideration of motives can plainly have no
bearing on it. There remain the cases (1) of reflection
on past actions of our own, (2) of consideration whether an
act should be presently done, which it rests with ourselves
to do or not to do. In both these cases the question of the
character or state of will which an action represents may
be raised with a possibility of being answered. Given an
ideal of virtue, such as has been delineated above, a man
may ask himself, Was I, in doing so and so, acting as a
good man should, with a pure heart, with a will set on the
objects on which it should be set?—or again, Shall I, in
doing so and so, be acting as a good man should, goodness
being understood in the same sense? The question may be
reasonably asked, and there is nothing in the nature of the
case to prevent a true answer being given to it. It remains

to be considered, however, whether it can be raised with advantage; whether our ideal of virtue can in this way be practically applied with the result of giving men either truer views of what in particular they ought to do, or a better disposition to do it.

297. The habit in a man of raising such questions about himself as those just indicated, is what we have mainly in view when we call him conscientious. Now it must certainly be admitted that there have been men, great in service to their kind, to whom we should not naturally apply this epithet; and again that although, in most cases where a man is complained of as 'over-conscientious,' the complaint merely indicates his superiority to the level of moral practice about him, it may sometimes indicate a real fault. There is a kind of devotion to great objects or to public service, which seems to leave a man no leisure and to afford no occasion for the question about himself, whether he has been as good as he should have been, whether a better man would not have acted otherwise than he has done. And again there is a sense in which to be always fingering one's motives is a sign rather of an unwholesome preoccupation with self than of the eagerness in disinterested service which helps forward mankind. A man's approach to the ideal of virtue is by no means to be measured by the clearness or constancy of his reflection upon the ideal. A prevalent interest in some work which tends to make men what they should be may be found in those who seldom entertain the question whether they are themselves what they should be, and who in those regions of their life which lie off the line of the prevailing interest—perhaps also in their choice of means by which to give effect to that interest—are the worse for not entertaining it. With all their sins of omission and commission such men may be nearer the ideal of virtue than others, who pride themselves on conformity to a standard of virtue (which cannot be the highest, or they would not credit themselves with conforming to it), and who so hug

[handwritten marginal note: This is something like the view of Carlyle in his Characterish i.e. conscious + unhealthy; + unconscious + healthy.]

their reputation with themselves for acting conscientiously that in difficult situations they will not act at all.

298. This admission made, it remains true that the comparison of our own practice, as we know it on the inner side in relation to the motives and character which it expresses, with an ideal of virtue, is the spring from which morality perpetually renews its life. It is thus that we 'lift up our hearts, and lift them up unto the Lord.' It is thus alone, however insufficient, however 'dimly charactered and slight,' the ideal, that the initiative is given in the individual—and it can be given nowhere else—to any movement which really contributes to the bettering of man. It is thus that he is roused from acquiescence in the standard of mere respectability. No one, indeed, who recognises in their full extent the results of disinterested spiritual effort on the part of a forgotten multitude, which the respectability of any civilised age embodies, or who asks himself what any of us would be but for a sense of what respectability requires, will be disposed to depreciate its value. But the standard of respectability by which any age or country is influenced could never have been attained, if the temper which acquiesces in it had been universal—if no one had been lifted above that acquiescence—in the past. It has been reached through the action of men who, each in his time and turn, have refused to accept the way of living which they found about them, and to which, upon the principle of seeking the greater pleasure and avoiding the greater pain, they would naturally have conformed. The conception of a better way of living may have been on a larger or a smaller scale. It may have related to some general reformation of society, or to the change of some particular practice in which the protesting individual had been concerned. But if it has taken effect in any actual elevation of morality, it is because certain men have brought it home to themselves in a contrast between what they should be and what they are, which has awakened the sense of a personal responsibility for improvement.

In so doing they may not have raised the question of personal goodness, in the form in which it presents itself to the self-examining conscience of one who lives among a highly moralised society and conforms as a matter of course to its standards. They may not have asked themselves, Have we, in doing what was expected of us, been doing it from the right motives? In that form the question pre-supposes the establishment of a definite standard of conventional morality. In the days when such morality was still in making, and in the minds of the forgotten enthusiasts to whom we owe it, this would scarcely be the way in which the contrast between an ideal of virtue and current practice would present itself. Under such conditions it would present itself less as a challenge to purify the heart than as a call to new courses of overt action, the relation of which to motives and character it would not occur to any one to consider. But in principle it is the same operation in the individual of an idea of a perfect life, with which his own is contrasted, whether it take the form of a consciousness of personal responsibility for putting an end to some practice which, to a mind awakening to the claims of the human soul, seems unjust or unworthy, or the form of self-interrogation as to the purity of the heart from which a walk and conduct, outwardly correct, proceeds.

299. It may be objected, however, that in thus identifying the motive power at work in the practical reformer of morality with that which sets the introspective conscience upon the enquiry whether the heart is as pure as it should be, we are obscuring the real question as to the practical value of the latter. No one doubts that a man who improves the current morality of his time must be something of an Idealist. He must have an idea, which moves him to seek its realisation, of a better order of life than he finds about him. That idea cannot represent any experienced reality. If it did, the reformer's labour would be superfluous; the order of life which he seeks to bring about would be already in existence. It is an idea to which nothing real as yet corresponds, but which, as actuating the reformer, tends to bring into being a reality corresponding to itself. It is in this sense that the reformer must be an Idealist. But the idea which he seeks to realise is an idea of definite institutions and arrangements of life, of courses of action, each producing their outward sensible effects. What real identity is there between the influence of such an idea—an ideal of virtue, if we like to call it so—producing a visible alteration in man's life, and that of an ideal which sets a man upon asking, not what there is which he ought to do and is not doing, but whether, in that which he has been doing and will (as he ought) continue to do, his heart has been sufficiently pure?

The identity will appear, when we reflect that it is not a 'mere idea' of a better order of life that ever set any one upon a work of disinterested moral reform, in that sense of the term in which one of us might have 'an idea' of the Lord Mayor's show, or of a debate in Parliament, without having been present at them. The idea which moves the reformer is one that he feels a personal responsibility for realising. This feeling of personal responsibility for its execution is part and parcel of the practical idea itself, of the form of consciousness which we so describe. It is that which distinguishes it as a *practical* idea. The reformer cannot bear to think of himself except as giving effect, so far as may be, to his project of reform ; and thus, instead of merely contemplating a possible work, he does it. He presents himself to himself on the one hand as achieving, so far as in him lies, the contemplated work, on the other hand as neglecting it for some less worthy object; and he turns with contempt and aversion from the latter presentation. Now it is because, to the real reformer, the thought of something which should be done is thus always at the same time the thought of something which he should be and seeks to be, but would not be if he did not do the work, that there is a real unity between the spiritual principle which animates him, and that which appears in the self-questioning of the man who, without charging himself with the neglect of any outward duty, without contemplating any particular good work which he might do but has not done, still asks himself whether he has been what he should be in doing what he has done.

300. But, granted the unity of the spiritual principle at work in the two supposed cases, is there any real unity in the effects which it produces in the person of the moral reformer and in the person of the self-questioning 'saint'? In the one case the effect is the recognition and fulfilment of certain specific duties, previously not recognised or not fulfilled, by the moral reformer and those whom he influences. He and they come to deal differently with their fellow-men. But in the other case, if we enquire what specific performance follows from the self-questioning as to purity of heart, we find it difficult to answer. Among the respectable classes of a well-regulated society there is little in outward walk and conduct to distinguish the merely respectable from the most anxiously conscientious. As a rule, it will only be to a man already pretty thoroughly moralised by the best social influences that it will occur to reproach himself with having unworthy motives even in irreproachable conduct; and, as a rule, when such a man comes thus to reproach himself in presence of some ideal of a perfect Will, he will already have been fulfilling, under the feeling that it is expected of him, all the particular duties which the consciousness of such an ideal might otherwise challenge him to fulfil. Unless he has leisure for philanthropy, or a gift of utterance, there will be little in outward act to distinguish his converted state—if we may so describe the state in which he learns to contrast his personal unworthiness with an ideal of holiness—from that of moral self-complacency, in which he may have previously been living, and which is the state of most of the dutiful citizens about him.

301. If we could watch him closely enough, indeed, even in outward conduct there would appear to be a difference. Doing the work expected of him 'not with eye-service, as

a man-pleaser, but in singleness of heart, as unto the Lord,' he will rise to a higher standard of doing it. Into the duties which he is expected to fulfil he will put much more meaning than is put by those who claim their fulfilment, and will always be on the look-out for duties which no one would think the worse of him for not recognising. But in so doing, he probably will not seem to himself to be acting according to a higher standard than those about him. And in fact, although in a certain sense he transcends the 'law of opinion,' of social expectation, he only does so by interpreting it according to its higher spirit. That law, being, as we have seen, the result of the past action in human consciousness of an ideal of conduct, will yield different rules according as it is or is not interpreted by a consciousness under the same influence. It speaks with many voices according as men have ears to hear, and the spirit of the conscientious man shows itself in catching the purest of them. He is like a judge who is perpetually making new law in ostensibly interpreting the old. He extracts the higher meaning out of the recognised social code, giving reality to some requirements which it has hitherto only contained potentially. He feels the necessity of rules of conduct which, though they necessarily arise out of that effort to make human life perfect which has brought conventional morality into existence, are not yet a recognised part of that morality, and thus have no authority with those whose highest motive is a sense of what is expected of them.

302. This is true; but it is not merely on this account—not merely on account of certain effects in outward conduct which, upon sufficient scrutiny, it might be found to yield—that we claim for the temper of genuine self-abasement in presence of an ideal of holiness an intrinsic value, the same in kind with that which all would ascribe to a zeal for moral reform. We claim such a value for it—a value independent of any that it might possess as a means to a good other than itself—on the ground that it is a component influence in the perfect human life; on the ground that, whatever the universe of activities in which that life displays itself may prove to be, the self-abasing, which is also the aspiring or God-seeking, spirit, must always be their source and spring. The character exhibited by the moral reformer has a like value, in so far as it is not merely a means to the perfect life, but a phase of the same spiritual principle as must govern that life. But whereas we cannot but suppose that, if the perfect life of mankind were attained, this spiritual principle must have passed out of the phase in which it can appear as a reforming zeal—for in that event there could no longer be wrongs to redress, or indulged vices to eradicate—on the other hand we cannot suppose that, while human life remains human life, it can even in its most perfect form be superior to the call for self-abasement before an ideal of holiness.

There is no contradiction in the supposition of a human life purged of vices and with no wrongs left to set right. It is indeed merely the supposition of human life with all its capacities realised. In such a life the question of the reformer, What ought to be done in the way of overt action that is not being done? would no longer be significant. But so long as it is the life of men, *i.e.* of beings who are born and grow and die; in whom an animal nature is the vehicle through which the divine self-realising spirit works; in whom virtue is not born ready-made but has to be formed (however unfailing the process may come to be) through habit and education in conflict with opposing tendencies; so long the contrast must remain for the human soul between itself and the infinite spirit, of whom it must be conscious, as present to itself but other than itself, or it would not be the human soul. The more complete the realisation of its capacities, the clearer will be its apprehension at once of its own infinity in respect of its consciousness of there being an infinite spirit—a consciousness which only a self-communication of that spirit could convey—and of its finiteness as an outcome of natural conditions; a finiteness in consequence of which the infinite spirit is for

ever something beyond it, still longed for, never reached.
Towards an infinite spirit, to whom he is thus related, the
attitude of man at his highest and completest could still be
only that which we have described as self-abasement before
an ideal of holiness; not the attitude of knowledge, for
knowledge is of matters of fact or relations, and the infinite
spirit is neither fact nor relation ; not the attitude of full and
conscious union, for that the limitation of human nature
prevents ; but the same attitude of awe and aspiration which
belongs to all the upward stages of the moral life.   He
must think of the infinite spirit as better than the best that
he can himself attain to, but (just for that reason) as having
an essential community with his own best.   And, as his own
best rests upon a self-devoted will, so it must be as a will,
good not under the limitations of opposing tendencies but in
some more excellent, though not by us positively conceivable, way, that he will set before himself the infinite spirit.

303. The spiritual act, then, which in different aspects
may be described either as self-abasement or self-exaltation—
the act in which the heart is lifted up to God, in which the
whole inner man goes forth after an ideal of personal holiness—this act, while it is in principle one with the whole
course of man's moral endeavour, may be deemed in
a certain sense its most final form, because, in that rest
from the labour of baffled and disappointed endeavour
which a perfectly ordered society might be supposed to
bring, it would still not be superseded.   Its value is an
intrinsic value, not derived from any result beyond itself to
which it contributes.   In this respect, indeed, it does not
differ from any other expression of the good will.   If it differs
apparently from the more obviously practical expressions
of such a will, the reason is that these, while sharing its
intrinsic value, have also a further value, as means, which it
does not seem to possess.   They issue in sensible ameliorations of human society.   But these very ameliorations are
relative to that intrinsic good, the perfection of the human
soul, of which the heart at once self-abased and aspiring is

itself a lasting mode.   Whether such a heart, in this person or that, itself issues in outward 'transient' action of a noticeably beneficent kind, will depend mainly on the social surroundings, and on the intellectual and other qualifications of the particular person.   If these in any case are such as to call for and to favour a large amount of useful social activity, we are apt under the impression of the outward effect to overlook the spiritual principle which yields it, and which may be the same in another person otherwise circumstanced and gifted, by whom no such apparent effect is produced.   We praise the successful reformer, and forget that he is but what the man of unnoticed conscientious goodness might be in another situation and with other opportunities.

If the end by reference to which moral values are to be judged were anything but the perfect life itself, as resting on a devoted will, it would be right to depreciate the obscure saint by the side of the man to whose work we can point in the redress of wrongs and the purging of social vices.   But if the supreme value for man is what we take it to be—man himself in his perfection—then it is idle to contrast the more observably practical type of goodness with the more self-questioning or consciously God-seeking type.   The value of each is intrinsic and identical; for each rests on a heart or character or will which, however differently it may come to be exhibited as human capacities come to be more fulfilled, must still be that of the perfect man.   The distinction between them, as looked at from the point of view from which moral values are properly estimated, is mainly accidental.   It is a distinction of the circumstances under which the same principle of action is exercised.   Under certain conditions of society, of individual temperament and ability, it takes the one form, under other conditions the other.   In neither form is it barren of effects; but in one form its effects are more overt and 'transient,' in the other more impalpable and 'immanent.'   But the one order of effects no less than the other has its value as a means to that perfect life, to which the obscure saint and the true social reformer alike are not merely related as a means, but which each in his own person, under whatever limitations, represents.

304. From these considerations we return to the enquiry out of which they have arisen. Having distinguished the question, What ought to be done? — a question to be answered in detail by examination of the probable effects of contemplated action—from the question, What should I be? —a question of motives and character—we pointed out that the latter question might properly be raised by a man with reference to his own actions, past or prospective. In regard to others he cannot fully know what the motives and character represented by any particular action have been or will be, and in the absence of such knowledge he certainly cannot be blamable for declining to guess. But as to himself any one may ask, Was I what I should have been in doing so and so? or, Shall I in doing so and so be what I should be? He may ask such a question reasonably, because it does not depend on the amount of his information, or on his skill in analysis, but on his honesty with himself, whether the answer shall be virtually a true one. But will he for raising such questions, and raising them with such an ideal of virtue before him as has been above indicated, be any the wiser as to what he ought to do, or any the more disposed to do it?

305. Now it is obvious that, though he put such questions to himself with all possible earnestness, he will not for doing so, directly at any rate, be the better judge of what he should do, so far as the judgment depends on correct information or inference as to matters of facts, or on a correct analysis of circumstances. But a man's doubts as to his own conduct may be of a kind which such information and analysis are principally needed to resolve. He may be asking himself such questions as these: Was I right in relieving that beggar yesterday? Was I right in making the declaration required on taking orders? Was I right in voting against the Coercion Act last session? And he *may* be asking these questions about himself in the same sense in which he might ask them about the actions of any one else, or in which they might be discussed by a debating society, without any reference to the motives or character represented by the acts in question. The supposition that any one should ask such questions about his own conduct solely in this sense, is no doubt an extreme one. He could not really detach himself from the consideration of the state of mind, better or worse, which led him to act as he did. In relieving the beggar was he not merely compounding with his conscience for his self-indulgence in shirking the trouble which a more judicious exercise of benevolence would have cost him ; or merely giving himself the pleasure of momentarily pleasing another, or of being applauded for generosity, at the cost of encouraging a mischievous practice? In making the declaration referred to, was his motive a pure desire to do good and teach the truth, or was he affected by any desire to lead a comfortable life, combining a maximum of reputation for usefulness with a minimum of wear and tear? In voting against the Coercion Act was he at all influenced by the wish to please an important fraction of his constituents, or by a pique against ministers? It is scarcely possible that any one, at all honest with himself, should consider his own conduct in the cases supposed without testing it by some such questions of motive as these.

But when the fullest and most honest consideration has been given them, they do not supersede the questions of fact and circumstance which the supposed cases necessarily involve. The man could not measure the value of his conduct in almsgiving, in taking orders, in voting against Coercion, without taking account of the effect of almsgiving in general and in the particular case ; of the circumstances on which the usefulness of the Church, and the relative truth of the declarations required by it, depend ; of those conditions of social life in general, and in Ireland specially, which make Coercion a necessity or a political evil. For though he may do what is good in result without being good, he cannot have been good unless he has done what is good in result.   The question whether he has done what he ought in any particular case may be answered in the affirmative without its following that he has been what he ought to be in doing it ; but unless it can be so answered he may not assume that he has been what he ought to be. And in order to answer it in such cases as we have been supposing, with due reference to circumstances and effects, that sort of knowledge and penetration is required which the most anxious self-interrogation, the most genuine self-abasement, will not directly supply.

306. But, it will be objected, this admission is inconsistent with the statement just now made, that a true answer to the question, Was I what I should have been in doing so and so? depends not on the amount of a man's information, but on his honesty with himself.   It now appears that a man cannot have been what he should have been in doing any action, unless the action was of a kind to yield good results, and that the correctness of a man's judgment in certain cases on this latter point depends not on his honesty with himself, but on his knowledge and powers of analysis. How are the two statements to be reconciled?   An explanation of this point will bring out the true function and value of the self-questioning conscience.

If the function of the conscience in challenging me with the question, Was I what I should have been in doing this or that? were to arrive at a precise estimate of the worth of my conduct in the particular case, the consideration of the effects of the action could be as little dispensed with as that of its motives.   To make my conduct perfectly good, it would be necessary that the effects of the act should be purely for good, according to the true standard of good, as well as that my interest in doing it should be purely an interest in that good.   It is obvious, however, that the exact measure in which my conduct has fallen short of this unattainable perfection, till we can see all moral effects in their causes, cannot be speculatively ascertained;

nor is it of practical importance to attempt its ascertainment. What is of importance is that I should keep alive that kind of sense of shortcoming in my motives and character, which is the condition of aspiration and progress towards higher goodness. And to this end, while the question whether I have been duly patient and considerate and unbiassed by passion or self-interest in taking account of the probable consequences of my act, is an essential question—a question which it only needs that I should be honest with myself, not clever or well-informed, to answer — the question how the action has turned out in respect of consequences which I had not the requisite knowledge or ability to foresee, may be left aside without practical harm.   If indeed the question as to motives and character, honestly dealt with, could leave me under the impression that in doing so and so I was all that I should have been, it would be important for me to be reminded that the action may have had evil consequences which I did not foresee—perhaps in my dulness and ignorance could not foresee—but which yet are part of my act. But just because the question of motives and character, honestly dealt with, is incompatible with self-complacency in the contemplation of any piece of past conduct, its moral function is fully served without supplementary enquiry into unforeseen consequences of the conduct.   It is a sufficient spring for the endeavour after a higher goodness that I should be ashamed of my selfishness, indolence, or impatience, without being ashamed also of my ignorance and want of foresight.   Without the former sort of shame, the latter, if it could be engendered, would be morally barren ; while, given that personal endeavour after the highest which is the other side of self-abasement, this will turn the products of intellectual enlightenment and scientific discovery, as they come, to account in the way of contribution to human perfection.   It will do this, and nothing else will.

307. If we are called on to say, then, whether a man will be any the wiser as to what he ought to do, or any the more disposed to do it, for applying an ideal of virtue to his own conduct in the form of the question, Was I in this or that piece of conduct what I should be? we must point out that this question itself expresses the source of all wisdom as to what we ought to do. It expresses the aspiration, the effort, in man to be the best that he has it in him to be, from which is ultimately derived the thought that there is something which ought to be done, and the enquiry what in particular it is. It represents the quest for right conduct, as carried on by the individual under that sense of personal responsibility for doing the best, for attaining the highest, which can alone make him a reformer of his own practice or of the practice of others. It is true indeed that no recognition of an ideal of virtue, however pure and high, no such incitement to the reform of oneself and one's neighbour as a comparison of the ideal with current practice can afford, will enlighten us as to the effect of different kinds of action upon the welfare of society, whether that welfare be estimated with reference to a maximum of possible pleasure, or to an end which the realisation of a good will itself constitutes. As it stands before the mind of any particular person, the ideal will not directly yield an injunction to do anything in particular which is not in his mind already associated with good results, nor to abstain from anything which is not already associated with evil results. But while it will not immediately instruct him as to the physical or social consequences of action, and through such instruction yield new commands, it will keep him on the look-out for it, will open his mind to it, will make him ready, as soon as it comes, to interpret the instruction into a personal duty. The agents in imparting the instruction may be analysts and experimenters, to whom the ideal of virtue is of little apparent concern—who seldom trouble themselves with the question whether they are what they should be—though, unless in their intellectual employment they were controlled by an ideal of perfect work, they would not prove the instructors of mankind. But when the instruction has been conveyed, the self-imposed imperative to turn it to account for the bettering of life remains to be given; and it is only from a conscience responsive to an ideal of virtue that it can proceed. The lesson, for instance, of the mischief done by indiscriminate almsgiving, or by the sale of spirits, may have been most plainly taught by social or physical analysis, but it would be practically barren unless certain persons, each under a consciousness of responsibility for making the best of himself as a social being, charged themselves with the task of getting the lesson put into practice by society.

308. The notion that an ideal of virtue must be barren in the suggestion of particular duties previously unrecognised, has probably arisen from the necessity of expressing it verbally in the form of a definition or of a general proposition. From such a proposition as 'the true good for man is the realisation of his capabilities, or the perfecting of human life,' or 'the good will is a will which has such perfection for its object,'—or, again, from a definition of any particular form of the good will, of any specific virtue —we may be fairly challenged to deduce any particular obligation but such as is already included in the notions represented by the terms which stand as the subjects of these several propositions. From a knowledge that the true good, the good will, the specific virtues, are as defined, no one will come to be aware of any particular duties of which he was not aware before he arrived at the definitions. The most that can be said (of which more below) will be that such definitions may put him on his guard against self-sophistications, which might otherwise obscure to him the clearness of admitted duties. If the practical consciousness, which we name an ideal of virtue, were no more than the speculative judgment embodied in a definition of the ideal, or than speculative reflection upon the ideal, the same admission would have to be made in regard to it. But it is much more than this; or, rather, it does not primarily involve any such speculative judgment at all, but only comes to involve such a judgment as a secondary result of that aspiration in men after a possible best of life and character, which primarily constitutes the consciousness of the ideal. Before a definition of the ideal can be possible, this aspiration must have taken effect in the ordering of life; and it is reflection on the product which it has thus yielded that suggests general statements as to the various virtues, and as to some supreme virtue; ultimately, as intellectual needs increase, formal definitions of virtue and the virtues.

But the acquaintance of educated men with such definitions, the employment of the analytical intellect upon them, is very different from what we mean by the practical consciousness of the moral ideal. This implies the continued action in the individual of the same spiritual principle that has yielded those forms of life and character which form the subject of our moral definitions; its continued action as at once compelling dissatisfaction with the imperfection of those forms, and creating a sensibility to the suggestions of a further perfecting of life which they contain. A definition of virtue, a theory of the good, is quite a different thing, in presence of such a living inward interpreter, from what it would be as an abstract proposition. A proposition of geometry, from which by mere analysis no truth could be derived which was not already contained in it, becomes fertile of new truth when applied by the geometer to a new construction. A rule of law, barren to mere analysis, yields new rules when interpreted by the judge in application to new cases. And thus a general ethical proposition, which by itself is merely a record of past moral judgments, and from which by mere analysis no rules of conduct could be derived but such as have been already accepted and embodied in it, becomes a source of new practical direction when applied by a conscience, working under a felt necessity of seeking the best, to circumstances previously not existent or not considered, or to some new lesson of experience.

309. Our conclusion, then, is that the state of mind which is now most naturally expressed by the unspoken questions, Have I been what I should be, shall I be what I should be, in doing so and so? is that in which all moral progress originates. It must have preceded the formation of definite ideals of character, as well as any articulation of the distinction between outward action and its motives. It is no other than the sense of personal responsibility for making the best of themselves in the family, the tribe, or the state, which must have actuated certain persons, many or few, in order to the establishment and recognition of any moral standards whatever. Given such standards, it is the spirit which at once demands from the individual a loyal conformity to them, and disposes him, upon their suggestion, to construct for himself an ideal of virtue, of personal goodness, higher than they explicitly contain. The action of such an ideal, in those stages of moral development with which we are now familiar, is the essential condition of all further bettering of human life. Its action is of course partial in various degrees of partiality. It may appear as a zeal for public service on the part of some one not careful enough about the correctness of his own life, or on the other hand in the absorbed religious devotion of the saintly recluse. In the average citizen it may appear only as the influence which makes him conscientious in the discharge of work which he would not suffer except in conscience for neglecting, or as the voice, fitfully heard within, which gives meaning to the announcement of a perfect life lived for him and somehow to be made his own. Taking human society together, its action in one mode supplements its action in another, and the whole sum of its action forms the motive power of true moral development; which means the apprehension on our part, ever widening and ever filling and ever more fully responded to in practice, of our possibilities as men and of the reciprocal claims and duties which those possibilities imply.

CHAPTER II

310. SUPPOSING the considerations with which the last chapter ended to be admitted, we have still only convinced ourselves of the supreme value which belongs to an ideal of personal goodness, as a principle of action. The value of a certain *theory* of the ideal, of such a doctrine of the good and of goodness as has been previously sketched in this treatise, is a different question. It was this that we undertook to consider, and this we have so far not directly touched. Having taken the ideal to be a devotion of character and life in some form or other to the perfecting of man; having insisted that this perfection is to be understood as itself consisting in a life of such self-devoted activity on the part of all persons; we undertook to enquire what available criterion of right and wrong such a theory could afford; how, applied to the circumstances of life, it could be construed into particular duties, so as to give us some general guide to the line of conduct we should adopt where conventional morality fails us. This enquiry, it may be fairly said, is not met by dwelling on the effect of a moral ideal, which need not be, and generally is not, accompanied by any clear theory of itself, in awakening the individual to a recognition of new duties, as new situations arise and new experience is acquired. The most genuine devotion to the highest ideal of goodness will not save a man from occasional perplexity as to the right line of action for him to take. If it seems to do so, it will only be because, not being the highest kind of devotion, it makes him confident in merely traditional or inconsiderate judgments. If the perplexity were one which admitted of being put in the form, Shall I be acting according to my ideal of virtue, or as a good man should, in doing so and so? a true devotion to the ideal might guide him through it. But in that case, it may be argued, the practical action of the ideal itself is enough. A theory about it, a philosophy of the true good, is superfluous. But if, on the other hand, the conscientious man's perplexity arises either from a conflict between two authorities which seem to have equal claims on his obedience, or from doubt as to the effect of different courses of contemplated action, while mere devotion to the ideal will not clear his path before him, of what avail will be any instruction that we could give him in accordance with our theory of the good and of goodness?

311. The discussion of this question has been advisedly postponed till we had considered the practical effect of an ideal of goodness, as possessing a man who may as yet be unacquainted with any philosophical theories about it. Any value which a true moral theory may have for the direction of conduct depends on its being applied and interpreted by a mind which the ideal, as a practical principle, already actuates. And it will be as well at once to admit that the value must in any case be rather negative than positive; rather in the way of deliverance from the moral anarchy which an apparent conflict between duties equally imperative may bring about, or of providing a safeguard against the pretext which in a speculative age some inadequate and mis-applied theory may afford to our selfishness, than in the way of pointing out duties previously ignored. This latter service must always be rendered by the application of a mind, which the ideal possesses, to new situations, to experience newly acquired or newly analysed, rather than by reflection on any theory of the ideal. Whether a mind so possessed and ap-plied is philosophically instructed or no, is in most circum-stances matter of indifference. One is sometimes, indeed, tempted to think that Moral Philosophy is only needed to remedy the evils which it has itself caused; that if men were not constrained by a necessity of their intellectual nature to give abstract expression to their ideals, the particular mis-leading suggestions, against which a true philosophy is needed to guard, would not be forthcoming.

For these suggestions chiefly arise from the inadequacy of the formulae in which requirements imposed by a really valuable ideal have found intellectual expression. Under influence of such an ideal institutions and rules of life are formed, essential for their time and turn, but not fitted to serve as the foundation of a universally binding prescription. The generalising intellect, however, requires their embodiment in universal rules; and when these are found to conflict with each other, or with some demand of the self-realising spirit which has not yet found expression in a recognised rule, the result is an intellectual perplexity, of which our lower nature is quite ready to take advantage. Blind passion is enlisted in the cause of the several rules. Egoistic interests are ready to turn any of them to account, or to find an excuse for indulgence in what seems to be their neutralisation of each other. Meanwhile perhaps some nobler soul takes up that position of self-outlawry which Wordsworth expresses in the words put into Rob Roy's mouth :—

> We have a passion—make a law,
> Too false to guide us or control !
> And for the law itself we fight
> In bitterness of soul.

> And, puzzled, blinded thus, we lose
> Distinctions that are plain and few ;
> These find I graven on my heart ;
> *That* tells me what to do.

For deliverance from this state of moral anarchy, which in various forms recurs whenever a sufficient liberation of the intellectual faculties has been attained, there is needed a further pursuit of the same speculative processes which have brought it about. As has just been said, no good will come of this, unless under the direction of a genuine interest in the perfecting of man ; but, given this interest, it is only through philosophy that it can be made independent of the conflicting, because inadequate, formulae in which duties are presented to it, and saved from distraction between rival authorities, of which the injunctions seem at once absolute and irreconcilable, because their origin is not understood.

312. But philosophy itself in its results may yield opportunity to a self-excusing egoism. The formulae in which it expresses conceptions of moral ends and virtues must always be liable to prove misleading, in the absence of that living interest in a practically true ideal which can alone elicit their higher significance. They are generated in intellectual antagonism and must always probably retain the marks of their origin. Those which have served the purpose of enabling men to see behind and beyond their own moral prejudices or some absolute authoritative assertion of a merely relative duty, have not themselves conveyed complete and final truth. If they had done so, it would still have been a truth that could only be made instructive for men's guidance in their moral vocation, if applied to the particulars of life by a mind bent on the highest. But in fact the best practical philosophy of any age has never been more than an assertion of partial truths, which had some special present function to fulfil in the deliverance or defence of the human soul. When they have done their work, these truths become insufficient for the expression of the highest practical convictions operating in man, while the speculative intellect, if enlisted in the service of the pleasure-seeking nature, can easily extract excuses from them for evading the cogency of those convictions. But the remedy for this evil is still not to be found in the abandonment of philosophy, but in its further pursuit. The spring of all moral progress, indeed, can still lie nowhere else than in the attraction of heart and will by the ideal of human perfection, and in the practical convictions which arise from it ; but philosophy will still be needed as the interpreter of practical conviction, and it can itself alone provide for the adequacy of the interpretation.

313. This general account of the practical function which a philosophy of conduct has to serve will probably carry more conviction, if we consider some particular forms of perplexity as to right conduct in which philosophy might be of service, and again some instances of the opportunity which an inadequate philosophy may offer to egoistic tendencies. A previous reminder, however, may be needed that a case of perplexity as to right conduct, if it is to be one in which philosophy can serve a useful purpose, must be one of *bona fide* perplexity of conscience. Now the margin within which such perplexities can arise in a Christian society is not really very large. The effort after an ideal of conduct has so far taken effect in the establishment of a recognised standard of what is due from man to man, that the articulation of the general imperative, 'Do what is best for mankind [1],' into particular duties is sufficiently clear and full for the ordinary occasions of life. In fulfilling the duties which would be recognised as belonging to his station in life by any one who considered the matter dispassionately, without bias by personal inclination—in fulfilling them loyally, without shirking, 'not with eye-service as menpleasers,'—we can seldom go wrong ; and when we have done this fully, there will seldom be much more that we can do. The function of bringing home these duties to the consciences of men—of helping them to be honest with themselves in their recognition and interpretation of them— is rather that of the preacher than of the philosopher. *Speculatively* there is much for the philosopher to do in examining how that ordering of life has arisen, to which these duties are relative ; what is the history of their recognition ; what is the rationale of them ; what is the most correct expression for the practical ideas which underlie them. And, as we shall see, there may be circumstances which give this speculative enquiry a practical value. These circumstances, however, must always be exceptional. Ordinarily it will be an impertinence for the philosopher to pretend either to supplement or to supersede those practical directions of conduct,

---

[1] I use this as a fair popular equivalent of Kant's formula—'Treat humanity, whether in your person or in that of another, never merely as a means, always at the same time as an end.'

which are supplied by the duties of his station to any one who is free from any selfish interest in ignoring them.

314. Perplexity of conscience, properly so called, seems always to arise from conflict between different formulae for expressing the ideal of good in human conduct, or between different institutions for furthering its realisation, which have alike obtained authority over men's minds without being intrinsically entitled to more than a partial and relative obedience ; or from the incompatibility of some such formula or institution, on the one side, with some moral impulse of the individual on the other, which is really an impulse towards the attainment of human perfection, but cannot adjust itself to recognised rules and established institutions. From the perplexities thus occasioned we must distinguish those that arise from difficulty in the analysis of circumstances or in the forecast of the effects of actions. These are to be met, no doubt, by an exercise of the intellect, but by its exercise rather in the investigation of matters of fact than by that reflection upon ideas which is properly called philosophy.

From both kinds of practical perplexity again are to be distinguished those self-sophistications which arise from a desire to find excuses for gratifying unworthy inclinations. Such self-sophistications, we know, will often dignify themselves with the title of cases of conscience ; and the disrepute which has fallen upon 'casuistry' has been partly due to its having often been employed in their service. A man will pretend to be perplexed with a case of conscience, when really he is wishing to make out that some general rule of conduct does not apply to him, because its fulfilment would cause him trouble, or because it conflicts with some passion which he wishes to indulge. Most cases in which we argue that circumstances modify for us the obligation to veracity are of this kind. When such is the source of the 'perplexity,' it is not the most perfect philosophy, the completest possible theory of the moral ideal, that will be of avail for deliverance from it. Just so far as the character is formed to disinterested loyalty to the moral law, however

imperfectly the law may be conceived, it will brush aside
the fictitious embarrassment.   As Kant puts it, that emotion
which on one side is 'Achtung' for the moral law, on the
other is 'Verachtung' for one's selfish inclinations.   Such an
emotion may not save a man from many concessions to his
own weakness, but it will make him refuse with contempt to
resort to casuistry for their justification.   He may be enlightened enough to appreciate the relativity of most general
rules of conduct, to understand that they admit of exceptions
according to circumstances, but he will despise the suggestion
of an exception to them in his own favour—an exception in
order to save himself pain or gain himself pleasure.   This
sort of self-contempt affords a short method of settling questions to which the speculative intellect, if once it so far enlists
itself in the service of passion as to treat them seriously, will
'find no end, in wandering mazes lost.'

315. There may be cases, however, in which the difficulty
felt in adhering to a general rule, such as that of veracity,
arises from an impulse entitled in itself to as much respect
as the conscientious injunction to adhere to the rule.   A
famous example is the temptation of Jeannie Deans to give
false evidence on a single point for the sake of saving her
sister, of whose substantial innocence she is assured.   In
such a case would Moral Philosophy, if it could gain a hearing, have any direction to give to the perplexed person?   He
is asking himself, Shall I in this case be acting as I ought,
as a good man should, in adhering to the strict rule of veracity,
or in departing from it to save the beloved person from
a punishment which I know to be undeserved?   Whatever
the principle of our Moral Philosophy, can it help in answering the question?   The Utilitarian theory, which is apt to
take credit to itself for special practical availability, can here
have no counsel to give.   For by what possible calculus could
the excess, on the whole, of pleasure over pain or of pain over
pleasure, to be expected from adherence to the rule of veracity, be balanced against the excess of pleasure over pain or
of pain over pleasure, to be expected in the particular case

from its violation? But if we suppose the question to be dealt with according to the principles advocated in this treatise, we do not escape embarrassment. How shall the perplexed person say whether the motive which suggests adherence to the rule of veracity, or that which suggests departure from it, is the worthier of the two? A true Moral Philosophy does not recognise any value in conformity to a universal rule, simply as such, but only in that which *ordinarily* issues in such conformity, *viz.* the readiness to sacrifice every lower inclination in the desire to do right for the sake of doing it. But in the case supposed, may not the desire to save the beloved person, known to be substantially innocent, claim to be a disinterested desire to do right equally with a determination to adhere to the strict rule of veracity?

316. If the moral philosopher were called on to answer this question as a matter of general speculation, not for the guidance of a particular person in a particular case, he would have to say that it did not admit of being answered with a simple 'yes' or 'no.' For purposes of moral valuation neither the desire to save the life of the beloved person, nor the determination at any cost to adhere to the rule of strict veracity, can be detached from the relation which it bears to the whole history of a life, to the universe of a character; and this relation is not in any case ascertainable by us. Of two men, placed in precisely similar perplexities, one might adhere to the rule of veracity at the cost of sacrificing the life of a beloved and innocent person, the other might save the person at the cost of violating the rule of veracity, and it would be impossible for the moral philosopher to say which action were the better or the worse of the two; because he would not know in regard to either that spiritual history upon which its moral value depends.

If on the other hand (an unlikely supposition) he had to assist the perplexed conscience [1] in deciding between the

---

[1] [The expression 'perplexed *conscience*' would probably have been modified on revision, in accordance with the distinctions laid down in § 321.]

alternative actions in such a case as that supposed, he would have to press the question whether it is not at bottom some personal weakness which suggests the departure from the ordinary moral rule ; whether it is really a greater devotion to the beloved person that suggests a falsehood for her sake, and not perhaps a backwardness to serve her in some more difficult and dangerous way, in which she might still be served though she had to bear the consequence of the truth being told.   If that consequence should prove to be her painful and undeserved death, 'What are you,' the doubter must be asked, 'what is the victim whom your untruth might save, that the suffering of either should be set against the duty of adherence to a rule, of which the universal observance is a prime condition of the perfect ordering of social life, and therefore morally necessary ?   Each of you, no doubt, has an absolute value which no rule, as such, can have.   Rules are made for man, not man for rules.   But the question is not really between the value of either of you and the value of a rule, but between the importance to be attached on the one hand to your pain or deliverance from pain, and that to be attached on the other to the moral life of society which every lie must injure, and to the integrity of your character as a person self-subordinated to the requirements of social good.   Let the worst come from your truth-speaking ; still it is not that which is of absolute value, either in you or in the victim of the law, which will suffer loss. Your devotion to the beloved person is indeed truly a good ; but that devotion is not set aside by, but carried on into, the larger devotion which includes it, and which forbids your departure from the rule of veracity.   As to the beloved person herself, the question is more dark, for she is passive in the matter ; it is not any action to be done by her that is under consideration, and no one can gain directly in intrinsic worth by the action of another.   But it is certain that her deliverance from suffering through your wrong-doing could not be really for her good ; it would not make her heart purer, or direct her will to higher objects ; and you may trust on the other hand (though unable to foresee how such a result should come about) that in taking that consequence of her conduct, which only your wrong-doing could avert, she will gain in that spiritual capability which is alone to her a source of abiding good.'

317. The suggestion of such counsel being offered to any one under such trial as we have supposed, inevitably strikes us as inappropriate. We know that in fact under such circumstances the soul would not be at leisure for philosophical reflection. Its conduct must be determined by influences that act more swiftly and decisively ; if in the severe path for which we have supposed the philosopher to be arguing, by an inbred horror of falsehood, which does not wait to give an account of itself, or by sense of the presence of a divine onlooker, whose disapproval, not for fear of penal consequences but for very shame, cannot be faced. According to the distinction previously drawn, it is the action of an ideal of virtue itself, not any theory about the ideal, that can alone be efficient in such a case. Though not in the emergency itself, however, yet in preparing the soul for it, a true philosophy may have an important service to render. It will be a service, indeed, rather of the defensive and negative than of the actively inciting kind—a service which in a speculative and dialectical age needs to be rendered, lest the hold of the highest moral ideas on the mind should be weakened from apparent lack of intellectual justification.

Those ideas, as we have often pointed out, are not abstract conceptions. They actuate men independently of the operations of the discursive intellect. They rather direct those operations than are their result. The idea, in its various forms, of something that human life should be, of a perfect being for whom this 'should be' already 'is,' cannot proceed from observation of matters of fact or from inference founded on such observation, though in various ways (on which we cannot here dwell) it regulates that observation and inference. Such ideas or principles of action, at work before they are understood, not only give rise to institutions and modes of life, but also express themselves in forms of the imagination. In complication with effects of passion and force, they produce the laws, whether enforced by opinion or by the magistrate, which form the essential and permanent element in the fabric of social obligation; and they also yield the imagination of a supreme invisible but all-seeing ruler, to whom service is due, from whom commands proceed as from an earthly superior—the head of a family or the sovereign of a state—and who punishes the violation of those commands. It is in the form of this imagination that, in the case at least of all ordinary good people, the idea of an absolute duty is so brought to bear on the soul as to yield an awe superior to any personal inclination. In sudden calls upon the will, when the sustaining force of habit is of no avail, when no rewards or penalties, either under the law of the state or the law of opinion, are to be looked for, whatever the course of action adopted, can any of us be sure that, except under the impression of the 'great task-master's eye' upon him, he would do the work which upon reflection he would admit should be done?

318. It is a necessity, however, of our rational nature that these forms of imagination, in which our highest practical ideas have found expression, should be subject to criticism. Is there really a divine ruler, who issues commands which we can obey or disobey; who somehow sees and hears us, though not through eye or ear; whom it is possible for us to please or offend? Now there is undoubtedly a sense in which these questions, once asked, can only be answered in the negative. The most convinced Theist must admit that God is as unimaginable as He is unperceivable,—unimaginable because unperceivable, for that which we imagine (in the proper sense of the term) has the necessary finiteness of that which we perceive; that statements, therefore, which in any strict sense could only be applied to an imaginable finite agent, cannot in any such sense be applied to God. As applied to Him, they must at any rate not be reasoned from as we reason from state-

ments about matters of fact. The practice of treating them as if they were such statements, with the confusions and contradictions to which it inevitably leads, only enhances doubt as to the reality of the divine Spirit; of which we must confess that it is inexpressible in its nature by us, though operative in us through those practical ideas of a possible perfect life, of a being for whom this perfect life is already actual, which, acting upon imagination, yield the language of ordinary religion.

319. Now when criticism comes to do its inevitable work upon the language of imagination in which our fundamental moral ideas have found expression, a counter-work is called for from philosophy, which has an important bearing upon conduct. It has to disentangle the operative ideas from their necessarily imperfect expression, and to explain that the validity of the ideas themselves, as principles of action, is not affected by the discovery that the language, in which men under their influence naturally express themselves, has not the sort of truth which belongs to a correct statement of matters of fact. It has to show when and how—these ideas not being matters of fact or obtained by abstraction from matters of fact—the figures of speech employed in expressing the aspirations and endeavours to which they give rise, being derived by metaphor from sensible matters of fact, are liable to mislead us if we argue from them as though they conveyed literal truth. It has to point out what is the sense in which alone the question as to the truth of such language can be properly asked or answered. If the question is asked, for instance, whether there is truth in the language, habitual to the religious conscience, in which God is represented as giving us certain commands and seeing whether we perform them or no, the philosopher will remind us that to enquire whether such language is true, in the same sense in which it might be true that I ordered my servant to do certain things this morning and took notice whether he did them, is as inappropriate as it would be to enquire (according to an example employed by Locke in another connection) whether sleep is swift or virtue square. It can only be reasonably asked whether it is true in the sense that it naturally expresses, in terms of imagination, an emotion arising from consciousness of a relation which really subsists between the human soul and God. If the infinite Spirit so communicates itself to the soul of man as to yield the idea of a possible perfect life, and that consequent sense of personal responsibility on the part of the individual for making the best of himself as a social being from which the recognition of particular duties arises, then it is a legitimate expression by means of metaphor—the only possible means, except action, by which the consciousness of spiritual realities can express itself—to say that our essential duties are commands of God. If again the self-communication of the infinite Spirit to the soul of man is such that man is conscious of his relation to a conscious being, who is in eternal perfection all that man has it in him to come to be, then it is a legitimate expression of that conscious relation by means of metaphor to say that God sees whether His commands are fulfilled by us or no, and an appropriate emotion to feel shame as in His presence for omissions or violations of duty incognisable by other men.

320. The above must not be taken to mean that it is to be considered the business of philosophy to justify the language of religious imagination universally and unconditionally. Even as that language is current in Christendom, there may be much in it that a true moral philosophy will have to condemn as inconsistent with the highest kind of moral conviction. Objection may properly be taken, for instance, to the ordinary representation of God as a source of rewards and penalties; as rewarding goodness with certain pleasures bestowed from without, as punishing wickedness with pains inflicted from without. The objection to it, however, is not that it represents God under a figure which is not a statement of fact (for the same objection would apply equally to all the language of religion), but that the figure is one which interferes with the true idea of goodness as its own reward, of vice as its own punishment.   It is an important function of philosophy to examine the current language of religious imagination, not with the unreasonable view of testing its speculative truth, as we might test the truth of some doctrine about natural phenomena, but in order to satisfy ourselves whether it worthily expresses the emotions of a soul in which the highest moral ideas have done their perfect work.

With such an application of philosophy, however, we are not at present concerned.   Our present purpose is merely to point out the service which philosophy may render to practical morality in counteracting the advantage which scepticism may otherwise give to passion against duty.   It is true, of course, that when the soul is suddenly called upon to face some awful moment, to which are joined great issues for good or evil in its moral history, it is not by 'going over the theory of virtue in one's mind,' not by any philosophical consideration of the origin and validity of moral ideas, that the right determination can be given. A judgment of the sort we call intuitive—a judgment which in fact represents long courses of habit and imagination founded on ideas—is all that the occasion admits of.   But even in such cases it may make a great difference to the issue, whether the inclination to the weaker or less worthy course is or is not assisted by a suggestion from the intellect that the counter-injunction of conscience is illusory.   And in such an age as ours this suggestion is likely to be forthcoming, if scepticism has been allowed to pull to pieces the imaginative vesture in which our formative practical ideas have clothed themselves, without a vindication by philosophy of the ultimate authority of the ideas themselves, and of so much in the language of religious imagination as is their pure and (to us) necessary expression.

321. We have still, however, to consider the service which philosophy may render in what we distinguished above as *bona fide* perplexities *of conscience ; bona fide* perplexities, as distinct from those self-sophistications, born of the pleasure-seeking impulse, in dealing with which philosophy would be misapplied; perplexities *of conscience*, as distinct from cases like that of Jeannie Deans, where conscience speaks without ambiguity but is opposed by an impulse in itself noble and disinterested. In cases of this latter kind philosophy may, as we have seen, under special conditions of intellectual culture, have an important service to render; but it will not be in the way of setting aside apparent contradictions in the deliverance of conscience. It will rather be in the way of vindicating the real authority of that deliverance against a scepticism which might otherwise take advantage of the discovery that the forms of imagination, in which the deliverance is clothed, are not the same as statements of speculative truth. The kind of practical perplexity which we have now to consider arises not from any doubt as to the authority of conscience, nor from any attempt of selfish inclination to 'dodge' conscience by assuming its disguise, but from the fact that the requirements of conscience seem to be in conflict with each other. However disposed to do what his conscience enjoins, the man finds it difficult to decide what its injunction is.

In the crisis, for instance, through which several European states have recently passed, such a difficulty might naturally occur to a good Catholic who was also a loyal subject. His conscience would seem to enjoin equally obedience to the law of the State, and obedience to the law of the Church. But these laws were in conflict. Which then was he to obey? It is a form of the same difficulty which in earlier days must have occurred to Quakers and Anabaptists, to whom the law derived from Scripture seemed contradictory to that of the State, and to those early Christians for whom the law which they disobeyed in refusing to sacrifice retained any authority. In still earlier times it may have arisen in the form of that conflict between the law of the family and the law of the State, presented in the 'Antigone.' Nor is the case really different when the modern citizen, in his capacity

as an official or as a soldier, is called upon to help in putting
down some revolutionary movement which yet presents itself
to his inmost conviction as the cause of 'God and the People.'
This case may indeed appear different from those previously
noticed, because, while those were cases of conflict between
acknowledged authorities, this may seem rather to be one of
conflict between private opinion and authority.   But if the
private opinion is more than a conceit which it is pleasant
to air ; if it is a source of really conscientious opposition to
an authority which equally appeals to the conscience ; if, in
other words, it is an expression which the ideal of human
good gives to itself in the mind of the man who entertains
it ; then it too rests on a basis of social authority.   No individual can make a conscience for himself. He always needs
a society to make it for him.   A conscientious ' heresy,'
religious or political, always represents some gradually
maturing conviction as to social good, already implicitly
involved in the ideas on which the accepted rules of conduct
rest, though it may conflict with the formulae in which those
ideas have been hitherto authoritatively expressed, and may
lead to the overthrow of institutions which have previously
contributed to their realisation.

322. In preparation for the times when conscience is thus
liable to be divided against itself, much practical service may
be rendered by a philosophy which, without depreciating
the authority of conscience as such, can explain the origin
of its conflicting deliverances, and, without pronouncing unconditionally for either, can direct the soul to the true end
to which each in some qualified way is relative.   In order to
illustrate this in more detail, we will suppose a philosopher,
holding the doctrines previously stated in this treatise, to be
called upon for counsel in difficulties of the kind just noticed.
It will of course occur to every one that the counsel given
goes too far back in its reasons, and in its conclusions is of
too neutral a kind, to command attention in times of social
or religious conflict and revolution.   But, though this is so,
it might have its effect upon the few who lead the many, in

preparing the mind through years of meditation for the days when prompt practical decision is required.

The philosopher, then, will begin by considering how the seeming contradiction in the deliverances of conscience comes about. He will point out that, though there would be no such thing as conscience at all but for the consciousness on the part of the individual that there is an unconditional good which, while independent of his likes and dislikes, is yet *his* good—though this consciousness is as irremovable as morality—yet it does not follow that all the judgments which arise out of this consciousness are unconditionally valid. The several dicta of conscience have had their history. Passing beyond the stage of mere conformity to custom, of mere obedience to persons and powers that be—a conformity and obedience which themselves arise out of an operative, though inarticulate, idea of common good—men have formed more or less general notions of the customs and powers, as entitled to their conformity and obedience. Certain formulae, expressing the nature of the authorities to which obedience is due, and their most familiar requirements, have become part of 'the *a priori* furniture' of men's minds, in the sense that they are accepted as valid independently of those lessons of experience which men are conscious of acquiring for themselves. Such are what are commonly called the 'dicta of conscience.' Certain injunctions of family duty, of obedience to the law of the State, of conformity to a law of honour or opinion, have assumed this character. So too in Christendom have certain ordinances of the Church, notwithstanding much variety of opinion as to what constitutes the Church.

323. Now in all such deliverances of conscience the content of the obligation is blended with some conception or imagination of an authority imposing the obligation, in a combination which only the trained analytical intellect can disentangle. Just as to children the duty of speaking the truth seems inseparable from the parental command to do so, so to many a simple Catholic, for instance, the fact that the Church commands him to live cleanly and honestly seems the source of the obligation so to live. To give just measure and to go to Mass are to him homogeneous duties; just as to unenlightened persons in a differently ordered religious community to give just measure and to observe the Sabbath may be so. An abrogation of the authority which imposes the ceremonial obligation would seem to imply a disappearance of the moral obligation as well; because this too in the mind of the individual has become associated with the imagination of an imponent authority, the same as that which enjoins the ceremonial observance. This does not arise from the existence of a Church as a co-ordinate institution with the State. Were there no Church, the difference would only be that, as in the Græco-Roman world, the State would gather to itself the sentiments of which, as it is, the Church seems the more natural object. Moral duties would still be associated with the imagination of an imponent authority, whose injunctions they would be supposed to be, though the authority might be single instead of twofold.

Nor would any considerate member of modern society, even the most enlightened, venture to say that his sense of moral duty was independent of some such imagination of an imponent, however resolutely he might refuse to recognise either the Church or any particular personage as the imponent. If he has ceased to describe himself naturally as a good Catholic or good Churchman, he may still attach significance to the description of himself as a good Christian; and this probably implies to him the recognition of an imponent of obligation in the founder of the Christian society or the author of a Christian revelation. Or if he has ceased to recognise such an imponent, he probably still calls himself a loyal subject; and in so doing expresses the fact that he presents to himself some personal external source—some source other than a spirit working in him—of the law which he obeys; and that he obeys the law, not from fear of pains and penalties, but from reverence for the authority from which he believes it to proceed—as much, therefore, when he might evade it with impunity as when he runs the risk of punishment. Perhaps there may be no ostensible person, no emperor or king, whom he regards as the author of the law which he obeys, and he may accordingly prefer to describe himself as a loyal citizen rather than as a loyal subject, but he is very exceptional if he does not still think of some association of persons, a 'sovereign people,' as the authority from which law proceeds. If he ceased to present such an authority to himself, having previously discarded the imagination of Church or King or Divine Lawgiver as imponents of duty, he would be apt to find the obligation, not only of what is local and temporary in positive law, but of what is essential in the moral law, slipping away from him.

324. This imagination of an external imponent, however, is not intrinsically necessary to the consciousness of what we call metaphorically [1] moral law, while it is the source of apparent conflict between different injunctions of conscience. It is the very essence of moral duty to be imposed by a man on himself. The moral duty to obey a positive law, whether a law of the State or of the Church, is imposed not by the author or enforcer of the positive law, but by that spirit of man—not less divine because the spirit of man—which sets before him the ideal of a perfect life, and pronounces obedience to the positive law to be necessary to its realisation. This actual imposition, however, of duties by man upon himself precedes and is independent of a true conception of what duty is. Men who are really a law to themselves, in the sense that it is their idea of an absolute 'should be,' of some perfection to be realised in and by them, that is the source of the general rule of life which they observe, are yet unable to present that rule to themselves as anything else than the injunction of some external authority. It is this state of mind

---

[1] I say 'metaphorically,' because what we primarily understand by 'law' is some sort of command, given by a superior in power to one whom he is able to punish for disobedience; whereas it is the essence of moral 'law' that it is a rule which a man imposes on himself, and from another motive than the fear of punishment.

that renders them liable to the perplexities of conscience described, in which duties appear to conflict with each other.

There is no such thing really as a conflict of duties. A man's duty under any particular set of circumstances is always one, though the conditions of the case may be so complicated and obscure as to make it difficult to decide what the duty really is. That which we are apt to call a conflict of duties is really a competition of reverences for imagined imponents of duty, whose injunctions, actual or supposed, do not agree. A woman perhaps finds herself directed to act in one way by her father, in another by her confessor. A citizen may find himself similarly distracted between the law of the State and that of the Church; or between the ordinance of an ostensible sovereign and that of a revolutionary committee, claiming to act in the name of God and the People. In such cases, if the conscience were clear of prepossession in favour of this authority or that, and were simply prepared to recognise as duty the course which contributes most to the perfect life, it might yet be difficult enough to ascertain what this course of action would be, though there would be no doubt that the one duty was to pursue that course of action when ascertained. But the actual perplexity of conscience in such cases commonly arises not from this difficulty, but from the habit of identifying duty with injunctions given by external authorities, and from the fact that in the supposed case the injunctions so given are inconsistent with each other.

325. Now the task of the moral philosopher in regard to such cases would be a comparatively easy one, if it simply consisted in trying to rid a man of his illusions of conscience; if he had merely to point out the work of imagination in ascribing the essential duties which conscience enjoins to an external imponent, and to show that the apparent conflict of duties is in fact merely a conflict between certain external authorities which are wrongly supposed to impose duties, whereas all that a purely external authority can impose is

a command enforced by fear. If the philosopher aims at
no more than this, he may succeed in his work, but its value
will be doubtful. It may prove easier to convince men that
duties, in the moral sense, cannot be imposed from without
than, when this has been shown, to maintain the conviction
that they exist at all. If the result of the philosopher's work
is to popularise the notion that the authorities to which men
have chiefly looked as imponents of duties, are merely powers
able to induce obedience to their commands by threat of
punishment for disobedience, without substitution of any
new reverence for that which must be withdrawn from the
authorities so regarded, we shall have nothing to thank him
for. In truth the phrase 'external authority,' as applied to
the imagined imponents of duty, involves something of a
contradiction. If they were merely external, they would
not be authorities, for an authority implies, on the part of
the man to whom it is an authority, a conception of its
having a claim upon his obedience; and this again implies
that his obedience to it is a self-imposed obedience—an
obedience which commends itself to his reason as good,
irrespectively of penalties attached to disobedience. The
authority, in being recognised as an authority, has ceased to
be a mere source of commands, enforced by fear of punishment for their violation, and in that sense to be merely
external. Its injunctions now commend themselves to the
subject of them, not indeed as proceeding from a spirit
which is his own or himself, but as directed to the attainment of an end in which the subject is interested on his
own account; which is, and is known by him to be, his true
good. How the several injunctions in detail contribute to
such an end he does not see; but he trusts the authority
from which they proceed to have it more completely in view
than he can himself. It is thus that the Church is an authority to the good Catholic, the State to the good citizen,
the Bible to the orthodox Protestant. In each case the
acknowledgment of the authority has become one and the
same thing with the individual's presentation to himself of

a true good, at once his own and the good of others, which it is his business to pursue.

326. Now it would be a blundering and reckless procedure on the part of the moral philosopher, if he were first to construe too literally the language in which these authorities are described, so to speak, from without for rhetorical or logical purposes,—to take it as if it represented their true spiritual import for those who acknowledge them—and then, in his hurry to assert the truth that a moral obligation cannot be imposed from without, were to seek to dethrone them from their place in the moral imagination, and to substitute for them an improvised conscience that should make its own laws *de novo* from within. It must rather be his object, without setting aside any of the established authorities which have acquired a hold on the conscience, to awaken such an understanding of the impulse after an ideal of conduct which, without being understood, has expressed itself in these authorities, as may gradually render men independent of the mode of its authoritative expression. One who has learnt this lesson will have a rationale of the various duties presented to him in the name of Cæsar or of God, which will help him to distinguish what is essential in the duties from the form of their imposition, and to guide himself by looking to the common end to which they are alike relative. Should an occasion arise when the duties seem to conflict, he will be prepared for the discovery that the conflict is not really between duties, but between powers invested by the imagination with the character of imponents of duty. He will be able to stand this discovery without moral deterioration, because he has learnt to fix his eye on the moral end or function—the function in the way of furthering perfection of conduct—served by the authorities which he has been bred to acknowledge. He can thus find in that end, or in the Spirit whose self-communication renders him capable of seeking it, a fit object for all the reverences claimed by those authorities, and which he now discovers to be due to them only by a derived and limited title.

327. It may thus fall to the moral philosopher, under

certain conditions of society and of intellectual movement, to render an important practical service. But he will render it simply by fulfilling with the utmost possible completeness his proper work of analysis. As a *moral* philosopher he analyses human conduct; the motives which it expresses, the spiritual endowments implied in it, the history of thought, habits and institutions through which it has come to be what it is. He does not understand his business as a philosopher, if he claims to do more than this. He will not take it for a reproach to be reminded that no philosopher can supply a 'moral dynamic.' The pretension to do so he would regard as a great impertinence. He finds moral dynamic enough in the actual spiritual nature of man, when that nature is regarded, as it is his business to regard it, not merely in its hitherto performance, but in its intrinsic possibilities. If he cannot help wishing for more, that is an incident of the very aspiration after perfection of conduct which constitutes the dynamic. His immediate business as a philosopher is not to strengthen or heighten this aspiration, much less to bring it into existence, but to understand it. As a man and a citizen, indeed, it is his function to serve as its organ; to give effect to it in his own conduct, to assist in communicating it to others. And since in being a philosopher he does not cease to be a man and a citizen, he will rejoice that the analysis, which alone forms his employment as a philosopher, should incidentally serve a purpose subordinate to the 'moral dynamic'—that it should help to remove any obstacle to the effort of the human soul after a perfect life.

The distraction of conscience caused, as we have seen, by competition of reverences for authorities whose injunctions come into conflict with each other, may form such an obstacle. Its outward effect may sometimes be a paralysis of action; sometimes, on the other hand, hasty and embittered action in opposition to one of the causes or authorities between the claims of which conscience is perplexed—action hasty and embittered for the very reason that the agent is afraid to face the consequence of dispassionate enquiry into the validity of the claims to which he blindly submits.   So far as the impediment to the highest living, to the free development of human capabilities, is of this kind, the philosopher by mere thoroughness and completeness of ethical analysis may help to remove it.   By giving the most adequate account possible of the moral ideal; by considering the process through which the institutions and rules of life, of which we acknowledge the authority, have arisen out of the effort, however blindly directed, after such an ideal, and have in their several measures contributed to its realisation; by showing that conscience in the individual, while owing its education to those institutions and rules, is not properly the mere organ of any or all of them, but may freely and in its own right apprehend the ideal of which they are more or less inadequate expressions; by thus doing his proper work as a philosopher of morals, he may help the soul to rise above the region of distraction between competing authorities, or between authorities and an inner law, to a region in which it can harmonise all the authorities by looking to the end to which they, or whatever is really authoritative in them, no less than the inner law, are alike relative.

328. That the soul, however, should derive any such benefit from philosophy implies a previous discipline, which cannot be derived from philosophy, but only from conduct regulated by the authorities which philosophy teaches it to understand.   It is a complaint as old as the time of Plato that, in learning to seek for the rationale of the rules which they are trained to obey—to enquire what is the ideal of human good, which these rules serve and are justified by serving—men come to find excuses for disregarding them. And, no doubt, as Plato saw, till the character is set in the direction of the ideal, a theory of the ideal can be of no value for the improvement of conduct in any sense.   It may be doubted, indeed, whether the apparent mischief, which arises in a speculative age from the habit of asking a reason why for the rules of respectability, does more than affect the excuses made for acts of self-indulgence of which men, innocent of criticism or speculation, would equally be guilty. But, however this may be, it remains true that the value of the Dialectic which asks and gives such an account of ideal good as at once justifies and limits obedience to practical authorities, is conditional upon its finding in the individual a well-formed habitual morality.

When it does so, it may influence life for good, by enlisting in the real service of mankind the zeal which would otherwise become a mis-directed loyalty or a spirit of unprofitable rebellion. It will teach a man to question the absoluteness of the authorities which speak in the name of Cæsar and of God—not with a view to shirking the precepts of either in the interest of his own pleasures, but in order that he may not be led by either into a 'conscientious' opposition to the other, obstructive to the work of which the promotion in different ways is the true function of each. When he finds that the requirements of Church or State, the observances of conventional morality or conventional religion, are in conflict with what some plead as their conscientious convictions, it will make him watchful to ascertain whether these new convictions may not represent a truer effort after the highest ideal than that embodied in the authorities which seek to suppress them. On the other hand, when he finds some conviction of his own in conflict with authority, it will teach him not indeed to conceal it for fear of inconvenient consequences, but to suppress all pride in it as if it were an achievement of his own; to regard it as proceeding, so far as it is good for anything, from the operation of the same practical reason in society which has given rise to the authorities with which his conviction brings him into collision. So regarding it, he will be respectful of the prejudices which he offends by expressing it; careful to eschew support which might be due not to an appreciation of what is good in the new conviction, but to mere aversion from the check put upon self-will by the authorities impugned; patient of opposition, and, in case of failure, ready to admit that there is more wisdom than he understood in the conventions which have been too strong for him.

CHAPTER III

329. THE chief theory of conduct which in Modern
Europe has afforded the conscientious citizen a vantage-
ground for judging of the competing claims on his obedience,
and enabled him to substitute a critical and intelligent for
a blind and unquestioning conformity, has no doubt been
the Utilitarian. What we are now considering, it must be
borne in mind, is the practical value of theories in regard
to the moral ideal, as distinct from the possession of the
character by the ideal itself. It is not to the purpose, therefore, to notice the work of religious reformers. It is probable
indeed that every movement of religious reform has originated in some clearer conception of the ideal of human conduct, arrived at by some person or persons ; a conception,
perhaps, towards which many men have been silently working, but which finally finds in some one individual the
character which can give decisive practical expression to it.
But in the initiation of religious reforms the new theory of
the ideal, as a theory, always holds a secondary place. It is
not absent, but it is, so to speak, absorbed in a character—
a character to which the speculative completeness of the
theory is of little interest—and it is this character which
gives the new conception of the ideal its power in the world.
The influence exercised by Utilitárianism, on the other hand,
has been specially the influence of a theory. Whatever the
errors arising from its Hedonistic psychology, no other theory
has been available for the social or political reformer, combining so much truth with such ready applicability. No
other has offered so commanding a point of view from which
to criticise the precepts and institutions presented as authoritative. When laws of the Church, or of the State, or of

'opinion,' have become antagonistic to each other; when any of them, again, has been found to conflict with one of those convictions of tender consciences, or of enthusiasts for humanity, which are a 'law of opinion' in the making, Utilitarianism furnishes a test by which the competing claims of the different laws, or those of law on one side and individual conviction on the other, may be put to the test.

330. All persons having a private interest in the maintenance of the law or custom which the Utilitarian theory calls in question ; all who shrink from the trouble of having to examine established rules of conduct; others who are rightly persuaded that the service rendered to mankind by rules that have become sacred is not to be measured by any account of their usefulness which the most enlightened observer can make out—these withstand Utilitarian criticism in the name of principle against expediency. Generally, however—at any rate when the question is one, not of conduct in private relations, but of laws or institutions, or of political conduct—that view of the right course to take which pleads 'principle,' as against suggestions said to be founded on 'expediency,' really only differs from the latter in respect of the more limited range of consequences which it takes into account. The 'principle' alleged has originally derived its authority from reference to some social good which it has been found to serve. The 'expediency,' for the sake of which a departure from the established rule is pressed for, is equally founded on a conception of social good, but on the conception of a good in which a wider range of persons is contemplated as partaking.

The ill-repute which attaches to considerations of expediency, so far as it is well founded, is chiefly due to the fact that, when the question of conduct at issue is one which the person debating it has a private interest in deciding one way or the other—when he himself will gain pleasure or avoid pain by either decision—the admission of expediency as the ground of decision is apt to give him an excuse for deciding in his own favour. And, even when this personal bias is not

operative, the man who looks to 'expediency' may be apt to
trust to some limited view of consequences, which is all that
his own vision can command, while if he had 'stuck to principle' he would really have been guided by a more complete
view, gathered from the wisdom of ages. Neither of these
mischiefs, however, arises from the Utilitarian principle of
practical judgment, as fairly applied, but from that mis-
application of it by interested or hasty individuals to which
all principles are liable. Nor must it be forgotten that, when
private interest affords a motive for deciding a practical
question in a particular way, 'principle' will sometimes
furnish a more convenient excuse than 'expediency.' Slave-
holders, for instance, have never found any difficulty in
justifying slavery 'on principle.'

331. On the whole there is no doubt that the theory of an
ideal good, consisting in the greatest happiness of the greatest
number, as the end by reference to which the claim of all
laws and powers and rules of action on our obedience is to
be tested, has tended to improve human conduct and character. This admission may be made quite as readily by
those who consider such conduct and character an end in
itself, as by those who hold that its improvement can only
be measured by reference to an extraneous end, consisting
in the quantity of pleasure produced by it; perhaps, when
due account has been taken of the difficulty of deciding
whether quantity of pleasure is really increased by 'social
progress,' *more* readily by the former than by the latter. It
is not indeed to be supposed that the Utilitarian theory, any
more than any other theory of morals, has brought about the
recognition or practice of any virtues that were not recognised
and practised independently of it; or that any one, for being
a theoretic Utilitarian, has been a better man—*i.e.* one more
habitually governed by desire for human perfection in some
of its forms—than he otherwise would have been. But it
has helped men, acting under the influence of ideals of
conduct and rules of virtuous living, to fill up those ideals
and apply those rules in a manner beneficial to a wider

range of persons—beneficial to them in the sense of tending to remove certain óbstacles to good living in their favour. It has not given men a more lively sense of their duty to others—no theory can do that—but it has led those in whom that sense has already been awakened to be less partial in judging who the 'others' are, to consider all men as the 'others,' and, on the ground of the claim of all men to an equal chance of 'happiness,' to secure their political and promote their social equality. To do this is not indeed directly to advance the highest living among men, but it is to remove obstacles to such living, which in the name of principle and authority have often been maintained.

332. The practical service, however, thus rendered by Utilitarianism has been independent of its analysis of well-being or good. It has been by insisting that it is 'the greatest number' whose highest good is to be taken into account, not by identifying that highest good with a greatest nett quantity of pleasure, that it has improved the organisation of human life. It is thus that it has given a wider and more impartial range to public spirit, to the desire to do good. It is thus that it has made men watchful of customary morality, lest its rules should be conceived in the interest of some particular class of persons, who—probably without being fully aware of it—have been concerned in establishing and maintaining them. It is thus that it has afforded men ground for enquiring, when laws, alike pleading the highest authority, were found to make conflicting claims on their obedience, whether either claim represented the real good of society, and which represented the good of the largest body of persons.

Very often this question may be sufficiently answered without any thorough analysis of what the good of society consists in, and thus the truth of the answer is independent of the truth of the theory which measures good by the quantity of pleasure experienced on the whole. In none of the great struggles between privileged and unprivileged classes, through which modern society has passed, would a man have been helped to a sounder judgment as to the part which he should take by a more correct definition of the good. The essential thing for his right guidance has been that, whatever might be the definition of good which he would accept, he should admit the equal title of all men to it in the same sense; that account should be taken of the widest possible range of society that can be brought into view, and that whatever is deemed good for any class or individuals in the society should be deemed good for all its members. In the struggle, for instance, through which the United States of America lately passed, a conscientious Virginian, divided in his mind between allegiance to his State and allegiance to the Union, could have found no useful direction in the truest possible analysis of the nature of ultimate good. The kind of well-being ostensibly served by the laws of his State for those who had the benefit of the laws, was not a different kind from that served by the maintenance of the Union. The question was whether secession or maintenance of the Union would promote that well-being most impartially, and for the widest range of society.

Again, in most cases where a man has to decide how he may best promote the greatest good of others, it makes little practical difference in regard to the line of action to be taken, whether he considers their greatest good to lie in the possession of a certain character, as an end not a means, or in the enjoyment of the most pleasure of which they are capable. No one can convey a good character to another. Every one must make his character for himself. All that one man can do to make another better is to remove obstacles, and supply conditions favourable to the formation of a good character. Now, in a general way and up to a certain point, the line of action directed to this removal of obstacles and supply of conditions favourable to goodness, will also tend to make existence more pleasant for those whose good is being sought. For instance, healthy houses and food, sound elementary education, the removal of temptations to drink, which are needed in order to supply conditions favourable to good character, tend also to make life more pleasant on the whole. The question at issue between Hedonistic Utilitarians and their opponents as to the nature of ultimate good cannot affect their importance.

333. So far we have seen how a philosophy of morals may prevent the perplexity of conscience, and consequent paralysis or misdirection of spiritual energy, arising from a conflict between authorities which have alike some sacredness for the imagination, or between such an authority and some unauthorised conviction of the individual; how it may do this by directing the devotion, hitherto supposed to be due to certain imponents of duty, explicitly to the end from reference to which all true authority, without distinction, must be derived; how the form of philosophy which in the modern world has most conspicuously rendered this service has been the Utilitarian, because it has most definitely announced the interest of humanity, without distinction of persons or classes, as the end by reference to which all claims upon obedience are ultimately to be measured. We may pay this homage to Utilitarianism without admitting that Hedonistic interpretation of the interest of humanity which has in fact generally been adopted by Utilitarians, especially by those who count themselves scientific. Impartiality of reference to human well-being has been the great lesson which the Utilitarian has had to teach. That 'unscientific' interpretation of well-being which the men most receptive of the lesson, on the strength of their own unselfish wishes and aspirations, have been ready to supply, has made them practically independent of any further analysis of it, when once the equality of claim to it had been thoroughly recognised. We may give Utilitarianism, therefore, full credit for the work it has done in rationalising the order of social and political life, while holding at the same time that its Hedonistic interpretation of well-being, if logically carried out, would deprive it of any practical influence for good; and that, as this interpretation in a speculative age comes to be more dwelt upon by the individual, it may itself induce practical evils, from which deliverance must be sought in a truer analysis of the ultimate good for man. It remains for us then to consider, whether there is any practical service—any service in the way of a direction of conduct—to be rendered in particular by such a theory of the good, of the moral ideal, as has been set forth above in opposition to the Hedonistic view. Are there any questions in regard to the right line to be taken in life, upon which men are liable to *bona fide* perplexity [1], and upon which this theory might offer a guidance that Utilitarianism, as a theory, could not supply? And, again, can it claim any useful office, simply in virtue of its being a philosophy of morals more adequate to the moral capability of man, as a counteracting influence to that weakening of conduct and lowering of aims, which in a speculative age a less adequate, and therefore misleading, philosophy may bring about?

334. Hitherto the practical effects of Utilitarianism, as a generally accepted theory, have been chiefly seen in its application to public policy rather than to private conduct. It has been the question, Ought such and such laws or institutions to be maintained or altered? rather than the question, Ought I to do this or that? which it has in fact generally been employed to settle. Philosophic Utilitarians, of course, have always held that the ultimate criterion of right and wrong in the actions of individuals, as much as in laws and institutions, is to be sought in the balance of resulting pleasure or pain, but they have not generally been forward to press the application of this criterion by individuals to their own actions. They have seldom, indeed, taken the same line as Mr. Henry Sidgwick, who, while he holds that no other scientific test of right conduct is possible than that derived from calculating the quantity of pleasure produced by any course of action to all sentient beings capable of being affected by it, yet explicitly rejects the doctrine that pleasure is the sole object of desire ; and who, even when he has thus cleared the Utilitarian motive from the liability

---

[1] ' *Bona fide* perplexity,' as having its origin really in intellectual difficulties, not in any selfish interest.

to be identified with the pleasure of the person moved by it, still admits that the moral sentiments are in fact independent of it, and expressly guards himself against being supposed to mean that the desire of producing the utmost possible pleasure is the only right or best motive of action[1]. Such Utilitarianism has more of Butler and Hutcheson in it than of Bentham and Mill. But there are probably few even among the more strictly Hedonistic Utilitarians who hold that our ordinary judgments of actions, as right or wrong, are formed upon any estimate by the individual of the effects of the actions in the way of producing pleasure or pain, or who would wish them to be so formed. Even when, as is commonly the case, they retain the psychological doctrine that pleasure—which must mean pleasure to oneself—is the sole object of desire, pain the sole object of aversion, they would deny that in his best actions the individual was actually influenced by what we naturally describe as interested motives, or by a calculation of pleasure-yielding consequences. They would admit that such actions are done from interest in others, or from a feeling that they ought to be done; and they would reconcile this admission with their doctrine as to pleasure being the sole object of desire, by supposing that it is aversion from some specific pain of shame, desire for some specific pleasure in doing nobly or in contemplating the pleasure of others—by whatever process of evolution these sensibilities may have arisen—that form the motives to such actions. And, just as they would thus qualify their view of the kind of desire for pleasure which is the motive to an admirable action, so they would admit that in most cases the question, whether an action was right or wrong, was most likely to be correctly decided by the individual on the strength of judgments which we call intuitive, which may perhaps represent prolonged observation by his ancestors of the pleasure-giving and pain-giving effects of actions, but are independent of any such observation on his own part.

335. It is not to be expected, however, in an age of

[1] Methods of Ethics, Bk. I. Chap. iv, and Bk. IV. Chap. i.

intellectual emancipation, when a scientific test of right action has been announced which is in itself easily intelligible (whatever upon thorough enquiry may turn out to be the difficulties of its application), that educated men will fail to employ it in their judgments of what they individually should do and should not do. Having got to the water, the ducklings will swim. The habit of calling authorities in question cannot be limited to philosophers; and, having once learned to call them in question, men will not stop short with the authorities that have regulated their civil and political relations. They will seek a rationale of their most intimate moral obligations; and when the Utilitarian philosopher offers them a scientific test of right and wrong, they will not be slow to apply it to the question which interests them most—the question how they may best conduct their own lives. In the European nations a constantly increasing number of persons find themselves in circumstances, in which a large option is allowed them as to the plan on which they will conduct their lives. The necessities of providing for a family, or of fulfilling the requirements of some employment without which they could not live, no longer determine the whole course of their existence. They can 'please themselves' in regard to a large part of their action; and they are naturally interested in finding a theory which, though it will probably have much less influence than they ascribe to it in really directing even their more optional conduct, will always give them a basis for arguing with themselves and others, whether that conduct is justifiable or otherwise.

How prevalent such argument has become, at least in 'cultivated circles,' need not be said. Hedonism has become not only a serious topic in the study, but often the babble of the drawing-room. Good people, of the sort who fifty years ago would have found in the law of their neighbours' opinion, or in the requirements of their church or sect, or in the precepts of Scripture as interpreted by church or sect, sufficient direction for so much of their walk and conduct as it would have occurred to them to think in need of any direction, may now be heard arguing whether this occupation or that, this or that habit of action, this or that way of spending their time, conveys the greater amount of pleasure and is therefore the more to be approved. That they attach serious importance to the question, that they suppose its decision to go for a great deal in the actual guidance of their lives, may be inferred from the surprise and displeasure with which they would receive a suggestion that, after all, their action is pretty much independent of it. They may not be very clear whether it is pleasure to themselves or to others that they have in view ; they may not have appreciated the distinction between 'egoistic' and 'universalistic' Hedonism ; but there can be no doubt of two things : (1) that to an extent unknown in previous generations they are seeking a theoretical direction for individual conduct, and seeking it in a consideration of the natural consequences of conduct, as causing pleasure or pain; and (2) that they seem to themselves to be largely influenced in conduct by this theoretical direction.

336. Those who are glad of a topic for denunciation may, if they like, treat the prevalence of such opinions among educated men as encouraging the tendency to vicious self-indulgence in practice. No such unfairness will here be committed. There is no good reason to apprehend that there is relatively more—we may even hope that there is less—of such self-indulgence than in previous generations ; though, for reasons just indicated, it has a wider scope for itself, talks more of itself and is more talked about, than at times when men were more tied down by the necessities of their position. We are no more justified in treating what we take to be untrue theories of morals as positive promoters of vice, than in treating what we deem truer theories as positive promoters of virtue. Only those in whom the tendencies to vicious self-indulgence have been so far overcome as to allow the aspiration after perfection of life to take effect, are in a state to be affected either for better or

for worse by theories of the good.   The worst that can truly be objected against the prevalence of Hedonistic theory, just noticed, is that it may retard and mislead those who are already good, according to the ordinary sense of goodness as equivalent to immunity from vice, in their effort to be better ; and the most that can be claimed for the theory which we deem truer, is that it keeps the way clearer of speculative impediments to the operation of motives, which it seeks to interpret but does not pretend to supply.   The grounds for this objection and this claim are what we have now to consider.

337. We have already explained the reasons to which we ascribe the general acceptance of Hedonistic theory by persons who are themselves by no means habitual pleasure-seekers.   They seem to be chiefly two.   One is the confused notion that the pleasure incidental to the satisfaction of desire, or to the consciousness of work done, is itself the object of the desire, or the end to which the work is directed. Simply for want of thorough reflective analysis, men whose main interest is in the achievement of objects quite different from any enjoyment of pleasure, are ready to admit that their object is always some pleasure or other, because they are conscious of always anticipating pleasure in the achievement of their objects.   The other reason is the impossibility of adequately defining an end that consists in the realisation of human capabilities, until the realisation is accomplished. When we say that the 'summum bonum,' by reference to which the value of men's actions is to be measured, is the perfection of human life, as consisting in the full realisation of human capabilities, some more detailed account of this realisation, and of the perfection which it constitutes, is naturally asked for.   But such an account cannot be given in a way that is likely at first to satisfy the questioner.   We can point indeed to a great realisation of human capabilities, which has actually been achieved.   Men have been in large measure civilised and moralised ; nature has been largely subdued to their use ; they have learnt to express themselves in the fine arts.   The ordinary activity of men,

regulated by law and custom, has its value as contributing to this realisation. But it is not for this ordinary activity, so regulated, that those who are seeking practical direction in a theory of the good need any guidance. It does not occur to them that they have any option in regard to it. They play their part in it as a matter of course. It is an aspiration after some further perfection than that already attained in those actual arrangements of life, which they have no choice but to accept and help to maintain, that makes them enquire into the ends of living. If the philosopher can only tell them to try to be better and to make others better ; to seek a more complete fulfilment of the capabilities of human nature in themselves and in others ; to make this the object of their lives and the end by reference to which they measure the value of actions ; if he cannot at the same time tell them what this greater perfection will positively mean for themselves and others ; they will be apt to think that he has told them nothing, and to contrast the emptiness of the end to which he professes to direct them, with the definite intelligibility of that which is explained to consist in a greatest possible quantity of pleasure for all sentient beings. For does not every one know what pleasure is and desire it, and cannot every one compare a greater with a less quantity of it ?

338. For the moment we will suppose this contrast between the two ways of conceiving the chief good—between the definiteness of the one and the vagueness of the other— to be valid, as it is, no doubt, generally accepted. We will suppose the view that the 'summum bonum' is the greatest possible nett quantity of pleasure to be adopted by some one, who has no inducement to find in it excuses for self-indulgence of that kind which, as we have seen, though it may find excuses for itself in theoretical Hedonism, is never really occasioned by it. We will suppose it to be disinterestedly applied by such an one to the direction of his life, in those respects in which he is likely to feel the need of direction. We have previously explained the grounds on which, as a matter of speculation, we reject this view, and need not

here repeat them.   The question now to be discussed is
whether it is likely to have any effects which may make
a reconsideration of it, and a more thorough insight into the
truth of the view opposed to it, practically desirable.   Is not
its intrinsic unavailability for supplying motive or guidance
to a man who wishes to make his life better, likely to induce
a practical scepticism in reflecting persons who have adopted
it, which tends to paralyse the effort after a better life?

To speak of it as thus intrinsically unavailable is a statement which will probably be thought to need prompt
vindication.   It will be remembered that we are supposing
a man to be in search of some guidance of conduct which
mere conformity to established usage, and the fulfilment of
the duties of his station according to what is expected of him,
will not afford.   As regards duties recognised by the law of
opinion—those of common veracity and fair dealing, and of
beneficence in its more obvious forms, family duties and
those imposed by State or Church—it is easy to show that
an overbalance of pain would on the whole result from their
neglect to those capable of being affected by it, whether or
no we consider this to constitute the reason why they should
be fulfilled.   We cannot doubt that a general desire to avoid
pain has had much to do with the establishment of such
duties, though we may think that alone it could not suffice
for their establishment.   And it is certain that any disturbance of the established order, simply as disturbance, must
cause much pain.   On the other hand, there is no considerable balance of pleasure to one who violates such duties, or
to other exceptional persons to whom his act may be an
occasion of pleasure, to be set against the general pain caused
by it.   From the nature of the case the pangs of fear and
shame must go far to neutralise any access of pleasure to
such persons.   In such cases, therefore, if the test of felicific
consequences is to be applied, there is no doubt as to the
result that it will yield.   But then these are not the cases in
which the application of such a test is ever likely to be called
for.   It is for direction in cases where the rules of conven-

tional morality fail them, or in the attempt to remedy the defects of that morality, that enlightened and conscientious persons look to their theory of the good. A man wishes to satisfy himself, for instance, whether he is justified in spending so much of his time, without neglect of any recognised duty, in the gratification of his taste for music, or of his curiosity in literature ; in conforming to the expectation of his class by accepting a challenge to a duel, or by running race-horses, or by being a party to the purchase of votes at an election ; whether he ought not, in consideration of the state of society, to give up his habit of moderate drinking, or apply less of his wealth to private enjoyments and more to public purposes. Or perhaps he finds himself in some situation, such as that which we illustrated from the 'Heart of Midlothian,' in which, for the sake of others as well as himself, there seems to be strong reason for departing from some ordinary rule of morality, and in which, having emancipated himself from those influences of imagination which might govern the conduct of less enlightened persons, he requires some rule of reason to direct him. When the problem is of this kind, how far will the Hedonistic theory really help to its solution ?

339. In the first order of instances just suggested, the question before the individual, speaking generally, is whether he should depart from the course of action to which custom or inclination, or the sense of what the opinion of his class requires of him, would naturally lead him, with a view to some higher good ; and this, on the principles of Hedonistic Utilitarianism, must mean, with a view to the production of a quantity of pleasure greater on the whole than that to be expected from the course of action which, but for the sake of this higher good, he would naturally follow. We will suppose the Hedonistic calculation, then, to be undertaken by an enlightened and dispassionate person in order to the settlement of this question. How is he to assure himself that the proposed immediate and undoubted sacrifice on his own part will be compensated by an addition to the

sum of human enjoyments on the whole? We say *human* enjoyments, in order not to complicate the question at the outset by recognising the necessity of taking the pleasures of all sentient beings into account, though it is difficult to see how upon Hedonistic principles that necessity can be ignored; for if it is pleasure, as such, and not the person enjoying it, that has intrinsic value, all pleasures alike, by whatever beings enjoyed, must be considered in making up the main account. Though confining his view, however, to the pains and pleasures of men, our enquirer, if he refuses to be put off with answers which really imply non-Hedonistic suppositions, will find it difficult to assure himself that, by any interference with usage or resistance to his own inclination, he can make the balance of human pleasures as against human pains greater than it is.

340. And in the process of dealing with this difficulty he is likely to find himself in the presence of one still more formidable, because more closely affecting the springs of his own conduct. He will have to face the question whether, upon the principles which have generally been taken as the foundation of philosophic Utilitarianism, the supposition that it is possible for him to do anything else than follow his pleasure-seeking impulses can be other than an illusion. In the first place he will be likely to call in question the common assumption that the aggregate of pleasures at any time enjoyed might, *under the circumstances*, be greater than it is. He will see that this assumption conflicts with the principles on which 'the proof of Utilitarianism' has been generally founded. These principles are that every one acts from what is for the time his strongest desire or aversion, and that the object of a man's strongest desire is always that which for the time he imagines as his greatest pleasure, the object of his strongest aversion that which for the time he imagines as his greatest pain. Now we have clearly no title to say that any one is mistaken in such imagination; that anything else would be a greater pleasure or pain *to him at the time* than that which, being what he is and under the given circumstances, he looks forward to as a greatest pleasure or pain. Of his present capacity for pleasure we have, on the hypothesis, no test but his desire, and of his desire no test but his action.

It will be objected, perhaps, that a man is really capable of other pleasure than that which at any time he imagines as his greatest and consequently desires, since his imagination of pleasure is founded on past experience of pleasure, and this is not the measure of what he is capable of receiving. Now of course the pleasure which has been is not exactly that which shall be. A more intense pleasure may from time to time come in a man's way than any he has before experienced; and this may affect his imagination, and consequent desire, of pleasure for the future. But it does not follow from this that any one at any given time, possessed by imagination of a particular pleasure and by desire for it, is capable of any other pleasure than that. He may come to be so capable, but for the present he is not. The pleasure may turn out to be much less in enjoyment than in imagination; it may in the sequel lead to the most intense pain; but it remains true that for the time, if it is the pleasure which the man imagines as then for him the greatest, and which by inevitable consequence (on the given hypothesis) he most strongly desires, it is in fact the greatest pleasure of which he is capable. And, *mutatis mutandis*, the same will be true of pain. Our enquirer then will conclude that, supposing his principles to be true, the aggregate balance of pleasures at any time enjoyed by mankind is as great as it is possible for it to be, the persons and the circumstances being what they are; and that, since in each of his actions a man obtains the greatest pleasure or avoids the greatest pain which is at the time possible for him, there is no ground for saying that in the total result he obtains a less sum of pleasure than any which it was really possible for him to obtain, except through some good fortune independent of his own action.

341. This conclusion must at least suggest a reconsideration of the sense in which it is commonly said that such or such an action ought or ought not to be done. The Utilitarian who does not probe his Hedonistic principles to the bottom, has no difficulty in saying of any one that he ought to do what he does not, because, while he takes for granted that the largest balance of possible pleasure is the chief good, he does not question that it is open to the man who 'does what he ought not' to obtain a larger quantity of pleasure for himself and for others than he in fact obtains by acting as he does. But upon Hedonistic principles, as we have just seen, it is clearly not possible for a man, as his desires and aversions at any time stand, to obtain at the time by his own act more pleasure, or avoid more pain, than he in fact does. We cannot therefore, consistently with these principles, tell the man whom we count vicious that, according to the common Utilitarian language, he wilfully disregards his own true interest and throws away his own greatest happiness. At the most we can only tell him that more pleasure on the whole would have resulted from another course of action than that to which an inevitable strongest desire for pleasures, from time to time imagined as the greatest, has in fact led him. But even this, when the matter is looked into, will not seem so certain. It is not to be denied, of course, that if some instrument could be invented, by which the degrees of intensity of successive pleasures and pains could be registered, and then the sum added up, in many cases where a man had led an immoral life the balance would be found much less on the side of pleasure, or much more on the side of pain, than would have resulted had the man led a different life; though on each occasion, according to the Hedonistic hypothesis, he must have obtained the most pleasure of which for the time he was capable. This is plainly the case where the man's actions have made his life much shorter, or much more painful in its later period, than it would have been had he acted differently. But here everything must depend on the nature of the individual case. For a man with a very strong constitution a certain course of action will have a different bearing on his future capacity for enjoyment from that which it has for a weaker man. On the other hand, if a man has some germ of disease in his system which must kill him before he is old, the method of seeking a rapid succession of intense pleasures, without reference to the effects they may have in later life, will be the right one for him to adopt with a view to enjoying the largest sum possible for him on the whole, while it would be the wrong one for a man who, with care, was sure to live to old age.

342. Even in regard to modes of living, then, which at first sight seem certain to yield a man more pain and less pleasure on the whole than he might have had, if he could have lived differently, we shall find that we have to make an indefinite number of exceptions. Even in regard to them, so far as the goodness or badness of a particular course of action is to depend on its relation to the nett sum of pleasure possible for the individual so acting, we shall have to say that it may be good for one and bad for another, according to physical conditions which we are not competent to ascertain. In other cases where, looking on from the outside, we are apt to think that the enjoyment of certain pleasures, the most intense of which the individual is for the time capable, diminishes the whole sum possible for him, we are arguing from our own conditions and susceptibilities. We argue that the enjoyment of certain pleasures brings a preponderance of pain in the long run, because it brings poverty or dishonour or the pangs of conscience, or deprives a man of the pleasures of friendship or family affection or a cultivated taste. But, as to these pleasures which we suppose to be forgone, we have no means of measuring their intensity, as enjoyed by one man, against the intensity of pleasures which we count vicious, as enjoyed by another man. We cannot tell to what degree they would have been pleasures to the man whom we suppose to have deprived himself of them. As to the pains, again, which we suppose the immoral man to incur, their incidence depends largely on his position, the length of his purse, and a multitude of circumstances which vary with the individual case. We are not entitled to hold that, if incurred at all, they are to him what they would be to a man who had lived differently. The very pursuit of pleasures of sense may so dull the moral sensibilities that the pain, which an onlooker associates with those pleasures as their natural consequence, does not really follow for the person who has enjoyed them. It would thus seem that, though there are doubtless many men who by their manner of life make the balance of pleasures and pains, number and duration being duly set against intensity, less favourable to themselves than it might have been if they could have lived differently, yet we cannot with certainty tell any particular person that he is living such a life, and are not entitled to identify those in whose case the balance will turn out favourable with those whom we in fact count virtuous, nor those in whose case it will turn out unfavourable with those whom we count vicious.

343. It may be objected here perhaps that, although we cannot say with certainty of any particular course of action, as pursued by a particular person, that it diminishes the sum of pleasures open to him, we may be quite sure that action of that kind has a general tendency to diminish pleasure for the persons pursuing it. Does this mean, however, that the supposed course of action would diminish the sum of pleasures if generally pursued, or that it does so for the majority of those who pursue it? The former meaning is not to the purpose, when we are considering the question whether the lives actually lived by men bring them less pleasure on the whole than the same men would experience if they lived differently. Supposing a moral obligation upon the individual to act according to general rules, it will of course be his duty to consider whether any course of action which, as adopted by himself, is productive of a preponderance of pleasure, would have a like result if generally adopted. But no such consideration can affect the question whether the line of action, actually pursued by this man or that, is consistent with the attainment by those persons of the maximum of pleasure possible for them.   On this question the fact that the same line of action, if pursued by other people than those who do in fact pursue it, would diminish the balance of pleasure possible for those other people, has simply no bearing at all.   In this regard each particular action or course of action must stand upon its own merits.   If the morality of the action—the question whether it is morally good or bad—depends on the balance of pleasure or pain that will result from it—not from apparently similar actions done by other men, but from that particular action as done by the person who does it, and under the circumstances under which it is done; and if we cannot be sure that the particular action diminishes the balance of pleasures which, given the circumstances of the case and the desires and aversions of the agent, was really possible, as little can we be sure whether that particular action is morally good or bad, whether it should be done or should not be done.

344. It may be objected, however, that this uncertainty can only continue, so long as we confine our consideration to the consequences of the particular action to the agent himself; that it must disappear when we take into account its consequences to society in general, as on Utilitarian principles we are bound to do.   But is this so?   It must be remembered that we are supposing the principles of Hedonistic Utilitarianism to be strictly carried out.   According to them ultimate value lies in pleasures as such, not in the persons enjoying them.   A pleasure of a certain intensity, enjoyed by three persons, is of no more value than a pleasure of threefold intensity enjoyed by one.   It must be remembered also that the question relates to the pleasure-giving effects of particular actions, not of kinds of action.   Now actions are no doubt sometimes done, in regard to which it would be idle to doubt that the pain, or loss of pleasure, which they cause to others far outweighs any pleasure, or relief from pain, which they bring to those concerned in doing them. But is this the case with the every-day actions which men of a high moral standard would condemn, and to which the moral reformer would seek to put an end? Is it really possible to measure the addition to the pleasure of others, or diminution of their pains, that would be caused by the agent's abstaining from any such an act—which, on the hypothesis, yields him the most intense pleasure of which for the time he is capable, or it would not be done—against the loss of pleasure which he would thereby undergo? The loss of pleasure would vary indefinitely with different persons; it would be different in the same person at different times, according to the degree of that susceptibility upon which the intensity of the pleasure which is for the time most intense for the individual depends. How can we be sure that, in all or in most cases where such actions are done, the certain loss of pleasure or increase of pain to each individual, which, taking him as he is on occasion of each action, would be implied in his acting otherwise than he does, would be so overbalanced by increase of pleasure or decrease of pain to others, that the total sum of pleasure enjoyed by the aggregate of men, taking them as they are, would be greater than it is?

345. If our supposed Hedonistic enquirer follows out these considerations to their legitimate conclusion, they are likely at least to have a modifying influence on any zeal which may have possessed him for reforming current morality in himself and others. They will at least make him less confident in judging that men, as they are, should act otherwise than they do, less confident in any methods of increasing the enjoyments of mankind, and in consequence more ready to let things take their course. 'But after all,' it may be said, 'this may mean no more than that they will make him less censorious, more patient of the failings of mankind, more alive to the slowness of the process by which alone any amelioration of the human lot can be achieved. The conclusion supposed to be arrived at amounts to no more than this, that, if we would increase the sum of enjoyments at any time open to men, we must first change their desires and their surroundings. The enquirer who is in doubt whether or no he should interfere with some custom, or resist some inclination of his own, with a view to increasing human enjoyments, may admit that by so doing he cannot make the balance of pleasure greater than it at any time happens to be, so long as men and circumstances remain what at the time they are; but he may hope that his personal sacrifice, his disturbance (necessarily painful in itself) of mischievous class conventions, will so alter men and circumstances as to make the balance of enjoyments greater in the future than it at present is. This hope should be enough to induce any one, who does not need to be attracted by the glory of present recognised success, "to spurn delights and live laborious days." '

Now it is quite true that there is nothing in his acceptance of the supposed principles, however logically he applies them, to prevent our enquirer, if he is of sanguine temper, from hoping for an increase in the nett sum of human enjoyments. The question is whether they warrant him in believing that by any self-denial or reforming energy on his part the result can be affected. The 'vulgar' Utilitarian notion, of course, is that it is men's own fault that they are not happier on the whole than they are; that it is open to them by their own action to increase the sum of their enjoyments; that they ought to do so; that every one is responsible for contributing as much as he can, according to his lights and powers, to the stock of human happiness. But our enquirer, following out the principles of philosophical Utilitarianism, will be apt to doubt the justification of this belief, whatever he may think of its origin and serviceableness. 'The course of a man's action,' he will say, 'depends on the pleasures and pains that have happened to come in his way, through a chain of events over which he has had no control. These determine his desires and aversions, which in turn determine his actions and through them to some extent the pleasures and pains of his future. No *initiative* by the individual anywhere occurs.

Desires indeed may arise in a man which he has not felt before, and may lead to action which increases the stock of human enjoyment; but they can only arise because some pleasures have fallen to his lot that he had not experienced before. Clearly then there is no alternative but to let the world have its way, and my own inclinations have their way. I may indulge the hope that the result will be some diminution of the misery of mankind. There may be observable tendencies which encourage this hope. New pleasures may arise for men in the natural course of events, which will so modify their action as in the future to yield more pleasure on the whole than they have had in the past. The inclinations which I find in myself, and which arise from pleasures that I have experienced, may contribute to this result. It may turn out that I have a taste which renders me a medium of increased pleasure to mankind. But, whether it prove so or no, that I should follow my tastes and inclinations is the only possibility.'

346. There is no ground for surmising that any so distinct conclusion is consciously arrived at even by the most thorough-going speculative Hedonists, except under the influence of self-indulgent habits which are quite independent of their theories, and may be common to them with men who in theory are 'Ascetics.' But if it is the logical issue of their theory, though a real consciousness of duty, which the theory fails to interpret, may prevent its distinct avowal even in the most secret dialogue of the soul with itself, it can scarcely fail to weaken their actual initiative in good works. In a man of strong speculative interest a suspicion that his theory does not justify his practice cannot go for nothing. Now that the above conclusion is the logical issue of the Hedonistic theory is what no one, aware of the extent to which that theory is adopted, and superior to the temptation of scoring a dialectical victory, would wish to make out if he could help it. But how is the conclusion to be avoided? If men at any given time are getting as much pleasure as under the conditions is possible for them—and that this is the case seems the necessary inference from the Hedonistic principles stated—the only way of increasing the sum will be by altering their possibilities of pleasure; by changing the conditions in the way of imagination and desire, which determine the greatest sum of pleasure possible for men as they are, in such a way that a larger sum shall be possible for them in the future. The Hedonist may hope that such an alteration will come about, either through some beneficence of nature, or through the effort of every man to compass means of attaining the pleasures which he most desires and avoiding the pains which he most dislikes. But how, according to his doctrine, should any one try to change the course of life to which habit and inclination lead him, in order to produce such an alteration? Such an attempt would imply that an alteration of what pleases or pains him most can be an object to a man, to whom yet, upon the hypothesis, desire for the pleasure which most attracts him, aversion from the pain which most repels him in imagination, is the only possible motive; and is not this a contradiction?

347. If the speculative Hedonist, then, anxious about his duty in the world, once comes to put to himself the question, why he should trouble himself about a duty in the world at all, it would seem that he can logically answer the question in only one way; however inconsistent the answer may be with the fact that he cannot help asking the question. He must conclude that he has no duty in the world, according to the sense in which he naturally uses the word—no duty other than a necessity of following the inclination for that which from time to time presents itself to him as his greatest pleasure, or the aversion from what presents itself as his greatest pain. He must explain the seeming consciousness of duty as best he can, by supposition of its arising from antagonism between aversion from some apprehended pain of punishment or shame, and inclination to some anticipated pleasure. As the vulgar understand the phrases 'should do' or 'ought to do'—as he himself understands them in his unphilosophical moments—he must count it absurd to say that any-

thing ought to be done by himself or any one else, which is not done ; absurd, that is, if it is taken to imply that any one has any real option of acting otherwise than as, under imagination of a greatest pleasure or a greatest pain, he in fact does act, or that there is a happiness actually open to men as they are, which by their own fault they throw away. The whole phraseology of obligation, in short, upon Hedonistic principles can best be explained by a theory which is essentially the same as that of Hobbes, and which in Plato's time was represented by the dictum of certain Sophists that ' Justice is the interest of the stronger.' A few words will explain the form in which such a theory would naturally present itself to one who made the legitimate deductions from the principles in question.

348. The contemplation of certain actions by the individual, as actions which he ought to do, implies at once that they can be done, and that they are such as the individual, if left to his natural desire for pleasure and aversion from pain, would not do. But, upon Hedonistic principles, except through *some* desire for pleasure or aversion from pain they could not be done. The distinction of them, then, must lie in the kind of pleasure or pain which the individual contemplates as his inducement to do them. It must be a pleasure or pain which he looks for from the agency of others, who have power to reward or punish him —to reward or punish him, if with nothing else, yet with an approval or disapproval to which he is so sensitive that the approval may in his imagination outweigh every other pleasure, the disapproval every other pain. Thus the consciousness ' I ought to do this or that ' must be interpreted as equivalent to the consciousness that it is expected of me by others, who are ' stronger ' than I am in the sense that they have power to reward or punish me—whether these ' others ' are represented by the civil magistrate or by some public opinion, whether the rewards and punishments proceeding from them are in the nature of what we call physical, or what we call mental, pleasure and pain. It is their interest which is the ultimate foundation of the judgment, on the part of the individual, that he ought or ought not. This judgment only represents the interest of the individual, in so far as that which he presents to himself as his greatest pleasure or pain has come to depend upon his forecast of the will or sentiment of the others, who are stronger than he. The better and worse ἁπλῶς, or simply, being equivalent to the greater pleasure and greater pain simply, the *morally* better and worse are the greater pleasure and pain of those who have power to reward and punish, and who through that power are able so to affect the imagination of individuals as to make it seem a greatest pleasure to please them, a greatest pain to displease them. So far as in any society this power rests, directly or indirectly, with the majority, the morally better for any member of that society will be the greater pleasure of the greater number; not however because that greater number is the greater number, but because it possesses the power described. The action of the individual will be morally good, according as the greater pleasure of the individual—which is his only possible motive—corresponds with the greater pleasure of the stronger, in the sense explained, and thus leads him to do what is expected of him by the stronger. He is counted a good man when this is habitually the case with him. His conscience is that sympathy with the feeling of the stronger, in virtue of which an action that would displease the stronger, and therefore be morally bad, becomes painful to him on the contemplation. An action which a man does 'from sense of duty,' irrespectively, as it seems, of anticipated pleasure or pain, really represents a sympathetic sense of what is expected of him, which makes the contemplated pain of not doing it outweigh any pleasure to be gained by a contrary course. Perhaps he has no definite notion of any particular persons who expect it of him; perhaps there are no such persons; but his feeling about it is the result of a like feeling on the part of his ancestors, which, as felt by them, was directed to some definite source of hope or fear. Between fear of the sword

or stick, and the sort of conscience which is said neither to
fear punishment nor hope for reward, the gap seems wide,
but it may not perhaps be too wide for evolution and hereditary transmission to fill.

349. Some such account of the 'phenomena of morality'
seems the most logical which, upon Hedonistic principles,
can be arrived at. If we admit that the only possible motive
to action is desire for some pleasure or aversion from some
pain, it offers the most consistent method of explaining that
which all must admit to be the distinguishing thing in
morality—the appearance, namely, of there being another
standard of value than pleasure, of there being actions that
proceed from another motive than desire for pleasure. If
the question is asked, how that which is said to be the moral
good and criterion, *viz.* the greatest nett sum of pleasures
for the greatest number, can be a good or object of desire to
the individual, who on the hypothesis can only desire his
own pleasure, it may be replied that we are not called upon
to consider it such an object of desire to him at all. On
the contrary, in calling an action *morally* good we imply some
element of repugnance to the desire of the person for whom
it is *morally* good. It is not good as satisfying any *natural*
desire for pleasure on his part, *i. e.* any such desire as he
would have if left to himself. It is as causing pleasure to
others, not to him, that it has come to be reckoned good.
His interest in doing it is merely the result of the relation in
which the action stands to others, as a source of pleasure to
them and therefore approved by them. He does it as a
means of gaining the pleasure of their approval, or of avoiding
the pain of punishment or shame—the pleasure and pain to
which for the time he happens to be most sensitive.

Again, upon this theory, we are saved the embarrassment
of having to explain how, if the individual always chooses
what pleases him best, he can miss a moral good which
consists in or implies the greatest sum of pleasure possible
for him. According to it, that which is morally best for
the individual is not *his* greatest pleasure, but the greatest

pleasure for those who can reward and punish him ; who can make their approval and disapproval objects of his desire and aversion. Thus, though he always chooses the greatest imagined pleasure, the individual's acts may conflict with the morally best, unless desire for reward or approval, aversion from punishment or disapproval, keep his action in constant correspondence with the interest of those who make morality. There is no need then to attempt any impossible 'moral arithmetic,' any balance of the extent and durability of certain pleasures against the intensity of others, with a view to showing that the immoral man misses the greatest sum of pleasure possible to him. It is not *his* greatest pleasure, but the greatest pleasure of 'the stronger,' which forms the issue in all questions of morality. No question need be raised between what 'seems' good and what 'is' good. That which in the long run seems to those who wield the forces of society most conducive to their pleasure, is really so, and the strongest force in society tends to become equivalent, directly or indirectly, to that of the majority : so that a man's duty—that which he 'ought to do,' or which he feels is expected of him—tends to be that sort of action which conduces to the greatest happiness of the greatest number. But as there is no fixedness or finality either in the ruling influence of society, or in the modes of action which those who exercise this influence find most for their pleasure, no final or absolute judgment can be given as to the morally better or worse. Within certain limits the standard of morality fluctuates.

350. So much for the course of speculation which a logical mind, starting from the principles on which Utilitarianism has generally been founded, is likely to follow. In order to illustrate more definitely the weakening of moral initiative likely to result from it, we will suppose our enquirer, having been touched by a scruple as to his continuance in some practice in which, like others of his class, he has indulged, and which is not condemned either by law or public opinion, to be examining this scruple in the light of his Hedonistic philosophy. Let the enquirer be some one so circumstanced as was C. J. Fox, and let gambling be the practice in question. Let us suppose a dialogue within the soul, excited by the suggestion that the practice is *morally* bad and ought to be given up.

'How can it be morally bad? I have come to the conclusion that the morally bad means that which conflicts with the will of the stronger, or, as the Utilitarians say, with a law enforced by some sanction, either the legal sanction or the popular sanction; but no such law is broken by the practice in question.'

'You forget the other sanctions, the religious and the natural.'

'If I forget the religious sanction, this shows that to me it is not a sanction. It is a purely subjective sanction, consisting in fear of the pains of another world. As a matter of fact, I do not find any ostensibly divine prohibition of gambling, sanctioned by the threat of such pains ; but, if I did, it would not affect me, for it cannot be proved that such pains will ever be endured, and I do not happen to be afraid of them.'

'But the natural sanction? In gambling you are violating a law enforced by a natural sanction, as you will find when the painful consequences of your gambling propensities in due course of nature come to be felt.'

'Here at any rate we are shifting our ground. The first suggestion was that the practice was *morally* bad, and it would not be so if it were contrary to a law enforced by *natural* sanctions ; if, in the natural course of things and without the intervention of any social force, it led to an over-balance of pain. But how can it be shown that in gambling I violate a law enforced by a natural sanction? There is no doubt about the intense pleasure I find in gambling, as measured, according to our principles, by my intense desire to gamble. The pleasures that I am supposed to forgo by gambling might not be pleasures to me ; and, as for any future pains likely to result from the practice, they will scarcely be so intense, when my skin is hardened against many pangs which would be formidable if inflicted now, as to be compared with the pleasure I now find in following my bent.'

'Ah, but think of the long succession of them; how much they will amount to, when all put together.'

'But they never will be put together. I may fairly hope that one will be over, and relieved by some interval of pleasure, before another begins. Unbroken continuance of even slight pain is, no doubt, awful to anticipate. But there is no reason to think that the pain consequent on this indulgence will be unbroken, or that, if there were nothing to relieve it, I need live to endure it. If I found it becoming unbearable, I should have the remedy in my own hands.'

'Perhaps we have been arguing the question upon wrong grounds. The practice of gambling may not be demonstrably productive of more pain than pleasure to you individually, but there can be no doubt that it is so to society generally. It is true that, in the present state of law and of opinion, it does not violate any rule enforced by the political or by the popular sanction, and thus, in the restricted sense of the word, is not morally bad. But this state of law and opinion is itself in violation of a law having a *natural* sanction—the sanction consisting in the excess of pain above pleasure produced by gambling to society in general. It is thus bad in the sense of being pernicious, just as Hobbes admitted that a law, though it could not be unjust, might be pernicious. It ought to be changed, and you ought to refuse to conform to it, in deference to a higher law than that enforced by the state or public opinion, a law having the natural sanction which belongs to any rule necessary to the greatest happiness of the greatest number.'

'Here are three propositions, each more doubtful than the other. It is not very easy to show that the practice is pernicious in that sense of the word which alone, as Hedonists, we can admit; *viz.* that more pleasure, after deduction for counterbalancing pain, would at any time be felt by more persons if the practice were changed. You cannot dictate

to people what their pleasures shall be.   If the practice is so
predominantly unpleasant in its consequences to the majority
as you say, why have they not found that out and stopped
it?   But granting that it is so, what do you mean by saying
that it ought to be changed?   This apparently is an obligation on the part of society, but to whom is it an obligation?
An obligation on the part of the several members of the
society to each other and to the whole society is intelligible.
But in the absence of any law either of the state or of opinion
against the practice, it cannot be said that any such obligation is violated by the practice.   An obligation of society to
itself is unintelligible.   You say indeed that society ought
to change the practice, because it violates a law enforced by
a natural sanction.   But here you are the victim of a figure
of speech.   You are personifying 'nature' as an imponent
of obligation.   Stripped of figures of speech, this proposition
is merely a repetition of that already shown to be doubtful,
that the practice is pernicious—productive of more pain
than pleasure.   If it is so, that is a reason for expecting that
society with increasing experience will see fit to refuse to
tolerate it, but none for saying that it ought to do so.   Even
less is it a ground for saying that, while the practice continues to be sanctioned by society, I ought not to indulge
in it.   My taste for gambling does not conflict either with
positive law or with what is expected of me by society.   To
whom then am I under any obligation to renounce it?   It
cannot be held that it is a duty which I owe to myself; for,
if there is any meaning in that phrase, it can only mean,
according to our principles, that the practice tends more to
my pain than to my pleasure, and this we have seen there
is no reason for holding.   If society with further experience
changes its mind on the matter, it may then make it more
painful for me to indulge my taste than to abstain; but
there is no reason why I should anticipate the result of
social conflict in this or in any other case.   Indeed, according to Hedonistic principles, I could not if I would.   For
the present from time to time a strongest desire—strongest

because excited by imagination of what is for the time my most intense pleasure—moves me to gamble, and I act accordingly. If society will furnish me with a stronger motive for abstaining, let it do so. I can only await the change of law or social opinion that will bring such a deterrent to bear on me.'

351. This sort of Hedonistic fatalism seems to be logically inherent in all Utilitarian philosophy which founds itself on the principle that pleasure is the sole object of desire. That this principle may be rejected by one who yet accepts the Utilitarian doctrine of ultimate good, we know from the example of Mr. Henry Sidgwick. Whether his rejection of it is not really inconsistent with his view of the 'Summum Bonum' is a point to be considered later. What concerns us here is the fact that the principle stated is taken as the foundation of their Ethical doctrine alike by Bentham, J. S. Mill and Mr. H. Spencer, and that, the more the Utilitarian philosophy is applied to the direction of private conduct, the more practically important this principle is likely to become, and the more likely are speculative men to draw from it those legitimate inferences which we have been considering, to the embarrassment of their own higher impulses. That in the most illustrious spokesmen of Utilitarianism no such tendency has really appeared, is explained by their pre-occupation with great projects of political and social amelioration, which made their theoretical reduction of the good to pleasure of quite secondary importance. They had the great lesson to teach, that the value of all laws and institutions, the rectitude of all conduct, was to be estimated by reference to the well-being of all men, and that in the estimate of that well-being no nation or class or individual was to count above another. It mattered little for practical purposes that they held the well-being of society to consist simply of the nett aggregate of pleasures enjoyed by its members, and that they founded this view on the principle that some pleasure or other is the sole object of every desire. The mischief latent in this principle could only appear if it occurred to them to ask the question, which their reforming zeal was too strong to allow them to ask, why they should trouble themselves to alter their tastes and habits, or those of other people.   It is only when this question has come to be commonly asked by men at once sufficiently free from the mastery either of the lower or of the higher passions, and with sufficient command over the circumstances of their lives, for the answer to have real influence over their conduct, that the theoretical consequences which we have seen to be involved in the Hedonistic principle become of serious practical import.

We have then to consider, not so much whether the principle that pleasure is the sole object of desire is itself tenable —on that enough has been already said in this treatise—as whether the doctrine which, having rejected this view of desire, professes to find the absolutely desirable or 'Summum Bonum' for man in some perfection of human life, some realisation of human capacities, is of a kind, not only to save speculative men from that suspicion of there being an illusion in their impulses after a higher life which Hedonism naturally yields, but also to guide those impulses in cases of honest doubt as to the right line of action to adopt.

CHAPTER IV

THE PRACTICAL VALUE OF UTILITARIANISM COMPARED
WITH THAT OF THE THEORY OF THE GOOD
AS HUMAN PERFECTION

352. ACCORDING to the doctrine of this treatise, as we have previously endeavoured to state it, there is a principle of self-development in man, independent of the excitement of new desires by those new imaginations, which presuppose new experiences, of pleasure. In virtue of this principle he anticipates experience. In a certain sense he makes it, instead of merely waiting to be made by it. He is capable of being moved by an idea of himself, as becoming that which he has it in him to be—an idea which does not represent previous experience, but gradually brings an experience into being, gradually creates a filling for itself, in the shape of arts, laws, institutions and habits of living, which, so far as they go, exhibit the capabilities of man, define the idea of his end, afford a positive answer to the otherwise unanswerable question, what in particular it is that man has it in him to become. The action of such an idea in the individual accounts for two things which, upon the Hedonistic supposition, are equally unaccountable. It accounts for the possibility of the question, Why should I trouble about making myself or my neighbours other than we are? and, given the question, it accounts for an answer being rendered to it, in the shape of a real initiation of effort for the improvement of human life.

The supposition, therefore, of a free or self-objectifying spiritual agency in human history is one to which a fair analysis of human history inevitably leads us. But it remains to be asked by what rule the effort is to be guided, which we suppose the idea of a possible human perfection thus to initiate. That idea, according to our view, is primarily in man unfilled and unrealised; and within the experience of men it is never fully realised, never acquires a content adequate to its capacity. There are arts and institutions and rules of life, in which the human spirit has so far incompletely realised its idea of a possible Best; and the individual in whom the idea is at work will derive from it a general injunction to further these arts, to maintain and, so far as he can, improve these institutions. It is when this general injunction has to be translated into particulars that the difficulty arises. How is the essential to be distinguished from the unessential and obstructive, in the processes through which an effort after the perfection of man may be traced? How are the arts to become a more thorough realisation of the ideal which has imperfectly expressed itself in them? How are the institutions of social life, and the rules of conventional morality, to be cleared of the alien growths which they owe to the constant co-operation of selfish passions with interest in common good, and which render them so imperfectly organic to the development of the human spirit? Above all, how is this or that individual—circumstanced as he is, and endowed, physically and mentally, as he is—to take part in the work? When he is called upon to decide between adherence to some established rule of morality and service to a particular person, or to face some new combination of circumstances to which recognised rules of conduct do not seem to apply, how is he to find guidance in an idea which merely moves him to aim at the best and highest in conduct? In short, as we put the difficulty after first stating the doctrine which finds the basis of morality in such an idea (§ 198)—'So far as it can be translated into practice at all, must not its effect be either a dead conformity to the code of customary morality, anywhere and at any time established, without effort to reform or expand it, or else unlimited licence in departing from it at the prompting of any impulse which the individual may be pleased to consider a higher law?'

Unless these questions can be satisfactorily answered, it

would seem that our theory of the basis of morality, though its adoption might save some speculative persons from that distrust of their own conscience to which Hedonism would naturally lead them, can be of no further practical value. It may still serve to dispel the notion that the inclination to take one's ease and let the world have its way is justified by philosophy. It may still have an important bearing on that examination by the individual of his own walk and conduct, in which the question of motive should hold the first place; for it recognises, as the one motive which should be supreme, a desire which the Hedonist must ignore. But it will have no guidance to offer to the impulse which it explains, and of which it asserts the importance. In those cases in which, as we have previously pointed out, the question, Ought this or that to be done? has to be answered irrespectively of motive and with reference merely to the effects of actions, it will be of no avail. For that purpose we need some conception of a 'Summum Bonum' or ultimate good, definite enough to enable us to enquire whether the effects of a particular action contribute to that end or no. But if the idea of a possible perfection of life cannot be translated into any definite conceptions of what contributes to the attainment of that life, except such as are derived from existing usage and law, it cannot afford such a criterion as we want of the value of possible actions, when we are in doubt which of them should be done; for we want a criterion that shall be independent of law and usage, while at the same time it shall be other than the casual conviction of the individual.

353. Now, as we have more than once admitted, we can form no positive conception of what the ultimate perfection of the human spirit would be; what its life would be when all its capabilities were fully realised. We can no more do this than we can form a positive conception of what the nature of God in itself is. All the notions that we can form of human excellences or virtues are in some way relative to present imperfections. We may say perhaps, with the Apostle, that Faith, Hope and Charity '*abide*;' that they are not merely passing phases of a life which may come to enter on conditions in which they would cease to be possible ; and there may be a sense in which this is true. But when we come to speak of the functions in which those virtues manifest themselves, we find that we are speaking of functions essentially relative to a state of society in which it is impossible to suppose that the human spirit has reached its full development. 'Charity beareth all things, believeth all things, hopeth all things ;' but if all men had come to be what they should be, what would there be for Charity to bear, to hope, and to believe?

Though the idea of an absolutely perfect life, however, cannot be more to us than the idea that there must be such a life, as distinct from an idea of what it is—and we may admit this while holding that this idea is in a supreme sense formative and influential—it does not follow that there is any difficulty in conceiving very definitely a life of the individual and of society more perfect, because more completely fulfilling the vocation of individual and society, than any which is being lived. There may have been a period in the history of our race when the idea of a possible perfection was a blindly moving influence ; when it had not yet taken sufficient effect in the ordering of life and the formation of virtues for reflection on these to enable men to say what it would be to be more perfect. But we are certainly not in that state now. We all recognise, and perhaps in some fragmentary way practise, virtues which both carry in themselves unfulfilled possibilities, and at the same time plainly point out the direction in which their own further development is to be sought for. It has already been sought in this treatise to trace the ideal of the cardinal virtues, as recognised by the conscience of Christendom. In none of these would the man who came nearest the ideal 'count himself to have attained,' nor would he have any difficulty in defining the path of his further attainment. No one is eager *enough* to know what is true or make what is beautiful ; no one ready *enough* to endure pain and forgo pleasure in the service of his fellows; no one impartial *enough* in treating the claims of another exactly as his own. Thus to have more 'intellectual excellence;' to be more brave, temperate and just, in the sense in which any one capable of enquiring what it is to be more perfect would now understand these virtues, is a sufficient object for him to set before himself by way of answer to the question, so far as it concerns him individually; while a state of society in which these virtues shall be more generally attainable and attained, is a sufficient account of the more perfect life considered as a social good.

354. It would seem then that, though statements at once positive and instructive as to the absolutely Best life may be beyond our reach, yet, by help of mere honest reflection on the evidence of its true vocation which the human spirit has so far yielded in arts and sciences, in moral and political achievement, we can know enough of a better life than our own, of a better social order than any that now is, to have an available criterion of what is good or bad in law and usage, and in the tendencies of men's actions. The working theory of the end, which we derive from the doctrine that the ultimate good for man must be some full development of the human spirit in character and conduct, may be represented by some such question as the following: Does this or that law or usage, this or that course of action—directly or indirectly, positively or as a preventive of the opposite—contribute to the better-being of society, as measured by the more general establishment of conditions favourable to the attainment of the recognised excellences and virtues, by the more general attainment of those excellences in some degree, or by their attainment on the part of some persons in higher degree without detraction from the opportunities of others? In order to put this question we must, no doubt, have a definite notion of the direction in which the 'Summum Bonum' is to be sought, but not of what its full attainment would actually be; and this, it will be found, is all that we need or can obtain for our guidance in estimating the value of laws and institutions, actions and usages, by their effects.

It will do nothing indeed to help us in ascertaining what the effects of any institution or action really are.   No theory whatever of the 'Summum Bonum,' Hedonistic or other, can avail for the settlement of this question, which requires analysis of facts and circumstances, not consideration of ends.   But it will sufficiently direct us in regard to the kind of effects we should look out for in our analysis, and to the value we should put upon them when ascertained.

In all cases then in which, according to the distinction previously explained, the question at issue is not, What ought I to be? but, What ought to be done? the criterion just stated should be our guide in answering it.   As we have seen, the question, What ought I to be ? includes the question, What ought to be done? for I am not what I ought to be—my character and motives are not what they should be—unless my actions, in virtue of their effects, are such as ought to be done.   But, as we have also seen, for that purpose which the question, Am I what I ought to be ? mainly serves in ethical development—the purpose, namely, of self-reproval and consequent incitement of the effort to be better —no elaborate enquiry into the effects of actions done is commonly needed.   So far, however, as such an enquiry is involved in the process of self-examination, the criterion to be employed in the valuation of effects will be such as we have described.   It will have to be employed, again, in all cases where we are judging the actions of others, whose state of character is incognisable by us, or considering whether outward action of a certain kind, irrespectively of motives, is good or bad, whether certain institutions or practices of society should be maintained or given up—these being all questions solely of effect.   It is a criterion, indeed, which will seldom come to the front, even in the minds of those who are most clearly aware that it is their criterion, because in all ordinary cases of disinterested doubt as to the value of institutions and usages, and of actions in which we are not ourselves concerned, the question which occupies us is, What under all the conditions of the case are the effects actually produced? not, What is the value of the effects? But it should be, and (as we hold) with all men who have assimilated the higher moral culture of Christendom really is, the measure of value which is kept in view in the effort to ascertain the effects of action, and which is tacitly applied in the estimate of all ascertained effects that are susceptible of moral valuation.

355. The Utilitarian, if he can bring himself to attend to what is here advanced, will probably say that in ordinary cases and for practical purposes he can accept our criterion, but that he cannot regard it as ultimate or scientific, and that it fails us just in those cases where an ultimate or scientific criterion is needed, because in them the rules of established morality are insufficient or inapplicable. He will not object to measure the better-being of society in an ordinary way 'by the more general establishment of conditions favourable to the attainment of the recognised excellences and virtues, by the more general attainment of those excellences in some degree, or by their attainment on the part of some persons in higher degree without detraction from the opportunities of others,' because he will hold that these recognised virtues and excellences represent an incalculable accumulation of experience as to the modes in which the largest balance of pleasure may be obtained. Their exercise according to him does not constitute the 'Summum Bonum,' but under ordinary conditions it is an ascertained means to it. 'Is there then,' the reader may ask us, 'any practical difference between the Utilitarian criterion and yours? You say that the effects of actions, institutions, etc., are to be valued according to their relation to the production of personal excellence, moral and intellectual. The Utilitarian does not deny this; but whereas, according to you, the excellence is itself the ultimate end, according to the Utilitarian it has its value only as a means —speaking generally, a necessary and unfailing means—to the production of the largest possible sum of pleasure. Since you are both agreed, then, that the effects to be looked at in all ordinary moral valuation are effects that have a bearing on meritorious character, whether there be a further end beyond that character or no, the several criteria come to pretty much the same thing. It will only be in exceptional cases that any difference between the two views of the criterion need appear; in the estimation, for instance, of some practice (such as vivisection may perhaps be reckoned) which stands in no ascertained relation, direct or indirect, to the maintenance, advancement, or diffusion of meritorious conduct; or in the estimation of some exceptional act to which the general rule, that the nett maximum of possible pleasure is only to be reached by following the paths of recognised virtue, is rendered inapplicable by some peculiarity in the circumstances of the case or in the position of the agent. Here the Utilitarian must apply his ultimate criterion directly. He must seek to ascertain the balance of pleasure or pain resulting from the particular practice or action, without the help of those records of prolonged observation upon pleasure-giving and pain-giving consequences which the established rules of morality in effect supply. This is no doubt a difficult task; but, upon the theory which rejects the Hedonistic calculus as criterion on the ground that virtuous character and conduct is an end in itself, is any criterion in such cases available at all?'

356. Now it is satisfactory to acknowledge that the theory of the criterion for which we are arguing does not for practical purposes differ much from the Utilitarian, so long as the Utilitarian view of the criterion is not founded—as it generally has been, and perhaps logically should be—on the Hedonistic theory of motives. The doctrine that pleasure is the only possible object of desire logically excludes the possibility of aspiration for personal holiness, of effort after goodness for its own sake. According to it the state of will and character which we have previously used the phrase 'purity of heart' to describe, is not only an unrealisable ideal, but an ideal which cannot excite desire for its attainment at all. This theory of motives, therefore, is incompatible in principle with the whole view of the nature of virtue, as issuing from a character in which the interest in being good is dominant, already set forth in this treatise. But if the Utilitarian is committed to no more than a certain doctrine of the criterion of morality—the doctrine that the value of actions and institutions is to be measured in the last resort by their effect on the nett sum of pleasures enjoyable by all human, or perhaps by all sentient, beings, the difference between him and one who would substitute for this 'nett sum, etc.' 'the fulfilment of human capacities' may be practically small. A desire for the enjoyment of pleasure by others—whether in the largest quantity possible, or in some more positively conceivable form—is so entirely different from desire for a pleasure that, if the Utilitarian considers his 'Summum Bonum,' or any limited form of it, to be a possible object of desire to the individual, he clears himself practically, even though it be at the sacrifice of consistency, from chargeability with any such theory of motives as would exclude the possibility of a 'pure heart.'

We are brought, then, to this point. The Utilitarian theory of ultimate good, if founded upon the Hedonistic theory of motives, we have found to be 'intrinsically unavailable for supplying motive or guidance to a man who wishes to make his life better,' because that theory of motives, when argued out, appears to exclude, not indeed the hope on the part of the individual that his own life and that of mankind may become better, *i.e.* more pleasant, but the belief that it can rest with him to exercise any initiative, whether in the way of resistance to inclination or of painful interference with usage, which may affect the result. We saw reason to think that this logical consequence of the theory tended to have at least a weakening influence upon life and conduct, and that there was accordingly a practical reason for seeking a substitute in another theory of ultimate good. But the question now arises whether this substitute shall be sought, according to the previous argument of this treatise, in a theory which would place the 'Summum Bonum' in a perfection of human life, not indeed positively definable by us, but having an identity with the virtuous life actually achieved by the best men, as having for its principle the same will to be perfect; or rather in a revision of the Utilitarian theory, which shall make it independent of the Hedonistic theory of motives, while retaining the account of the 'Summum Bonum' as a maximum of possible pleasure. We will endeavour to consider candidly what the latter alternative has to recommend it.

357. It is noticeable in the first place that, if the Utilitarian doctrine of the chief good as criterion—the doctrine that the greatest possible sum of pleasures is the end by reference to which the value of actions is to be tested—is dissociated from the Hedonistic doctrine of motives, though it may be cleared from liability to bad practical effects, it has also lost what has been in fact its chief claim to the acceptance of ordinary men. The process of its acceptance has been commonly this. Because there is pleasure in all satisfaction of desire, men have come to think that the object of desire is always some pleasure; that every good is a pleasure. From this the inference is natural enough that a greatest possible sum of pleasures is a greatest possible good—at any rate till it is pointed out that the possibility of desiring a sum of pleasures, which never can be enjoyed as a sum, would not follow from the fact that the object of desire was always some imagined pleasure. But once drop the notion that pleasure is the sole thing desired, and the question arises why it should be deemed that which 'in our calm moments' is to be counted the sole thing desirable, so that the value of all which men do or which concerns them is to be measured simply by its tendency to produce pleasure. We suppose ourselves now to be arguing with men who admit the possibility of disinterested motives, who value character according as it is habitually actuated by them; who neither understand by such motives desires for that kind of pleasure of which the contemplation of another's pleasure is the condition, nor allow themselves to suppose that, granting benevolence to be always a desire to produce pleasure, it is therefore a desire for (*i. e.* to enjoy) pleasure. Why, we ask such persons, do you take that to be the one thing ultimately desirable, which you not only admit to be not the sole thing desired, but which you admit is not desired in those actions which you esteem the most?

358. It may be surmised that the chief attraction which the Hedonistic criterion has had for such persons has lain in its apparent definiteness. The conception of the 'Summum Bonum,' as consisting in a greatest possible nett sum of pleasures, has seemed to afford a much more positive and intelligible criterion than the conception of a full realisation of human capacities, which we admit to be only definable by reflection on the partial realisation of those capacities in recognised excellences of character and conduct. It promises an escape, too, from the circle in which, as already observed, we seem to move, when we say that we ought to do so and so because it is virtuous or noble to do it, and then have to explain what is virtuous or noble as what we ought to do. A 'Summum Bonum' consisting of a greatest possible sum of pleasures is supposed to be definite and intelligible, because every one knows what pleasure is. But in what sense does every one know it? If only in the sense that every one can imagine the renewal of some pleasure which he has enjoyed, it may be pointed out that pleasures, not being enjoyable in a sum— to say nothing of a greatest possible sum—cannot be imagined in a sum either. Though this remark, however, might be to the purpose against a Hedonist who held that desire could only be excited by imagined pleasure, and yet that a greatest sum of pleasure was an object of desire, it is not to the purpose against those who merely look on the greatest sum of pleasures as the true criterion, without holding that desire is only excited by imagination of pleasure. They will reply that, though we may not be able, strictly speaking, to imagine a sum of pleasures, every one knows what it is. Every one knows the difference between enjoying a longer

succession of pleasures and a shorter one, a succession of
more intense and a succession of less intense pleasures,
a succession of pleasures less interrupted by pain and one
more interrupted. In this sense every one knows the
difference between enjoying a larger sum of pleasures and
enjoying a smaller sum. He knows the difference also
between a larger number of persons or sentient beings and
a smaller one. He attaches therefore a definite meaning
to the enjoyment of a greater nett amount of pleasure by
a greater number of beings, and has a definite criterion for
distinguishing a better action from a worse, in the tendency
of the one, as compared with the other, to produce a greater
amount of pleasure to a greater number of persons.

359. The ability, however, to compare a larger sum of
pleasure with a smaller in the sense explained—as we might
compare a longer time with a shorter—is quite a different
thing from ability to conceive a greatest possible sum of
pleasures, or to attach any meaning to that phrase. It seems,
indeed, to be intrinsically as unmeaning as it would be to
speak of a greatest possible quantity of time or space. The
sum of pleasures plainly admits of indefinite increase, with
the continued existence of sentient beings capable of pleasure. It is greater to-day than it was yesterday, and, unless
it has suddenly come to pass that experiences of pain outnumber experiences of pleasure, it will be greater to-morrow
than it is to-day ; but it will never be complete while sentient
beings exist. To say that ultimate good is a greatest possible sum of pleasures, strictly taken, is to say that it is an
end which for ever recedes ; which is not only unattainable
but from the nature of the case can never be more nearly
approached ; and such an end clearly cannot serve the
purpose of a criterion, by enabling us to distinguish actions
which bring men nearer to it from those that do not. Are
we then, since the notion of a greatest possible sum of
pleasures is thus unavailable, to understand that in applying
the Utilitarian criterion we merely approve one action in
comparison with another, as tending to yield more pleasure

to more beings capable of pleasure, without reference to a 'Summum Bonum' or ideal of a perfect state of existence at all? But without such reference is there any meaning in approval or disapproval at all? It is intelligible that without such reference the larger sum of pleasures should be desired as against the less; on supposition of benevolent impulses, it is intelligible that the larger sum should be desired by a man for others as well as for himself. But the desire is one thing, the approval of it—the judgment 'in a calm hour' that the desire of the action moved by it is reasonable—is quite another thing. Without some ideal— however indeterminate—of a best state of existence, with the attainment of which the approved motive or action may be deemed compatible, the approval of it would seem impossible. Utilitarians have therefore to consider whether they can employ a criterion of action, as they do employ it, without some idea of ultimate good; and, since a greatest possible sum of pleasures is a phrase to which no idea really corresponds, what is the idea which really actuates them in the employment of their criterion.

360. When, having duly reflected on these points, we try (if the expression may be pardoned) to make sense of the Utilitarian theory—bearing in mind at once its implication of the conception of a 'Summum Bonum,' and the impossibility that of pleasures, so long as sentient beings continue to enjoy themselves, there should be any such greatest sum as can satisfy the conception—we cannot avoid the conclusion that the 'Summum Bonum' which the Utilitarian contemplates is not a sum of pleasures, but a certain state of existence; a state in which all human beings, or all beings of whose consciousness he supposes himself able to take account, shall live as pleasantly as is possible for them, without one gaining pleasure at the expense of another. The reason why he approves an action is not that he judges it likely to make an addition to a sum of pleasures which never comes nearer completion, but that he judges it likely to contribute to this state of general enjoyable existence. If he says that the right object for a man is to increase the stock of human enjoyments, it is presumable that he is not really thinking of an addition to a sum of pleasant experiences, however large, which might be made and yet leave those who had had the experiences with no more of the good in possession than they had before.   He does not mean that a thousand experiences of pleasure constitute more of a good than nine hundred experiences of the same intensity, or less of a good than six hundred of a double intensity.   He is thinking of a good consisting in a certain sort of social life, of which he does not particularise the nature to himself further than by conceiving it as a pleasant life to all who share in it, and as one of which all have the enjoyment, if not equally, yet none at the cost of others.   By increasing the stock of enjoyments he means enabling more persons to live pleasantly, or with less interruption from pain.   The good which he has before him is not an aggregate of pleasures but a pleasant life—a life at all times and for all persons as pleasant, as little marred by pain, as possible ; but good, *qua* a life in which the persons living are happy or enjoy themselves, not *qua* a life into which so many enjoyments are crowded.

361.   Now the objection to this conception of a chief good is not that, so far as it goes, it is otherwise than true.   According to our view, since there is pleasure in all realisation of capacity, the life in which human capacities should be fully realised would necessarily be a pleasant life [1].   The objection is that, instead of having that definiteness which, because all know what pleasure is, it seemed at first to promise, it turns out on consideration to be so abstract and indefinite.   It tells us nothing of that life, to the attainment of which our actions must contribute if they are to be what they should be, but merely that it would be as pleasant as possible for all persons, or for all beings of whose consciousness we can take account.   The question is whether in thinking of an absolutely desirable life, as the end by refer-

[1] [Cf. however § 276.]

ence to which the effects of our actions are to be valued,
our view must be confined to the mere quality of its universal pleasantness, and whether in consequence productivity
of pleasure is the ultimate ground on which actions are to
be approved. The view for which we plead is that the
quality of the absolutely desirable life, which renders it such
in man's thoughts, is that it shall be the full realisation of
his capacities ; that, although pleasure must be incidental to
such realisation, it is in no way distinctive of it, being equally
incidental to any unimpeded activity, to the exercise of
merely animal functions no less than to those that are properly human ; that, although we know not in detail what
the final realisation of man's capacities would be, we know
well enough, from the evidence they have so far given of
themselves, what a fuller development of them would be ;
and that thus, in the injunction to make life as full a realisation as possible of human capacities, we have a definiteness
of direction, which the injunction to make life as pleasant as
possible does not supply.

362. Such definiteness of direction as is derivable from
the latter injunction really depends on the assumption that,
with a view to the general enjoyment of life, conduct should
follow the paths of recognised virtue. On supposition that
the requirements of conventional morality represent a great
mass of experience as to the social behaviour by which life
is rendered more generally pleasant, we may be sure that as
a rule their violation is not the way to help men on the
whole to live more pleasantly. The supposition need not
be disputed. But how did these requirements, or what is
really beneficent in them, come to be formed ? There was
a time when they did not yet amount to the requirements of
a conventional morality—when a large part of them were as
yet only the convictions of a few peculiar people as to what
was needed in the interest of a better social being. Whence
then did these few derive direction for those efforts to make
social life what it should be, which our present conventional
morality was not there to guide, and which any conventional

morality then current would have discountenanced? Would not the mere injunction to make human life as pleasant as possible, failing the interpretation which our present conventional morality may supply, but which it was not then there to supply, have had either no significance for them or a misleading one—a misleading significance if taken to be interpreted by the then recognised standards of meritorious conduct, and otherwise none? Has not the spirit in which the better being of society has in fact been promoted been generally that which Mr. Browning puts into the mouth of his Rabbi Ben Ezra?—

> Then, welcome each rebuff
> That turns earth's smoothness rough,
> Each sting that bids nor sit nor stand but go!
> Be our joys three-parts pain!
> Strive, and hold cheap the strain;
> Learn, nor account the pang; dare, never grudge the throe![1]

And would this spirit ever have found its inward law in an injunction to produce as much pleasure as possible—to seek as its supreme object to obtain that for others which it would reject for itself? Does not the same spirit still find such an injunction unmeaning or repellent, in those cases where it needs, owing to the felt insufficiency of the rules of conventional morality, to resort for direction to some conception of ultimate good?

363. It may be retorted, however, that by our own confession the injunction to realise the capacities, to make the most and best, of the human soul, derives its definite content from reference to the recognised virtues and excellences of life. It is an injunction to attain these more fully, to render

---

[1] [The following passage from the Epilogue to 'Romola,' which the author intended to quote at some point in this chapter, may be added here: 'We can only have the highest happiness, such as goes along with being a great man, by having wide thoughts, and much feeling for the rest of the world as well as ourselves; and this sort of happiness often brings so much pain with it, that we can only tell it from pain by its being what we would choose before everything else, because our souls see it is good.']

them more generally attainable, to give further realisation to the spirit which has expressed itself in them. If it on the one hand, and the injunction to make life as pleasant as possible on the other, have alike need of this reference in order to acquire definite meaning, what advantage has the former over the latter? Its advantage we take to be this. The former injunction does, while the latter does not, correspond to the inward law by which men have been governed in the effort and aspiration that have yielded the various excellences in the way of art and knowledge, no less than of conduct, which now determine our ideal of further perfection. Accordingly in those cases—very exceptional, as we have all along pointed out—where the difference between the two injunctions would make itself practically apparent, the one would, while the other would not, suggest a manner of life, a standard of achievement in knowledge and art, higher than that which current expectations call for. A man who interprets the recognised virtues and excellences as having been arrived at with a view to the increase of pleasure, who holds them to be valuable only as means to that end, has not the clue to guide him in cases where it is no longer enough to follow the 'law of opinion' or social expectation, but where it behoves him to act in the higher spirit of those virtues and excellences—a spirit which he must interpret for himself. The question whether it would conduce more to general pleasure that he should set up for being better than his neighbours, instead of swimming with the stream; that he should follow the severer path of duty, where his departure from it would be unknown or uncondemned, and where it would save himself and those whom he loves from much suffering; that he should seek the highest beauty in art, the completest truth in knowledge, rather than conform to popular taste and opinion—this is a question which he will find for ever unanswerable; and, in presence of its unanswerability, the fact that his own pleasure will undoubtedly be served by deciding it in the easier way is likely to have considerable weight. If, on the other hand, he were governed by the conviction that the recognised virtues and excellences are ends in themselves, because in them the human spirit in some measure fulfils its divine vocation, attains something of the perfection which it lies in it to attain, he would find in reflection on them an indication of the ends to be kept in view, where the rule of being virtuous according to some established type of virtue is insufficient, as well as a constant direction to estimate at its highest the claim on his personal devotion to the further perfecting of man.

364. Before we attempt finally to illustrate the manner in which these different conceptions of ultimate good, and the different injunctions founded on them, would be likely under certain conditions to affect the practical judgment, it will be well to remove one more possible misapprehension as to the distinction between them.   They are not to be distinguished as if according to one the 'Summum Bonum' were a state of desirable consciousness, while according to the other it was not.   It is agreed that in presenting a 'Summum Bonum' to ourselves we present it as a state of desirable consciousness.   Except as some sort of conscious life it can be to us nothing ; and to say that we think of it as desirable is the same thing as to say that we think of it as good.   The question is whether we think of it as good or desirable because we anticipate pleasure in it, or because and so far as we already desire it, knowing that there must be pleasure in the satisfaction of a desire, though pleasure be not the object of the desire.   Utilitarians, however—even such Utilitarians as Mr. Henry Sidgwick [1]—are apt to argue as if to hold that the ultimate standard of moral valuation is something else than the productivity of pleasure, was to hold that it is something else than productivity of desirable consciousness.   So to argue is quite consistent in those who take pleasure to be the sole object of desire ; for with them, if any kind of conscious life admits of being desired—and

[1] Methods of Ethics, Book III. chap. xiv. § 2. pp. 368–370 (2nd Edition).

unless it admits of being desired, it cannot be desirable—it must be on the ground of the pleasure anticipated in it. But if this view is rejected, as it is rejected by Mr. Sidgwick, it does not appear why a state of consciousness should not be desired for another reason than for the sake of the pleasure anticipated in it, or why it should not be for another reason that 'when we sit down in a calm hour' we deem it desirable.

The present writer holds as strongly as Mr. Sidgwick could do that it is only in some form of conscious life—more definitely, of self-conscious life—that we can look for the realisation of our capacities or the perfection of our being; in other words, for ultimate good. While regarding Truth, Freedom, Beauty, etc., as constituent elements of the highest good, not as means to a good beyond them, he would understand by them, in Mr. Sidgwick's words [1], the 'relations of conscious minds which we call cognition of Truth, contemplation of Beauty, Independence of action, etc.' He admits further that desire for perfection of being—the desire of which the operation in us gives meaning to the statement that the attainment of such perfection is supremely desirable—carries with it some anticipation of the pleasure there would be in satisfaction of the desire, an anticipation which renders the description of the highest state as one of happiness or bliss natural to us. His contention is that to suppose pleasure on that account to be the object of our desire for supreme or ultimate good, is to repeat the mistake, to which Mr. Sidgwick is so thoroughly alive, of confusing the pleasure which attends the satisfaction of a desire with the object of the desire, and the anticipation of that pleasure with the desire itself. It is not because looked forward to as pleasant, that the form of conscious life in which our capacities shall be fully realised is an object of desire to us;

[1] *Methods of Ethics*, p. 368. Mr. Sidgwick writes, ' the objective relations of conscious minds.' I have omitted ' objective' from not being quite sure of its significance in this connection. Nor am I sure that I could accept ' Independence of action' as an equivalent for ' Freedom,' in that sense in which I look upon ' Freedom' as a constituent of the highest good.

it is because, in such self-conscious beings as we are, a desire for their realisation goes along with the presence of the capacities, that the form of conscious life in which this desire shall be satisfied is looked forward to as pleasant. And it is because the object of this desire, when reflected on, from the nature of the case presents itself to us as absolutely final, not because we anticipate pleasure in its attainment as we do in that of any and every desired object, that 'in a calm hour' we pronounce it supremely desirable.

365. Now it would be unfair to convey the impression that Mr. Sidgwick, in identifying that 'desirable consciousness,' which he holds that ultimate good must be, simply with pleasure, is chargeable with confusion between the object of a desire and the pleasure anticipated in its satisfaction. The result of such a confusion, unless avoided by a further one, would be 'Egoistic' Hedonism, not the 'Universalistic' Hedonism which he himself adopts. In the common Hedonistic ratiocination—we always anticipate pleasure in the satisfaction of desire, therefore pleasure is the sole thing desired, therefore the sole thing desirable—pleasure must throughout mean pleasure for the person supposed to desire it. Since it is not pretended that it means anything else in the two former steps of the ratiocination, it must mean it also in the last. It can be taken to mean the pleasure of others, or of all men, only through a confusion between desire to enjoy pleasure and desire to produce it, from which Mr. Sidgwick keeps quite free. It is not upon any such ratiocination that he founds his own conclusion that 'desirable feeling' (by which he understands pleasure) 'for the innumerable multitude of living beings, present and to come [1],' is the one end 'ultimately and intrinsically desirable;' but on an appeal to what he calls 'common sense.' 'As rational beings we are manifestly bound to aim at good generally, not merely at this or that part of it [2],' and in the last resort we can give no meaning to good but happiness, which = desirable consciousness, which = pleasure. Reason

---

[1] Methods of Ethics, p. 371.   [2] Ibid. p. 355.

therefore bids us aim at a supreme good, made up of the goods (or happinesses) of all sentient beings; at the good of one sentient being equally with another, 'except in so far as it is less, or less certainly knowable or attainable.'

Now in this theory it is clear that an office is ascribed to Reason which in ordinary Utilitarian doctrine, as in the philosophy of Locke and Hume on which that doctrine is founded, is explicitly denied to it. To say that as *rational* beings we are bound to aim at anything whatever *in the nature of an ultimate end*, would have seemed absurd to Hume and to the original Utilitarians. To them reason was a faculty not of ends but of means. As a matter of fact, they held, we all do aim at pleasure as our ultimate end; all that could properly be said to be reasonable or unreasonable was our selection of means to that end. They would no more have thought of asking why pleasure ought to be pursued than of asking why any fact ought to be a fact. Mr. Sidgwick, however, does ask the question, and answers that pleasure ought to be pursued because reason pronounces it desirable; but that, since reason pronounces pleasure, if equal in amount, to be equally desirable by whatever being enjoyed, it is universal pleasure—the pleasure of all sentient beings— that ought to be pursued. It is not indeed an object that every one ought at all times to have consciously before him[1], but it is the ultimate good by reference to which, 'when we sit down in a calm hour,' the desirability of every other good is to be tested.

366. In this procedure Mr. Sidgwick is quite consistent with himself. His rejection of 'Egoistic' in favour of 'Universalistic' Hedonism rests upon a ground which in Mr. Mill's doctrine it is impossible to discover. His appeal to reason may be made to justify the recognition of an obligation to regard the happiness of all men or all animals equally, which, upon the doctrine that pleasure is the one thing desirable because the one thing desired, can only be logically justified by the untenable assumption that the only

[1] *Methods of Ethics*, p. 381.

way to obtain a maximum of pleasure for oneself is to have an equal regard for the pleasure of everyone else. But Mr. Sidgwick's way of justifying his Altruism constrains us to ask him some further questions. What does he understand by the 'reason' to which he ascribes the office of deciding what the one 'ultimately and intrinsically desirable end' is; not on the means to it, but on the nature of the end itself? In saying that it is reasonable to pursue desirable consciousness, is he not open to the same charge of moving in a circle which he brings against those who say that it is reasonable to live according to nature, or virtuous to seek perfection, while after all they have no other account to give of the life according to nature but that it is reasonable, or of perfection but that it is the highest virtue [1]? What does he mean by desirable consciousness but the sort of consciousness which it is reasonable to seek?

He apparently avoids the circle, no doubt, by describing the desirable consciousness as pleasure; but the escape is only apparent. A statement that it is reasonable to seek pleasure would not itself be chargeable with tautology, but, unless it meant that it was reasonable to seek pleasure for the sake of some chief good other than pleasure (in which sense the statement is not likely to be made), it would be absurd. If we hold pleasure to be itself the good, because the object of all desire, and if we are careful about our words, we may call it reasonable to seek certain means to it, but not to seek pleasure itself. Mr. Sidgwick himself, as we have seen, is not guilty of this absurdity, because he carefully distinguishes the desired from the desirable. His doctrine is not that it is reasonable to seek pleasure in that sense in which Hedonistic writers take it to be the one thing desired, *i.e.* as the pleasure of the person seeking it, but that it is reasonable to seek to convey pleasure to all sentient beings, because this universal enjoyment, though it is only in certain exceptional 'calm hours' *desired*, is intrinsically and ultimately *desirable* or good. Now does he mean anything else

[1] Methods of Ethics, p. 352.

by 'desirable' in this connection than 'reasonably to be desired'? If not, does not his doctrine come to this, that it is reasonable to seek as ultimate good that form of conscious life which is reasonably to be desired?

367. It will be understood that, in thus criticising Mr. Sidgwick's account of ultimate good, our object is not to depreciate it, but to show how much more truth there is in it, from our point of view, than in the common statement of Utilitarianism. We have previously explained how it comes about that any true theory of the good will present an appearance of moving in a circle. The rational or self-conscious soul, we have seen, constitutes its own end; is an end at once to and in itself. Its end is the perfection of itself, the fulfilment of the law of its being. The consciousness of there being such an end expresses itself in the judgment that something absolutely should be, that there is something intrinsically and ultimately desirable. This judgment is, in this sense, the expression of reason; and all those who, like Mr. Sidgwick, recognise the distinction between the absolutely desirable and the *de facto* desired, have in effect admitted that reason gives—is the source of there being—a supreme practical good. If we ask for a reason why we should pursue this end, there is none to be given but that it is rational to do so, that reason bids it, that the pursuit is the effort of the self-conscious or rational soul after its own perfection. It is reasonable to desire it because it is reasonably to be desired. Those who like to do so may make merry over the tautology. Those who understand how it arises—from the fact, namely, that reason gives its own end, that the self-conscious spirit of man presents its own perfection to itself as the intrinsically desirable—will not be moved by the mirth. They will not try to escape the charge of tautology by taking the desirableness of ultimate good to consist in anything else than in the thought of it as that which would satisfy reason—satisfy the demand of the self-conscious soul for its own perfection. They will not appeal to pleasure, as being that which in fact we all desire, in order to determine our notion of what reason bids us desire. They will be aware that this notion cannot be determined by reference to anything but what reason has itself done ; by anything but reflection on the excellences of character and conduct to which the rational effort after perfection of life has given rise. They will appeal to the virtues to tell them what is virtuous, to goodness to tell them what is truly good, to the work of reason in human life to tell them what is reasonably to be desired ; knowing well what they are about in so doing, and that it is the only appropriate procedure, because only in the full attainment of its end could reason learn fully what that end is, and only in what it has so far attained of the end can it learn what its further attainment would be.

368. It is perhaps unjustifiable to ascribe to any one a course of thought which he would himself disavow ; but we naturally ask for a reason why Mr. Sidgwick, having accepted principles, as it would seem, so antagonistic to those of the philosophic Utilitarians, should end by accepting their conclusion. When we consider on the one hand his implied admission that it is reason which presents us with the idea of ultimate good, and on the other his profession of inability to look for that good in anything but the pleasure of all sentient beings, the conjecture suggests itself that, while really thinking of the ultimately desirable as consisting in the satisfaction of reason, he shrank from a statement seemingly so tautological and uninstructive as that the end which reason bids us seek is the satisfaction or perfection of the rational nature itself. He was thus led to cast about for an account of the supreme good in terms which should not imply its essential relation to reason. 'Pleasure of all sentient beings' does not imply any such relation, for there is nothing in the enjoyment of pleasure which reason is needed to constitute ; and no one, except under constraint of some extravagant theory, denies that pleasure is good. Thus the statement that universal pleasure is the ultimate good which reason bids us seek, seems on the one hand to avoid the admitted absurdity of saying that reason bids us seek our own pleasure, and, on the other, the tautology of saying that reason bids us seek the satisfaction of reason.

But why does no one deny that pleasure is good? Because every one is conscious of desiring pleasure for himself. That is to say, pleasure is good, not as = the desirable, but as = the desired ; and the pleasure which is *thus* good is not universal pleasure but the pleasure of the subject desiring it, as related to his desire. Thus between the proposition that pleasure is good as = the desired, and the proposition that universal pleasure is good as = the rationally desirable, the connection (as Mr. Sidgwick is too acute not to perceive) is merely verbal. The latter can only be derived from the former on supposition that reason presents to itself as the *desirable*— as good in *this* sense—the enjoyment by every sentient being of the pleasure which he in fact desires, and which is good for him in *that* sense. Even if this supposition be granted, it will still be the satisfaction of reason that constitutes the good in the sense of the ultimately desirable, though reason will be supposed to satisfy itself in the contemplation of the enjoyment by every being of that which is good in the sense of being desired, viz. pleasure. The question will then be whether reason can thus satisfy itself. Is it in contemplation of the enjoyment of unbroken pleasure by all sentient beings that we are to think of the rational soul as saying to itself that at length its quest for ultimate good has found its goal ?

369. To this question—which, it will of course be understood, is not put by Mr. Sidgwick himself, but to which, in our view, his doctrine leads—his answer seems ambiguous. He holds indeed that a maximum of possible pleasure for all sentient beings is the ultimate good at which reason bids us aim, but he explains that by pleasure he means 'desirable consciousness.' Now unless we are to forget the distinction between the desired and the desirable which we might learn from Mr. Sidgwick himself[1], we cannot suppose that the

[1] *Methods of Ethics*, p. 361.

rational soul, in presenting a *desirable* consciousness on its own part as involved in ultimate good, presents it simply as so much pleasure. The very fact that it asks for a consciousness which is desirable or *should be* desired, shows that it cannot satisfy itself with that which every one naturally desires, but of which for that reason no one can think as what he should desire. The presentation of an object as one that *should be* desired implies that it is not desired *as a pleasure* by the person to whom it so presents itself. A man may speak significantly of another person's pleasure as desirable, but not of his own. The desirableness *of a pleasure* must always express its relation to some one else than the person desiring the enjoyment of the pleasure. Thus to suppose a consciousness to be at once desired as a pleasure, and contemplated as desirable by the same person, is a contradiction. To the man who 'in a calm hour' sets before himself a certain form of conscious life as the object which reason bids him aim at, though it is not impossible that pleasure should be the desirable quality in that life as he seeks to bring it about for other people, it cannot be the desirable quality in it as he seeks to obtain it for himself. When we are told, therefore, that ultimate good is desirable consciousness or pleasure for all sentient beings, we reply that, though it may be sought as pleasure for all sentient beings, it cannot be sought as his own pleasure by one who also contemplates it as the consciousness desirable for himself. The description of ultimate good as pleasure, and the description of it as desirable (not desired) consciousness, are incompatible descriptions, so far as they are descriptions of a state of being which the rational soul seeks as its own.

370. Now, according to the view already stated in this treatise, the rational soul in seeking an ultimate good necessarily seeks it as a state of its own being. An ultimate, intrinsic, absolute good has no meaning for us, except that which it derives from the effort of the rational soul in us to become all that it is conscious of a capacity for becoming. As the rational soul is essentially the principle of self-con-

sciousness, so the idea of ultimate good on the part of every one capable of it is necessarily the idea of a perfect self-conscious life for himself. The desirableness of that life is its desirableness as his own life. But to any one actuated by it the idea of a perfection, of a state in which he shall be satisfied, for himself will involve the idea of a perfection of all other beings, so far as he finds the thought of their being perfect necessary to his own satisfaction. Moral development, as has been previously explained more at large, is a progress in which the individual's conception of the kind of life that would be implied in his perfection gradually becomes fuller and more determinate; fuller and more determinate both in regard to the range of persons whose participation in the perfect life is thought of as necessary to its attainment by any one, and in regard to the qualities on the part of the individual which it is thought must be exercised in it. In the most complete determination within our reach, the conception still does not suffice to enable any one to say positively what the perfection of his life would be; but the determination has reached that stage in which the educated citizen of Christendom is able to think of the perfect life as essentially conditioned by the exercise of virtues, resting on a self-sacrificing will, in which it is open to all men to participate, and as fully attainable by one man, only in so far as through those virtues it is attained by all. In thinking of ultimate good he thinks of it indeed necessarily as perfection for himself; as a life in which he shall be fully satisfied through having become all that the spirit within him enables him to become. But he cannot think of himself as satisfied in any life other than a social life, exhibiting the exercise of self-denying will, and in which 'the multitude of the redeemed,' which is all men, shall participate. He has other faculties indeed than those which are directly exhibited in the specifically moral virtues—faculties which find their expression not in his dealings with other men, but in the arts and sciences—and the development of these must be a necessary constituent in any life which he presents to himself as one in which he can find satisfaction. But 'when he sits down in a calm hour' it will not be in isolation that the development of any of these faculties will assume the character for him of ultimate good. Intrinsic desirableness, sufficiency to satisfy the rational soul, will be seen to belong to their realisation only in so far as it is a constituent in a whole of social life, of which the distinction, as a social life, shall be universality of disinterested goodness.

371. We should accept the view, then, that to think of ultimate good is to think of an intrinsically desirable form of conscious life ; but we should seek further to define it. We should take it in the sense that to think of such good is to think of a state of self-conscious life as intrinsically desirable for oneself, and for that reason is to think of it as something else than pleasure—the thought of an object as pleasure for oneself, and the thought of it as intrinsically desirable for oneself, being thoughts which exclude each other. The pleasure anticipated in the life is not that which renders it desirable ; but so far as desire is excited by the thought of it as desirable, and so far as that desire is reflected on, pleasure comes to be anticipated in the satisfaction of that desire. The thought of the intrinsically desirable life, then, is the thought of something else than pleasure, but the thought of what ? The thought, we answer, of the full realisation of the capacities of the human soul, of the fulfilment of man's vocation, as of that in which alone he can satisfy himself—a thought of which the content is never final and complete, which is always by its creative energy further determining its own content, but which for practical purposes, as the mover and guide of our highest moral effort, may be taken to be the thought of such a social life as that described in the previous paragraph. The thought of such a life, again, when applied as a criterion for the valuation of the probable effects of action, may be taken to be represented by the question stated in § 354 :—'Does this or that law or usage, this or that course of action—directly or indirectly, positively or as preventive of the opposite—contribute to the better

being of society, as measured by the more general establishment of conditions favourable to the attainment of the
recognised virtues and excellences, by the more general
attainment of those excellences in some degree, or by their
attainment on the part of some persons in higher degree
without detraction from the opportunities of others?' It
remains for us now finally to consider the availability of the
injunctions and criteria founded on such a theory of ultimate
good, as compared with those derivable from the identification of ultimate good with a universal enjoyment of pleasure,
in those exceptional cases in which their comparative availability is likely to be put to the test.

372. As has been already remarked, these cases will be
exceptional owing to the efficiency of the direction for outward conduct which conventional morality now commonly
affords. The origin of that morality is not here in question.
If there is reason to hold, as it has been previously sought
to show, that the progressive principle in morality, through
which the recognised standard of virtuous living among us
has come to be what it is, has not been an interest either in
the enjoyment or in the production of pleasure, there is so
far a presumption against general pleasure being the ultimate
good to which we should look for direction when conventional morality fails us. But the reader naturally asks for
a conclusion more definite than this presumption. He will
wish to satisfy himself whether, in the settlement of real
questions of conduct, our theory of ultimate good has any
advantage over that which Mr. Sidgwick describes as Universalistic Hedonism—whether under any conditions it might
afford other and better guidance. In discussing this point
we must suppose the person who resorts to either theory for
guidance to have accepted the direction of conventional
morality, so far as it goes—the one on the ground that it
represents a decisive amount of transmitted experience as to
the pleasure-giving or pain-giving effects, on the whole, of
different kinds of action ; the other on the ground that its

observance, unless the contrary can be shown, must be taken as at least a condition of the social well-being which he would measure by the prevalence of a virtuous will.

We must also keep out of sight difficulties that do not relate to the *valuation* of the anticipated effects of actions, but to the question what effects are to be anticipated from them. In many cases the whole practical difficulty of deciding whether a contemplated action ought or ought not to be done, is the difficulty of deciding what effects are likely to follow from it ; not of valuing the effects if once they could be ascertained, but of ascertaining what they will be. No theory of ultimate good has an advantage over another in dealing with this difficulty, since none rather than another can claim to give us knowledge of facts, or to make us clear-sighted and patient in the analysis of circumstances. Any difference in respect of influence upon the practical judgment between the two theories in question must arise from the different value which they severally lead us to put upon effects ascertained or expected, not from any different methods which they suggest of ascertaining the effects of action, nor from any difference in the importance which they lead us to attach to doing so.

373. In a previous paragraph (§ 338) examples have been given of the kind of question in regard to personal conduct, in his answer to which a speculative person might be affected for the worse by a logical application of the Utilitarian theory of good, so far as that theory is founded on the principle that pleasure is the only possible object of desire. We are now supposing this principle to be dropped, but the Utilitarian doctrine of the chief good to be retained. We are dealing with a theory in which the action of disinterested motives, in the natural sense of the words (as desires which have not pleasure directly or indirectly for their object), is fully recognised, and the identification of ultimate good with a maximum of universal pleasure is accepted on the ground of its supposed intrinsic reasonableness. The question is whether, in cases of the kind supposed, a logical application of this conception of ultimate good, as a criterion of what should be done, will be of any avail. The cases are of a kind in which it has to be decided whether, in words already used (§ 363), a man 'should set up for being better than his neighbours or should swim with the stream; whether he should follow the severer path of duty where his departure from it would be unknown or uncondemned, and where it would save himself and those whom he loves from much suffering; whether he should seek the highest beauty in art, the completest truth in knowledge, rather than conform to popular taste and opinion.' For the purposes of such a decision our contention is not that of itself the theory of Universalistic Hedonism would yield a wrong answer, but that it would yield none at all, and would thus in effect leave the decision to be made by the enquirer's inclination to the course of action which is most pleasant or least painful to him individually.

374. We have already seen how, when the question before the individual is whether for the sake of some higher good he should depart from the course of action to which custom or inclination, or the sense of what the opinion of his class requires of him, would naturally lead him, the logical tendency of the doctrine that pleasure is the sole object of desire must be to entangle him in a Hedonistic fatalism, which would mean paralysis of the moral initiative. Universalistic Hedonism, as Mr. Sidgwick conceives it, is not chargeable with this tendency. It justifies the question, What should I do for the bettering of life? for it recognises the possibility of an initiative not determined by imagination of pleasure or pain. But for doubts of the kind we are considering, where conventional morality cannot be appealed to as representing accumulated experience of consequences in the way of pleasure and pain, it seems to afford no solution. We have supposed a man in doubt whether, in consideration of the claims of society, he is justified in spending so much of his time in the gratification of his taste for music or of his curiosity in literature, or in continuing a habit of 'moderate drinking.' Let such an one translate 'in consideration of the claims of society' into 'with a view to producing as much pleasure as possible to all beings capable of it.' Must it not be apparent to him, just so far as he really apprehends the nature of the problem which he professes to set before himself, that it is wholly insoluble? What knowledge has he, or from the nature of the case can he obtain, either of the conditions on which the pleasures of all other beings, present and to come, depend or will depend, or of the various degrees to which other men—to say nothing of the animals—are susceptible of pleasure, that he should be able to judge whether the suggested breach of custom, the suggested resistance to personal inclination, is likely to contribute to the 'Summum Bonum' which he adopts as his criterion? Unless he has really some other conception of ultimate good to fall back upon, will he not inevitably take refuge in the justification which the theory of Universalistic Hedonism affords him for attaching most importance to the most certainly known pleasures, and let custom and inclination decide him?

375. In fact, the man who is challenged by doubts of the kind described, who asks himself whether he is duly responding to claims which conventional morality does not recognise, always has another standard of ultimate good to fall back upon, however much his Hedonistic philosophy may obscure it to him. That standard is an ideal of a perfect life for himself and other men, as attainable for him only through them, for them only through him; a life that shall be perfect, in the sense of being the fulfilment of all that the human spirit in him and them has the real capacity or vocation of becoming, and which (as is implied in its being such fulfilment) shall rest on the will to be perfect. However unable he may be to give an account of such an ideal, it yet has so much hold on him as to make the promotion of goodness for its own sake in himself and others an intelligible end to him. The reader, however, will be weary of hearing of this ideal, and will be waiting to know in what particular way it can afford guidance in cases of the kind supposed, where conventional morality and Utilitarian theory alike fail to do so. We have argued that no man could tell whether, by denying himself according to the examples given, he would in the whole result increase the amount of pleasant living in the world, present and to come. Can he tell any better whether he will further that realisation of the ideal just described, in regard to which we admit the impossibility of saying positively what in its completeness it would be?

376. We answer as follows. The whole question of sacrificing one's own pleasure assumes a different aspect, when the end for which it is to be sacrificed is not an addition to a general aggregate of pleasures, but the harmonious exercise of man's proper activities in some life resting on a self-sacrificing will. According to the latter view, the individual's sacrifice of pleasure does not—as so much loss of pleasure—come into the reckoning at all; nor has any balance to be attempted of unascertainable pains and pleasures spreading over an indefinite range of sentient life. The good to be sought is not made up of pleasures, nor the evil to be avoided made up of pains. The end for which the sacrifice is demanded is one which in the sacrifice itself is in some measure attained—in some measure only, not fully, yet so that the sacrifice is related to the complete end, not as a means in itself valueless, but as a constituent to a whole which it helps to form. That realisation of the powers of the human spirit, which we deem the true end, is not to be thought of merely as something in a remote distance, towards which we may take steps now, but in which there is no present participation. It is continuously going on, though in varying and progressive degrees of completeness; and the individual's sacrifice of an inclination, harmless or even in its way laudable, for the sake of a higher good, is itself already in some measure an attainment of the higher good.

Thus, whereas according to any Hedonistic doctrine of true good, though it be 'Universalistic' Hedonism not 'Egoistic,' the certain present loss of pleasure to the individual himself and to his intimates, involved in sacrifices of the kind we are considering, is so much deduction from true good, only to be justified by a larger accession of pleasure in other quarters or at other times—an accession from the nature of the case less certain to the man meditating the sacrifice than the loss—upon the other view, while the loss of pleasure implied in the sacrifice to the person who makes it, and to any others whom he can induce willingly to accept any like loss that arises out of it for them, is morally, or relatively to the true good, matter of indifference, the exercise of a devoted will in the sacrifice, on the part of all concerned in it, is an actual and undoubted contribution to true good. The degree of its value will only be doubtful, so far as there may be uncertainty in regard to its tendency to yield more or less further good of the same kind in the sequel. We say 'more or less,' for that it tends to yield some further good of the same kind can never be really doubtful. Self-sacrifice, devotion to worthy objects, is always self-propagatory. If the question is asked,—

> Of love that never found his earthly close,
> What sequel?

there is at least the answer,

> But am I not the nobler through thy love?
> O, three times less unworthy [1]!

In like manner, upon the view that of the life which forms the true and full good the self-devoted will must be the principle, if the question is asked, What comes of any particular act of self-sacrifice? there is at least the answer that the act does not need anything further to come of it, in order to be in itself in little the good. But it is only if we falter in that view of the good, on the strength of which we give this answer, that we can doubt the beneficent result, in whatever manner or degree, of the act in itself good. The good will in one man has never failed to elicit or strengthen such a will in another.

377. But it will be said that we are so far dealing only in

---

[1] Tennyson's 'Love and Duty.'

generalities. It may be admitted that an act or habit of self-sacrifice is a good in itself, but there are many ways in which a man may sacrifice himself, and he is responsible for choosing the most useful. It is of little profit to tell him of the intrinsic nobility of self-sacrifice, unless we can give him some means of judging for what sort of objects he in particular should be prepared to give up his tastes and inclinations, or to run the gauntlet of established custom. To revert to one of the examples employed, no one would think of saying absolutely that there was merit in sacrificing a taste for music. On the contrary, there may be a duty to cultivate it. The question whether it should be sacrificed or cultivated must depend on the position and general capabilities of the individual, on the circumstances of his time, on the claims of surrounding society. Some direction therefore is needed for the individual in making his sacrifices; some criterion of the ends which he should keep before him in deciding for this sacrifice rather than for that. How can the view of the good for which we have been pleading afford such direction or criterion?

The answer lies in a consideration of that unity of the human spirit throughout its individual manifestations, in virtue of which the realisation of its possibilities, though a personal object to each man, is at the same time an object fully attainable by one only in so far as it is attained by the whole human society. The statement that the act of self-sacrifice has its value in itself is not to be understood as denying that it has its value in its consequences, but as implying that those consequences, to be of intrinsic value, must be of a kind with the act itself, as an exercise of a character having its dominant interest in some form of human perfection. The injunction that would be founded on the view of that perfection as the end would never be 'Sacrifice inclination' simply, but 'Sacrifice inclination in so far as by so doing you may make men better;' but the bettering of men would mean their advance in a goodness the same in principle as that which appears in the sacrifice enjoined, and this sacrifice itself would be regarded as already an instalment of the good to be more largely attained in its consequences. The direction to the individual, in doubt whether he should deny himself some attractive pursuit or some harmless indulgence, would be, not that he should make the sacrifice for the sake of making it, but that he should be ready to make it, if upon honest consideration it appear that men would be the better for his doing so.

378. Universalistic Hedonism might give the same direction; but in the interpretation of the direction there would be a great difference—a difference which might very well amount to that between demanding the sacrifice and allowing the indulgence. The Hedonist, understanding by the bettering of men an addition to the pleasures enjoyed by them, present and to come, has at any rate an obscure computation before him. In such cases as we are now considering he would not have the presumption, afforded by a call of conventionally recognised duty, that obedience to it, however painful to the individual, would be felicific in the general result. The presumption from his point of view must always be against the 'reasonableness' of making the sacrifice, till the probability of an excess of pleasure from its ulterior consequences over the pain more immediately produced by it could be clearly made out. Such a probability must generally be very difficult to arrive at. It does not at all follow, as is apt to be assumed, because an observance of conventional morality may be required in the interest of general pleasure, that an advance upon conventional morality is so. Upon the view that the exercise of a virtuous will is an end in itself, the question about a possible 'too much' of virtue cannot arise. But it is otherwise if an opposite view is taken. If virtue is of value only as a means to general pleasure, it becomes necessary to enquire what is the degree of it which so contributes—to what extent an increase in the number of self-devoted persons, and a more intense and constant self-devotion on their part, is desirable, in order to an increase in the sum of pleasures for all human, or all sentient, beings. Thus in his forecast of the 'felicific' results to be looked for from any advance upon the 'law of opinion' in the way of self-denying virtue, the Hedonistic Utilitarian may not avail himself of the short method that would be represented by the maxim, 'The more virtue, the more pleasure.' He may not assume that, because the suggested self-denial would tend to increase virtue among men, it would tend to increase pleasure. The pleasure-increasing tendency must be made out on its own account ; and, unless the self-denial in question is one that upon physiological evidence can be proved likely in its consequences to cause some decisive reduction in physical suffering, it is not easy to see how this should be done. When it had been done, the balance between the remoter and less certain gain and the proximate loss would have still to be struck. Upon such principles the case against making the 'uncalled for' sacrifice, even though dispassionately conducted, would generally be invincibly strong.

379. From the other point of view, even though the precise nature and strength of the call for the sacrifice could not clearly be made out, the presumption would still be in favour of its being made, on the ground of the intrinsic value attaching alike to the exercise of the self-denying character, and to those results, of a kind with itself, which through the influence of example it is sure to produce among men. It is true that this general presumption will not help a man to decide which of many particular courses of self-denying action, which it is open to him to pursue but which he would not be thought the worse of for not pursuing, is the one which it is best for him to pursue. It is his duty not to waste himself among various efforts, each of which might be well-intentioned and involve real self-denial, but none of them in the direction in which he in particular under the circumstances of the case might do most good. For deciding, however, whether any particular sacrifice is one that he ought to make, he has much more available guidance, according to our view, than a computation of the total range of pleasures and pains to be looked for as a consequence of the sacrifice. He has to ask, according to the terms in which the question has been above put, whether the suggested sacrifice on his part is one by which he may best contribute to the well-being of society, 'as measured by the more general establishment of conditions favourable to the attainment of the recognised virtues and excellences, by the more general attainment of those excellences in some degree, or by their attainment on the part of some persons in higher degree without detraction from the opportunities of others.' It is not to be disguised, of course, that with such an end before him as this question represents, he may find it difficult to ascertain, by analysis of circumstances and enquiry into facts, in what degree the various forms of self-denying activity open to him are likely to contribute to the end. As has already been pointed out, such analysis and enquiry are not to be dispensed with upon one theory of the end any more than upon another. The question is of the object with reference to which the analysis and enquiry are to be conducted ; whether in order to ascertain tendencies to produce a maximum of pleasure over all time to all beings capable of it, or in order to ascertain tendencies to produce a perfection of human society, resting on the universal prevalence of the will to be perfect. When the point at issue is whether some sacrifice should be made which is uncalled for by social convention, while its tendency in the former direction will generally be found unascertainable, its tendency in the latter will be within the ken of any dispassionate and considerate man.

380. A man asks himself—to revert once more to that instance—whether he is justified in giving so much of his time to the gratification of his taste for music ; which must mean, whether there are not claims upon him for the service of mankind which cannot be satisfied while he does so. Now it may really be a difficult question for him to settle whether he cannot serve mankind more effectually by giving more of his time to music rather than less. It is a question for the settlement of which there may be needed careful analysis of his own faculties, of the needs of society about him, of his particular opportunities and powers of meeting those needs ; and in settling it the truest conception of ulti-

mate good will not prevent the mistakes to which hastiness, prejudice, and self-conceit naturally lead. Still there is all the difference between approaching the question with some definite conception of the claims of mankind, of the good to be sought for them, and without any such conception. The Hedonistic theory, as we have tried to show, affords no such conception. It insists indeed on the claim of every man to have as much pleasure as is compatible with the attainment of the greatest possible amount on the whole, but this claim cannot be translated into a claim to be or to do, or to have the chance of being or doing, anything in particular. We cannot found upon it even a claim of every man to be free; for who can be sure that the freedom of all men, when the whole range of the possibilities of pleasure is taken into account, tends to an excess of pleasure over pain? Still less can we found upon it a claim of every one to be helped to be good, according to our present standard of goodness. Hedonistic theory can only bid us promote the received virtues and excellences among men with an *if* which makes the injunction of no avail in such a case as we are considering. They are to be promoted up to the limit at which their promotion still certainly yields more pleasure than pain to the universe of human or sentient beings; and it is impossible to say what this limit is.

It is otherwise when the exercise of the recognised virtues and excellences, as resting upon a self-devoted will or will to be perfect, is considered to be an end in itself—to be itself, if not in completeness yet in principle and essence, the ultimate good for man. The general nature of the claim of other men upon him is plain to every one who contemplates it with reference to such an end. It is a claim for service in the direction of making the attainment of those virtues and excellences, by some persons and in some form, more possible. The question for the individual will still remain, how he in particular may best render this service, and it may be one of much difficulty. He may easily deceive himself in answering it, but he will not have the excuse for answering it in favour of his own inclination, which is afforded by reference to a 'Summum Bonum' of which the most readily ascertainable constituent must always be his own pleasure.

381. As to the particular instance we have been considering, while intrinsic value will not be denied to excellence in music as having a place in the fulfilment of man's vocation, it is a question, so to speak, of spiritual proportion, whether the attainment of such excellence is of importance in any society of men under the given conditions of that society. For, like all excellence in art, it has its value as an element in a whole of spiritual life, to which the moral virtues are essential; which without them would be no realisation of the capacities of the human soul. In some Italian principality of the last century, for instance, with its civil life crushed out and its moral energies debased, excellence in music could hardly be accounted of actual and present value at all. Its value would be potential, in so far as the artist's work might survive to become an element in a nobler life elsewhere or at a later time. Under such conditions much occupation with music might imply indifference to claims of the human soul which must be satisfied in order to the attainment of a life in which the value of music could be actualised. And under better social conditions there may be claims, arising from the particular position of an individual, which render the pursuit of excellence in music, though it would be the right pursuit for others qualified as he is, a wrong one for him. In the absence of such claims the main question will be of his particular talent. Has he talent to serve mankind—to contribute to the perfection of the human soul—more as a musician than in any other way? Only if he has will he be justified in making music his main pursuit. If he is not to make it his main pursuit, the question will remain, to what extent he may be justified in indulging his taste for it, either as a refreshment of faculties which are to be mainly used in other pursuits—to be so used, because in them he may best serve mankind in the sense explained—or as enabling him to share in that intrinsically valuable lifting up of the soul which music may afford.

382. Such questions are not to be answered by 'intuition,' nor do they arise under conditions under which our guidance in duty needs to be intuitive—needs to be derived from convictions which afford immediate direction independently of any complicated consideration of circumstances. They only arise for persons who have exceptional opportunity of directing their own pursuits, and who do not need to be in a hurry in their decisions. To most people sufficient direction for their pursuits is afforded by claims so well established in conventional morality that they are intuitively recognised, and that a conscience merely responsive to social disapprobation would reproach us for neglecting them. For all of us it is so in regard to a great part of our lives. But the cases we have been considering are those in which some 'counsel of perfection' is needed, which reference to such claims does not supply, and which has to be derived from reference to a theory of ultimate good. In such cases many questions have to be answered, which intuition cannot answer, before the issue is arrived at to which the theory of ultimate good becomes applicable; but then the cases only occur for persons who have leisure and faculty for dealing with such questions. For them the essential thing is that their theory of the good should afford a really available criterion for estimating those further claims upon them which are not enforced by the sanction of conventional morality, and a criterion which affords no plea to the self-indulgent impulse. Our point has been to show, in the instance given, that such a criterion is afforded by the theory of ultimate good as a perfection of the human spirit resting on the will to be perfect (which may be called in short the theory of virtue as an end in itself), but not by the theory of good as consisting in a maximum of possible pleasure.

Oxford : Printed at the Clarendon Press by HORACE HART, M.A.